THEORIES OF
SMALL GROUPS

This book is dedicated to our mentor, Joseph E. McGrath, whose path-breaking research and conscientious cultivation of the field of group research has inspired and encouraged several generations of group researchers.

THEORIES OF
SMALL GROUPS

Interdisciplinary Perspectives

Editors

Marshall Scott Poole
Texas A&M University

Andrea B. Hollingshead
University of Illinois at Urbana-Champaign

SAGE Publications
Thousand Oaks ▪ London ▪ New Delhi

For information:

Sage Publications, Inc.
2455 Teller Road
Thousand Oaks, California 91320
E-mail: order@sagepub.com

Sage Publications Ltd.
1 Oliver's Yard
55 City Road
London EC1Y 1SP
United Kingdom

Sage Publications India Pvt. Ltd.
B-42, Panchsheel Enclave
Post Box 4109
New Delhi 110 017 India

Printed in the United States of America

Library of Congress Cataloging-in-Publication Data

Theories of small groups : interdisciplinary perspectives / edited by Marshall Scott Poole and Andrea B. Hollingshead.
    p. cm.
Includes bibliographical references and index.
ISBN 0-7619-3075-2 (cloth) — ISBN 0-7619-3076-0 (pbk.)
  1. Small groups. I. Poole, Marshall Scott, 1951- II. Hollingshead, Andrea B.
HM736.T47 2005
302.3′4—dc22

                              2004011263

05   06   07   08   09   10   9 8 7 6 5 4 3 2 1

Acquisitions Editor:	Todd R. Armstrong
Editorial Assistant:	Deya Saoud
Production Editor:	Kristen Gibson
Copy Editor:	Jackie Tasch
Typesetter:	C&M Digitals (P) Ltd.
Proofreader:	Annette Pagliaro
Cover Designer:	Janet Foulger

Contents

Preface

The purpose of this book is to draw together the threads that unify the field of group research. Currently, group scholars are spread across a number of academic fields, each with its own particular set of interests, problems, methods, and issues. Common theories and research streams, however, have the potential to bind group research into a more comprehensive discipline.

Theories of Groups: Interdisciplinary Perspectives attempts to summarize the current state of group theory and research in a relatively brief volume. It is not a traditional handbook that presents comprehensive reviews of all the research on various subjects. Instead, the chapters of this book are designed to define and describe distinctive theoretical perspectives on groups and to highlight select research findings within those perspectives. They chart the main currents in the past 20 years of group research and suggest where group research should go in the future.

This book is written for graduate courses on group research and for practicing scholars. We hope it gives graduate students perspective on their own disciplines, along with knowledge of useful and relevant research in other disciplines. We hope it inspires them to look beyond their individual fields and to develop the broader field of group research, a truly interdisciplinary field. We also hope it gives established group scholars insight into different theoretical approaches that might inform and enrich their own research, as well as a better understanding of the overall field of group research. Almost every current line of research on groups resonates with work in other fields, and we hope this volume helps to bring out these connections.

We would like to acknowledge a number of contributions. The list of authors in the Contents is literally "the tip of the iceberg" of those who made this book possible. To best explain their contributions, we will introduce them in the context of a brief history of the larger project from which this book springs, "Evaluating Theory and Research on Groups: What Do We Know and What Do We Need to Know?"

The project started in 1998 when John Rohrbaugh had the idea that, in honor of the new millennium, the community of group scholars should do an extensive inventory of theory and research on groups across disciplinary boundaries. Rohrbaugh talked to Scott Poole about his idea, and the two of them contacted Joe McGrath and Dick Moreland. All four agreed it was an opportune time to take stock of the current state of knowledge about groups and concluded that the best way to accomplish the task was to hold two conferences to convene group scholars from a number of fields to identify common theories and significant findings. The first conference would be about theory, and the second would be about future directions.

Rohrbaugh et al. then convened a planning committee that added Deborah Ancona, Janet Fulk, Charles Hermann, Poppy McLeod, Rick Kettner-Polley, and Cecilia Ridgeway to the original group. These 10 met in Pittsburgh in February 1999 to define the scope of the project and to generate a plan of action. It was at this meeting, facilitated by Sandy Schuman, that the initial list of seven interdisciplinary perspectives on groups was finalized. The list included the functional; psychodynamic; symbolic interpretive; status, conflict, and power; social identity; social evolutionary; and temporal perspectives. A steering committee consisting of Hermann, McGrath, McLeod, Moreland, Poole, and Rohrbaugh was charged with refining the ideas behind the conference and gathering resources to support it.

In May 1999, the George Bush School of Government and Public Service at Texas A&M committed funds to help support the two conferences. In late 1999, the decision, risk, and management science and social psychology programs of the National Science Foundation funded a grant to support the conferences and the preparation of this book, as well as other projects designed to foster the interdisciplinary field of group research. During 2000, the steering committee continued to work on the conferences and identified coleaders for "perspective groups," interdisciplinary working groups of scholars who would summarize theory and research for each of the seven perspectives.

The planning committee and cochairs convened in January 2001 at the Nag's Head Conference Center in Boca Raton, Florida. This meeting focused on the format and schedule for the first conference and on clarifying the seven perspectives. Those attending this meeting included Dom Abrams, Holly Arrow, Linnda Caporael, Larry Frey, Michael Hogg, Andrea Hollingshead, Bibb Latane, and David Wilson, in addition to most members of the planning committee.

In the Spring of 2001, the coleaders recruited scholars from multiple disciplines to join their perspective groups, and the groups were fairly well constituted by May 2001, although members continued to join and leave the perspective groups. The perspective groups worked during the Summer and early Fall of 2001 to define the core concepts of their perspective, the theoretical variants within it, and the key empirical findings of research in the perspective. Some of this work was conducted in special meetings funded by the project, but most was done over the Internet. Most participants used e-mail, but a few groups used Andromeda, a Web-based conferencing space provided by Cogos, Incorporated. Special thanks are due to Brad Jackson of Cogos, who made the software available to us and provided excellent technical support.

Scholars who participated in the perspective groups, in addition to those mentioned previously, included: Gary Alan Fine, Brooke Harrington, Charlotte Hemelrijk, Kelly Henry, Randy Hirokawa, Michael Lovaglia, Elizabeth Mannix, Sabine Otten, Ray Ozley, Paul Paulus, Randall Peterson, Charles Samuelson, Kennon Sheldon, Jane Sell, Sunwolf, Susan Wheelan, Gwen Wittenbaum, Rick Wilson, Wendy Wood, and Kay Yoon. We want to remember in particular Steve Hinkle, who tragically passed away prior to the conference.

The first conference was held in October 2001 at Texas A&M University in College Station, Texas. Local arrangements were handled by a large group of interested scholars and graduate students from Texas A&M. We would like to thank Rachel Hull, Jon Iuzzini, Toby Kyte, Minda Orina, Jeff Quinn, Kevin Real, Dan ("The Van Man") Ryan, Jill Teubner, Sisi Tran, Jyotsna Vaid, Kristen Watrous, Carol Wilson, Melissa Witt, and Wendy Wood for their help in making the conference a reality.

The tragic events of September 11, 2001, unfortunately prevented travel for all of our international scholars and many within the United States. The conference was smaller than we had hoped it would be, but the initial presentations of the perspective groups and the ensuing discussions convinced us that these interdisciplinary integrations were viable theoretical positions. The perspective groups continued to work on papers laying out the seven perspectives.

As drafts of the papers were passed back and forth, the editors of this volume, Scott Poole and Andrea Hollingshead, searched for additional perspectives that might be added to the original seven. This search was initiated based on comments from the College Station conference about perspectives that had been omitted from consideration. We decided that the network and feminist perspectives should be added to the project and commissioned author teams to write chapters on these theoretical positions.

The perspective groups eventually produced two sets of papers. One set focused primarily on theoretical assumptions of the nine perspectives. These relatively brief descriptions were published in *Small Group Research*, 2004, issues 1 and 3. Longer descriptions of the perspectives along with key research findings make up the chapters of this book. We are grateful to the members of the perspective groups, who persisted through round after round of reviews to produce chapters that exhibited sufficient consistency to make the perspectives comparable, yet captured the unique features and concerns of each perspective.

We would like to thank Todd Armstrong, our editor at Sage Publications for seeing the potential of this project and helping us to realize it; Deya Saoud, the editorial assistant on the book, and our copy editor, Jacqueline Tasch. It is a much better book due to their efforts.

In addition to the National Science Foundation and the George Bush School at Texas A&M University, we would like to acknowledge financial support for this project from the Rockefeller College of Public Affairs and Policy at State University of New York, Albany, the Department of Psychology at the University of Pittsburgh, Bibb Latane and the Nags Head Research Institute, and the Office of the Vice President for Research and Departments of Communication, Psychology, and Sociology at Texas A&M University. Their generous support enabled the project to accomplish results that many of its participants were not certain could be obtained.

Marshall Scott Poole
College Station, Texas

Andrea B. Hollingshead
Urbana, Illinois

1

Interdisciplinary Perspectives on Small Groups

Marshall Scott Poole, Andrea B. Hollingshead, Joseph E. McGrath, Richard Moreland, and John Rohrbaugh

Abstract

This book attempts to assess, synthesize, integrate, and evaluate the body of theory on small groups across disciplinary boundaries. In this introduction, we identify and briefly describe nine general theoretical perspectives from which small groups have been examined: the psychodynamic, functional, temporal, conflict-power-status, symbolic-interpretive, social identity, social-evolutionary, social network, and feminist perspectives. We conclude with some general observations about the nine perspectives and an overview of the book.

The study of groups has been an important endeavor in psychology, sociology, education, communication, management, social work, political science, public policy, urban planning, and information science. Since 1940, literally thousands of studies on every aspect of groups have been published. Countless literature reviews, handbooks, and "state of the field" articles attempt to pull together what is known about groups within distinct disciplines.

Although it has been pursued actively within individual disciplines and subdisciplines, as a whole, group research remains fragmented and discipline bound. There have been few attempts to integrate theory and research across disciplinary boundaries. Theorists and researchers often are not aware of relevant work in other fields. Even within fields, lines of research proceed unconnected to other potentially relevant work. To capitalize on the advances of the past 50 years and on the present energy directed to group research, it is important to link disparate areas and to foster integration among diverse theoretical traditions. The advances in the understanding of groups that have appeared in individual fields provide a firm foundation for an interdisciplinary integration of theory and research on groups. This book represents one of the first efforts to bring together across disciplinary boundaries scholars who view groups from a common theoretical lens.

The major objective of this edited book is to summarize the current state of group theory and research in a brief volume that can be used by researchers and in the graduate courses that will train the next generation of group scholars. The book describes where group research has been and will suggest where it should go in the future. The goals of describing, explaining, predicting, and improving groups reflect an aspiration to develop broader and more general theories of groups than now exist.

Background

This book is the culmination of a National Science Foundation-supported project to promote integrative thinking about group theory and research, "Assessing Theory and Research on Groups: What Do We Know and What Do We Need to Know," which was launched in 1998.[1] The goal of this project was to conduct an assessment and evaluation of the current state of knowledge on small groups and to link disparate areas and foster integrative positions in group theory and research.[2] Group researchers from diverse fields met together at Texas A&M University in October 2001 to assess the current status of theory and to take stock of the major findings in group research. A second conference was held in November 2002 at Case Western Reserve University.

Prior to the conferences, the project-planning teams distilled a set of general theoretical perspectives from the multitude of models and theories advanced by various disciplines on small groups. Each general perspective had to meet the following criteria:

1. The perspective focused on purposive groups, broadly construed to include any type of group that has a goal. This included traditional work groups, such as factory and field crews, committees, teams, and task forces. It also included less traditional groups, such as support and therapy groups, educational groups, and clubs.

2. The perspective advanced a distinctive view of groups, group processes, and group outcomes.

3. Research on the perspective had been conducted in more than one discipline.

4. The perspective had the potential for application in multiple disciplines, even some that had not previously employed it.

5. Contemporary scholars working with the perspective could be identified.

Seven interdisciplinary perspectives were defined in advance of the first conference held at Texas A&M University: the functional perspective, the psychodynamic perspective, the social identity perspective, the power-status-conflict perspective, the evolutionary perspective, the symbolic-interpretive perspective, and the change-dynamics perspective. Subsequent discussion among the editors of this volume suggested that two additional perspectives, which have emerged in recent years, should be added: the feminist and network perspectives.[3]

Organization of This Volume

The book is organized around the nine theoretical perspectives. Each of these perspectives is described in a chapter written by an author team composed of experts who have conducted independent research within that perspective. Each expert represents a different "take" on that perspective, and several fields are represented within most author teams. Each author team prepared a chapter that describes their theoretical perspective and the various theories that the perspective subsumes and summarizes relevant research findings from that perspective. These chapters form the core of this book. In addition to this introductory chapter, there is also a concluding chapter on touchstone themes that run through the chapters, unifying and differentiating them.

In the remainder of this chapter, we will introduce the nine broad theoretical perspectives on groups. We will briefly summarize the general approach to the study of groups taken by each perspective. We will then offer some observations about the theoretical perspectives as a whole.

Theoretical Perspectives on Groups

The dictionary defines *perspective* as "a specific point of view in under-standing things or events" (Guralnik, 1980, p. 1062). Each of the nine perspectives offers the mind's eye a different view of groups. Just as each spectator may notice different aspects of the landscape from the same over-look, so specific theories within each perspective may differ to some degree. On the whole, however, theories within each perspective bear a distinct resemblance in their basic assumptions about what is important in groups and in the explanations and understandings they offer. The nine perspectives can be characterized in terms of how they explain group processes and out-comes; in terms of the types of inputs, processes, and outcomes they focus on; and in terms of the relative emphasis they place on input, process, and outcome variables.

The *functional perspective* is "a normative approach to describing and predicting group performance that focuses on the functions of inputs and/or processes" in groups (Chapter 2, this volume). It is characterized by the assumption that groups are goal oriented and that group performance in meeting goals varies and can be evaluated. Functional researchers attempt to identify the group behaviors and activities that promote and detract from effective performance. Inputs that influence group functions include the nature of the group's task, the internal structure of the group, group cohesiveness, group composition, and the group's environment. In some theories, these inputs are contingencies that influence the specific functions required for group effectiveness, whereas in others, the inputs determine which functions or activities the group enacts. Outputs consid-ered in functional theories include group effectiveness as measured by pro-ductivity, efficiency, and quality; leadership effectiveness; and satisfaction with the group outcomes. The functional perspective accords equal prior-ity to all terms in the input-process-output chain. This is understandable, because the input-process-output formulation was first applied in func-tional research.

The functional perspective has produced a greater number of studies than any other. Theories and lines of research developed within this perspective include the functional theory of group decision making (Gouran & Hirokawa, 1996), social combination models of group decision making (Davis, 1973), groupthink (Janis, 1982), collective information processing (Stasser & Titus, 1985), and group boundary spanning (Ancona & Caldwell, 1992).

The *psychodynamic perspective* is an approach to the study of groups that focuses on the relationship between the emotional, nonconscious processes and the conscious, rational processes of interpersonal interaction. It assumes that the existence of any group can be explained by the human instinct to combine spontaneously with others as a means to ensure species survival through protection and procreation. These primitive instincts are driven by emotions, and the resulting emotional dynamics remain part of all human social interaction. Key inputs for this perspective are the history of the group and its members, particularly unresolved problems or projects. Important processes include: leader-member dynamics revolving around dependence, independence, interdependence, and counterdependence; member attempts to position themselves in the group to address problems or needs; the development of group fantasies; and group orientations such as fight, flight, and engagement behaviors. As these processes suggest, the affective and emotional side of groups is a main focus of the psychodynamic perspective. Meaningful outcomes for psychodynamic theories include member and group growth and development and satisfaction of member and group needs. Psychodynamic theories tend to emphasize process and outcomes and place inputs in a secondary position. Given the multitude of factors that can shape group dynamics, these theories tend to work backward from process and outcomes to inputs, deducing which inputs are important from analysis of group processes and their link to outcomes.

Research in this perspective can be traced back to the writings of Freud (1920) and his followers. Bales (Bales & Cohen, 1979) incorporated psychodynamic elements, particularly the concept of group fantasy, into a functional theory of groups, culminating in the development of SYMLOG (Systematic Multilevel Observation of Groups) system and theory. Research using SYMLOG continues to flourish. Building on Bales's work, Bormann (1996) developed another type of fantasy theme analysis that emphasized the role of symbolism and rhetorical processes in the constitution of groups. Bion's (1961) *Experiences in Groups and Other Papers* proved to be another watershed work in this area, outlining a dynamic analysis of group orientations in terms of fight-flight behavior and engagement with core issues. A large group of scholars built on this work, combining Bion's insights with those of the later Freudians.

The *social identity perspective* explains groups in terms of members' sense of the social groups to which they belong, their identification with these groups, the social identity they construct based on this identification, and the dynamics between ingroups and outgroups driven by social identity.

The primary focus of social identity theory is the relations between different social groups, but it has also proven useful for understanding within-group dynamics. Important inputs for social identity theory include the structure of the surrounding society, culture, member characteristics, and cues that make group versus individual identity salient. Key processes include self-categorization, depersonalization, inclusion/exclusion, social influence, stereotyping, and intergroup conflict. Relevant outputs for social identity theory include member self-concept, group cohesiveness, loyalty, turnover, conformity, and social loafing.

Social identity theory has generated a large body of research focused on individual processes such as prejudice and social judgment as shaped by large social categories, such as gender, racial groups, and nations. Most social identity research focuses on intergroup relations, and it has important implications for understanding small groups. Social identity scholars have investigated social identity processes involved in deindividuation (Reicher, Spears, & Postmes, 1995), group cohesion (Abrams, Marques, Bown, & Henson, 2000), social influence (Turner, 1991), leadership (Hogg, Hains, & Mason, 1998), decision making (Hogg, 1996), and computer-mediated communication (Spears & Lea, 1994).

The *conflict-power-status perspective* explains groups in terms of the dynamics of power, status, resources, and social relationships and the group structures associated with these processes. Theories in this perspective generally assume there are inequalities among members in terms of resources, status, and power and focus on how these inequalities are generated and reproduced and how they influence group processes and outcomes. Influence, conflict management, negotiation, consensus building, and distribution of resources are important processes studied by the theories within this perspective. Important inputs include status outside the group, resources, existing status and power structures in the group, and the type of interdependence among members. Key outputs include distribution of valued resources among members, realization of members' interests, group performance, member satisfaction, and changes in status and resource control. Input and process are the two elements most emphasized by theories in this perspective. Inputs determine members' initial positions (e.g., their initial status, their tendency to compete versus cooperate) and influence group processes. Group processes often have their own dynamics and determine outcomes, which may include changes in the input structures.

A variety of theories and research streams in political science, social psychology, and sociology exemplify the conflict-power-status perspective, including social exchange theory (Thibaut & Kelley, 1959), social dilemma research (Komorita & Parks, 1995; Ostrom, 1990), expectation states theory (Berger, Wagner, & Zelditch, 1992; Knottnerus, 1997), and power dependence theory (Emerson, 1962). These theories focus on phenomena such as mixed-motive situations, coalitions, conflict management, and the impact of diversity. In Chapter 5 of this volume, Lovaglia, Mannix, Samuelson, Sell, and Wilson advance a model of institutional rules as a possible route to integrating the work within this broad perspective.

The symbolic-interpretive perspective focuses on the social construction of groups and offers explanations based on the meaning groups have for their members. Social interaction, language, symbols, and individual and collective interpretative schemes are common elements in symbolic-interpretive theories. These theories posit that processes such as fantasy chaining, structuration, dialectics, and sense making underlie the creation, growth, maintenance, and demise of groups. They argue that such processes frame and shape other group phenomena, including work, conflict, power and status dynamics, and stability and change. Inputs are viewed primarily as conditions or stimuli for symbolic and interpretive processes and are thus accorded less attention in these theories than processes. Outcomes in these theories include some directly related to symbolic-interpretive processes, such as a common vision, group identity, internal group structures, and group boundaries, as well as effectiveness, group cohesion, and member satisfaction. These latter outcomes are mediated by the former; for example, the cohesiveness of the group depends on its developing a coherent identity and vision.

Theories subsumed under the symbolic-interpretive perspective include symbolic convergence theory (Bormann, 1996), dialectical theory of groups (Smith & Berg, 1987), the bona fide group perspective (Putnam & Stohl, 1996), and structuration theory (Poole, Seibold, & McPhee, 1996). Symbolic-interpretive studies have focused on group decision-making, leader-member relations (e.g., Bennis & Shepard, 1975), the social construction of "meetings" (Schwartzman, 1989), and groups as communities (Adelman & Frey, 1997).

The *feminist perspective* challenges traditional approaches to studying groups by investigating and theorizing how power and privilege are enacted through interactions that favor one gender over another. The theories within this broad perspective trace group dynamics and outcomes to differences in male and female motivations in social situations, their views of groups, and their different life experiences. There is an assumption that typical social structures and conditions are tilted toward male standpoints and privilege them over female views, although participants may be unaware that this is the case. The result is a tendency among both researchers and groups to emphasize rational, task-focused concerns over relationships and community. The most important input for this perspective is the gender composition of the group. Some studies focus on the proportions of men and women in a group—of whatever size—as in notions about a "tipping point" beyond which the group culture changes. Others pay attention to specific numbers of men and women in the group, as in concerns with "token" or single representatives of one sex or the other. Some mainly contrast all-male with all-female groups. All these formulations use a feminist perspective to examine variations in how roles and statuses get distributed, what kind of group "culture" develops and how that development comes about, and how different aspects of group process play out (e.g., how group members interact with one another to carry out group work) in groups of different gender composition. Most feminist scholars are concerned not only with explaining how gender impacts groups but also with the elimination of relations of domination in all groups. It is important, these scholars say, to give voice to all points of view in groups without privileging any. This can be accomplished only by a redefinition of group interaction that emphasizes surfacing and acknowledging different points of view, without insisting that they be compromised. This quest for a different way of working in groups has suggested novel structures and processes that can be applied in group settings.

Scholars from a variety of disciplines have conducted research on groups informed by the feminist perspective. Research has focused on topics such as gender and competitive and cooperative behavior in groups (Walters, Stuhlmacher, & Meyer, 1998), gender composition effects (Wood & Rhodes, 1992), gender differences in the use of computer-mediated communication systems (Gopal, Miranda, Robichaux, & Bostrom, 1997), and group performance as a function of gender (Bowers, Pharmer, & Salas, 2000). Feminist researchers have also discussed in some depth the methods appropriate for conducting feminist studies of groups.

The *social network perspective* considers groups as interlinked structures embedded in larger social networks. Groups, their properties, and their processes are conceptualized in terms of patterns of relationships among members. Important input variables for the network perspective include member attributes, properties of preexisting networks such as density, centralization, and structural holes; and resource distributions and interdependencies. Processes within networks include affiliation, exchange, influence, information flow, diffusion, and reticulation of the network. Key outcomes include task effectiveness and efficiency, cohesiveness, attitude and belief convergence, and change in the network. In the social network perspective, groups are treated not as free-standing entities but rather as part of larger networks in which they relate to other groups and individuals. As such, groups are subject to effects depending on their position in the larger social network. The network perspective offers a clear model regarding how patterns of relations between members and attributes and patterns of relationships among members affect functioning at the group level. The network perspective accords inputs—most important, network structure and properties—the most significant place. Processes are also important, although they tend to be secondary to the structures within which they occur.

Research has focused on the effects of communication networks on group performance (Bavelas, 1950; Cummings & Cross, 2003), factors influencing centralization in group networks (Argote, Turner, & Fichman, 1989), and how ties external to a group influence group performance (Hansen, 1999). A number of researchers are also focusing on how multiple networks within groups relate to each other, for instance, how networks of roles relate to task networks (Arrow, McGrath, & Berdahl, 2000).

The *temporal perspective* explains groups in terms of how they change or develop over time. Some theories in this perspective focus on development, assuming that there is a direction to the group's change—that is, that the group progresses toward a definite goal or end state—whereas others focus on change per se without assuming any particular direction or pattern. Time is a hallmark of the theories in this perspective. These theories view time variously: as a context, a resource, a mediator of other processes, and a moderator of other processes. Time is context when used as a metric for other processes, which are the central focus. For example, studies of group development focus on substantive changes in groups, using time as part of the context in which these changes occur. Time is also viewed as a resource that groups work with, distributing time to tasks and speeding up work when time is short. When time is a mediator, time itself becomes a variable in the theory, as in studies of punctuated equilibrium in groups, which posit reorganization of the group at a mid-point transition. Time is a moderator when it interacts with other variables, for example, in studies that propose that effects of the communication medium differ in new and established groups. The theories in this perspective emphasize process over inputs and outputs. Inputs function primarily as contingencies that influence how the process unfolds. Outputs are products of the process and, in some cases, also feedback to influence it.

A broad array of theories and research is subsumed under the temporal perspective. The perspective includes studies of group development (Bennis & Shepard, 1975; Wheelan, 1994), decision development (Poole & Baldwin, 1996), social entrainment (McGrath & Kelly, 1986), socialization (Moreland & Levine, 1982), punctuated equilibrium (Gersick, 1988), and complexity models of groups (Arrow et al., 2000).

The *evolutionary perspective* posits that group structure and interaction reflect evolutionary forces that have shaped human social behaviors over tens of thousands of years. Theorists within this perspective argue that human preferences for certain types of groups and general norms that govern group behavior (e.g., cooperation) have evolved since the advent of humankind through a process of variation, selection, and retention (natural selection). This requires them to extend evolutionary theory into the realm of group behavior. Social evolutionary theories differ in how they conceptualize groups. Some theorists treat groups simply as aggregates of individuals and view group behavior primarily at the level of the individual; in this view, group behavior is a product of individual behavior that scales up to the group level (Palmer, Fredrickson, & Tilley, 1997). Others view groups as meaningful entities that have evolved along with cultures through group selection at the cultural level, and they focus on cultural variation in group behavior (Boyd & Richerson, 1985). A few theorists posit that the small group is a basic unit through which human society has evolved (Caporael, 1997; Dunbar, 1993). The evolutionary perspective regards inputs as paramount: People (or in some cases the cultures in which people live) have inherent tendencies toward group behavior that have evolved because they are functional. Processes and outcomes are influenced by these tendencies. The evolutionary perspective on groups is currently evolving (so to speak). Only recently have psychologists and biologists turned their attention to groups and away from populations of individuals. Studies on the evolutionary basis of prosocial behavior (Wilson & Sober, 1994), cooperation and its spread through collectives (Axelrod, 1984), and egalitarianism in groups (Boehm, 2000) exemplify work in this area. A particularly interesting hypothesis is that social evolution has resulted in several archetypal groups, each with a characteristic size and function (Caporael, 1997; Dunbar, 1993).

Key Findings

In addition to describing the major theories and theoretical variants within each perspective, each of the nine perspective chapters summarizes key findings of research within the perspective. To provide some consistency across chapters, authors were asked to address seven key questions regarding findings, insofar as their perspective allowed them to do so:

1. What facets of group composition (group size, members' abilities, values, traits, demographics) affect the group's interaction and performance?

2. How do the group's projects (what it is trying to do—its tasks, goals, intentions)—affect its interaction and performance?

3. How are groups structured (e.g., norms, roles, networks), what tools and technologies do they have access to, and how do those structures and technologies affect group interaction and performance?

4. What kinds of group interaction processes do the group carry out (e.g., communication, information processing, conflict management, coordination of action), and how do these functions affect other factors and performance?

5. What results from group action (e.g., performance evaluation, impacts on group, impacts on members, assessment of consequences)?

6. How does the group change over time (e.g., formation, development, dissolution)?

7. How does the group's ecology, including its physical, social, organizational, and technical environment, as well as intergroup relations, affect its interaction and performance?

Several of the chapters explicitly address the seven questions, and each chapter has a table summarizing findings relevant to the questions.

The seven questions have a functional bias: They are organized around the input-process-output framework that underlies the functional model and focuses on "moves" and effects in interactions. Perspectives significantly different from the functional perspective may not address some of these questions, and on the other hand, they may focus on questions not in this list. Hence, several chapters do not directly address the seven questions and may raise additional issues not included in the original list. The questions addressed by a perspective tell us much about the priorities and direction of the perspective.

Some General Observations

When this project commenced, we believed that we would be able to identify several interdisciplinary perspectives on small groups, and we have been gratified to find nine. Common themes across disciplines may reflect the increasingly cosmopolitan nature of the field, or they may be a product of general intellectual trends that influence several fields. It is to be hoped that crystallizing the perspectives can stimulate theory development and more research, both within and across disciplines.

In the concluding chapter of this book, Fulk and McGrath identify and discuss common themes or "touchstones" running through the perspectives. Here, we will advance several of our own observations. First, the same theories and scholars are often claimed by more than one perspective. For example, Robert F. Bales is mentioned in connection with the psychodynamic, functional, and time-change-development perspectives. This reflects a long career that generated many diverse studies and much in-depth theoretical thinking. It also highlights the fact that individual theories and models, such as Bales's SYMLOG framework, may combine aspects of two or more perspectives. Thinking in terms of theoretical perspectives directs our attention away from theories developed by individuals or small groups of scholars and toward broader theories that transcend individual scholars. It invites synthesis and awareness of basic assumptions and of different ways of viewing groups.

The same topics are often studied by more than one perspective. For example, conflict has been studied by scholars working in the functionalist perspective (which emphasizes consensus and resolution of conflict) and by scholars working in the conflict-power-status perspective (which emphasizes how conflict and competition develop group structures and distribute rewards and resources among members). Obviously, the different perspectives illuminate different facets of the same phenomena, and this is valuable for more than the diverse understandings it offers. Trying to make sense of such disparate accounts of the same thing can direct our attention to previously overlooked elements. For instance, the development of status hierarchies (emphasized by the conflict-power-status perspective) serves to stabilize the group and to give members a common reference point (the consensus emphasized by the functional perspective). This highlights the functional nature of conflict, something that tends to be overlooked by functional researchers.

Some theoretical perspectives are more consolidated—in the sense that they have developed a coherent theoretical center that unifies theories and research in the area—than others. The functional, social identity, and psychodynamic perspectives enjoy a common explanatory scheme that is compact and easy to articulate. The time-change-development, symbolic-interpretive, and network perspectives seem to be evolving toward a common framework that can consolidate thinking in these areas. The conflict-power-status perspective is less coherent, although the theories within it clearly share a common focus. Consolidation of the three lines of work on conflict, power, and status, however, will take a major theoretical reformulation. The evolutionary and feminist perspectives are interesting in that they both have a common general perspective, but the theories and theorists within them are fundamentally divided on some central issues, such as the proper evolutionary unit or the appropriate stance of feminism vis-à-vis society as a whole. It will be interesting to see how these perspectives mature.

Well-consolidated perspectives are valuable because they offer a common reference point for theory development and for explanation. We can question and refine them, as in the debates over what constitutes a satisfactory functional explanation. However, less consolidated and looser perspectives are valuable because they are flexible and suggestive, offering scholars more alternatives than well-defined canonical explanatory schemes. Will the less consolidated perspectives eventually become tighter through successive refinement, through a blazing integrative insight, or through breaking them into clearer, more circumscribed perspectives? The progress of theory development in the social sciences suggests that they will do so, that the looser perspectives delineated here offer challenges for future generations of researchers.

However, there is also reason to suspect that less consolidated general perspectives such as evolutionary theory, which has been applied in quite different ways in various branches of biology, economics, and organization studies, will defy specification precisely because the aspects encompassed are extremely complex, variegated, and difficult to test. Taking a more focused look at these phenomena may move important aspects out of our field of vision, just as focusing a microscope moves us quickly past gross features that may be the key to understanding.

We can also differentiate the perspectives on three conceptual continua: whether they adopt an objective or social constructionist view of groups, whether they are primarily single or multilevel in approach, and their normative stance on groups.

Some theoretical perspectives treat the group as a natural entity. These theories approach the group as a freestanding phenomenon to be studied from the researcher's point of view and privilege the researcher's constructs and models of the group. Other theories, in contrast, place great emphasis on the social construction of groups and assume that the goal of group research is to understand these social constructions and the process by which they are created, sustained, and changed. Social constructionist theories take as their starting point the member's point of view, and theoretical constructs and models are built on the foundation of member constructs and models. The contrast between objectivist and social constructionist approaches has been discussed by Burrell and Morgan (1979) and represents a major divide in social scientific research in general between post-positivistic and interpretive/ critical approaches (e.g., Miller, 2002).

The functional, conflict-status-power, network, and socioevolutionary perspectives adopt an objectivist stance toward groups. They approach groups "from the outside" and give primacy to the researcher's concepts and models. In contrast, the psychodynamic, symbolic-interpretive, and feminist perspectives take a social constructionist stance. Although these perspectives advance powerful theories of group processes, they give primacy to the members' social construction of their groups. The starting point for analysis in these perspectives is always interpretation of members' meanings. The social identity and temporal perspectives offer a mixture of objective and constructionist positions. Theories within the temporal perspective vary: phase theories, complex adaptive systems theory, and theories of time as a resource take an objective approach, whereas social construction of time research and structurational perspectives incorporate social constructionist assumptions. Social identity theory is a unique combination of the two approaches in that it takes an objective approach to the study of the social construction of identity in group settings.

In terms of levels of analysis, most theories of groups have been single-level theories, focusing primarily on the group level and making indirect references to the individual level in terms of characteristics or motivations of members. In these theories, the individual level is underemphasized, and most of the action occurs at the group level. However, some theories study groups at multiple levels, considering the group as part of the larger organization or offering an explicit treatment of how individual and group levels interact through membership dynamics and role definition (e.g., Moreland & Levine, 1982).

The nine theoretical perspectives differ in the degree to which they explicitly incorporate multiple levels of analysis. Most theories within the functional, psychodynamic, conflict-status-power, symbolic-interpretive, and temporal perspectives are single-level theories. Although theories within these perspectives may refer to other social levels, as in functional boundary-spanning research (which concerns how the group deals with people and organizations outside the group) and group development studies (which often focus on individual needs as drivers of the development process), their primary focus is not on the relationship between levels but on the group itself. The network, evolutionary, social identity, and feminist perspectives, on the other hand, explicitly consider multiple levels of analysis. The network perspective explicitly looks at groups as patterns of relations among members or as part of larger social networks, whereas the evolutionary perspective sees groups as a basic unit of evolution operating within larger social organizations and populations. The social identity and feminist perspectives consider how large-scale social groups and categories are reconstructed within and influence small group dynamics.

Having made these gross distinctions, however, it is important to recognize that group research in general increasingly recognizes the role of multiple levels of analysis. Theories such as complex systems theory, structuration theory, individual socialization theory within the temporal perspective, and bona fide groups theory within the symbolic interpretive perspective, among others, attempt to expand those perspectives by considering multiple levels of analysis. In the future, we expect to see an increasing number of multi-level theories of groups.

A final distinction among the perspectives can be drawn by considering the degree to which they are premised on normative assumptions about groups. The study of groups is closely linked with the practice of working in groups, and as a result, some perspectives on groups are built around normative presumptions. These can be contrasted with perspectives focused solely on the descriptive study of groups.

The functional, feminist, psychodynamic, and social identity perspectives have clear normative bases. Functional theory is concerned with what makes groups effective. All notions of effectiveness are normative in that they define effectiveness with respect to a particular point of view, that of management or of the group's members, for example. The feminist perspective takes a critical approach to groups and seeks to uncover previously unacknowledged imbalances in power and privilege, under the implicit assumption that members of groups should be on equal footing. Psychodynamic theories presume that some dynamics are helpful (e.g., achieving beneficial interdependence) while others (e.g., scapegoating) are harmful. In the social identity perspective, there is an assumption that hostility and conflict between groups is counterproductive and should be reduced through unmasking and potentially correcting the underlying social dynamics. In all four perspectives, the values of the theorist as judge of effectiveness, critic of domination and prejudice, or analyst of productive/destructive group dynamics play a critical role in the nature of the theories advanced and the types of conclusions drawn.

The network and conflict-power-status perspectives exhibit less emphasis on normative considerations. They seek to describe groups in terms of networks and differentiation of members, without necessarily judging whether these are salutary or harmful. Although the values of a particular researcher may well reveal themselves in research within these perspectives, the perspectives themselves are relatively agnostic in terms of values.

The other three perspectives have normative implications, but the inherent influence of norms is less clear. In evolutionary theory, variations that promote survival are favored. In effect, survival and growth of the species is a value underlying evolutionary theory, but its status as a norm is unclear. Is survival a value or a factual outcome? In the temporal perspective, movement through a development sequence is often regarded as progress, in which later stages are judged to be advances over earlier ones. However, not all temporal theories make such assumptions. Some argue that temporal progressions follow cycles, and some do not posit developmental mileposts at all. Symbolic-interpretive theorists clearly identify positive and negative dynamics in many symbolic processes, but normative evaluation is not central to the theories within this perspective. Symbolic interpretive theorists vary widely in the normative frames they bring to their work and in the vigor with which they apply them.

Acknowledged or not, human values play a role in social scientific research. However, some theories lead with their values, others incorporate values less directly, and still others attempt to minimize the role of values. None of these approaches is inherently superior to any other, but it is important to understand the specific role values play in theories of groups.

This is only a partial look at the complex web of relations among the nine theoretical perspectives introduced in this volume. Chapter 11 explores five more touchstones on which the theories can be compared in greater depth than this chapter has allowed.

Conclusion

Interdisciplinary linkages cannot be created top down. They will grow best from serious and intensive interaction among group scholars from many fields. This should facilitate the breakdown of barriers imposed by the jargon that has developed around field-centric studies, the methodologies favored by specific disciplines, and the out-group biases honed by reinforcing the values of one discipline through implicit or explicit criticisms of others. Although these barriers retard diffusion of ideas across disciplines, they also reflect constructive and positive development within disciplines that have had to address the challenges posed by their particular history and context. Gradual growth of an interdisciplinary field is the best way to ensure that the positive features of each discipline are maintained while arbitrary and incidental barriers are dissolved. If researchers scattered across multiple fields could all link together to form an interdisciplinary field of group research, it would not only give voice to an important research area but also help to nurture and vitalize research in the various disciplines (Poole, 1994). We hope that this book will provide the foundation of a new phase for group theory and research.

Notes

1. We gratefully acknowledge support for this project from the National Science Foundation (SES-9986562, Social Psychology and Decision, Risk & Management Sciences Program); the George Bush School of Government and Public Service, the Vice President for Research, and the Departments of Communication, Psychology, and Sociology at Texas A&M University; the Weatherhead School of Management at Case Western Reserve University; the Rockefeller College of Public Affairs and Policy at SUNY-Albany; the Department of Psychology at the University of Pittsburgh; and the Nag's Head Conference Center.

2. The initial planning team for this effort consisted of Joe McGrath, Dick Moreland, Scott Poole, and John Rohrbaugh. An expanded planning group included the original four members with the addition of Deborah Ancona, Janet Fulk, Charles Hermann, Poppy McLeod, Rick Kettner-Polley, and Cecilia Ridgeway. Sandy Schuman was facilitator for the meeting of this group in Cleveland, Ohio, in the Fall 2000. This group identified additional scholars to represent the seven perspectives defined during the planning effort, and they convened at the Nag's Head Conference Center in January 2001. The scholars added to the expanded planning group for the Nag's Head meeting included Dominic Abrams, Holly Arrow, Linnda Caporael, Larry Frey, Andrea Hollingshead, Michael Hogg, Bibb Latane, and David Wilson. The group of scholars involved in this project has continued to evolve.

3. A special double issue of *Small Group Research* (Hollingshead & Poole, 2004) was devoted to this project. The articles in that special issue were shorter and focused on theory. Seven of the nine perspectives were reviewed in that special issue: functional, conflict, temporal, psychodynamic, symbolic-interpretive, social identity, and network.

References

Abrams, D., Marques, J. M., Bown, N. J., & Henson, M. (2000). Pro-norm and anti-norm deviance within in-groups and out-groups. *Journal of Personality and Social Psychology, 78,* 906–912.

Adelman, M. B., & Frey, L. R. (1997). *The fragile community: Living together with AIDS.* Mahwah, NJ: Lawrence Erlbaum.

Ancona, D. G., & Caldwell, D. F. (1992). Bridging the boundary—external activity and performance in organizational teams. *Administrative Science Quarterly, 37,* 634–665.

Argote, L., Turner, M. E., & Fichman, M. (1989). To centralize or not to centralize: The effects of uncertainty and threat on group structure and performance. *Organizational Behavior and Human Decision Processes, 43,* 58–74.

Arrow, H., McGrath, J. E., & Berdahl, J. L. (2000). *Small groups as complex systems: Formation, coordination, development, and adaptation.* Thousand Oaks, CA: Sage.

Axelrod, R. (1984). *The evolution of cooperation.* New York: Basic Books.

Bales, R. F., & Cohen, S. P. (1979). *SYMLOG: A system for multiple level observation of groups.* New York: Free Press.

Bavelas, A. (1950). Communication patterns in task-oriented groups. *Journal of the Acoustical Society of America, 22,* 723–730.

Bennis, W. G., & Shepard, H. A. (1975). A theory of group development. In G. S. Gibbard, J. J. Hartman, & R. D. Mann (Eds.), *Analysis of groups: Contributions to theory, research, and practice* (pp. 127–153). San Francisco: Jossey-Bass.

Berger, J., Wagner, D. G., & Zelditch, M., Jr. (1992). A working strategy for constructing theories: State organizing processes. In G. Ritzer (Ed.), *Metatheorizing: Key issues in sociological theory* (Vol. 6, pp. 107–23). Newbury Park, CA: Sage.

Bion, W. R. (1961). *Experiences in groups and other papers.* New York: Basic Books.

Boehm, C. (2000). *Hierarchy in the forest: The evolution of egalitarian behavior.* Cambridge, MA: Harvard University Press.

Bormann, E. G. (1996). Symbolic convergence theory and communication in group decision making. In R. Y. Hirokawa & M. S. Poole (Eds.), *Communication and group decision making* (2nd ed., pp. 81–113). Thousand Oaks, CA: Sage.

Bowers, C. A., Pharmer, J. A., & Salas, E. (2000). When member homogeneity is needed in work teams: A meta-analysis. *Small Group Research, 31,* 305–327.

Boyd, R., & Richerson, P. J. (1985). *Culture and the evolutionary process.* Chicago: University of Chicago Press.

Burrell, G., & Morgan, G. (1979). *Sociological paradigms and organisational analysis: Elements of the sociology of corporate life.* London: Heinemann.

Caporael, L. R. (1997). The evolution of truly social cognition: The core configurations model. *Personality and Social Psychology Review, 1,* 276–298.

Cummings, J. N., & Cross, R. (2003). Structural properties of work groups and their consequences for performance. *Social Networks, 25,* 197–210.

Davis, J. H. (1973). Group decision and social interaction: A theory of social decision schemes. *Psychological Review, 80,* 97–125.

Dunbar, R. I. M. (1993). Coevolution of neocortical size, group size, and language in humans. *Behavioral and Brain Sciences, 16,* 681–735.

Emerson, R. M. (1962). Power-dependence relations. *American Sociological Review, 27,* 31–41.

Freud, S. (1920). *Group psychology and the analysis of the ego* (J. Strachey, Trans.). New York: Boni & Liveright.

Gersick, C. J. G. (1988). Time and transition in work teams: Toward a new model of group development. *Academy of Management Journal, 31*, 9–41.

Gopal, A., Miranda, S. M., Robichaux, B. P., & Bostrom, R. P. (1997). Leveraging diversity with information technology: Gender, attitude, and intervening influences in the use of group support systems. *Small Group Research, 28*, 29–71.

Gouran, D. S., & Hirokawa, R. Y. (1996). Functional theory and communication in decision-making and problem-solving groups: An expanded view. In R. Y. Hirokawa & M. S. Poole (Eds.), *Communication and group decision-making* (2nd ed., pp. 55–80). Thousand Oaks, CA: Sage.

Guralnik, D. B. (Ed.). (1980). *Webster's new world dictionary of the American language* (2nd ed.). New York: Simon & Schuster.

Hansen, M. T. (1999). The search-transfer problem: The role of weak ties in sharing knowledge across organization subunits. *Administrative Science Quarterly, 44*, 82–111.

Hogg, M. A. (1996). Social identity, self-categorization, and the small group. In E. H. Witte & J. H. Davis (Eds.), *Understanding group behavior: Vol. 2. Small group processes and interpersonal relations* (pp. 227–253). Mahwah, NJ: Lawrence Erlbaum.

Hogg, M. A., Hains, S. C., & Mason, I. (1998). Identification and leadership in small groups: Salience, frame of reference, and leader stereotypicality effects on leader evaluations. *Journal of Personality and Social Psychology, 75*, 1248–1263.

Hollingshead, A. B., & Poole, M. S. (Eds.). (2004). Interdisciplinary perspectives on groups [Special issues]. *Small Group Research, 35*(1, 3).

Janis, I. L. (1982). *Groupthink: Psychological studies of policy decisions* (2nd ed.). Boston: Houghton-Mifflin.

Knottnerus, J. D. (1997). Social structural analysis and status generalization: The contributions of potential of expectation states theory. In J. Szmatka, J. Skvoretz, & J. Berger (Eds.), *Status, network, and structure: Theory development in group processes* (pp. 119–136). Stanford, CA: Stanford University Press.

Komorita, S. S., & Parks, C. D. (1995). Interpersonal relations: Mixed-motive interaction. In *Annual review of psychology* (pp. 183–207). Stanford, CA: Annual Reviews.

McGrath, J. E., & Kelly, J. R. (1986). *Time and human interaction: Toward a social psychology of time.* New York: Guilford.

Miller, K. (2002). *Communication theories: Perspectives, processes, and contexts.* Boston: McGraw-Hill.

Moreland, R. L., & Levine, J. M. (1982). Socialization in small groups: Temporal changes in individual-group relations. In L. Berkowitz (Ed.), *Advances in experimental social psychology* (Vol. 15, pp. 137–192). New York: Academic Press.

Ostrom, E. (1990). *Governing the commons: The evolution of institutions for collective actions.* New York: Cambridge University Press.

Palmer, C. T. , Fredrickson, B. E., & Tilley, C. F. (1997). Categories and gatherings: Group selection and the mythology of cultural anthropology. *Evolution and Human Behavior, 18*, 291–308.

Poole, M. S. (1994). Breaking the isolation of small group research. *Communication Studies, 45,* 20–29.

Poole, M. S., & Baldwin, C. L. (1996). Developmental processes in group decision-making. In R. Y. Hirokawa & M. S. Poole (Eds.), *Communication and group decision-making* (2nd ed., pp. 215–241). Thousand Oaks, CA: Sage.

Poole, M. S., Seibold, D. R., & McPhee, R. D. (1996). The structuration of group decisions. In R. Y. Hirokawa & M. S. Poole (Eds.), *Communication and group decision making* (2nd ed., pp. 114–146). Thousand Oaks, CA: Sage.

Putnam, L. L., & Stohl, C. (1996). Bona fide groups: An alternative perspective for communication and small group decision making. In R. Y. Hirokawa & M. S. Poole (Eds.), *Communication and group decision making* (2nd ed., pp. 179–214). Thousand Oaks, CA: Sage.

Reicher, S. D., Spears, R., & Postmes, T. (1995). A social identity model of deindividuation phenomena. *European Journal of Social Psychology, 6,* 161–198.

Schwartzman, H. B. (1989). *The meeting: Gatherings in organizations and communities.* New York: Plenum.

Smith, K. K., & Berg, D. N. (1987). *Paradoxes of group life: Understanding conflict, paralysis, and movement in group dynamics.* San Francisco: Jossey-Bass.

Spears, R., & Lea, M. (1994). Panacea or panopticon? The hidden power in computer-mediated communication. *Communication Research, 21,* 427–459.

Stasser, G., & Titus, W. (1985). Pooling of unshared information in group decision making: Biased information sampling during discussion. *Journal of Personality and Social Psychology, 48,* 1467–1478.

Thibaut, J. W., & Kelley, H. H. (1959). *The social psychology of groups.* New York: John Wiley.

Turner, J.C. (1991). *Social influence.* Buckingham, UK: Open University Press.

Walters, A. E., Stuhlmacher, A. F., & Meyer, L. L. (1998). Gender and negotiator competitiveness: A meta-analysis. *Organizational Behavior and Human Decision Processes, 76,* 1–29.

Wheelan, S. (1994). *Group processes: A developmental perspective.* Boston: Allyn & Bacon.

Wilson, D. S., & Sober, E. (1994). Re-introducing group selection to the human behavioral sciences. *Behavioral and Brain Sciences, 17,* 585–654.

Wood, W., & Rhodes, N. (1992). Sex differences in interaction style in task groups. In C. L. Ridgeway (Ed.), *Gender, interaction, and inequality* (pp. 97–121). New York: Springer-Verlag.

2

A Look at Groups From the Functional Perspective

Andrea B. Hollingshead,
Gwen M. Wittenbaum, Paul B. Paulus,
Randy Y. Hirokawa, Deborah G. Ancona,
Randall S. Peterson, Karen A. Jehn, and Kay Yoon

Abstract

This chapter discusses theory and research on small groups from the functional perspective. We define, present the underlying theoretical assumptions of, and review seven representative areas of research from the functional perspective. The seven areas include group decision-making, social combination approach, groupthink, collective information sharing, group brainstorming, conflict management, and an external view of groups. Our review of research from the functional perspective also covers how group composition, projects, structures, and ecology affect group interactions and outcomes. The functional perspective is strong in predicting and explaining task-oriented group performance but is more limited in predicting and explaining the

Authors' Note: We would like to thank J. Richard Hackman for his helpful and insightful comments.

behavior of groups with socioemotional or multiple goals outside normative boundaries. We present other debates and challenges to the functional perspective and suggest future research directions.

M ost people who have worked in groups can say that some of their groups functioned better than others. They can identify which groups created outstanding products, better than expected initially, and which groups performed much worse than expected, given group members' individual skills and abilities. They can also distinguish between groups that worked well together and those that did not (Hackman, 1990). Scholars who study groups from the functional perspective aim to understand the factors and processes that help and hurt the quality of group performance.[1]

The Functional Perspective Defined

Which leadership styles facilitate good group decision-making? What group size is ideal for creative idea generation? How does the manner in which team members communicate and manage conflict affect their productivity? The answers to these and other questions regarding group task performance lie at the heart of the functional perspective. The functional perspective is defined as a normative approach to describing and predicting group behavior and performance that focuses on the functions of inputs and/or processes.

Most theory and research pertaining to group performance effectiveness has used the lens of the functional perspective. Four core assumptions define the functional perspective: (1) groups are goal oriented; (2) group behavior and performance varies in quality and quantity and can be evaluated; (3) interaction processes have utility and can be regulated; (4) internal and external factors influence group behavior and performance via interaction. Each assumption is described below in more detail.

1. *Groups are goal oriented.* According to the functional perspective, groups have one or more goals. These goals may be social-emotional (e.g., to provide support to members), group oriented (e.g., to obtain resources for the group to continue), or task oriented (e.g., to produce a product, idea, or decision) (cf. Cartwright & Zander, 1968; McGrath, 1991). Much of the research from the functional perspective has focused on the effective

accomplishment of task-oriented goals. Task-oriented goals include production in the cognitive realm (reaching a good group decision, generating creative ideas, solving a problem, remembering information) or physical world (building widgets, performing a song). Although groups may hold other goals related to their task (e.g., to get along well, to maintain the prestige of the group, to keep meetings short), the functional perspective largely focuses on groups' ability to satisfy a primary group task goal.

2. Group behavior and performance varies and can be evaluated. The functional perspective assumes that group performance is evaluated by some standard. That standard could be how well the group reaches its goals, but it is often how effectively or efficiently the group performs a task-related goal. When group performance falls short of this normative standard, interventions are generated to help groups reach their potential. Most of these interventions involve tinkering with the interaction process and are described in the next section.

3. Interaction processes have utility and can be regulated. The functional perspective prescribes that certain interaction processes are more useful to groups for achieving their goals than others and that interaction processes can be controlled and regulated. Theories that fit into the functional perspective suggest that certain actions or activities are required of groups during their interaction for successful goal attainment. The functions of required actions or activities can be procedural or rhetorical and can include information processing, conflict management, or even the development of a group culture (Hirokawa & Poole, 1996). When the goal is task oriented, such as making a good decision, the requisite actions or activities are often based on a rational model (e.g., members should communicate and optimally weigh all task-relevant information) (Hirokawa, 1985).

To increase the likelihood that groups will meet their goals, functionalists often design interventions to control and regulate interaction, interventions that make the desired pattern of actions and activities during group interaction more likely. These interventions may include the development of procedural rules (such as brainstorming instructions), communication technologies (such as a feature that provides anonymity to members), or restructuring of the group's task (having groups rank-order alternatives rather than choose the best one).

4. Internal and external factors influence group performance via interaction. According to the functional perspective, factors emanating from within the group (e.g., member composition, group size) and external

Table 2.1   The Functional Perspective

Definition of perspective	A normative approach to describing and predicting group performance that focuses on the functions of inputs and/or processes
Key assumptions	<ul><li>Groups are goal oriented</li><li>Group performance is evaluated</li><li>Interaction processes have utility and can be regulated</li><li>Internal and external factors influence group performance via interaction</li></ul>
Types of groups	Task-performing groups
Key theories	Functional theory, groupthink, social decision scheme theory, collective information sampling theory, transactive memory, goal setting
Dominant research methodologies	Primarily laboratory experiments, with a few exceptions
Strengths	<ul><li>Ability to predict and explain group performance via static inputs and processes</li><li>Empirical base for the development of interventions to improve group performance</li></ul>
Weaknesses	<ul><li>Does not address groups that have a socioemotional purpose</li><li>Difficulty in defining and measuring "effective" performance</li><li>Task-performing groups may have goals other than effective performance</li><li>Cannot detect or explain nonlinear processes</li></ul>

circumstances (e.g., outside threat, time pressure) affect how the group performs. Thus, group performance is a causal outcome of these internal and external inputs. But that is not a simple, isomorphic translation. A given input can lead to many different outcomes; likewise, one outcome can be produced by many different inputs. Moreover, inputs may interact with each other to produce a group outcome. The input-output relation is mediated by processes that occur during group interaction (e.g., communication patterns, conflict management). These interaction processes influence group outcomes causally. Thus, the functional perspective assumes a sequential, causal string: Input factors influence interaction processes, which influence group performance outcomes. See Table 2.1.

Research Areas in the Functional Perspective

Functionalist thinking extends far back in the intellectual history of both psychology and sociology and remains influential in both fields today. William James, John Dewey, Robert Merton, and Talcott Parsons were among the early social scientists responsible for developing and advancing functionalist approaches for explaining and prescribing behavior in individuals and in society.

The functional perspective has been very influential and has guided much, if not most, of small group research. This body of research has explored many topics and has been conducted by researchers from many disciplines. In this section, we show how seven central areas that span topics in classic and contemporary group performance and decision-making group research have been approached from the functional perspective. These seven central areas include: the functional theory of group decision-making, the social combination approach to group decision-making, groupthink, collective information sharing, group brainstorming, conflict management, and an external view of groups.

These seven topics represent research from a variety of disciplines including communication, psychology, organizational behavior, political science, and sociology. They also reflect the areas of expertise of the coauthors. In each section, we provide a brief historical overview, show how that area encompasses the key assumptions of the functional perspective previously identified, and discuss several key findings in some detail. It is important to note that the seven topics described here are meant to be representative and are not an exhaustive set of topics that has been investigated through the functional perspective. For example, one topic that is glaringly missing is the functional perspective of leadership, one of the oldest and longest-standing lines of group research. See Bass (1990) for an excellent summary of this work and Hackman (2002) for a current take on it.

The Functional Theory of Group Decision-Making

The question of why some groups arrive at better decisions than others has long been of interest to group and organizational scholars in a variety of academic disciplines. Efforts to address this question have led to the widely held view that variations in the quality of group decisions can, in many cases, be attributed to the quality of interaction, or communication, that precedes choice making in the group (e.g., Collins & Guetzkow, 1964; Hackman & Morris, 1975; Hirokawa, 1982; Janis & Mann, 1977; McGrath, 1984; Roby & Lanzetta, 1958).

According to some scholars (e.g., Cragan & Wright, 1990; Griffin, 2000; Pavitt, 1994), one of the most influential theories accounting for the relation between communication and group decision-making effectiveness is the functional theory of group decision-making (Gouran & Hirokawa, 1983, 1986, 1996; Gouran, Hirokawa, Julian, & Leatham, 1993; Hirokawa, 1980a, 1980b, 1982, 1983, 1985, 1988; Hirokawa & Rost, 1992; Hirokawa & Scheerhorn, 1986). As the name implies, this theory models group decision-making, using the functional perspective. The core notion of the functional theory is that effective group decision-making is contingent on interactions contributing to the satisfaction of critical task requirements.

Over the years, the functional theory of group decision-making effectiveness has undergone change, with slight variations in the proposed critical functions necessary to reach an effective decision. In general, however, empirical tests of the functional theory have usually focused on the relations between group decision-making effectiveness (performance) and a group's ability to satisfy five requisite functions during its decision-making interaction (Hirokawa, 1999). The communication functions include:

1. Developing a thorough and accurate understanding of the problem. Given the information available to it, the group needs to arrive at an accurate (i.e., reasonable) understanding of (1) the nature of the problem, (2) the extent and seriousness of the problem, (3) the likely cause(s) of the problem, and (4) the possible consequences of not dealing effectively with the problem.

2. Achieving an appropriate understanding of the requirements for an acceptable choice. The group must recognize the specific standards that the choice must satisfy to be judged acceptable by evaluators of that decision.

3. Marshaling and, if necessary, developing a range of realistic and acceptable alternatives. The group must generate, or be aware of, a number of appropriate and feasible alternatives among which an acceptable choice is assumed to exist.

4. Assessing thoroughly and accurately the positive consequences associated with alternative choices. Given the information available to it, the group needs to be fully cognizant of the relative merits of all available choices.

5. Assessing thoroughly and accurately the negative consequences associated with alternative choices. Given the information available to it, the group needs to be fully cognizant of the relative disadvantages associated with each alternative.

Empirical tests have yielded general support for the functional theory of group decision-making effectiveness. However, comparisons of findings across studies indicate that group decision-making performance is inconsistently related to requisite functions. Methodological limitations notwithstanding, the cross-study variability of empirical support for the functional theory has raised the issue of whether contingency variables affect the performance of the five critical communication functions. The one contingency variable that has attracted most attention is the nature of the task. Hirokawa (1990) asserted that when the task is complex (e.g., having unclear goals or barriers to effective performance), a group would have a greater need for problem analysis, procedural orientation, and planning. In other words, finding solutions to simple problems does not require the kind of communicative interdependence necessitated by complex tasks.

A recent meta-analysis of empirical research testing the functional theory showed that group members' assessment of negative consequences of various alternative solutions was the most important communication function (Orlitzky & Hirokawa, 2001). This finding supports Janis's (1982) emphasis on the necessity of critical evaluators in a group. Arguments for the benefits of devil's advocacy and dialectical inquiry in small group decision-making have been in a similar vein (Valacich & Schwenk, 1995). However, recent data indicates that it can actually be hazardous to assign a devil's advocate in a group (Nemeth, Brown, & Rogers, 2001). Genuine diversity tends to bring out the best performance; staged diversity brings out a smug attitude of having discussed issues that can lead to worse outcomes than doing nothing. The effect of this communication function seems to be moderated by whether the task is equivocal. Assessment of negative consequences seems more important for equivocal tasks (i.e., multiple acceptable choices; nonobvious criteria; correct choice is difficult to establish) than for unequivocal tasks.

In sum, the functional theory predicts that the effects of communication functions on group decision quality are moderated by task features (e.g., how equivocal or complex the task). The influence of input variables (e.g., group composition) on communication functions and subsequent group performance depends largely on the nature of the group's task.

A Social Combination View of Group Decision-Making

The goals of the social combination approach are to predict or to explain how group members combine their individual preferences into a single group response for a given type of task. Baron, Kerr, and Miller (1992) made an important distinction between the social combination and social communication approaches to group decision-making. The social communication approach "assumes that the best way to analyze how a group reaches its decision is to listen to what the group members say to one another" (p. 93). The question of interest is who says what to whom in what situations with what effect. The functional theory of group decision-making previously described is an example of a social communication approach. In contrast, for the social combination approach, the basic unit of analysis is not a spoken thought or argument but rather the actual pre-meeting preferences of the group members (Baron et al., p. 94). The fundamental assumption is that group interaction may be modeled as a mapping process from members' preferences to a single collective decision.

The study of group task performance from the social combination approach demonstrates all of the assumptions of the functional perspective. Although the social combination approach has been used for predicting or describing how groups combine their individual preferences into a single group response for a given type of task, it could also be used for prescribing the best way to do that. The social combination approach assumes that groups are goal oriented and that their goal is to reach consensus on the best alternative. It also assumes that some group choices are better than others and that performance standards vary depending on properties of the group task. This approach also assumes that group discussion is the means by which group members combine their preferences into a single group response. It represents an input-process-output approach to studying group performance. (For discussions of the social decision scheme theory, formal methods, and applications to various group decision tasks, see Davis, 1973, 1980, and 1982.)

Social combination models, also called social decision schemes, formalize the processes by which a group maps a distribution of member preferences (e.g., the number of jurors who believe the defendant is guilty and not guilty before group discussion) into a collective group decision (the jury's verdict). Laughlin and Hollingshead (1995) postulated five ways that group members can resolve disagreement to reach consensus on a collective group response: voting, turn taking, demonstration, random selection, and generation of a new alternative.

Each of these ways of resolving disagreement can be represented probabilistically by a different social combination model. For example, voting can be represented as a majority-wins model. Turn taking can be represented as a proportionality process that assigns a probability to each alternative in proportion to the number of its advocates. Demonstration can be represented as a truth-wins or truth-supported-wins model (cf. Lorge & Solomon, 1955). Random assignment can be represented by a model that assigns equal probability to any alternative advocated by at least one group member. Different social combination models can be tested by comparing the actual proportion of groups selecting each alternative to the expected proportion for each social combination model. These analyses take into account the observed distributions of individual preferences across the set of alternatives.

One major finding discovered by researchers using the social combination approach is that groups rarely consider alternatives that are not advocated by at least one member prior to the group discussion (cf. Hollingshead, 1996b; Laughlin, 1999). Another is that group processes vary depending on the nature of the task (Davis, 1982; Laughlin, 1980). Cooperative group tasks may be ordered on a continuum anchored by intellective and judgmental tasks (Laughlin, 1980). Intellective tasks are problems or decisions for which there exists a demonstrably correct response within a verbal or quantitative conceptual system (Laughlin & Ellis, 1986). The objective for the group is to determine the correct answer; the criterion of success is whether the correct response is adopted. Truth-wins or truth-supported-wins models best predict the probability that the group will select the correct answer for intellective tasks. Judgmental tasks are evaluative, behavioral, or aesthetic judgments for which there is no demonstrably correct solution. For these tasks, the group objective is to achieve consensus; the criterion of group success is whether consensus is reached. Majority or plurality models best predict the probability of the group choice for judgmental tasks.

This approach has been applied to many group tasks including jury decisions (Davis, Kameda, Parks, Stasson, & Zimmerman, 1989), group memory performance (Hinsz, 1990), mathematical problems (Laughlin & Ellis, 1986), collective induction (Laughlin, 1988), and group decision-making (Stasser & Titus, 1985). This approach greatly influenced group research conducted by social psychologists in the 1970s, 1980s, and 1990s due to its great predictive and explanatory power.

Groupthink

The literature on groupthink is another example of research coming from the functional perspective on groups. Groupthink is a collective striving for unanimity that supersedes group members' efforts for thorough information processing (Janis, 1972, 1982). Because groupthink promotes quick compromises and avoidance of disagreements in group decision-making, this consensus-seeking tendency leads to an incomplete survey of alternative courses of action, poor information search, selective bias in processing information, and failure to evaluate alternatives realistically. Groupthink takes place when the group is highly cohesive, is insulated from other influences outside the group boundary, and is in highly stressful situations (e.g., competitive environment, time constraints).

Janis's (1972, 1982) groupthink model makes all of the assumptions implicit in functional research. First, it assumes groups are goal oriented. Each of the political and business decision-making groups Janis (e.g., 1982,

1985, 1989) studied had clear policy and public relations goals. For example, the Nixon White House wanted to contain any information about the Watergate break-in, and the Kennedy Executive Committee wanted to initiate a popular revolution to overthrow the Castro regime in Cuba.

Janis's (1989) work also provided a clear normative standard by which to judge groups and their interaction processes. Janis called this "vigilant decision making," which included (a) carefully surveying the range of objectives the groups wants to achieve, (b) carefully reviewing and formulating action alternatives, (c) rigorously searching for information bearing on the likely consequences of each alternative, (d) analyzing incoming information bearing on the likely consequences of each alternative, (e) analyzing incoming information dispassionately and thoughtfully, (f) reconsidering once-rejected action alternatives when new information comes to light, (g) confronting trade-offs that arise as a result of the conflicting costs and preferred options, and (h) making the effort to complete detailed contingency plans to be enacted should key assumptions underlying the preferred plan fail to hold. Specific advice for leaders includes accepting criticism and providing impartial leadership. Janis specifically argued that groups ought to be evaluated by this standard. He directly tested and confirmed this notion by comparing the number of vigilance aspects characterizing the group with an historical evaluation of its success (Herek, Janis, & Huth, 1987).

Third, Janis's groupthink work clearly implicates group process as the primary mechanism by which good and bad outcomes are reached. To illustrate this point, groupthink occurs when group cohesiveness and a provocative situational context work together such that the members like each other and want to draw social support from one another in the highly stressful situation. Groupthink teams place such a high priority on supporting each other emotionally that they choose not to challenge one another (i.e., concurrence seeking). This lack of rigorous information search leads to poor-quality information processing and a high probability that outcomes will not meet goals. In short, the group process of drive for consensus is the primary group process mechanism by which outcomes occur. (For a review of the groupthink literature and alternative explanations for the phenomenon, see the February/March 1998 issues of *Organizational Behavior and Human Decision Processes,* which take a retrospective look at groupthink theory and research over 25 years.)

Collective Information Sharing

In 1985, Stasser and Titus published the first paper that examined collective information sharing in groups. This study initiated research designed to understand how group members share information during discussion and how such information pooling affects group decisions. The discussion bias revealed by this research shows that decision-making groups tend to discuss shared information that is commonly known by all members more than unshared information that is known by a single member (see Stasser, 1999; Wittenbaum & Stasser, 1996, for reviews). Failure to discuss unshared information can affect the quality of group decisions when the information is distributed among members as a hidden profile (e.g., Stasser & Stewart, 1992). In a hidden profile distribution, information supporting a less desirable decision alternative is largely shared, whereas information supporting the optimal decision alternative is predominantly unshared. Thus, members must communicate their unshared information to discover the best option.

The study of collective information sharing has exemplified all of the assumptions of the functional perspective on groups. First, all groups studied in this tradition have been given the explicit goal of reaching a good group decision. In most cases, groups are led to believe that one of the decision alternatives is the best. For example, groups have been instructed to choose the one suspect among three who is guilty of murder (e.g., Stasser & Stewart, 1992), select the best candidate for a job or political position (e.g., Stasser & Titus, 1987), identify the correct diagnosis for hypothetical medical cases (e.g., Larson, Christensen, Abbott, & Franz, 1996), select the best company for investment (e.g., Hollingshead, 1996b), or choose the best drug to market (Kelly & Karau, 1999). In rare cases, and as a goal manipulation, researchers have instructed groups to select a preferred decision alternative, given that information was insufficient for identifying a correct solution (e.g., Stewart & Stasser, 1998). In all studies, groups were given a clear task goal to reach a decision that was either optimal or preferred.

Second, collective information sharing and subsequent group performance has been evaluated in comparison to a normative standard of achievement. A benefit of group decision-making, as compared to individual decision making, is that group members can make a more informed decision collectively by pooling their unique information. Thus, mentioning unshared information and emphasizing it during discussion (e.g., through repetition) is considered to be evidence of good performance. When members neglect unshared information in favor of shared information, they are viewed as not pooling information effectively. When information is distributed among members as a hidden profile, failure to disseminate unshared information can result in the group choosing a less desirable decision alternative. In this case, successful performance results when group members communicate their unshared information in sufficient quantities to identify and choose the best option (Winquist & Larson, 1998).

Third, much of the collective information-sharing research has attempted to uncover conditions that facilitate unshared information use and thus the discovery of the optimal option in a hidden profile. Various inputs that originate from within the group (e.g., leadership, member status, expertise) have been shown to influence information sharing. For example, leaders (Larson et al., 1996), high-status members (Wittenbaum, 2000), and experts (Stasser, Stewart, & Wittenbaum, 1995) communicate unshared information to a greater extent than nonleaders, low-status members, and non-experts. Some internal inputs (expertise, member acquaintance, task demonstrability) affect the quality of group decisions in a hidden profile because of the mediating role of information sharing. For example, when members know one another's expert roles (Stasser et al., 1995), are personally acquainted with one another (Gruenfeld, Mannix, Williams, & Neale, 1996), and think the task is solvable (Stasser & Stewart, 1992), they are more likely to discuss unshared information and thus discover the correct option in a hidden profile. One study showed that when groups have a norm to be critical, they are more likely to put a positive value on unshared information and thus correctly solve the hidden profile (Postmes, Spears, & Cihangir, 2001). Thus, both discussing and positively evaluating unshared information are critical processes that influence group decision quality.

In one of the few studies to examine the impact of external inputs on collective information sharing and decision making, Kelly and Karau (1999) found that the effect of members' initial preferences on their ability to solve a hidden profile depended on the amount of time pressure imposed on the group. This study illustrates that both internal (e.g., initial preferences) and external (e.g., time pressure) inputs, either independently or in combination, affect the quality of group decisions.

Group Brainstorming

The group brainstorming literature is concerned with the goals of generating as many ideas as possible. In fact, the procedures suggested by Osborn (1953) were designed to "liberate" groups to be highly productive. The brainstorming rules do lead to an increase in the number of ideas generated. However, contrary to Osborn's expectations, brainstorming groups were found to be less productive than similar-size sets of individuals (Diehl & Stroebe, 1987). Quality of ideas is not an explicit goal of brainstorming, but it is presumed that generation of a larger number of ideas will also lead to more good ideas. This is in fact the case, although the proportion of good ideas does not seem to change (Paulus, Larey, & Dzindolet, 2000). Interestingly, when groups are given a quality goal, this actually reduces productivity (Bartis, Szymanski, & Harkins, 1988).

One goal of groups may be satisfaction. Groups and teams seem to have positive perceptions of their productivity (Paulus, Larey, & Ortega, 1995). However, these positive perceptions are often inconsistent with the actual performance of groups (Paulus, Dzindolet, Poletes, & Camacho, 1993). In other words, groups may have an illusion of productivity.

A major concern in the brainstorming literature has been the evaluation of group performance or productivity relative to nominal groups (the total performance scores of a similar number of individuals performing alone). Face-to-face brainstorming groups perform worse than nominal groups (Paulus, 2000). When groups exchange ideas by means of writing or computer technology, groups may actually generate more ideas than comparable nominal groups (Pinsonneault, Barki, Gallupe, & Hoppen, 1999). Group size seems to be negatively correlated with idea generation in face-to-face groups (e.g., Mullen, Johnson, & Salas, 1991) and positively correlated with idea generation in computer groups (Valacich, Dennis, & Connolly, 1994).

Much of the literature on group brainstorming has been concerned with factors that inhibit or facilitate idea sharing in groups (Paulus, Dugosh, Dzindolet, Coskun, & Putman, in press). Among the reasons cited for this production loss are production blocking or interference, social loafing, and social anxiety (Diehl & Stroebe, 1987). Each of these factors may combine with others to produce low performance norms and a tendency to use low performers as a point of reference (Camacho & Paulus, 1995). However, if groups have trained facilitators who try to counteract some of the tendencies of groups, it may be possible for them to perform at the level of nominal groups (Kramer, Fleming, & Mannis, 2001).

Recent studies have been concerned with social and cognitive factors that can actually produce group synergy (higher performance than nominal groups). Presumably, if groups elicit competitive feelings and a concern with high levels of performance, upward comparison processes could occur (Paulus, Larey, Putman, Leggett, & Roland, 1996). In other words the groups will be motivated toward self-improvement. Exposure to productive models may be one way to achieve this aim (Kramer et al., 2001). Intergroup competition can also enhance performance of brainstorming groups (Coskun, 2000).

Several models have been developed to describe the cognitive processes that occur in brainstorming groups (Dugosh, Paulus, Roland, & Yang, 2000; Nijstad, Diehl, & Stroebe, in press; Paulus et al., in press). It is assumed that exposure to others' ideas will enhance the association processes conducive to ideational creativity. That is, discussing ideas with others should increase the number of ideas, the range of idea categories, and the quality of ideas

(Larey & Paulus, 1999). However, it is important that group members be able to process the ideas of others. For example, providing brief breaks throughout the brainstorming session to reflect on the shared ideas, structuring the idea-sharing process by focusing on one aspect of the problem at a time, and alternating individual and group brainstorming are some techniques that appear to be helpful (Paulus, in press). Idea sharing should be most helpful if the group members have knowledge sets that are complementary (Diehl & Stroebe, 1987). However, the emotional conflicts that may occur in diverse groups and difficulty in understanding one another's ideas may limit the benefits of cognitive diversity (Milliken, Bartel, & Kurtzberg, 2003).

Team Conflict Management

The discussion about the association between group conflict and outcomes has taken shape over nearly 50 years, dating back to Guetzkow and Gyr (1954). In this discussion, the experience of relationship or emotional conflict has long been associated with poor group performance (e.g., Deutsch, 1969). The experience of task conflict has often but not always been associated with improved group performance (e.g., Hoffman & Maier, 1961). (See Pruitt and Carnevale, 1993, for a review of this earlier research.)

Research on conflict in groups and teams is often based on social-psychological theory regarding group activity, member interaction, and social processes (e.g., communication, trust building). This perspective, however, often ignores the task environment and the focus on problem solving and task performance that the functional perspective takes into account in predicting group activity and outcomes. In fact, social psychology has moved away from anything "social" and into the realm of individual cognition, often ignoring the interaction processes of individuals in a group setting. This is also the direction one aspect of conflict management—negotiation research—has followed (with a few exceptions; see Weingart and Jehn, 2000, for a review).

Given the task performance and outcome evaluation focus of the functional perspective, much research and theorizing in the conflict arena have focused on organizational groups and teams. It is assumed that these work groups are goal oriented and that members, while also having individual goals (i.e., wages, satisfaction), have a common group goal. From a conflict-management perspective, social interaction inherently leads to conflict, even in common goal groups. There will be conflict over task distribution and resource allocation, differing viewpoints, and often interpersonal problems as well.

Three types of group conflict have been recognized and researched in the last decade in organizational settings: task conflict, relationship conflict, and process conflict (Jehn, 1995). Relationship conflict is defined as disagreement over personal issues not related to work. Relationship conflicts frequently reported are about social events, gossip, clothing preferences, political views, and hobbies (Jehn, 1997). These conflicts deplete energy and effort that could be expended toward task completion and consolidation around mutual goals. It has been shown that relationship conflict has negative effects and is responsible for outcomes such as increased turnover, high rates of absenteeism, decreased satisfaction, low levels of perceived performance, poor objective performance, and low commitment (Amason, 1996; Baron, 1991; Jehn, 1995; Jehn, Chadwick, & Thatcher, 1997).

Task conflict is defined as disagreement about work-related issues. Task conflict, which is focused on content-related issues, can enhance performance quality. For example, critical debate among members and open discussion regarding task issues increase group performance because members are more likely to offer and evaluate various solutions, thus reaching optimal decisions and outcomes (Cosier & Rose, 1977; Schweiger, Sandberg, & Rechner, 1989). However, conflict in any form can create an uncomfortable environment, decreasing individuals' motivation and satisfaction (Amason & Schweiger, 1994).

Process conflict refers to disagreement over delegation of duties and resources. Jehn (1997) delineates between task and process conflict based on findings of an ethnographic study of work groups. Process conflict is usually associated with the resource allocation and distribution of responsibilities within the group. These processes are normally tied to group members' compensation and can promote competition over limited or scarce resources. This is likely to result in tension within a group. Once the tension is increased, employees are likely to become less satisfied.

Process conflicts among members about logistical and delegation issues—how task accomplishment should proceed in the work unit, who is responsible for what, and how things should be delegated—have been less researched (Jehn, 1997). Jehn and Mannix (2001) found that to best understand the effects of process conflict, group processes must be examined over time. High-performing teams were found to have a conflict profile that included moderate process conflict during the early stage of group formation (i.e., arguments deciding who is best qualified to perform a specific task), low process conflict during the middle of group task performance while members focus on the task, and a slight increase in process conflict toward completion of the task as members again discuss roles and duties to efficiently and effectively finish the task (Jehn & Mannix, 2001).

A main input to group processes, especially conflict, is member demographics and the resulting diversity within the group. Because of negative categorization processes, members of demographically heterogeneous groups are likely to experience frustration, discomfort, hostility, and anxiety that can result in animosity and annoyance between individuals and, hence, relationship conflict is likely to emerge within the group (Tajfel & Turner, 1986). As salience of members' differences increases, polarization among members is likely to grow as well, which can result in more fights over non-task-related issues. Variety in knowledge and experiences can lead to disagreement among members about group tasks, and such disagreement is often linked to better decisions and group performance but not always to higher satisfaction (Jackson, 1992). This is consistent with the research on groupthink. One interesting finding regarding educational differences among members is the formation of hierarchy and status differentials within the group, which rather than improving group processes tends to cause resentment, loss of motivation, and lower performance (Jehn, Northcraft, & Neale, 1999).

The type of task the group performs, as well as the norms the group develops, moderates the relations between conflict and performance. If the group task is complex, nonroutine, and creative, a moderate level of task conflict is more effective in producing high-quality decisions than no task conflict. If the task is routine, has standard operating procedures, and is repetitive, low levels of task conflict are more effective for task completion (Jehn, 1995). If groups have norms that encourage task debates but discourage personal attacks, the group is more likely to be a high-functioning team with members more likely to be satisfied with the interaction and likely to remain in the group (Simons & Peterson, 2000).

Much of the past research and theorizing on conflict examines individual and group outcomes such as performance and satisfaction. Lacking is research connecting conflict management to creativity and innovation, a necessary output to examine in today's competitive, fast-changing environment in which new products, creative decisions, and integrative outcomes are necessary (De Dreu & West, 2001).

An External View of Groups

The external view of teams explores how the boundary activities that link the team to its external environment impact performance and how the external context in which a team resides influences the team's process and performance. This work fits squarely in the functionalist perspective in that its quest is to discover what makes teams more effective. Furthermore, the predictors of effectiveness include input factors (e.g., the context), and process dimensions (e.g., boundary activity), following the input-process-output model. The story of the evolution of the external view and its relation to the functionalist perspective follow.

Much of the work on the external view of teams has at its roots some of the original ideas presented by the seminal creators of the functional perspective. For example, George Homans (1950) posited both an internal and external system that enables the group to survive in its environment. He saw the environment as presenting some initial and subsequent conditions to which a team must adapt. Team behavior was not a one-time event but rather cycles of interaction between the team and its environment that could enter either positive or negative feedback cycles. One of Kurt Lewin's (1948) contributions to the external view was the prediction that a team's ability to adapt is related to the permeability of its boundaries and the nature of the interactions across those boundaries. These ideas are all based on some of the core assumptions of the functional perspective: an interest in team goals, a focus on team effectiveness, and the notion of interplay among inputs, process, and outputs. What differentiated these ideas was the focus on the external environment and cross-boundary processes.

One of the major predictions of this external view is that boundary activity is a key component of group process and one that plays a central role in predicting performance. In a study of 100 sales teams in the telecommunications industry, Gladstein (1984) showed that group process broke not into the traditional categories of task and maintenance behaviors (Philip & Dunphy, 1959) but rather into the categories of intragroup processes and boundary management. Thus, team members view the behaviors necessary to interact with the environment as separate and distinct from internal behaviors.

At this point, there is a fair amount of evidence that these boundary behaviors are related to the performance of teams (Ancona & Caldwell, 2000). Those studying innovation have focused on the transfer of technical information across team boundaries (Aldrich & Herker, 1977; Allen, 1984; Hansen, 1999; Katz, Tushman, & Allen, 1995). In general, these studies show that when the task is uncertain or when the outside information needed is complex, then boundary activity is positively related to performance (cf. Scott, 1997). Teams that are able to capitalize on diverse external networks have a greater learning capability than those that cannot leverage diversity (Reagans & Zuckerman, 2001).

Studies of consulting teams, product-development teams, and drug-development teams (Ancona, 1990; Ancona, Bresman, & Kaufer, 2002; Ancona & Caldwell, 1992) show it is not simply the amount of external communication that determines team performance, as information-processing theorists had posited (Thompson, 1967), but rather it is the nature of that interaction. More specifically, teams whose members engaged in ambassadorial activity (behaviors aimed up the organizational hierarchy to gain resources, convince others to support the team, and protect the team), task coordinator activity (behaviors aimed laterally throughout the organization to get feedback on product design and coordinate and negotiate with outside groups), and appropriate amounts of scouting activity (behaviors aimed within and outside the firm to scan the technological and market environment) were higher performers than those who remained isolated or engaged in other forms of activity.

The external view also emphasizes the role of inputs in shaping team process and performance. Inputs have included the physical environment, team composition, team structure, organizational structure, resources, rewards, and leadership (cf. Becker & Baloff, 1969; Hackman, 1987; Kiesler, 1978; Perrow, 1967; Sundstrom, 1999). Recent work on time and timing has also emphasized the temporal context of teams. Building on the work of McGrath and Rotchford (1983), it has been argued that temporal variables—pace, cycles, and rhythms—are key aspects of the environment that exert influence on teams. Using this temporal lens, the context is seen to play the role of external pacer, rhythm setter, creator of windows of opportunity, source of interrupts, and a key influence on the meaning of time (Ancona & Chong, 1996, 1999).

Answers to the Seven Questions

As described in the introductory chapter, a set of questions can be used as a means to compare and contrast the different theoretical perspectives. Here are the seven questions and the seven answers from the functional perspective. See Table 2.2 for a summary of major points.

What Facets of Group Composition Affect the Group's Interaction and Performance?

It is quite clear that group composition has a significant impact on group and team performance. Group size has a major impact on group interaction and performance on a variety of tasks (see Bonito & Hollingshead, 1997, for review). Larger group size can increase social loafing and interference/blocking and thereby diminish performance, but larger group size also increases the chance of a greater range of abilities. Equality of participation is inversely related to group size in face-to-face groups. However, there is

Table 2.2   Key Findings of Functional Perspective Research

Group composition	• Increased group size is negatively related to effective processes (e.g., social loafing and blocking) and equality of participation, and positively related to range of abilities • History among group members improves group performance • High-status group members participate more and are more influential in group discussions • Personality traits of group members affect group performance, contingent on task and organizational culture • The effect of demographic and characteristic diversity on performance is moderated by task • Group members' external connections are helpful to group performance
Group structure	• Technologies can enhance or constrain group processes and performance depending on the type of task. • Leadership, expert roles, and self-management influence patterns of interaction in groups. • Status, hierarchy, and power affect group interaction and performance. • Effects of network structure on group performance are moderated by group size and the type of task.
Group projects	The type of task determines interdependence, boundary activities with external environment, and cooperation/competition
Interaction	Group interaction serves information processing, analytical, procedural, goal-setting, rhetorical, conflict management/negotiation, controlling, and group maintenance functions
Group action/outcomes	• Outcomes of task-oriented groups include a product of some kind (decision, solution, etc.), rules of engagement, interpersonal relationships, and beliefs about the group and its members • Group discussion results in biases in social judgment (e.g., ingroup/outgroup distinction, task competence, credibility) • Group actions develop group cohesiveness
Change over time	• Phases and activities in different phases serve different functions over time • There is no universal order of group development that predicts success or failure of group decision making

(Continued)

Table 2.2 (Continued)

	• Group development is not uniform, and movement of stages is often dramatic, quick, and unpredictable
Ecology	• The physical environment (e.g., crowding, proximity, privacy) influences group interaction and performance
	• The temporal environment determines opportunities, rhythms, and pacing of the team
	• Dynamism in the environment and the rate of external change determines group members' need for external boundary activity
	• Time pressure reduces quality of group performance and decision

evidence that larger groups increase performance in electronic brainstorming groups (Valacich et al., 1994).

There are many studies of ability composition in groups (Devine, 1999; Devine, Clayton, Philips, Dunford, & Melner, 1999). The most intriguing aspect of that literature is that there is often not a straightforward relation between the abilities of group members and the performance of the group. Group interaction may interfere with the clear expression of individual abilities. However, groups composed of people who know each other well or who have worked together in the past solve problems better than comparable groups of strangers. One explanation for this phenomenon is that experienced groups make better use of each individual's expertise (Moreland, 1999).

Status differences among group members affect interaction and performance. In group discussions, high-status members participate more and are more influential than low-status members (Dovidio, Brown, Heltman, Ellyson, & Keating, 1988; Kirchler & Davis, 1986). These effects are present even in computer-mediated settings (Hollingshead, 1996a, 1996b; Weisband, Schneider, & Connolly, 1995).

A growing body of research shows that personality traits are related to group interaction and performance (see Moynihan & Peterson, 2001, for a review). The relations generally take one of three forms. The first is universal: Certain traits always predict group performance and process. For example, high levels of agreeableness and emotional stability in groups are generally associated with cohesive group process, and conscientiousness is generally associated with task focus (e.g., Barrick, Stewart, Neubert, &

Mount, 1998; Bond & Shiu, 1997; LePine, Hollenbeck, Ilgen, & Hedlund, 1997). Extraversion may also be related to group performance (Barry & Stewart, 1997). The second form is contingent: Certain traits predict group process and performance depending on the task or organizational culture. For example, high levels of conscientiousness are associated with team performance, except on creative tasks (e.g., Waung & Brice, 1998). Finally, the third form is configurational: Group process and performance are predicted by the mix of traits within a group. For example, personality heterogeneity is generally beneficial for task-related outcomes, and homogeneity is beneficial for relationship-orientated outcomes (e.g., Hoffman & Maier, 1961).

Quite a few studies examine gender effects (same-sex groups versus mixed-sex groups; and all male versus all female groups) on group interaction and performance, with mixed results (see Eagly, Karau, & Makhijani, 1995; Eagly, Wood, & Diekman, 2000, for reviews). However, we know very little about differences in composition based on demographics other than gender (see Jackson, 1992, for review). Few studies have examined the effect of racial composition on group interaction (Filardo, 1996) or the effects of cultural diversity or homogeneity on group performance (Watson, Kumar, & Michaelsen, 1993).

Diversity that increases task-relevant skills and knowledge can be helpful to performance. However, too much of that diversity may not be helpful because of group members' failure to understand one another. Diversity on characteristics not related to the task may be problematic in that it may elicit negative emotional reactions or attitudes and increase turnover (Jackson, 1992). To the extent that diversity inhibits cohesion or task commitment, it can be harmful for groups with certain types of tasks. A recent meta-analysis suggests that the homogeneity or heterogeneity of group composition has little effect on group performance (Bowers, Pharmer, & Salas, 2000). The effect of diversity on performance appears to be moderated by task difficulty.

If one assumes that boundary activity is related to performance (cf. Ancona & Caldwell, 1992) and that external ties bring in crucial information (Reagans & Zuckerman, 2001), then composition is helpful to team performance to the extent that the team members have the necessary external connections. Thus, members should be chosen not solely with respect to who they are and how they will interact but also with respect to whom they know outside their group.

Research on group composition has often been restricted to looking at group members' average level on a particular characteristic and investigating only one characteristic at a time rather than multiple characteristics simultaneously. The study of group composition has been slowed by the difficulty of assembling a large number of groups with different configurations on a particular set of traits and by the lack of powerful statistical techniques for detecting statistical differences in small sample sizes. Berdahl (1998) described potential advantages of using computational modeling for studying group composition dynamics.

How Do the Group's Projects Affect Its Interaction and Performance?

As previously indicated, the type of task is important in determining the impact of a host of social and personal variables. There is a considerable body of literature on the main effects of task on group process and performance (Hackman & Morris, 1975) which continues to contemporary research on work teams that gives prominence to the design of team tasks (Hackman, 1987).

Roby and Lanzetta (1958) proposed one of the first meaningful task classification schemes, suggesting that tasks had objective properties and modal properties, which represent typical behaviors that groups exhibit while working on the task. Later task classification systems include: disjunctive/ conjunctive/compensatory/additive (Steiner, 1972) and intellective/judgmental (Laughlin, 1980).

McGrath's (1984) circumplex model is the most often cited way to categorize group tasks. The research emphasis has been on cognitive tasks (problem solving, decision making, idea generation) rather than on behavioral tasks in the physical realm (such as sports teams and musical bands). The nature and degree of interdependence that group members have while working on tasks and projects have large and direct impacts on group interaction and performance (Thompson, 1967). In addition, tasks can also affect relations between the group and its external environment: The greater the external interdependence with others, the greater the need for boundary activity (Ancona & Caldwell, 1992).

Group interaction is directly linked to group tasks. The demands of group tasks dictate the important functions that have to be performed interactively for a group to be successful. The performance of those functions shapes the structure of interaction development. Task type mediates the relations between the performance of functions and group performance (see Orlitzky & Hirokawa, 2001, for the meta-analysis of the functional perspective).

Group goals are also important in determining task success. There is an extensive literature on intragroup cooperation or competition (Mulvey & Ribbens, 1999; Pate, Watson, & Johnson, 1998; Stanne, Johnson, & Johnson, 1999). A less extensive literature discusses the effects of intergroup cooperation or competition on the performance of small groups (cf. Tajfel, 1982).

How Are Groups Structured, What Tools and Technologies Do They Have Access to, and How Do Those Structures and Technologies Affect Group Interaction and Performance?

In the last decade, considerable interest in groups and technology has emerged. Many features of technologies (members distributed or co-located, synchronous or asynchronous communication, anonymous or identified members, the presence of decision support or a facilitator) can enhance or constrain group processes and task performance (see McGrath & Hollingshead, 1994, for a review). Very few studies have demonstrated that groups communicating via computer perform better than groups interacting face to face, although many have demonstrated that computer-mediated groups perform less well than or as well as face-to-face groups. Even though computer-mediated groups generate less communication and use less information in their decisions, they take longer to make decisions. Although groups interacting via computer may perform worse on tasks initially than face-to-face groups, the performance advantages of face-to-face groups diminish over time (Hollingshead, McGrath, & O'Connor, 1993). These findings suggest that groups can adapt to their technology.

There seems to be an interaction effect of task and technology on the quality of group performance. Electronic groups produce more ideas of higher quality on idea-generation tasks. Face-to-face groups tend to have higher quality products on intellective and negotiation tasks. Some studies have found that computer-mediated groups exchange less information and are less likely to repeat information in their decisions than face-to-face groups. In some cases, this reduction can lead to poorer outcomes for newly formed groups. However, the structure that is imposed by the technology rather than the technology itself may be responsible for this effect (Hollingshead et al., 1993).

Different patterns of interaction have led to classifications of group member roles (Stogdill, 1974). The role of leader has been studied most. Many theories of emergent leadership and effective leadership have developed over the decades (see Bass, 1990, for review). More recently, the collective information-sharing area has examined the influence of expert roles on information sharing and decision making (e.g., Stasser et al., 1995). There has also been a recent emphasis on teamwork, with the presumption that this will increase group motivation and performance. Some case study evidence suggests that self-managed teams can be effective (Hackman, 2002; Manz & Sims, 1993). However, there is a general lack of well-controlled research studies to determine exactly what aspects of teamwork structure in organizations are the critical factors (for exception, see Wageman, 2001).

Status, hierarchy, and power are aspects of the group's structure that affect group influence and performance (see Chapter 5, this volume, for a more detailed analysis). Performance norms can also be influential (Postmes et al., 2001). Group norms influence the development of cohesiveness, which can be thought of as a component of the group's structure. Much research has examined the effects of cohesiveness on group decision-making and performance (see Mullen & Copper, 1994, for review). Too much or too little cohesiveness can have a negative impact on group performance.

Although no network structure is universally superior in facilitating group performance, some network structures appear to be more facilitative for certain types of tasks. Leavitt (1951), for example, used a simple symbol-identification task and found that centralized structures (such as the wheel) produced higher quality group performance than did decentralized structures (such as the circle; see Chapter 8, this volume, for a more detailed analysis). Shaw (1964) obtained the opposite findings using a more complicated mathematical problem. He concluded that the influence of network structures on group performance is limited by the size of the group, the subject population, and the kind of task. Of these, Shaw (1964) viewed task as the most crucial variable.

What Kinds of Group Interaction Processes Does the Group Carry Out and How Do These Processes Affect Other Factors and Performance?

Different types of group interaction have been studied relatively independently. Interaction process includes both content (what is said) and patterning (how it is said). The emphasis has been on the former, but the latter has received some attention (Bonito & Hollingshead, 1997).

Hirokawa and Poole (1996) argued that group communication performs at least nine sets of functions in groups:

1. Information processing (the analysis and combination of information, as well as the generation, elaboration, and evaluation of ideas)

2. Analytical processing (the assessment of circumstances and contingencies surrounding the choice-making situation)

3. Procedural functions (the establishment and maintenance of procedures and rules)

4. Goal-oriented functions (the establishment of group goals and values)

5. Synergistic functions (the coordination and motivation of the activities of group members)

6. Rhetorical, encompassing persuasion, social influence, and leadership

7. Conflict management and negotiation

8. Control

9. Creation and maintenance of group cultures and climates

Much of the recent research on groups conducted from the functional perspective has investigated information-processing functions. Hinsz, Tindale, and Vollrath's (1997) article in *Psychological Bulletin* on "groups as information processors" summarizes this body of research. Conflict-management processes have been studied more by negotiation researchers than by group researchers (see Pruitt & Carnevale, 1993, for review). However, some research examines conflict management as an input-group performance mediator (e.g., Jehn & Shah, 1997), and other recent research studies the effect of constructive controversy (effective conflict management) on group performance (e.g., Alper, Tjosvold, & Law, 1998). Wittenbaum, Vaughan, and Stasser (1998) presented a model of group coordination, including how members tacitly or explicitly coordinate their actions in task-oriented groups.

Hackman (1990) and McGrath (1991) discuss the importance of group viability over time. If the group accomplishes its present task but is unable to continue its work into the future, then it is not a high-performing team.

What Results From Group Action?

Research from the functional perspective has focused heavily on the evaluation of group performance and much less on aspects such as group viability, member satisfaction, and organizational-level outcomes. What "results" from group interaction largely depends on the type of group. But in regard to task-oriented groups, the "outcomes" of groups include: (1) a product of some kind (decision, solution, etc.), (2) agreed upon rules of engagement, (3) interpersonal relationships among members, and (4) lasting attitudes and beliefs about the group and its members—some that are shared by some or all members of the groups and others that are unique to individual group members.

During the 1990s, some research examined the effect of group discussion on biases in social judgment (e.g., fundamental attribution error, base rate fallacy, consensus overutilization effect; see Tindale, 1993, for a review). For these tasks, there is a normative standard for assessing good group judgment. The output of groups in many of those studies consists of social judgment about target people outside of the group. Wittenbaum, Hubbell, and Zuckerman's (1999) research on mutual enhancement has examined the influence of information sharing in groups on members' task-related social perceptions (e.g., task competence, credibility) of one another and themselves (Wittenbaum, 2000). Members who discuss shared information evaluate one another as more task capable than members who discuss unshared information.

Cohesiveness can also be a result of group action. Some studies have examined the factors that influence the development of cohesiveness in groups (Hurst, Stein, Korchin, & Soskin, 1978; McClure & Foster, 1991). Performing well may result in members feeling attracted to one another.

How Does the Group Change Over Time?

This is another understudied area in the group-performance domain. A body of research on time and change in groups rests on a functional analysis: namely, that phases and activities serve different functions over time. Work that fits into this category includes: interaction process analysis (Bales & Strodtbeck, 1951), phasic models of interaction (Fisher, 1970; Tuckman, 1965), decision development (Poole & Roth, 1988, 1989), and time, interaction, and performance (TIP) theory (McGrath, 1991; see Chapter 9, this volume for more detail).

However, much of the research conducted from the functional approach is normative rather than descriptive and emphasizes the factors and processes leading to effective group performance. Hirokawa (1983) showed that group development is related to group performance. However, Hirokawa (1985, 1988) later found no universal sequences of phases that were associated with either group success or failure.

How Does the Group's Ecology, Including Its Physical, Social, Organizational, and Technical Environment as well as Intergroup Relations, Affect Its Interaction and Performance?

The role of the physical environment on group interaction has not been sufficiently addressed by the functional perspective. A few studies examine environmental factors and group performance (crowding, privacy, personal space, presence of posters), and some literature emphasizes design to encourage group interaction (sociopetal design) (cf. Shaw, 1964). Burgoon (1992) discusses proximity and its effects on relationships in groups. Recently, there has been an interest in studying the impact of the natural environment on performance and group interaction.

The literature on teamwork has documented the importance of organizational structure, leadership, and support (e.g., Hackman & Morris, 1975).

A few studies have examined how accountability to others outside of the group affects group performance and decision making (Lerner & Tetlock, 1999). Ancona and Caldwell's work (1992) examines environmental adaptation, particularly in organizational settings. The more dynamism there is in the environment and the greater the rate of external change, the greater the need for external boundary activity.

Much research has shown that time pressure hurts group performance and decision quality (e.g. Karau & Kelly, 1992; Kelly, Jackson, & Hutson-Comeaux, 1997; Kelly & Karau, 1999). In that research, time pressure is typically imposed from outside the group.

Challenges and Debates for the Functional Perspective

As the prior sections illustrate, the functional perspective explains many group decision-making and performance dynamics. Its strength lies in its ability to predict and explain task-oriented group performance as influenced by static inputs and processes. As a result of research and theory guided by the functional perspective, the group dynamics literature is filled with lessons about how group composition, structure, task-related goals, and interaction processes influence the effectiveness of groups and organizations. Managers and team leaders may use these lessons to implement interventions and training to help groups function more successfully. If a group's goal is optimal task performance at one point in time, then the functional perspective is an ideal lens through which to understand, predict, and assist group functioning.

The features that make the functional perspective attractive are also the qualities that contribute to its weaknesses. First, research and theory from the functional perspective typically ignore groups whose main purpose is to attain goals that are not task-related but rather social-emotional, or groups that have both task and socioemotional goals. To the extent that the functional perspective views effective task accomplishment as the main group goal, then interesting processes regarding how groups satisfy multiple goals during task completion are not well understood.

Therapy groups, social support groups, clubs, and Greek organizations are examples of groups that have largely social-emotional goals. Members of therapy groups seek collective psychological well-being; social support groups aim to provide an outlet for acceptance, validation, and healing; and members of Greek organizations want to achieve camaraderie, inclusion, and friendship. Researchers could use the framework of the functional perspective to develop a set of requisite behaviors or activities during interaction for the attainment of socioemotional goals.

By researching and specifying the functions necessary for attaining different socioemotional goals, researchers may be able to extend the functionalist framework to groups that have multiple goals. A key function in groups with multiple goals would be the balancing, sequencing, and prioritizing of multiple goals. This extension may even provide leverage in analyzing complex dynamic systems.

A related weakness is the manner in which functionalists assess effective group action. Scholarship within the functional perspective evaluates group performance against some standard. The standard consists of normative criteria that identify how groups should perform. These criteria are typically based on a rational model that assumes that members should act in a manner informed by logic, facts, reason, and conscious deliberation. To the extent that group action reflects unconscious processes, social or political interests, incomplete information use, or irrational thinking, group performance is considered defective. Researchers in the functional tradition generally assume that they understand the best group processes and outcomes better than group members. However, such an approach fails to understand group processes from the perspective of the goals and interests of the group members.

Because the functional perspective views group outcomes as the linear function of inputs and processes, it cannot explain cyclical, nonlinear group dynamics, or reverse causality. Group action is presumed to result from a chainlike series of events, with outcomes representing an endpoint in the chain. However, certain inputs and processes might contribute to outcomes, which then contribute to different inputs and group processes. The functional perspective cannot account for complex, adaptive, dynamic systems over time. McGrath, Arrow, and Berdahl (2000) recently advocated that group scholarship in the future should move away from a simple functional perspective and toward one that allows for the study of groups as complex, dynamic systems. See Stohl and Holmes (1993) for another critique of the functional perspective.

Future Research Directions

Although the majority of small group research has been conducted from the functional perspective, many pertinent research questions remain unanswered. In this section, we expand on some weaknesses of this perspective and suggest three promising directions for future research: (1) expanding the types of inputs, processes, and outputs studied and exploring more complex relations among them; (2) using more and varied research methods; and (3) studying continuing groups at multiple time points.

Expanding the Types of Inputs, Processes, and Outputs

Research from the functional perspective has focused on some inputs, processes, and outcomes to the exclusion of others. Regarding input factors, much research has examined the effects of composition diversity or homogeneity on group performance. However, composition diversity has largely been limited to differences in gender, ability, and motivation. Little is known about how variation in member composition based on race, cultural background, or personality affects group outcomes. Also, existing research has been biased toward examining cognitive tasks. Most studies within the functional perspective examine decision making, idea generation, negotiation, or problem solving rather than behavioral tasks that require a physical performance or the execution of a plan or decision. Knowledge of groups from the functional perspective would be improved if studies examined a wider range of group task and composition variables within the same design.

Regarding group processes, much is known about the content of group discussion (i.e., what members say to one another), but less is known about discussion patterns (i.e., the structure of talk). Dabbs and Ruback (1987) advocated that discussion patterns such as onset, offset, delays, interruptions, sequencing, simultaneous speech, speaking-turn length, and distribution of talk time across members can predict important group outcomes such as leadership emergence and idea generation. The process of conflict management has received much attention among researchers who study dyadic negotiations. However, more research is needed to understand this process in larger groups. Finally, the functional perspective largely focuses on outcomes related to group task performance. Group maintenance and member satisfaction are other goals that might be served by functions (McGrath, 1991), but most of the perspectives that are reviewed here emphasize production and effectiveness goals. Additional research is needed to explore other outcomes such as member satisfaction and learning, group solidarity and viability, and organizational-level consequences.

More research is needed that explores greater complexity between input variables and processes. Many of the studies within the functional perspective examine simple input-process, input-output, or process-output relationships. More studies should incorporate all three steps in the chain (i.e., inputs, processes, and outputs). Too often, research studies focus on one type of task goal to the exclusion of others. Research that examines the interrelations among processes involved in negotiation, decision making, and idea generation would be invaluable.

Using More and Varied Research Methods

The laboratory experiment is the most commonly used method for examining groups within the functional perspective. If identifying causal connections between inputs, processes, and outcomes is of primary importance, then the experimental method is an ideal method. However, other research methods can be used to address some holes in understanding groups from the functional perspective. Despite the bias toward laboratory experimentation, there is some (largely nonexperimental) research examining groups in natural contexts. For example, Peterson, Owens, and Martorana (1999) developed an Organizational Group Dynamics Q-sort, a 100-item instrument designed to assess group process across a wide variety of data sources. Unfortunately, there is often a significant gap between basic and applied research in methods that are used and inputs, processes, and outcomes that are examined. The development of more sophisticated methods for studying groups in organizational and political settings may help to close the gap between basic experimental research and applied research in natural settings.

In addition, meta-analysis can be a useful tool for aggregating general effects of inputs and processes. Single studies only address a few inputs and processes. Meta-analyses can find patterns across the primary studies that will allow researchers to better identify and apply the fundamental principles of small groups from the functional perspective.

Studying Continuing Groups at Multiple Time Points

With few exceptions, researchers from the functional perspective have examined the antecedents and processes associated with effective performance of ad hoc groups working together on one task at one point in time. Clearly, more research from the functional perspective needs to investigate groups embedded in larger social systems and how effective and ineffective groups adjust in response to changes in their environment.

We need to find out whether our theories about effective group performance also apply to continuing groups. Some research suggests that groups perform better when members know something about one another's knowledge (e.g., Hollingshead, 2001; Wegner, 1987). However, experience can also lead to a lack of innovation and poor responses to nonroutine events (Waller, Conte, Gibson, & Carpenter, 2001). When and under what conditions will group experience lead to improved group performance? Studying groups in their natural settings at multiple points in time will enable researchers to begin to answer that question and to develop interventions for experienced groups that are performing poorly.

Note

1. We use the terms *groups* and *teams* interchangeably in this chapter.

References

Aldrich, H., & Herker, D. (1977). Boundary spanning roles and organizational structure. *Academy of Management Review, 2*, 217–230.

Allen, T. J. (1984). *Managing the flow of technology transfer and the dissemination of technological information within R & D organization.* Cambridge: MIT Press.

Alper, S., Tjosvold, D., & Law, K. S. (1998). Interdependence and controversy in group decision making: Antecedents to effective self-managing teams. *Organizational Behavior & Human Decision Processes, 74*, 33–52.

Amason, A. C. (1996). Distinguishing the effects of functional and dysfunctional conflict on strategic decision making: Resolving a paradox for top management teams. *Academy of Management Journal, 39*, 123–148.

Amason, A. C., & Schweiger, D. M. (1994). Resolving the paradox of conflict, strategic decision making, and organizational performance. *International Journal of Conflict Management, 5*, 239–253.

Ancona, D. (1990). Outward bound: Strategies for team survival in the organization. *Academy of Management Journal, 33*, 334–365.

Ancona, D., Bresman, H., & Kaufer, K. (2002). The comparative advantage of X-teams. *Sloan Management Review, 43*, 33–39

Ancona, D., & Caldwell, D. (1992). Bringing the boundary: External activity and performance in organizational teams. *Administrative Science Quarterly, 37*, 634–665.

Ancona, D., & Caldwell, D. (2000). Compose teams to assure successful boundary activity. In E. A. Locke (Ed.), *The handbook of principles of organizational behavior* (pp. 199–210). Oxford, UK: Blackwell.

Ancona, D., & Chong, C. (1996). Entrainment: Pace, cycle, and rhythm in organizational behavior. In B. M. Staw & L. L. Cummings (Eds.), *Research in organizational behavior: An annual series of analytical essays and critical reviews* (Vol. 18, pp. 251–284). Greenwich, CT: JAI Press.

Ancona, D., & Chong, C. (1999). Cycles and synchrony: The temporal role of context in team behavior. In R. Wageman (Ed.), *Research on managing groups and teams: Groups in context* (Vol. 2, pp. 33–48). Stamford, CT: JAI Press.

Bales, R. F., & Strodtbeck, F. L. (1951). Phases in group problem-solving. *Journal of Abnormal and Social Psychology, 46,* 485–495.

Baron, R. A. (1991). Positive effects of conflict: A cognitive perspective. *Employee Responsibilities and Rights Journal, 4,* 25–36.

Baron, R. S., Kerr, N. L., & Miller, N. (1992). *Group process, group decision, group action.* Buckingham, UK/Bristol, PA: Open University Press.

Barrick, M. R., Stewart, G. L., Neubert, M. J., & Mount, M. K. (1998). Relating member ability and personality to work-team processes and team effectiveness. *Journal of Applied Psychology, 83,* 377–391.

Barry, B., & Stewart, G. L. (1997). Composition, process, and performance in self-managed groups: The role of personality. *Journal of Applied Psychology, 82,* 62–78.

Bartis, S. P., Szymanski, K., & Harkins, S. G. (1988). Evaluation and performance: A two-edged knife. *Personality and Social Psychology Bulletin, 14,* 242–251.

Bass, B. (1990). *Bass & Stogdill's handbook of leadership: Theory, research, and managerial applications.* New York: Free Press/Macmillan.

Becker, S. W., & Baloff, N. (1969). Organization structure and complex problem solving. *Administrative Science Quarterly, 14,* 260–271.

Berdahl, J. L. (1998). The dynamics of composition and socialization in small groups: Insights gained from developing a computational model. In M. A. Neale, E. A. Mannix, & D. H Gruenfeld (Eds.), *Research on managing in groups and teams* (Vol. 1, pp. 209–227). Greenwich, CT: JAI Press.

Bond, M. H., & Shiu, W. Y. (1997). The relationship between a group's personality resources and the two dimensions of its group process. *Small Group Research, 28,* 194–217.

Bonito, J. A., & Hollingshead, A. B. (1997). Participation in small groups. In B. R. Burleson & A. W. Kunkel (Eds.), *Communication yearbook* (Vol. 20, pp. 227–261). Thousand Oaks, CA: Sage.

Bowers, C. A., Pharmer, J. A., & Salas, E. (2000). When member homogeneity is needed in work teams: A meta-analysis. *Small Group Research, 31,* 305–327.

Burgoon, J. K. (1992). Spatial relationships in small groups. In R. S. Cathcart & L. A. Samovar (Eds.), *Small group communication: A reader* (pp. 287–300). Dubuque, IA: William C. Brown.

Camacho, L. M., & Paulus, P. B. (1995). The role of social anxiousness in group brainstorming. *Journal of Personality and Social Psychology, 68,* 1071–1080.

Cartwright, D., & Zander, A. W. (1968). *Group dynamics research and theory* (3rd ed.). New York: Harper & Row.

Collins, B. E., & Guetzkow, H. (1964). *A social psychology of group processes for decision-making.* New York: John Wiley.

Cosier, R. A., & Rose, G. L. (1977). Cognitive conflict and goal conflict effects on task performance. *Organizational Behavior and Human Performance, 19,* 378–391.

Coskun, H. (2000). *The effects of outgroup comparison, social context, intrinsic motivation, and collective identity in brainstorming groups.* Unpublished doctoral dissertation, the University of Texas at Arlington.

Cragan, J. W., & Wright, D. W. (1990). Small group communication research of the 1980s: A synthesis and critique. *Communication Studies, 41,* 212–236.

Dabbs, J. M., Jr., & Ruback, R. B. (1987). Dimensions of group process: Amount and structure of group interaction. In L. Berkowitz (Ed.), *Advances in experimental social psychology* (Vol. 20, pp. 123–169). San Diego, CA: Academic Press.

Davis, J. H. (1973). Group decision and social interaction: A theory of social decision schemes. *Psychological Review, 80,* 97–125.

Davis, J. H. (1980). Group decision and procedural justice. In M. Fishbein (Ed.), *Progress in social psychology* (pp. 157–229). Hillsdale, NJ: Lawrence Erlbaum.

Davis, J. H. (1982). Social interaction as a combinatorial process in group decision. In H. Brandstatter, J. H. Davis, & G. Stocker-Kreichgauer (Eds.), *Group decision making* (pp. 27–58). London: Academic Press.

Davis, J. H., Kameda, T., Parks, C., Stasson, M., & Zimmerman, S. (1989). Some social mechanics of group decision making: The distribution of opinion, polling sequence, and implications for consensus. *Journal of Personality and Social Psychology, 57,* 1000–1012.

De Dreu, C. K., & West, M. A. (2001). Minority dissent and team innovation: The importance of participation in decision making. *Journal of Applied Psychology, 86,* 1191–1201.

Deutsch, M. (1969). Conflicts: Productive and destructive. *Journal of Social Issues, 25,* 7–41.

Devine, D. J. (1999). Effects of cognitive ability, task knowledge, information sharing, and conflict on group decision-making effectiveness. *Small Group Research, 30,* 608–634.

Devine, D. J., Clayton, L. D., Philips, J. L., Dunford, B. B., & Melner, S. B. (1999). Teams in organizations: Prevalence, characteristics, and effectiveness. *Small Group Research, 30,* 678–711.

Diehl, M., & Stroebe, W. (1987). Productivity loss in brainstorming groups: Toward the solution of a riddle. *Journal of Personality and Social Psychology, 53,* 497–509.

Dovidio, J. F., Brown, C. E., Heltman, K., Ellyson, S. L., & Keating, C. F. (1988). Power displays between women and men in discussions of gender-linked tasks: A multichannel study. *Journal of Personality and Social Psychology, 55,* 580–587.

Dugosh, K. L., Paulus, P. B., Roland, E. J., & Yang, H. C. (2000). Cognitive stimulation in brainstorming. *Journal of Personality and Social Psychology, 79,* 722–735.

Eagly, A. H., Karau, S. J., & Makhijani, M. G. (1995). Gender and the effectiveness of leaders: A meta-analysis. *Psychological Bulletin, 117,* 125–145.

Eagly, A. H., Wood, W., & Diekman, A. B. (2000). Social role theory of sex differences and similarities: A current appraisal. In T. Eckes & H. M. Trautner (Eds.), *The developmental social psychology of gender* (pp. 123–174). Mahwah, NJ: Lawrence Erlbaum.

Filardo, E. K. (1996). Gender patterns in African American and white adolescents' social interactions in same-race, mixed-gender groups. *Journal of Personality and Social Psychology. 71*, 71–82.

Fisher, B. A. (1970). The process of decision modification in small group discussion groups. *Journal of Communication, 20*, 51–64.

Gladstein, D. (1984). Groups in context: A model of task group effectiveness. *Administrative Science Quarterly, 29*, 499–517.

Gouran, D. S., & Hirokawa, R. Y. (1983). The role of communication in decision-making groups: A functional perspective. In M. S. Mander (Ed.), *Communications in transition* (pp. 168–185). New York: Praeger.

Gouran, D. S., & Hirokawa, R. Y. (1986). The counteractive functions of communication in effective group decision-making. In R. Y. Hirokawa & M. S. Poole (Eds.), *Communication and group decision-making* (pp. 81–90). Beverly Hills, CA: Sage.

Gouran, D. S., & Hirokawa, R. Y. (1996). Functional theory and communication in decision-making and problem-solving groups: An expanded view. In R. Y. Hirokawa & M. S. Poole (Eds.), *Communication and group decision-making* (2nd ed., pp. 55–80). Thousand Oaks, CA: Sage.

Gouran, D. S., Hirokawa, R. Y., Julian, K. M., & Leatham, G. B. (1993). The evolution and current status of the functional perspective on communication in decision-making and problem-solving groups: A critical analysis. *Communication Yearbook, 16*, 573–600.

Griffin, E. A. (2000). *A first look at communication theory* (4th ed.). New York: McGraw-Hill.

Gruenfeld, D. H., Mannix, E. A., Williams, K. Y., & Neale, M. A. (1996). Group composition and decision making: How member familiarity and information distribution affect process and performance. *Organizational Behavior and Human Decision Processes, 67*, 1–15.

Guetzkow, H., & Gyr, J. (1954). An analysis of conflict in decision-making groups. *Human Relations, 7*, 367–381.

Hackman, J. R. (1987). The design of work teams. In J. W. Lorsch (Ed.), *Handbook of organizational behavior* (pp. 315–342). Englewood Cliffs, NJ: Prentice Hall.

Hackman, J. R. (1990). *Groups that work (and those that don't): Creating conditions for effective teamwork.* San Francisco: Jossey-Bass.

Hackman, J. R. (2002). *Leading teams.* Cambridge, MA: Harvard Business Press.

Hackman, J. R., & Morris, C. G. (1975). Group tasks, group interaction process, and group performance effectiveness: A review and proposed integration. In L. Berkowitz (Ed.), *Advances in experimental social psychology* (Vol. 8, pp. 45–99). New York: Academic Press.

Hansen, M. (1999). The search-transfer problem: The role of weak ties in sharing knowledge across organization subunits. *Administrative Science Quarterly, 44*, 82–111.

Herek, G., Janis, I. L., & Huth, P. (1987). Decision making during international crises: Is quality of process related to outcome? *Journal of Conflict Resolution, 31*, 203–226.

Hinsz, V. B. (1990). Cognitive and consensus processes in group recognition memory performance. *Journal of Personality and Social Psychology, 59*, 705–718.

Hinsz, V. B., Tindale, R. S., & Vollrath, D. A. (1997). The emerging conceptualization of groups as information processes. *Psychological Bulletin, 121*, 43–64.

Hirokawa, R. Y. (1980a). A comparative analysis of communication patterns within effective and ineffective decision-making groups. *Communication Monographs, 47*, 312–321.

Hirokawa, R. Y. (1980b). *A function-oriented analysis of small group interaction within effective and ineffective decision-making groups: An exploratory investigation.* Unpublished doctoral dissertation, University of Washington, Seattle.

Hirokawa, R. Y. (1982). Group communication and problem-solving effectiveness I: A critical review of inconsistent findings. *Communication Quarterly, 30*, 134–141.

Hirokawa, R. Y. (1983). Group communication and problem-solving effectiveness II: An exploratory investigation of procedural functions. *Western Journal of Speech Communication, 47*, 59–74.

Hirokawa, R. Y. (1985). Discussion procedures and decision-making performance: A test of a functional perspective. *Human Communication Research, 12*, 203–224.

Hirokawa, R. Y. (1988). Group communication and decision-making performance: A continued test of the functional perspective. *Human Communication Research, 14*, 487–515.

Hirokawa, R. Y. (1990). The role of communication in group decision-making efficacy: A task-contingency perspective. *Small Group Research, 21*, 190–204.

Hirokawa, R. Y. (1999). *From the tiny pond to the big ocean: Studying communication and group decision-making from a functional perspective.* Lecture conducted at B. Aubrey Fisher Memorial, University of Utah, Salt Lake City.

Hirokawa, R. Y., & Poole, M. S. (Eds.). (1996). *Communication and group decision making.* Thousand Oaks, CA: Sage.

Hirokawa, R. Y., & Rost, K. M. (1992). Effective group decision making in organizations: Field test of the vigilant interaction theory. *Management Communication Quarterly, 5*, 267–288.

Hirokawa, R. Y., & Scheerhorn, D. R. (1986). Communication in faulty group decision-making. In R. Y. Hirokawa & M. S. Poole (Eds.), *Communication and group decision-making* (pp. 63–80). Beverly Hills, CA: Sage.

Hoffman, L.R., & Maier, R.F. (1961). Quality and acceptance of problem solving by members of homogenous and heterogeneous groups. *Journal of Abnormal and Social Psychology, 62*, 401–407.

Hollingshead, A. B. (1996a). Information suppression and status persistence in group decision making: The effects of communication media. *Human Communication Research, 23*, 193–219.

Hollingshead, A. B. (1996b). The rank-order effect in group decision making. *Organizational Behavior and Human Decision Processes, 68*, 181–193.

Hollingshead, A. B. (2001). Cognitive interdependence and convergent expectations in transactive memory. *Journal of Personality and Social Psychology, 81*, 1080–1089.

Hollingshead, A. B., McGrath, J. E., & O'Connor, K. M. (1993). Group task performance and communication technology: A longitudinal study of computer-mediated versus face-to-face work groups. *Small Group Research, 24*, 307–333.

Homans, G. C. (1950). *The human group*. Cambridge, MA: Harvard University Press.

Hurst, A. G., Stein, K. B., Korchin, S. J., & Soskin, W. F. (1978). Leadership style determinants of cohesiveness in adolescent groups. *International Journal of Group Psychotherapy, 28*, 263–277.

Jackson, S. E. (1992). Team composition in organizational settings: Issues in managing an increasingly diverse work force. In S. Worchel, W. Wood, & J. A. Simpson (Eds.), *Group process and productivity* (pp. 138–173). Newbury Park, CA: Sage.

Janis, I. L. (1972). *Victims of groupthink*. Boston: Houghton-Mifflin.

Janis, I. L. (1982). *Groupthink: Psychological studies of policy decisions* (2nd ed.). Boston: Houghton Mifflin.

Janis, I. L. (1985). Sources of error in strategic decision making. In J. M. Pennings (Ed.), *Organizational strategy and change* (pp. 157–197). San Francisco: Jossey-Bass.

Janis, I. L. (1989). *Crucial decisions: Leadership in policy-making and management*. New York: Free Press.

Janis, I. L., & Mann, L. (1977). *Decision making: A psychological analysis of conflict, choice, and commitment*. New York: Free Press.

Jehn, K. A. (1995). A multimethod examination of the benefits and detriments of intragroup conflict. *Administrative Science Quarterly, 40*, 256–282.

Jehn, K. A. (1997). A qualitative analysis of conflict types and dimensions in organizational groups. *Administrative Science Quarterly, 42*, 520–557.

Jehn, K. A., Chadwick, C., & Thatcher, S. M. (1997). To agree or not to agree: The effects of value congruence, individual demographic dissimilarity, and conflict on workgroup outcomes. *International Journal of Conflict Management, 8*, 287–305.

Jehn, K. A., & Mannix, E. A. (2001). The dynamic nature of conflict: A longitudinal study of intragroup conflict and group performance. *Academy of Management Journal, 44*, 238–251.

Jehn, K. A., Northcraft, G., & Neale, M. (1999). Why differences make a difference: A field study of diversity, conflict, and performance in workgroups. *Administrative Science Quarterly, 44*, 741–763.

Jehn, K. A., & Shah, P. P (1997). Interpersonal relationships and task performance: An examination of mediation processes in friendship and acquaintance groups. *Journal of Personality & Social Psychology, 72*, 775–790.

Karau, S. J., & Kelly, J. R. (1992). The effects of time scarcity and time abundance on group performance quality and interaction process. *Journal of Experimental Social Psychology, 28,* 542–571.

Katz, R., Tushman, M., & Allen, T. J. (1995). The influence of supervisory promotion and network location on subordinate careers in a dual ladder RD & E setting. *Management Science, 41,* 848–863.

Kelly, J. R., Jackson, J. W., & Hutson-Comeaux, S. L. (1997). The effects of time pressure and task differences on influence modes and accuracy in decision-making groups. *Personality and Social Psychology Bulletin, 23,* 10–22.

Kelly, J. R., & Karau, S. J. (1999). Group decision making: The effects of initial preferences and time pressure. *Personality and Social Psychology Bulletin, 25,* 1342–1354.

Kiesler, S. (1978). *Interpersonal processes in groups and organizations.* Arlington Heights, IL: AHM Publishing.

Kirchler, E., & Davis, J. H. (1986). The influence of member status differences and task type on group consensus and member position change. *Journal of Personality and Social Psychology, 51,* 83–91.

Kramer, T. J., Fleming, G. P., & Mannis, S. M. (2001). Improving face-to-face brainstorming through modeling and facilitation. *Small Group Research, 32,* 533–557.

Larey, T. S., & Paulus, P. B. (1999). Group preference and convergent tendencies in small groups: A content analysis of group brainstorming performance. *Creativity Research Journal, 12,* 175–184.

Larson, J. R., Christensen, C., Abbott, A. S., & Franz, T. M. (1996). Diagnosing groups: Charting the flow of information in medical decision-making teams. *Journal of Personality and Social Psychology, 71,* 315–330.

Laughlin, P. R. (1980). Social combination processes of cooperative problem-solving groups on verbal intellective tasks. In M. Fishbein (Ed.), *Progress in social psychology* (pp. 127–155). Hillsdale, NJ: Lawrence Erlbaum.

Laughlin, P. R. (1988). Collective induction: Group performance, social combination processes, and mutual majority and minority influence. *Journal of Personality and Social Psychology, 54,* 254–267.

Laughlin, P. R. (1999). Collective induction: Twelve postulates. *Organizational Behavior and Human Decision Processes, 80,* 50–69.

Laughlin, P. R., & Ellis, A. L. (1986). Demonstrability and social combination processes on mathematical intellective tasks. *Journal of Experimental Social Psychology, 22,* 177–189.

Laughlin, P. R., & Hollingshead, A. B. (1995). A theory of collective induction. *Organizational Behavior and Human Decision Processes, 61,* 94–107.

Leavitt, H. J. (1951). Some effects of certain communication patterns on group performance. *Journal of Abnormal and Social Psychology, 46,* 38–50.

LePine, J. A., Hollenbeck, J. R., Ilgen, D. R., & Hedlund, J. (1997). Effects of individual differences on the performance of hierarchical decision-making teams: Much more than g. *Journal of Applied Psychology, 82,* 803–811.

Lerner, J. S., & Tetlock, P. E. (1999). Accounting for the effects of accountability. *Psychological Bulletin, 125,* 255–275.

Lewin, K. (1948). *Resolving social conflicts* (Rev. ed.). New York: Harper & Brothers.

Lorge, I., & Solomon, H. (1955). Two models of group behavior in the solution of Eureka-type problems. *Psychometrika, 20,* 139–148.

Manz, C., & Sims, H. (1993). *Business without bosses: How self-managing teams are building high-performing companies.* New York: John Wiley.

McClure, B. A., & Foster, C. D. (1991). Group work as a method of promoting cohesiveness within a women's gymnastics team. *Perceptual and Motor Skills, 73,* 307–313.

McGrath, J. E. (1984). *Groups: Interaction and performance.* Englewood Cliffs, NJ: Prentice Hall.

McGrath, J. E. (1991). Time, interaction, and performance (TIP): A theory of groups. *Small Group Research, 22,* 147–174.

McGrath, J. E., Arrow, H., & Berdahl, J. L. (2000). The study of groups: Past, present, and future. *Personality and Social Psychology Review, 4,* 95–105.

McGrath, J. E., & Hollingshead, A. B. (1994). *Groups interacting with technology: Ideas, evidence, issues, and an agenda.* Thousand Oaks, CA: Sage.

McGrath, J. E., & Rotchford, N. L. (1983). Time and behavior in organizations. In L. L. Cummings & B. M. Staw (Eds.), *Research in organizational behavior* (Vol. 5, pp. 57–101). Greenwich, CT: JAI Press.

McLeod, P. L., Baron, R. S., Marti, M. W., & Yoon, K. (1997). The eyes have it: Minority influence in face-to-face and computer-mediated group discussion. *Journal of Applied Psychology, 82,* 706–718.

Milliken, F. J., Bartel, C. A., & Kurtzberg, T. R. (2003). Diversity and creativity in work groups: A dynamic perspective on the affective and cognitive processes that link diversity and performance. In P. B. Paulus & B. Nijstad (Eds.), *Group creativity: Innovation through collaboration* (pp. 32–62). New York: Oxford University Press.

Moreland, R. L. (1999). Transactive memory: Learning who knows what in work groups and organizations. In L. Thompson, J. Levine, & D. Messick (Eds.), *Shared cognition in organizations: The management of knowledge* (pp. 3–31). Mahwah, NJ: Lawrence Erlbaum.

Moynihan, L. M., & Peterson, R. S. (2001). A contingent configuration approach to understanding the role of personality in organizational groups. *Research in Organizational Behavior, 23,* 327–378.

Mullen, B., & Copper, C. (1994). The relation between group cohesiveness and performance: An integration. *Psychological Bulletin, 115,* 210–227.

Mullen, B., Johnson, C., & Salas, E. (1991). Productivity loss in brainstorming groups: A meta-analytic integration. *Basic and Applied Social Psychology, 12,* 3–23.

Mulvey, P. W., & Ribbens, B. A. (1999). The effects of intergroup competition and assigned group goals on group efficacy and group effectiveness. *Small Group Research, 30,* 651–677.

Nemeth, C. J., Brown, K., & Rogers, J. (2001). Devil's advocate versus authentic dissent: Stimulating quantity and quality. *European Journal of Social Psychology, 31*, 707–720.

Nijstad, B. A., Diehl, M., & Stroebe, W. (2003). Cognitive stimulation and interference in idea generating groups. In P. B. Paulus & B. A. Nijstad (Eds.), *Group creativity* (pp. 137-159). New York: Oxford University Press.

Orlitzky, M., & Hirokawa, R. Y. (2001). To err is human, to correct for it divine: A meta-analysis of research testing the functional theory of group decision-making effectiveness. *Small Group Research, 32*, 313–341.

Osborn, A. F. (1953). *Applied imagination* (2nd ed.). New York: Scribner.

Pate, S., Watson, W. E., & Johnson, L. (1998). The effects of competition on the decision quality of diverse and non-diverse groups. *Journal of Applied Social Psychology, 28*, 912–923.

Paulus, P. B. (2000). Groups, teams, and creativity: The creative potential of idea generating groups. *Applied Psychology: An International Review, 49*, 237–262.

Paulus, P. B. (in press). Fostering creativity in groups and teams. In C. Ford (Ed.), *Handbook of organizational creativity*. Mahwah, NJ: Lawrence Erlbaum.

Paulus, P. B., Dugosh, K. L., Dzindolet, M. T., Coskun, H., & Putman, V. L. (2002). Social and cognitive influences in group brainstorming: Predicting production gains and losses. *European Review of Social Psychology, 12*, 299–325.

Paulus, P. B., Dzindolet, M. T., Poletes, G., & Camacho, L. M. (1993). Perception of performance in group brainstorming: The illusion of group productivity. *Personality and Social Psychology Bulletin, 19*, 78–89.

Paulus, P. B., Larey, T. S., & Dzindolet, M. T. (2000). Creativity in groups and teams. In M. Turner (Ed.), *Groups at work: Advances in theory and research* (pp. 319–338). Hillsdale, NJ: Lawrence Erlbaum.

Paulus, P. B., Larey, T. S., & Ortega, A. H. (1995). Performance and perceptions of brainstormers in an organizational setting. *Basic and Applied Social Psychology, 17*, 249–265.

Paulus, P. B., Larey, T. S., Putman, V. L., Leggett, K. L., & Roland, E. J. (1996). Social influence process in computer brainstorming. *Basic and Applied Social Psychology, 18*, 3–14.

Pavitt, C. (1994). Theoretical commitments presupposed by functional approaches to group discussion. *Small Group Research, 25*, 520–541.

Perrow, C. (1967). A framework for the comparative analysis of organizations. *American Sociological Review, 32*, 194–208.

Peterson, R. S., Owens, P. D., & Martorana, P. V. (1999). The group dynamics q-sort in organizational research: A new method for studying familiar problems. *Organizational Research Methods, 2*, 107–136.

Phillip, H., & Dunphy, D. (1959). Developmental trends in small groups. *Sociometry, 22*, 162–174.

Pinsonneault, A., Barki, H., Gallupe, R. B., & Hoppen, N. (1999). Electronic brainstorming: The illusion of productivity. *Information Systems Research, 10,* 110–133.

Poole, M. S., & Roth, J. (1988). Decision development in small groups: IV. A typology of group decision paths. *Human Communication Research, 15,* 323–356.

Poole, M. S., & Roth, J. (1989). Decision development in small groups: V. Test of a contingency model. *Human Communication Research, 15,* 549–589.

Postmes, T., Spears, R., & Cihangir, S. (2001). Quality of decision making and group norms. *Journal of Personality and Social Psychology, 80,* 918–930.

Pruitt, D. G., & Carnevale, P. J. (1993). *Negotiation in social conflict.* Pacific Grove, CA: Brooks/Cole.

Reagans, R., & Zuckerman, E. W. (2001). Networks, diversity, and productivity: The social capital of corporate R & D teams. *Organization Science, 12,* 502–517.

Roby, T. B., & Lanzetta, J. T. (1958). Considerations in the analysis of group tasks, *Psychological Bulletin, 55,* 88–101.

Schweiger, D. M., Sandberg, W. R., & Rechner, P. L. (1989). Experiential effects of dialectical inquiry, devil's advocacy, and consensus approaches to strategic decision making. *Academy of Management Journal, 32,* 745–772.

Scott, S. (1997). Social identification in product and process development teams. *Journal of Engineering and Technology Management, 14,* 97–127.

Shaw, M. E. (1964). Communication networks. In L. Berkowitz (Ed.), *Advances in experimental social psychology* (Vol. 1, pp. 111–147). Orlando, FL: Academic Press.

Simons, T. L., & Peterson, R. S. (2000). Task conflict and relationship conflict in top management teams: The pivotal role of intragroup trust. *Journal of Applied Psychology, 85,* 102–111.

Stanne, M. B., Johnson, D. W., & Johnson, R. T. (1999). Does competition enhance or inhibit motor performance: A meta-analysis. *Psychological Bulletin, 125,* 133–154.

Stasser, G. (1999). The uncertain role of unshared information in collective choice. In L. L. Thompson, J. M. Levine, & D. M. Messick (Eds.), *Shared cognition in organizations: The management of knowledge* (pp. 49–69). Hillsdale, NJ: Lawrence Erlbaum.

Stasser, G., & Stewart, D. (1992). Discovery of hidden profiles by decision-making groups: Solving a problem versus making a judgment. *Journal of Personality and Social Psychology, 63,* 426–434.

Stasser, G., Stewart, D. D., & Wittenbaum, G. M. (1995). Expert roles and information exchange during discussion: The importance of knowing who knows what. *Journal of Experimental Social Psychology, 31,* 244–265.

Stasser, G., & Titus, W. (1985). Pooling of unshared information in group decision making: Biased information sampling during discussion. *Journal of Personality and Social Psychology, 48,* 1467–1478.

Stasser, G., & Titus, W. (1987). Effects of information load and percentage of shared information on the dissemination of unshared information during group discussion. *Journal of Personality and Social Psychology, 53,* 81–93.

Steiner, I. D. (1972). *Group process and productivity.* San Diego, CA: Academic Press.

Stewart, D. D., & Stasser, G. (1998). The sampling of critical, unshared information in decision-making groups: The role of an informed minority. *European Journal of Social Psychology, 28,* 95–113.

Stogdill, R. M. (1974). *Handbook of leadership: A survey of theory and research.* New York: Free Press.

Stohl, C., & Holmes, M. (1993). A functional perspective for bona fide groups. *Communication Yearbook, 16,* 601–614.

Sundstrom, E. (1999). *Supporting work team effectiveness.* San Francisco: Jossey-Bass.

Tajfel, H. (1982). The social psychology of intergroup relations. *Annual Review of Psychology, 33,* 1–39.

Tajfel, H., & Turner, J. C. (1986). The social identity theory of intergroup behavior. In W. G. Austin & S. Worchel (Eds.), *Psychology of intergroup relations* (2nd ed., pp. 7–24). Chicago: Nelson-Hall.

Thompson, J. D. (1967). *Organizations in action: Social science bases of administration therapy.* New York: McGraw-Hill.

Tindale, R. S. (1993). Decision errors made by individuals and groups. In N. J. Castellan (Ed.), *Individual and group decision making: Current issues* (pp. 109–124). Hillsdale, NJ: Lawrence Erlbaum.

Tuckman, B. W. (1965). Developmental sequence in small groups. *Psychological Bulletin, 63,* 384–399.

Valacich, J. S., Dennis, A. R., & Connolly, T. (1994). Idea generation in computer-based groups: A new ending to an old story. *Organizational Behavior and Human Decision Processes, 57,* 448–467.

Valacich, J. S., & Schwenk, C. (1995). Devil's advocate and dialectical inquiry effects on face-to-face and computer-mediated group decision-making. *Organizational Behavior and Human Decision Processes, 63,* 158–173.

Wageman, R. (2001). How leaders foster self-managing team effectiveness: Design choices versus hands-on coaching. *Organization Science, 12*(5), 559–578.

Waller, M. J., Conte, J. M., Gibson, C. A., & Carpenter, M. A. (2001). The effect of individual perceptions of deadlines on team performance. *Academy of Management Review, 26,* 586–600.

Watson, W. E., Kumar, K., & Michaelsen, L. K. (1993). Cultural diversity's impact on interaction process and performance: Comparing homogeneous and diverse task groups. *Academy of Management Journal, 36,* 590–602.

Waung, M., & Brice, T. S. (1998). The effects of conscientiousness and opportunity to caucus on group performance. *Small Group Research, 29,* 624–634.

Wegner, D. M. (1987). Transactive memory: A contemporary analysis of the group mind. In B. Mullen & G. R. Goethals (Eds.), *Theories of group behavior* (pp. 185–208). New York: Springer-Verlag.

Weingart, L. R., & Jehn, K. (2000). Managing intra-team conflict through collaboration. In E. A. Locke (Ed.), *The handbook of principles of organizational behavior* (pp. 226–238). Oxford, UK: Blackwell.

Weisband, S. P., Schneider, S. K., & Connolly, T. (1995). Electronic communication and social information: Status salience and status differences. *Academy of Management Journal, 38,* 1124–1151.

Winquist, J. R., & Larson, J. R., Jr. (1998). Information pooling: When it impacts group decision making. *Journal of Personality and Social Psychology, 74,* 371–377.

Wittenbaum, G. M. (2000). The bias toward discussing shared information: Why are high status group members immune? *Communication Research, 27,* 379–401.

Wittenbaum, G. M., Hubbell, A. P., & Zuckerman, C. (1999). Mutual enhancement: Toward an understanding of the collective preference for shared information. *Journal of Personality and Social Psychology, 77,* 967–978.

Wittenbaum, G. M., & Stasser, G. (1996). Management of information in small groups. In J. L. Nye & A. M. Brower (Eds.), *What's social about social cognition? Social cognition research in small groups* (pp. 3–28). Thousand Oaks, CA: Sage.

Wittenbaum, G. M., Vaughan, S. I., & Stasser, G. (1998). Coordination in task-performing groups. In R. S. Tindale & L. Heath (Eds.), *Theory and research on small groups: Social psychological applications to social issues* (Vol. 4, pp. 177–204). New York: Plenum.

3

Psychodynamic Perspectives on Small Groups

Poppy Lauretta McLeod and Richard Kettner-Polley

Abstract

The psychodynamic perspective is defined as an approach to the study of group behavior that focuses on the relationship between the emotional nonconscious processes and the conscious rational processes of interpersonal interaction. This perspective is divided here into two broad approaches: psychoanalytic and humanistic. Both approaches share the fundamental assumptions that nonconscious emotional processes shape interpersonal behavior in groups, that the lack of awareness of these processes inhibits effective work groups, and that bringing such processes to members' awareness will help remove this inhibition. Psychoanalytic approaches assume that social behavior has biological bases and is governed by a medical model. Its early development traces back to the psychoanalytic theory of Freud. Humanistic approaches are governed by an education and human development model and trace their roots to the early social psychological theories of Lewin. Psychodynamic perspectives have influenced the study of groups widely, most notably in major contributions to theories of group development. Directions of future inquiry include the concepts from positive psychology of flow and emotional intelligence.

The distinction between emotional behaviors and task-oriented behaviors has been the object of much attention in the small-group literature for nearly a century. The prevailing ethos within the literature has treated this distinction as an uneasy alliance, one that must be accepted as characteristic of groups. Psychodynamic perspectives, however, challenge the prevailing characterization of this distinction—or even its existence. From these perspectives, a group's understanding of its emotional processes *is* its task, or is crucial for accomplishing its task.

Psychodynamic perspectives have been applied primarily to small, face-to-face interacting groups, but applications to large groups, organizations, and societies are also well represented (for examples, see Alderfer, 1998; Hirschhorn, 1999; Jarrett & Kellner, 1996; Kernberg, 1984, 1998; Kets de Vries & Miller, 1984; Miller & Rice, 1967; Morgan & Thomas, 1996; Paul, Strbiak, & Landrum, 2002; Seel, 2001; Smith, 1982; Smith & Berg, 1987; Vogler, 2000; Volkan, 1999a, 1999b). Furthermore, the vast majority of this literature has focused on groups whose function is therapy, learning, or personal development. The work within these groups, therefore, generally is learning about the group, improving the group's functioning, or restoring its members to health.

The following vignette will illustrate the phenomena that lie within the purview of psychodynamic perspectives and will lead to the formal definition of the perspective.

The weekly meeting was half over. Wilfred, who had been managing this team for 6 months, had just finished presenting what he thought was a perfectly reasonable proposal for how the team could respond to the CEO's request for company-wide cost-cutting. He had been very careful to show how his proposal included inputs given by members of the team. Yet, he was surprised by the reactions he was sensing—reactions that seemed to include both hostility and indifference. His request for feedback was initially met with silence, and then the members who usually were the outspoken ones said they thought Wilfred's ideas were great. One or two others in the room nodded, seeming to agree. Still, Wilfred felt they were only humoring him, and he wondered how committed the team would be to implementing the plans.

If we apply a psychodynamic perspective to this vignette, we might focus on the context of organizational cost-cutting and the consequent anxiety this likely produced among organizational members. We would then look for the psychological defenses against this anxiety that might be manifested. For example, a psychodynamically oriented theorist might explore whether the members of Wilfred's team projected their anxiety onto him, their leader, and then reacted with hostility to the weakness they now perceive in him. Or reactions of indifference might stem actually from fear of being let down by the leader on whom they had depended. Other questions would include the emotional reasons behind the members' apparent reluctance to tell the team leader their true feelings about his ideas. If Wilfred were knowledgeable about the psychodynamics of groups, he might be able to try an intervention in the meeting in which he would describe explicitly the undercurrents he sensed and then facilitate a discussion about the members' emotional reactions to the company situation and the effects of those reactions on their work. Psychodynamic theorists would argue that discussions such as this ultimately would benefit the group's work on its organizational tasks. We will return briefly to this vignette as we discuss the formal definition and fundamental assumptions of psychodynamic perspectives.

Psychodynamic Perspectives Defined

As the title of the chapter implies, there is more than one version of the psychodynamic perspective. We focus here on two major approaches— *psychoanalytic* (Bion, 1961; Foulkes, 1964; Freud, 1920; Kernberg, 1984; Klein, 1959; Miller, 1998; Slater, 1966; Yalom, 1995), and *humanistic* (Back, 1972; Golembiewski & Blumberg, 1977; Lewin, 1943; Maslow, 1970; Moreno, 1953; Rogers, 1970; Shaffer & Galinsky, 1989). Both approaches have in common a focus on the relationship between nonconscious and conscious processes in groups.[1] Furthermore, the roots of the various versions are based almost exclusively within the disciplines of psychotherapy and social and organizational psychology. The definition that unifies them is:

> an approach to the study of group behavior that focuses on the relationship between the emotional nonconscious processes and the conscious rational processes of interpersonal interaction.

The various psychodynamic perspectives share in common three broad assumptions. The first is that emotional and nonconscious processes exist within all human groups. This assumption is based on the argument that the universal psychological processes by which humans develop in terms of emotions and personality form the foundations of social behaviors (Klein, 1959). Examples of these individual-level processes include defense mechanisms and identification processes. One of the debates among psychodynamic perspectives is whether groups as a whole manifest such processes (e.g., Bion, 1961) or whether these processes are only meaningful as individual-level phenomena manifested in a group context (e.g., Foulkes, 1964). Put in the language of therapy, one of the roots of this field, the question is whether psychoanalysis is performed on individuals in a group setting or on the whole group.

The second assumption is that despite the fact that these processes are largely outside of group members' conscious awareness, they nevertheless affect the quality of interpersonal interaction and task performance, no matter the specific domain or definition of the task. Much of the literature within these perspectives focuses on therapeutic and personal development groups, whose explicit task is an increase in understanding of these processes. But performance on other kinds of tasks is affected as well. The previously presented vignette contains a suggestion that group members may not be fully committed to implement a plan, even though the plan was developed through a functionally effective decision process. The psychodynamic perspective opens a window through which the unresolved anxiety within the team can be seen—an emotional state that may well attenuate the amount of effort they put forth to implement the plan. Moreover, psychodynamically oriented theorists would note that the members of this group may not be conscious of reducing their work efforts.

The third assumption is that bringing nonconscious processes to group members' conscious awareness is necessary for increasing group effectiveness. The path to learning is through dispassionate analysis of the connections between the nonconscious and the conscious dynamics within a group. Presumably, if the team in our vignette could learn to recognize how the nonvisible phenomena at work in their group affect them, they would eventually return to high morale and effective task performance. Table 3.1 summarizes these definitions and assumptions.

Varieties of Psychodynamic Perspectives

Psychoanalytic Approaches

It might reasonably be argued that the most fundamental assumption of psychoanalytic approaches is that group behavior has biological origins. The theories from this perspective rest on evolutionary arguments related to adaptiveness and survival. The existence of any group ultimately can be explained by the human instinct to combine spontaneously with others as a means to ensure species survival through protection and procreation. These

Table 3.1   The Psychodynamic Perspective

Definition of perspective	An approach to the study of group behavior that focuses on the relations between emotional and nonconscious processes and the conscious and rational processes of interpersonal interaction
Key assumptions	• Social behavior has roots in biological instincts • Existence of a group mind • Unawareness of emotional processes inhibits effectiveness; bringing these processes to awareness removes inhibition
Types of groups	• Therapy • Personal development • Work teams
Key theories	• Psychoanalysis • Field theory • Psychodrama • Humanistic and positive psychology
Dominant research methodologies	• Case study/clinical observations • Field and quasi-experiments • Correlational survey studies
Strengths	• Compelling and enduring • Intuitively appealing • Despite variations in the theory, there is good deal of consistency • Applicability to many types of groups • Theory has been fruitful source of research
Weaknesses	• Pervasive focus on "dark" processes • Subjectivity of interpretations • Sexism • Subjective research methods, problems of generalizability

primitive instincts are driven by emotions, and the resulting emotional dynamics remain part of all human social interaction.

The emotional dynamics in groups lead to the formation of the "group mind," a concept that has been at the root of this perspective for close to a century. Le Bon (1920) and McDougall (1922) presented theories of how small and large groups come to act as if they were single organisms. Freud later adopted this concept as he began to apply his theories of human development to the group level.

Consistent with a biological approach is the observation that a medical model, specifically psychotherapeutic, is the main paradigm guiding theory and research under this perspective. Psychotherapy includes a large number of techniques for the purpose of treating emotional and psychological disturbances (see Anderson, Anderson, & Glanze, 2001). Thus psychoanalytic approaches have a problem-solving orientation. Perhaps because of the traditional medical focus on disease, there is a decided bias toward a "dark" view of the role that emotions play in groups. We intend here both the literal meaning of dark—as in the absence of, or away from light—and the figurative meaning, as in mysterious or sinister. These processes are dark because they are not directly observable and because they are seen as the source of the problems to be solved. Not surprising, virtually all of the key theorists whose work has shaped psychoanalytic approaches to groups— Sigmund Freud, Melanie Klein, Wilfred Bion, Michael (Siegmund) Foulkes, A. K. Rice and Elliott Jacques—were psychotherapists.

Early Roots: Sigmund Freud and Melanie Klein

Freud developed his theory and method of psychoanalysis initially for working with individual patients suffering from neuroses. He himself, however, was among the first to recognize the potential application of his theories to the social arena. As mentioned earlier, he embraced the concept of the singular group mind presented by Le Bon (1920) and McDougall (1922). Freud characterized the emotional processes that formed the group mind as libidinal and defensive in nature, relating to the fundamental instincts of procreation and survival (see Ettin, Cohen, & Fidler, 1997; Long, 1992).

Freud characterized the development of personality as a series of fixed stages, each stage characterized by a particular conflict between the libidinous instincts and societal expectations. He viewed personality as consisting of three structures: the *id,* which operates at the unconscious level and is the source of instincts and emotions; the *superego,* which also operates at the unconscious level and is the repository of values and moral sense; and the *ego,* which is the seat of rational and conscious thought. The developmental stages describe the growth of the ego and its ability to control the unconscious impulses and processes of the id and the superego. The idea of developmental stages characterized by resolution of inherent tensions is central to psychoanalytic approaches to groups. As will be seen in the coming discussion of Wilfred Bion, a group could be said to act at any given time as if it were in a particular stage of psychosexual development.

Melanie Klein's (1946, 1959) work, particularly in her departures from Freud's views, paved the way for significant advancement in psychoanalytic theories of group behavior. Consistent with Freud, Klein argued that the development of the higher order elements of personality (ego and superego) evolved through processes of defending the psyche against anxiety. Both Freud and Klein postulated that the earliest emotion experienced in the human psyche is aggression and that the child's inchoate ego is too fragile to contain the full measure of its own aggressive impulses. Klein argued that the infant resorts to the primitive ego defense mechanism of *splitting,* which involves separating its positive and negative emotions and then *projecting* these emotions onto different objects. The infant thus eventually comes to experience its world as populated by various objects toward which it has negative or positive feelings. These objects, which Klein recognizes as being at a fantasy level of experience, form structures that help the infant develop a sense of reality about its world (Long, 1992). She departed from Freud in postulating that these processes occur at a much younger age than he contended, and she believed that the sexual instincts played a less prominent role in development. Unlike Freud, Klein worked directly with children and thus arguably had a firmer empirical basis for her version of the theory.

The splitting and projection processes are theorized to take place at the level of fantasy, but Klein postulated that these processes affect behavior and relations in reality, through the process of *projective identification.* Klein referred to this as a "process where fantasized, split off parts of the self are projected into others, so that those others are seen to possess these parts, and so that the individual becomes identified with the other" (quoted in Long, 1992, p. 28). An example of how splitting and projection might persist in social situations could be illustrated in the vignette presented earlier. Certain members of Wilfred's group might find it threatening to feel resentment toward their boss. Those members might instead begin to perceive another member of the group as possessing negative characteristics and, accordingly, project resentment toward that other member rather than toward Wilfred, the leader.

Although Klein herself did not apply these ideas to groups, it can be readily seen how subsequent followers of her ideas, most notably Bion (1961), would take this step. Klein's idea of projective identification suggests that interaction between people can occur on a nonconscious level. She suggested that the basic structures formed by the primitive ego defenses of splitting and projection, and the more developed mechanism of projective identification, form the basis for patterns that continue to manifest themselves in interpersonal interactions throughout life. This argument has been the cornerstone of the most important theoretical developments in the psychoanalytic perspective. Otto Kernberg (1998), a contemporary proponent of Klein's ideas, reports that "impressive clinical evidence indicates that regardless of the individual's maturity and psychological integration, certain group conditions tend to bring on regression and activate primitive psychological levels" (p. 7).

Wilfred Bion

Arguably, Wilfred Bion is the single most important theorist across all versions of psychodynamic perspectives on groups (Kernberg, 1998). His theory and method have been applied to groups of all sizes, within just about every setting imaginable. The most widely taught and cited theories of group development, which we will discuss explicitly in a later section of this chapter, are built on the skeleton of Bion's theory. We will accordingly discuss his theory and contributions at some length here.

Bion's work was directly influenced by Klein, who was both his mentor and his analyst. She was also a founding member of the Tavistock Institute, where she and Bion were colleagues. Bion's experiments with conducting psychotherapy in group settings, which eventually became known as "the Tavistock method," began at a British military hospital with neurotic patients (Bion, 1961). Following his psychoanalytic heritage, Bion accepted the idea of a group acting as a single entity, but he took it a step further. He argued that there was a distinction between psychotherapy on individuals conducted in a group setting and psychotherapy on the group as a whole. He thus contributed methods and theories that allowed for the study and treatment of groups as entities in their own right. We will describe the Tavistock method in more detail in the later section on methodology.

One of the qualities unique to the group-as-a-whole perspective is group culture. Bion described two types of cultures: one that characterizes groups engaged in sophisticated, rational work (*the work group culture*) and another that characterizes groups acting as if they were assembled for some reason other than the overt task (*basic assumption group cultures*). These basic assumption groups are shadows, existing in a parallel but nonconscious level as the work group. For Bion, the basic assumption groups are the *biogenetic core* universal to all human groups.

Miller (1998) presents a very useful elaboration of the biological basis of Bion's basic assumption groups. Miller shows that there are two fundamental biological instincts: survival and reproduction. The survival instinct can be divided into the instincts to seek pleasure and to avoid pain. The instinct to seek pleasure is associated with the nurturing received from the mother's breast (or substitute) and the accompanying dependency on her care taking. This dependency is associated with the conflicting emotions of aggression, also directed toward the caretaker because of anxiety aroused by the dependency, and rage when the breast is removed. These emotions of aggression and rage are associated with the instinct to avoid pain. The role of these two survival instincts is to increase the chances of the third instinct—to reproduce the species. This instinct is associated with the libidinal emotions of love and attraction.

Bion described three kinds of basic assumption cultures, each having an emotional character derived from one of the three instincts: pain avoidance, pleasure seeking, and reproduction. Miller argued that the conflict described between the pleasure derived from one's caretaker, on the one hand, and the rage and aggression that results from depending on that caretaker, on the other, leaves an imprint that is manifested in the basic assumptions of *dependency* and of *fight-flight*. Groups operating under the emotions of the dependency assumption behave *as if* they are in need of nurturing. They look for or expect a leader to show them what to do, to reassure them, or in short, to take care of them. Groups operating under the fight-flight basic assumption behave emotionally *as if* they face an enemy or are on the verge of battle. They look for a leader either to lead them into battle or to lead their retreat from the battle. And according to Miller, the libidinal energy associated with the reproductive instinct is the basis for the emotional character of Bion's *pairing* basic assumption culture. Groups operating under a pairing basic assumption are characterized by the emotions of expectation and hope. The group's attention is drawn to the relationship between two of its members, whom the group expects to produce a "messiah" who will deliver them from their problems. What is important is maintaining the sense of expectation. The messiah must therefore remain hoped-for and unborn.

The work group culture, in contrast to the basic assumption cultures, is governed by rationality and task orientation rather than by emotions. The work group

> has an organization appropriate to its task; it operates on the basis of rationality; members are valued for their contribution rather than for their status, and they recognize their disagreements; it can tolerate turnover of members without fear of losing its identity, and it can recognize and face the need for change. (Miller, 1998, p. 1497)

The work group is conscious; the basic assumption groups are nonconscious and parallel to the work group. Bion's biogenetic hypothesis asserts that humans are genetically predisposed to operate under the group culture of the basic assumptions: "Participating in basic-assumption activity requires no training, experience, or mental development. It is instantaneous, inevitable, and instinctive" (Bion, 1961, p. 138). There have been suggestions of additional basic assumption cultures (e.g., Hopper, 1997; Turquet, 1985) and criticisms of Bion's conceptualization (e.g., Brown, 2000; Shambaugh, 1985), but the three cultures originally formulated by Bion remain the ones generally accepted in this literature.

Bion's basic assumption cultures are analogous to the instinct-driven id from Freudian theory. Growth and maturity involve learning to control the impulses originating in the id; analogously, maturity of a group represents that group's ability to control the impulse to operate under a basic assumption culture. The basic assumption groups represent regressive forces within a group that threaten progress on the group's overt work task (Karterud, 2000). For example, the group presented in the earlier vignette could be considered to be acting under the basic assumption of fight-flight. The members seem to behave *as if* the group is under siege; some of them appear to be running from the battle through apathy, whereas others are preparing for it through antagonism. A rational description of these emotions might ultimately help this group to increase its capacity to overcome the regressive effects of basic assumptions.

In the same way that there is a positive aspect to the id's role in individual personality, the basic assumption is that cultures have a positive role to play in groups. The emotions that underlie the dependency culture, for example, are important for the work of institutions such as schools or hospitals, whose role is essentially a nurturing one. The aggressiveness of the fight-flight culture has value within organizations such as businesses or armies, which are engaged in competition. The expectant hopeful outlook characteristic of the pairing basic assumption culture might be useful for organizations such as arts institutions, which are engaged in generative or creative endeavors. Emotionally healthy groups know how to channel the emotions into task progress.

A final concept of Bion's theory we present here is his notion of *valency*. He defined valency as

> the individual's readiness to enter into combination with the group in making and acting on basic assumptions; if his capacity for combination is great, I shall speak of a high valency, if small, of low valency; he can have, in my view, *no* valency only by ceasing to be human. (Bion, 1961, p. 103; emphasis in original)

Bion's definition of valency further illustrates his belief that basic assumptions are fundamental to human nature. This particular belief, that emotions are fundamental to human nature and are part of all social interactions, represents one of the assumptions that is common across all traditions of psychodynamic perspectives. We turn now to a discussion of the humanistic tradition.

Humanistic Approaches

The chief difference between the humanistic and psychoanalytic approaches is that the humanistic approach focuses on the unleashing of potential rather than the curing of pathology. Thus, whereas a medical model characterizes psychoanalytic approaches, a model based on education and development is the hallmark of humanistic approaches. The most prominent theorists whose work formed the foundations for this tradition included social psychologists and educators as well as clinicians (e.g., Kurt Lewin, Abraham Maslow, Carl Rogers, Jacob Moreno).

The institution most closely associated with humanistic approaches is the National Training Laboratory (NTL) (Back, 1972; Bradford, Gibb, & Benne, 1964; Cooper & Mangham, 1971; Golembiewski & Blumberg, 1977; Shaffer & Galinsky, 1989), where the T-group (T for *training*) method was born in 1946. In contrast to Tavistock groups, which have remained closely affiliated with the Tavistock Institute, T-groups spread wildly beyond the confines of the NTL and took on the proportions of a social movement. Training workshops became variously known by the labels of human relations training, sensitivity training, and encounter group training (Faith, Wong, & Carpenter, 1995; Weigel, 2002). Even the titles given to group facilitators reflect to some extent the contrast between the Tavistock and T-group traditions. Tavistock group facilitators usually are referred to as *consultants*, emphasizing their role of diagnosing and helping to solve problems. T-group facilitators are usually called *trainers*, emphasizing their role of education and development. The distinction between specific methods of the T-group and Tavistock will be addressed when we discuss methodological issues.

Despite these differences, the Tavistock Institute and the NTL share the psychodynamic focus on emotions and nonconscious processes in groups and the notion that an explicit focus on these processes is beneficial for the development of groups. The Tavistock Institution predated NTL by nearly 20 years, and we know that the NTL founders were influenced by Bion's work. There is also evidence that the Tavistock practitioners knew of and respected the work of the early NTL contributors, Kurt Lewin in particular.

Kurt Lewin and the First Training Workshop

A remarkable fact about the history of the T-group movement is that the time of its origin, almost to the very moment, is clear. There is no debate about the widely told story (see Back, 1972; Shaffer & Galinsky, 1989; and www.ntl .org for excellent accounts of the history). In 1946, Kurt Lewin directed a conference in New Britain, Connecticut, designed to train leaders to handle intergroup tensions in their home communities. Three learning groups were formed, facilitated respectively by Ronald Lippitt, Kenneth Benne, and Leland Bradford. In addition, each of the groups was assigned a research staff member, who collected observation data during the group sessions. Nightly debriefing sessions were held with the facilitators and research observers to discuss what had happened in the groups during the day's sessions.

One evening, three of the conference participants asked if they could sit in on the debriefing, and Lewin granted this request. Eventually, the conversation among the facilitators made reference to one of the participants there present, who then reacted to what had been said by offering her own interpretation of what had happened earlier in the group. Lewin, in particular, grew very interested and excited by what he saw as this additional data, and eventually, the other two group members were also drawn into the discussion. After word spread throughout the conference about this exciting session, all the participants showed up for the debriefing meeting the next night and every night for the remainder of the conference. These evening *feedback* sessions became the focal point of the conference.

Lewin and his colleagues, recognizing the learning benefit of these feedback sessions, decided to schedule another conference for the following year, this time building in feedback sessions as a formal part of the conference design. The feedback sessions became known as training groups, eventually abbreviated to the familiar T-group. The 1947 conference, held in Bethel, Maine, was christened the first National Training Laboratory in Group Dynamics. Tragically, Kurt Lewin died before this conference took place.

The origins of the humanistic approach show another aspect of its contrast with the psychoanalytic approach. The humanistic approach began with a focus on groups, whereas the psychoanalytic approach started with a focus on individuals. Lewin and his colleagues had founded the Research Center for Group Dynamics at MIT (later moved to the University of Michigan after Lewin's death), and it was this center that sponsored the 1946 Connecticut conference.

Lewin's earliest contributions to the field of group dynamics had been a series of studies showing the effects of group discussion on attitude change (e.g., Lewin, 1943, 1958). The objective of these studies was to change consumer eating habits during World War II. The strategy of combining systematic data collection with effecting behavior change introduced one of Lewin's great contributions to all of social science: the action research paradigm (Lewin, 1947, 1948). A central aspect of the action research paradigm is feedback, from researcher to participant back to researcher. It is, therefore, not surprising that Lewin quickly recognized the important role of feedback in those first impromptu sessions.

Whereas the biological sciences informed Bion and other psychoanalysts, the physical sciences informed the work of Lewin and those influenced by him. In particular, his field theory (Lewin, 1951) relied on ideas and language from physics to describe and explain the dynamics governing human social interaction. The German tradition of Gestalt psychology (e.g., Koffka, 1935; Kohler, 1969) was a key foundation to his work. The ideas from field theory have been applied to the dynamics of small (e.g., Bales, Cohen, & Williamson, 1979) and large (e.g., Rice, 1965) groups. In Lewin's view, non-conscious processes produce forces that control the patterns of interactions among individuals within a social context, just as physical forces control the relative movement of objects within a field. Bales et al. (1979), for example, theorized that interpersonal behaviors could be defined as vectors, each having a measurable force and direction. Patterns of polarization and unification, therefore, could be predicted through vector analysis. Furthermore, the operation of vectors could occur also at the nonconscious levels of fantasy or of values.

The Spread Beyond NTL

In this discussion we will use the terms *humanistic* and *T-group* interchangeably. By the 1960s and 1970s, the interest in the T-group movement in the United States was extensive. From its headquarters in Bethel, NTL opened offices elsewhere in the United States, most notably in California. Perhaps due to the early loss of its central figure, Kurt Lewin, a core definition of T-group and a strict adherence to a particular methodology did not hold. Meetings, workshops, conferences, and independent consulting practices proliferated, carrying the different labels mentioned earlier. It has also been argued that the culture of the United Sates, characterized by relative affluence and a high degree of mobility among its population, was also a factor in the diffuse spread of the T-group movement (Back, 1972).

A source of controversy and tension surrounding the explosive proliferation of laboratory training during the 1960s and 1970s was whether T-groups were becoming therapy groups (e.g., Back, 1972; Golembiewski & Blumberg, 1977). Furthermore, the perceived blurring of the boundaries between T-group training and therapy was also the source of the questions raised about the legitimacy of T-groups (Alderfer, 1998; Back, 1972; Golembiewski & Blumberg, 1977; Walton & Warwick, 1973; Weigel, 2002). On balance, however, T-group methodology has been viewed as valuable, especially within the organizational sector (e.g., Campbell & Dunnette, 1968; House, 1967). We will return to a discussion of the empirical evidence of T-group effectiveness.

Abraham Maslow (1970) raised an important counterpoint to psychoanalytic approaches. He argued not only that those approaches were flawed, with their focus on disease, but also that the general medical model held the same flaw. His view was that the route to health, both physical and mental, was through the study of healthy people. Although Maslow dealt very little with groups, his perspective was extended and adapted to the group level by

Clayton Alderfer (1987). Also, his views converged with those of Lewin and the T-Group movement in the work of Douglas McGregor (1960). Today's burgeoning work in the area of positive psychology continues this tradition, and we will review some of the work in a later section.

The Maslovian perspective suggests that the lower-level needs are based in biology but that the higher needs transcend the biological. Particularly problematic for the group literature is the place of affiliative needs in the hierarchy. In Maslow's scheme, these lie between the biologically based physiological and safety needs and the higher-order esteem and self-actualization needs. Bion's basic assumption of pairing suggests, for example, that affiliation within groups is a reflection of biological (reproductive) needs, albeit at the level of fantasy. Yet, group members' affiliations with one another can also be linked to self-esteem and even self-actualization.

The essence of the T-group approach is personal development. It is generally agreed that the objectives of this approach are "1) self insight . . . 2) understanding the conditions which inhibit or facilitate effective group functioning, 3) understanding interpersonal operations in groups, and 4) developing skills for diagnosing individual, group and organizational behavior" (Bennis, 1977, p. 18). Thus, the objective of T-groups is not to solve specific problems. Rather, individual group members learn to take what they have learned from the T-group experience to solve their problems for themselves.

Moreno's psychodramatic perspective could also be classified as humanistic in that it focuses on unleashing rather than overcoming emotion. The psychodramatic approach first appeared in Moreno's 1934 book, *Who Shall Survive? A New Approach to the Problem of Human Interrelations* (revised and retitled, 1953). It represents the triumph of emotion over analysis and promotes the view that the individual and the group need to be liberated through spontaneity and the expression of repressed emotion. Formally, psychodrama can be defined as "a method that uses dramatizations of personal experiences through role-playing and enactment under a variety of simulated conditions, which include at least one scene and one psychodramatic technique" (Kipper & Ritchie, 2003, p. 14). Examples of psychodramatic techniques will be described in the following section on methods.

Moreno's second main contribution to the group literature was sociometry. Sociometric methods are used to define groups that exist in larger collectives as well as to highlight interconnections among groups. The individual can be seen as lying at the intersection of overlapping groups, defined by networks of social relationships. This is a concept that has its origins in the work of Georg Simmel (1908/1955). The original German title of his extended essay, "The Web of Group Affiliation," translates as "Intersecting Social Circles." Polley and Eid (1994) combined Moreno's concept of the social atom, Lewinian field theory, and Simmel's intersecting social circles into the notion of social molecules, an extension of the physical science metaphor that pervades this branch of the psychodynamic tradition.

The impact of both Lewin and Moreno on theory and practice is paradoxical. Lewin's major theoretical contribution was field theory, and yet few of the attempts to develop this theory have borne much fruit. On the other hand, Lewin's model of action research, although much less theoretically rich, has been embraced by organizational development practitioners as well as by social workers. Moreno's psychodramatic perspective represents a small niche in the practice of group psychotherapy, whereas his basic sociometric concepts led to a number of major lines of research on networks of affiliation. Both Lewin and Moreno started significant lines of theoretical development rich with psychodynamic origins, but what grew out of their work was the pragmatic—a method of change in Lewin's case and a method of measuring and organizing interpersonal bonds in the case of Moreno.

Finally, we would like to note that despite the different philosophical orientations underlying the psychoanalytic and humanistic approaches to psychodynamic theory, the earlier history shows that these two traditions influenced each other significantly. The design of the early T-groups certainly borrowed some of the techniques from Bion's Tavistock method. The consulting practice of the Tavistock Institute, in turn, was influenced by Lewin's action research techniques. A. K. Rice's (Rice, 1965; Miller & Rice, 1967) development of open systems theory, in particular, represents a conjunction between these two traditions. We now turn to a discussion of methodological issues.

Methodological Issues

The work within all versions of psychodynamic perspectives is dominated by practice over theoretically driven research. The area is rich with theory, but the theories have been more frequently applied directly to the field of practice than to systematic data collection. Even the well-crafted and theoretically driven research of Kurt Lewin was tied closely to producing social change. Thus, it might be said that an interest in producing change—at the level of individual, group, and organization—characterizes methodological choices within this perspective. Because the work is so heavily practice driven, we must talk about two classes of methodology. The first contains the techniques and tools of practice, such as the design of a T-group conference or the tools involved in psychodrama. The second contains tools, traditionally thought to be research methods, that are used to collect systematic data on various questions related to psychodynamic perspectives in groups. In making the distinction between these two classes, however, we do not intend to imply that the methods of practice do not constitute research. Indeed, the tradition of action research that is foundational within this perspective provides the means for linking practice to research. We discuss each of these classes separately.

Methods Used in Practice

As mentioned near the beginning of the chapter, an assumption that all varieties of psychodynamic perspectives share is the beneficial effects of bringing nonconscious and emotional processes to the conscious awareness of group members. The differences between the various approaches lie in the objectives and the techniques for bringing forth nonconscious processes. Although there are many variations of group practice based on psychodynamic theories, the three techniques of the Tavistock method, T-group laboratory training, and psychodrama are the most representative. The general format that all these techniques share in common is that the group experience itself is often part of a larger training or therapy workshop. The duration of the groups can range from one single session to multiple sessions spanning many weeks. A format particularly popular during the height of the T-group encounter movement in the 1960s and 1970s was the 2- to 3-day marathon session, with T-group experiences interspersed with other learning activities such as lectures (Weigel, 2002). The average size of a group is between 7 and 10 members, although groups as large as 20 are not uncommon. A trainer or consultant works with the group, as will be described later.

The major contribution that Bion made by his development of the Tavistock method was to provide a way of treating the group-as-a-whole, in contrast to treating individuals within a group setting. The most famous aspect of the Tavistock method is perhaps the behavior of the therapist or consultant. The consultant decidedly does not act as a leader, organizer, or facilitator of the group. The ambiguity inherent in the situation that ensues is central to the technique; it provides the occasion for primitive regressive emotions associated with the basic assumption cultures to manifest and thereby to become available for analysis (Whitman, 1964).

The consultant to a group, as he or she observes the evidence of the particular culture operating in a group, will make *interpretations* that may describe directly what he or she sees or that may be designed to get group members to recognize the evidence themselves. Keeping the focus on the group, even interpretations about the behavior of a particular individual member are interpretations about the group. The psychoanalytically oriented therapist or consultant attempts to present an emotionally neutral face to the group so that the intrapsychic processes, such as projection and identification, that form the basic assumption cultures will emerge. Because the Tavistock technique is oriented toward solving or curing problems, the therapist or consultant will tailor interpretations to the specific problem(s) facing a particular patient or client group. In this way, the Tavistock method can be thought of as a prescription to help with a particular issue (Back, 1972).

The T-group laboratory training shares some common surface characteristics with the Tavistock method. The group trainer similarly adopts an explicit non-leading role, also with the result of creating a situation filled with ambiguity. As in the Tavistock method, it is expected that removing accustomed social structures will make salient for people their emotional reactions to those structures. The T-group trainer also makes interpretations of participants' reactions with regard to what those reactions reveal about nonconscious processes. Departing from the Tavistock psychoanalytic tradition, the T-group approach does not attempt to relate participants' emotional reactions to deeper intrapsychic structures and history. The nonconscious processes that come to light are examined for what participants can learn from them about their own behaviors or about groups generally (Bennis, 1977). Finally, the stance of the trainer is more one of collaboration than of neutrality.

Psychodrama techniques are also designed to bring nonconscious process into conscious awareness. The methods used rely on social and personal identities. The characters that are taken on through the various techniques represent specific identities or aspects of identity. Examples of psychodrama techniques include *role reversal,* where two group members begin by portraying particular roles and then switch the roles; *role playing,* where group members enact roles but without changing their identities, for example when members play the role of being themselves; and *doubling,* where one group member portrays him- or herself while another group member also plays the role of that first member. Unlike leaders in the Tavistock and T-group methods, the group trainer may take an active and literally director's role. In common with the T-group trainer role, the psychodramatist collaborates with the group members. On the other hand, psychodrama is closer to the Tavistock method in that it was developed as a method of conducting psychotherapy, although over the history of its development, its uses have not been limited to therapy.

Methods Used in Research

The vast majority of the data collected by those interested in psychodynamic perspectives in groups focuses on how group members change. Therefore, most empirical research in this area investigates the efficacy of the techniques used in practice. The literature exploring this question includes examinations of what specific aspects of personality or behavior are affected, the processes through which effects occur, the means by which the effects can be measured, and the factors that explain differences in patterns and rates of change.

The most frequent methods used are case studies and quasi-experimental field studies. Case study methodology, so characteristic of the clinical approach, dominated the early literature in this area. Bion's (1961) landmark book is actually a series of case reports from his therapy groups, gathered together in a single volume. Bion's case studies provided systematic descriptions of behavior patterns as evidence for the existence of the constructs he theorized. Lion and Gruenfeld (1993), Stock and Thelen (1958), and Thelen (2000) also describe, through their personal experiences as participants and researchers in group laboratories, the operation of Bion's constructs. This use of case study to provide evidence that theorized concepts can be perceived in reality is also a feature of studies from both psychoanalytic and humanistic perspectives. The other primary application of case study methodology, also equally applicable to all psychodynamic perspectives, is to show evidence of the effects on participants in the group experience. Casey and Solomon (1971), for example, reported evidence from a case study that seating arrangements in a T-group affected the network of interaction among the group members.

Field studies designed to examine the outcomes of the group experience on the participants tend to use either a pre- and posttest design (e.g., Danish, 1971; Hipple, 1976; Smith, 1983) or a treatment, nontreatment control group design (e.g., Bunker, 1965). The outcome measures examined include changes in individual traits such as self-control and neuroticism (e.g., Anderson & Slocum, 1973) and behaviors such as communication and interpersonal skills (e.g., Hipple, 1976). Qualitative reviews of the literature generally conclude that participation in a T-group leads to behavior change (e.g., Campbell & Dunnette, 1968; Forsyth, 1991; Hartman, 1979; Highhouse, 2002; House, 1967; Lieberman, 1976; Smith, 1975). Two meta-analyses provide quantitative support for this general claim (Burke & Day, 1986; Faith et al., 1995). In another meta-analysis, focused specifically on psychodrama, Kipper and Ritchie (2003) examined 25 studies. They reported average effect sizes larger than for other forms of group psychotherapy. They also found that the specific psychodrama techniques of role reversal and doubling were the most effective. We are not aware of qualitative or quantitative review studies specifically focused on the effectiveness of the Tavistock method.

Another approach found in field studies is to compare or vary different factors. Differences in the style or characteristics of the group consultant or trainer have been one such interest. Lundgren and Knight (1977), for example, found a positive relation between T-group trainers' needs for control and affection and group members' attitudes toward the trainers. Morrison (1984) compared leaders behaving as Tavistock method consultants and as T-group trainers in terms of their effect on groups. He reported that group leaders were more positively valued and seen as more competent and more emotionally supportive when behaving as T-group trainers than as Tavistock consultants. In an interesting follow-up study, Morrison and Stein (1985) added the factor of gender. Male and female leaders behaved as either Tavistock consultants or as T-group trainers. T-group trainers overall were seen as more emotionally supportive, but female T-group trainers were seen as least competent and potent. Morrison and Stein found further that male trainers were most highly valued overall.

Courter (1999) added to the gender difference literature by varying the gender composition of the groups, but holding the gender of the consultants constant. Using all-female consultants of Tavistock groups, he found that all-female groups were most resistant to the consultant. Courter's study is also an example of field studies that examine differences in characteristics of the groups or the group members.

A frequent research question is how do the characteristics of individual group members account for differences in the effect of a group experience. Danish (1971), for example, found a positive relation between participant motivation to change and measures of actual behavioral change following a T-group experience. McConnell (1971), as another example, reported that the individual traits of flexibility, tolerance, independence, and decisiveness predicted success in a T-group experience. Anderson and Slocum's (1973) review of the role of individual traits on T-group outcomes presented results consistent with these findings. Anderson and Slocum also noted that although T-group training seemed to be associated with changes in behaviors and attitudes, changes in personality were unlikely to occur.

The methods of data collection include self- and other-report measures, frequently using established instruments such as Schutz's (1966) FIRO-B. Moreno's (1953) sociometric methods, however, are probably the most enduring methodological advance to come out of the psychodynamic perspective. The method is simple, although often misused. Members of a large group are asked very specific questions: Who would you like to room with?

Who would you like to work with? Who would you least like to work with? In the early years of sociometry, the answers to these questions were recorded by plotting the network of connections on paper. People would then be moved from group to group on the diagram in an attempt to maximize the number of ties within a group, such as a housing unit or work group. This method was used in both a wartime resettlement camp in Hungary and a girls' school in New York. When sociometry was rediscovered decades later, various computer algorithms were used to achieve the same result, leading to the development of network analysis. In practice, much of the work in network analysis has involved the sort of vague choice questions that Moreno railed against: Who do you like? Who do you dislike? The field of network analysis would do well to return to Moreno's original guidelines. Networks of affiliation are complex and multidimensional and not easily captured by a single like-dislike continuum.

The other systematic methodological approach to stem from the psychodynamic perspective is Bales's methods of observation and interpersonal rating. These began with interaction process analysis (IPA) (Bales, 1950), a relatively objective measurement instrument that involved trained scorers who recorded interaction within 12 categories (6 on the task side and 6 on the emotional side). The theoretical basis was Parsonian functionalism (see Parsons, Bales, & Shils, 1953), but the nature of the self-analytic groups that were observed (at the Harvard Business School and later in Harvard undergraduate classes) quickly led Bales to integrate the methodology with psychodynamic theory. *Personality and Interpersonal Behavior* (Bales, 1970) laid the groundwork, based on Arthur Couch's (1960) dissertation study relating a wide variety of personality tests to observed interpersonal behavior. From there, SYMLOG (Bales et al., 1979) explicitly integrated psychodynamic concepts by asking observers to infer values from fantasy content in group discussion.

The methodology employed by this branch of researchers began as purely observational (IPA) and then moved to direct observation using SYMLOG supplemented by questionnaire-based interpersonal ratings. IPA records only behavior, and all coding is done by outside observers. This observational information is supplemented by a battery of psychological tests administered to group participants. SYMLOG records both behavior and the content of imagery. In some cases, outside observers are employed, but paralleling the earlier shift by NTL to participant observation and analysis, group members have been trained in SYMLOG observation methods, and small subsets of participants rotate out of the interacting group to observe and provide feedback.

Typically, two sessions are observed each week, and a third session is used for feedback. SYMLOG scoring codes all references to people and events outside the "here and now" of the group as "fantasy" and treats these fantasy images—from history, literature, current events, and so forth—as reflections of processes occurring in the group. Retrospective interpersonal ratings at both the behavioral and image levels supplemented these direct observations. At this point, very few researchers are using the direct observation methods, and practice has shifted to the interpersonal ratings. There are two reasons for this shift. First, direct observation is costly and time consuming, and second, the rating method allows for all members to provide their perceptions of each other member, yielding richer information about biases and motivated perceptions. What is lost is much of the detailed information about imagery and the fine-grained analysis of group development that is only possible with observational methods.

Key Findings of Psychodynamic Research

What Facets of Group Composition Affect the Group's Interaction and Performance?

Table 3.2 summarizes the findings reviewed in this section. The facets receiving the most attention within psychodynamic perspectives have been personality traits (e.g., Anderson & Slocum, 1973; Boller, 1974; Danish, 1971; Lion & Gruenfeld, 1993; Lundgren, 1973; McConnell, 1971; Poland & Jones, 1973) and demographic characteristics (e.g., Courter, 1999; Hafsi, 1997; Morrison, 1984; Morrison & Stein, 1985; Takahashi, 1991). The psychoanalytic approaches tend to focus on how facets of composition lead to variations in basic patterns of social interaction that are assumed to be the universal consequences of biological instincts. Bion's basic assumption groups are examples of such universal patterns. Human development is about learning to respond in socially acceptable ways to the pulls of instinct, according to the psychoanalytic view. Personality and demography are two socially relevant factors that can explain individual differences in responses.

For example, Moxnes (1998, 1999) argued for the existence of a specific set of archetypal roles in groups, which have a biogenetic basis. He thus sees these roles as universal. The roles he proposes have strong gender identities (e.g., father, mother, son, daughter, king, queen), and Moxnes attributes traditionally gender-appropriate characteristics to them. He is careful to describe these specific roles as social constructions that have biological origins. The origins, he argues, are rooted in the universal human experience of "unity with a mother" (1999, p. 1438).

Table 3.2   Key Findings From Psychodynamic Perspective Research

Group composition	Groups generally are small; characteristics of individual members are rarely direct focus of research attention; rather, the interpersonal dynamics that might be triggered by personal characteristics is the focus of attention
Group structure	The boundaries of the groups should be clear, firm, yet permeable; interpsychic structures, analogous to but not the same as intrapsychic structures, are thought to exist; specific roles are thought to exist
Group projects	The group itself is typically the project; improvement of its functioning; greater understanding of group processes is general aim
Interaction	Interaction takes place at conscious and nonconscious levels; nature and pattern of interpersonal interaction is significant focus of attention within this perspective; overt, conscious interaction is thought to contain evidence about the interaction also taking place at the deeper, nonconscious level; group trainers' practice of interpretation is unique form of interaction
Group action/outcomes	Most important outcome is insight and understanding of group function and actual improvement of group functioning; an area of debate is whether improvement of individuals is explicit goal
Change over time	Based on biological model, groups are thought to be organisms that mature over time; the process of maturity unfolds in a set series of stages or phases; these phases are frequently modeled after phases of human infant development along the dimensions of emotional and psychosexual maturity
Ecology	Group boundaries are important; groups are thought to be entities that stand apart from their backgrounds; identity derives partly from position in the environment relative to other groups and entities in that environment

Moxnes (1999) presents some suggestions that the emergence of these deep, archetypal roles may not be universal. In some research he did in Japan, which he characterized as a collectivist culture, he did not observe the emergence of deep roles. Moxnes speculated that the deep roles might exist in such cultures at the level of inter- rather than intragroup. Another possibility that he did not consider was that his own observation approach may not have allowed him to discern roles relevant to that culture.

The approach to group composition from a humanistic orientation can be described as more factorial in nature, in keeping with the reliance on experimental design that is characteristic of this approach. This research has consisted largely of field-based experiments examining the effects of specific factors relevant to group composition. Examples of the personality or demographic factors that have been examined include group members' social status and dominance hierarchies (Lundgren, 1973; Plutchik & Landau, 1973), need for control (Lundgren & Knight, 1977), and self-concept (Serok & Bar, 1984).

Differences in social status, as conceptualized in sociology, have received surprisingly little attention within this literature. Social status has largely been treated as an emergent property at an intragroup level, as a function of the behavior and roles exhibited by the members in the group (e.g., Lundgren, 1973). But the extent to which societally defined indicators of status affect the psychodynamics of groups is a question that has largely not been addressed. Blackwell (2002), for example, presents an analysis of how encounters in groups between people from different social classes (defined by relation to the means of production in society) mirror the societal-level conflicts between those classes. Szonyi (2002) reported that social distance, based on differences in societally defined roles, affects the processes within therapy groups. Given the relative paucity of psychodynamic work on social status, this would seem to be a fruitful area for future inquiry.

How Do the Group's Projects Affect Its Interaction and Performance?

We need to reconsider the wording of this question for psychodynamic perspectives. As originally formulated, the question frames the group's projects as being *in relation to* its processes. In contrast, psychodynamic perspectives treat the group's processes *as* its projects (Hirschhorn, 1999). This is true for both psychoanalytic and humanistic approaches. Group tasks, as treated in a functional sense of accomplishments or outcomes, are almost incidental within the psychodynamic literature. A work task may present the occasion for the study of psychodynamic processes, but there is very little systematic examination of task *qua* task in this perspective. Even for Bion, who characterizes the basic assumption groups as interfering with the *work* of a group, the work is gain of insight and sophistication about the group's functioning. Thus, we believe the most useful issues to address with respect to group task, as conceptualized by the psychodynamic theorists, is to discuss the variations in approaches to the task—defined as gaining insight and maturity and improving group functioning.

Despite the roots of this perspective in therapy and its focus on group process, the importance of organizational and work contexts has long been recognized within the literature (e.g., Alderfer, 1998; Burke & Day, 1986; Campbell & Dunnette, 1968; Highhouse, 2002; House, 1967; John, 2000; Kernberg, 1984; Kets de Vries & Miller, 1984; Menzies, 1959; Miller & Rice, 1967; Rice, 1965). But even within the literature describing organization settings, the focus of inquiry and analysis is on nonconscious and emotional processes. Indeed, it is reasonable to argue that an important contribution of the psychodynamic perspective is to bring attention to the pervasive existence of these processes and their impact on behavior within all social settings. Psychodynamic perspectives have been applied to a broad variety of organizational topics, such as the functioning of top management teams (e.g., Jarrett & Kellner, 1996; Noran, 1996; Paul et al., 2002), organizational conflict (e.g., Smith, 1982), and the change of organizations as a whole (e.g., Jaques, Klein, & Heimann, 1955; Kernberg, 1984, 1998).

How Are Groups Structured? What Tools and Technologies Do They Have Access To? How Do Those Structures and Technologies Affect Group Interaction and Performance?

As already described in the section on methods, both the Tavistock and T-group methods rely on the technique of not establishing formal structures for groups. The result is, thus, to make group structure the object of study. The psychoanalytic tradition assumes that groups will act as if structures, modeled from intrapsychic processes, were present. The humanistic tradition similarly assumes that structures will emerge; such structures also are based on participants' pre-existing expectations but do not necessarily stem from intrapsychic forces. Psychodynamically oriented research has examined the emergence of elements of structure such as the evidence for the presence of basic assumption cultures (e.g., Karterud, 1989a, 1989b, 2000) or the emergence of specific role structures (e.g., Casey & Solomon, 1971; Hafsi, 1998; Lundgren, 1973).

Finally, T-group and Tavistock methods can be considered "technologies" developed out of the psychodynamic perspective. In fact, the NTL founders have themselves employed the label "educational technology" (Bradford et al., 1964) for the T-group technique.

What Kinds of Group Interaction Processes
Does the Group Carry Out and How Do These
Processes Affect Other Factors and Performance?

Psychoanalytic approaches consider interaction between members to occur at both conscious and nonconscious levels. The intrapsychic processes of projection and transference can be considered to be types of interaction. Team members stimulate emotionally based reactions in each other that can be manifested and observed in patterns of overt, conscious communication. Long (1992), for example, defines groups in terms of unconscious motivations that guide "transindividual processes." Humanistic approaches generally do not dispute the nonconscious aspect of interpersonal communication. The focus of humanistically oriented work, however, is on increasing the authenticity and quality of communication (e.g., Bennis, 1977).

The roots of interaction at the nonconscious level can again be traced to Melanie Klein's theory of object-relations. Over time, infants come to view their world as populated by a variety of objects to which they have positive or negative relationships. Thus, from infancy into adulthood, humans are predisposed to think of themselves as in relationship with "others," and they have a posture of interacting with these others, regardless of whether they are physically present. Classic psychoanalytic theory postulates that interaction patterns developed from the earliest family constellation continue to operate at the nonconscious level within all social situations.

A form of interaction unique to psychodynamic perspectives is the practice of interpretation on the part of the group trainer or consultant. As described earlier, this practice involves making the usually invisible and nonconscious processes in a group visible and available for rational, conscious awareness and discussion. The impact of a group trainer's interpretations depends on individual members' ego ideal identification with a leadership figure (Kernberg, 1998; Paul et al., 2002). We argue here that even outside of the specific context of therapeutic or personal development groups, the interpersonal behavior of interpreting the emotional and nonrational significance of overt behaviors to the group is an important leadership role.

What Results From Group Action?

The result of group action that is the main focus of psychodynamic perspectives is change. For psychoanalytic approaches, change means solving a particular problem, and for humanistic approaches, change means personal development. The concern about work task performance and outcomes is generally secondary to concerns about psychological and emotional outcomes. Task performance is relevant only insofar as it indicates the emotional health of the group and individual members. Thus, as has already been reviewed in the method section, the focus of the vast majority of the research across all approaches is on the effectiveness of the group experience in bringing out positive change (see reviews by Campbell & Dunnette, 1968; Faith et al., 1995; Highhouse, 2002; House, 1967; Kipper & Ritchie, 2003).

How Does the Group Change Over Time?

It might reasonably be argued that theorizing about developmental stages in groups is the single most important contribution of psychodynamic perspectives to the general literature on groups. The change in groups over time has been of considerable research interest across all versions of psychodynamic perspectives (e.g., Aiello, 1973; Glassman & Kates, 1983; Koortzen & Cilliers, 2002; Lundgren & Knight, 1978; Woodman & Sherwood, 1980). An interest in identifying phases of group development was a motivation behind the group training conference that eventually led to the development of the T-group technique and the founding of NTL (Back, 1972).

The classic and most frequently cited theories of group development (e.g., Bennis & Shepard; 1956; Tuckman, 1965; Tuckman & Jensen, 1977; Wheelan, 1990, 1994; Wheelan, Davidson, & Tilin, 2003) can be traced back to Bion's theory of basic assumption and work group cultures and further still to Klein's object-relations theory. Early stages are characterized by orientation behaviors and members' seeking guidance and support from a leader. These early stages can be compared to Bion's dependency basic assumption groups. Later stages, as members grapple with how they will work on their task and as individual members assert ideas about work on the task, are characterized by conflict (see also Bales, 1953). This phase can be compared to the fight-flight basic assumption groups described by Bion. This stage is followed by reconciliation and overriding concern for harmony and cohesiveness. This could be compared to Bion's pairing basic assumption (with respect to the feeling of hope and optimism for the future of their projects). Finally, most models describe members' moving into a routine of rational and effective work, which can be compared to Bion's work group.

The most significant challenge to this general, linear theory of group development was put forward by Connie Gersick (1991), who proposed a *punctuated equilibrium* model of group development. She argued that groups develop, not through a fixed set of linear phases, but rather in a more evolutionary manner characterized by periods of stability interrupted by very short periods of transition. Interestingly, her model has in common with the psychodynamically derived theories a foundation in the biological sciences. Chang, Bordia, and Duck (2003) reported results from a laboratory experiment showing that both types of development patterns can operate simultaneously within a group. Despite Gersick's and others' (e.g., Poole & Roth, 1988, 1989) criticisms, linear models of group development phases continue to be accepted as the standard, cited in nearly every textbook of organizational psychology.

How Does the Group's Ecology, Including Its Physical, Social, Organizational, and Technical Environment, as well as Intergroup Relations, Affect Its Interaction and Performance?

A. K. Rice's contribution of open systems theory addresses the ecology of groups (Miller & Rice, 1967; Rice, 1965). A key tenet of this theory is that systems must make exchanges with their environments in order to survive. At the group level, the balance of task focus and focus on primitive object relations in its social field depends on such factors as the extent to which the task is clear and defined and the adequacy of task leadership (see Kernberg, 1998). A group's relationship to its environment—with respect to how well it obtains resources, how well it receives direction for a task, and what task is to be carried out—is a relevant issue; so is how well the group receives accurate feedback on how well it is fulfilling its purpose.

Exchanges between groups and their environment are transacted across the groups' boundaries. Rice posits that boundaries should be clear and firm, but permeable. Rioch (1981) described some of the practices that Rice used during Tavistock conferences to reinforce institutional boundaries. For example, he was careful to start and end sessions on time to emphasize time-based boundaries. He maintained separate physical spaces for conference participants and staff members, reinforcing role boundaries. His goal was to ensure that conference participants understood the role of boundaries, as they defined a group within its environment. Rice saw this rational approach to boundaries as part of the work group culture, as defined in Bion's sense.

Areas for Future Inquiry

Margaret Rioch (1981), who worked directly with both Bion and Rice at the Tavistock Institute, makes the following observation about their work:

> Lacking in both their works is the concept of the activity called play . . . neither . . . has given a great deal of thought to the purely esthetic aspect of life. . . . Perhaps it is characteristic of the Protestant ethic that the ideal group for both Bion and Rice is a "working" group. (p. 672)

Rioch's comment refers most specifically to the study of groups such as orchestras or sports teams, whose "work" is what most of us think of as play. Her observation, however, also offers a counterpoint to the generally negative undertone characteristic of much of the psychodynamic literature. Playful or lighthearted behaviors within groups typically are treated as representing flight from the group's task, collusion, or indulgence in fantasy. Bion's and Rice's treatment of emotional processes is to find ways to harness them to serve the needs of the group task. Rioch questions whether it might not be possible to find in the concept of play "a true synthesis of mature, scientific and primitive fantasy elements without the one being subservient to the other" (p. 673).

For example, the emerging work in positive psychology, with its emphasis on the role of positive emotions, might offer the theoretical basis for achieving the synthesis that Rioch suggests. Both the work of Csikszentmihalyi on the concept of flow (Csikszentmihalyi & Csikszentmihalyi, 1988; Jackson & Csikszentmihalyi , 1999) and Goleman's (1995) work on emotional intelligence stress the importance of understanding the role that emotions play in all aspects of social life, including the workplace, schools, families, and small groups.

Bion sees humans as "hard-wired" to enter into basic assumption cultures. Goleman agrees with Bion that our most basic instincts are to act from emotions—either to avoid pain or to seek pleasure—and the process of maturity involves the struggle of sublimating those instincts into socially appropriate behavior and responses. Goleman takes a philosophical stance toward this struggle similar to that of Bion. That is, emotionally intelligent groups (sophisticated work groups, in Bion's terms) should harness emotions in the service of rational task accomplishment. At the same time, both Goleman and Csikszentmihalyi recognize the inherent value of positive emotions that may not be immediately applied to a task—that is, play. In fact, Goleman (1995) cites the phenomenon of flow as "emotional intelligence at its best." Rather than treating emotions as instruments for task accomplishment, in flow, the emotions are a part of the experience, and valued for their own sake. Goleman writes:

[The] experience is a glorious one: the hallmark of flow is a feeling of spontaneous joy, even rapture . . . it is intrinsically rewarding . . . it interrupts flow to reflect too much on what is happening . . . while in flow [people] are unconcerned with thoughts of success or failure—the sheer pleasure of the act itself is what motivates them. (p. 91)

While the result of flow can be high-quality outcomes on a given task, emotions are not treated as either obstacles or stepping stones to the outcomes;

rather, they are a part of the actual experience. In this way, Goleman can be seen as having much in common with the humanistically oriented approaches to psychodynamics, especially the work on psychodrama. We propose here that the approach to emotions represented in the work of Goleman, Csikszentmihalyi, and Rioch provides the theoretical bridge between the psychoanalytic and humanistic approaches to psychodynamic perspectives in groups.

Note

1. We use the term *nonconscious* to include subconscious, preconscious, and unconscious processes.

References

Aiello, T. J. (1973). Studying the group process: T-groups. *Group Process, 5,* 129–143.

Alderfer, C. P. (1987). An intergroup perspective on group dynamics. In. J. Lorsch (Ed.), *Handbook of organizational behavior* (pp. 190–222). Englewood Cliffs, NJ: Prentice Hall.

Alderfer, C. P. (1998). Group psychological consulting to organizations: A perspective on history. *Consulting Psychology Journal: Practices and Research, 50,* 67–77.

Anderson, C., & Slocum, J. W. (1973). Personality traits and their impact on T-group training success. *Training & Development Journal, 27,* 18–25.

Anderson, D., Anderson, K., & Glanze, W. (Eds.). (2001). *Mosby's medical dictionary* (6th ed.). New York: Elsevier Science.

Back, K. W. (1972). *Beyond words: The story of sensitivity training and the encounter movement.* New York: Russell Sage.

Bales, R. F. (1950). *Interaction process analysis: A method for the study of small groups.* Cambridge, MA: Addison-Wesley.

Bales, R. F. (1953). The equilibrium problem in small groups. In T. Parsons, R. F. Bales, & E. Shils (Eds.), *Working papers in the theory of action* (Chapter 4). New York: Free Press.

Bales, R. F. (1970). *Personality and interpersonal behavior.* New York: Holt, Rinehart & Winston.

Bales, R. F., Cohen, S. P., & Williamson, S. (1979). *SYMLOG: A system for the multi-level observation of groups.* New York: Free Press.

Bennis, W. G. (1977). Goals and meta-goals of laboratory training. In R. T. Golembiewski & A. Blumberg (Eds.), *Sensitivity training and the laboratory approach: Readings about concepts and applications.* (pp. 18–24). Itasca IL: F. E. Peacock.

Bennis, W. G., & Shepard, H. A. (1956). A theory of group development. *Human Relations, 9,* 415–437.

Bion, W. R. (1961). *Experiences in groups and other papers.* New York: Basic Books.

Blackwell, D. (2002). Out of their class: Class colonization and resistance in analytic psychotherapy and group analysis. *Group Analysis, 35,* 367–381.

Boller, J. D. (1974). Differential effects of two T-group styles. *Counselor Education & Supervision, 14,* 117–123.

Bradford, L. P., Gibb, J. R., & Benne, K. D. (Eds.). (1964). *T-group theory and laboratory method: Innovation in re-education.* New York: John Wiley.

Brown, D. G. (2000). Bion and Foulkes: Basic assumptions and beyond. In M. Pines (Ed.), *Bion and group psychotherapy* (pp. 192–219). Philadelphia: Jessica Kingsely.

Bunker, D. R. (1965). Individual applications of laboratory training. *Journal of Applied Behavioral Science, 1,* 131–147.

Burke, M. J., & Day, R. R. (1986). A cumulative study of the effectiveness of managerial training. *Journal of Applied Psychology, 71,* 232–245.

Campbell, J. P., & Dunnette, M. D. (1968). Effectiveness of T-group experiences in managerial training and development. *Psychological Bulletin, 70,* 73–104.

Casey, N. A., & Solomon, L. (1971). The effect of seating arrangement of T-group interaction and sociometric choices. *Interpersonal Development, 2,* 9–20.

Chang, A., Bordia, P., & Duck, J. (2003). Punctuated equilibrium and linear progression: Toward a new understanding of group development. *Academy of Management Journal, 46,* 106–117.

Cooper, C. L., & Mangham, I. L. (Eds.). (1971). *T-groups: A survey of research.* New York: Wiley-Interscience.

Couch, A. D. (1960). *Psychological determinants of interpersonal behavior.* Unpublished doctoral dissertation, Harvard University, Cambridge, MA.

Courter, M. L., Jr. (1999). *Reactions to female leadership: The influence of small group gender composition in the context of two Tavistock group relations conferences.* Unpublished doctoral dissertation, Northwestern University, Evanston, IL.

Csikszentmihalyi, M., & Csikszentmihalyi, I. S. (Eds.). (1988). *Optimal experience: Psychological studies of flow in consciousness.* New York: Cambridge University Press.

Danish, S. J. (1971). Factors influencing changes in empathy following a group experience. *Journal of Counseling Psychology, 18,* 262–267.

Ettin, M. F., Cohen, B. D., & Fidler, J. W. (1997). Group-as-a-whole theory viewed in its 20th-century context. *Group Dynamics: Theory, Research, and Practice, 1,* 329–340.

Faith, M. S., Wong, F. Y., & Carpenter, K. M. (1995). Group sensitivity training: Update, meta-analysis, and recommendations. *Journal of Counseling Psychology, 42,* 390–399.

Forsyth, D. R. (1991). Change in therapeutic groups. In C. R. Snyder & D. R. Forsyth (Eds.), *Handbook of social and clinical psychology* (pp. 664–680). New York: Pergamon Press.

Foulkes, M. (1964). *Therapeutic group analysis.* New York: International Universities Press.

Freud, S. (1920). *Group psychology and the analysis of the ego* (J. Strachey, Trans., 1959). New York: Boni & Liveright.

Gersick, C. J. (1991). Revolutionary change theories: A multilevel exploration of the punctuated equilibrium paradigm. *Academy of Management Review, 16,* 10–36.

Glassman, U., & Kates, L. (1983). Authority themes and worker-group transactions: Additional dimensions to the stages of group development. *Social Work With Groups, 6,* 33–52.

Goleman, D. (1995). *Emotional intelligence.* New York: Bantam Books.

Golembiewski, R. T., & Blumberg, A. (Eds.). (1977). *Sensitivity training and the laboratory approach: Readings about concepts and applications.* Itasca IL: F. E. Peacock.

Hafsi, M. (1997). Valency and its measurement: Validating a Japanese version of the Reaction to Group Situation Test (RGST). *Psychologia: An International Journal of Psychology in the Orient, 40,* 152–162.

Hafsi, M. (1998). Experimental inquiry into the psychodynamics of the relationship between the group's dominant basic assumption type and scapegoating. *Psychologia: An International Journal of Psychology in the Orient, 41,* 272–284.

Hartman, J. J. (1979). Small group methods of personal change. *Annual Review of Psychology, 30,* 453–476.

Highhouse, S. (2002). A history of the T-group and its early applications in management development. *Group Dynamics, 6,* 277–290.

Hipple, J. L. (1976). Effects of differential human relations laboratory design on personal growth. *Small Group Behavior, 7,* 407–422.

Hirschhorn, L. (1999). The primary risk. *Human Relations, 52,* 5–23.

Hopper, E. (1997). Traumatic experience in the unconscious life of groups: A fourth basic assumption. *Group Analysis, 30,* 439–470.

House, R. J. (1967). T-group education and leadership effectiveness: A review of the empirical literature and a critical evaluation. *Personnel Psychology, 20,* 1–32.

Jackson, S. A., & Csikszentmihalyi, M. (1999). *Flow in sports: The keys to optimal experiences and performances.* Champaign, IL: Human Kinetics.

Jaques, E., Klein, M., & Heimann, P. (1955). Social systems as a defence against persecutory and depressive anxiety. In R. E. Morey-Kyrle (Ed.), *New directions in psychoanalysis.* London: Tavistock.

Jarrett, M., & Kellner, K. (1996). Coping with uncertainty: A psychodynamic perspective on the work of top teams. *Journal of Management Development, 15,* 54–68.

John, K. (2000). Basic needs, conflict, and dynamics in groups. *Journal of Individual Psychology, 56,* 419–434.

Karterud, S. W. (1989a). A comparative study of six different inpatient groups with respect to their basic assumption functioning. *International Journal of Group Psychotherapy, 39,* 355–376.

Karterud, S. W. (1989b). A study of Bion's basic assumption groups. *Human Relations, 42,* 315–335.

Karterud, S. W. (2000). The group emotionality rating. In A. P. Beck & C. M. Lewis (Eds.), *The process of group psychotherapy: Systems for analyzing change* (pp. 113–134). Washington, DC: American Psychological Association.

Kernberg, O. F. (1984). The couch at sea: Psychoanalytic studies of group and organizational leadership. *International Journal of Group Psychotherapy, 34,* 5–23.

Kernberg. O. F. (1998). *Ideology, conflict, and leadership in groups and organizations.* New Haven, CT: Yale University Press.

Kets de Vries, M. F. R., & Miller, D. (1984). Group fantasies and organizational functioning. *Human Relations, 37,* 111–134.

Kipper, D. A., & Ritchie, T. D. (2003). The effectiveness of psychodramatic techniques: A meta-analysis. *Group Dynamics, 7,* 13–25.

Klein, M. (1946). Notes on some schizoid mechanisms. In M. Klein (Ed.), *Developments in psychoanalysis.* London: Hogarth Press.

Klein, M. (1959). Our adult world and its roots in infancy. *Human Relations, 12,* 291–303.

Koffka, K. (1935). *Principles of Gestalt psychology.* New York: Harcourt, Brace.

Kohler, W. (1969). *The task of Gestalt psychology.* Princeton, NJ: Princeton University Press.

Koortzen, P., & Cilliers, F. (2002). The psychoanalytic approach to team development. In. R. L. Low (Ed.), *The California school of organizational studies: Handbook of organizational consulting psychology: A comprehensive guide to theory, skills, and techniques.* (pp. 260–284). San Francisco: Jossey-Bass.

Le Bon, G. (1920). *The crowd: A study of the popular mind.* London: Fisher Unwin.

Lewin, K. (1943). Forces behind food habits and methods of change. *Bulletin of the National Research Council, 108,* 35–65.

Lewin, K. (1947). Frontiers in group dynamics: II. Channels of group life; social planning and action research. *Human Relations, 1,* 143–153.

Lewin, K. (1948). *Resolving social conflicts.* New York: Harper & Row.

Lewin, K. (1951). *Field theory in social science.* New York: Harper.

Lewin, K. (1958). Group decision and social change. In E. Maccoby, T. Newcombe, & E. Hartley (Eds.), *Readings in social psychology.* New York: Holt Rinehart.

Lieberman, M. A. (1976). Change induction in small groups. *Annual Review of Psychology, 27,* 217–250.

Lion, C., & Gruenfeld, L. W. (1993). The behavior and personality of work group and basic assumption group members. *Small Group Research, 24,* 236–257.

Long, S. (1992). *A structural analysis of small groups.* New York: Routledge.

Lundgren, D. C. (1973). Attitudinal and behavioral correlates of emergent status in training groups. *Journal of Social Psychology, 90,* 141–153.

Lundgren, D. C., & Knight, D. J. (1977). Trainer style and member attitudes toward trainer and group in T-groups. *Small Group Behavior, 8,* 47–64.

Lundgren, D. C., & Knight, D. J. (1978). Sequential stages of development in sensitivity training groups. *Journal of Applied Behavioral Science, 14,* 204–222.

Maslow, A. H. (1970). *Motivation and personality* (3rd ed.). New York: Harper Collins.

McConnell, H. K. (1971). Individual differences as mediators or participant behavior and self-descriptive change in two human relations training programs. *Organizational Behavior & Human Decision Processes, 6,* 550–572.

McDougall, W. (1922). *The group mind.* Cambridge, UK: Cambridge University Press.

McGregor, D. (1960). *The human side of the enterprise.* New York: McGraw-Hill.

Menzies, I. E. P. (1959). The functioning of social systems as a defence against anxiety: A report on a study of the nursing service of a general hospital. *Human Relations, 13,* 95–121.

Miller, E. J. (1998). A note on the protomental system and "groupishness": Bion's basic assumptions revisited. *Human Relations, 51,* 1495–1508.

Miller, E. J., & Rice, A. K. (1967). *Systems of organization.* London: Tavistock.

Moreno, J. (1953). *Who shall survive?* New York: Beacon House.

Morgan, H., & Thomas, K. (1996). A psychodynamic perspective on group processes. In M. Wetherell (Ed.), *Identities, groups, and social issues* (pp. 63–117). London: Sage.

Morrison, T. L. (1984). Member reactions to a group leader in varying leadership roles. *Journal of Social Psychology, 122,* 49–53.

Morrison, T. L., & Stein, D. D. (1985). Member reaction to male and female leaders in two types of group experience. *Journal of Social Psychology, 125,* 7–16.

Moxnes, P. (1998). Fantasies and fairy tales in groups and organizations: Bion's basic assumptions and the deep roles. *European Journal of Work and Organizational Psychology, 7,* 283–298.

Moxnes, P. (1999). Deep roles: Twelve primordial roles of mind and organization. *Human Relations, 52,* 1427–1443.

Noran, A. R. (1996). Avoiding the perils of management by groups: The contributions of Bion, Tavistock, and social work theorists. *Social Work With Groups, 19,* 53–65.

Paul, J., Strbiak, C. A., & Landrum, N. E. (2002). Psychoanalytic diagnosis of top management team dysfunction. *Journal of Managerial Psychology, 17,* 381–393.

Parsons, T., Bales, R. F., & Shils, E. (Eds.). (1953). *Working papers in the theory of action.* New York: Free Press.

Plutchik, R., & Landau, H. (1973). Perceived dominance and emotional states in small groups. *Psychotherapy: Theory, Research & Practice, 10,* 341–342.

Poland, W. D., & Jones, J. E. (1973). Personal orientations and perceived benefit from a human relations laboratory. *Small Group Behavior, 4,* 496–502.

Polley, R. B., & Eid, J. (1994). First among equals: Leaders, peers, and choice. *Journal of Group Psychotherapy, Psychodrama & Sociometry, 47,* 59–76.

Poole, M. S., & Roth, J. (1988). Decision development in small groups IV: A typology of group decision paths. *Human Communication Research, 15,* 323–356.

Poole, M. S., & Roth, J. (1989). Decision development in small groups V: Test of a contingency model. *Human Communication Research, 15,* 549–589.

Rice, A. K. (1965). *Learning for leadership: Interpersonal and intergroup relations.* London: Tavistock.

Rioch, M. J. (1981). The influence of Wilfred Bion and the A. K. Rice group relations conferences. In. J. S. Grotstein (Ed.), *Do I dare disturb the universe? A memorial to Wilfred R. Bion* (pp. 668–673). London: Maresfield Library.

Rogers, C. R. (1970). *Carl Rogers on encounter groups.* New York: Harper.

Schutz, W. (1966). *FIRO: The interpersonal underworld.* Palo Alto, CA: Science and Behavior Books.

Seel, R. (2001). Anxiety and incompetence in the large group: A psychodynamic perspective. *Journal of Organizational Change Management, 14,* 493–503.

Serok, S., & Bar, R. (1984). Looking at a Gestalt group impact: An experiment. *Small Group Behavior, 15,* 270–277.

Shaffer, J. B. P., & Galinsky, M. D. (1989). *Models of group therapy.* Englewood Cliffs, NJ: Prentice Hall.

Shambaugh, P. W. (1985). The mythic structure of Bion's groups. *Human Relations, 38,* 937–951.

Simmel, G. (1955). *Conflict and the web of group affiliations* (K. H. Wolff & R. Bendix, Trans.). New York: Free Press. (Original work published 1908.)

Slater, P. E. (1966). *Microcosm: Structural, psychological and religious evolution in groups.* New York: Wiley & Sons.

Smith, K. K. (1982). *Groups in conflict: Prisons in disguise.* Dubuque IA: Kendall/Hunt.

Smith, K. K., & Berg, D. N. (1987). *Paradoxes of group life: Understanding conflict, paralysis, and movement in group dynamics.* San Francisco: New Lexington Press.

Smith, P. B. (1975). Controlled studies of the outcome of sensitivity training. *Psychological Bulletin, 4,* 597–622.

Smith, P. B. (1983). Back-home environment and within-group relationships as determinants of personal change. *Human Relations, 36,* 53–67.

Stock. D., & Thelen, H. (1958). *Emotional dynamics and group culture.* New York: New York University Press.

Szonyi, G. (2002). A group of group conductors as mirror of social stratification conflicts. *Group Analysis, 35,* 390–206.

Takahashi, T. (1991). A comparative study of Japanese and American group dynamics. *Psychoanalytic Review, 78,* 49–62.

Thelen, H. A. (2000). Research with Bion's concepts. In M. Pines (Ed.), *Bion and group psychotherapy* (International Library of Group Analysis, Vol. 15, pp. 114–138). London: Jessica Kingsley.

Tuckman, B. W. (1965). Development sequence in small groups. *Psychological Bulletin, 63*, 384–399.

Tuckman, B. W., & Jensen, M. A. C. (1977). Stages in small group development revisited. *Group and Organizational Studies, 2*, 419–427.

Turquet, P. M. (1985). Leadership: The individual and the group. In A. D. Coleman & M. Geller (Eds.), *Group relations reader* (Vol. 2, pp. 87–144). Washington DC: A. K. Rice Institute.

Vogler, C. (2000). Social identity and emotion: The meeting of psychoanalysis and sociology. *The Sociological Review, 48*, 19–42.

Volkan, V. D. (1999a). Psychoanalysis and diplomacy: Part I. Individual and large group identity. *Journal of Applied Psychoanalytic Studies, 1*, 29–55.

Volkan, V. D. (1999b). Psychoanalysis and diplomacy Part II: Large group rituals. *Journal of Applied Psychoanalytic Studies, 1*, 223–247.

Walton, R. E., & Warwick, D. (1973). The ethics of organization development. *Journal of Applied Behavioral Science, 9*, 681–698.

Weigel, R. G. (2002). The marathon encounter group—vision and reality: Exhuming the body for a last look. *Consulting Psychology Journal: Practice and Research, 54*, 186–198.

Wheelan, S. A. (1990). *Facilitating training groups: A guide to leadership and verbal intervention skills.* New York: Praeger.

Wheelan, S. A. (1994). *The group development questionnaire: A manual for professionals.* Provincetown, MA: GDQ Associates.

Wheelan, S. A., Davidson, B., & Tilin, F. (2003). Group development across time: Reality or illusion? *Small Group Research, 34*, 223–245.

Whitman, R. M. (1964). Psychodynamic principles underlying T-group processes. In L. P. Bradford, J. R. Gibb, & K. D. Benne (Eds.), *T-group theory and laboratory method: Innovation in re-education* (pp. 310–335). New York: John Wiley.

Woodman, R. W., & Sherwood, J. J. (1980). The role of team development in organizational effectiveness: A critical review. *Psychological Bulletin, 88*, 166–186.

Yalom, I. D. (1995). *The theory and practice of group psychotherapy* (4th ed.). New York: Basic Books.

4

The Social Identity Perspective on Small Groups

Dominic Abrams, Michael A. Hogg,
Steve Hinkle, and Sabine Otten

Abstract

This chapter describes the historical development, metatheoretical background, and current state of the social identity perspective. The theory developed as an analysis of intergroup relations among large-scale social categories and has evolved a strong social cognitive emphasis. In this chapter, we show that the social identity perspective is intended to be a general analysis of group membership and group processes that focuses on the generative relationship between collective self-conception and group phenomena. We describe several applications of the social identity perspective to small groups including: differentiation within groups; leadership; deviance; group decision-making; computer-mediated communication; mobilization, collective action, and social loafing; and group culture. We conclude with a discussion of the strengths and weaknesses of the perspective and of future directions.

Authors' Note: Very sadly, Steve Hinkle died suddenly on October 19, 2001. He worked enthusiastically and closely with us on the early preparation of this chapter, writing particularly on the cross-cultural aspects.

The social identity approach holds that people's salient identity can be characterized on a continuum from very personal (unique) to highly shared (social) attributes. Personal identity as an individual may be based on idiosyncratic characteristics. Social identity is based on attributes shared among members of particular social groups and categories. The approach holds that people categorize themselves and others according to salient differences in a social comparative context. Group behavior happens when people act in terms of a shared social categorization—a common social identity. This identity-based definition of a social group makes the social identity approach distinctive because it shifts the conceptualization of groups from a focus on particular features of physical entities, such as group size, interaction, interdependence, proximity, or contact. In a nutshell, the social identity approach starts from the premise that the group is in the individual, rather than vice versa.

Social identity theory (Tajfel & Turner, 1979) and the perspective that frames it (Abrams & Hogg, 1990b; Hogg & Abrams, 1988) have been characterized as a distinctively European social psychology (see Jaspars, 1980; Tajfel, 1972). Numerous collections of social identity research have been published subsequently (e.g. Abrams & Hogg, 1990b, 1999; Capozza & Brown, 2000; Ellemers, Spears, & Doojse, 1999; Robinson, 1996; Worchel, Morales, Páez, & Deschamps, 1998). The field is too large to summarize in a single chapter. Therefore, we concentrate on conveying the key aspects, including its historical and metatheoretical roots, and several important developments within the perspective.

Most social identity research has concentrated on intergroup relations. However, the perspective also speaks directly to processes within small groups. This chapter (see also Hogg, Abrams, Otten, & Hinkle, in press) describes the principle features and development of the social identity perspective. We summarize evidence relating to group status, power and action, deindividuation and depersonalization, social influence, decision making, cohesiveness, leadership, motivation, and responses to deviance. We consider questions that remain problematic for the perspective, such as how social identity is best conceptualized, its flexibility, and how it is manifested in group behavior in different cultural contexts. Table 4.1 (pp. 103–104) sets out some of the key features of the approach, and Table 4.2 (pp. 105–107) distills what the perspective brings to bear on the way groups are characterized. Our discussion necessarily leaves out important but less relevant areas of intergroup relations research on social identity (e.g., stereotyping, prejudice, discrimination, and collective protest research).

The Social Scientific Context
of the Social Identity Approach

When the *European Journal of Social Psychology* was first published in 1971, it heralded a self-conscious effort on the part of European social psychologists to establish a distinctive approach to theory and research that better reflected the historical and cultural context of Europe. The quest was to develop a social psychology that was nonreductionist and that recognized the role of the social in psychological processes and vice versa (cf. F. H. Allport, 1924; G. W. Allport, 1954). One central theme was that social conflict between groups could not be understood solely by examination of psychological processes within individuals. Rather, the problem was to understand how and why individuals embody the social reality defined by collectives or groups. How do the group's concerns become the individual's concern? The flavor of the debates in Europe is readily apparent from reading some of the influential edited collections published in the 1970s and 1980s (e.g., Tajfel, 1978; Turner & Giles, 1981; see Hogg & Abrams, 1988, for a detailed account of reductionist approaches to intergroup relations). The goal was set out clearly by Tajfel and his colleagues in the introduction to their two-volume series, *The Social Dimension*:

> Social psychology can and must include in its theoretical and research preoccupations a direct concern with the relationship between human psychological functioning and the large-scale social processes and events which shape this functioning and are shaped by it. (Tajfel, Jaspars, & Fraser, 1984, p. 3)

Social relations between groups were considered fundamental to an explanation of group members' psychology (e.g., Moscovici & Doise, 1994). The study of group and intergroup relations became increasingly prominent (see Abrams & Hogg, 1998, 2004; Moreland, Hogg, & Hains, 1994). Two major theoretical approaches developed within the European tradition. Alongside the social identity perspective is the social representations perspective, which has also generated a large volume of research but has been much slower to cross over into mainstream social psychology in North America (see Deaux & Philogene, 2001; Farr & Moscovici, 1984). Both perspectives offer useful insights into intergroup and intragroup relations (see Tindale & Kameda, 2000).

There remain strong proponents of the primacy of an individual self (e.g., Gaertner & Schopler, 1998). However, there is also a substantial set of researchers from North America who explicitly incorporate the social identity perspective into their work (e.g., see Bourhis, 1994; Brewer & Brown,

1998; Deaux, 1996; Gaertner & Dovidio, 2000; Hinkle & Brown, 1990) and many who accept many of the premises of the approach. Thus, although differences of theoretical emphasis remain important, the social identity perspective is now strongly represented in the general upsurge in social psychological research on groups (see Abrams & Hogg, 1998) as well as in social cognition research (Abrams & Hogg, 1999).

Features of the Social Identity Perspective

Some parameters of the social identity perspective are set out in Table 4.1. The perspective defines the group as a subjective entity. A group exists to the extent that its members have a sense of shared identity. There is no formal definition of how many people are required to form a group (although Brown, 2000, suggests three is an appropriate minimum). Rather, the issue is whether a person feels and acts as a group member. The perspective is relevant to all groups that are bound by a common identity, including competitive teams; ethnic groups and minority social groups; organizational units, such as departments or teams; and ad hoc groups that serve common interests (e.g., political or leisure activities). It is perhaps useful to define the groups to which it may not apply. These include social aggregates (e.g., people in a shopping mall), populations defined as groups externally but not subjectively (e.g., socioeconomic and consumer stratifications used by market researchers), sets of people who individually and independently suffer a common fate (e.g., people who get the flu virus), people who spend a lot of time together in the same place (e.g., an office building), and networks of friends. Although such collections of individuals are unlikely to be groups, the social identity perspective allows that any of them *could* become a group under certain conditions.

The social identity perspective assumes that group processes are driven by inter- and intragroup social comparisons through which members strive to clarify their group's distinctiveness, positivity, and validity. An important aspect is that these comparisons focus on dimensions that are relevant to the group as a whole, rather than on attributes of the individual members. The perspective makes a clear distinction between people engaged in activities together but as a set of individuals and people engaged in activities framed by a shared social identity. Only the latter would be defined as a group.

The remainder of this chapter explains the development of social identity theory, providing the metatheoretical context for the approach. We then consider some of the relevant evidence and variants and related theories that have emerged. We also touch on various questions about the limits of the social identity approach.

Table 4.1   Social Identity Perspective

Definition of perspective	The social identity perspective is largely rooted in the European social psychological literature on intergroup relations. The approach is avowedly nonreductionist. Groups have a shared psychological reality, which produces collective processes that transcend personal motives and interpersonal relationships or interaction. Thus, the uniformity and coherence of group behavior is explicable in terms of the shared identity that the group provides for its members. Social identity is considered as both a cause and an outcome of intergroup behavior and numerous other group phenomena.
Key assumptions	<ul><li>Groups provide a source of identity common to all members: social identity</li><li>Group members are motivated to sustain a positive social identity, achieved through positive intergroup differentiation</li><li>Group goals, norms, stereotypes, and influence are defined by the implicit or explicit intergroup context</li><li>The coherence of groups is based on shared identity more than by variables such as goal relations, conflict, deprivation, status, interpersonal attraction, conformity pressure, and so on</li><li>Group action is mobilized around the prototypical group position rather than particular individuals; this means face-to-face interaction is not necessary for social influence to occur within a group</li></ul>
Types of groups	Most research focuses on large-scale social category memberships, or small groups defined in terms of ad hoc categorizations. Some research examines organizational teams and levels. However, the small/large group distinction is not central to this perspective. Rather, the perspective applies to any group that can serve as a basis for self-categorization. Different theoretical elements in the social identity approach focus on different parts of the process, ranging from the purely cognitive to the macrosocial. Groups studied range from completely artificial minimal groups to transitory task groups (e.g., a team in an experiment or an organization) to contextual groups (e.g., being a psychology student, which has relevance only in the context of other students) to major demographic categories (e.g., gender, ethnicity).

(Continued)

Table 4.1 (Continued)

Key theories	• Social identity theory • Self-categorization theory • Variants and developments of the above, for example, optimal distinctiveness theory, social attraction model, social self-regulation model, social identity-deindividuation model, uncertainty reduction model, common in-group identity model, intergroup emotions theory, subjective group dynamics model, ethnolinguistic vitality model, interactive acculturation model, dual model of collective action
Dominant research methodologies	• Experimental and quasi-experimental studies of effects of social categorization on prejudice, stereotyping, discrimination, social influence etc. • Field studies of identification in naturally occurring groups • Laboratory simulations of effects of structural intergroup inequalities
Strengths	• Provides an overarching metatheory for understanding what groups do and why • Provides an account for the coordination of group action that does not depend on face-to-face or one-to-one communication • Provides a mechanism for immediate social influence • Always considers the social context of the group • Provides an account of the relationship between groups and the self-concept • Offers well-developed research paradigms and techniques for both laboratory and survey-based studies
Weaknesses	• Does not theorize how interpersonal relations articulate with intergroup relations • Offers a relatively limited perspective on motivation • Lacks precision in predicting microlevel processes within small groups • Vulnerable to post-hoc explanation of inconsistent evidence • Does not yet offer a coherent developmental account of groups or social identity • Has provided a more detailed account of intergroup behavior and motivation than of intragroup behavior

Table 4.2   Key Findings of Social Identity Perspective Research

Group composition	• Change in composition is defined psychologically; the group is the set of people with whom a person shares a salient social category • Composition is defined by the comparative context; often the group boundaries and membership are obvious, but sometimes they emerge in response to salient events (e.g., external threat, opportunities) from the environment or other groups • Membership may be many or few • Psychologically, most members are interchangeable • Intragroup relations are determined by the relative prototypicality of different group members • More prototypical group members are more attractive and influential than others
Group structure	• Status is based on prototypicality (e.g., leaders are perceived as most prototypical) • Norms are prototypical positions, defined either rapidly or slowly through comparison with the norms of relevant comparison groups • Group status is defined through intergroup comparison on different dimensions • Group cohesiveness is generally likely to be weakened by lower group status (which causes dis-identification), but this effect is moderated by perceptions of the stability and legitimacy of intergroup differences and the perceived centrality or relevance of the dimensions on which comparisons are made • Cohesion is based on social attraction, which may wax and wane depending on the comparative context; more stable contexts result in a more stable basis for group cohesiveness • Threat mobilizes identity maintenance strategies, which may result in strengthened or weakened social identity
Group projects	If a group of people share a social identity in terms of that group, they will share motives to enhance the status, power, and esteem of that group, and to ensure that the group's definition of reality is valid and clear; generally, these goals are attained by establishing positive distinctiveness for the group in comparison with relevant outgroups

(Continued)

Table 4.2 (Continued)

Interaction	• More depersonalized as social identity becomes more salient; dwells on the relationship between group members in terms of how prototypical they are of the group rather than in terms of their personal qualities or other characteristics • Likely to center on more prototypical members (who will be most influential) • More favorable to ingroups than to outgroups • Interpersonal differences tolerated, but strong reactions to group members who do not conform to in-group norms • Regulated in terms of group norms
Group action/outcomes	• Social identity salience increases conformity to ingroup norms • Group-based attitude formation (e.g., prejudice/preference for individuals based entirely on which group they belong to) • Group-based emotion (e.g., commitment to the group as a whole rather than to individual members) • Group-serving behavior (e.g., loyalty to the group as a whole rather than to particular individuals, turnover intention within organizations) • Collective action (e.g., protest) arises through activation of common social identity and judgment of need for change in intergroup structure, rather than intragroup interaction • Group decisions likely to reflect needs for positive social identity • Low-status groups may respond creatively to find new dimensions on which they can define themselves positively
Change over time	• In principle, social identification can move rapidly from one category membership (e.g., gender) to another (e.g., work group), depending on comparative context • Self-defining social categories may remain stable, but content may change over time as a result of different intergroup comparisons • Group mobilization and protest may move through sequences from purely personal to purely collective action • Recategorization or decategorization may mean the group is psychologically absorbed or dissolved

	• Salient cross-cutting categorizations will weaken the psychological coherence of the group
Ecology	• Comparative context determines which group memberships and social identifications are salient
	• Social identity salience is increased by competition, conflict, status insecurity, but also by simple comparison and fit to a situation
	• Mergers, takeovers, changes in social comparative context all create potential threats to social identity distinctiveness, resulting either in reassertion of identity or identification with a new level/category
	• Subordinate and superordinate levels of identity provide opportunities for distinctiveness and status enhancement, raising possibility that people may identify at the same time with different levels of abstraction of group memberships (e.g., both the organization and a team within it)

The Development of Social Identity Theory

Tajfel's research on physical perception (e.g., Tajfel & Wilkes, 1963) explored the accentuation principle. Once categorized, differences among stimuli that share a category are perceptually reduced, and differences between stimuli in different categories are accentuated. Moreover, when the categorization or the correlated dimension is important or valued, this accentuation effect is increased. Tajfel (1981) extended his analysis of these effects and applied them to social stimuli, providing a powerful analysis of stereotyping. Whereas the North American social cognition approach treated stereotypes as inaccurate, biased, faulty judgments, perhaps resulting from information-processing errors (e.g., Hamilton, 1981), Tajfel stressed the shared nature of stereotypes and their social functions. These functions included social differentiation between groups, attribution or explanation for differences between groups, and justification for differential status or treatment of groups. These functions are rooted not only in individual motivation, but also in social structural relationships between groups. The fascinating problem was how these social functions are ingrained in the psychology of individuals.

The minimal group research conducted by Tajfel's group at Bristol demonstrated powerfully that the mere process of assigning different category memberships to anonymous individuals was sufficient to generate ingroup favoritism and intergroup discrimination (Tajfel, 1970). Among the more intriguing findings was that individuals would sacrifice self-interest and absolute gain for their group, so as to ensure their group achieved relative gain in comparison with the outgroup. Moreover, ingroup bias occurred even when the gain was symbolic rather than material. The minimal group paradigm has subsequently been adopted widely as a baseline condition for intergroup relations research (Bourhis, 1994).

Tajfel and Turner's (1979) explanation for minimal intergroup discrimination rested on the idea that identity could be defined along a continuum from personal identity (the individual aspects of oneself) at one extreme and social identity (self-defined by one's group memberships) at the other. The two ends of the continuum corresponded to qualitatively different behavior: interpersonal behavior and intergroup behavior, respectively. When social identity is salient, group members strive for positive distinctiveness for their group. By ensuring that their ingroup is positively distinctive from outgroups, the ingroup, and hence the self, is imbued with positive value. In a minimal group, the most meaningful definition of self is as a group member. The explanation for intergroup discrimination in a minimal group setting was, therefore, that ingroup bias was a means of sustaining or increasing the positivity of social identity as a group member.

Along with their cognitive-motivational explanation for intergroup discrimination, Tajfel and Turner (1979) provided an analysis of the macrosocial framework that could explain different forms of intergroup behavior. People's understanding of intergroup relationships was thought to be critical in determining how they maintained their social identity. Tajfel and Turner specifically considered the impact of beliefs about the legitimacy and stability of intergroup status relations and beliefs about the permeability of intergroup boundaries. When the status differences between groups appear to be stable and legitimate but the boundaries between groups are permeable, it is likely that low-status group members may adopt a social mobility strategy, to disidentify with the low-status group and to move to the higher status group. However, group boundaries are often impermeable (e.g., when group membership is defined by skin color), in which case the low-status group members may adopt a collective strategy of social creativity (finding new dimensions of comparison on which to establish positive distinctiveness from the higher-status group). When status differences are insecure (illegitimate or unstable), lower-status groups may adopt a social competition strategy—to challenge the higher-status group directly on dimensions that define its superiority. These macrosocial features and accompanying belief systems are directly relevant to relationships within groups because they bear on the members' likely commitment to group goals and to the group itself. Subsequently, a large volume of research has been dedicated to these macrosocial aspects of social identity theory (e.g., Ellemers et al., 1999; Skevington & Baker, 1989; Tajfel, 1978).

What distinguishes the social identity approach from other approaches is that not only the theorists but also the subjects reflect on the social structure and its meaning for group membership. People's naïve theories of society (or of particular intergroup relationships) meaningfully affect the way they regard themselves and others as group members within a social structure (see Abrams & Hogg, 2004).

Self-Categorization Theory

The cognitive aspects of the social identity approach developed by Turner and his colleagues were published in their book, *Rediscovering the Social Group: A Self-Categorization Theory* (Turner, Hogg, Oakes, Reicher, & Wetherell, 1987). Self-Categorization Theory (SCT) concentrates more directly on the mechanisms by which the self becomes transformed from an individual to a group member.

According to SCT, identities are simply self-categorizations that operate at different levels of abstraction. In a particular social context, people apply the categorization that best makes sense of what is happening, so that people categorize the self and others in ways that fit the context. For example, at an airport, we generally categorize people into passengers versus staff, or passengers for this flight versus those for other flights. Differences within the categories may be enormous, but they are functionally irrelevant because they cannot meaningfully make sense of the situation. Thus, categorization implies shared membership at a particular level of inclusiveness, and it is applied flexibly to maximize the comparative and normative fit of individuals to their categories. At the airport, we may assume that all uniformed people are staff, who can be distinguished easily from passengers (high comparative fit). However, if a large number of uniformed people are intermingled among the lines waiting to check in, normative fit would be low (there is a poor correspondence between the categorization and expected behavior). In that case, we might try to find an alternative basis for categorization (e.g., those in front versus those behind the check-in desk). The level of inclusiveness that we use to categorize people can range from the relatively particular (e.g., business class versus economy class passengers) to the relatively general (e.g., travelers versus ground staff), depending on what best fits the situation or task at hand. At the extremes, the categorizations become the individual self and self as a human being.

A key consequence of social categorization is polarization of the ingroup and outgroup defining prototypes to which group members are assimilated.

Consequently, perceptions of group members and of the self become depersonalized. Group members are judged in terms of their closeness to their group prototype and not as distinct individuals. Likewise, the self is perceived and experienced with reference to the ingroup prototype. The more salient and meaningful a social categorization becomes, the more group members and the self will be depersonalized.

Depersonalization is a powerful psychological vehicle for many familiar group processes. Depersonalization means a person takes the ingroup prototype as a norm, the ingroup stereotype as a self-description; the ingroup's interests as self-interest, and a threat to the ingroup as a threat to the self. This conception of the individual as a depersonalized group member helps to make sense of a wide range of phenomena associated with group membership.

Motivation and Social Identity

The prediction of the effect of social identity ultimately depends on the underlying motivational processes. Group motivation (Hogg & Abrams, 1993) is obviously multifaceted, but the motivational elements of social identification boil down to a few likely candidates. First, group members seem motivated to ensure their social identity is comparatively positive (Abrams & Hogg, 1988; see also Baumeister, 1998). The proposal in social identity theory that intergroup bias serves self-esteem needs was subsequently disaggregated by Abrams and Hogg (1988) into the distinct hypotheses that ingroup favoritism should enhance self-esteem and that low self-esteem should enhance a striving for positive ingroup distinctiveness. Despite relatively consistent evidence in line with the first hypothesis, the second has received only partial support (Rubin & Hewstone, 1998). Second, group members seem to seek greater distinctiveness when their group is in a strong position but greater assimilation or inclusiveness when their group is in a weaker position (Brewer, 1991). That is to say, the optimal level of self-categorization depends on the relative size and status of the groups with which a person may identify. Third, people seem motivated to maximize the meaningfulness of their group memberships (Abrams, 1992) and social situations by establishing a coherent social identity within them (Hogg & Abrams, 1993). Such clarity can be achieved through locating and conforming to group norms, eliminating intragroup conflict, and evaluatively differentiating one's own group from others (Marques, Abrams, Páez, & Hogg, 2001). Both self-categorization theory (Turner et al., 1987) and the uncertainty reduction model (Hogg, 2000; Hogg & Abrams, 1993) conceptualize self-construal as a group member as a function of a search for meaning and clarity in a given social context. This motivational process also has a more obvious application to small group contexts, within which meaning and interpretation might be actively constructed through interaction.

Ellemers, Spears, and Doojse (2002) propose that social contexts provide a source of both potential threat and potential resources to deal with threat. They conceptualize a taxonomy with group commitment along a continuum from high to low and situations as posing either no threat, individual-directed threat, or group-directed threat. In different combinations of threat and commitment, there will be different identity concerns and motives. In the absence of threat, the primary identity concerns for low- and high-committed group members are accuracy and social meaning, and the accompanying motives are either noninvolvement or identity expression, respectively. In the presence of threats to individual identity, increasing group commitment should cause group members to be more concerned with the categorization of self as part of the group and motivated less for self-affirmation and more for acceptance by the group. Finally, when threat is directed at the group, members with low commitment are likely to want to distance themselves from the group and pursue individual mobility strategies, whereas those who are highly committed are likely to be concerned about the distinctiveness and positive value of the group and to pursue group affirmation strategies. This framework represents a fairly direct extension of Tajfel and Turner's original formulation of social identity theory, perhaps substituting threat for status security. As such, the taxonomy presents a unidirectional model in which the impact of threat on outcome is moderated by commitment. The model does not account for processes that affect group commitment both at the individual level and situationally. As Ellemers et al. (2002) note, "the strategic functions of the responses we have been discussing only make sense in a temporal context in which there is hope and scope to change an unfavorable status quo" (p. 180). Moreover, we think an important question to explore is how small face-to-face groups respond to threats when different members perceive those threats in different ways and when they differ in levels of commitment. These more dynamic processes could be a very fruitful avenue for future research.

Social Identity and Small Groups

Social Influence

The social identity perspective describes the social influence process associated with conformity as *referent informational influence* (Turner et al., 1987).

In group contexts, people attend to information about the context-specific group norm. Typically, the most immediate and best source of this information is identity-consistent behavior of core group members; however, outgroups can also provide relevant information (whatever they are, we are not). Once the norm has been recognized or established, it is internalized as the context-specific ingroup prototype and conformed to via the self-categorization process. Contextual norms serve at least two functions: (1) to express ingroup similarities and ingroup identity and (2) to distance the ingroup from all that the outgroup stands for. Therefore, the contextual norms tend to be polarized away from outgroup norms and thus to be more extreme than any central normative tendency of the ingroup.

Referent informational influence has been offered as a single process alternative to dual-process models of influence (e.g., normative versus informational influence). For example, people are influenced more by ingroup than outgroup sources, and when social identity is salient or when the ingroup is a minority, group members are more likely to adopt ingroup norms, both privately and publicly (Abrams & Hogg, 1990a; DeDreu & DeVries, 2001; Marques, Abrams, & Serodio, 2001; Turner, 1991).

Deindividuation Versus Depersonalization in Groups

One powerful example of depersonalization is the impact of anonymity on group behavior. Early crowd research and deindividuation research (e.g., Diener, 1980) supported the conclusion that anonymity and lack of accountability within a crowd resulted in a loss of self-regulation. Under the cover of groups, it seemed, people were likely to succumb to all kinds of influences that, as individuals, they would normally resist. The social identity interpretation of crowd behavior, and of deindividuation research, is quite different. First, it is evident that even when people are highly self-aware, their group membership may be salient, and indeed increased self-awareness can result in increased self-regulation in terms of group norms and goals (see Abrams, 1994; Abrams & Brown, 1989). Moreover, even when groups prevent self-focused attention, social identity can still provide the normative framework for action. According to the Social Identity Deindividuation (SIDE) model (Reicher, Spears, & Postmes, 1995), crowd behavior may be extreme and dramatic because members of the crowd quickly establish a social identity and common norms in relation to other groups. For example, during the St Pauls' Riots in Bristol, UK, the crowd members mobilized violently against the police. Reicher (1984) argued that rather than being disinhibited or chaotic, the crowd's behavior was highly organized around focal group norms. A meta-analysis of deindividuation research by Postmes and Spears (1998) concluded that supposedly anti-normative behavior in deindividuation experiments could more readily be accounted for in terms of conformity to situation-specific norms when social identity was salient.

Recent research on group anonymity has considered the context of computer-mediated communication within virtual groups, a frequent medium for decision making in organizations (Hollingshead, 2001). The SIDE model (Spears & Lea, 1994) explains what may go on in such groups. Computer-mediated communication potentially has a participation equalization effect, which evens out many of the status effects that occur in face-to-face groups, and so people may feel less inhibited because they are less personally identifiable. However, disinhibition depends on how effectively identity and status markers are concealed by the electronic medium. If people feel anonymous in the presence of a highly salient social identity, they will be depersonalized but not deindividuated. Therefore, they will conform strongly to identity-congruent norms and be easily influenced by group leaders and normative group members (Postmes, Spears, & Lea, 1998). For example, Lea, Spears, and de Groot (2001) demonstrated that visual anonymity in computer-mediated communication groups increased group-based self-categorization and stereotyping of and attraction to the group. Postmes, Spears, Sakhl, and de Groot (2001) then demonstrated that when a common group identity was made salient, anonymity increased social influence within groups (conformity to norms of either efficiency or prosocial task solutions). In another study, Postmes and Spears (2001) showed that males behaved more gender stereotypically on stereotype-relevant tasks when they were depersonalized (anonymous and not individuated). Thus, contrary to traditional models of group decision-making and influence, the evidence suggests that groups may become more coherent and constrained by group norms when members are less able to distinguish among one another as individuals.

Decision Making, Cohesion, and Attraction

The small groups in which people spend most time are likely to involve face-to-face interaction and familiarity with individual members. As a whole, the social identity perspective would expect that many small group processes including group decision processes (Hogg, 1996) are generally framed by the intergroup context. Therefore, group members who express opinions reflecting prototypical differences that distinguish their group from outgroups would be predicted to be especially influential (Abrams, Hulbert, & Davis,

1996). For example, once an intergroup context is salient, the perceived norm for a group may be polarized away from the opposing group's norm. This identity-based displacement of the norm may arise prior to any inter-action within the group. The tendency for groups to focus on shared rather than unshared features was demonstrated by Stasser and Titus's (1985) work on hidden profiles in decision-making groups. Moreover, Wittenbaum, Hubbell, and Zuckerman (1999) found that members who discuss shared information are perceived as more competent. Likewise Kameda, Ohtsubo, and Takezawa (1997) found that members who hold information that over-laps more with others are also perceived to be more central to the group. These findings suggest that, at least initially, group members may seek con-sensus by focusing on prototypical opinions and members. Conversely, groups that are more diverse internally (perhaps with cross-cutting catego-rizations internally) appear likely to make better decisions than homoge-neous groups because there is a less obviously prototypical position for them to adopt (Tindale, Kameda, & Hinz, 2003).

A further branch of research that illuminates social identity processes in decision-making groups is the work on shared task representations (Tindale & Kameda, 2000). When tasks are complex, it appears that members depend more on shared ground rules for tackling them, even when these are not optimal. This implies that members of small groups may seek a common frame of reference for their decisions and the common frame may be provided by shared social identity (see also Kerr & Tindale, 2004).

More direct evidence for a distinctive role for social identity is that it pro-vides a basis for group cohesion and solidarity. Attraction to group members is affected more strongly by shared identity than by interpersonal similarity or attractiveness (Abrams, Marques, Bown, & Henson, 2000). Hogg (1992) distinguished between personal attraction, which is based on interpersonal similarities, and social attraction, which is based on similarities to the group prototype. A group may happen to stick together because pairs of individu-als like one another (personal attraction), but it is much more likely to stick together if members share a common basis for mutual attraction. Social attraction is a function of how much one identifies with the group and how prototypical the other person is: It is positive regard or liking for the proto-type as it is embodied by real group members. Social attraction tends to be relatively consensual and unidirectional: If membership is salient and group members agree on the prototype, then more prototypical members tend to be consensually "popular" and less prototypical members tend to be con-sensually socially unpopular. For example, Hogg and Hardie (1991) found, among members of Australian football teams, that perceived prototypicality and norms were related to measures of social but not personal attraction among the team. These relationships were stronger among members who identified more with the team. Bown and Abrams (2003) demonstrated that evaluations of workers in a commercial organization were affected (negatively) independently by being personally unlikable and being nonprototypical. Taken together, the evidence seems consistent with the idea that depersonalized prototype-based liking within a salient group represents a powerful basis for the affective aspects of group cohesiveness—the warm feeling of oneness with fellow members.

Exclusion and Inclusion of Deviant Group Members

Increasingly, the social identity perspective has been used to consider the conditions under which people deviate, break ranks, or withdraw from a larger inclusive group (see Abrams, Hogg, & Marques, in press; Williams, Forgas, & von Hippel, in press). For example, involvement in delinquency can be traced to the reputation and social identity conferred by such action (Emler & Reicher, 1995). However, the common reaction to deviant members within small groups (Schachter, 1959; Shaw, 1976) is modified substantially by whether people are judging ingroup or outgroup deviants. Specifically, there is a so-called "black sheep effect" (see Marques & Páez, 1994) such that unlikable ingroup members are derogated more than equally unlikable outgroup members.

This often-replicated finding suggests that when group members judge one another, they are more concerned with the implications of the behavior for their group's validity and cohesiveness than with the objective nature of the deviant's behavior. In particular, Abrams and Marques's subjective group dynamics model (e.g., Abrams et al., 2000) proposes that group members seize on evidence that subjectively establishes the validity of their own group's norms. As a result, they are quite forgiving of deviants in their own group who adopt extreme attitudes that go beyond the group norm, but they are disparaging of deviants who adopt more moderate or conciliatory attitudes toward other groups. Ingroup loyalty is a valued attribute among group members (see also Zdaniuk & Levine, 2001).

Conversely, group members are quite accepting of outgroup members whose deviance implies exaggerated support for ingroup norms (Abrams, Marques, Bown, & Dougill, 2002). These effects are larger when group members identify more highly with the group. The model, therefore, extends social identity theory to predict how intergroup contexts affect intragroup relations. Abrams, Rutland, and Cameron (2003) extended their analysis to consider how subjective group dynamics develop. Although young children show ingroup bias and are able to detect deviant members of their groups, it is only as they get older that evaluations of these deviants become systematically related to intergroup evaluations and social identity.

Marques, Abrams, and Serodio (2001) demonstrated that reactions to deviant group members are more extreme when the group is otherwise heterogeneous and when the intergroup context is more competitive. Hogg, Fielding, and Darley (in press) suggest some further motivational components. They argue that the reaction of members to a deviant depends on (1) whether the deviant occupies a position on the boundary with the outgroup or remote from the outgroup, (2) whether there is a threat to the group's valence or its entitativity, and (3) whether the deviant publicly attributes his or her deviance to self or to the group. Other perspectives on deviance focus on deviants as ingroup critics (e.g., Hornsey & Imani, 2004) or as minority groups that challenge the accepted wisdom of the majority (e.g., Nemeth & Staw, 1989). In both these cases, as discussed previously, deviance is viewed as a constructive contribution to group life—minorities and critics are effectively trying to change the group's identity from inside.

Social Identity and Social Dilemmas in Groups

Social dilemmas pit individual interests against those of the ingroup. From a social identity perspective, it can be predicted that as group members and social identity become more salient, the interests of self and group become one, thereby resolving the dilemma (Brewer & Schneider, 1990; de Cremer & van Vugt, 1999). However, it may not always be possible to increase social identification with the group. (Indeed, the attractions of personal gain may be so salient that group identity has little impact.) In these circumstances, groups may need to impose additional sanctions or rewards to constrain their members (see Foddy, Smithson, Schneider, & Hogg, 1999). In practice, a means by which members may be motivated to serve the group rather than themselves is through the presence of a trusted and prototypical group leader (e.g., van Vugt & de Cremer, 1999).

Leadership

Research also shows that social identity is quite central to the way leaders are judged and have influence within groups and organizations (e.g., Hogg, Hains, & Mason, 1998; Morris, Hulbert, & Abrams, 2000). For example, Hains, Hogg, and Duck (1997) showed that when group membership was salient, experimental participants rated potential leaders more highly based on how prototypical the group's leader was than on the basis of whether the person showed stereotypically good leader qualities (Lord, 1985). In a similar vein, de Cremer and van Vugt (1999) have shown that among members who identify highly with the group, leaders in social dilemma situations are preferred more if they share the group's values. Moreover, leaders that are more prototypical are likely to have higher influence and attract more confidence among group members. The social identity analysis of leadership (see Hogg & van Knippenberg, 2003) holds that as group membership salience increases, members judge one another increasingly in terms of prototypicality. The most prototypical members are figural against the background of the rest of the group, and this provides them with the status and ability to gain compliance from others. As a result, their behavior is attributed internally, and they are likely to be accorded leadership status.

Integrative and Disintegrative Consequences of Social Identity in Organizations and Multiple Group Settings

Organizations provide a highly meaningful basis for social identity. Ashforth and Mael (1989) first applied social identity theory to organizational settings, and there has been a significant upsurge in research in this area (e.g., Haslam, 2004; Hogg & Terry, 2001; van Knippenberg & Hogg, 2001). Some work has examined organizational commitment and turnover (e.g., Abrams, Ando, & Hinkle, 1998; Ellemers et al., 1999; Moreland, Levine, & McMinn, 2001). Other work has concentrated on broader organizational dynamics that flow from a social identity analysis (Haslam, 2004). The research demonstrates that identification with the organization is strongly related to other forms of commitment, such as team and organizational citizenship, loyalty, turnover, and related constructs (also see Tyler & Blader, 2000). Tyler and Blader's (2003) Group Engagement Model highlights the importance of procedural justice for the valuing of social identity within organizations and the way people then engage with others.

When social identity is salient, stereotypes are applied more strongly to others (Leyens, Yzerbyt, & Schadron, 1994) and to the self (Simon & Hamilton 1994; Spears, Oakes, Ellemers, & Haslam, 1997). In addition to the descriptive content of group membership, the affective associations with different groups are applied strongly when social identity is salient (Smith, 1999). Within organizations, mergers and competition both seem to heighten sensitivity to social identity concerns (Hogg & Terry, 2001). Social identity processes can be a basis for problematic relationships in organizations. For example, Hennessey and West (1999) found that strong team identification within an organization was associated with ingroup favoritism against other work groups. Thus, even though identification may be good for commitment to a team, it may also result in other less desirable outcomes for the organization as a whole.

Organizational diversity has been conceptualized as bringing both advantages and disadvantages for self-categorization and social identity (Brewer, 1996). A related problem facing organizations is how to deal with internal structuring and restructuring, on either a temporary or permanent basis (Terry, Carey, & Callan, 2001; van Knippenberg, van Knippenberg, Monden, & Lima, 2002; van Leeuwen, van Knippenberg, & Ellemers, 2003). For example, different teams or subgroups within organizations often have to work together and may even be merged. Therefore, an interesting question is how the social identity of the members of the originating groups changes. The common ingroup identity model (Gaertner & Dovidio, 2000) holds that relations between subgroups (e.g., two 6-person groups) become more harmonious when they perceive that they share a common superordinate category. Other forms of recategorization can help to promote positive cross-group relationships. For example, groups can also be internally structured into nested subgroups (Brewer, 1996; Hogg & Hornsey, in press), such as sales and marketing in an organization. They may also be intersected by wider cross-cutting categories (e.g., psychologists and physicists in a university; see Crisp, Ensari, Hewstone, & Miller, 2003). Moreover, it appears that where continuation of identity into the merged organization is perceived, the new superordinate identity may be strengthened rather than reduced (van Leeuwen, van Knippenberg & Ellemers, 2003). Each of these approaches may increase group members' openness to positive relationships with other parts of the organization.

The likely success of recategorizing groups into a common superordinate category has been questioned. For example, Hewstone and Brown (1986) argue that groups must be able to sustain their subgroup distinctiveness, and others propose that positive attitudes to the superordinate group involve a dual level of identification (sub- and superordinate) or projection of their own group's characteristics onto the superordinate category (Hornsey & Hogg, 2000; Marques, Abrams, & Serodio, 2001; Wenzel, Mummendey, Weber, & Waldus, 2003). When groups or organizations merge, the new merged organization may compromise the identities of members of both originating organizations (e.g., Terry et al., 2001).

Aside from cognitive effects of recategorization, organizations are also likely to have to contend with difference in the power and status of merged subgroups. These differences have implications for how satisfactory the superordinate level will be for each subgroup. Wenzel et al. (2003) argue that in almost all nested group situations, one group's attributes are more fully represented in the overarching group, and thus, one nested group appears to occupy a dominant position. Subordinate subgroups can often feel that their distinct identity within the larger collective is threatened, which can cause them to fight strongly for their independence within the wider collective.

In a further complexity, as highlighted by Brewer's (1991) optimal distinctiveness theory, individuals may actively seek group memberships that provide them with both a comfortable level of inclusiveness (within the group) and distinctiveness (from other groups). Thus, imposed mergers or de-mergers may disrupt an identity equilibrium and result in new schisms. For example, Sani and Reicher (2000) provide a social identity analysis of schisms in groups; they argue that a schism is most likely to arise under conditions of identity threat and intolerance of diverse views within the overarching group.

Contextual, Temporal, and Cultural Context of Social Identity

A Variable Self-Concept?

At the intraindividual level, social identity research has examined the dynamics of identity salience (Oakes, 1987) and the self-concept (Abrams, 1999; Abrams & Hogg, 2001). The hallmark of the social identity approach is that social identity may be highly flexible. That is, from situation to situation, different social identifications (identification with different social categories) may become salient. Social identity is not restricted to a particular size or type of group; it is *self-conception* as sharing a category membership with a set of other people. They may be people one does not know (e.g., supporters of a particular cause), or they may be members of a well-established, long-standing social group (e.g., a research team or department). Although existing interpersonal relationships may be important, they are not necessary, and they do not determine the content of social identity. The same individual can readily be recategorized as an ingroup or as an outgroup member, depending on the comparison categories that are salient at the time. It follows that much of the apparent inconsistency of individual behavior may be associated with the particular self-inclusive category that is salient at a given time. For example, one may be critical of an opponent's cheating but forgiving of cheating by one's own team (Abrams, Randsley de Moura, Hutchison, & Viki, in press). This idea of flexibility has been subject to some criticism from those who argue that structural and motivational processes produce consistency and stability in the self-concept (Abrams, 1999; Brewer, 1991; Deaux, 1996). However, there is agreement that the self acts in a flexible and adaptive way to engage meaningfully with different roles and group memberships.

The question of whether the self is a continuous and flexible process or has a relatively stable structure that partitions group identity from other forms of identity is relevant for small groups. It may be difficult to imagine how a small group could sustain its coherence over time if the identities of its members were constantly in flux. Reid and Deaux (1996) acknowledge a basic difference between collective and individual selves and suggest that the cognitive organization of self-structure involves a significant amount of linkage between certain identities and certain attributes. Deaux, Reid, Mizrahi, and Ethier (1995) have also suggested that although social and personal identities differ qualitatively from one another, there are also important qualitative differences among types of social identity (e.g., ethnicity/religion, stigma, political).

Trafimow, Triandis, and Goto (1991) suggested that the self could be divided into different structural parts (specifically, private and collective), which are stored in different locations in memory. However, this idea has several problems when considering small groups. After all, small groups involve both a categorical level (the group) and apparently unique interpersonal relationships. A further refinement was proposed by Brewer and Gardner (1996), who distinguish between three aspects of the self: *individual self* (personal traits that differentiate self from all others), *relational self* (defined by dyadic relationships that assimilate self to significant other people), and *collective self* (group memberships that differentiate "us" from "them").

Brewer (2001) went on to distinguish four general types of social identity. Person-based social identities emphasize how properties of groups are internalized by individual group members as part of the self-concept. Relational social identities define self in relation to specific other people with whom one interacts in a group context (see also Markus & Kitayama's 1991 description of the interdependent self). Group-based social identities are equivalent to the collective self or social identity as traditionally defined. Collective identities refer to a process whereby group members not only share self-defining attributes but also engage in social action to forge an image of what the group stands for and how it is represented and viewed by others.

Henry, Arrow, and Carini (1999) also proposed that there may be different forms of collective identity. They proposed that social identity is too broad a concept to capture identification with an interacting group. They prefer to use the term *group identification,* and they provided measurement evidence for three components of group identification: social categorization (a cognitive process), interpersonal attraction (an affective process), and interdependence (a behavioral component). This approach may help to capture much of the variance in psychological processes that bind individuals to groups. In common with Brewer's refinement of the personal-social identity distinction to include relational social identities, Henry et al.'s ideas introduce multiple levels of psychological linkage with the group. Overall, we think it certainly likely that the social identity perspective on small groups is enriched by consideration of the nature of relationships among members within groups (see also Abrams, 1992). However, we are also aware that increasing scope across levels of analysis may detract from more fine-grained analysis of processes within levels. For example, social identity theory itself already distinguishes among the cognitive, affective, and behavioral components of social identity (see Hinkle, Taylor, Fox-Cardomone, & Crook, 1989).

Group in the Self or Self in the Group?

The idea that the group is introjected into the self implies that all members of a particular group are likely to share the *same* understanding of the group, centering on the group prototype. This assumption helps to explain the coherence and sustained coordination of behavior among members of groups. However, recently there have been suggestions that the idea of functional antagonism between levels of self-categorization (individual versus group), as postulated by SCT, may not fully capture the relationship between defining features of the ingroup (social identity) and defining features of the individual self (personal identity) (see Spears, 2001). Indeed, there is some evidence that people's perceptions of their groups are in fact simple extensions of the self. In some situations (e.g., categorization into a minimal or transitory group), a person has virtually no knowledge about the group and therefore is dependent on extrapolation of knowledge of the self to infer the group's attributes. Such possibilities are inherent in Cadinu and Rothbart's (1996) self-anchoring model, as well as the model of asymmetrical egocentric social projection as discussed and tested by Krueger and Clement (Clement & Krueger, 2000; Krueger, 1998).

In the minimal group setting, evidence suggests that self-ratings are used as a means to define the ingroup (i.e., the self is used as a heuristic), whereas there is no similar evidence for self-stereotyping (i.e., the ingroup as anchor for the judgment). Hence, self-anchoring might contribute considerably to the formation of ingroup representations. This evidence implies that each member of a group may have quite egocentric, possibly idiosyncratic views of the group's characteristics and relationships with other groups (see Otten, 2002). Future research should explore the conditions that enable social identity based on self-anchoring to become transformed into a social identity based on a consensually shared group prototype. Three obvious sources of such transitions are highly salient contrasts with outgroups, high levels of within-group interaction and information exchange, and the age and shared history of the group (Otten & Wentura, 2001).

The increasing interest in analyzing the relationship between personal and social identity maps on to the similar interest in the relationship between intragroup and intergroup processes. It is clear that we are observing a street with traffic in both directions. We know that group identification increases ingroup bias. Conversely, Brewer and Roccas (2001), for example, present evidence that individual value orientations can affect social identifications. Simon and Kampmeier (2001) showed that an individual striving for distinctiveness can well combine with identification with a minority, whereas individual independence might be combined with majority membership. In sum, there is evidence that intergroup and intragroup processes function in a dynamic interrelationship, and much is to be gained by analyzing the way the two sets of processes operate together (see Abrams et al., 2000; Marques, Abrams, Páez, & Martinez-Taboada, 1998; Spears, 2001).

Culture and Small Groups

Hofstede's (1980) examination of values amongst IBM employees in more than 40 national cultures resulted in four dimensions that organized the observed cross-cultural variation: power distance, individualism-collectivism, cultural masculinity-femininity, and uncertainty avoidance. The individualism-collectivism construct has received the greatest scrutiny and criticism (e.g., Kagitcibasi, 1997; Oyserman, Coon, & Kemmelmeier, 2002; Rhee, Uleman, & Lee, 1996; Triandis & Gelfand, 1998). Hofstede viewed individualism-collectivism as a bipolar dimension contrasting cultures where ties between the individual and groups are loose, the self is conceived primarily as an independent entity, and conflicts between individual and group goals are generally resolved in favor of individual goals with those cultures where group memberships are influential aspects of the self and individual goals are subordinate to those of the collective. The construct suggests significant differences in terms of the relative import of social and personal identities, the emphasis on task versus socioemotional considerations, conformity versus independence, equity versus equality and need in the allocation of resources, and preferences for direct versus mediated forms of dispute resolution. From a social identity perspective, if there are cultural differences in the way people understand their group memberships (e.g., the generic norms that accompany group membership), there will also be identity-based differences between cultures in what people do within small groups.

Bond and Smith's (1996) meta-analysis revealed higher conformity in collectivist than individualist national cultures. There also appears to be less social loafing in collectivist relative to individualist cultures, even including reversals of the usual social loafing effect in collectivist cultures (Earley, 1993; Gabrenya, Wang, & Latane, 1985), a phenomenon labeled *social striving* by Gabrenya et al. Group norms appear to be a stronger predictor of employee turnover intentions in a collectivist (Japan) relative to an individualist (Britain) national culture (Abrams et al., 1998; see also Morris, Podolny, & Ariel, 2001). Bierbrauer (1992) observed that whereas guilt mediated the effects of norms among a sample of Germans (individualistic culture), both guilt and shame proved to be important mediators among the more collectivist Kurds and Lebanese.

There is also evidence for cultural differences in group polarization (Carlson & Davis, 1971), emphases on equality and need versus equity as resource allocation principles (van den Heuval & Poortinga, 1999), preferences for approaches to conflict resolution (Leung, Bond, Carment, Krishnan, & Liebrand 1990; Markus & Lin, 1999), and leadership behavior (Offermann & Hellmann, 1997; Schmidt & Yeh, 1992). In summary, small groups appear to behave differently in more collectivist cultures than in more individualistic cultures. From a social identity perspective, regardless of culture, identification with the group should be the process that determines the *extent* to which group membership determines behavior, but not the particular form behavior. For example, given that self-esteem may be achieved in different means in independent versus more interdependent cultures (Heine, Lehman, Markus, & Kitayama, 1999), it is likely that higher and lower levels of group identity will also manifest themselves differently in different cultures.

Numerous studies have tested and supported the hypothesis that social identities are of greater import for the self in collectivist than in individualist cultures (Bochner, 1994; Bond & Cheung, 1983; Markus & Kitayama, 1991). Cousins (1989) demonstrated that whether Japanese respondents manifested a greater or lesser number of self-descriptions indicative of social identities relative to U.S. respondents depended on the social context in which the self was assessed. Current research also suggests that a group norm of individualism can be activated in individualistic cultures. This implies that people in small groups with a strongly individualistic norm or local culture would, paradoxically, behave more individualistically as a function of increased identification (e.g., Abrams et al., 1998; Jetten, Postmes, & McAuliffe, 2002; McAuliffe, Jetten, Hornsey, & Hogg, in press).

A more complex social identity hypothesis was advanced by Hinkle and Brown (1990). They proposed that the relationship between ingroup identification and ingroup favoritism would be strongest among collectivists with a relational orientation to making group evaluations, that is, an approach based on ingroup versus outgroup comparison. This prediction was advanced relative to individualists and those with an autonomous orientation to group evaluation, that is, an approach based on comparison to past ingroup circumstances or abstract evaluative bases. Although it is not without criticism from within the social identity and self-categorization traditions (Turner, 1999), the hypothesis has been supported at the individual level of analysis, as has a parallel hypothesis concerning the relationship between ingroup favoritism and self-esteem (Hinkle, Taylor, Fox-Cardamone, & Ely, 1998). Support for the former hypothesis has also been reported at the cross-cultural level of analysis by Torres (1996) and in a meta-analysis by Aharpour (1998), although Capozza, Voci, and Licciardello's (2000) comparison between northern (individualist) and southern (collectivist) Italians directly opposed the hypothesis. In summary, cross-cultural differences in group phenomena such as conformity, social loafing, and the influence of norms suggest that group and intergroup processes reflect a *combination* of cultural variables and varying degrees of social identification with relevant groups.

Research Methods

The dominant research method in social identity research has been the minimal intergroup paradigm (see Bourhis, 1994; Hogg & Abrams, 1988; Tajfel, 1970). The critical features of this are that individuals are categorized randomly into two or more groups, but on the basis of an apparently meaningful criterion. They remain anonymous, and they have no idea which other individuals are in each category. Participants are usually then asked to assign rewards or points to up to 12 different pairs of anonymous members of each group using a set of reward matrices. These matrices are designed to detect the pull of different motivational strategies, including displaying fairness, maximizing the difference in favor of the ingroup, maximizing joint outcomes, maximizing ingroup profit, and so on. Part of the attraction of this paradigm is that it allows investigation of group behavior that is uncontaminated by group history, interpersonal relations, realistic conflict, familiarity, or any of the other factors that had traditionally been used to account for intergroup relations. The paradigm demonstrates how mere (self) categorization is sufficient to generate ingroup bias.

Over the last 15 years or so, the paradigm has been adapted quite extensively to explore and simulate how specific features of intergroup context, such as power and status differences or unjust inequalities, can affect levels of bias (e.g., Bourhris, 1994) and self-categorization (see Otten & Wentura, 2001). The use of minimal categorization is now quite extensive and is used to study all kinds of intergroup and intragroup phenomena, ranging from cohesion to social influence (see Haslam, 2004).

Social identity research has also employed real social category memberships, focusing more on the mediating processes, such as the level or degree of identification, identity threat, and self-esteem to see how these affect the impact of group membership on behavior (see Ellemers et al., 2002). Manipulation of the level of abstraction at which members categorize themselves and others has also been used increasingly to explore how intra- and intergroup attitudes and behavior are responsive to different levels of categorization (Gaertner & Dovidio, 2000). In addition, recent research has independently manipulated the salience of intergroup categorization and intragroup differences simultaneously, and in conjunction with other factors such as accountability (e.g., Marques et al., 1998). The predominant methodology is quantitative and hypothesis-led rather than qualitative or exploratory (although both of these are represented in the literature).

Dependent variables tend to focus on group-level attributes (e.g., allocation of resources to the group; feelings of cohesiveness or attraction to the group; agreement with group norms or values; identification with the group; collective self-esteem; evaluations of the group's status; stereotypes of ingroup, outgroup, and the self; and so on). However, a substantial body of the research directly contrasts group-level and individual-level processes, such as interpersonal attraction versus social attraction, interpersonal similarity versus group prototypicality. Therefore, the measures used are drawn from a wide range of research approaches within social psychology.

Strengths, Weaknesses, and Conclusions

To conclude, the social identity approach or perspective emerged as a part of an intellectual challenge to the individualistic theorizing that prevailed in social psychology throughout the latter part of the 20th century. The social identity approach has been applied to a very wide variety of group phenomena, particularly intergroup phenomena. The approach relates individual cognition to the social context and social structure in which it operates and offers a psychological level of analysis for understanding how individuals function as group members. Thus, a key strength is that it provides an overarching metatheory for understanding groups (Abrams & Hogg, 2004). This non-reductionist metatheory does not depend on face-to-face communication or interpersonal relationships but accounts for the psychological mediation of social structures on the self-concept and on social action. It highlights the context in which groups exist and explains the connection between that context and identity. The approach emphasizes the dynamics of intergroup relationships and how these dynamically affect intragroup relations and the self. The approach has generated an enormous volume of research, particularly in intergroup relations, and employs a wide range of robust research techniques.

The impact of the social identity perspective on small group decision research has lagged behind its substantial embodiment within mainstream intergroup relations research. Currently, more attention is being paid to the implications of this perspective for intragroup processes (Abrams & Hogg, 1998). In addition, much of the evidence we have described is from experimental or quasi-experimental research involving conceptual rather than actual groups, although some very rich qualitative evidence in the social identity area does fill some of these gaps (see Reicher & Hopkins, 2001).

There are unquestionably some gaps and weaknesses to be addressed in the social identity approach. The theorizing of motivation is rather limited, relying heavily on a few basic ideas such as self-esteem and uncertainty reduction. These may be fundamental motives, but greater attention needs to be paid to transitory and proximal motivations and emotions that exist within specific groups (e.g., loyalty, social exchange/dependency, fear, greed, and so on). The approach also has relatively little to say about the aspects of group behavior that are independent of perceptions of the group prototype or norms, such as close intragroup and intergroup friendships, contractual obligations, and interdependence. We are also aware that the analysis of group structure is primarily oriented toward issues of group and individual status rather than specific roles within groups (apart from leadership). We believe there is much to be gained by developing a more detailed account of the ways intergroup, intragroup, and interpersonal processes are interrelated and coordinated.

One of the charges often made is that social identity and self-categorization theories are difficult to falsify because it is relatively easy to provide post-hoc explanations for the presence or absence of social identity effects in terms of the salience or relevance of particular social categorizations in particular contexts (cf. Abrams, 1992; Hinkle & Brown, 1990; Turner, 1999). A further task is to provide a more developmental theory with regard to the way social identity changes over the course of both a group's life and a person's life (cf. Bennett & Sani, 2004; Moreland et al., 2001).

Overall, we are optimistic that the social identity approach has much to offer the analysis of small groups, and we hope we have pointed toward some interesting avenues. The study of organizations is an obvious arena, but the social identity approach should be equally valuable in other contexts in which differences in social choice, opportunity, and action are associated with social category memberships (e.g., education, health, politics, sports). The social identity approach provides an overarching conceptual framework for understanding groups. However, we recognize that social identity is only a part of the story and that it must be set in the context of individual, relational, and cultural elements in groups.

References

Abrams, D. (1992). Processes of social identification. In G. Breakwell (Ed.), *Social psychology of identity and the self-concept* (pp. 57–99). San Diego, CA: Academic Press.

Abrams, D. (1994). Social self-regulation. *Personality and Social Psychology Bulletin, 20,* 473–483.

Abrams, D. (1999). Social identity, social cognition, and the self: The flexibility and stability of self-categorization. In D. Abrams & M. A. Hogg (Eds.), *Social identity and social cognition* (pp. 197–229). Oxford, UK: Blackwell.

Abrams, D., Ando, K., & Hinkle, S. W. (1998). Psychological attachment to the group: Cross-cultural differences in organizational identification and subjective norms as predictors of workers' turnover intentions. *Personality and Social Psychology Bulletin, 24,* 1027–1039.

Abrams, D., & Brown, R. J. (1989). Self-consciousness and social identity: Self-regulation as a group member. *Social Psychology Quarterly, 52,* 311–318.

Abrams, D., & Hogg, M. A. (1988). Comments on the motivational status of self-esteem in social identity and intergroup discrimination. *British Journal of Social Psychology, 18,* 317–334.

Abrams, D., & Hogg, M. A. (1990a). Social identification, self-categorization, and social influence. *European Review of Social Psychology, 1,* 195–228.

Abrams, D., & Hogg, M. A. (Eds.). (1990b). *Social identity theory: Constructive and critical advances.* London: Harvester Wheatsheaf.

Abrams, D., & Hogg, M.A. (1998). Prospects for research in group processes and intergroup relations. *Group Processes and Intergroup Relations, 1,* 7–20.

Abrams, D., & Hogg, M. A. (Eds.). (1999). *Social identity and social cognition.* Oxford, UK: Blackwell.

Abrams, D., & Hogg, M. A. (2001). Collective self. In M. A. Hogg & S. Tindale (Eds.), *Blackwell handbook of social psychology: Vol 3. Group processes* (pp. 425–461). Oxford, UK: Blackwell.

Abrams, D., & Hogg, M. A. (2004). Metatheory: Lessons from social identity research. *Personality and Social Psychology Review, 8,* 97–105.

Abrams, D., Hogg, M. A., & Marques, J. (Eds.). (in press). *Social psychology of inclusion and exclusion.* New York: Psychology Press.

Abrams, D., Hulbert, L. G., & Davis, J. H. (1996, October 16). *Social context and group decisions.* Paper presented at Society of Experimental Social Psychology Annual Conference, Sturbridge, MA.

Abrams, D., Marques, J. M., Bown, N. J., & Dougill, M. (2002). Anti-norm and pro-norm deviance in the bank and on the campus: Two experiments on subjective group dynamics. *Group Processes and Intergroup Relations, 5,* 163–182.

Abrams, D., Marques, J. M., Bown, N. J., & Henson, M. (2000). Pro-norm and anti-norm deviance within in-groups and out-groups. *Journal of Personality and Social Psychology, 78,* 906–912.

Abrams, D., Randsley de Moura, G. R., Hutchison, P., & Viki, G. T. (in press). When bad becomes good (and vice versa): Why social exclusion is not based on difference. In D. Abrams, M. A. Hogg, & J. M. Marques (Eds.), *Social exclusion and inclusion.* Philadelphia: Psychology Press.

Abrams, D., Rutland, A., & Cameron, L. (2003). The development of subjective group dynamics: Children's judgments of normative and deviant in-group and out-group individuals. *Child Development, 74,* 1840–1856.

Aharpour, S. (1998). *Social identity theory and group diversity: An analysis of functions of group identification.* Unpublished PhD thesis, University of Kent at Canterbury, UK.

Allport, F. H. (1924). *Social psychology.* Boston: Houghton Mifflin.

Allport, G. W. (1954). *The nature of prejudice.* London: Addison-Wesley.

Ashforth, B. E., & Mael, F. A. (1989). Social identity theory and the organization. *Academy of Management Review, 14,* 20–39.

Baumeister, R. F. (1998). The self. In D. T. Gilbert, S. T. Fiske, & G. Lindzey (Eds.), *The handbook of social psychology* (Vol. 1, pp. 680–740). New York: McGraw-Hill.

Bennett, M., & Sani, F. (Eds.). (2004). *The development of the social self.* Philadelphia: Psychology Press.

Bierbrauer, G. (1992). Reactions to violation of normative standards: A cross-cultural analysis of shame and guilt. *International Journal of Psychology, 27,* 181–193.

Bochner, S. (1994). Cross-cultural differences in the self concept: A test of Hofstede's individualism/collectivism distinction. *Journal of Cross Cultural Psychology, 25,* 273–283.

Bond, M. H., & Cheung, T. (1983). College students' spontaneous self-concept: The effect of culture among respondents in Hong Kong, Japan, and the United States. *Journal of Cross Cultural Psychology, 14,* 153–171.

Bond, R., & Smith, P. B. (1996). Culture and conformity: A meta-analysis of studies using Asch's (1952b, 1956) line judgment task. *Psychological Bulletin, 119,* 111–137.

Bourhis, R. Y. (1994). Power, gender, and intergroup discrimination: Some minimal group experiments. In M. P. Zanna & J. M. Olson (Eds.), *The psychology of prejudice: The Ontario symposium* (Vol. 7, pp. 119–135). Hillsdale, NJ: Lawrence Erlbaum.

Bown, N., & Abrams, D. (2003). Despicability in the workplace: Effects of behavioural deviance and unlikeability on the evaluation of in-group and out-group members. *Journal of Applied Social Psychology, 33,* 1–14.

Brewer, M. B. (1991). The social self: On being the same and different at the same time. *Personality and Social Psychology Bulletin, 17,* 475–482.

Brewer, M. B. (1996). Managing diversity: The role of social identities. In S. Jackson & M. Ruderman (Eds.), *Diversity in work teams* (pp. 47–68). Washington, DC: American Psychological Association.

Brewer, M. B. (2001). The many faces of social identity: Implications for political psychology. *Political Psychology, 22,* 115–125.

Brewer, M. B., & Brown, R. J. (1998). Intergroup relations. In D. T. Gilbert, S. T. Fiske, & G. Linzdey (Eds.), *The handbook of social psychology* (Vol. 2, pp. 554–594). New York: McGraw-Hill.

Brewer, M. B., & Gardner, W. (1996). Who is this "we"? Levels of collective identity and self-representations. *Journal of Personality and Social Psychology, 71,* 83–93.

Brewer, M. B., & Roccas, S. (2001). Individual values, social identity, and optimal distinctiveness. In C. Sedikides & M. B. Brewer (Eds.), *Individual self, relational self, collective self* (pp. 219–237). Philadelphia: Psychology Press.

Brewer, M. B., & Schneider, S. (1990). Social identity and social dilemmas: A double-edged sword. In D. Abrams & M. A. Hogg (Eds.), *Social identity theory: Constructive and critical advances* (pp. 169–184). London: Harvester Wheatsheaf.

Brown, R. (2000). *Group processes: Dynamics in and between groups.* Oxford, UK: Blackwell.

Cadinu, M. R., & Rothbart, M. (1996). Self-anchoring and differentiation processes in the minimal group setting. *Journal of Personality and Social Psychology, 70,* 661–677.

Capozza, D., & Brown, R. J. (Eds.). (2000). *Social identity processes.* London: Sage.

Capozza, D., Voci, A., & Licciardello, O. (2000). Individualism, collectivism, and social identity theory. In D. Capozza & R. J. Brown (Eds.), *Social identity processes* (pp. 62–80). London: Sage.

Carlson, J., & Davis, D. M. (1971). Cultural values and the risky shift: A cross cultural test in Uganda and the United States. *Journal of Personality and Social Psychology, 20,* 392–399.

Clement, R. W., & Krueger, J. (2000). The primacy of self-referent information in perceptions of social consensus. *British Journal of Social Psychology, 39,* 279–299.

Cousins, S. D. (1989). Culture and self-perception in Japan and the United States. *Journal of Personality and Social Psychology, 56,* 124–131.

Crisp, R., Ensari, N., Hewstone, M., & Miller, N. (2003). A dual-route model of crossed categorization effects. In W. Stroebe & M. Hewstone (Eds.),

Euorpean review of social psychology (Vol. 13, pp. 35–74). New York: Psychology Press.

Deaux, K. (1996). Social identification. In E. T. Higgins & A. W. Kruglanski (Eds.), *Social psychology: Handbook of basic principles* (pp. 777–798). New York: Guilford.

Deaux, K., & Philogene, G. (Eds.). (2001). *Representations of the social.* Oxford, UK: Blackwell.

Deaux, K., Reid, A., Mizrahi, K., & Ethier, K. A. (1995). Parameters of social identity. *Journal of Personality and Social Psychology, 68,* 280–291.

de Cremer, D., & van Vugt, M. (1999). Social identification effects in social dilemmas: A transformation of motives. *European Journal of Social Psychology, 29,* 871–893.

DeDreu, C. K. W., & DeVries, N. K. (2001). *Group consensus and minority influence.* Oxford, UK: Blackwell.

Diener, E. (1980). Deindividuation: The absence of self-awareness and self-regulation in group members. In P. B. Paulus (Ed.), *Psychology of group influence* (pp. 209–242). Hillsdale, NJ: Lawrence Erlbaum.

Earley, P. C. (1993). East meets West meets Mideast: Further explorations of collectivistic and individualistic work groups. *Academy of Management Journal, 36,* 319–348.

Ellemers, N., Spears, R., & Doojse, B. (Eds.). (1999). *Social identity.* Oxford, UK: Blackwell.

Ellemers, N., Spears, R., & Doojse, B. (2002). Self and social identity. *Annual Review of Psychology, 53,* 161–186.

Emler, N., & Reicher, S. D. (1995). *Adolescence and delinquency: The collective management of reputation.* Oxford, UK: Blackwell.

Farr, R. M., & Moscovici, S. (Eds.). (1984). *Social representations.* Cambridge, UK: Cambridge University Press.

Foddy, M., Smithson, M., Schneider, S., & Hogg, M. A. (Eds.). (1999). *Resolving social dilemmas: Dynamic, structural, and intergroup aspects.* Philadelphia: Psychology Press.

Gabrenya, W. K., Wang, Y., & Latane, B. (1985). Social loafing on an optimizing task: Cross-cultural differences among Chinese and Americans. *Journal of Cross Cultural Psychology, 16,* 223–242.

Gaertner, L., & Schopler, J. (1998). Perceived ingroup entitativity and intergroup bias: An interconnection of self and others. *European Journal of Social Psychology, 28,* 963–980.

Gaertner, S. L., & Dovidio, J. F. (2000). *Reducing intergroup bias.* Philadelphia: Psychology Press.

Hains, S. C., Hogg, M. A., & Duck, J. M. (1997). Self-categorization and leadership: Effects of group prototypicality and leader stereotypicality. *Personality and Social Psychology Bulletin, 23,* 1087–1100.

Hamilton, D. L. (Ed.). (1981). *Cognitive processes in stereotyping and intergroup behavior.* Hillsdale, NJ: Lawrence Erlbaum.

Haslam, S. A. (2004). *Psychology in organizations: The social identity approach* (2nd ed.). London: Sage.

Heine, S. H., Lehman, D. R., Markus, H. R., & Kitayama, S. (1999). Is there a universal need for positive self-regard? *Psychological Review, 106,* 766–794.

Hennessey, J., & West, M. (1999). Intergroup behavior in organizations: A field test of social identity theory. *Small Group Research, 30,* 361–382.

Henry, K. B., Arrow, H., & Carini, B. (1999). A tripartite model of group identification: Theory and measurement. *Small Group Research, 30,* 558–581.

Hewstone, M., & Brown, R. J. (1986). Contact is not enough: An intergroup persepective on the "Contact Hypothesis." In M. Hewstone & R. J. Brown (Eds.), *Contact and conflict in intergroup encounters* (pp. 1–44). Oxford, UK: Blackwell.

Hinkle, S. W., & Brown, R. J. (1990). Intergroup comparisons and social identity: Some links and lacunae. In D. Abrams & M. A. Hogg (Eds.), *Social identity theory: Constructive and critical advances* (pp. 48–70). Hemel Hempstead, UK: Harvester Wheatsheaf.

Hinkle, S., Taylor, L. A., Fox-Cardamone, D. L., & Crook, K. F. (1989). Intragroup identification and intergroup differentiation: A multi-component approach. *British Journal of Social Psychology, 28,* 305–317.

Hinkle, S., Taylor, L. A., Fox-Cardamone, D. L., & Ely, P. (1998). Social identity and aspects of social creativity: Shifting to new dimensions of intergroup comparison. In S. Worchel, J. F. Morales, D. Páez, & J.-C. Deschamps (Eds.), *Social identity: International perspectives* (pp. 166–179). London: Sage.

Hofstede, G. (1980). *Culture's consequences.* Beverly Hills, CA: Sage.

Hogg, M. A. (1992). *The social psychology of group cohesiveness: From attraction to social identity.* Hemel Hempstead, UK: Harvester Wheatsheaf.

Hogg, M. A. (1996). Social identity, self-categorization, and the small group. In E. H. Witte & J. H. Davis (Eds.), *Understanding group behavior: Vol. 2. Small group processes and interpersonal relations* (pp. 227–253). Mahwah, NJ: Lawrence Erlbaum.

Hogg, M. A. (2000). Subjective uncertainty reduction through self-categorization: A motivational theory of social identity processes. *European Review of Social Psychology, 11,* 223–255.

Hogg, M. A., & Abrams, D. (1988). *Social identifications: A social psychology of intergroup relations and group processes.* London: Routledge.

Hogg, M. A., & Abrams, D. (1993). Towards a single-process uncertainty-reduction model of social motivation in groups. In M. A. Hogg & D. Abrams (Eds.), *Group motivation: Social psychological perspectives* (pp. 173–190). London: Harvester Wheatsheaf.

Hogg, M. A., Abrams, D., Otten, S., & Hinkle, S. (2004). The social identity perspective: Intergroup relations, self-conception, and small groups. *Small Group Research, 35,* 243–245.

Hogg, M. A., Fielding, K. S., & Darley, J. (in press). Deviance and marginalization. In D. Abrams, M. A. Hogg, & J. M. Marques (Eds.), *The social psychology of inclusion and exclusion.* New York: Psychology Press.

Hogg, M. A., & Hardie, E. A. (1991). Social attraction, personal attraction, and self-categorization: A field study. *Personality and Social Psychology Bulletin, 17,* 175–180.

Hogg, M. A., Hains, S. C., & Mason, I. (1998). Identification and leadership in small groups: Salience, frame of reference, and leader stereotypicality effects on leader evaluations. *Journal of Personality and Social Psychology, 75,* 1248–1263.

Hogg, M. A., & Hornsey, M. J. (in press). Self-concept threat and multiple categorization within groups. In R. J. Crisp & M. Hewstone (Eds.), *Multiple social categorization: Processes, models, and applications.* New York: Psychology Press.

Hogg, M. A., & Terry, D. (Eds.). (2001). *Social identity processes in organizational contexts.* Philadelphia: Psychology Press.

Hogg, M. A., & van Knippenberg, D. (2003). Social identity and leadership processes in groups. In M. P. Zanna (Ed.), *Advances in experimental social psychology* (Vol. 35, pp. 1–52). San Diego, CA: Academic Press.

Hollingshead, A. B. (2001). Communication technologies, the Internet, and group research. In M. A. Hogg & R. S. Tindale (Eds.), *Blackwell handbook of social psychology: Vol. 3. Group processes* (pp. 557–573). Oxford, UK: Blackwell.

Hornsey, M., & Hogg, M. A. (2000). Subgroup relations: Two experiments comparing subgroup differentiation and common ingroup identity models of prejudice reduction. *Personality and Social Psychology Bulletin, 28,* 242–256.

Hornsey, M. J., & Imani, A. (2004). Criticising groups from the inside and the outside: An identity perspective on the intergroup sensitivity effect. *Personality and Social Psychology Bulletin, 30,* 365–383.

Jaspars, J. M. F. (1980). The coming of age of social psychology in Europe. *European Journal of Social Psychology, 10,* 421–428.

Jetten, J., Postmes, T., & McAuliffe, B. J. (2002). We're all individuals: Group norms of individualism and collectivism, levels of identification, and identity threat. *European Journal of Social Psychology, 32,* 189–207.

Kagitcibasi, C. (1997). Whither multiculturalism? *Applied Psychology: An International Review, 46,* 44–49.

Kameda, T., Ohtsubo, Y., & Takezawa, M. (1997). Centrality in sociocognitive network and social influence: An illustration in a group decision-making context. *Journal of Personality and Social Pshychology, 73,* 296–309.

Kerr, N., & Tindale, R. S. (2004). Group performance and decision making. *Annual Review of Psychology, 55,* 623–655.

Krueger, J. (1998). Enhancement bias in the description of self and others. *Personality and Social Psychology Bulletin, 24,* 505–516.

Lea, M., Spears, R., & de Groot, D. (2001). Knowing me knowing you: Anonymity effects on social identity processes within groups. *Personality and Social Psychology Bulletin, 27,* 526–537.

Leung, K., Bond, M. H., Carment, D. W., Krishnan, L., & Liebrand, W. (1990). Effects of cultural femininity on preference for methods of conflict processing:

A cross-cultural study. *Journal of Experimental Social Psychology, 26,* 373–388.

Leyens, J. P., Yzerbyt, V., & Schadron, G. (1994). *Stereotypes and social cognition.* London: Sage.

Lord, R. G. (1985). An information processing approach to social perception, leadership, and behavioral measurement in organizations. *Research in Organizational Behavior, 7,* 87–128.

Markus, H. R., & Kitayama, S.(1991). Culture and the self: Implications for cognition, emotion, and motivation. *Psychological Review, 98,* 224–253.

Markus, H. R., & Lin, L. R. (1999). Conflictways: Cultural diversity in the meanings and practices of conflict. In D. A. Prentice & D. T. Miller (Eds.), *Cultural divides: Understanding and overcoming group conflict* (pp. 302–333). New York: Russell Sage Foundation.

Marques, J., Abrams, D., Páez, D., & Hogg, M. A. (2001). Social categorization, social identification, and rejection of deviant group members. In M. A. Hogg & S. Tindale (Eds.), *Blackwell handbook of social psychology: Vol 3. Group processes.* (pp. 400–424). Oxford, UK: Blackwell.

Marques, J., Abrams, D., Páez, D., & Martinez-Taboada, C. (1998). The role of categorization and in-group norms in judgments of groups and their members. *Journal of Personality and Social Psychology, 75,* 976–988.

Marques, J. M., Abrams, D., & Serodio, R. (2001). Being better by being right: Subjective group dynamics and derogation of in-group deviants when generic norms are undermined. *Journal of Personality and Social Psychology, 81,* 436–447.

Marques, J. M., & Páez, D. (1994). The black sheep effect: Social categorization, rejection of ingroup deviates, and perception of group variability. *European Review of Social Psychology, 5,* 37–68.

McAuliffe, B. J., Jetten, J., Hornsey, M. J., & Hogg, M. A. (in press). The impact of individualist and collectivist group norms on evaluations of dissenting group members. *Journal of Experimental Social Psychology.*

Moreland, R. L., Hogg, M. A., & Hains, S. C. (1994). Back to the future: Social psychological research on groups. *Journal of Experimental Social Psychology, 30,* 527–555.

Moreland, R. L., Levine, J. M., & McMinn, J. G. (2001). Self-categorization and work group socialization. In M. A. Hogg & D. Terry (Eds.), *Social identity processes in organizational contexts* (pp. 87–100). Philadelphia: Psychology Press.

Morris, L., Hulbert, L., & Abrams, D. (2000). An experimental investigation of group members' perceived influence over leader decisions. *Group Dynamics, 4,* 157–167.

Morris, M. W., Podolny, J. M., & Ariel, S. (2001). Culture, norms, and obligations: Cross-national differences in patterns of interpersonal norms and felt obligations toward coworkers. In W. Wosinska & R. B. Cialdini (Eds.), *The practice of social influence in multiple cultures: Applied social research.* (pp. 97–123). Mahwah, NJ: Lawrence Erlbaum.

Moscovici, S., & Doise, W. (1994). *Conflict and consensus: A general theory of collective decisions.* London: Sage.

Nemeth, C., & Staw, B. M. (1989). The tradeoffs of social control and innovation in groups and organizations. In L. Berkowitz (Ed.), *Advances in experimental social psychology* (Vol. 22, pp. 175–210). San Diego, CA: Academic Press.

Oakes, P. J. (1987). The salience of social categories. In J. C. Turner, M. A. Hogg, P. J. Oakes, S. D. Reicher, & M. S. Wetherell (Eds.), *Rediscovering the social group: A self-categorization theory* (pp. 117–141). Oxford, UK: Blackwell.

Offermann, L. R., & Hellmann, P. S. (1997). Culture's consequences for leadership behavior: National values in action. *Journal of Cross Cultural Psychology, 28,* 342–351.

Otten, S. (2002). "Me" and "us" or "us" and "them"? The self as heuristic for defining novel ingroups. *European Review of Social Psychology, 13,* 1–33.

Otten, S., & Wentura, D. (2001). Self-anchoring and ingroup favoritism: An individual-profiles analysis. *Journal of Experimental Social Psychology, 37,* 525–532.

Oyserman, D., Coon, H. M., & Kemmelmeier, M. (2002). Rethinking individualism and collectivism: Evaluation of theoretical assumptions and meta-analyses. *Psychological Bulletin, 128,* 3–72.

Postmes, T., & Spears, R. (1998). Deindividuation and antinormative behavior: A meta-analysis. *Psychological Bulletin, 123,* 238–259.

Postmes, T., & Spears, R. (2001). Quality of decision making and group norms. *Journal of Personality and Social Psychology, 80,* 918–930.

Postmes, T., Spears, R., & Lea, M. (1998). Breaching or building social boundaries? SIDE-effects of computer-mediated communication. *Communication Research, 25,* 689–715.

Postmes, T., Spears, R., Sakhl, K., & de Groot, D. (2001). Social influence in computer mediated communication: The effects of anonymity on group behavior. *Personality and Social Psychology Bulletin, 27,* 1243–1254.

Reicher, S. D. (1984). Social influence in the crowd: Attitudinal and behavioral effects of deindividuation in conditions of high and low group salience. *British Journal of Social Psychology, 23,* 341–350.

Reicher, S. D., & Hopkins, N. (2001). *Self and nation.* London: Sage.

Reicher, S. D., Spears, R., & Postmes, T. (1995). A social identity model of deindividuation phenomena. *European Journal of Social Psychology, 6,* 161–198.

Reid, A., & Deaux, K. (1996). Relationship between social and personal identities: Segregation or integration. *Journal of Personality and Social Psychology, 71,* 1084–1091.

Rhee, E., Uleman, J. S., & Lee, H. (1996). Variations in collectivism and individualism by ingroup and culture: Confirmatory factor analysis. *Journal of Personality and Social Psychology, 71,* 1037–1054.

Robinson, W. P. (Ed.). (1996). *Social groups and identities: Developing the legacy of Henri Tajfel.* Oxford, UK: Butterworth-Heinemann.

Rubin, M., & Hewstone, M. (1998). Social identity theory's self-esteem hypothesis: A review and some suggestions for clarification. *Personality and Social Psychology Review, 2*, 40–62.

Sani, F., & Reicher, S. D. (2000). Contested identities and schisms in groups: Opposing the ordination of women as priests in the Church of England. *British Journal of Social Psychology, 39*, 95–112.

Schachter, S. (1959). *The psychology of affiliation.* Stanford, CA: Stanford University Press.

Schmidt, S. M., & Yeh, R. (1992). The structure of leader influence: A cross-national comparison. *Journal of Cross Cultural Psychology, 23*, 251–264.

Shaw, M. E. (1976). *Group dynamics* (2nd ed.). New York: McGraw Hill.

Simon, B., & Kampmeier, C. (2001). Revisiting the individual self: Toward a social psychological theory of the individual self and the collective self. In C. Sedikides & M. B. Brewer (Eds.), *Individual self, relational self, collective self* (pp. 199–218). Philadelphia: Psychology Press.

Simon, B., & Hamilton, D. L. (1994). Self-stereotyping and social context: The effects of relative in-group size and in-group status. *Journal of Personality and Social Psychology, 66*, 699–711.

Skevington, S., & Baker, D. (Eds.). (1989). *The social identity of women.* London: Sage.

Smith, E. R. (1999). Affective and cognitive implications of a group becoming part of the self: New models of prejudice and of the self-concept. In D. Abrams & M. A. Hogg (Eds.), *Social identity and social cognition* (pp 183–196). Oxford, UK: Blackwell.

Spears, R. (2001). The interaction between the individual and the collective self: Self-categorization in context. In C. Sedikides & M. B. Brewer (Eds.), *Individual self, relational self, collective self* (pp. 171–198). Philadelphia: Psychology Press.

Spears, R., & Lea, M. (1994). Panacea or panopticon? The hidden power in computer-mediated communication. *Communication Research, 21*, 427–459.

Spears, R., Oakes, P. J., Ellemers, N., & Haslam, S. A. (Eds.). (1997). *The social psychology of stereotyping and group life.* Oxford, UK: Blackwell.

Stasser, G., & Titus, W. (1985). Pooling of unshared information in group decision making: Biased information sampling during discussion. *Journal of Personality and Social Psychology, 48*, 1467–1478.

Tajfel, H. (1970). Experiments in intergroup discrimination. *Scientific American, 223*, 96–102.

Tajfel, H. (1972). Some developments in European social psychology. *European Journal of Social Psychology, 2*, 307–322.

Tajfel, H. (Ed.). (1978). *Differentiation between social groups: Studies in the social psychology of intergroup relations.* London: Academic Press.

Tajfel, H. (1981). *Human groups and social categories: Studies in social psychology.* Cambridge, UK: Cambridge University Press.

Tajfel, H., Jaspars, J. M. F., & Fraser, C. (1984). The social dimension in European social psychology. In H. Tajfel (Ed.), *The social dimension: European developments in social psychology* (Vol. 1, pp. 1–5). Cambridge, UK: Cambridge University Press.

Tajfel, H., & Turner, J. C. (1979). An integrative theory of intergroup conflict. In W. G. Austin & S. Worchel (Eds.), *The social psychology of intergroup relations* (pp. 33–47). Monterey, CA: Brooks/Cole.

Tajfel, H., & Wilkes, A. L. (1963). Classification and quantitative judgement. *British Journal of Psychology, 54,* 101–114.

Terry, D. J., Carey, C. J., & Callan, V. J. (2001). Employee adjustment to an organizational merger: An intergroup perspective. *Personality and Social Psychology Bulletin, 27,* 267–280.

Tindale, R. S., & Kameda, T. (2000). Social sharedness as a unifying theme for information processing in groups. *Group Proceses and Intergroup Relations, 3,* 123–140.

Tindale, R. S., Kameda, T., & Hinz, V. B. (2003). Group decision making. In M. A. Hogg & J. Cooper (Eds.), *The Sage handbook of social psychology* (pp. 381–403). London: Sage.

Torres, A. R. R. (1996). *Exploring group diversity: Relationships between ingroup identification and ingroup bias.* Unpublished PhD thesis, University of Kent at Canterbury, UK.

Trafimow, D., Triandis, H. C., & Goto, S. G. (1991). Some tests of the distinction between the private self and the collective self. *Journal of Personality and Social Psychology, 60,* 649–655.

Triandis, H. C., & Gelfand, M. J. (1998). Converging measurement of horizontal and vertical individualism and collectivism. *Journal of Personality and Social Psychology, 74,* 118–128.

Turner, J. C. (1991). *Social influence.* Buckingham, UK: Open University Press.

Turner, J. C. (1999). Some current issues in research on social identity and self-categorization theories. In N. Ellemers, R. Spears, & B. Doojse (Eds.), *Social identity* (pp. 6–34). Oxford, UK: Blackwell.

Turner, J. C., & Giles, H. (Eds.). (1981). *Intergroup behavior.* Oxford, UK: Blackwell.

Turner, J. C., Hogg, M. A., Oakes, P. J., Reicher, S. D., & Wetherell, M. S. (1987). *Rediscovering the social group: A self-categorization theory.* Oxford, UK: Blackwell.

Tyler, T. R., & Blader, S. L. (2000). *Cooperation in groups: Procedural justice, social identity, and behavioral engagement.* Philadelphia: Psychology Press.

Tyler, T. R., & Blader, S. L. (2003). The group engagement model: Procedural justice, social identity, and cooperative behavior. *Personality and Social Psychology Review, 7,* 349–361.

van den Heuvel, K., & Poortinga, Y. H. (1999). Resource allocation by Greek and Dutch students: A test of three models. *International Journal of Psychology, 34,* 1–13.

van Knippenberg, D., & Hogg, M. A. (Eds.). (2001). *Social identity processes in organizations* [Special issue]. *Group Processes and Intergroup Relations, 4(3).*

van Knippenberg, D., van Knippenberg, B., Monden, L., & Lima, F. (2002). Organizational identification after a merger: A social identity perspective. *British Journal of Social Psychology, 41*, 233–252.

van Leeuwen, E., van Knippenberg, D., & Ellemers, N. (2003). Continuing and changing group identities: The effects of merging on social identification and ingroup bias. *Personality and Social Psychology Bulletin, 29*, 679–690.

van Vugt, M., & de Cremer, D. (1999). Leadership in social dilemmas: The effects of group identification on collective actions to provide public goods. *Journal of Personality and Social Psychology, 76*, 587–599.

Wenzel, M., Mummendey, A., Weber, U., & Waldus, S. (2003). The ingroup as pars pro toto: Projection from the ingroup onto the inclusive category as a precursor to social discrimination. *Personality and Social Psychology Bulletin, 29*, 561–573.

Williams, K. D., Forgas, J. P., & von Hippel, W. (Eds.). (in press). *The social outcast: Ostracism, social exclusion, rejection, and bullying.* New York: Psychology Press.

Wittenbaum, G. M., Hubbell, A. P., & Zuckerman, C. (1999). Mutual enhancement: Toward an understanding of collective preference for shared information. *Journal of Personality and Social Psychology, 77*, 967–978.

Worchel, S., Morales, J. F., Páez , D., & Deschamps, J. C. (Eds.). (1998). *Social identity: International perspectives.* London: Sage.

Zdaniuk, B., & Levine, J. M. (2001). Group loyalty: Impact of members' identification and contributions. *Journal of Experimental Social Psychology, 37*, 502–509.

5

Conflict, Power, and Status in Groups

Michael Lovaglia, Elizabeth A. Mannix,
Charles D. Samuelson, Jane Sell,
and Rick K. Wilson

Abstract

We investigate the concepts and perspectives of conflict, power, and status developed across the disciplines of political science, psychology, and sociology. Although the different disciplines, at times, have different assumptions about actors and interactions, we find a great deal of similarity. This similarity allows us to uncover some general principles that apply to group behavior. In particular, we ask: How are power and status used to maintain or resolve conflict? To address this question, we use institutional rules to analyze the research within and across areas.

Managing conflict is fundamental to the existence of society. Individuals compete with one another for the material goods needed to survive and for the power and status that advantage some individuals over others. Even when material needs have been satisfied, competition for power and status continues, ensuring continued conflict. Hierarchies of power and status emerge from that conflict and serve to manage it, allowing individuals to cooperate and their groups to survive.

We address three concepts central to social science—conflict, power, and status—within the context of group processes, using research and theory primarily from psychology, political science, and sociology. (For a statement of this perspective that focuses on theory, see Sell, Lovaglia, Mannix, Samuelson, & Wilson, 2004.) Organizing such large bodies of literature within each discipline and then across disciplines is a daunting task. The authors represent the three different disciplines but probably do not represent all the many methodologies that characterize these disciplines. In fact, one of the commonalities among us is that we use experimental approaches (perhaps not exclusively but certainly commonly). Our methodological approach also, rather naturally, coincides with our interest and focus on theory building or theory testing.

One way to organize these substantive areas is to view conflict as a result of differences in power or status. Thus, we aim to address the general question: How are power and status used to maintain or resolve conflict? In the sections that follow, we discuss some general assumptions used in the theories of power, status, and conflict, define important concepts, and then review the major findings in each of the three areas separately. See Table 5.1 and Table 5.2 (pp. 142–143) for a summary and integration of the theories and findings across the three areas.

We try to emphasize what we do know and, just as important, to uncover what we do not know. Finally, we offer some avenues for future theorizing and testing. To further organize our discussion, we will use institution and institutional rules as a framework. Such a framework is most often found in political science discussions, but we find that the framework helps uncover commonalities and expose disjuncture. Even when the different disciplines address the same issues, they may use different language. To clarify our discussion, we first define the terms conflict, power, and status and then discuss how we use the institutional framework.

Orienting Assumptions and Definitions

The general approach taken across the disciplines is to define the attributes of the group and then investigate how certain attributes may affect the fundamental operations of the group. So, for example, groups vary from dyads to a great number of actors, and to actors nested within different types and levels of structures. The actors can be individuals or they can be collective actors who represent an entire group, organization, or structure.

Table 5.1   The Conflict-Power-Status Perspective

Definition of perspective	The conflict, power and status perspective examines the underlying causes and effects of preference, choice, and resource asymmetries among actors in groups
Key assumptions	<ul><li>Actors want to maximize their own or their groups' outcomes</li><li>Interdependence drives group interactions</li><li>Many group interactions are mixed-motive</li><li>Actors often have different preferences, resources, and choices</li><li>As a result, conflict, power, and status differences among actors are inevitable</li></ul>
Types of groups	Groups range from small intimate groups to alliances of nation states
Key theories	<ul><li>Power-dependence theory</li><li>Network exchange theory</li><li>Bargaining and coalition theories</li><li>Game theory</li><li>Expectation states theory</li><li>Dominance theory</li><li>Status construction theory</li><li>Institutional choice theories</li></ul>
Dominant research methodologies	<ul><li>Small group studies have been primarily laboratory or field studies</li><li>Larger group studies have been primarily historical</li></ul>
Strengths	<ul><li>Rigorously tested theoretical development of fundamental ideas</li><li>Theoretical development within particular fields is cumulative</li></ul>
Weaknesses	<ul><li>Lack of theoretical integration across subareas</li><li>Change in power structures over time has been little studied</li></ul>

The conflict, power, and status perspective examines the underlying causes and effects of preference and resource asymmetries among actors in small groups. The assumptions underlying this perspective are that: (1) actors want to maximize their own outcomes or the outcomes of their groups; (2) interdependence among actors drives group interactions (i.e., actors are dependent on one another to achieve outcomes); (3) many group interactions are mixed-motive (i.e., there is a trade-off between the best

Table 5.2   Key Findings of Conflict-Power-Status Perspective Research

Group composition	• Larger size is often, although not always, related to poorer coordination ability in conflict over resources • Diversity (including demographic characteristics, expertise, values, and individual difference variables) has been linked to lower levels of cooperation and to conflict in many types of group interactions, affecting group process and performance; these effects are moderated by a number of structural and individual difference variables • Power is often based on structural position rather than characteristics of group members • Status is defined relative to others in the group; consequently, changes in group composition can cause dramatic interaction changes
Group structure	• The institutional rules for position, information, and interaction have large effects on the amount of cooperation and can reinforce or contradict status differences • Power is based on alternatives, alliances, and norms determined by the initial interactions • Task structures (e.g., cooperative versus competitive) can change status dynamics and amount of conflict
Group projects	• Relationship and process conflict in particular can negatively affect project completion • Task conflict can lead to better quality projects
Interaction	• Exchanges between equal power positions produce positive emotional reactions • Initial status differences are usually reproduced within interaction • Some interactions can change initial status differences if those interactions enable demonstration of different skills, abilities, or statuses
Group action/outcomes	Brief but frequent conflict tends to improve performance, but multiple temporal patterns can yield equally good performance outcomes
Change over time	• Expectation of future interaction tends to increase cooperation • Longitudinal research indicates that different patterns of conflict are likely to result in different group outcomes

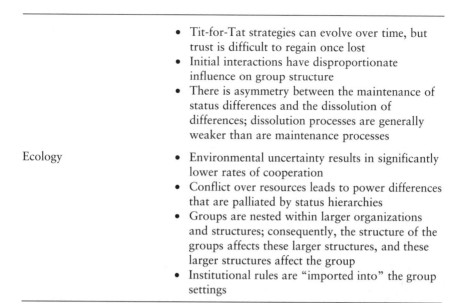

	• Tit-for-Tat strategies can evolve over time, but trust is difficult to regain once lost
	• Initial interactions have disproportionate influence on group structure
	• There is asymmetry between the maintenance of status differences and the dissolution of differences; dissolution processes are generally weaker than are maintenance processes
Ecology	• Environmental uncertainty results in significantly lower rates of cooperation
	• Conflict over resources leads to power differences that are palliated by status hierarchies
	• Groups are nested within larger organizations and structures; consequently, the structure of the groups affects these larger structures, and these larger structures affect the group
	• Institutional rules are "imported into" the group settings

choice for the individual and the best choice for the group); (4) actors often have different preferences, choices, and resources; and (5) as a result, conflict, power, and status differences among actors are inevitable.

Different disciplines tend to focus on different aspects of group phenomena. Psychology and economics tend to focus on the individual decision maker or actor, whereas political science and sociology tend to emphasize the structures or constraints that surround the actors. The intersection of the disciplines provides the focus for this article. This intersection defines much of the research on conflict, power, and status and addresses how the actor or actors and the structures and constraints change through the process of interactions. The interactions are typically viewed as exchanges within or among groups and are motivated by actors wishing to increase or maintain their collective or individual resources. These motivations may or may not be conscious.

Conflict

Conflict can be defined as awareness by the parties involved of differences, discrepancies, incompatible wishes, or irreconcilable desires (Boulding, 1962). Conflict can also be created when each member of a group is confronted with a choice between the motive to compete and the motive to cooperate with other group members. Schelling (1960) coined the term *mixed-motive game* to define this latter form of intragroup conflict. In this chapter, we include both of these aforementioned definitions of conflict.

There has been a debate in organizational research regarding whether agreement or disagreement within groups is advantageous (Eisenhardt & Zbaracki, 1992). One key to unlocking this complex relationship lies in the differentiation of conflict as either relationship or task related. Relationship conflict is an awareness of *interpersonal* incompatibilities. Relationship conflict often includes personality clashes, animosity, and annoyance between individuals. Studies show that relationship conflict is detrimental to individual and group performance, member satisfaction, and the likelihood the group will work together in the future (Jehn & Mannix, 2001). When group members have interpersonal problems or feel friction with one another, they may be distracted from the task, work less cooperatively, and produce suboptimal products (Roseman, Wiest, & Swartz, 1994).

Task or *cognitive conflict* is an awareness of differences in viewpoints and opinions pertaining to the group's task. Examples are disagreement among group members' ideas about the task being performed, disagreement regarding an organization's current hiring strategies, and conflict about the information to include in an annual report. In contrast with relationship conflict, moderate levels of task conflict have been shown to be beneficial to many kinds of group performance. Teams performing complex cognitive tasks benefit from differences of opinion about the work being done (Bourgeois, 1985; Eisenhardt & Schoonhoven, 1990; Jehn, 1994; Jehn & Mannix, 2001; Shah & Jehn, 1993).

A third type of conflict, labeled *process conflict*, has also been identified. Process conflict concerns disagreements over how the task will be accomplished, who will do what, or how the group will proceed. A relatively small amount of research has been done on this type of conflict. However, it has been proposed that high levels of process conflict can decrease the group's focus on the task and lead to lower levels of satisfaction and performance (Jehn, 1992; Jehn, Northcraft, & Neale, 1999).

Power

Often the resolution of conflict involves power. Social power can arise from exchange processes, as often studied by sociologists, or from redistribution of resources, often studied by political scientists.

Social power, as it has come to be defined in recent research, is the ability to gain favorable outcomes at another's expense (Willer, Lovaglia, & Markovsky, 1997). This definition of power is similar to Weber's (1968) definition and to French and Raven's (1959) development of power and its different bases. It also has been noted that power does not need to involve direct interaction; it can involve indirect relations (see Willer, 2003).

Thibaut and Kelley's (1959) social psychology of groups advanced the concept that social power is produced by the dependence of some group members on others. More specifically, they proposed that individuals in a group compare their expected outcomes within the group with alternative outcomes that may be available to them, an idea that was termed the *comparison level of alternatives* (CL_{alt}). An important proposition from this research is that those individuals with more attractive alternatives were less dependent on the group and thus had more power. Homans (1974) termed this the *principle of least interest:* "The person who is perceived by the other as the less interested, the more indifferent, to the exchange is apt to have the greater power" (p. 74).

Emerson's (1962, 1964) *power dependence theory* of social relations also specifies social power as relational. To have power is to have power *over* someone rather than a more general conception of power as the capacity *to accomplish* something. Power dependence theory united behaviorist conceptions of social behavior as exchange with the idea that dependence is produced by the availability of alternatives or their lack. The more dependent an individual is on a social relationship, the less power that individual has.

Power at its most fundamental involves redistribution rather than just social or economic exchange. (As Linda Molm, 1997a, points out, many of the early exchange theorists did not consider such redistribution or coercion, which put them at odds with most political theorists.) Indeed, for some early political theorists, coercion *is* power (see, e.g., for example, Bacharach & Baratz, 1963; Bierstedt, 1950; Lasswell & Kaplan, 1950). That is, redistribution is integrally linked to a basic concept of power in which Person A is assigned the right not only to take the surplus but also to take what Person B has. B may not agree to being made worse off, but differences in power may give B no choice. The source of power is usually found in *institutional mechanisms* or rules that assign the right to make a decision, the right to enforce a decision, or the right to private information that grants advantage. Typically, those institutional mechanisms support Person A's rights and punish those who do not recognize A's rights. As we note later, there are other institutional rules that are important for defining characteristics of groups as well as the kinds of power relations that emerge within groups (see Crawford & Ostrom, 1995, for an excellent discussion of the grammar of institutional rules).

Status

Intimately related to power is status. Status is defined as a position in a social network. This is a purposely broad definition because it includes status such as mother or sister as well as status such as socioeconomic status or minority status. It is important to see that these statuses involve beliefs about the social worth of the individuals who occupy them, called *status beliefs,* such that a person who occupies one position is "better than" a person who occupies another position (e.g., Sewell, 1992).

Status often provides an "organization" function for groups in that it defines a structure in which power use (and the lack of power use) is acceptable. The acceptable use of power can make a group function relatively smoothly but may at the same time generate an acceptance of inequality. In addition, power use can generate negative sentiment and interrupt the process by which power use translates to status (or further status distinctions, see Lovaglia & Houser, 1996; Walker et al., 2000; Willer, Troyer, & Lovaglia, 2001).

Many social scientists (e.g., Weber) have suggested that status significance is acquired through resources. In a well-developed articulation of one process through which nominal characteristics, such as race and sex category, might acquire status value and status beliefs, Ridgeway (1991) developed and then tested aspects of status construction theory. This theory posits one mechanism through which a characteristic previously not status-valued might acquire status value. According to the theory, members differ in the level of material resources they possess, they differ on an unordered nominal characteristic, and resources are correlated with the "state" or category of the characteristic (Ridgeway, 1997).

Because power can be used to acquire resources and control of resources confers power, Ridgeway's (1991, 1997) analysis implies that power and status are related concepts. We conceive of power as an ability to extract advantage from others despite their resistance. Thus, power is largely independent of the expectations and attitudes of group members. Status, however, is conferred to an individual based on the expectations group members have for contributions to valued group goals. Thye (2000) has also shown that high status increases the resources that individuals acquire through exchange. Power use, however, often produces resistance and conflict, which can interfere with status attainment (Lovaglia, 1997; Willer et al., 1997).

Institutional Rules

How are power and status used to resolve or maintain conflict? Because the research within and across the research areas of power, status, and conflict, is so incredibly varied, we will address and organize this question within the general context of institutions. Four institutional "rules" are particularly important for understanding small groups. These include boundary rules, aggregation rules, position rules, and information rules.

The *boundary rules* define who is and who is not in the group. Although this seems commonsensical, it provides enormous leverage in analysis. The boundary rules can detail the permeability of the group—whether members can easily enter or exit. Both features help determine whether the group will be stable. If the boundaries are permeable, it has implications for how many different members come into the group, the extent to which norms built within the group carry forward and are shared, and the extent to which sanctions can successfully be imposed by the group. If anyone can join the group at any time, then the membership is likely to change constantly. Often, groups attract like-minded individuals (individuals who share the same preferences). However, if anyone can join, then individual preferences are more likely to be heterogeneous. In addition, it will be difficult to sustain any kind of group norms or group memory if there is high turnover in membership. Finally, the threat of sanction will be very weak if individuals can easily exit. (For a useful, general explanation of the nature of exit, see Hirschman, 1970).

In addition, the strength of boundaries is important for characterizing in-group and out-group identity. (See Chapter 4, this volume, for a description of the social identity perspective.) The social categorization that automatically accompanies insiders versus outsiders creates ingroup and outgroup dichotomies. When a particular status becomes salient, it is activated, and individuals will respond on the basis of their group membership rather than their personal identity (Brewer & Miller, 1984). Although reacting based on ingroup identity can include a negativity toward outgroups, it is not a necessary condition of such identity (see discussion in Brewer, 1999; Feshback, 1994). Many forms of discrimination and bias may develop not because outgroups are hated but because positive emotions such as admiration, sympathy, and trust are reserved for the ingroup and withheld from the outgroup (Brewer, 1999). However, if there are few constraints on who can enter, the degree to which group categories are used and create ingroup and outgroup dichotomies is decreased.

The *aggregation rules* define how the group decides on a collective choice. Many rules can be used, and only three will be discussed. Almost all groups need to make decisions about how the members will jointly proceed. Aggregating the individual preferences of the group members, then, is crucial. Groups often settle on simple majority rule, in which everyone agrees to abide by the desires of the majority. However, this is not the only model. In fact, small groups could easily use a unanimity rule, in which everyone is required to agree before the group settles on a choice. In small groups, this decision rule is often used. The costs for such a rule, however, are quite high. If anyone objects, then the task of negotiating an acceptable choice can take some time. Such a rule creates important incentives for people to hold out—especially if they fundamentally disagree with a proposed group decision. It is easy to see how such a rule can quickly lead to paralysis. Groups also use an "anyone" rule, in which any actor can impose a group choice. For small groups, in which preferences are widely shared, this is a very efficient rule for making decisions. But it may also imply that decisions are made too quickly, and the decisions may not adequately reflect what the group would do if it spent some time deliberating (e.g., Riker, 1962).

The *position rules* define who gets to act at any point. These rules cut to the heart of authority. The best means of understanding this point is to think about a position within the group and to think of it independently of the individual occupying the position. In most groups, certain positions are granted authority over other positions. If the group has a leader, that position is endowed with certain actions that cannot be taken by other members of the group. Position rules can easily be used to develop lines of hierarchy in a group. Likewise, a nonhierarchical group is one in which all members occupy an identical position. Position rules are useful for understanding status differences that are derived from admissible actions within the group (of course, status characteristics often accompany individuals across groups and are interesting in themselves).

The *information rules* describe how information is shared and what each actor can know. The information linkages determine the extent to which each member knows what the others have done (or what they are planning). In most settings, individuals within the group react and respond to others. If the information conditions are complete (everyone sees what everyone else has done to the point), then it is easy to formulate an action that constitutes a best response. However, what happens when information is hidden? This makes a response uncertain. It also means that those holding one-sided information gain important control over others.

We will use these institutional rules to examine how the three subject areas of conflict, power, and status relate to each other. Although the institutional rules are examined independently, it is clear that the effects of any given rule can be increased or decreased by its juxtaposition with another rule or other rules.

Conflict: Theory and Findings

As noted earlier, the literature on conflict in small groups can be roughly divided into conflict over resources and conflict over information (DeDreu,

Harinck, & Van vianen, 1999). Research on conflict over resources includes such topics as bargaining and negotiation, coalition formation, and social dilemmas. The outcome variables most often analyzed in these studies are joint profit, coalition size or composition, and proportion of cooperative choices. In contrast, research on conflict over information has focused on either intellective or evaluative issues and tends to emphasize the relationship between intragroup conflict and group performance.

Among organizational scholars, the work on conflict in groups and teams can be characterized as stemming from two traditions. One research stream comes from negotiation researchers who have expanded their work on dyadic negotiations to the group level. In this tradition, the emphasis has been placed on classic negotiation concepts, such as distributive versus integrative solutions, BATNAs (best alternative to a negotiated agreement), and reservation prices. At the same time, economists and political scientists have been very concerned with the institutional structure within which small groups negotiate. Integral to these approaches have been considerations of coalition formation, aggregation rules, and agenda mechanisms. The bulk of this work has been conducted in the laboratory using negotiation simulations. In these studies, conflict is seen as inevitable, and the level of conflict is seen as the dependent variable.

The other research stream comes from scholars studying teams more broadly, usually within organizational settings. The goal here is to understand how group input variables (e.g., diversity, skill) lead to various group processes (e.g., communication, conflict) and thus affect group outcome variables (e.g., satisfaction and performance). As such, in this research, conflict is often treated as a mediating variable. As noted earlier, the effects of conflict on team performance are mixed, depending on the type of conflict.

Conflicts Over Resources

Coalition Formation

One of the most obvious and important differences between multiparty as compared to dyadic negotiation is the potential to exclude group members from final agreement through coalition formation (Caplow, 1956; Gamson, 1961; Murnighan, 1986). In other words, the boundary rules can be changed to invoke different distributions of resources. Two very different traditions have emerged. One, which predominates in the political science and economics literatures, finds that coalitional instability is rooted in the conflict over individual preferences and relies heavily on noncooperative models of game theory. The second approach, derived from cooperative models of game theory and found in the bargaining literature drawn from social psychology, points to processes that lead people to join together.

The noncooperative literature has its origins in work by Arrow (1951), in which individuals have no opportunity to bind themselves to an allocation over resources. As a consequence, coalitions will be unstable and will often rely on a collective choice mechanism (e.g., majority voting). Unfortunately, there is no mechanism that gives a consistent social choice: Different procedures can lead to different outcomes, even though no individual changes preferences for outcomes. Work by Fiorina and Plott (1978) demonstrates this in a laboratory setting with small groups, showing that instability over final choices is common and that coalitions quickly form and dissolve, without much impact on outcomes.

Instability over outcomes is mitigated in predictable ways by institutional rules imposed on the negotiation setting. If an actor is given the right to veto divisions of a good, then there is substantial stability over outcomes (Wilson & Herzberg, 1987). The way in which an agenda is ordered affects outcomes (Wilson, 1986). Who gets to construct the agenda is also crucial (see the survey by McKelvey & Ordeshook, 1990). Many institutional features relating to aggregation rules and position rules have an impact on the types of coalitions that form and the kinds of outcomes that are chosen. Many of these rules have been mathematically modeled and thoroughly tested in the laboratory.

The cooperation literature, most often the focus of social psychologists, finds that as the negotiating unit increases from two to three or more individuals, several variables interact to determine the integrative value of the final agreement, as well as individual outcomes (Ancona, Friedman, & Kolb, 1991). In determining individual outcomes, the power balance of the group is clearly one of the most important variables; indeed, power has been called the "essence of bargaining" (Bacharach & Lawler, 1981). However, research has shown that factors such as distribution norms, discount rates, and expectations of future interaction, as well institutional rules, interact with the negotiator's power to affect the ability of a group member to maximize his or her outcome (Bettenhausen & Murnighan, 1985; Komorita & Hamilton, 1984; Thompson, Mannix, & Bazerman, 1988). For example, when institutional position and allocation rules favor low-power players (i.e., norms based on need rather than equity), and when the structure of the interaction emphases cooperation (i.e., a joint meeting arrangement rather than separate caucusing), empirical findings indicate that high-power players find their outcomes greatly reduced (Mannix, 1993, 1994).

The opportunity for coalition formation (i.e., the type of position rule) can also affect the overall efficiency of the group's negotiated agreement.

Mannix (1991, 1993) demonstrated that members of unequal-power groups were more likely to reject collaborative group decision-making, and move toward more competitive and distributive negotiation strategies. As a result, the overall performance of the team was reduced because some individuals were denied a level of resources needed to perform effectively.

Recent work in political science has returned to examining coalition formation using cooperative game theory. The impetus for this work has been with understanding how ministerial portfolios are allocated in coalition governments (Laver, 1998). The empirical finding is that minority coalition partners usually get more than they should, given their strength (Diermeier & Stevenson, 2000; Stevenson & Martin, 2001). A similar finding routinely arises under the minimal choice paradigm in social psychology (for a review, see Ellemers, Spears, & Doojse, 1997). Here the weakest players always get too much, compared to their "value" to the group.

Polzer, Mannix, and Neale (1995, 1998) drew from the coalition, negotiation, and social categorization literatures to propose that when coalitions form because of compatible preferences on one issue, they are likely to remain intact to influence outcomes on other issues, even those for which the coalition members *do not* have compatible preferences. Resistance from parties outside the coalition tends to strengthen the bond between the coalition members, making it more likely for them to continue to identify and cooperate with each other and compete with the noncoalition members.

Group Composition

Negotiation researchers have examined diversity by focusing on factors such as values (Jehn & Mannix, 2001) and motivational orientation (Weingart, Bennett, & Brett, 1993). Jehn (1994) demonstrated that teams with low levels of value similarity had higher levels of conflict than groups with higher levels of value similarity. Weingart and associates (1993) demonstrated that groups composed of members with a cooperative social orientation, who also considered issues simultaneously, had higher quality outcomes than groups composed of individualistic negotiators. They also demonstrated that cooperative groups were more trusting and engaged in less argumentation than individualistic groups.

Social Dilemmas and Trust Games

Social dilemmas are perhaps the most studied phenomena within investigations of conflict over resources. Social dilemmas are settings in which an actor's short-term self-interest competes with the group interest (see Dawes,

1980; Ostrom, 1990, 2000). Especially influential theoretical formulations of social dilemmas include Olson (1965) on free-riding, Hardin (1968) on the tragedy associated with the commons, and Ostrom (1990) on governing the commons.

Historically, rational choice models of decision making have dominated the study of mixed-motive conflict in small groups (Kerr, 1989; Komorita & Parks, 1995). Specifically, largely due to the impact of classic statements by von Neumann and Morgenstern (1944) and Luce and Raiffa (1957), game theory has been an important explanatory framework. (See Schroeder, 1995, for a brief historical overview.)

Group Composition. In the social dilemmas literature, the composition variable that has received the most attention is group size. The traditional theoretical view has been that group size and cooperation are inversely related: As group size increases, cooperation declines (Messick, 1973; Olson, 1965). However, Franzen (1994) noted that a significant number of studies find no differences in cooperation rate as a function of group size. He suggested that the mixed results may be related to variability in two factors: (1) type of experimental game and (2) whether the game is "one-shot" or iterated (multiple trials). Another methodological and theoretical complication is that changes in group size are often confounded with other independent variables that are difficult to hold constant simultaneously with increases in group size (e.g., payoff size, anonymity and/or de-individuation, perceived self- or collective efficacy) (see Isaac & Walker, 1988).

However, Kerr (1989) has conducted a series of experiments that was able to successfully manipulate group size independently of perceived self-efficacy (i.e., a group member's subjective expectation that his or her own contribution will make a significant difference to the group's chances of providing the public good). Kerr's research suggests the possibility that group size exerts its effect on cooperation through systematic changes in group members' perceptions of their own self-efficacy and the group's collective efficacy. This line of research also suggests the intriguing possibility that illusions of self- and collective efficacy can be exploited by reframing large-group social dilemmas in terms of smaller collective units (see Weick, 1984).

For reasons that are unclear, social dilemma researchers generally have not focused much attention on the composition question. Most research has examined the impact of individual differences such as social value orientation (e.g., Samuelson, 1993) or interpersonal trust (Brann & Foddy, 1987; Yamagishi, 1986a). However, very little empirical work has investigated the effects of different configurations of group composition (gender, age, ethnic status, etc.) on cooperation in social dilemmas (see, however, Espinoza & Garza, 1985). One exception to this general trend is a set of experiments on gender composition (Sell, 1997; Sell, Griffith, & Wilson, 1993). Information about gender, only when paired with information about choices, activated differences in levels of cooperation. Sell (1997) explained the gender composition effect in terms of expectation states theory (Berger, Wagner, & Zelditch, 1992). Group members with high status (males) will contribute more resources to the public good than low-status members (females) because they expect that they can exert greater strategic influence on others within the group.

A different model has been used in economics, where experiments have focused on ultimatum and trust games. The groups generally examined in these contexts are dyads, and the groups have little history or interaction. They differ from groups considered in the social dilemma context in that coordination is not generally at issue; thus, the incentive structure can be highlighted. These games feature different sources of conflict and have focused on the diversity of subjects to explain persistent behavioral regularities. In the ultimatum game, an individual is given the opportunity to allocate money or resources. That proposed allocation is then sent to a second individual, who can either accept or reject it. If rejected, neither party gets any money. If accepted, the allocations are awarded. In the trust game, one player is given the opportunity to keep an amount of money or pass it to another player. If kept, the decision ends. If passed, the amount is doubled or tripled, and the second player decides how to allocate the increased amount. The first player, when passing the money, must trust the second player to allocate the money so that the first player is not left worse off. In both games, there is economic equilibrium: In the ultimatum game, the first mover should take almost all of the money, and the second player should never reject the allocation. In the trust game, the first player should never trust the second player and, as a consequence, should never pass the money. In fact, subjects routinely allocate more than a trivial amount, and second players reject allocations (see Guth & Tietz, 1990). In addition, there is plenty of trusting behavior (see Berg, Dickhaut, & McCabe, 1995).

Predicting when people will allocate fairly or when they will trust has not been settled. A good deal of research points out that individuals use their counterpart's characteristics when deciding how to act. Eckel and Grossman (2001) find that women are likely to give more to their counterpart, women are less likely to reject allocations, and offers from women are less likely to be rejected.

Eckel and Wilson (2002) find that whites are less likely to trust minorities (African Americans and Hispanics, but not Asian Americans) when viewing a photograph of their counterpart. Even something as simple as a counterpart smiling in a photograph is enough to invite trust (Scharlemann, Eckel, Kacelnik, & Wilson, 2001). Numerous other research projects are working to dissect the social cues used in making strategic decisions in small groups.

Institutional Structure. Early research on social dilemmas emphasized the effects of reward structure on cooperative behavior (Komorita & Parks, 1995). For example, Komorita (1976) proposed the K' index as an extension of Rapoport's (1966) K-index (two-person PDG) to the N-person Prisoner's Dilemma game. This index was developed to make predictions about how cooperation rate should change as a function of changes in the relative pay-offs for cooperative versus competitive choices. Specifically, Komorita (1976) showed that cooperation and K' should be positively related: As K' increases, cooperation rate increases. Subsequent research on reward structure has investigated how variations in the presentation of payoff matrices affect cooperation. In this regard, Komorita and Barth (1985) demonstrated that rewards for cooperation are more effective in increasing cooperation than are punishments for competitive choices.

However, other research work has concluded that sanctioning systems that punish noncooperative behavior can be effective structural mechanisms for eliciting high levels of cooperation (Ostrom, Walker, & Gardner, 1992; Sato, 1987; Sell & Wilson, 1999; Yamagishi, 1986a). Recently, concern has been expressed that sanctioning systems may be inherently problematic because such rules can have unintended consequences (e.g., increasing pessimism among group members about eliciting cooperation from others, which may serve to exacerbate the very problem the sanctioning system was designed to correct; e.g., Tenbrunsel & Messick, 1999). In addition, the initial establishment of a sanctioning system is no trivial task because raising resources from group members to support the system represents a "second order" social dilemma (Yamagishi, 1986b).

Since the mid-1980s, social dilemma researchers have been investigating how and why certain structurally equivalent social dilemma tasks elicit different levels of cooperation. The most common contrast has been between resource dilemma and public goods paradigms (see Komorita & Parks, 1995). Brewer and Kramer (1986), using prospect theory (Kahneman & Tversky, 1979) to motivate their analysis of framing effects, stimulated much of this research by reporting that the cooperation rate was significantly lower in a public goods dilemma task than the corresponding resource dilemma version, particularly in larger groups. Some subsequent research failed to replicate these results (Aquino, Steisel, & Kay, 1992; Fleishman, 1988, Messick, Allison, & Samuelson, 1988; Rutte, Wilke, & Messick, 1987). This inconsistent pattern has caused some researchers to doubt the applicability of prospect theory to decision making in social dilemmas (Schwartz-Shea & Simmons, 1995). Son and Sell (1995) and Sell and Son (1997) maintain that differences in the types of decision-making contexts can easily lead to differences in framing. Whether framing effects were apparent throughout the groups' decision making depended on the kind of good and the information available. One instance in which prospect theory differences are maintained and lead to greater contributions in resource dilemma settings was demonstrated in a cross-cultural test (Sell, Chen, Hunter-Holmes, & Johansson, 2002).

Institutional Choice. While most social dilemma research has focused on the effects of various structural variables on cooperation within a defined set of institutional rules, other research has examined the conditions under which group members voluntarily prefer to *change* the institutional rules (Samuelson & Messick, 1995). Two variables that have been studied in detail are efficiency and equity. The most robust experimental finding is that group members prefer structural change (e.g., superordinate authority, sanctioning system, privatization of common resource pool) to the status quo rule structure (i.e., free access, no sanctioning system) when the group experiences negative outcomes from resource overuse or excessive free riding (e.g., Messick & Brewer, 1983; Samuelson, Rutte, & Wilke, 1984; Sato, 1987).

The picture is equivocal with respect to inequities in the distribution of resources across group members. Most experiments have found that resource inequity is *not* a sufficient condition for structural change (Samuelson & Messick, 1995), however, cultural differences appear to moderate this effect (Samuelson et al., 1984). Other factors that shape preferences for structural change are the type of alternative rule system (Samuelson & Messick, 1986a), differences in resource access (Samuelson & Messick, 1986b), causal attributions for negative group outcomes (Samuelson, 1991), and individual differences in social value orientation (Samuelson, 1993). A multiattribute utility model that incorporates these empirical results has been proposed by Samuelson and Messick (1995) and supported by experimental results reported by Samuelson (1993). Alternative theoretical frameworks for understanding structural change decisions have also been developed by others, including Yamagishi (1986b).

Interaction Processes. One process variable that has attracted considerable theoretical and empirical attention in social dilemma research is communication (Sally, 1995). The robust empirical result from 25 years of research is that group discussion about the social dilemma problem results in significantly higher rates of cooperation compared to no-discussion control conditions (e.g., Dawes, McTavish, & Shaklee, 1977; Liebrand, 1984.). Recent research has focused on understanding why this communication effect occurs.

Orbell, van de Kragt, and Dawes (1988) have argued that group discussion about the dilemma activates a sense of group identity (Brewer & Kramer, 1986), which increases the weight given to the collective interest relative to individual self-interest. Both Orbell and associates (1988) and Kerr and Kaufman-Gilleland (1994) have also proposed that group discussion offers opportunities for members to make commitments to cooperate with one another. Researchers also debate whether universal consensus (Orbell et al., 1988) or perceived general consensus (Bouas & Komorita, 1996) is a sufficient condition for the communication effect to occur. It has also been shown that communication can help reduce egocentric cognitive biases that often decrease cooperation in resource dilemmas (Wade-Benzoni, Tenbrunsel, & Bazerman, 1996.) Related to this, there is evidence that simply being able to send "signals" or "cheap talk" messages to other participants does not increase cooperation in the same way that actual discussion does (Wilson & Sell, 1997), although the ability to monitor others through communication is important (Sell & Wilson, 1991).

A second process variable is reciprocal strategy effects in social dilemmas. Much of this line of research stems from Axelrod's (1984) finding that the Tit-for-Tat (TFT) strategy performed the best overall when paired against a wide variety of more complex strategies in a two-person Prisoner's Dilemma game. Laboratory studies by Komorita and colleagues sought to establish the generality of Axelrod's (1984) computer simulation results under social dilemma conditions involving three or more players. For example, Komorita, Hilty, and Parks (1991) examined timing effects and found that reciprocating cooperation *immediately* was more important to long-term cooperation than immediate reciprocation of defection. These researchers also reported that contrary to Axelrod (1984), TFT's "niceness" in its opening cooperative choice resulted in less cooperation from others over time. It has also been shown that TFT's effectiveness decreases with increases in group size (Komorita, Parks, & Hulbert, 1992) and loses much of its efficacy when rewards for cooperation are minimal (Komorita & Chan, 1993).

Ecology. The intergroup context in which social dilemmas are often embedded outside the laboratory has been investigated systematically in recent years. The research question is framed as: What factors influence cooperation in a situation where one group must compete with another group to obtain a public good? Rapoport and Bornstein (1987) developed a new research paradigm called the Intergroup Public Goods (IPG) game to explore this question. Several studies have documented that preplay discussion *within* each group increases the number of contributors (Bornstein, Rapoport, & Kerpel, 1989; Rapoport & Bornstein, 1989). However, although allowing between-group communication improves collective outcomes in the IPG, it results in suboptimal group outcomes when combined with within-group discussion (Bornstein et al., 1989). Bornstein (1992) also developed a continuous public goods version of the IPG game (Intergroup Prisoner's Dilemma game) and found that the pattern of within- and between-group communication effects observed in the IPG game may be limited to step-level public goods in which an external provision point is established. Finally, relative differences in group size do not appear to influence contribution rates in the IPG game, assuming that payoff differences are held constant (Rapoport, Bornstein, & Erev, 1989).

Social dilemma researchers have identified environmental uncertainty as an important ecological context variable (Messick et al., 1988). Environmental uncertainty refers to the fact that in many resource dilemmas in the natural environment, it is not known with certainty how much of the resource is available for consumption or its rate of natural replenishment (e.g., fish stocks, water reservoirs). In contrast, most research studies on resource dilemmas have assumed that participants have full knowledge of the state of the common resource pool. Researchers have demonstrated that high environmental uncertainty results in significantly lower rates of cooperation (i.e., resource overconsumption) compared to conditions of low environmental uncertainty (Budescu & Wallsten, 1990; Hine & Gifford, 1996). The explanation for *why* this effect occurs is less clear. One hypothesis is that individuals under high uncertainty tend to overestimate resource pool size and hence overharvest based on this biased judgment (Budescu & Wallsten 1990). Subsequent research has revealed that the effects of environmental uncertainty on cooperation are moderated by task structure (van Dijk, Wilke, & Wilke, 1999) and the social value orientation of decision makers (Roch & Samuelson, 1997).

Conflicts Over Information

Researchers in social psychology and organizational behavior have a long tradition of studying the effects of conflict on the quality of decision making in small groups. The primary dependent variable in these studies is group performance.

Group Composition

Many scholars have argued that diversity enhances decision quality in groups through the presence of the cognitive conflict that is created (Damon, 1991; Levine & Resnick, 1993). For example, a devil's advocate can reduce the incidence of groupthink (Janis, 1982) by surfacing faulty assumptions and disconfirming evidence. Similarly, a vocal deviate who proposes unusual and even incorrect solutions during problem solving can lead groups to generate more arguments (Smith, Tindale, & Dugoni, 1996), apply more strategies (Nemeth & Wachtler, 1983), detect more novel solutions (Nemeth & Kwan, 1987), use multiple perspectives simultaneously (Gruenfeld, 1995; Peterson & Nemeth, 1996), and generally outperform groups without this type of influence.

Much of this work showing the benefits of diversity for constructive conflict has tended to take place in the laboratory using ad hoc groups (cf. Williams & O'Reilly, 1998). That alone is not terribly problematic; the real difficulty is the tendency of this research to treat multiple types of diversity as though they had the same effects on group process and performance. Diversity in groups can be a function of a variety of attributes, including demographics, experience, expertise, values, interpersonal style, and access to information (McGrath, Berdahl, & Arrow, 1996).

Recent work, in both the field and the laboratory, has begun to disentangle the different types of compositional diversity and their effects on process and performance. For example, recent research has shown that gender and racial/ethnic diversity are most often linked to affective or relationship conflict in teams. As a result, the link between diversity and performance, mediated by conflict, is a negative one. By contrast, when institutional rules exist that promote position diversity in terms of roles, there can be increased cognitive or task conflict, a result that often enhances performance in the team (Jehn et al., 1999; Pelled, Eisenhardt, & Xin, 1999).

Another form of diversity might be identified in considering the relationship ties among group members and the effects of friendship and familiarity on group processes and performance. Shah and Jehn (1993) found that groups composed of friends exhibited greater task and emotional conflict while working on a decision task than groups of strangers. Because the task required critical inquiry and analysis of assumptions, the conflict gave groups of friends a performance advantage (see also Murnighan & Conlon, 1991). Jehn and Shah (1997) examined the interaction process among groups of friends and groups of strangers performing different types of tasks. They found that friendship groups outperformed stranger groups due to a higher level of group commitment, cooperation, critical evaluation, task monitoring, and positive communication. Gruenfeld, Mannix, Williams and Neale (1996) found that when team members had uniquely held critical information, teams with positive relationship ties outperformed teams of strangers. Groups of strangers were most likely to aggregate their individual, prediscussion suspect choices and simply adopt the majority preference for the final group decision. By contrast, teams with relationship ties rarely adopted the majority preference. Instead, their relationships permitted them to go beyond the simple aggregation of task-relevant information.

The institution rules about aggregation and information in small groups have become important in political science, albeit in a slightly different manner. There the focus has been on the Condorcet jury theorem and the size of the group that is needed in order to pool the information so as to come up with an objectively true answer. The usual way of telling the story is that an individual is either guilty or not. A group of people has bits and pieces of information about the nature of guilt or innocence. What, then, is the optimal size of a group for a majority to get it right? This issue has been thoroughly modeled by Austen-Smith and Banks (1996), who find interesting problems with the assumption that people will sincerely reveal their information. Behaviorally, however, people in small groups are able to aggregate highly uncertain information and reach correct conclusions (see Bottom, Ladha, & Miller, 2002). The same problem has been of interest to people thinking about very large groups—such as voters who are deciding on a referendum and hold very limited pieces of information (Lupia & McCubbins, 1998).

Temporal Dynamics. Some early efforts in the study of groups had an inherently temporal dimension, notably the work on group dynamics and the related study of phases in group problem solving. Many stage models have been proposed—for example, Tuckman (1965): forming, storming, norming, and performing— and often include some period of group conflict.

McGrath and associates conducted a long-term analysis of group process and performance over time, published as a special issue of *Small Group Research*. Among the findings relevant to this chapter, they found that in continuing work groups, those with stable membership experienced conflict more frequently than groups for which membership was characterized by instability and change (Arrow & McGrath, 1993). O'Connor, Gruenfeld, and McGrath (1993) found that a number of factors affected the experience of conflict over time. The type of task affected conflict, with mixed-motive tasks creating the most conflict and collaborative tasks creating the least conflict. Changes in the communication media tended to increase conflict, whereas changes in group membership tended to decrease conflict.

Jehn and Mannix (2001) measured not only the type of conflict experienced by project groups but also the time it occurred in the life of the team. They found that high team performance was associated with moderately high levels of task conflict during the middle of the group process, moderate levels of procedural conflict that peak toward completion of the group project, and low levels of relationship conflict across all time periods. Their results also indicated that teams with higher levels of *group value consensus*— that is, a higher similarity of work-related values—were more likely to develop beneficial patterns of conflict over time.

Power: Theory and Findings

Power stems from the conflict over access to resources: material, social, and informational. In the coalition formation research discussed in the previous section, power is studied as the perceived capacity to form a successful coalition. In political science, power is the capacity to redistribute resources, wresting them from one individual or group and granting them to another. Exchange researchers see power as the ability to gain favorable outcomes at another's expense, a process that can be more or less voluntary.

Political Power as Redistribution

Political scientists have been interested in the ways in which the design of specific institutional rules affects the ways in which groups redistribute resources. Unlike much of the research on public goods, in which individual incentives lead to everyone being made worse off, the focus by many political scientists has been with individuals' private incentives to use rules that make themselves better off at the expense of other group members. Early work by Fiorina and Plott (1978) demonstrated that differing voting rules or institutions could have a dramatic impact on the types of outcomes chosen by a group. The same point was made in work by Wilson and Herzberg (1987) and Wilson (1986).

In a particularly striking applied experiment, Plott and Levine (1978) note how they tested for the preferences of fellow members of a flying club. The committee on which they served was charged with finding a mix of airplanes to add to their fleet. Plott and Levine detail how they then designed a very specific agenda to gain their own preferred fleet mixture—one that was not widely shared by other group members. That agendas can be manipulated is of little surprise to scholars steeped in studying legislative behavior. Yet, the extent to which institutional rules can advantage some over others is striking. Knight (1992) delves into the ways in which institutional change typically rewards those making the change at the expense of others. Much of the study of political science concerns the ways in which rules redistribute outcomes.

Social Power as Exchange

Exchange relations are usually conceived by group process researchers as voluntary, resulting in benefit to both parties to an exchange (Emerson, 1972; Homans, 1961). Punishment or coercion occurs when one individual is less well-off after an interaction than he or she was before, a robbery victim, for example. A qualitative distinction between exchange and coercion, however, may not be theoretically relevant (Molm, 1997a, 1997b). After coercion, people may be better off having submitted than they would have been had they refused. Coercion can be seen as the end of a continuum on which reward levels between exchange partners become increasingly unequal past the point where one partner's reward becomes negative; that is, a cost. Coercive power can then be analyzed in the same kinds of exchange settings that were used to investigate reward power (Willer, 1987). Thus, the conception of power used by political scientists—as the appropriation of resources—can be fitted into the exchange perspective.

Molm (1989, 1991, 1997a, 1997b) uses a non-negotiated exchange setting to investigate coercive power. In it, individuals have opportunities to reward or punish others, but there is no way to change the given institutions. Molm finds that coercive power must be intentionally used, unlike reward power, in which unequal rewards can be passively accepted. Coercion is more likely to be used when the prospect of mutually rewarding exchange is low, possibly because coercion is risky, jeopardizing future opportunities for mutually beneficial exchange. Negative emotional reactions that accompany power use also link power to conflict (Molm, 1997a). Consonant with two established theories of conflict, bilateral deterrence and conflict spiral, punishment promotes conflict (Lawler, 1986; Lawler, Ford, & Blegen, 1988). And because unequal power in exchange relations can produce negative emotion, even without punishment or coercion, power differences in exchange relations may often promote conflict.

Emerson's Power-Balancing Mechanisms

In Emerson's (1962, 1964) power-dependence theory of social relations, the more dependent an individual is on a social relationship, the less power that individual has. In the theory, dependence results in two ways. First, the more a person values resources controlled by another, the more dependent that person is. Second, the more available those valued resources are outside the relationship, the less dependent that person is.

Power-dependence theory also assumes that power use prompts those subjected to power to mitigate its negative consequences. In Emerson's (1969) most memorable statement, "To have a power advantage is to use it, and to use it is to lose it" (p. 391). Emerson (1962) presented four power-balancing mechanisms through which power use leads eventually to equal or balanced power. The power-balancing mechanisms follow logically from the desire of low-power individuals to improve their access to valued resources or reduce the costs of unequal exchange: (1) low-power individuals can reduce the value they place on resources controlled by others; (2) low-power individuals can cultivate alternative sources of valued resources currently controlled by others; (3) high-power individuals can increase the value they place on resources controlled by others; (4) high-power individuals can be denied alternative sources of valued resources currently controlled by others. Low-power individuals commonly use strategies to promote power balance. The theory has found wide application, especially in business and the study of organizations (Bacharach & Lawler, 1980, 1981; Pfeffer, 1981, 1992).

Although power-dependence theory is elegant and logically coherent, power-dependence theory has a dangerous weakness. It fails to explain why social relations characterized by power use and dominance are so widespread and why social inequality appears to be a major factor in social relations for the foreseeable future. Whereas the first part of Emerson's (1969) famous statement— "to have power is to use it" (p. 391)—has been supported by research even when a high-power actor has no intention of using it (Willer & Skvoretz, 1997), the second part—"to use it is to lose it"—defies common observation. Powerful people not only seldom lose power but also often seem to use their power to gain more power. Explaining the discrepancy between the implications of Emerson's theory for social equality and the continuation of social inequality is a major project for future theory and research.

One approach is to investigate power-*un*balancing mechanisms overlooked by the theory. While low-power individuals actively seek to balance power, high-power individuals may just as actively seek to maintain or increase power imbalance. Furthermore, high-power individuals may be able to exploit their power advantage to block attempts to balance power (Molm, 1997a). Examples of power unbalancing mechanisms include colonization to develop alternative sources of valued resources and political repression to reduce opportunities for low-power individuals to form coalitions (Lovaglia, Skvoretz, Markovsky, & Willer, 1999).

Values and Preferences

Emerson (1987) had argued that a comprehensive theory of value was necessary for the further development of power dependence theory. Two recent attempts to examine and develop theories of value and preferences are Chai (2001) and Kanazawa (2001).

Power in Exchange Networks

Emerson's second proposition, that dependence is related to alternative sources of valued resources, began a major subfield of research that attempts to explain and predict the power held by occupants of positions in an exchange network. Analysis of even small networks of five or six positions can be difficult due to a complex pattern of exchange relations. As the number of network positions increases linearly, the number of potential patterns of network relations increases exponentially.

Relative power of positions in simple networks constrained to a single type of exchange relationship can be analyzed by successively estimating the alternatives available to each position in a series of exchange opportunities. For example, strong power positions are those in which actors can exchange with other actors, but those other actors cannot exchange among themselves. Members in strong power positions often acquire nearly all available resources (Cook, Emerson, Gillmore, & Yamagishi, 1983; Markovsky, Willer, & Patton, 1988). Subsequent research has also examined weak power networks (Markovsky, Skvoretz, Willer, Lovaglia, & Erger, 1993).

Finding a workable general formula for predicting power in networks of increasing size and complexity has proven an attractive challenge for researchers in several analytical traditions: a graph-theoretic approach (Lovaglia, Skvoretz, Willer, & Markovsky, 1995), a game theory approach (Bienenstock & Bonacich, 1993), a self and identity approach (Burke, 1996), Friedkin's (1992) expected value model, and Yamaguchi's (1996) rational choice model. Although the different approaches have had varying degrees of success in predicting the power of positions in the simple exchange networks that have been experimentally investigated, a general solution for a broad range of complex larger networks remains elusive (Lucas, Younts, Lovaglia, & Markovsky, 2001).

Power and Emotion in Exchange Relations

Conceptualizing coercion in an exchange setting dramatizes the connections between power and emotions in group processes. Power can produce strong negative emotion in those on whom it is used, both coercively (Molm, 1991) and in exchange (Willer et al., 1997). Exchange relations, in contrast, are characterized by commitment and positive emotional bonds that increase with repeated exchange (Lawler & Yoon, 1993, 1996). In resolving these contrasting effects, Lawler and Yoon (1998) showed that positive emotion results from exchange relations characterized by mutual dependence: that is, when the stakes are high for both parties, but also when both parties are equally dependent on each other for a successful exchange outcome. Lawler and Yoon (1998) found *no* increase in commitment or positive emotion when power was unequal, allowing one partner to use power *over* another.

Emotion mediates the effects of status on influence. An individual's negative emotion decreases the influence of a partner; and the effects of emotion combine with other status information to determine influence (Lovaglia & Houser, 1996). Willer et al. (1997) showed that power use can produce those negative emotions that had been found to decrease influence. They conclude that power use could increase influence if the negative emotional reactions that accompany power use could be contained.

Status: Theory and Findings

Perspectives on Status

Status has been examined from a number of different perspectives. One of the most developed research programs in sociology that focuses on status is expectation states theory. As Knottnerus (1997) states, expectation states theory has a metatheoretical concept of a *state organizing process*, which provides a general framework for the constructing of theories of the interpersonal process (Berger et al., 1992). Knottnerus argues that there are several different models underlying expectation states theories, some quite different than others.

Status characteristics theory is one of the oldest and best developed of the research areas within expectation states. The general question addressed is: How do status characteristics generate and then sustain inequalities of power and prestige? These dependent variables, power and prestige, are usually conceptualized in terms of the influence one member has over another, the rate of participation of any given group member, the opportunities given to act, and, finally, compliance. Compliance is the most subtle of these four and is evidenced by the lack of any challenge. Summary statements of the theory involved in this process can be found in Berger, Conner, and Fisek (1974, 1982), Berger, Fisek, Norman, and Zelditch (1977); Berger and Zelditch (1985); and Humphreys and Berger (1981).

Two types of status characteristics within the status characteristics theory—diffuse and specific—correspond to an expectation or assessment of how the individual will perform on the completion of a task. Diffuse status characteristics are readily apparent and are often based on category membership, such as sex, race, or age. Specific status characteristics are those associated with a specific ability, such as the ability to do needlepoint or mathematical ability.

Briefly, the process is described as a burden of proof process; that is, *unless* some characteristic or event intervenes, status characteristics organize our interactions such that those who are higher on social status garner higher amounts of power and prestige than those lower in status. The burden of proof rests on a demonstration that status should *not* be used. The process occurs in several steps, none of which are posited to necessarily be conscious. Status characteristics theory, although not specifying institutions or rules, does specify that the theory applies only to settings in which the group is motivated to succeed on a group task and group members are willing to consider others' choices or opinions in the completion of the task. This implies that the boundary conditions are well-defined, while the specification of aggregation, position, and information rules is unclear. One could argue that this enables the importation of more general societal rules and institutions. In fact, a branch of expectation states theory, legitimation theory, does explicitly consider this importation idea by consideration of how the surrounding society supports the valuation of certain types of characteristics over others.

There are other formulations that address the role of status. Dominance theorists propose that humans display behaviors that simply signal their interpersonal dominance and submission (Mazur, 1973, 1983; Mazur et al., 1980; Ofshe & Lee, 1981). These theorists have demonstrated parallels between patterns in human groups and the dominance patterns or pecking orders seen in many nonhuman social species. Other formulations have also addressed the idea that some status characteristics are derived from evolutionary processes by which some groups were faced with very different problems than others faced. This argument is most often associated with evolutionary psychology (Buss & Kenrick, 1998; Cosmides & Tooby, 1994). In addition, social role theory (see Eagly, 1987; Eagly & Johnson, 1990; Eagly & Karau, 1991; Eagly & Wood, 1999) argues that some status characteristics are prompted by the characteristics of the situation and that these characteristics are primarily based on the structure of role and resources existent in society.

Status Composition of Groups

One focus of status characteristics theory is the composition of the group and how this affects the manner in which status organizes interaction. As previously mentioned, many studies have been conducted on the burden of proof process and how this relates to differing status characteristics.

In terms of diffuse status characteristics, there has been a great deal of research done on the role of gender. Ridgeway and Smith-Lovin (1999) summarize this work as involving three broad conclusions:

1. People perceive gender differences to be pervasive in interaction.

2. Examinations of interaction among equal-status group members demonstrate relatively few gender differences in behavior. The differences that do appear seem related to socioemotional behaviors (e.g., women smile more than men) and less related to actual task outcomes. Evidence—for example, from Johnson (1994); Johnson, Clay-Warner, and Funk (1996) and Walker, Ilardi, McMahon, and Fennell (1996)—demonstrates that when women are in leadership roles, many of the gender differences disappear. Such evidence supports the conclusions that the four institutional rules specifying boundary, aggregation, position, and information either contribute to or interrupt the maintenance of status distinctions.

3. Because so many gendered interactions occur within unequal power settings, gender and power become intertwined at multiple levels so that there is a relatively constant reinforcement of gender differences. That is, the institutional rules enable and sustain these status differences.

The work in this area then, emphasizes that it is not necessarily the status characteristics of the individual group members per se that are important in predicting and explaining the interaction and consequences of the group, but rather the composition of the group—the differentials in status. So, when the status characteristics are clear, it is important to separate out the effect of the status of an individual from the effect of the status composition of a particular group. A characteristic attracts more attention as the discrepancy in its distribution increases (Kanter, 1977; Moreland & Levine, 1992). For example, the greater divergence between the number of women and the number of men, the greater the salience of gender.

The burden of proof process is exceptionally resilient, but can that process be decreased or changed? This question has been raised in a few formulations that specifically consider the process or dynamic of generalization processes.

What Process Is Involved in Status Generalization?

Once status characteristics are activated within a group, there is an effect on subsequent points in time. Once deference is granted on Time 1, it acts as reinforcement for the person to whom the deference was granted and an indicator to the others in the group that the behavior is expected. In this manner, initial status differences cumulate in a self-fulfilling fashion. So, this indicates that initial interactions are particularly important for groups because they begin a trajectory for behavior. This would especially be the case for groups in which boundaries are fixed.

Another aspect of process is related to this: Once the burden of proof process starts or has been historically supported by institutions (as in the case of many diffuse status characteristics such as race/ethnicity and gender), it becomes more and more difficult to deter or even diminish. One long-term research and application program headed by Elizabeth Cohen tried different kinds of interventions to help diminish status differences between majority and minority children at school (Cohen, 1982, 1993; Cohen & Roper, 1972). One effective strategy was termed the "inconsistency" intervention in which a minority child learned a specific skill or ability and then taught this skill to a majority child. This inconsistency principle dampened the effect of the diffuse status characteristics by introducing specific status characteristics that contradicted the state or evaluation of the diffuse status characteristics. Other interventions included norms of cooperation and equal participation and a curriculum that emphasized children working together on tasks that involve many different abilities. This last strategy, in particular, was not one emphasized within the expectations states traditions and suggests a whole line of research.

Structure of the Group

The structure of a group is determined, in large part, by the institutional rules that govern the group. For example, Lucas and Lovaglia (1998) examined how leadership status based on appointment and demonstrated competence affected group behavior. Norms of equal participation also diminished status differences, but there are other aspects as well. One relevant part of the structure of a group is the task in which it is engaged. Again, the status of sex category or gender seems to have received a disproportionate amount of attention in this area. Research by Dovidio, Brown, Heltmann, Ellyson, and Keating (1988), for example, indicates that whether a task is stereotypically female (e.g., sewing or child care) or stereotypically male (e.g., fixing a car) affects the degree to which gender is salient and therefore the degree to which gender organizes interaction. Whereas women might be somewhat more influential on tasks perceived as feminine, males are quite a bit more influential on both stereotypical male and neutral tasks. One interesting question in this research rests with the social value of those tasks. So, for example, there is evidence that women's tasks are devalued, in part because they *are* women's tasks. The generalization of this sex-stereotypical task relation can be made to other diffuse status characteristics as well. So, for example, older people might defer to children if they are trying to solve a problem associated with children's cartoons, but they are also likely to devalue such a task.

Elizabeth Cohen's development of the idea of the multiability task relates to this question. By changing the task of the group, the importance of status characteristics should change. Apparently inspired by Cohen's work, Fisek (1991) developed a formal graph theory emphasizing how tasks with multiple aspects might be important in the status generalization process. Lovaglia et al. (1998) expanded the traditional approach to status generalization and developed and then tested a formulation positing that status processes formed within a group interaction context might generalize to individual tasks, such as IQ tests. This broadening of task also involves a consideration of sequencing or time.

As indicated, this issue has not received the attention it deserves. In part, the lack of consideration may stem from the common scope conditions of expectation states formulations that specify collective task orientation without analysis of what the particular task might be.

The issues of sentiment and affect are related to both structure and process. As we have indicated, most status formulations have been concerned with task-oriented groups and have addressed specific or diffuse status characteristics. In these cases, the concern has been with performance evaluations and the observable power and prestige components of action rates, action opportunities, compliance, and influence. Some earlier literature had suggested that those with status disadvantage could become more influential if they "balanced" their assertive task behavior with positive, group-oriented statements (see Meeker & Weitzel-O'Neill, 1977; Ridgeway, 1982). Driskell and Webster (1997) found that low-status group members who disliked their task partners rejected influence at higher rates than those who did not dislike their partner, and somewhat related to this, Lovaglia and Houser (1996) and Lovaglia (1997) show that participants' negative emotion increased resistance to influence. Shelly (2001) presented evidence that sentiment can organize interactions in much the same way as status characteristics.

Promising areas of study include specification of when sentiment or affect might be expected to have a greater or lesser effect. Specifying an institutional framework, as we have advocated, would force researchers to delineate more completely the specific rules and tasks involved in the group. It is likely, for example, that if rules are imposed on group members or are designed to coerce or constrain, different kinds of affect result and different kinds of status processes may also result. As indicated earlier, threats of punishment may undermine group morale, but it is also likely that positive affect can be generated though certain institutional rules (cf. Lawler & Yoon, 1993, 1996, 1998).

Another area that concerns emotion relates to how established hierarchies might be affected by the introduction of emotion. It is likely that both how the emotion is interpreted and what effect it has on the group would be conditioned by the status composition. So, for example, suppose a group status hierarchy is well established and a new entrant to the group is very angry. How does the group respond to this emotion? Is the hierarchy threatened or maintained?

Conclusion

This chapter demonstrates that there is an enormous breadth in the research concerning power, status, and conflict. One of the glaring weaknesses of research within these areas is the lack of theoretical integrations across disciplines and research areas. We focused on empirical research that uses the experimental method. Effective research programs, however, will incorporate a variety of methods to demonstrate the usefulness of knowledge produced through experimentally validated theory. For example, ethnographies have explored how power, status, and conflict are manifested in friendship structures (Anderson, 1999; MacLeod, 1987) and how institutional rules are seldom questioned (see Vaughan, 1995). Survey studies have been important for detailing how people think about conflict, power, and status and how these attitudes, opinions, and beliefs have changed over time (Schuman, Steeh, Bobo, & Krysan, 1997). Historical evidence has been critical for highlighting how different points in time and space dramatically affect the interplay among status, power, and conflict (e.g., Diamond, 1997; Ostrom, 1990).

There are also methods and techniques that provide new kinds of conceptualizations. Such work involves the use of simulations that help organize theoretical assumptions and how such assumptions might translate to differing outcomes (see, e.g., Faust & Skvoretz, 2002; Fossett, 1999). A relatively new area of investigation, both theoretically and methodologically, is the relationship between physiology and social behavior. Usually accessed within an experimental design, various measurement devices or techniques have been used within psychology to study individual behavior. Recently, however, the instruments have become more powerful and have turned toward understanding social processes (e.g., McCabe, Houser, Ryan, Smith, & Trouard, 2001). These instruments include PET (positive electron tomography), EEG (electro-encephalogram) and fMRI (fast magnetic resonance imaging).

Using the institutional rules has provided a way to conceptualize across three disciplines and across three concepts. It has also uncovered the nested nature of questions about group processes. Groups are interacting within particular environments, and these environments allow, enable, or prohibit certain patterns of behavior. In answering how power and status relate to conflict, knowledge of the institutional rules is indispensable. These rules legitimize some kinds of behavior and as a consequence delegitimize others.

Sometimes, the institutional rules are clearly specified, but that is not always the case. Status formulations suggest that even when there are no explicitly written or defined rules, there are informal, sometimes unconscious, but clearly patterned rules about decision making. These involve the burden of proof process, and the statuses involved could vary from position (e.g., position in an exchange network) to occupational status (e.g., doctor versus garbage collector) to diffuse status (e.g., man versus woman).

This new perspective combining power, status, and conflict within institutional rules has also prompted us to examine what we don't know and what we need to know. Now we pose some questions that seem to arise naturally from our discussion throughout the chapter.

How can institutional rules be used to intervene in both coordination and incentive problems of groups in social dilemma settings? A large literature in economics is directed toward incentive problems, and we have discussed some other social psychological research, which addresses changing incentives. But there is much less work on the coordination problem. This question implicates power, status, and conflict. This issue is critical because, even if the incentive problem is solved perfectly (that is, a solution is apparent that is in the interests of all group members), the problem of coordination remains. The applied importance of this question/issue is seen all too often, in settings where panic occurs. The "objective" incentive problem is solvable, but the lack of coordination dictates catastrophic outcomes.

How does the type or structure of a group's task change the dynamics of status and power organization? As indicated in our discussion, this issue has not received much attention, even though the few studies that do investigate it have yielded important and sometimes surprising results. This question forces researchers to examine different questions from those traditionally considered. Rather than asking how status and power organize interaction within the task group, questions would be: How does the structure of the task affect the dynamics of the status and power? What kinds of tasks and institutional rules decrease hierarchy?

Why are the same individuals altruistic in one context and competitive in different contexts? How is trust developed and maintained? We have mentioned issues related to the maintenance and dissolution of social categorization; this question highlights its importance. These categorizations seem fundamental to understanding the creation and maintenance of conflict within groups as well as between groups. They form the basis for status distinctions and seem intimately related to acquisition and dissolution of power. Sociological investigations tend to emphasize how such a subset of these categorizations (specific status characteristics and diffuse status characteristics) is perpetuated and how the subset's effects might be dampened. Psychologists have examined how such ingroup, outgroup categorizations lead to differential attributions and subsequent performance or allocation differences. Political scientists have examined categorizations in terms of more or less likely partnerships or coalitions. Putting all of these insights together and developing principles that bridge different levels of investigation (dyads, within groups, across groups) holds promise for more theoretical power.

How do different kinds of social interaction affect individuals' physiology? What kinds of physiological responses accompany experiences of subordination and domination? How long-lasting are the effects, and how do these effects then condition subsequent behaviors? These questions indicate that even more interdisciplinary research is needed to address how the social and the biological are or are not interdependent. Furthermore, this question challenges the commonly held lay assumption that biology precedes social interaction. Here we ask how social interaction might create and sustain biological difference.

How are the negative reactions of power use overcome, resulting in the respect and admiration conferred on the powerful? Power use produces negative reactions in those on whom it is used. Those negative reactions often result in conflict. Yet, the powerful are likely to be supported by people who are afraid that power will be used on them. Also, the powerful are held in generally high regard, gaining the respect and admiration of many. How are the negative reactions of power use overcome, resulting in the respect and admiration conferred on the powerful?

Finally, we hope that this chapter sparks interdisciplinary interest in these intertwined areas. There is an irony to the study of power, status, and conflict in that, all too often, the differing disciplines investigating these concepts fall into conflict themselves. The conflict is sometimes simply a conflict over terminology that leads to misunderstanding, but at times the conflict seems to escalate to the protection of a particular discipline's "turf." When such conflicts arise, it becomes easier to simply ignore the other disciplines. As we mentioned in the beginning of our discussion, we hope this chapter "manages" the potential conflict by proposing some overarching themes, new directions, and fundamental questions.

References

Ancona, D., Friedman, R., & Kolb, D. (1991). The group and what happens on the way to "Yes." *Negotiation Journal, 7,* 155–174.

Anderson, E. (1999). *Code of the street.* New York: W. W. Norton.

Aquino, K., Steisel, V., & Kay, A. (1992). The effects of resource distribution, voice, and decision framing on the provision of public goods. *Journal of Conflict Resolution, 36,* 665–687.

Arrow, H., & McGrath, J. E. (1993). Membership matters: How member change and continuity affect small group structure, process, and performance. *Small Group Research, 24,* 337–361.

Arrow, K. J. (1951). *Social choice and individual values.* New York: John Wiley.

Austen-Smith, D., & Banks, J. S. (1996). Information aggregation, rationality, and the Condorcet Jury Theorem. *American Political Science Review, 90,* 34–45.

Axelrod, R. (1984). *The evolution of cooperation.* New York: Basic Books.

Bacharach, P. A., & Baratz, M. S. (1963). Decisions and nondecisions: An analytical framework. *American Political Science Review, 57,* 641–651.

Bacharach, S. B., & Lawler, E. J. (1980). *Power and politics in organizations.* San Francisco: Jossey-Bass.

Bacharach, S. B., & Lawler, E. J. (1981). *Bargaining: Power, tactics, and outcomes.* San Francisco: Jossey-Bass.

Berg, J., Dickhaut, J. W., & McCabe, K. A. (1995). Trust, reciprocity, and social history. *Games and Economic Behavior, 10,* 122–142.

Berger, J., Conner, T. L., & Fisek, M. H. (1974). *Expectation states theory: A theoretical research program.* Cambridge, MA: Winthrop.

Berger, J., Conner, T. L., & Fisek, M. H. (1982). *Expectation states theory: A theoretical research program* (Rev. ed.). Lanham, MD: University Press of America.

Berger, J., Fisek, M. H., Norman, R. Z., & Zelditch, M., Jr. (1977). *Status characteristics and social interaction: An expectation-status approach.* New York: Elsevier Scientific.

Berger, J., Wagner, D. G., & Zelditch, M., Jr. (1992). A working strategy for constructing theories: State organizing processes. In G. Ritzer (Ed.), *Metatheorizing: Key issues in sociological theory* (Vol. 6, pp. 107–123). Newbury Park, CA: Sage.

Berger, J., & Zelditch, M., Jr. (1985). *Status, rewards, and influence: How expectations organize behavior.* San Francisco: Jossey-Bass.

Bettenhausen, K., & Murnighan, J. K. (1985). The emergence of norms in competitive decision-making groups. *Administrative Science Quarterly, 30,* 350–372.

Bienenstock, E. J., & Bonacich, P. (1993). Game theory models for exchange networks: Experimental results. *Sociological Perspective, 36,* 117–135.

Bierstedt, R. (1950). An analysis of social power. *American Sociological Review, 15,* 730–738.

Bornstein, G. (1992). The free-rider problem in intergroup conflicts over step-level and continuous public goods. *Journal of Personality and Social Psychology, 62,* 597–606.

Bornstein, G., Rapoport, A., & Kerpel, L. (1989). Within and between-group communication in intergroup competition for public goods. *Journal of Experimental Social Psychology, 25,* 422–436.

Bottom, W. P., Ladha, K., & Miller, G. (2002). Propagation of individual bias through group judgment error in the treatment of asymmetrically informative signals. *Journal of Risk and Uncertainty, 25,* 147–163.

Bouas, K. S., & Komorita, S. S. (1996). Group discussion and cooperation in social dilemmas. *Personality and Social Psychology Bulletin, 22,* 1144-1150.

Boulding, K. E. (1962). *Conflict and defense.* New York: Harper.

Bourgeois, L. J. (1985). Strategic goals, perceived uncertainty, and economic performance in volatile environments. *Academy of Management Journal, 28,* 548–573.

Brann, P., & Foddy, M. (1987). Trust and the consumption of a deteriorating common resource. *The Journal of Conflict Resolution, 31,* 615–630.

Brewer, M. B. (1999). The psychology of prejudice: Ingroup love or outgroup hate? *Journal of Social Issues, 55,* 429–444.

Brewer, M., & Kramer, R. M. (1986). Choice behavior in social dilemmas: Effects of social identity, group size, and decision framing. *Journal of Personality and Social Psychology, 50,* 543–549.

Brewer, M., & Miller, N. (1984). Beyond the contact hypothesis: Theoretical perspectives on desegregation. In N. Miller & M. Brewer (Eds.), *The psychology of desegregation* (pp. 89–111). Orlando, FL: Academic Press.

Budescu, D. V., & Wallsten, T. S. (1990). Dyadic decisions with numerical and verbal probabilities. *Organizational Behavior and Human Decision Processes, 46*, 240–263.

Burke, P. J. (1996). An identity model of network exchange. *American Sociological Review, 62*, 134–150.

Buss, D. M., & Kenrick, D. T. (1998). Evolutionary social psychology. In D. Gilbert, S. Fiske, & G. Lindzey (Eds.), *The handbook of social psychology* (pp. 982–1026). New York: Random House.

Caplow, T. A. (1956). A theory of coalitions in the triad. *American Sociological Review, 21*, 489–493.

Chai, S. K. (2001). *Choosing an identity: A general model of preferences and belief formation.* Ann Arbor: University of Michigan Press.

Cohen, E. G. (1982). Expectation states and interracial interaction in school settings. *Annual Review of Sociology, 8*, 209–235.

Cohen, E. G. (1993). From theory to practice: The development of an applied research program. In J. Berger & M. Zelditch, Jr. (Eds.), *Theoretical research programs: Studies in the growth of theory* (pp. 385–415). Stanford, CA: Stanford University Press.

Cohen, E. G., & Roper, S. (1972). Modifications of interracial interaction disability: An application of status characteristics theory. *American Sociological Review, 37*, 643–665.

Cook, K. S., Emerson, R. M., Gillmore, M. R., & Yamagishi, T. (1983). The distribution of power in exchange networks: Theory and experimental results. *American Journal of Sociology, 89*, 275–305.

Cosmides, L., & Tooby, J. (1994). Better than rational: Evolutionary psychology and the invisible hand. *The American Economic Review, 84*, 327–332.

Crawford, S. E. S., & Ostrom, E. (1995). A grammar of institutions. *American Political Science Review, 89*, 582–600.

Damon, W. (1991). Problems of direction in socially shared cognition. In L. B. Resnick, J. M. Levine, & S. D. Teasley (Eds.), *Perspectives on socially shared cognition* (pp. 384–397). Washington, DC: American Psychological Association.

Dawes, R. M. (1980). Social dilemmas. *Annual Review of Psychology, 32*, 169–193.

Dawes, R. M., McTavish, J., & Shaklee, H. (1977). Behavior, communication, and assumptions about other people's behavior in a commons dilemma situation. *Journal of Personality and Social Psychology, 35*, 1–11.

DeDreu, C. K. W., Harinck, F., & Van vianen, A. E. M. (1999). Conflict and performance in groups and organizations. In C. L. Cooper & I. Robertson (Eds.), *International review of industrial and organizational psychology* (pp. 369–414). New York: John Wiley.

Diamond, J. (1997). *Guns, germs, and steel: The fates of human societies.* New York: W.W. Norton.

Diermeier, D., & Stevenson, R. T. (2000). Cabinet survival and competing risks. *American Journal of Political Science, 43,* 1051–1068.

Dovidio, J. F., Brown, C. E., Heltmann, I., Ellyson, S. L., & Keating, C. F. (1988). Power displays between women and men in discussion of gender-linked tasks: A multichannel study. *Journal of Personality and Social Psychology, 55,* 580–587.

Driskell, J. E., Jr., & Webster, M., Jr. (1997). Status and sentiment in task groups. In J. Szmatka, J. Skvoretz, & J. Berger (Eds.), *Status, network, and structure: Theory construction and theory development* (pp. 179–200). Stanford, CA: Stanford University Press.

Eagly, A. H. (1987). *Sex differences in social behavior: A social-role interpretation.* Hillsdale, NJ: Lawrence Erlbaum.

Eagly, A. H., & Johnson, B. (1990). Gender and the emergence of leaders: A meta-analysis. *Psychological Bulletin, 108,* 233–256.

Eagly, A. H., & Karau, S. (1991). Gender and the emergence of leaders: A meta-analysis. *Journal of Personality and Social Psychology, 60,* 685–710.

Eagly, A. H., & Wood, W. (1999). The origins of sex differences in human behavior: Evolved dispositions versus social roles. *American Psychologist, 54,* 408–423.

Eckel, C. C., & Grossman, P. J. (2001). Chivalry and solidarity in ultimatum games. *Economic Inquiry, 39,* 171–188.

Eckel, C. C., & Wilson, R. K. (2002, March 21–23). *Conditional trust: Sex, race, and facial expressions in a trust game.* Paper presented at the annual meeting of the Public Choice Society, San Diego, CA.

Eisenhardt, K. M., & Schoonhoven, C. B. (1990). Organizational growth: Linking founding team, strategy, environment, and growth among U.S. semiconductor ventures, 1978–1988. *Administrative Science Quarterly, 35,* 504–529.

Eisenhardt, K. M., & Zbaracki, M. J. (1992). Strategic decision making. *Strategic Management Journal, 13,* 17–37.

Ellemer, N., Spears, R., & Doojse, B. (1997). *Social identity: Context, commitment, content.* Oxford, UK: Blackwell.

Emerson, R. M. (1962). Power-dependence relations. *American Sociological Review, 27,* 31–41.

Emerson, R. M. (1964). Power-dependence relations: Two experiments. *Sociometry, 27,* 282–298.

Emerson, R. M. (1969). Operant psychology and exchange theory. In R. L. Burgess & D. Bushnell, Jr. (Eds.), *Behavioral sociology* (pp. 379–405). New York: Columbia University Press.

Emerson, R. M. (1972). Exchange theory, Part I: A psychological basis for social exchange. In J. Berger, M. Zelditch, Jr., & B. Anderson (Eds.), *Sociological theories in progress* (Vol. 2, pp. 58–87). Boston: Houghton Mifflin.

Emerson, R. M. (1987). Toward a theory of value in social exchange. In K. S. Cook (Ed.), *Social exchange theory* (pp. 11–58). Newbury Park, CA: Sage.

Espinoza, J. A., & Garza, R. T. (1985). Social group salience and interethnic cooperation. *Journal of Experimental Social Psychology, 21,* 380–392.

Faust, K., & Skvoretz, J. (2002). Comparing networks across space and time, size and species. *Sociological Methodology, 32,* 267–299.

Feshback, S. (1994). Nationalism, patriotism, and aggression: A clarification of functional differences. In L. R. Huesman (Ed.), *Aggressive behavior: Current perspectives* (pp. 275–291). New York: Plenum.

Fiorina, M. P., & Plott, C. R. (1978). Committee decisions under majority rule: An experimental study. *American Political Science Review, 72,* 575–598.

Fisek, H. M. (1991). Complex task structures and power and prestige orders. In E. J. Lawler, B. Markovsky, C. L. Ridgeway, & H. Walker (Eds.), *Advances in group processes* (Vol. 8, pp. 64–81). Greenwich, CT: JAI Press.

Fleishman, J. A. (1988). The effects of decision framing and others' behavior on cooperation in a social dilemma. *The Journal of Conflict Resolution, 32,* 162–180.

Fossett, M. (1999, August). *Ethnic preferences, social distance dynamics, and residential segregation: Results from simulation analyses.* Paper presented at the American Sociological Association, Chicago.

Franzen, A. (1994). Group size effects in social dilemmas: A review of experimental literature. In U. Schulz, W. Albers, & U. Mueller (Eds.), *Social dilemmas and cooperation* (pp. 117–146). New York: Springer-Verlag.

French, J. R., Jr., & Raven, B. H. (1959). The bases of social power. In D. Cartwright (Ed.), *Studies in social power* (pp. 150–167). Ann Arbor, MI: Institute for Social Research.

Friedkin, N. (1992). An expected value model of social power: Predictions for selected exchange networks. *Social Networks, 14,* 213–229.

Gamson, W. A. (1961). A theory of coalition formation. *American Sociological Review, 26,* 373–382.

Gruenfeld, D. H. (1995). Status, ideology, and integrative complexity on the U.S. Supreme Court: Rethinking the politics of political decision making. *Journal of Personality and Social Psychology, 68,* 5–20.

Gruenfeld, D. H., Mannix, E. A., Williams, K. Y., & Neale, M. A. (1996). Group composition and decision-making: How member familiarity and information distribution affect process and performance. *Organizational Behavior and Human Decision Processes, 67,* 1–15.

Guth, W., & Tietz, R. (1990). Ultimatum bargaining behavior: A survey of comparison of experimental results. *Journal of Economic Psychology, 11,* 417–449.

Hardin, G. (1968). The tragedy of the commons. *Science, 162,* 1243–1248.

Hine, D. W., & Gifford, R. (1996). What information do we use in social dilemmas? Environmental uncertainty and the employment of coordination rules. *Journal of Applied Social Psychology, 26,* 993–1009.

Hirschman, A. O. (1970). *Exit, voice, and loyalty: Responses to decline in firms, organizations, and states.* Cambridge, MA: Harvard University Press.

Homans, G. C. (1961). *Social behavior: Its elementary forms.* New York: Harcourt Brace Jovanovich.

Homans, G. C. (1974). *Social behavior: Its elementary forms* (Rev. ed.). New York: Harcourt Brace Jovanovich.

Humphreys, P., & Berger, J. (1981). Theoretical consequences of the status characteristics formulation. *American Journal of Sociology, 86,* 958–983.

Isaac, M. R., & Walker, J. M. (1988). Group size effects in public goods provision: The voluntary contributions mechanism. *Quarterly Journal of Economics, 103,* 179–199.

Janis, I. L. (1982). *Victims of groupthink* (2nd ed.). Boston: Houghton Mifflin.

Jehn, K. (1992). The impact of intragroup conflict on effectiveness: A multimethod examination of the benefits and detriments of conflict. *Dissertation Abstracts International, 53,* 2005.

Jehn, K. (1994). Enhancing effectiveness: An investigation of advantages and disadvantages of value-based intragroup conflict. *International Journal of Conflict Management, 5,* 223–238.

Jehn, K., & Mannix, E. A. (2001). The dynamic nature of conflict: A longitudinal study of intragroup conflict and group performances. *Academy of Management Journal, 44,* 238–251.

Jehn, K., Northcraft, G. B., & Neale, M. A. (1999). Why differences make a difference: A field study of diversity, conflict, and performance in workgroups. *Administrative Science Quarterly, 44,* 741–763.

Jehn, K., & Shah, P. (1997). Interpersonal relationships and task performance: An examination of mediating processes in friendship and acquaintance groups. *Journal of Personality and Social Psychology, 72,* 775–790.

Johnson, C. (1994). Gender, legitimate authority, and leader-subordinate conversations. *American Sociological Review, 59,* 122–135.

Johnson, C., Clay-Warner, J., & Funk, S. J. (1996). Effects of authority structures and gender on interaction in same-sex task groups. *Social Psychology Quarterly, 59,* 221–236.

Kahneman, D., & Tversky, A. (1979). Prospect theory: An analysis of decision under risk. *Econometrica, 47,* 263–291.

Kanazawa, S. (2001). De gustibus est disputandum. *Social Forces, 79,* 1131–1162.

Kanter, R. (1977). *Men and women of the corporation.* New York: Basic Books.

Kerr, N. L. (1989). Illusions of efficacy: The effects of group size on perceived efficacy in social dilemmas. *Journal of Experimental Social Psychology, 25,* 287–313.

Kerr, N., & Kaufman-Gilleland, C. (1994). Communication, commitment, and cooperation in social dilemmas. *Journal of Personality and Social Psychology, 66,* 513–529.

Knight, J. (1992). *Institutions and social conflict.* Cambridge, UK: Cambridge University Press.

Knottnerus, J. D. (1997). Social structural analysis and status generalization: The contributions of potential of expectation states theory. In J. Szmatka, J. Skvoretz, & J. Berger (Eds.), *Status, network, and structure: Theory development in group processes* (pp. 119–136). Stanford, CA: Stanford University Press.

Komorita, S. S. (1976). A model of the N-person dilemma-type game. *Journal of Experimental Social Psychology, 12,* 357–373.

Komorita, S. S., & Barth, J. M. (1985). Components of reward in social dilemmas. *Journal of Personality and Social Psychology, 48,* 364–373.

Komorita, S. S., & Chan, D. K. S. (1993). The effects of reward structure and reciprocity in social dilemmas. *Journal of Experimental Social Psychology, 29,* 252–267.

Komorita, S. S., & Hamilton, T. P. (1984). *Research in the sociology of organizations: Vol. 3. Power and equity in coalition bargaining.* Greenwich, CT: JAI Press.

Komorita, S. S., Hilty, J., & Parks, C. (1991). Reciprocity and cooperation in social dilemmas. *The Journal of Conflict Resolution, 35,* 494–518.

Komorita, S. S., & Parks, C. D. (1995). Interpersonal relations: Mixed-motive interaction. *Annual Review of Psychology, 46,* 183–207.

Komorita, S. S., Parks, C. D., & Hulbert, L. G. (1992). Reciprocity and the induction of cooperation in social dilemmas. *Journal of Personality and Social Psychology, 62,* 607–617.

Lasswell, H. D., & Kaplan, A. (1950). *Power and society: A framework for political inquiry.* New Haven, CT: Yale University Press.

Laver, M. (1998). Models of government formation. *Annual Review of Political Science, 1,* 1–25.

Lawler, E. J. (1986). Bilateral deterrence and conflict spiral: A theoretical analysis. In E. J. Lawler (Ed.), *Advances in group processes* (Vol. 3, pp. 107–130). Greenwich, CT: JAI Press.

Lawler, E. J., Ford, R., & Blegen, M. A. (1988). Coercive capability in conflict: A test of bilateral deterrence versus conflict spiral theory. *Social Psychology Quarterly, 51,* 93–107.

Lawler, E. J., & Yoon, J. (1993). Power and the emergence of commitment behavior in negotiated exchange. *American Sociological Review, 58,* 465–481.

Lawler, E. J., & Yoon, J. (1996). Commitment in exchange relations: Test of a theory of relational cohesion. *American Sociological Review, 61,* 89–108.

Lawler, E. J., & Yoon, J. (1998). Network structure and emotion in exchange relations. *American Sociological Review, 63,* 871–894.

Levine, J. M., & Resnick, L. B. (1993). Social foundations of cognition. *Annual Review of Psychology, 44,* 585–612.

Liebrand, W. B. G. (1984). The effects of social motives, communication, and group size on behavior in an n-person multi-state mixed-motive game. *European Journal of Social Psychology, 14,* 239–264.

Lovaglia, M. J. (1997). Status, emotion, and structural power. In J. Szmatka, J. Skvoretz, & J. Berger (Eds.), *Status, network, and structure: Theory development in group processes* (pp. 159–178). Stanford, CA: Stanford University Press.

Lovaglia, M. J., & Houser, J. (1996). Emotional reactions and status in groups. *American Sociological Review, 61,* 867–883.

Lovaglia, M. J., Skvoretz, J., Markovsky, B., & Willer, D. (1999). An automated approach to the theoretical analysis of difficult problems. In D. Willer (Ed.), *Network exchange theory* (pp. 259–269). Westport, CT: Praeger.

Lovaglia, M. J., Skvoretz, J., Willer, D., & Markovsky, B. (1995). Negotiated exchanges in social networks. *Social Forces, 74,* 123–155.

Lucas, J. W., & Lovaglia, M. J. (1998). Leadership status, gender, group size, and emotion in face-to-face groups. *Sociological Perspectives, 41*(3), 617–637.

Lucas, J. W., Younts, C. W., Lovaglia, M. J., & Markovsky, B. (2001). Lines of power in exchange networks. *Social Forces, 80,* 185–214.

Luce, R. D., & Raiffa, H. (1957). *Games and decision: Introduction and critical survey.* New York: John Wiley.

Lupia, A., & McCubbins, M. D. (1998). *The democratic dilemma: Can citizens learn what they need to know?* Cambridge, UK: Cambridge University Press.

MacLeod, J. (1987). *Ain't no makin' it: Leveled aspirations in a low-income neighborhood.* Boulder, CO: Westview Press.

Mannix, E. A. (1991). Resource dilemmas and discount rates in organizational decision making groups. *Journal of Experimental Social Psychology, 27,* 379–391.

Mannix, E. A. (1993). Organizations as resource dilemmas: The effects of power balance on group decision making. *Organizational Behavior and Human Decision Processes, 55,* 1–22.

Mannix, E. A. (1994). Will we meet again? The effects of power, distribution norms, and the scope of future interaction in small group negotiation. *International Journal of Conflict Management, 5,* 343–368.

Markovsky, B., Skvoretz, J., Willer, D., Lovaglia, M. J., & Erger, J. (1993). The seeds of weak power: An extension of network exchange theory. *American Sociological Review, 58,* 197–209.

Markovsky, B., Willer, D., & Patton, T. (1988). Power relations in exchange networks. *American Sociological Review, 53,* 220–236.

Mazur, A. (1973). Cross-species comparison of status in established small groups. *American Sociological Review, 38,* 513–529.

Mazur, A. (1983). Hormones, aggression, and dominance in humans. In B. Svare (Ed.), *Hormones and aggressive behavior.* New York: Plenum.

Mazur, A., Rosa, E., Faupel, M., Heller, J., Leen, R., & Thurman, B. (1980). Physiological aspects of communication via mutual gaze. *American Journal of Sociology, 86,* 50–74.

McCabe, K., Houser, D., Ryan, L., Smith, V., & Trouard, T. (2001). A functional imaging study of cooperation in two-person reciprocal exchange. *Proceedings, National Academy of Science, 98,* 11832–11835.

McGrath, J. E., Berdahl, J. L., & Arrow, H. (1996). Traits, expectations, culture, and clout: The dynamics of diversity in work groups. In S. E. Jackson & M. N. Ruderman (Eds.), *Diversity in work teams: Research paradigms for a changing workplace* (pp. 17–45). Washington, DC: American Psychological Association.

McKelvey, R. D., & Ordeshook, P. C. (1990). A decade of experimental research on spatial models of elections and committees. In J. M. Enelow & M. J. Hinich (Eds.), *Advances in the spatial theory of voting.* Cambridge, UK: Cambridge University Press.

Meeker, B. F., & Weitzel-O'Neill, P. A. (1977). Sex roles and interpersonal behavior in task oriented groups. *American Sociological Review, 42,* 91–105.

Messick, D. M. (1973). To join or not to join: An approach to the unionization decision. *Organizational Behavior and Human Performance, 10,* 145–156.

Messick, D. M., Allison, S. T., & Samuelson, C. D. (1988). Framing and communication effects on group members' responses to environmental and social uncertainty. In S. Maital (Ed.), *Applied behavioral economics* (Vol. 2, pp. 677–700). New York: New York University Press.

Messick, D. M., & Brewer, M. B. (1983). Solving social dilemmas: A review. L. Wheeler & P. Shaver (Eds.), *Review of personality and social psychology* (pp. 11-44). Beverly Hills, CA: Sage.

Molm, L. D. (1989). Punishment power: A balancing process in power-dependence relations. *American Journal of Sociology, 94,* 1392–1418.

Molm, L. D. (1991). Affect and social exchange: Satisfaction in power-dependence relations. *American Sociological Review, 56,* 475–493.

Molm, L. D. (1997a). *Coercive power in social exchange.* Cambridge, UK: Cambridge University Press.

Molm, L. D. (1997b). Risk and power use: Constraints on the use of coercion in exchange. *American Sociological Review, 62,* 113–133.

Moreland, R. L., & Levine, J. M. (1992). The composition of small groups. In E. Lawler, B. Markovsky, C. Ridgeway, & H. Walker (Eds.), *Advances in group processes* (Vol 9., pp. 237–280). Greenwich, CT: JAI Press.

Murnighan, J. K. (1986). Organization coalitions: Structural contingencies and the formation process. In R. Lewicki, B. Sheppard, & M. Bazerman (Eds.), *Research on negotiation in organizations.* Greenwich, CT: JAI Press.

Murnighan, J. K., & Conlon, D. (1991). The dynamics of intense workgroup: A study of British string quartets. *Administrative Science Quarterly, 36,* 165–186.

Nemeth, C. J., & Kwan, J. L. (1987). Minority influence, divergent thinking, and detection of correct solutions. *Journal of Applied Social Psychology, 17,* 788–799.

Nemeth, C. J., & Wachtler, J. (1983). Creative problem solving as a result of majority vs. minority influence. *European Journal of Social Psychology, 13,* 45–55.

O'Connor, K., Gruenfeld, D., & McGrath, J. (1993). The experience and effects of conflict in continuing workgroups. *Small Group Research, 24,* 362–382.

Ofshe, R., & Lee, M. T. (1981). Reply to Greenstein. *Social Psychology Quarterly, 44,* 383–385.

Olson, M. (1965). *The logic of collective action.* Cambridge, MA: Harvard University Press.

Orbell, J. M., van de Kragt, A. J. C., & Dawes, R. M. (1988). Explaining discussion-induced cooperation. *Journal of Personality and Social Psychology, 54,* 811–819.

Ostrom, E. (1990). *Governing the commons: The evolution of institutions for collective actions.* New York: Cambridge University Press.

Ostrom, E. (2000). Collective action and the evolution of social norms. *Journal of Economic Perspectives, 14,* 137–158.

Ostrom, E., Walker, J., & Gardner, R. (1992). Covenants with and without a sword: Self-governance is possible. *The American Political Science Review, 86,* 404–417.

Pelled, L. H., Eisenhardt, K. M., & Xin, K. R. (1999). Exploring the black box: An analysis of work group diversity, conflict, and performance. *Administrative Science Quarterly, 44,* 1–28.

Peterson, R. S., & Nemeth, C. J. (1996). Focus versus flexibility: Majority and minority influence can both improve performance. *Personality and Social Psychology Bulletin, 22,* 14–23.

Pfeffer, J. (1981). *Power in organizations.* Mansfield, MA: Pitman.

Pfeffer, J. (1992). *Managing with power: Politics and influence in organizations.* Boston: Harvard Business School Press.

Plott, C. R., & Levine, M. E. (1978). A model of agenda influence on committee decisions. *American Economic Review, 68,* 146–160.

Polzer, J., Mannix, E. A., & Neale, M. (1995). Multi-party negotiation in its social context. In R. Kramer & D. Messick (Eds.), *Negotiation as a social process* (pp. 123–142). Thousand Oaks, CA: Sage.

Polzer, J., Mannix, E. A., & Neale, M. A. (1998). Interest alignment and coalitions in multi-party negotiation. *Academy of Management Journal, 41,* 42–54.

Rapoport, A. (1966). *Two-person game theory.* Ann Arbor: University of Michigan Press.

Rapoport, A., & Bornstein, G. (1987). Integroup competition for the provision of binary public goods. *Psychological Review, 94,* 291–299.

Rapoport, A., & Bornstein G. (1989). Solving public goods problems in competition between equal and unequal size groups. *The Journal of Conflict Resolution, 33,* 460–479.

Rapoport, A., Bornstein, G., & Erev, I. (1989). Intergroup competition for public goods: Effects of unequal resources and relative group size. *Journal of Personality and Social Psychology, 56,* 748–756.

Ridgeway, C. L. (1982). Status in groups: The importance of motivation. *American Sociological Review, 47,* 76–88.

Ridgeway, C. L. (1991). The social construction of status value: Gender and other nominal characteristics. *Social Forces, 70,* 367–386.

Ridgeway, C. L. (1997). Where do status beliefs come from? New developments. In J. Szmatka, J. Skvoretz, & J. Berger (Eds.), *Status, network, and structure* (pp. 137–158). Stanford, CA: Stanford University Press.

Ridgeway, C. L., & Smith-Lovin, L. (1999). The gender system and interaction. *Annual Review of Sociology, 25,* 191–216.

Riker, W. H. (1962). *The theory of political coalitions.* New Haven, CT: Yale University Press.

Roch, S. G., & Samuelson, C. D. (1997). Effects of environmental uncertainty and social value orientation in resource dilemmas. *Organizational Behavior and Human Decision Processes, 70,* 221–235.

Roseman, I. J., Wiest, C., & Swartz, T. S. (1994). Phenomenology, behaviors, and goals differentiate discrete emotions. *Journal of Personality and Social Psychology, 67,* 206–221.

Rutte, C. G., Wilke, H. A. M., & Messick, D. M. (1987). The effects of framing social dilemmas as give-some or take-some games. *British Journal of Social Psychology, 26,* 103–108.

Sally, D. (1995). Conversation and cooperation in social dilemmas: A meta-analysis of experiments from 1958 to 1992. *Rationality and Society, 7,* 58–92.

Samuelson, C. D. (1991). Perceived task difficulty, causal attributions, and preference for structural change in resource dilemmas. *Personality and Social Psychology, 17,* 181–187.

Samuelson, C. D. (1993). A multiattribute evaluation approach to structural change in resource dilemmas. *Organizational Behavior and Human Decision Processes, 55,* 298–324.

Samuelson, C. D., & Messick, D. M. (1986a). Alternative structural solutions to resource dilemmas. *Organizational Behavior and Human Decision Processes, 37,* 139–155.

Samuelson, C. D., & Messick, D. M. (1986b). Inequities in access to and use of shared resources in social dilemmas. *Journal of Personality and Social Psychology, 51,* 960–967.

Samuelson, C. D., & Messick, D. M. (1995). Let's make some new rules: Social factors that make freedom unattractive. In R. Kramer & D. M. Messick (Eds.), *Negotiation as a social process* (pp. 48–68). Thousand Oaks, CA: Sage.

Samuelson, C., D., Rutte, C. G., & Wilke, H. (1984). Individual and structural solutions to resource dilemmas in two cultures. *Journal of Personality and Social Psychology, 47,* 94–104.

Sato, K. (1987). Distribution of the cost of maintaining common resources. *Journal of Experimental Social Psychology, 31,* 19–31.

Scharlemann, J. P., Eckel, C. C., Kacelnik, A., & Wilson, R. W. (2001). The value of a smile: Game theory with a human face. *Journal of Economic Psychology, 22,* 617–640.

Schelling, T. C. (1960). *The strategy of conflict.* Oxford, UK: Oxford University Press.

Schroeder, D. A. (1995). *Social dilemmas: Perspectives on individuals and groups.* Westport, CT: Praeger.

Schuman, H., Steeh, C., Bobo, L., & Krysan, M. (1997). *Racial attitudes in America: Trends and interpretations* (Rev. ed.). Cambridge, MA: Harvard University Press.

Schwartz-Shea, P., & Simmons, R. T. (1995). Social dilemmas and perceptions: Experiments on framing and inconsequentiality. In D. A. Schroeder (Ed.), *Social dilemmas: Perspectives on individuals and groups* (pp. 87–103). Westport, CT: Praeger.

Sell, J. (1997). Gender, strategies, and contributions to public goods. *Social Psychology Quarterly, 60,* 252–265.

Sell, J., Chen, Z. Y., Hunter-Holmes, P., & Johansson, A. (2002). A cross-cultural comparison of public good and resource good settings. *Social Psychology Quarterly, 65,* 285–297.

Sell, J., Griffith, W. I., & Wilson, R. K. (1993). Are women more cooperative than men in social dilemmas? *Social Psychology Quarterly, 56,* 211–222.

Sell, J., Lovaglia, M. J., Mannix, E. A., Samuelson, C. D., & Wilson, R. K. (2004). Investigating conflict, power, and status within and among groups. *Small Group Research, 35,* 44–72.

Sell, J., & Son, Y. (1997). Comparing public goods with common pool resources: Three experiments. *Social Psychology Quarterly, 60,* 118–137.

Sell, J., & Wilson, R. K. (1991). Levels of information and public goods. *Social Forces, 70,* 107–124.

Sell, J., & Wilson, R. K. (1999). The maintenance of cooperation: Expectations of future interaction and the trigger of group punishment. *Social Forces, 77,* 1551–1570.

Sewell, W. H., Jr. (1992). A theory of structure: Duality, agency, and transformation. *American Journal of Sociology, 98,* 1–29.

Shah, P., & Jehn, K. (1993). Do friends perform better than acquaintances? The interaction of friendship, conflict, and task. *Group Decision and Negotiation, 2,* 149–166.

Shelly, R. K. (2001). How performance expectations arise from sentiments. *Social Psychology Quarterly, 64,* 72–87.

Smith, C. M., Tindale, R. S., & Dugoni, B. L. (1996). Minority and majority influence in freely interacting groups. *British Journal of Social Psychology, 35,* 137–149.

Son, Y., & Sell, J. (1995). Are the dilemmas posed by public goods and common pool resources the same? In L. Freese (Ed.), *Advances in human ecology* (Vol. 4, pp. 69–88). Greenwich, CT: JAI Press.

Stevenson, R., & Martin, L. (2001). Cabinet formation in parliamentary democracies. *American Journal of Political Science, 45,* 33–50.

Tenbrunsel, A. E., & Messick, D. M. (1999). Sanctioning systems, decision frames, and cooperation. *Administrative Science Quarterly, 44,* 684–707.

Thibaut, J. W., & Kelley, H. H. (1959). *The social psychology of groups.* New York: John Wiley.

Thompson, L. L., Mannix, E. A., & Bazerman, M. H. (1988). Group negotiation. *Journal of Personality and Social Psychology, 54,* 86–94.

Thye, S. R. (2000). A status-value theory of power in exchange. *American Sociological Review, 65,* 407–432.

Tuckman, B. W. (1965). Developmental sequences in small groups. *Psychological Bulletin, 63,* 384–399.

Van Dijk, E. V., Wilke, H., & Wilke, M. (1999). What information do we use in social dilemmas? Environmental uncertainty and the employment of coordination rules. *Journal of Experimental Social Psychology, 35,* 109–135.

Vaughan, D. (1995). *The Challenger launch decision: Risky technology, culture, and deviance at NASA.* Chicago: University of Chicago Press.

Von Neumann, J., & Morgenstern, O. (1944). *Theory of games and economic behavior.* Princeton, NJ: Princeton University Press.

Wade-Benzoni, K. A., Tenbrunsel, A. E., & Bazerman, M. H. (1996). Egocentric interpretations of fairness in asymmetric environmental social dilemmas: Explaining harvesting behavior and the role of communication. *Organization Behavior and Human Decision Processes, 67*, 111–126.

Walker, H. A., Ilardi, B. C., McMahon, A. M., & Fennell, M. L. (1996). Gender, interaction, and leadership. *Social Psychology Quarterly, 59*, 255–272.

Walker, H. A., Thye, S. R., Simpson, B., Lovaglia, M. J., Willer, D., & Markovsky, B. (2000). Network exchange theory: Recent development and new directions. *Social Psychology Quarterly, 63*, 324–337.

Weber, M. (1968). *Economy and society* (G. Roth & C. Wittich, Trans.). Totowa, NJ: Bedminister Press.

Weick, K. E. (1984). Small wins: Redefining the scale of social problems. *American Psychologist, 39*, 40–49.

Weingart, L., Bennett, R., & Brett, J. (1993). The impact of consideration of issues and motivational orientation on group negotiation process and outcome. *Journal of Applied Psychology, 78*, 504–517.

Willer, D. (1987). *Theory and the experimental investigation of social structures.* New York: Gordon & Breach.

Willer, D. (2003). Power at a distance. *Social Forces, 81*, 1295–1334.

Willer, D., Lovaglia, M. J., & Markovsky, B. (1997). Power and influence: A theoretical bridge. *Social Forces, 76*, 571–603.

Willer, D., & Skvoretz, J. (1997). Games and structures. *Rationality and Society, 9*, 5–35.

Willer, R. B., Troyer, L., & Lovaglia, M. J. (2001, August). *Using power to elevate status: Observers of power use.* Paper resented at the Annual Meeting of the American Sociological Association, Washington, DC.

Williams, K. Y., & O'Reilly, C. A. I. (1998). Demography and diversity in organizations: A review of 40 years of research. *Research in Organizational Behavior (Stamford, CT), 20*, 77–140.

Wilson, R. K. (1986). Forward and backward agenda procedures: Committee experiments on structurally-induced equilibrium. *Journal of Politics, 48*, 390–409.

Wilson, R. K., & Herzberg, R. Q. (1987). Negative decision powers and institutional equilibrium: Theory and experiments on blocking coalitions. *Western Political Quarterly, 40*, 593–609.

Wilson, R. K., & Sell, J. (1997). Cheap talk and reputation in repeated public goods settings. *Journal of Conflict Resolution, 41*, 695–717.

Yamagishi, T. (1986a). Motivational bases of the public goods problem. *Journal of Personality and Social Psychology, 50*, 67–73.

Yamagishi, T. (1986b). The provision of a sanctioning system as a public good. *Journal of Personality and Social Psychology, 51*, 110–116.

Yamaguchi, K. (1996). Power in networks of substitutable and complementary exchange relations: A rational-choice model and an analysis of power. *American Sociological Review, 61*, 308–332.

6

The Symbolic-Interpretive Perspective of Group Life

Larry Frey and Sunwolf

Abstract

Scholars who study groups from the symbolic-interpretive perspective seek to understand the nature, practices, and potential consequences of symbol usage in groups. This chapter first describes the key assumptions, theories, and methods of the symbolic-interpretive perspective and its approach to scholarship on small groups. We then examine representative research from this perspective that sheds light on the seven questions posed for this volume concerning (1) group composition; (2) group tasks and goals; (3) group tools, structures, and technologies; (4) group processes and interactions; (5) the results of group actions; (6) changes in groups over time; and (7) group ecology. For each question, we offer conclusions that can be drawn from the extant literature and pose a series of questions worth exploring in future research.

Humans have been characterized as the "symbol-using (symbol-making, symbol-misusing) animal" (Burke, 1966, p. 16). From such a perspective, a small group is viewed as a crucial site where the creation, exchange, and interpretation of symbols have important consequences at individual, relational, and collective levels. A *symbol* is an arbitrary word, object, or action that is deliberately created and agreed to by members of a collective (such as a group or culture) as representing the thing to which it refers but that bears no natural relationship to it, and it is usually differentiated from a *sign* or a *signal*, "something that stands for or represents something else and bears a natural, nonarbitrary relationship to it" (Infante, Rancer, & Womack, 2003, p. 354). As an example, the calloused hands of a group of people who have just physically moved furniture from one place to another is a natural sign/signal of the group's manual labor; the terms *group, furniture,* and *manual labor* are arbitrary symbols deliberately created to evoke shared meanings among group members. Members of a collective, thus, create and use symbols to stimulate meaning about abstract concepts; to be meaningful, symbols must be interpreted by members in a relatively similar manner.

Scholars who study groups from the symbolic-interpretive (S-I) perspective, thus, seek to understand the nature, practices, and potential consequences of significant symbol usage and interpretation by group members. Although the study of symbol usage and interpretation potentially excludes little from consideration, as shown in this chapter, those working from this perspective focus principally on the most significant symbols, those that make an important difference in the central activities that constitute group life (e.g., establishment of group boundaries, creation and maintenance of group identity, socialization of new group members, development of member relationships, and the accomplishment of group tasks). We start by defining the S-I perspective as applied to groups and examining its key assumptions. We then examine the study of groups from this perspective, including some theories and methods employed. We then devote the bulk of this chapter to examining what this perspective has to say about the seven questions posed for consideration for this volume.

Definition and Assumptions of the Symbolic-Interpretive Perspective

How do people's predispositions toward symbol usage influence their participation and interaction in groups? What symbolic practices do groups employ and for what purposes? How are symbolic practices and processes used in groups related to group products? These are the type of questions that lie at the heart of the S-I perspective as applied to small groups.

The S-I perspective, as applied to the study of groups, can be defined as:

> an approach concerned with understanding the nature, practices, and consequences of symbol usage within groups, as well as how groups and group processes are themselves products of symbolic activities.

The study of the nature, practices, and consequences (on individual, relational, and collective processes and products) of symbol usage constitutes a *symbolic-management focus;* an understanding of how groups and group processes are products of symbolic activity represents a *symbolic-constitutive focus* (Frey & Sunwolf, 2004).

The S-I perspective on groups is not a well-articulated perspective in the same sense as, for instance, the functional perspective (see Chapter 2, this volume). Indeed, to our knowledge, the term *S-I perspective,* at least as applied to groups, is a result of the first "Interdisciplinary Conference on Assessing Theory and Research on Groups: What Do We Know and What Do We Need to Know?" held in October 2001, which led to the creation of this volume. The S-I perspective, however, emerges from a relatively long history of scholarship associated with the "interpretive turn" (Geertz, 1973) toward the study of symbolic practices and sense making, a history that we have examined elsewhere (Frey & Sunwolf, 2004; see also Lindlof & Taylor, 2002). Here, we review the key assumptions of the perspective as applied to the study of small groups and explain the study of small groups from this perspective (see Table 6.1).

The S-I perspective makes the following key assumptions about small groups:

1. *A "group" is a significant symbol.* The term *group* is a significant symbol used to describe a relationship that people perceive exists among them. In defining a group, Socha (1997) listed as the first characteristic: "Three or more people who think of themselves as a group" (p. 7). The coach of a sports team, for instance, can exercise leadership over the team because the players perceive themselves as being a group; in contrast, a collection of individuals standing at a bus stop waiting for a bus to arrive would likely be confused if someone approached them and volunteered to "lead 'their group.'" The symbolic marker of a group, and its accompanying symbolic boundaries (e.g., between those considered to be inside and outside a group), creates, according to Smith and Berg (1987), "the possibility of relationship . . . [for] without boundary, there can be no relationship"; in this regard, symbolic boundaries "are at the base of everything in group life" (p. 103). Part of the task of the S-I perspective, therefore, is to reveal ways in which the significant symbol of "group" is created, sustained, and changed.

2. *The significant symbol of "group" is created through members' symbolic activities.* A group, and all that the term implies (e.g., a shared reality), is a socially constructed symbol, not a reified entity that exists in some objective sense. The notion that people's symbolic activities construct their reality

Table 6.1   The Symbolic-Interpretive Perspective

Definition of perspective	An approach concerned with understanding the nature, practices, and consequences of symbol usage within groups, as well as how groups and group processes are themselves products of symbolic activities
Key assumptions	• A *group* is a significant symbol • The significant symbol of *group* is created through members' symbolic activities • Symbolic activities in groups include symbolic predispositions, practices, processes, and products • Symbolic predispositions, practices, processes, and products are influenced by the environments in which groups are embedded
Types of groups	Naturally occurring, bona fide groups
Key theories	Rhetorical perspective, symbolic convergence theory, structuration theory, dialectical perspective, bona fide group perspective
Dominant research methodologies	Naturalistic paradigm, with research characterized by bona fide groups being studied in their natural contexts, induction, goal of holistic understanding of patterns and behaviors, emergent design, qualitative methods, and resulting in case studies
Strengths	• Potentially highly interdisciplinary • Broadens the landscape of groups studied (by investigating natural, bona fide groups) and the methods (specifically, qualitative methods) used to study them • Increases importance placed on understanding relational dynamics in groups • Foregrounds the voices of group members and their subjective interpretations and experiences of group dynamics
Weaknesses	• Acquiring access to natural, bona fide groups • Acquiring the dense data needed to make claims about symbol usage in groups • Context-bound findings applicable only to particular situations • Research is largely descriptive

(including perceiving themselves as a group) has been asserted by many philosophers. Dewey (1922) argued that ideas about the self, culture, and other matters are formed through communication; Heidegger's (1959) hermeneutic phenomenology viewed reality as being created through everyday language; Schutz's (1967) social phenomenology focused on how intersubjectivity was achieved through meaning created from social interaction; Mead (1934) asserted that social interaction creates and maintains the self, shared meanings, and social structures; and social constructionism argued that communication is the primary process that creates reality for social groups (see, e.g., Gergen, 1985; Pearce, 1995). From such a perspective, symbols are "not just a tool that group members use; groups are best regarded as a phenomenon that emerges from" symbol usage (Frey, 1994a, p. x). Part of the task of the S-I perspective, then, is to understand how members' conception of themselves as a group, and all that the term "group" implies, emerges from their symbolic practices.

3. *Symbolic activities in groups include symbolic predispositions, practices, and processes and products.* The S-I perspective focuses on three permeable and overlapping domains of symbolic activity in groups, each containing specific constructs of interest: symbolic (1) predispositions, (2) practices, and (3) processes and products (see Figure 6.1). *Symbolic predispositions* refer to tendencies that people have toward symbolic behavior, both in terms of practices in which they are predisposed to engage (e.g., their symbolic-management traits and values) and interpretations they make of others based on significant symbols (e.g., attributions based on gender and ethnicity symbols) and others' symbolic practices. Symbolic predispositions, thus, constitute the symbolic resources that people bring to groups—based, in large measure, on their experiences in previous groups and on their current membership in other groups—and draw on to guide their symbolic behavior and the interpretations they make of other people and their symbolic behavior. *Symbolic practices* refer to the specific forms of symbol usage employed by groups and their members, such as dress, gifts, humor, language, *metaphor* (a figure of speech in which a word or phrase that denotes one object is applied to another), *narratives* (stories that are used as organizing schemes), nonverbal behavior, *rites* ("a relatively elaborate, dramatic set of activities that consolidates cultural expressions into one event," Trice & Beyer, 1984, p. 655), *rituals* ("organized symbolic practices and ceremonial activities which serve to define and represent the social and cultural significance of particular occasions, events or changes," O'Sullivan, Hartley, Saunders, Montgomery, & Fiske, 1994, p. 267), and significant symbols. *Symbolic processes and products* refer to both macrolevel group dynamics (e.g., creating community, experiencing dialectical tensions, framing group tasks, establishing group boundaries, developing group climate/culture, promoting member relationships, and producing symbolic convergence) and to the specific outcomes of group symbolic activity (e.g., creating mission/vision

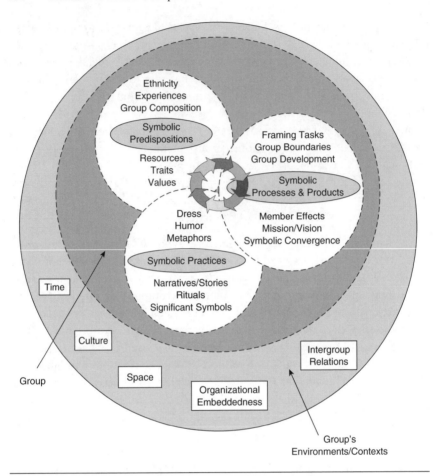

Figure 6.1   Symbolic-interpretive model of group predispositions, practices, processes, and products

SOURCE: Frey and Sunwolf (2004, p. 285). © 2004 Sage Publications, Inc. Reprinted by permission.

statements and making decisions). Processes and products are linked in the model to reflect their recursive and reflexive relationship (e.g., the creating of community in a group is both a process and a product that results from and influences symbolic activity). These three domains are also not mutually exclusive but overlap and influence one another (as indicated, respectively, by the overlapping circles and the bi-directional arrows between the circles in Figure 6.1); members' symbolic values, for instance, are a symbolic predisposition that may produce dialectical tensions in a group, tensions that need to be managed through symbolic practices (e.g., collective use of particular metaphors) that help members to symbolically converge around a group decision, a process that then may result in new or expanded symbolic values for those members. Part of the task of the S-I perspective, therefore, is to understand the nature of and relationships between symbolic predispositions, practices, processes, and products in groups.

4. *Symbolic predispositions, practices, processes, and products are influenced by the environments in which groups are embedded.* The S-I perspective views a group not as a container, a "distinct entity, located in a spatial relationship within a specific context and surrounded by a generalized backdrop called 'social context'" (Putnam & Stohl, 1996, p. 149), but as being interdependent with its relevant contexts (e.g., time, space, and culture). Relevant contexts affect internal group symbolic activity, which, in turn, can affect those contexts. Moreover, contexts are not objective entities independent of group interaction but are created and re-created through symbolic activity engaged in by group members; as Barge and Keyton (1994) explained, "How individuals communicate about their context and make reference to it constructs their view of the environment" (p. 95). Part of the task of the S-I perspective is, thus, to explain how symbolic activity in groups is influenced by and influences the environments within which groups are embedded.

The Study of Groups From the Symbolic-Interpretive Perspective

To do justice to these assumptions, the study of groups from the S-I perspective necessitates theories and methods that privilege the use and interpretation of symbols. These theories and methods demonstrate both unique strengths and weaknesses.

Theoretical Perspectives

The S-I perspective draws on a number of theories that highlight the nature, practices, and consequences of symbolic usage and interpretation in groups. Here, we examine five such theories: (1) the rhetorical perspective, (2) symbolic convergence theory, (3) structuration theory, (4) the dialectical perspective, and (5) the bona fide group perspective.

The *rhetorical perspective* has a long and distinguished history in Western culture. Traditionally, the word *rhetoric* is associated with Aristotle's definition of "discovering the available means of persuasion" (Cooper, 1960, p. 6). This classical conception of rhetoric as strategic, goal-oriented, persuasive messages designed to achieve agreement with the position of the communicator certainly applies to the group context; as Enos (1981) explained, group discussion is rhetorical "when its function is to resolve problems, secure agreements either as a means of promoting solidarity or attaining a particular task-oriented function" (p. 720). Black (1955), for example, showed how members' misuse of persuasive symbolic practices, such as examples and enthymemes, often led to breakdowns in group discussion. Contemporary views of rhetoric, however, have broadened to focus on rhetoric as an "emergent quality of human interaction which creates an intersubjective reality for participants and thus constitutes a way of knowing" (Alderton & Frey, 1986, p. 158). Johnson (1975), for instance, showed how rhetoric created a shared social reality for members of cabalist groups (people who define their enemies as conspirators).

Symbolic convergence theory (SCT) is a particular rhetorical perspective that focuses on how symbol usage creates a group consciousness among a set of people. Those working from this perspective seek to discover the "recurring communicative forms and patterns that indicate the evolution and presence of a shared group consciousness" and to explain "why group consciousnesses arise, continue, decline, and disappear, and the effects such group consciousnesses have in terms of meanings, motives, and communication within the group" (Bormann, 1996, p. 88). Specifically, scholars focus on the sharing of group *fantasies,* "creative and imaginative shared interpretation of events that fulfills a group psychological or rhetorical need" (Bormann, 1996, p. 88), which lead members to symbolically converge on a shared understanding of their group's purposes, practices, processes, and products. Bormann, Pratt, and Putnam (1978), for instance, showed how group members' shared understanding of whether a female should be the leader of the group was affected by the sharing of fantasies related to sex and power, including one fantasy about the tendency of black widow spiders to kill their mates, once fertilized. SCT, thus, explains how symbolic activity influences individuals to achieve shared symbolic ground that allows them to function together as a group.

Structuration theory seeks to explain the processes by which social systems, such as groups, become patterned with respect to collective practices. The theory starts by assuming that "the key to understanding group practices is through analysis of the structures that underlie them" (Poole, Seibold, & McPhee, 1996, p. 117). *Structures* are the *rules* (statements about how things are to be done) and *resources* (e.g., materials, knowledge, and skills) members create or appropriate from other group systems to generate and sustain the group system. *Structuration,* therefore, "refers to the *process by which systems are produced and reproduced through members' use of rules and resources*" (Poole et al., 1996, p. 117; italics in original). Witmer's (1997) ethnographic study of Alcoholics Anonymous, for instance, showed how the structures of the global organization were appropriated and reproduced in the local organizational setting through recursive group practices and individual actions. Hence, this perspective views symbolic activity as both the means of producing a group system and the dynamic product of such a system.

The inevitable and pervasive tensions experienced by group members (e.g., between independence and interdependence), as well as their management through symbolic means, are the focus of the *dialectical perspective.* A *dialectic* is a tension between seemingly contradictory elements (such as members wanting both closeness and distance from other members) that demands at least temporary resolution through symbolic activity. From such a perspective, "a group is constituted in the dynamic interplay of dialectical tensions, exigencies, and communicative responses among members of an assembly within its relevant contexts" (Johnson & Long, 2002, p. 31; see also Barge & Frey, 1997; Smith & Berg, 1987). Braithwaite, Baxter, and Harper (1998), for instance, examined the role of symbolic activities (specifically, rituals) in helping to manage the dialectical tensions experienced in step- or blended-family groups.

Finally, challenging the concept that a group is a fixed entity or container, the bona fide group (BFG) perspective argues that a group cannot be understood apart from the contexts and environments within which it is embedded (see Frey, 2003; Putnam & Stohl, 1990, 1996). A bona fide group demonstrates *permeable boundaries* (socially constructed, porous borders that are negotiated, defined, and redefined through members' interactions) and *interdependence with its contexts* (e.g., political and financial contexts). Lammers and Krikorian (1997), for instance, demonstrated how permeable boundaries, as reflected in changing group membership, and interdependence with relevant contexts, such as the institutional norms of the organization, affected the internal communication of medical surgical teams. The BFG perspective, thus, focuses on the symbolic construction of a group and the ways in which internal group communication is affected by and, in turn, affects the external environments in which a group is embedded.

Methodological Practices

Although much may be learned about symbol usage in groups, especially regarding symbolic management, via the use of positivistic research methods (e.g., quantitative laboratory studies), research from the S-I perspective, especially that directed toward a symbolic-constitutive understanding, tends to be consistent with the assumptions and practices of the naturalistic paradigm. Philosophically, proponents of the naturalistic paradigm believe that (1) realities are multiple and intersubjective (the ontological assumption), (2) there is an interdependent relationship between the researcher and that which is being researched (the epistemological assumption), and (3) research is value laden (the axiological assumption) (see, e.g., Lincoln & Guba, 1985).

According to Potter (1996), the research that emerges from these assumptions—*naturalistic inquiry*—demonstrates three general characteristics: (1) *naturalism*—phenomena are studied in their natural contexts (as opposed to researcher-created settings), (2) *phenomenological*—researchers set aside preconceived expectations to understand how participants make sense of their behavior, and (3) *interpretive*—observations made by participants and by researchers are woven together to produce rich descriptions and explanations. More specifically, research on groups from the S-I perspective (1) occurs *inductively* (moving from specific evidence to general explanations); (2) is driven by the goal of *holistic understanding of patterns and behaviors characterizing groups;* (3) employs an emergent design (taking advantage of opportunities occurring during the research process); (4) relies primarily on *qualitative methods* (data that take the form of symbols other than meaningful numbers acquired via participant observation, in-depth interviewing, and textual-analytic techniques such as discourse analysis); and (5) results in *case studies,* detailed examinations of a single subject, group, or phenomenon (see, e.g., Yin, 2003), that offer *context-bound findings* (applicable to the particular people, situation, and/or time period studied and applied tentatively to other, even similar, contexts) (see Frey, Botan, & Kreps, 2000; Lincoln & Guba, 1985; for application of these methods to the study of groups, see Frey, 1994b).

Strengths and Weaknesses of the Symbolic-Interpretive Perspective

The assumptions, theories, and methodological practices of the S-I perspective of group life, and the representative research reviewed in the next section of this chapter, demonstrate both strengths and weaknesses. With regard to strengths, first, although much of the work from the S-I perspective has taken place in only a couple of disciplines—namely, anthropology, communication, and sociology—the perspective is potentially highly interdisciplinary, with scholars from many disciplines being able to contribute to understanding symbol usage in groups. Second, the perspective broadens the landscape of groups studied (by investigating natural, bona fide groups) and the methods used to study them (specifically, via qualitative methods). Third, although group task work certainly remains of interest to scholars studying symbol usage in groups, understanding relational dynamics takes on increased importance, in part, because a group's task reality cannot be separated from the group's social reality, as relationships in groups significantly affect the tasks groups confront, and vice versa (see Frey, 1994b, 1996; Keyton, 1999). Moreover, meeting people's socioemotional needs in families, support groups, residential groups, children's or adolescents' groups, sports teams, social groups, consciousness-raising groups, covens, cults, gangs, and the other types of relationally oriented groups that S-I scholars often study requires extensive symbolic activity. Fourth, in uncovering people's symbol usage, S-I scholarship foregrounds the voices of group members and their (inter)subjective interpretations and experiences of group life.

There are, however, a number of weaknesses demonstrated by the S-I perspective of group life. First, scholars cannot always acquire access to the natural, bona fide groups they wish to study, either because the members are not interested in being studied or because they don't want their activities observed. Second, even when scholars gain access, they may not be able to engage in the type of longitudinal research that this perspective typically demands. Third, although S-I scholars seek a holistic understanding of group symbolic activity, they may ultimately be forced to focus on only a few key symbolic activities because of practical considerations such as time constraints. Fourth, although the analysis of qualitative data has recently received extensive treatment, there still remains a lack of standard ways to make sense of such data. Moreover, researchers must contend with different interpretations that might be made of the same symbolic activity by group members versus researchers or by other researchers who might observe the same phenomenon. Fifth, although the case studies of groups that result from this research are valuable (see Gouran, 1994), they yield only context-bound findings, applicable to the particular situation studied, leading to a slow process of knowledge accumulation and the lack of generalizability of findings across groups. Finally, perhaps because of these weaknesses, research from the S-I perspective has remained relatively descriptive of symbolic activity in groups, with little understanding of the predictive relationships between symbolic predispositions, practices, processes, and products and few prescriptive suggestions regarding how to facilitate symbolic activity in groups.

Answers to the Seven Questions

Given this understanding of the S-I perspective of group life, we use the remainder of this chapter to discuss what research conducted from this tradition reveals about the seven questions about groups posed for consideration for this volume. Although these are not necessarily the questions that would rise to the top from an S-I perspective (they probably are more appropriate for an alternative perspective, such as the functional perspective), for each question, we offer some conclusions that can be drawn from the extant literature (summarized in Table 6.2) and pose a series of questions worth exploring in future research.

What Facets of Group Composition Affect the Group's Interaction and Performance?

An S-I perspective sheds important light on how various facets of group composition might be conceived by researchers and how they potentially affect group formation, interaction, and performance. At both the individual and the collective level, group composition constitutes an important symbolic predisposition that can serve as both an impediment to symbolic activity and a symbolic resource.

First, although some of the characteristics that distinguish group members—such as demographics, traits, needs, beliefs, attitudes, and values (for overviews of relevant research, see, e.g., Haslett & Ruebush, 1999; Shaw, 1981)—have their genesis in physical or biological foundations (e.g., sex and race), from an S-I perspective, these characteristics constitute significant symbols whose importance is derived from a socially constructed process. This is true, in part, because these characteristics are conveyed largely through symbolic means, such as self-presentation style, with characteristics such as gender, race, and age each having its own distinct semaphore. At a deeper level, however, as Frey (2000) explained, "Diversity itself is not an inherent, predetermined condition per se; it is a symbolic concept that is created and sustained through interaction" (p. 226). Even the meaning or significance of traditional demographic variables changes over time (see Rodriguez, 1998), as evidenced, for example, by the broadened conceptualization of males and females to include the psychological sex-role orientations of male, female, and androgynous individuals (see Bem, 1981).

Second, member characteristics affect both an individual group member's behavior and a group's collective behavior. At the individual level, people often choose to become members of groups on the basis of perceived homogeneity of members. Blau (1977) and McPherson and Smith-Lovin

Table 6.2   Key Findings of Symbolic-Interpretive Research

Group composition	• Member characteristics constitute significant symbols whose importance is derived from a socially constructed process
	• Member characteristics affect both individual group members' behavior and a group's collective behavior
	• People enter groups with important predispositions that affect their view of group behavior and their symbolic behavior in groups, especially the communicative behavior in which they engage
	• Groups may take on personality and communication traits from the composition of their members
	• Group composition as a symbolic predisposition has important effects on group practices, processes, and products
	• Homogeneous groups often form strong ingroup identities that may unite members but prevent them from working effectively with other groups; in such instances, they may need symbolic practices to transcend their particular group identities
	• To manage the tensions created by diversity, heterogeneous groups often create symbols of the collectivity or engage in other symbolic practices to unify diverse members across competing identities
	• Tasks that demand more symbolic behavior tend to benefit from diverse member backgrounds
	• Positive or negative effects of group composition may reflect the extent to which groups are successful in managing diversity using symbolic practices
Group projects	• Group members symbolically frame and reframe their group's projects for a variety of purposes, often to create a shared sense of group purpose and identity
	• Symbolic framing of a group's tasks is particularly important for recruiting new members
	• In the most extreme instances, symbolic framing of a group's projects may create a group identity that does not tolerate individual autonomy
	• Symbolic management, including reframing, of a group's projects may be especially important when those projects are perceived negatively by members
	• Group projects vary in terms of their symbolic nature or the need for symbolic interaction, with some being relatively nonsymbolic and others being highly symbolic
	• The symbolic nature of the project influences the symbolic activity group members use to accomplish the project

(Continued)

Table 6.2 (Continued)

	• Symbolic framing of a group's projects affects group interaction and performance • Some group projects may be so powerfully framed, especially in terms of their consequences, that members must engage in symbolic activity to manage the potential tensions that could result from a disastrous group process
Group structure	• In some cases, people enter groups with symbolic conceptions of what structures (rules and resources that members use during their interaction to generate and sustain the group system) ought to guide group practices and processes • Although people may enter groups with some preexisting rules and resources and preferences for their use, structures are appropriated, produced, and reproduced through group symbolic activity; this ongoing process of structuration occurs through group members' interactions • Roles in general, and emergent leadership more specifically, are related to group members' symbolic behavior • Rites and rituals provide members with significant symbolic meaning regarding their group experience; they are especially important in creating and sustaining group identity and commitment and for managing the dialectical tensions of group life • Group structures are influenced, in part, by the medium through which groups communicate
Interaction	• Significant symbols (especially metaphors) and narratives (stories) are important symbolic practices that affect group members and group processes and products • Symbolic objects and gifts are a form of interaction that can create meaning for group members, especially in terms of fostering connections among members of a group or between groups, and they often become important symbols of a group's collective memory • Particular types of group interaction, such as discussion and dialogue, may have important consequences for group symbolic practices, processes, and products • Groups engage in a number of symbolic practices to frame and manage members' negative behaviors

Table 6.2 (Continued)

Group action/outcomes	• Group actions (practices and processes) can result in the creation of new and important symbols that help members to understand their lived experience, the society in which they live, and their worldviews • Participation in groups affects people at an emotional level, especially the emotions they have toward their group experience, with those emotions, in turn, affecting group processes and products [and, potentially, people's subsequent actions] in the world • People's experiences in groups can affect people's perceptions of and participation in future groups • Group actions often create unique symbols that bind members together into a group • Disenfranchised groups sometimes engage in symbolic reversal, reclaiming symbols that carry negative connotative meanings by inverting them so as to promote positive feelings and self-image • Collective group action can result in important effects in the world
Change over time	• Group development and the concepts relevant to it (e.g., stages and phases) are themselves ephemeral symbols constructed by scholars to reference phenomena that seemingly occur in groups • Group development is characterized by changes in symbolic practices and processes • Changes in symbolic practices over the course of group development occur in relation to the experience and management of dialectical tensions, tensions that are then managed by symbolic practices • Symbolic practices are used to weather changes within the group • Symbolic practices can be used to help members cope with the tensions associated with group endings
Ecology	• Group members symbolically construct a boundary that separates their group from its now-perceived external contexts • Boundaries between ingroup and outgroups often cause tensions that need to be managed via symbolic practices • Because group boundaries are interactionally created and re-created as an ongoing process, they can shift and change, often as a result of new members joining, new information obtained, and the creation of subgroups within a group

(Continued)

Table 6.2 (Continued)

- Although physical space is important, it is the symbolic meaning and contour that people give to space that transforms it into a "place," leading to place attachment, the emotional bonding of people and groups to particular spaces
- Groups symbolically construct time in different ways
- Discourse characterizing group interaction is often influenced by the external environments within which a group is embedded
- Groups may experience interactional difficulties because of participants' multiple memberships in various other groups, especially in cases where group members are representatives of other groups or constituencies
- Group products are significantly affected (both positively and negatively) by relevant contexts
- Because of the problems that groups experience due to the influence of their relevant contexts, they may try to isolate themselves from those contexts and become symbolic containers, but those external influences may still be felt, sometimes as a result of crisis
- Groups do need to insulate themselves from their relevant contexts so as to develop their own social space to a certain degree, which allows for the discovery of commonalities among members and promotes trust and relationship building
- Too much insulation can have negative effects on group processes and products, with insulated groups being less effective in accomplishing their projects than groups that reach out to their external environments

(1987), for instance, found that "birds of a feather flock together," with most people picking friendship groups that are similar to themselves in terms of members' gender, race, age, education, and other symbolically highlighted characteristics.

The S-I perspective also suggests that people enter groups with important predispositions that affect their view of groups and their symbolic behavior in groups. Bion (1961) was one of the first scholars to examine individuals' predispositions toward groups. Working from the classic distinction drawn between task and socioemotional dimensions of group life, Bion observed that group members sometimes focused too much on socioemotional activities and avoided working on the task because they were oriented toward certain "basic assumptions": (1) *dependency*—relying on other members, especially the leader, to provide direction and make decisions; (2) *fight-flight*—engaging in conflict with other members (fight) or physically or psychologically leaving the situation (flight); and (3) *pairing*—forming dyadic alliances. Lion and Gruenfeld (1993) showed a relationship between these predispositions and members' behavior in academic self-study groups, with those oriented toward a work mode being dominant, friendly, task oriented, and emotionally controlled; those oriented toward dependency or flight being submissive, friendly, and emotionally expressive; those oriented toward fight being dominant and unfriendly; and those oriented toward pairing being friendly.

A recent, intriguing approach to understanding people's orientations toward groups has to do with the negative predispositions that lead people to detest, loathe, or abhor working in groups. Freeman (1996), for instance, found that students' negative attitudes toward working in groups was associated with less success in the academic environment as measured by grades, whereas the opposite was the case for students who held positive attitudes. Keyton, Harmon, and Frey (1996) developed and tested a scale to measure "grouphate," finding that scores on the scale were related to members' evaluations of their work groups; specifically, as members' identification of more positive attributes about working in groups increased, their negative feelings about group work decreased. Grouphate may also affect members' active participation in group socialization and task-oriented activities (Keyton et al., 1996) and inhibit the effectiveness of formal structures (e.g., brainstorming) groups use to enhance their task outcomes (Keyton & Frey, 2002; Sunwolf & Seibold, 1998).

Group members' predispositions toward symbolic behavior have also been studied from the traditional perspective of *traits,* distinguishable and enduring ways in which people differ from one another (for a recent review of research on traits in groups, see Keyton & Frey, 2002). The S-I perspective is particularly concerned with those traits that affect people's tendencies toward symbolic behavior and their responses to others' symbolic behavior. For instance, the personality trait of *locus of control,* the extent to which people attribute responsibility for their own and others' behavior to internal or external forces (see Rotter, 1966), has been shown to affect individual and collective preferences for the way in which attribution-of-responsibility arguments are symbolically constructed, with "internals" preferring arguments that hold people accountable on the basis of personality, ability, effort, or motivation, and "externals" preferring arguments that attribute responsibility to external factors such as other people, the environment, fate, and luck (Alderton, 1980, 1982; Alderton & Frey, 1983). Scholars have also identified a number of *communication traits* that "account for enduring consistencies and differences in individual message-sending and message-receiving behaviors among individuals" (Infante et al., 2003, p. 77) in groups. For example, a summary by McCroskey and Richmond (1992) of the literature on *communication apprehension* (CA), "an individual's level of fear or anxiety associated with either real or anticipated communication with another person or persons" (McCroskey, 1977, p. 78), showed that CA had significant effects on group members' amount and type of talk and choice of seating, as well as on how they were perceived by other members with regard to credibility, the relevance of their contributions, and leadership.

At the collective level, groups may take on personality and communication traits from the composition of their members. Cattell (1948) was one of the first scholars to argue that groups possess personality traits that are analogous to individual personality traits and that can be inferred from group behavior, proposing the concept of *group syntality* to reference the personality of a group. Bion (1961) later claimed that group personality traits develop, in part, from members' individual predispositions, but even more important, from the patterns of interpersonal dynamics that occur in groups. Few scholars since, however, have investigated group traits (for relevant attempts, see van de Wetering's, 1996, articulation of authoritarianism as a group-level adaptation and Kraus's, 1997, theory of group aggression).

Group composition as a symbolic predisposition also has important effects on group practices, processes, and products. For instance, homogeneous groups often form strong ingroup identities that may unite members but prevent them from working effectively with other groups; in such instances, they may need symbolic practices to transcend their particular group identities. A classic study on intergroup relations conducted in the 1950s, called the "Robber's Cave Experiment," showed that two homogeneous groups of schoolboys created strong ingroup identities and expressed hostility toward the other group, especially under competitive conditions, but that these groups were later able to come together as a cohesive group when they were asked to orient themselves toward common, superordinate goals that included finding drinking water and securing a movie (see Sherif, Harvey, White, Hood, & Sherif, 1988).

Heterogeneous groups, in contrast, can create problems in interpersonal relations and communication among members that must be overcome (see, e.g., Kirchmeyer, 1993; Kirchmeyer & Cohen, 1992). Kanter's (1977) investigation of group diversity showed that the majority members (males, in this case) controlled the group and determined its culture, including the language used in communicating with minority members, with females viewed as "tokens." To manage the tensions created by diversity, heterogeneous groups often create symbols of the collectivity or engage in other symbolic practices to unify diverse members across competing identities. Schwalbe's (1996) ethnographic study of a men's group with little in common except for a feeling of alienation from traditional masculinity and feminism showed how the men forged a common bond through a pastiche of cultural symbols, including performing Native American rituals (sweat lodges) and sharing folktales from around the world.

Finally, the research on group composition is mixed with regard to group products. Some research suggests that heterogeneous groups—in terms of ethnicity (Ling, 1990), gender (Hoffman, Harburg, & Maier, 1962), and attitudes (Triandis, Hall, & Ewen, 1965)—produce higher quality solutions than do homogeneous groups, especially with regard to creative, innovative, and rapidly changing tasks (Eisenhart & Schoonhoven, 1990; Kono, 1988; Nemeth, 1986; Pelz & Andrews, 1976). In other cases, diversity has shown negative results for both group performance and member morale (Ancona & Caldwell, 1992; Wiersema & Bird, 1993). Perhaps the differences in these results reflect, in part, the type of task groups confront, with tasks that demand more symbolic behavior, such as generating ideas (Pelled, Eisenhardt, & Xin, 1999) or promoting therapy in adult psychotherapeutic groups (Kaplan & Sadock, 1993), tending to benefit from diverse member backgrounds. Perhaps these different results also reflect the extent to which groups are successful in managing diversity using symbolic practices. Watson, Kumar, and Michaelsen (1993) found that diverse groups are usually slower to reach their performance peak than their homogeneous counterparts due to the necessity of establishing a common symbolic framework for communication and other group actions.

The S-I perspective, thus, offers an interesting perspective on the nature and effects of group composition. We suggest the following questions as a research agenda: (1) What additional ways are there of conceiving of and assessing individual predispositions toward symbolic behavior in groups and understanding group composition in terms of symbolic predispositions? (2) How do various combinations of individuals' symbolic predispositions affect group practices, processes, and products? (3) In what types of groups (e.g., high- versus low-cohesive groups) would one expect to find more or less symbolic activity directed toward the creation of a common identity? (4) How do group symbolic practices, processes, and products influence members' predispositions? (5) How might groups themselves demonstrate symbolic traits?

How Do the Group's Projects Affect
Its Interaction and Performance?

From an S-I perspective, an important aspect of group life involves the need for a group to symbolically construct and interpret the nature of its projects. Even when these projects have been predetermined by the external environment, group members must interpret them and determine how to proceed. Such interpretive work takes place via symbolic behavior engaged in by members, and once a group reaches some shared understanding of its projects, their accomplishment occurs via symbolic behavior. Moreover, as explained previously, from an S-I perspective, group projects include not only traditional group tasks but also group identity formation, relationship development among members, and other aspects of the relational dimension of group life.

First, group members symbolically frame and reframe their group's projects for a variety of purposes. For instance, projects are often symbolically framed to create a shared sense of group purpose and identity and to influence group interaction and performance. In a series of case studies on symphonies, rescue teams, hospital teams, and groups in the military, computer industry, government, and crisis management, Lipman-Blumen and Leavitt (1999) described what they called "hot groups," whose members were intensely obsessed with symbolically redefining whatever tasks confronted them as personally ennobling missions and, thereby, creating for group members a sense of mission and commitment, no matter how trivial the original goal.

The symbolic framing of a group's projects is particularly important for recruiting new members. For instance, in investigating how individuals come to join cults, Snow, Zurcher, and Ekland-Olson (1980) found that the central mechanism is *frame alignment*, the rhetorical process of creating a shared ideology by persuading a recruit to see the world in the same way as does the group. The creation of a shared ideological stance—called *micromobilization* by Snow et al.—provides the basis for engagement between recruits and the group, as well as concerted action by the group. Some groups even manipulate symbols during member recruitment so as to be more attractive to target members. Martin and Thomas (2000) discussed strategies that counseling groups have for attracting "shy" college students, including advertisements that reframe "therapy group" to "clinic" to minimize any implication of psychopathology.

In the most extreme instances, such framing may create a group identity that does not tolerate individual autonomy. A study by Perloff (1993) of the Jonestown massacre, in which 910 individuals committed voluntary suicide together, indicates that a process of deindividuation narratives may have focused members away from themselves, stripping them of personal identity. Such extreme groups may be attractive to potential members because of their past experiences and because they perceive the group's projects in favorable ways. In a study of the Unification Church ("Moonies"), Galanter (1989) discovered that recruits who were most attracted to the Church were those who had previously experienced the greatest amount of emotional distress and saw the Church as a support group. Moreover, the symbolic framing of group projects can look quite different depending on whether one is a group member or an outsider. Conquergood's (1991, 1992, 1994) longitudinal ethnographic studies of street gangs in Chicago, for example, revealed that whereas outsiders viewed the goals of gangs in extremely negative terms, such as killing people and dealing drugs, gang members themselves perceived their group's goals to be creating family, enacting brotherhood, and protecting their community.

Symbolic management of a group's projects, including reframing, may be especially important when those projects are perceived negatively by members. Denison and Sutton (1990), for example, found that operating teams of doctors and nurses, faced with tasks that they often perceived to be boring, used humorous communication to reduce tension and relieve boredom, and Vinton (1989) reported that members of work groups used humor to draw social relationships into the task—via self-ridiculing jokes, for instance—particularly when the task was viewed as stressful, signaling to coworkers that one was willing to participate in a friendly, informal relationship. Moreover, in some cases, a group's projects may prove unobtainable, demanding either that the group engage in symbolic reframing or else disband. In an early, well-known study on cognitive dissonance, Festinger, Riecken, and Schacter (1956) penetrated a group (the Seekers) whose members believed that, on a specific date, a flood would destroy their hometown and the faithful few would be saved at midnight by a spaceship. When the group gathered on that fateful day and nothing happened, members were at first confused and disturbed, but one leader swiftly issued a new narrative, enthusiastically adopted by group members, that their faith had been so strong in waiting for the flood and the spaceship that the deities spared everyone. For awhile, this reframing renewed members' commitment to the group and even attracted some new members.

Second, group projects vary in terms of their symbolic nature or the need for symbolic interaction, with some being relatively nonsymbolic (e.g., a group physically moving furniture) and others being highly symbolic (e.g., a group engaging in spiritual practices). The symbolic nature of the project undoubtedly influences the symbolic activity group members use to accomplish it. Members of social support groups, for instance, consistently engage in extensive storytelling to establish commonality of experiences and emotions (e.g., Cawyer & Smith-Dupré, 1995), and certain cultural groups use indirect group storytelling rather than direct lecturing or moralizing to teach members the group's values, such as the storytelling displayed in African dilemma tales, Native American lesson stories, and Sufi wisdom tales (see Sunwolf, 1999a). Certain projects also seem to provoke symbolic practices and processes that affect group products. When a decision-making group decides to vote, for example, the symbolic influence of the voting process may influence subsequent outcomes, notwithstanding the group discussion or reasons for members' positions. Putnam (1986) concluded that voting procedures are symbolic methods a group may use to withdraw from conflict, but that those procedures can also be used to reduce uncertainty about group decisions and to equalize power in the group. The symbolic representation, through voting rules, of initial disagreement may affect a group's ability to reach consensus; for example, Kerr and MacCoun (1985) found that public polling rather than the use of a secret ballot increased the likelihood of a hung jury. Groups may even employ the wrong types of symbols for a particular project, with Johnson and Hackman (1995) reporting that groups may rely too much on words and mathematical symbols as problem-solving tools in situations where visualization or drawing may be better suited.

Third, the symbolic framing of a group's projects affects group interaction and performance. Adelman and Frey's (1994, 1997) study of an AIDS residence showed how the rhetorical framing of the residence as "a place to live with AIDS" and not a place to die (e.g., a hospice) influenced the types of interactions that occurred there. Adelman and Frey (1997) provided the following narrative and explanation to illustrate such influence:

> Terrance recounted his first day, sitting alone in his new room, wondering if he had made a good choice. Maria, another resident, knocked on the door, poked her head in, and said, "Well, I hope you came here to live and not to die," a reassurance that made him realize that things would be OK. This vision is more than a rhetorical veil; it not only emphasizes the importance of remaining active and healthy, it also wards off the shroud of inevitable and imminent mortality. (p. 35)

Some group projects like this may be so powerfully framed, especially in terms of their consequences (e.g., life and death), that members must engage in symbolic activity to manage the potential tensions that could result from a disastrous group process. Sunwolf (2001) identified a nonsummative, group-level process of real-world jurors deliberating in criminal trials, who engage in interactions characterized by "anticipatory group regret" that focused on anticipating the possibilities of a wrong verdict and the effects that might have on other people. To reduce their anxieties, jurors engaged in counterattitudinal (contrary to the known facts) storytelling, symbolically fantasizing about possible consequences of a guilty or not guilty verdict. Group processes were further affected as story battles ensued about the validity of the fictional narratives.

The S-I perspective, thus, demonstrates both the symbolic significance of a group's projects and the effects that significance can have on group practices, processes, and products. Questions that might profitably guide future research include: (1) How do groups and their members symbolically interpret and reinterpret their projects, and what factors affect such interpretations? (2) To what degree are groups successful in reframing their projects when the original framing is ineffective or unobtainable? (3) How do group symbolic practices, processes, and products differ depending on the type of group projects (e.g., providing social support versus making decisions)?

How Are Groups Structured, What Tools and Technologies Do They Have Access to, and How Do Those Structures and Technologies Affect Group Interaction and Performance?

The S-I perspective is particularly interested in how symbolic practices and processes, with regard to both group tasks and members' relationships, are structured. Tools and technologies that may affect group structures are conceived of both as external devices, processes, or resources that a group uses to enhance its interactional processes and as symbolic interpretations of meanings and individual resources that members bring to and create in groups. A number of relevant group structuring constructs emerge from the S-I perspective; these constructs are dynamic and fluid, changing over time because of perceived circumstances or varying contexts.

First, in some cases, people enter groups with symbolic conceptions of what structures ought to guide group practices and processes. Sunwolf and Seibold (1998), for instance, found that citizens waiting to be called for jury service in a courthouse brought with them, and were able to immediately describe and apply, specific structuring rules for their anticipated group verdict-rendering task, such as how time should be used and valued, how leadership should be created, what symbolic meaning should be contained in a "note" sent to the judge about the jury's competency to perform the task, and how dialectical tensions between loyalty to the group (jury) and loyalty to the organization (judicial system) should be resolved.

Second, although people may enter groups with some preexisting rules and resources and preferences for their use, as structuration theory maintains, structures are appropriated, produced, and reproduced through group symbolic activity. Scholars have explicated, for instance, the structuration of arguments in groups, including how arguments are sometimes produced by "tag-team" discourse among group members (see Canary, Brossman, & Seibold, 1987; Seibold, McPhee, Poole, Tanita, & Canary, 1981). As Meyers and Seibold (1990) concluded, group argument involves "the production of interactive messages in group discussion. These messages are patterned, rule governed, and collaboratively produced" (p. 287).

Third, one important structure that has been related to group members' symbolic behavior is roles, in general, and emergent leadership, more specifically. Sharf (1978), for instance, offered a rhetorical analysis of group leadership emergence, demonstrating in a detailed study of two task groups how emergent leaders used key symbols to create a rhetorical vision of the group that helped to dissipate tensions resulting from divisions within the group, create bonds of identification within the group, and induce cooperation among members. Schultz (1974, 1978, 1982, 1986) showed how emergent leadership could be predicted from the quality of the symbolic activity in which group members engaged, such as communicative behavior that set goals, gave directions, and summarized group discussion. Such results are in line with research showing that task group leaders participate at a higher rate than do other members (see Hare, Blumberg, Davies, & Kent, 1994), suggesting that leaders may assume a rule of communication entitlement and/or that nonleaders may behave in ways that defer communication opportunities as a result of bestowing the "symbol" of leadership on certain members.

Two especially intriguing structures from an S-I perspective are group rites and rituals. As "stylized, repetitive, communicative enactments" (Bruess & Pearson, 1997, p. 25) that occur routinely in groups, rites and rituals provide members with significant symbolic meaning regarding their group experience; they are especially important in creating and sustaining group identity and commitment (Kanter, 1972) and in managing the dialectical tensions of group life (see, e.g., Bell, 1992; Turner, 1969). Baxter and Clark (1996), for instance, showed how rituals practiced in both Asian-American and Euro-American families functioned to symbolize the well-being of the family group, create attachment and bonding between members, and reproduce group identity. Using symbolic convergence theory and fantasy theme analysis, Putnam, Van Hoeven, and Bullis (1991) demonstrated how rituals enacted by bargainers and team members during negotiations between administrators and teachers in two school districts functioned to frame the meaning of the bargaining rite quite differently, with one group viewing it as "the symbolic process of sharing unsolved problems, releasing tensions, and working with the other side on a document" and the other group viewing it as "'a necessary evil' or 'a distasteful process' forced on them by the law" (p. 100). The researchers interpreted this symbolic divergence between groups as providing support for Weick's (1979) contention that groups, especially those experiencing conflict, coalesce around means (symbolic practices and processes) rather than ends (symbolic products). Rites and rituals, however, may also result in shared symbolic products; for example, Adelman and Frey (1994, 1997) showed how the collective ritual of a balloon ceremony held for each member of the AIDS residence who died not only helped the remaining members to remember the deceased but also to "re-member" as a group through the "purposive, significant unification" that comes from the act of recollection (Myeroff, 1982, p. 111).

Finally, group structures are influenced, in part, by the medium through which groups communicate. Today, in large measure because of the dispersed nature of group work, many groups use technological means to communicate among members, including electronic meeting systems (e.g., videoconferencing) and various computer-supported group software (e.g., Lotus notes). These technologies serve as an infrastructure that affects group symbolic practices, processes, and products. For instance, a number of researchers, using structuration theory, have focused on how members appropriate technology in their group interactions and how such appropriations mediate the impact of that technology (see, e.g., DeSanctis & Poole, 1994; Poole & DeSanctis, 1990, 1992; Poole, Holmes, & DeSanctis, 1991). Poole and DeSanctis (1992) distinguished two aspects of technological structures: the structural features built into a particular technology (e.g., giving each group member one vote) and the symbolic "spirit" of a particular technology, the general goals and attitudes the technology promotes (e.g., democratic decision making). Poole, DeSanctis, Kirsch, and Jackson (1995) documented how different appropriations of the spirit of technology (group decision support systems) influenced the quality of team efforts. Even the technical features of technology may influence symbolic activity in groups: Meier's (2003) detailed analysis of a short episode recorded during a business meeting conducted via videoconferencing technology revealed that technical features such as time lag, unpredictable sound systems, and limited resolution of television screens led to different interpretations of the same discourse by the two groups involved, creating at each site a sense of "us" and "them."

The S-I perspective, thus, suggests the type of structures that groups create, ways in which those structures are created and re-created, and the effects of such structures on group symbolic practices, processes, and products. Questions that would usefully extend our knowledge include: (1) What theories might be developed to further understand, explain, and predict the relationship between symbol usage and group structures? (2) What are the effects of different tools and technologies on group symbolic practices, processes, and products? (3) How can group structuring practices and processes be manipulated (e.g., by facilitators, group leaders, and/or group members)?

What Kinds of Group Interaction Processes Does the Group Carry Out and How Do These Functions Affect Other Factors and Performance?

Group interaction processes are particularly germane to the S-I perspective, as such processes are accomplished through the use of symbols. The construction of mutual understanding is a central task of group work, and communication has long been assumed to rest on a foundation of shared understanding (see, e.g., Clark & Marshall, 1981; Fussell & Krauss, 1992; Krauss & Fussell, 1990). Clark (1985) has consistently pointed out that successful relational communication requires complex perspective taking, in which participants are able to identify their mutual knowledge and develop an awareness of the shared knowledge of relevant others. Communication in group discussions, of course, is more complex and necessarily requires more complex perspective taking than dyadic relationships. The S-I perspective, consequently, is particularly helpful for understanding how symbolic activities connect individuals to an entity larger than themselves, as symbols produce networks of shared reference points around which group members (who might otherwise have little in common) coalesce and, in so doing, create and sustain "groupness." Once in place, these networks generate new, meaningful symbols that further define, clarify, or change the boundaries and identities of a group, its interaction processes, and, potentially, its products. We have already discussed (and will discuss in the remaining questions) a number of symbolic practices and processes; here, we focus on some additional meaningful symbolic practices that groups employ.

First, significant symbols (especially metaphors) and narratives (stories) are important symbolic practices that affect group members and group processes and products. Adelman and Frey (1994, 1997), for instance, showed how the metaphor of "family" initially united relatively homogeneous members of an AIDS residence but subsequently became contested because of its hierarchical and patriarchal implications (e.g., staff as parents heading the household) as the amount of diversity increased in the residence, leading to the use of the significant symbol of "community," which better referenced that diversity. Adelman and Frey (1997) pointed out, however, that all symbols are open to being contested, as some residents saw community as a positive symbol (one said, "Community is like a forest. You've got to have a little bit of everything or the forest dies," p. 39), whereas others saw it negatively (with one member seeing the residence as "a jungle, a zoo sometimes," p. 39). Such symbolic practices potentially have important implications; for example, Frey, Adelman, Flint, and Query (2000) later found that residents' perceptions of the residence as a community (rather than as an institution or as a hospice), as well as their satisfaction in living there, could be predicted from the extent to which residents participated in the collective practices of the residence (specifically, governance/support practices, such as weekly house meetings and support groups, and everyday/special practices, such as prayer services and social events).

Another important and common form of discourse in groups is the production of narratives or stories (see, e.g., Bruner, 1987; Polkinghorne, 1988; Riessman, 1993; Sarbin, 1986). Narratives are used as organizing schemas (Mandler & Johnson, 1977) and as interpretive tools (Bennett, 1978), particularly when groups face complex decision-making tasks (Pennington & Hastie, 1986). Bennett (1992), for instance, found that mock jurors use story structures to organize and reorganize large amounts of constantly changing, complex evidence. Stories also often function as arguments for a given idea or proposal during group discussion or as a way to extend, interpret, or clarify a point of discussion (Meyers, Brashers, Winston, & Grob, 1997). Sunwolf (1999b), examining deliberation videotapes of criminal trials, found that group discussion was story laden, with jurors importing real-life narratives, as well as fictionalized trial evidence, by engaging in imaginative storytelling (e.g., what-if stories, if-only stories, and common knowledge stories). Furthermore, jurors engaged in symbolic story battles, arguing with one another about fantasized story possibilities that were not contained in the trial evidence.

When told in a group setting, stories help members to achieve symbolic convergence by communicating group norms and values, as well as by coordinating activities toward common goals (see Sunwolf & Frey, 2001); they are particularly effective for assimilating new members into a group's culture (Brown, 1985; Stohl, 1986) and for creating connections among group members. Creanza and McWhirter (1994), for instance, described how "narrative reminiscence" was used as a process strategy to enhance group effectiveness with elderly women. Women living in retirement communities were assigned the pregroup task of recovering memories of their childhood, working life, psychological stress, and gender; these "retrieved" narratives were then shared during group conversations and resulted in the formation of new and deeper connections among members.

Second, symbolic objects and gifts have long been recognized as a form of interaction that can create meaning for group members, especially in terms of fostering connection among group members or between groups. Polanyi (1944) and Sahlins (1972) showed how, until very recently in human history, the exchange of gifts was not about gaining profit but about forging and maintaining group solidarity. The "kula ring" of the Trobriand Islands is one of the most famous examples, in which kinship networks are maintained across a large archipelago by men who perform an annual circuit of ritual trade, paddling over to nearby islands in canoes to exchange shell necklaces and armbands. The "potlatch" ceremonies of the Native American tribes of the Pacific Northwest—in which a tribal leader threw a feast and inundated guests from associated tribes with gifts—served a similar purpose.

Objects and gifts often become important symbols of a group's collective memory. Adelman and Frey (1997) described the process of dispossession that took place as members of the AIDS residence they studied gave away their possessions just before they died; these objects functioned as symbols by which residents wished to be remembered by their fellow group members. As Adelman (1992) contended, "The symbolic meaning of the object itself and its use in facilitating interaction can serve as rituals for departing, as spiritual companions for those who survive, and as visible markers for reaffirming community purpose" (p. 401). Group memory may also be symbolized in photographs or preserved in scrapbooks that provide an important link between individuals and the group; for insiders, "going over the scrapbook together serves as a kind of intensification ritual, re-validating interpersonal bonds, and mutually enriching participants' perspectives on past events" (Katriel & Farrell, 1991, p. 13).

Third, scholars have differentiated particular types of group interaction that may have important consequences for group symbolic practices, processes, and products. Barge (2002), for example, working from a language game perspective in which "discourse among members of a community reflects their underlying view of reality and shared understandings" (p. 160), drew a distinction between *group discussion* and *group dialogue* as deliberative forms of group talk. Barge argued that group discussion focuses on problem talk and debate as the two forms of talk important for making effective group decisions; consequently, research from this language game articulates key functions or decision paths associated with effective group decisions (see, respectively, Gouran & Hirokawa, 1996; Poole et al., 1996; also see Chapter 2, this volume). In contrast, dialogue involves "collective and collaborative communication processes whereby people explore together their individual and collective assumptions and predispositions" for the purpose of "enhancing understanding and coordination among people" (Barge, 2002, pp. 168, 166). Barge showed how, among youth groups attending a day-long summit about community building, dialogue-oriented talk—such as "appreciative inquiry," in which group members ask questions of one another in a sincere attempt to value differences—promoted members' group communication competence, connection with other members, and some important outcomes, including subsequent increased volunteerism and a new mentoring and support program in the city of Waco, Texas.

Fourth, groups engage in a number of symbolic practices to frame and manage members' negative behaviors. Groups often engage, for instance, in symbolic scapegoating of a group member. Malekoff's (1994) study of a preadolescent boys' group in a community mental health center found that scapegoating of one of the members consisted of verbal insults, taunting, menacing, and an occasional chair pulled out from under the person; these behaviors stopped only when the scapegoat's role in the group was transformed through an exercise in self-disclosure that compelled the other children to view the target in a new way. Such negative symbolic scapegoating may actually serve positive functions for other group members. Fine (1987), studying preadolescent culture in boys' Little League baseball, using taped accounts of instances of preadolescent verbal combat, reported the utility of the unfortunate victim to the group, as the lad unwittingly enabled his attackers to impress one another with their negative verbal skills.

When group members demonstrate misconduct during interactions, the group often must engage in symbolic activity to manage that member. Stohl and Schell (1991), for instance, described a dynamic within dysfunctional groups called the *farrago*, which literally means "fodder for cattle," that occurs when a member exhibiting a specific set of dysfunctional characteristics leads the other members to engage in symbolic activity that revolves around trying to deal with that member. The researchers suggested that both habits of the problem individual (e.g., omnipotence and heroic stance) and properties of the group system contribute to the emergence of this dynamic. In such instances, the intervention most likely to be successful involves changing the symbolic practices of the group to focus "on the interactional tensions of the group and provide communication frames from within which the group can respond as a group" (Stohl & Schell, 1991, pp. 106–107).

An S-I perspective, thus, reveals the type of symbolic practices and processes that characterize group interaction and the potential effects of such activity on group products. Our understanding of group interaction processes would be informed by investigating questions that include: (1) What are the differential effects of highly symbolic activities that occur in groups? (2) How does the nature of the group influence the need for and types of symbols created and used during group interaction? (3) What types of events occurring during group interaction trigger the production and reproduction of symbolic activities? (4) What are the effects of "positive" and "negative" symbolic behaviors by members on group interaction processes and products, and what interventions can help groups to promote positive and avoid negative symbolic behaviors?

What Results From Group Action?

Many things, of course, result from group action; here, we focus on those results that are most relevant to the symbolic nature of group life. It should first be pointed out that the assessment of group products is not a straightforward matter (see Poole, Keyton, & Frey, 1999), especially from an S-I perspective, in which, as previously explained, processes and products are inherently intertwined. Multiple processes and products are also likely to result simultaneously, some serving positive ends and some causing harm (see Poole et al., 1999; Sunwolf & Seibold, 1998), and some of these processes and products, especially those at the individual member level, may not manifest themselves for quite some time. Many of the relevant processes and products that result from group (inter)action have been described in previous sections; here, we mention some additional ones that occur at the individual level and at the collective group level.

First, at the individual level, group actions (practices and processes) can result in the creation of new and important symbols that help members to understand their lived experience, the society in which they live, and their worldviews. Perhaps the best example of such effects are those that occur in self-help and support groups, which are typically employed to help people to deal with significant problems they face, especially those related to health. Indeed, more than 25 million U.S. Americans belong to a health-oriented support group (Kessler, Mickelson, & Zhao, 1997), and these groups are the most common way that individuals in this country attempt to change health behaviors (Davison, Pennebaker, & Dickerson, 2000). Cawyer and Smith-Dupré (1995), for instance, explained how the communication exchanged in a support group for people with HIV or AIDS helped members to prepare for what was to come and influenced their views of society. Humphreys (1996) showed that participation in Adult Children of Alcoholics/Al-Anon self-help groups affected participants' worldviews.

Participation in groups also affects people at an emotional level, especially the emotions they have toward their group experience, with those emotions, in turn, affecting group processes and products. We previously identified grouphate and anticipatory group regret as emotions that can result from and influence group actions. As another example, *group envy,* feelings of resentment or inferiority relative to other group members, has been found to result from participation in groups; it can subsequently affect members' behaviors and group outcomes. In a longitudinal study of 143 groups, Duffy and Shaw (2000) documented the sabotaging nature of envy, which was directly and negatively related to group performance and cohesion and indirectly influenced members' absenteeism and satisfaction with their group by increasing their social loafing.

The symbols and emotions produced by group experiences can also potentially affect people's subsequent actions in the world. Chesney and Chesler (1993), for instance, found that participation in support groups for parents of children with cancer was highly correlated with parents' increased activism (e.g., working with others to raise awareness about cancer issues in their community), use of active coping strategies, and seeking help. In addition, support group participation was negatively correlated with parents' subsequent use of passive coping strategies, especially a tendency to cope solely by themselves with their child's illness.

People's experiences in groups can also affect people's perceptions of and participation in future groups. Kantor and Lehr (1975), for instance, claimed that children acquire their initial understanding of groups from the interactions that occur in their families (see also Ebaugh, 1988; Socha, 1997, 1999). Indeed, Hall (1991) argued that one of the greatest problems facing contemporary organizations, especially with respect to creating effective teams, was dealing with those who could not work well in groups because of their experiences in dysfunctional families. Moreland (1985) explained how individuals' adjustment to new groups is influenced by their prior group experiences and existing social structures. Anderson, Riddle, and Martin's (1999) socialization model of groups suggests that individuals with many positive experiences in their library of group experiences approach new groups with more optimism than people whose group experiences have been primarily negative; as a result of their positive experiences, they may be more active in trying to accomplish both group task and relational goals (e.g., new member socialization). Although the effects of such predispositions toward groups are typically considered to be a symbolic predisposition (see the discussion of group composition), they are also a result of participating in groups.

Second, at the group level, group actions often create unique symbols that bind members together into a group. Barnlund (1988) noted that "every culture attempts to create a 'universe of discourse' for its members, a way in which people can interpret their experience and convey it to one another"

(p. 11). Such discourse includes nonverbal symbols (e.g., the color of clothing that gang members wear; see Conquergood & Siegel, 1990) and verbal symbols (e.g., terms such as *hollow* and *closed-out* used by surfer groups; see Scheerhorn & Geist, 1997). One result of using these ingroup symbols is that members come to identify with and become committed to the collective (see, e.g., Cheney & Tompkins, 1987).

One interesting group action engaged in by some disenfranchised groups involves *symbolic reversal* (Cohen, 1985), reclaiming symbols that carry negative connotative meanings by inverting them so as to promote positive feelings and self-image. An example of symbolic reversal was the slogan, "Black is beautiful," used by African American groups in the 1960s.

Finally, collective group action can result in important effects in the world. Brock and Howell (1994), for instance, examined the progression of a community-based political action group through five stages commonly used to analyze social movements, stages that reflect, in large measure, changes in a group's symbol usage (e.g., from symbols of identity to symbols of legitimacy). They found that the progression initially led the group to muster the resources to defeat a proposal for casino gambling in Detroit and, later, after members decided to remain together as a group, to serve as a powerful voice for a vision of the growth of that city in terms of neighborhood, community-based strategies rather than large-scale projects. Using the bona fide group perspective, symbolic convergence theory, and structuration theory, Howell, Brock, and Hauser (2003) later explained how a group of inner-city adult and youth volunteers were effective at the local level in confronting the issues of youth violence and urban decay in Detroit. These and other studies demonstrate that despite recent claims about U.S. citizens' inability to conceive of the public good (e.g., Bellah, Madsen, Sullivan, Swidler, & Tipton, 1991) and their supposed lack of participation in civic groups ("bowling alone," to use Putnam's, 2000, metaphor), there still exists a profound commitment to participation in community groups (see, e.g., Pitts, 1999).

The S-I perspective, thus, offers unique insights into the processes and products that result from group action at the individual and group levels and into the possible effects of those processes and products on the environments within which groups are embedded. Our understanding of the results of group action would be increased by research that addresses the following questions: (1) What are the effects of early childhood group experiences on how adults approach group life? (2) How do group experiences affect members' symbolic representations of, and emotions toward, themselves, others, and their environments? (3) How do different group discourses affect individual members and the group as a whole? (4) In addition to grouphate, anticipatory group regret, and group envy, what are some additional "darkside" effects of participating in groups?

How Does a Group Change Over Time?

An S-I perspective is helpful for understanding at both the macro- and the microlevel how groups change over time. At the macrolevel, *group development* and concepts relevant to it, such as *stages* and *phases,* are themselves ephemeral symbols constructed by scholars to reference phenomena that seemingly occur in groups. Such symbols are macrolevel interpretive concepts based on observation of microlevel practices. Perhaps this is one reason why scholars studying group development have moved away from macrolevel constructs to talk about microlevel practices, such as *activity tracks* (e.g., Poole, 1981, 1983a, 1983b; Poole & Roth, 1989a, 1989b). These microlevel practices themselves, of course, are symbolic practices; hence, the S-I perspective calls attention to the symbolic practices and processes that occur in groups over the course of time they meet.

First, group development is characterized by changes in symbolic practices and processes; indeed, virtually every stage model of group development is based on identifying differences in symbolic behaviors that characterize the stages conceived. Bennis and Shepard (1974), for instance, extending the work of Bion (1961), showed how self-analytic groups developed with regard to changes in symbolic behavior from a phase of dependence, filled with members' statements demonstrating dependency and flight, followed by counterdependence-fight (including the symbolic removal of the leader) and then resolution-catharsis statements, to a phase of interdependence, characterized by statements of enchantment-flight, disenchantment-flight, and, finally, consensual validation (see also Wheelan et al., 1994). Hartman and Gibbard (1974) traced the evolution of fantasy themes in the development of self-analytic group culture, showing how the fantasies that members shared progressed from those that focused on mystical fusion (the fear of being enveloped by the group) to deification (ascribing godlike powers to the leader) to utopianism (the group as a maternal, protecting entity) to bisexuality (pairing with masculine and feminine aspects of oneself, which arises when the group is threatened with dissolution) to messianism (the hope that a messiah will appear to save the group from disintegration).

Farrell (personal correspondence, October 15, 2001) proposed four stages of general group development, which involve changes in symbolic behavior: formation, social construction, routinization of activities, and disintegration. The formation stage revolves around members coming together to develop a collective consciousness, a shared set of sentiments and beliefs about what they are doing as a group. The social construction stage involves members constructing shared meanings about their meetings, frequent activities, their past, and their future. It is during this period that they develop catchphrases that capture their shared understanding about what type of people or behaviors are allowed "in" the group; out of this negotiation may emerge a name for the group. Farrell (2001) showed how authors C. S. Lewis, J. R. Tolkien, and their friends came to call their group of writers the "Inklings," a name that captured their sense of themselves as novices at creative writing at the early stage of their development. It is during this stage that group members also negotiate shared images of one another. Farrell, Schmitt, and Heinemann's (2001) study of interdisciplinary health care teams, using members' impressions of one another, found that as indicators of group development increased, members acquired more consensus about the images they had of each member in their group. As groups develop such shared meanings, they may encode their emerging meanings in narrative legends—stories that retell episodes involving their heroic members or outrageous deviants that convey the positive and negative boundaries of group membership (Farrell, 1986). The third stage involves routine cycles of work and play, which are recognized, for instance, by members of family groups with an alcoholic parent (Farrell, 2001). The fourth stage of disintegration demonstrates a predictable constellation of roles and meanings in the final stage of a group's existence.

Studies in social movements and community-based groups also demonstrate how different symbolic practices and processes characterize the developmental phases such groups experience. Chesebro, Cragan, and McCullough (1973), for instance, studied *consciousness raising* (face-to-face interaction that attempts to create new psychological orientations) in a group of people associated with the gay movement. They identified central symbols that characterized four stages of the consciousness-raising process: (1) self-realization of a new identity, in which members engaged in chains of fantasy sharing, "I-you" references, and open and noncombative communication, with a focus on the past; (2) creation of a group identity through polarized discourse, characterized by generalized "we-they" references between the movement and society, tension and hostility toward the external enemy, a somber social atmosphere among group members, and the emergence of a family discourse (frequent use of terms such as *brothers, sisters,* and *community*), with a focus on the present; (3) establishment of new group values, featuring contrast and comparison (between homosexual and heterosexual relationships), cooperative verbal interaction between members, and increased hostility toward the value structure of the external enemy, with a focus on the future; and (4) development of relationships with other revolutionary groups, with a return to "I-you" discourse, impersonal references to the "new minority group," and a competitive or argumentative atmosphere, with a move toward cooperation near the end of the stage.

Second, changes in symbolic practices over the course of group development occur in relation to the experience and management of dialectical tensions. Smith and Berg (1987) discussed three clusters of paradoxes that groups experience as they grow and develop: (1) paradoxes of belonging—centered on membership and themes of identity, involvement, individuality, and boundaries; (2) paradoxes of engaging—focused on participation and the dynamics of disclosure, trust, intimacy, and regression; and (3) paradoxes of speaking—concerned with influence and the themes of authority, dependency, creativity, and courage. The authors concluded that group development is dependent on members' ability to accept, understand, and manage the opposing forces active in their group and that groups become "stuck" or "frozen," unable to move forward, as a consequence of attempting to eliminate the paradoxical tensions they experience, not realizing that these tensions can never be eliminated. The chapters in Frey and Barge's (1997) text illuminate symbolic practices and processes that members can use to manage dialectical tensions so as to move forward in their development as a group.

Third, symbolic practices are used to weather changes that occur within groups. Volatile changes in group membership may constitute dissipative circumstances that threaten a group's survival, but the instability of those circumstances and the new resources they may produce also increase a group's creativity and viability (Smith & Gemmil, 1991). Lesch's (1994) study of a witches' coven, for instance, described the group's complex transition after the loss of one of its members. The group meetings that followed the member leaving featured exhaustive metacommunication rich with stories about the group's history, founding vision, core group values, group structure, and members' hopes for the future. Dramatic rhetorical acts (shared narratives) engaged in by coven members during this period cast them as protagonists, with forces antagonistic to the group depicted as threatening the group's existence and stability. Coven members also engaged in several symbolic strategies, such as a planned farewell ritual, to recognize the loss of the member and to preserve the group's identity and longevity. By directing symbolic activity toward addressing the turnover and rebuilding members' commitment to the group, the coven was able to engage in *group renewal,* "a rejuvenation of group identity" (Sinclair-James & Stohl, 1997, p. 315).

Fourth, there are, of course, times when groups end. Sinclair-James and Stohl (1997) identified four types of group endings—controlled, officiated, negotiated, and forced procedure—characterized by whether a group makes the decision to disband and whether the group can determine how it will end. Regardless of the type of ending, members often experience tensions related to termination, such as how to retain friendships with others from the group (Anderson et al., 1999). Scholars have suggested the use of symbolic practices to help members cope with these tensions, such as devoting a final meeting to evaluating the group experience and giving members a chance to say good-bye (Keyton, 1993). Group members also often stay in touch with one another after a group ends, symbolically reconstructing the group through shared memories; moreover, people often engage in symbolic behavior that references their membership in a prior group, such as wearing the letter jacket from their high school sports team or showing some other sign of previous affiliation (Sigman, 1991).

An S-I perspective, thus, offers a rich approach to understanding how groups change (or don't) over time. Our understanding of group development would benefit from research that addresses the following questions: (1) Do individual and collective meanings within groups change in systematic ways over time? (2) How are group changes over time influenced by external influences? (3) What are the developmental phases and symbolic practices and processes that emerge in different types of groups (e.g., task versus social groups)? (4) What effects might facilitators have on the use of symbolic practices and processes during various phases of group development?

How Does a Group's Ecology, Including Its Physical, Social, Organizational, and Technical Environment, as well as Intergroup Relations, Affect Its Interaction and Performance?

An S-I perspective, as previously explained, rejects the notion of a group as a "container"; instead, in line with a bona fide group perspective, as well as Alderfer's (1977, 1986, 1992) theory of embedded intergroup relations, which posits that groups are embedded in a suprasystem that contains interlocked subsystems, groups are viewed as interdependent with their relevant contexts, being affected by those contexts, and, in turn, affecting those contexts. Moreover, a group's relevant contexts are created and re-created through group members' interactions. As Schwartzman (1989) argued, based on her research about group meetings:

> Meetings do not merely exist *in* a sociocultural context because they frequently play an important role in constituting such systems for participants. At the same time, they provide individuals with multiple opportunities for making sense of such systems and negotiating as well as commenting on their place within it. (pp. 273–274)

She concluded that "in the broadest sense, it is in meetings that we come to know ourselves and our social systems" (p. 314).

First, group members symbolically construct a boundary that separates their group from its now-perceived external contexts. The symbolic construction of a boundary creates the possibility of relationships and entities, including small groups (Smith & Berg, 1987), a notion that can be traced back to Lewin's (1951) field theory. Such boundaries are both stable in the sense of being defined, yet fluid in that they are continuously negotiated, redefined, and changed through group members' interaction.

Boundaries not only create a group but also distinguish that group from other groups, a process that has important consequences. Tajfel's (1974, 1981) social identity theory argues that once a person becomes aware of belonging to one or more social groups, his or her social identity begins to form and is positive if the perceived group (ingroup) compares favorably to other relevant groups (outgroups). Positive ingroup cohesion may also involve the corresponding construction of negative symbolic attributions about outgroup members (see Conquergood's, 1991, 1992, 1994, work on gangs) and use of behaviors that prevent outsiders from joining the group. Sunwolf and Leets (2003, 2004), for instance, on the basis of narratives collected from 682 adolescents, found that symbolic group rules and practices were used to reject inclusion attempts made by outsiders, including symbolically ignoring and insulting them. The boundaries between ingroup and outgroups, thus, often cause tensions that need to be managed via symbolic practices. Buchalter (2003), for instance, showed how dialectical tensions associated with the borders separating a neighborhood in Philadelphia from the public housing project located within the neighborhood's formal boundaries were managed by residents, demonstrating how those borders were simultaneously both permeable and impermeable.

Because group boundaries are interactionally created and re-created as an ongoing process, they can shift and change, often as a result of new members joining, new information obtained, and the creation of subgroups within a group. Petronio, Jones, and Morr (2003), for instance, documented how family privacy dilemmas (e.g., a daughter finding love letters her mother wrote to someone other than the mother's husband) resulted in significant boundary shifts, subgroups, and symbolic activity designed to manage the reconstructed boundaries and subgroups within family groups.

Second, two important symbolic contexts within which groups are embedded are space and time. From an S-I perspective, although physical space is important, it is the symbolic meaning and contour that people give to space that transforms it into a "place," leading to *place attachment*, the emotional bonding of people and groups to particular spaces (see Altman &

Lowe, 1992). A number of scholars have shown that different groups sharing the same physical space create different meanings for and interpretations of that space as place (see, e.g., Agnew & Duncan, 1989; Harper, 1988; Massey, 1994).

The context of time can also be differentiated with respect to physical time versus people's symbolic conception of time, although even physical time is acted on symbolically, such as attempts to standardize time (e.g., by inserting leap years to "correct" for variations in the Earth's cycles) and different groups' use of physical time (e.g., some parts of the United States using daylight saving time whereas other parts do not). The symbolic construction of time has been well documented from a cultural group perspective, such as Hall's (1983) differentiation of *monochromic cultures*, in which time is highly structured primarily because work is privileged, and *polychromic cultures*, in which time is loosely structured and relationships and interactions are valued. Even in the same culture, groups may have different symbolic conceptions of time. Dubinskas's (1988) ethnographic study of scientists and managers in a genetic engineering firm showed that the two groups had contrasting conceptions of time based on their task demands, with scientists seeing time in terms of development, with extended time horizons, and managers viewing it in terms of planning, with shorter temporal horizons. Such differences in conceptions of time may be a result of the symbolic activity in which group members engage; Ballard and Seibold (2000), for instance, reported that members of work groups differed with regard to their time orientation and that their varied communication patterns may have contributed to these differences.

Third, the discourse characterizing group interaction is often influenced by the external environments within which a group is embedded. Geist and Chandler (1984), for instance, showed how the nature of the accounts forwarded by members during a decision-making staff meeting of a psychiatric health care team, such as the premises on which the accounts were based, could be traced back to sources within the organization (e.g., supervisors) to whom team members were prepared to explain and defend their actions. Groups embedded in organizations that relax constraints and instill a sense of urgent purpose may be consequently stimulated to thrive at intense levels of productivity. Lipman-Blumen and Leavitt (1999) reported that Apple Computer, Inc. was able to thrive in its time period (the 1970s) because it encouraged a group culture consistent with sensitivity groups, the Black Panthers, the uprisings at the University of California at Berkeley, and rebellion; in group meetings, members were encouraged to sit, stand, squat on the floor, or lie down, which resulted in lively listening and hot debate. A case study by Yep, Reece, and Negrón (2003) of a "closed" support group for

Asian Americans living with HIV infection revealed how the environment—specifically, culture and stigma—affected group boundaries and the context of group life: Culture influenced group members such that their discourse was consistent with Asian American cultural values; stigma affected internal group communication in that much of the support group members' interactions attempted to counteract social and cultural influences.

Knowing the relevant contexts within which a group is embedded may, in fact, be crucial to understanding the discourse that occurs in a group. Barge and Keyton's (1994) study revealed how knowledge of the historical and political contexts within which a city council operated was necessary for understanding the issues the council discussed; Tracy and Standerfer (2003) showed how much of the discourse exchanged during a school board's deliberations to select its next superintendent was directed toward influential constituencies beyond the seven-person board and how this discourse reframed even what the group should be deciding.

Fourth, groups may experience interactional difficulties precisely because of participants' multiple memberships in various other groups, especially in cases where group members are representatives of other groups or constituencies, such as in group collaboration (see Stohl & Walker, 2002). Case studies of environmental collaborations by Carpenter and Kennedy (1988) and Lange (2003), for instance, have shown that discussions and negotiations within these collaborations (e.g., between environmentalists and loggers) often proceeded more smoothly than expected until the agreements reached by the group were taken back to the members' constituency groups; the resulting problems that surfaced in the intraconstituency group communication subsequently affected the collaboration group members' ability to work together effectively.

Fifth, group products are significantly affected (both positively and negatively) by relevant contexts. Berteotti and Seibold (1994), for instance, found that allegiances to other groups among members of a hospice team and confusion regarding the positioning of the hospice team within larger administrative and organizational constraints prohibited effective role coordination and team building among the members, a situation that undermined effectiveness, creating information dissemination problems, flawed feedback, poor team meetings, dissatisfaction and alienation among team members, and ambiguous role descriptions. A study by Sherblom (2003) of international consulting teams working in multiple countries in Europe showed how the information focused on and the decisions made in one country were the result of a "bleed over" of having worked previously or simultaneously in another country. A case study by Broome (1995) of a facilitation that used interactive management (IM) with a Native American tribe to promote greater participation in tribal governance was deemed successful, in large measure, because important aspects of the procedure—the holistic approach of IM, its process orientation, and its ability to create a collaborative problem-solving environment—appeared to be congruent with several aspects of Native American culture.

Sixth, perhaps because of the problems that groups experience due to the influence of their relevant contexts, they may try to isolate themselves from those contexts and become symbolic containers, but those external influences may still be felt, sometimes as a result of a crisis. Houston's (2003) analysis of the infamous disaster that occurred on Mount Everest in May 1996, which cost the lives of 12 individuals, showed how members of the various teams climbing the mountain that day viewed themselves as separate and distinct expedition groups and, consequently, engaged in little intergroup communication or help. When the storm hit, however, the teams reorganized themselves into survival groups based on the larger shared group identity of "climbers."

Groups, of course, do need to insulate themselves from their relevant contexts to a certain degree so as to develop their own social space, which allows for the discovery of commonalities among members and promotes trust and relationship building, as Friedman (1994) showed in his study of labor-management teams. Indeed, Keyton and Stallworth (2003) found that the failure to create a unique and shared culture among group members led to credibility and trust problems for the members of a drug dealer eviction collaboration, prevented facilitative norms from developing, and resulted in members' loyalty to their organization rather than to the collaboration group.

However, too much insulation can have negative effects on group processes and products. A study by Oetzel and Robbins (2003) of highly insulated teams in a cooperative supermarket showed that the teams demonstrated significant intergroup relationship problems that prevented the supermarket from "living up" to the cooperative principles guiding the organization. This finding is not surprising, for insulated groups have consistently been shown to be less effective in accomplishing their projects than groups that reach out to their external environments (see, e.g., Ancona & Caldwell, 1988; Thornton, 1978). In fact, Ancona (1990) argued that group members' management of external relationships with constituencies is a better predictor of group performance than the quality of the internal communication of collaborating groups. A number of studies have documented ways in which groups manage their external environments, including a product team having its leader serve on key committees in other groups and inviting members of other groups to become part of the product team during peak times of coordination (Gladstein & Caldwell, 1985), exchanging agreements between groups to manage turf conflicts (Brett & Rognes, 1986), and teams probing the environment regarding proposals they developed (Ancona, 1990; Stohl, 1986, 1987). As Putnam and Stohl (1996) concluded, "Overall, these studies suggest that group members need to foster ambassador relationships with external groups . . . ; facilitate information processing across boundaries . . . ; and develop proposals consistent with values, norms, and changes in their environment" (p. 161). Of course, too much dependence on the external environment can also be problematic. In summarizing the various research findings, Putnam and Stohl (1996) argued:

> Neither total dependence on nor total isolation from external groups facilitates effective decision making. On the one hand, boundaries that are too amorphous hinder decision making through weak group identity, adversarial conflict among members, and strong representative roles. On the other hand, boundaries that are too impenetrable hinder decision making through strong group identity, avoidance of conflict, and absence of accountability to external groups. Thus, a balance seems necessary between overreliance on external units and too much dependence on the group itself in decision making. (p. 161)

An S-I perspective thus reveals important ways in which groups are affected by and, in turn, affect the contexts in which they are embedded. The following questions deserve researchers' attention: (1) How do group members form perceptions of which variables in their environments are relevant and then call on those variables as interpretive frames during group interaction? (2) How do members' relationships with outside groups, organizations, communities, and cultures facilitate or constrain their symbolic behavior in groups? (3) In what ways, and through what forms of representation, do groups include in their interaction processes the symbolic presence of specific outsiders? (4) How does the enactment of external contexts by members influence group symbolic practices, processes, and products? (5) How should outcomes (such as decision-making effectiveness) be symbolized (e.g., defined and operationalized) when relevant contexts and stakeholders must be taken into account?

Conclusion

The S-I perspective offers a rich framework for understanding how symbol usage in groups has important consequences at the individual, relational, and collective levels. By studying symbolic predispositions, practices, processes, and products, researchers uncover the symbols of group life, revealing both how groups and group members are symbol-using animals and how groups are created and sustained through symbolic activity.

References

Adelman, M. B. (1992). Rituals of adversity and remembering: The role of possessions for persons and community living with AIDS. In F. Sherry, Jr., & B. Sternthal (Eds.), *Advances in consumer research* (Vol. 19, pp. 201–403). Provo, UT: Association for Consumer Research.

Adelman, M. B., & Frey, L. R. (1994). The pilgrim must embark: Creating and sustaining community in a residential facility for people with AIDS. In L. R. Frey (Ed.), *Group communication in context: Studies of natural groups* (pp. 3–22). Hillsdale, NJ: Lawrence Erlbaum.

Adelman, M. B., & Frey, L. R. (1997). *The fragile community: Living together with AIDS.* Mahwah, NJ: Lawrence Erlbaum.

Agnew, J. A., & Duncan, J. S. (1989). *The power of place: Bringing together geographical and sociological imagination*s. Boston: Unwin Hyman.

Alderfer, C. P. (1977). Group and intergroup relations. In J. R. Hackman & J. L. Suttle (Eds.), *Improving life at work: Behavioral science approaches to organizational change* (pp. 227–296). Santa Monica, CA: Goodyear.

Alderfer, C. P. (1986). An intergroup perspective on group dynamics. In J. Lorsch (Ed.), *Handbook of organizational behavior* (pp. 190–222). Englewood Cliffs, NJ: Prentice Hall.

Alderfer, C. P. (1992). Contemporary issues in professional work with groups: Editor's introduction. *Journal of Applied Behavioral Sciences, 28,* 9–14.

Alderton, S. M. (1980). Attributions of responsibility for socially deviant behavior in decision-making discussions as a function of situation and locus of control. *Central States Speech Journal, 31,* 117–127.

Alderton, S. M. (1982). Locus of control-based argumentation as a predictor of group polarization. *Communication Quarterly, 30,* 381–387.

Alderton, S. M., & Frey, L. R. (1983). Effects of reactions to arguments on group outcome: The case of group polarization. *Central States Speech Journal, 34,* 88–95.

Alderton, S. M., & Frey, L. R. (1986). Argumentation in small group decision-making. In R. Y. Hirokawa & M. S. Poole (Eds.), *Communication and group decision-making* (pp. 157–173). Beverly Hills, CA: Sage.

Altman, I., & Lowe, S. M. (Eds.). (1992). *Place attachment.* New York: Plenum Press.

Ancona, D. G. (1990). Outward bound: Strategies for team survival in an organization. *Academy of Management Journal, 33,* 334–365.

Ancona, D. G., & Caldwell, D. F. (1988). Beyond task and maintenance: Defining external functions in groups. *Group and Organization Studies, 13,* 468–494.

Ancona, D. G., & Caldwell, D. F. (1992). Demography and design: Predictors of new product team performance. *Organization Science, 3*, 321–341.

Anderson, C. M., Riddle, B. L., & Martin, M. M. (1999). Socialization processes in groups. In L. R. Frey (Ed.), D. S. Gouran, & M. S. Poole (Assoc. Eds.), *The handbook of group communication theory and research* (pp. 139–163). Thousand Oaks, CA: Sage.

Ballard, D. I., & Seibold, D. R. (2000). Time orientation and temporal variation across work groups: Implications for group and organizational communication. *Western Journal of Communication, 64,* 218–242.

Barge, J. K. (2002). Enlarging the meaning of group deliberation: From discussion to dialogue. In L. R. Frey (Ed.), *New directions in group communication* (pp. 159–177). Thousand Oaks, CA: Sage.

Barge, J. K., & Frey, L. R. (1997). Life in a task group. In L. R. Frey & J. K. Barge (Eds.), *Managing group life: Communicating in decision-making groups* (pp. 29–51). Boston: Houghton Mifflin.

Barge, J. K., & Keyton, J. (1994). Contextualizing power and social influence in groups. In L. R. Frey (Ed.), *Group communication in context: Studies of natural groups* (pp. 85–105). Hillsdale, NJ: Lawrence Erlbaum.

Barnlund, D. C. (1988). Communication in a global village. In L. A. Samovar & R. E. Porter (Eds.), *Intercultural communication: A reader* (5th ed., pp. 5–14). Belmont, CA: Wadsworth.

Baxter, L. A., & Clark, C. L. (1996). Perceptions of family communication patterns and the enactment of family rituals. *Western Journal of Communication, 60,* 254–268.

Bell, C. (1992). *Ritual theory, ritual practice.* New York: Oxford University Press.

Bellah, R. N., Madsen, R. Sullivan, W. N., Swidler, A., & Tipton, S. M. (1991). *The good society.* New York: Knopf.

Bem, S. (1981). Gender schema theory: A cognitive account of sex typing. *Psychological Review, 88,* 354–364.

Bennett, W. L. (1978). Storytelling in criminal trials: A model of social judgment. *Quarterly Journal of Speech, 64,* 1–22.

Bennett, W. L. (1992). Legal fictions: Telling stories and doing justice. In M. L. McLaughlin, M. J. Cody, & S. J. Read (Eds.), *Explaining one's self to others: Reason-giving in a social context* (pp. 149–165). Hillsdale, NJ: Lawrence Erlbaum.

Bennis, W. G., & Shepard, H. A. (1975). A theory of group development. In G. S. Gibbard, J. J. Hartman, & R. D. Mann (Eds.), *Analysis of groups: Contributions to theory, research, and practice* (pp. 127–153). San Francisco: Jossey-Bass.

Berteotti, C. R., & Seibold, D. R. (1994). Coordination and role-definition problems in health-care teams: A hospice case study. In L. R. Frey (Ed.), *Group communication in context: Studies of natural groups* (pp. 107–131). Hillsdale, NJ: Lawrence Erlbaum.

Bion, W. R. (1961). *Experiences in groups and other papers.* New York: Basic Books.

Black, E. B. (1955). Consideration of the rhetorical causes of breakdown in discussion. *Speech Monographs, 22,* 15–19.

Blau, P. M. (1977). *Inequality and heterogeneity: A primitive theory of social structure.* New York: Free Press.

Bormann, E. G. (1996). Symbolic convergence theory and communication in group decision making. In R. Y. Hirokawa & M. S. Poole (Eds.), *Communication and group decision making* (2nd ed., pp. 81–113). Thousand Oaks, CA: Sage.

Bormann, E. G., Pratt, J., & Putnam, L. (1978). Power, authority, and sex: Male response to female leadership. *Communication Monographs, 45,* 119–155.

Braithwaite, D. O., Baxter, L. A., & Harper, A. M. (1998). The role of rituals in the management of the dialectical tension of "old" and "new" in blended families. *Communication Studies, 49,* 101–120.

Brett, J. M., & Rognes, J. K. (1986). Intergroup relations in organizations: A negotiations perspective. In P. S. Goodman & Associates (Eds.), *Designing effective work groups* (pp. 202–236). San Francisco: Jossey-Bass.

Brock, B. L., & Howell, S. (1994). Leadership in the evolution of a community-based political action group. In L. R. Frey (Ed.), *Group communication in context: Studies of natural groups* (pp. 135–152). Hillsdale, NJ: Lawrence Erlbaum.

Broome, B. J. (1995). The role of facilitated group process in community-based planning and design: Promoting greater participation in Comanche tribal governance. In L. R. Frey (Ed.), *Innovations in group facilitation: Applications in natural settings* (pp. 27–52). Cresskill, NJ: Hampton Press.

Brown, M. H. (1985). That reminds me of a story: Speech action in organizational socialization. *Western Journal of Speech Communication, 49,* 27–43.

Bruess, C. J. S., & Pearson, J. C. (1997). Interpersonal rituals in marriage and adult friendship. *Communication Monographs, 64,* 26–46.

Bruner, J. (1987). Life as narrative. *Social Research, 54,* 11–32.

Buchalter, R. (2003). Negotiating (im)permeable neighborhood borders. In L. R. Frey (Ed.), *Group communication in context: Studies of bona fide groups* (2nd ed., pp. 57–82). Mahwah, NJ: Lawrence Erlbaum.

Burke, K. (1966). *Language as symbolic action: Essays on life, literature, and method.* Berkeley: University of California Press.

Canary, D. J., Brossman, B. G., & Seibold, D. R. (1987). Argument structures in decision-making groups. *Southern Communication Journal, 53,* 18–37.

Carpenter, S. L., & Kennedy, W. J. D. (1988). *Managing public disputes: A practical guide to handling conflict and reaching decisions.* San Francisco: Jossey-Bass.

Cattell, R. B. (1948). Concepts and methods in the measurement of group syntality. *Psychological Review, 55,* 48–63.

Cawyer, C. S., & Smith-Dupré, A. (1995). Communicating social support: Identifying supportive episodes in an HIV/AIDS support group. *Communication Quarterly, 43,* 243–258.

Cheney, G., & Tompkins, P. (1987). Coming to terms with organizational identification and commitment. *Central States Speech Journal, 38,* 1–15.

Chesebro, J. W., Cragan, J. F., & McCullough, P. (1973). The small group technique of the radical revolutionary: A synthetic study of consciousness-raising. *Speech Monographs, 40,* 136–146.

Chesney, B. K., & Chesler, M. A. (1993). Activism through self-help group membership: Reported life changes of parents with children with cancer. *Small Group Research, 24,* 258–273.

Clark, H. H. (1985). Language use and language users. In G. Lindsey & E. Aronson (Eds.), *Handbook of social psychology* (pp. 179–231). New York: Random House.

Clark, H. H., & Marshall, C. E. (1981). Definite reference and mutual knowledge. In A. K. Joshi, B. L. Webber, & I. A. Sag (Eds.), *Elements of discourse understanding* (pp. 10–63). Cambridge, UK: Cambridge University Press.

Cohen, A. P. (1985). *The symbolic construction of community.* London: Routledge.

Conquergood, D. (1991). "For the nation!" How street gangs problematize patriotism. In R. Troester & C. Kelley (Eds.), *Peacemaking through communication* (pp. 8–21). Annandale, VA: Speech Communication Association.

Conquergood, D. (1992). Life in Big Red: Struggles and accommodations in a Chicago polyethnic tenement. In L. Lamphere (Ed.), *Structuring diversity: Ethnographic perspectives on the new immigration* (pp. 95–144). Chicago: University of Chicago Press.

Conquergood, D. (1994). Homeboys and hoods: Gangs and cultural space. In L. R. Frey (Ed.), *Group communication in context: Studies of natural groups* (pp. 23–55). Hillsdale, NJ: Lawrence Erlbaum.

Conquergood, D. (Producer), & Siegel, T. (Producer & Director). (1990). *The heart broken in half* [Motion picture]. New York: Filmmakers Library.

Cooper, L. (1960). *The rhetoric of Aristotle.* New York: Appleton-Crofts.

Creanza, A. L., & McWhirter, J. J. (1994). Reminiscence: A strategy for getting to know you. *Journal for Specialists in Group Work, 19,* 232–237.

Davison, K. P., Pennebaker, J. W., & Dickerson, S. S. (2000). Who talks? The social psychology of illness support groups. *American Psychologist, 55,* 205–217.

Denison, D. R., & Sutton, R. I. (1990). Operating room nurses. In J. R. Hackman (Ed.), *Groups that work (and those that don't): Creating conditions for effective teamwork* (pp. 293–308). San Francisco: Jossey-Bass.

DeSanctis, G., & Poole, M. S. (1994). Capturing the complexity in advanced technology use: Adaptive structuration theory. *Organization Science, 5,* 121–147.

Dewey, J. (1922). *Human nature and conduct.* New York: Henry Holt.

Dubinskas, F. (1988). Cultural construction: The many faces of time. In F. Dubinskas (Ed.), *Making time: Ethnographies of high-technology organizations* (pp. 180–232). Philadelphia: Temple University Press.

Duffy, M. K., & Shaw, J. D. (2000). The Salieri syndrome: Consequences of envy in groups. *Small Group Research, 31,* 3–23.

Ebaugh, H. R. F. (1988). *Becoming an ex: The process of role exit.* Chicago: University of Chicago Press.

Eisenhart, K., & Schoonhoven, C. (1990), Organizational growth: Linking founding team, strategy, environment, and growth among U.S. semiconductor ventures, 1978–1988. *Administrative Science Quarterly, 35,* 504–529.

Enos, R. L. (1981). Heuristic and eristic rhetoric in small group interaction: An examination of quasi-logical argument. In G. Zigelmueller & J. Rhodes (Eds.), *Dimensions of argument: Proceedings of the second summer conference on argumentation* (pp. 719–727). Annandale, VA: Speech Communication Association.

Farrell, M. P. (1986). Friendships between men. *Marriage and Family Review, 3/4,* 163–198.

Farrell, M. P. (2001). *Collaborative circles: Friendship dynamics and creative work.* Chicago: University of Chicago Press.

Farrell, M. P., Schmitt, M. H., & Heinemann, G. D. (2001). Informal roles and the stages of interdisciplinary team development. *Journal of Interprofessional Care, 15,* 281–295.

Festinger, L., Riecken, H. W., & Schacter, S. (1956). *When prophecy fails.* Minneapolis: University of Minnesota Press.

Fine, G. A. (1987). *With the boys: Little League baseball and preadolescent culture.* Chicago: University of Chicago Press.

Freeman, K. A. (1996). Attitudes toward work in project groups as predictors of group performance. *Small Group Research, 27,* 265–282.

Frey, L. R. (1994a). The call of the field: Studying communication in natural groups. In L. R. Frey (Ed.), *Group communication in context: Studies of natural groups* (pp. ix-xiv). Hillsdale, NJ: Lawrence Erlbaum.

Frey, L. R. (1994b). The naturalistic paradigm: Studying small groups in the postmodern era. *Small Group Research, 25,* 551–577.

Frey, L. R. (1996). Remembering and "re-membering": A history of theory and research on communication and group decision making. In R. Y. Hirokawa & M. S. Poole, (Eds.), *Communication and group decision making* (2nd ed., pp. 19–51). Thousand Oaks, CA: Sage.

Frey, L. R. (2000). Diversifying our understanding of diversity and communication in groups: Dialoguing with Clark, Anand, and Roberson (2000). *Group Dynamics: Theory, Research, and Practice, 4,* 222–229.

Frey, L. R. (2003). Group communication in context: Studying bona fide group. In L. R. Frey (Ed.), *Group communication in context: Studies of bona fide group* (2nd ed., pp. 1–20). Mahwah, NJ: Lawrence Erlbaum.

Frey, L. R., Adelman, M. B., Flint, L. J., & Query, J. L., Jr. (2000). Weaving meanings together in an AIDS residence: Communicative practices, perceived health outcomes, and the symbolic construction of community. *Journal of Health Communication, 5,* 53–72.

Frey, L. R., & Barge, J. K. (Eds.). (1997). *Managing group life: Communication in decision-making groups.* Boston: Houghton Mifflin.

Frey, L. R., Botan, C. H., & Kreps, G. L. (2000). *Investigating communication: An introduction to research methods* (2nd ed.). Boston: Allyn & Bacon.

Frey, L. R., & Sunwolf. (2004). The symbolic-interpretive perspective on group dynamics. *Small Group Research, 35,* 277–306.

Friedman, R. A. (1994). *Front stage, back stage: The dramatic structure of labor negotiations.* Cambridge, MA: MIT Press.

Fussell, S. R., & Krauss, R. M. (1992). Coordination of knowledge in communication: Effects of speakers' assumptions about what others know. *Journal of Personality and Social Psychology, 62,* 378–391.

Galanter, M. (1989). *Cults: Faith, healing, and coercion.* New York: Oxford University Press.

Geertz, C. (1973). *The interpretation of cultures: Selected essays.* New York: Basic Books.

Geist, P., & Chandler, T. (1984). Account analysis of influence in group decision-making. *Communication Monographs, 51,* 67–78.

Gergen, K. J. (1985). The social constructionist movement in model psychology. *American Psychology, 40,* 266–275.

Gladstein, D. L., & Caldwell, D. F. (1985). Boundary management in new product teams. In *Academy of Management Proceedings* (pp. 161–165). San Diego, CA: Academy of Management Association.

Gouran, D. S. (1994). Epilogue: On the value of case studies of decision-making and problem-solving groups. In L. R. Frey (Ed.), *Group communication in context: Studies of natural groups* (pp. 305–315). Hillsdale, NJ: Lawrence Erlbaum.

Gouran, D. S., & Hirokawa, R. Y. (1996). Functional theory and communication in decision-making and problem-solving groups: An expanded view. In R. Y. Hirokawa & M. S. Poole (Eds.), *Communication and group decision making* (2nd ed., pp. 55–80). Thousand Oaks, CA: Sage.

Hall, E. T. (1983). *The dance of life: The other dimension of time.* Garden City, NY: Anchor Press/Doubleday.

Hall, F. (1991). Dysfunctional managers: The next human resource challenge. *Organizational Dynamics, 20,* 48–57.

Hare, A. P., Blumberg, H. H., Davies, M. F., & Kent, M. V. (1994). *Small group research: A handbook.* Norwood, NJ: Ablex.

Harper, S. (1988). Rural reference groups and images of place. In D. C. D. Pocock (Ed.), *Humanistic approaches to geography* (pp. 32–49). Durham, NC: University of Durham, Department of Geography.

Hartman, J. J., & Gibbard, G. S. (1974). A note on fantasy themes in the evolution of group culture. In G. S. Gibbard, J. J. Hartman, & R. D. Mann (Eds.), *Analysis of groups: Contributions to theory, research, and practice* (pp. 315–336). San Francisco: Jossey-Bass.

Haslett, B. B., & Ruebush, J. (1999). What differences do individual differences in groups make? The effects of individuals, culture, and group composition. In L. R. Frey, D. S. Gouran, & M. S. Poole (Eds.), *The handbook of group communication theory and research* (pp. 115–138). Thousand Oaks, CA: Sage.

Heidegger, M. (1959). *An introduction to metaphysics* (R. Manheim, Trans.). New Haven, CT: Yale University Press.

Hoffman, L. R., Harburg, E., & Maier, N. R. F. (1962). Differences and disagreement as factors in creative group problem solving. *Journal of Abnormal and Social Psychology, 64,* 206–214.

Houston, R. (2003). In the mask of thin air: Intragroup and intergroup communication during the Mt. Everest disaster. In L. R. Frey (Ed.), *Group communication in context: Studies of bona fide groups* (2nd ed., pp. 137–156). Mahwah, NJ: Lawrence Erlbaum.

Howell, S., Brock, B., & Hauser, E. (2003). A multicultural, intergenerational youth program: Creating and sustaining a youth community group. In L. R. Frey (Ed.), *Group communication in context: Studies of bona fide groups* (2nd ed., pp. 85–107). Mahwah, NJ: Lawrence Erlbaum.

Humphreys, K. (1996). World view change in Adult Children of Alcoholics/ Al-Anon self-help groups: Restructuring the alcoholic family. *Interactional Journal of Group Psychotherapy, 46,* 255–263.

Infante, D. A., Rancer, A. S., & Womack, D. F. (2003). *Building communication theory* (4th ed.). Prospect Heights, IL: Waveland Press.

Johnson, B. M. (1975). Images of the enemy in intergroup conflict. *Central States Speech Journal, 26,* 84–92.

Johnson, C. E., & Hackman, M. Z. (1995). *Creative communication: Principles and applications.* Prospect Heights, IL: Waveland Press.

Johnson, S. D., & Long, L. M. (2002). "Being a part and being apart": Dialectics and group communication. In L. R. Frey (Ed.), *New directions in group communication* (pp. 25–42). Thousand Oaks, CA: Sage.

Kanter, R. M. (1972). *Commitment and community: Communes and utopias in sociological perspective.* Cambridge, MA: Harvard University Press.

Kanter, R. M. (1977). *Men and women of the corporation.* New York: Basic Books.

Kantor, D., & Lehr, W. (1975). *Inside the family.* San Francisco: Jossey-Bass.

Kaplan, H. I., & Sadock, B. J. (1993). Structured interactional group psychotherapy. In H. I. Kaplan & B. J. Sadock (Eds.), *Comprehensive group psychotherapy* (3rd ed., pp. 324–338). Baltimore: Williams & Wilkins.

Katriel, T., & Farrell, T. (1991). Scrapbooks as cultural texts: An American art of memory. *Text and Performance Quarterly, 11,* 1–17.

Kerr, N. L., & MacCoun, R. J. (1985). The effects of jury size and polling method on the process and product of jury deliberation. *Journal of Personality and Social Psychology, 34,* 282–294.

Kessler, R. C., Mickelson, K. D., & Zhao, S. (1997). Patterns and correlates of self-help group membership in the United States. *Social Policy, 27,* 27–46.

Keyton, J. (1993). Group termination: Completing the study of group development. *Small Group Research, 24,* 84–100.

Keyton, J. (1999). Relational communication in groups. In L. R. Frey, D. S. Gouran, & M. S. Poole (Eds.), *The handbook of group communication theory and research* (pp. 192–222). Thousand Oaks, CA: Sage.

Keyton, J., & Frey, L. R. (2002). The state of traits: Predispositions and group communication. In L. R. Frey (Ed.), *New directions in group communication* (pp. 99–120). Thousand Oaks, CA: Sage.

Keyton, J., Harmon, N., & Frey, L. R. (1996, November). *Grouphate: Implications for teaching group communication.* Paper presented at the meeting of the Speech Communication Association, San Diego, CA.

Keyton J., & Stallworth, V. (2003). On the verge of collaboration: Interaction process vs. group outcomes. In L. R. Frey (Ed.), *Group communication in context: Studies of bona fide groups* (2nd ed., pp. 235–260). Mahwah, NJ: Lawrence Erlbaum.

Kirchmeyer, C. (1993). Multicultural task groups: An account of the low contribution levels of minorities. *Small Group Research, 24,* 127–148.

Kirchmeyer, C., & Cohen, A. (1992). Multicultural groups: Their performance and reactions with constructive conflict. *Group and Organizational Management, 17,* 153–170.

Kono, T. (1988). Factors affecting the creativity of organizations: An approach from the analysis of new product development. In K. Urabe, J. Child, & T. Kagano (Eds.), *Innovation and management: International comparisons* (pp. 105–144). New York: Walter de Gruyter.

Kraus, G. (1997). The psychodynamics of constructive aggression in small groups. *Small Group Research, 28,* 122–125.

Krauss, R. M., & Fussell, S. R. (1990). Mutual knowledge and communicative effectiveness. In J. Galegher, R. E. Kraut, & C. Egido (Eds.), *Intellectual teamwork: Social and technical bases of collaborative work* (pp. 111–145). Hillsdale, NJ: Lawrence Erlbaum.

Lammers, J. C., & Krikorian, D. H. (1997). Theoretical extension and operationalization of the bona fide group construct with an application to surgical teams. *Journal of Applied Communication Research, 25,* 17–38.

Lange, J. I. (2003). Environmental collaboration and constituency communication. In L. R. Frey (Ed.), *Group communication in context: Studies of bona fide groups* (2nd ed., pp. 209–234). Mahwah, NJ: Lawrence Erlbaum.

Lesch, C. L. (1994). Observing theory in practice: Sustaining consciousness in a coven. In L. R. Frey (Ed.), *Group communication in context: Studies of natural groups* (pp. 57–82). Hillsdale, NJ: Lawrence Erlbaum.

Lewin, K. (1951). *Field theory in social science: Selected theoretical papers* (D. Cartwright, Ed.). New York: Harper.

Lincoln, Y. S., & Guba, E. G. (1985). *Naturalistic inquiry.* Beverly Hills, CA: Sage.

Lindlof, T. R., & Taylor, B. C. (2002). *Qualitative communication research methods* (2nd ed.). Thousand Oaks, CA: Sage.

Ling, S. C. (1990). *The effects of group cultural composition and cultural attitudes on performance.* Unpublished doctoral dissertation, University of Ontario, London, Canada.

Lion, C. L., & Gruenfeld, L. W. (1993). The behavior and personality of work group and basic assumption group members. *Small Group Research, 24,* 236–257.

Lipman-Blumen, J., & Leavitt, H. J. (1999). *Hot groups: Seeding them, feeding them, and using them to ignite your organization*. New York: Oxford University Press.

Malekoff, A. (1994). Moments and madness: Humanizing the scapegoat in the group. *Journal of Child and Adolescent Group Therapy, 4,* 171–176.

Mandler, J. M., & Johnson, N. S. (1977). Remembrance of things parsed: Story structure and recall. *Cognitive Psychology, 9,* 111–151.

Martin, V., & Thomas, M. C. (2000). A model psychoeducation group for shy college students. *Journal for Specialists in Group Work, 25,* 79–88.

Massey, D. (1994). *Space, place, and gender.* Minneapolis: University of Minnesota Press.

McCroskey, J. C. (1977). Oral communication apprehension: A summary of recent theory and research. *Human Communication Research, 1,* 78–96.

McCroskey, J. C., & Richmond, V. P. (1992). Communication apprehension and small group communication. In R. S. Cathcart & L. A. Samovar (Eds.), *Small group communication: A reader* (6th ed., pp. 361–374). Dubuque, IA: William C. Brown.

McPherson, J. M., & Smith-Lovin, L. (1987). Homophily in voluntary organizations: Status distance and the composition of face-to-face groups. *American Sociological Review, 52,* 370–379.

Mead, G. H. (1934). *Mind, self, and society.* Chicago: University of Chicago Press.

Meier, C. (2003). Doing "groupness" in a spatially distributed work group: The case of videoconferences at *Technics.* In L. R. Frey (Ed.), *Group communication in context: Studies of bona fide groups* (2nd ed., pp. 367–397). Mahwah, NJ: Lawrence Erlbaum.

Meyers, R. A., Brashers, D. E., Winston, L., & Grob, L. (1997). Sex differences and group argument: A theoretical framework and empirical investigation. *Communication Studies, 48,* 19–41.

Meyers, R. A., & Seibold, D. R. (1990). Perspectives on group argument: A critical review of persuasive arguments theory and an alternative structurational view. In J. A. Anderson (Ed.), *Communication yearbook* (Vol. 13, pp. 268–302). Newbury Park, CA: Sage.

Moreland, R. L. (1985). Social categorization and the assimilation of "new" group members. *Journal of Personality and Social Psychology, 48,* 1173–1190.

Myeroff, B. G. (1982). Life history among the elderly: Performance, visibility, and remembering. In J. Ruby (Ed.), *A crack in the mirror: Reflexive perspectives in anthropology* (pp. 99–117). Philadelphia: University of Pennsylvania Press.

Nemeth, C. (1986). Differential contributions of majority vs. minority influence. *Psychological Review, 93,* 23–32.

Oetzel, J. G., & Robbins, J. (2003). Multiple identities in teams in a cooperative supermarket. In L. R. Frey (Ed.), *Group communication in context: Studies of bona fide groups* (2nd ed., pp. 183–208). Mahwah, NJ: Lawrence Erlbaum.

O'Sullivan, T. Hartley, J., Saunders, D., Montgomery, M., & Fiske, J. (1994). *Key concepts in communication and cultural studies* (2nd ed.). London: Routledge.

Pearce, W. B. (1995). A sailing guide for social constructionists. In W. Leeds-Hurwitz (Ed.), *Social approaches to communication* (pp. 88–113). New York: Guilford.

Pelled, L. H., Eisenhardt, K. M., & Xin, K. R. (1999). Exploring the black box: An analysis of work group diversity, conflict, and performance. *Administrative Science Quarterly, 44,* 1–28.

Pelz, D. C., & Andrews, F. M. (1976). *Scientists in organizations: Productive climates for research and development* (Rev. ed.). Ann Arbor: University of Michigan, Institute for Social Research.

Pennington, N., & Hastie, R. (1986). Evidence evaluation in complex decision making. *Journal of Personality and Social Psychology, 51,* 242–256.

Perloff, R. M. (1993). *The dynamics of persuasion.* Hillsdale, NJ: Lawrence Erlbaum.

Petronio, S., Jones, S., & Morr, M. C. (2003). Family privacy dilemmas: Managing communication boundaries within family groups. In L. R. Frey (Ed.), *Group communication in context: Studies of bona fide groups* (2nd ed., pp. 23–55). Mahwah, NJ: Lawrence Erlbaum.

Pitts, E. T. (1999). *People and programs that make a difference in a multicultural society: Volunteerism in America.* Lewiston, NY: Edwin Mellon Press.

Polanyi, K. (1944). *The great transformation.* New York: Farrar & Rinehart.

Polkinghorne, D. E. (1988). *Narrative knowing and the human sciences.* Albany: State University of New York Press.

Poole, M. S. (1981). Decision development in small groups I: A comparison of two models. *Communication Monographs, 48,* 1–24.

Poole, M. S. (1983a). Decision development in small groups II: A study of multiple sequences in decision making. *Communication Monographs, 50,* 206–232.

Poole, M. S. (1983b). Decision development in small groups III: A multiple sequence model of group decision development. *Communication Monographs, 50,* 321–241.

Poole, M. S., & DeSanctis, G. (1990). Understanding the use of group decision support systems: The theory of adaptive structuration. In J. Fulk & C. Steinfield (Eds.), *Organizations and communication technology* (pp. 175–195). Newbury Park, CA: Sage.

Poole, M. S., & DeSanctis, G. (1992). Microlevel structuration in computer-supported group decision-making. *Human Communication Research, 19,* 5–49.

Poole, M. S., DeSanctis, G., Kirsch, L., & Jackson, M. (1995). Group decision support systems as facilitators of quality team efforts. In L. R. Frey (Ed.), *Innovations in group facilitation techniques: Applications in natural settings* (pp. 299–320). Cresskill, NJ: Hampton Press.

Poole, M. S., Holmes, M., & DeSanctis, G. (1991). Conflict management in a computer-supported meeting environment. *Management Science, 37,* 926–953.

Poole, M. S., Keyton, J., & Frey, L. R. (1999). Group communication methodology: Issues and considerations. In L. R. Frey, D. S. Gouran, & M. S. Poole (Eds.), *The handbook of group communication theory and research* (pp. 92–112). Thousand Oaks, CA: Sage.

Poole, M. S., & Roth, J. (1989a). Decision development in small groups IV: A typology of group decision paths. *Human Communication Research, 15,* 323–356.

Poole, M. S., & Roth, J. (1989b). Decision development in small groups V: A test of a contingency model. *Human Communication Research, 15,* 549–589.

Poole, M. S., Seibold, D. R., & McPhee, R. D. (1996). The structuration of group decisions. In R. Y. Hirokawa & M. S. Poole (Eds.), *Communication and group decision making* (2nd ed., pp. 114–146). Thousand Oaks, CA: Sage.

Potter, W. J. (1996). *An analysis of thinking and research about qualitative methods.* Mahwah, NJ: Lawrence Erlbaum.

Putnam, L. L. (1986). Conflict in group decision-making. In R. Y. Hirokawa & M. S. Poole (Eds.), *Communication and group decision-making* (pp. 175–196). Beverly Hills, CA: Sage.

Putnam, L. L., & Stohl, C. (1990). Bona fide groups: A reconceptualization of groups in context. *Communication Studies, 41,* 248–265.

Putnam, L. L., & Stohl, C. (1996). Bona fide groups: An alternative perspective for communication and small group decision making. In R. Y. Hirokawa & M. S. Poole (Eds.), *Communication and group decision making* (2nd ed., pp. 179–214). Thousand Oaks, CA: Sage.

Putnam, L. L., Van Hoeven, S. A., & Bullis, C. A. (1991). The role of rituals and fantasy themes in teachers' bargaining. *Western Journal of Speech Communication, 55,* 85–103.

Putnam, R. D. (2000). *Bowling alone: The collapse and revival of American community.* New York: Simon & Schuster.

Riessman, C. K. (1993). *Narrative analysis.* Newbury Park, CA: Sage.

Rodriguez, R. A. (1998). Challenging demographic reductionism: A pilot study investigating diversity in group composition. *Small Group Research, 29,* 744–759.

Rotter, J. B. (1966). Generalized expectancies for internal versus external control of reinforcement. *Psychological Monographs, 80,* 1–28.

Sahlins, M. (1972). *Stone age economics.* London: Tavistock.

Sarbin, T. R. (1986). *Narrative psychology: The storied nature of human conduct.* New York: Praeger.

Scheerhorn, D., & Geist, P. (1997). Social dynamics in groups. In L. R. Frey & J. K. Barge (Eds.), *Managing group life: Communicating in decision-making groups* (pp. 81–130). Boston: Houghton Mifflin.

Schultz, B. (1974). Characteristics of emergent leaders of continuing problem-solving groups. *Journal of Psychology, 88,* 167–173.

Schultz, B. (1978). Predicting emergent leaders: An exploratory study of the salience of communicative functions. *Small Group Behavior, 9,* 109–114.

Schultz, B. (1982). Argumentativeness: Its effect in group decision-making and its role in leadership perceptions. *Communication Quarterly, 30,* 368–375.

Schultz, B. (1986). Communication correlates of perceived leaders in the small group. *Small Group Behavior, 17,* 51–65.

Schutz, A. (1967). *The phenomenology of the social world* (G. Walsh & F. Lehnert, Trans.). Evanston, IL: Northwestern University Press.

Schwalbe, M. (1996). *Unlocking the iron cage: The men's movement, gender politics, and American culture.* New York: Oxford University Press.

Schwartzman, H. B. (1989). *The meeting: Gatherings in organizations and communities.* New York: Plenum Press.

Seibold, D. R., McPhee, R. D., Poole, M. S., Tanita, N. E., & Canary, D. J. (1981). Argument, group influence, and decision outcomes. In G. Ziegelmuller & J. Rhodes (Eds.), *Dimensions of argument: Proceedings of the second summer conference on argumentation* (pp. 663–692). Annandale, VA: Speech Communication Association.

Sharf, B. F. (1978). A rhetorical analysis of leadership in small groups. *Communication Monographs, 45,* 156–172.

Shaw, M. E. (1981). *Group dynamics: The psychology of small group behavior* (3rd ed.). New York: McGraw-Hill.

Sherblom, J. C. (2003). Influences on the recommendations of international business consulting teams. In L. R. Frey (Ed.), *Group communication in context: Studies of bona fide groups* (2nd ed., pp. 263–290). Mahwah, NJ: Lawrence Erlbaum.

Sherif, M., Harvey, O. J., White, B. J., Hood, E. R., & Sherif, C. W. (1988). *The Robbers Cave experiment: Intergroup conflict and cooperation.* Middleton, CT: Wesleyan University Press.

Sigman, S. J. (1991). Handling the discontinuous aspects of continuous social relationships: Toward research on the persistence of social forms. *Communication Theory, 1,* 106–127.

Sinclair-James, L., & Stohl, C. (1997). Group endings and new beginnings. In L. R. Frey & J. K. Barge (Eds.), *Managing group life: Communicating in decision-making groups* (pp. 308–334). Boston: Houghton Mifflin.

Smith, C., & Gemmil, G. (1991). Change in the small group: A dissipative structure perspective. *Human Relations, 44,* 697–716.

Smith, K. K., & Berg, D. N. (1987). *Paradoxes of group life: Understanding conflict, paralysis, and movement in group dynamics.* San Francisco: Jossey-Bass.

Snow, D., Zurcher, L., Jr., & Ekland-Olson, S. (1980). Social networks and social movements: A microstructural approach to differential recruitment. *American Sociological Review, 45,* 787–801.

Socha, T. J. (1997). Group communication across the life span. In L. R. Frey & J. K. Barge (Eds.), *Managing group life: Communicating in decision-making groups* (pp. 1–28). Boston: Houghton Mifflin.

Socha, T. J. (1999). Communication in family units: Studying the first "group." In L. R. Frey, D. S. Gouran, & M. S. Poole (Eds.), *The handbook of group communication theory and research* (pp. 475–492). Thousand Oaks, CA: Sage.

Stohl, C. (1986). The role of memorable messages in the process of organizational socialization. *Communication Quarterly, 34,* 231–249.

Stohl, C. (1987). Bridging the parallel organization: A study of quality circle effectiveness. In M. L. McLaughlin (Ed.), *Communication yearbook* (Vol. 10, pp. 416–429). Newbury Park, CA: Sage.

Stohl, C., & Schell, S. E. (1991). A communication-based model of a small-group dysfunction. *Communication Quarterly, 5,* 90–110.

Stohl, C., & Walker, K. (2002). A bona fide perspective for the future of groups: Understanding collaborative groups. In L. R. Frey (Ed.), *New directions in group communication* (pp. 237–252). Thousand Oaks, CA: Sage.

Sunwolf. (1999a). The pedagogical and persuasive effects of Native American lesson stories, African dilemma tales, and Sufi wisdom tales. *Howard Journal of Communications, 10,* 47–71.

Sunwolf. (1999b, November). *Telling tales in jury deliberations: Jurors' uses of fictionalized and factually-based storytelling in argument.* Paper presented at the meeting of the National Communication Association Convention, Chicago.

Sunwolf. (2001, November). *Decision regret theory: Reducing the anxiety of group decision making through shared counterfactual storytelling.* Paper presented at the meeting of the National Communication Association, Atlanta, GA.

Sunwolf, & Frey, L. R. (2001). Storytelling: The power of narrative communication and interpretation. In W. P. Robinson & H. Giles (Eds.), *The new handbook of language and social psychology* (pp. 119–135). New York: John Wiley.

Sunwolf, & Leets, L. (2003). Communication paralysis during peer group exclusion: Social dynamics that prevent children and adolescents from expressing disagreement. *Journal of Language and Social Psychology, 22,* 355–384.

Sunwolf, & Leets, L. (2004). Being left out: Rejecting outsiders and communicating group boundaries in childhood and adolescent peer groups. *Journal of Applied Communication Research, 32,* 195–223.

Sunwolf, & Seibold, D. R. (1998). Jurors' intuitive rules for deliberations: A structurational approach to communication in jury decision making. *Communication Monographs, 65,* 282–307.

Tajfel, H. (1974). Social identity and intergroup behavior. *Social Science Information, 13,* 65–93.

Tajfel, H. (1981). Social stereotypes and social groups. In J. C. Turner & H. Giles (Eds.), *Intergroup behavior* (pp. 144–167). Chicago: University of Chicago Press.

Thornton, B. C. (1978). Health care teams and multimethodological research. In B. D. Ruben (Ed.), *Communication yearbook* (Vol. 2, pp. 539–533). New Brunswick, NJ: Transaction Books.

Tracy, K., & Standerfer, C. (2003). Selecting a school superintendent: Sensitivities in group deliberation. In L. R. Frey (Ed.), *Group communication in context: Studies of bona fide groups* (2nd ed., 109–134). Mahwah, NJ: Lawrence Erlbaum.

Triandis, H. C., Hall, E. R, & Ewen, R. B. (1965). Member heterogeneity and dyadic creativity. *Human Relations, 17,* 33–35.

Trice, H. M., & Beyer, J. M. (1984). Studying organizational cultures through rites and ceremonials. *Academy of Management Review, 9,* 653–669.

Turner, V. (1969). *The ritual process: Structure and anti-structure.* Ithaca, NY: Cornell University Press.

van de Wetering, S. (1996). Authoritarianism as a group-level adaptation in humans. *Behavioral and Group Research, 19,* 780–781.

Vinton, K. L. (1989). Humor in the workplace: It's more than telling jokes. *Small Group Research, 20,* 151–166.

Watson, W. E., Kumar, K., & Michaelsen, L. K. (1993). Cultural diversity's impact on interaction process and performance: Comparing homogeneous and diverse task groups. *Academy of Management Journal, 36,* 590–602.

Weick, K. E. (1979). *The social psychology of organizing* (2nd ed.). Reading, MA: Addison-Wesley.

Wheelan, S. A., McKeage, R. L., Verdi, A. F., Abraham, M., Krasick, C., & Johnston, F. (1994). Communication and developmental patterns in a system of interacting groups. In L. R. Frey (Ed.), *Group communication in context: Studies of natural groups* (pp. 153–180). Hillsdale, NJ: Lawrence Erlbaum.

Wiersema, M. F., & Bird, A. (1993). Organizational demography in Japanese firms: Group heterogeneity, individual dissimilarity, and top management team turnover. *Academy of Management Journal, 36,* 996–1025.

Witmer, D. F. (1997). Communication and recovery: Structuration as an ontological approach to organizational culture. *Communication Monographs, 64,* 324–349.

Yep, G. A., Reece, S. T., & Negrón, E. L. (2003). Culture and stigma in a bona fide group: Boundaries and context in a "closed" support group for "Asian Americans" living with HIV infection. In L. R. Frey (Ed.), *Group communication in context: Studies of bona fide groups* (2nd ed., pp. 157–180). Mahwah, NJ: Lawrence Erlbaum.

Yin, R. K. (2003). *Case study research: Design and methods* (3rd ed.). Thousand Oaks, CA: Sage.

7

Understanding Groups
From a Feminist Perspective

Renee A. Meyers, Jennifer L. Berdahl, Dale Brashers,
Jennifer R. Considine, Janice R. Kelly, Celia Moore,
Jennifer L. Peterson, and Jennifer R. Spoor

Abstract

In this chapter, we first provide an overview of prominent theories in feminist scholarship. To simplify a very complex field, we divide the theories into two major categories: individual differences theories and structural inequality theories. The first set of theories focuses on the differences between women's and men's perspectives and values, whereas the second set of theories focuses on the societal structures that afford men power over women. We then review research that is relevant to these perspectives, organizing our review around four major foci of feminist-oriented research: (1) communal and agentic behavior, (2) power and leadership, (3) group tasks and performance, and (4) implications for changes in groups over time. Within this review, we address the seven questions pertaining to group structures, processes, outcomes, and practices. We then discuss feminist perspectives on research methodology and conclude by noting the strengths and weaknesses of a feminist perspective for continued scholarly inquiry in the group research domain.

Definitions, Assumptions, and Research Foci

One of the enduring concerns of early group research was ensuring the participation of all members in groups. Much attention was devoted to studying leadership styles and participatory processes that could facilitate the inclusion of all ideas in group decision-making and other activities. However, in some ways, this work was too simple because it presumed that simply by changing procedural rules, participation and fair inclusion of all perspectives would follow. It is clear that deep-seated individual differences and/or structures, many developed and sustained by the larger society, ultimately undermine attempts to broaden participation in groups. The contributions of women, minorities, and other marginalized groups are often downplayed and disadvantaged compared to the contributions of those in power in even the best-intentioned participatory processes. This has stimulated a growth in group research from the feminist perspective.

Scholarship from a feminist perspective seeks to understand and promote the elimination of oppression and domination and to replace them with relationships of equality. Feminist scholars are committed to resisting unfair social practices toward women and all other disenfranchised groups. Feminists assume that (1) men and women are equally capable and equally deserving, (2) proximal (intra- and interpersonal) and distal (societal, economic, political) factors influence gendered practices, and (3) gender plays an important role in every group. This final assumption reflects feminists' belief that to the extent that men and women differ in values or perspectives, and/or groups act as microcosms of embedding environments, gender impacts all group practice.

A feminist perspective is interested in investigating how relationships, interaction, power, and roles are constituted within groups based on sex and gender. In this chapter, *sex* refers to biological differences between men and women and *gender* refers to social, symbolic constructions that a society confers on biological sex. Relevant research questions within this perspective include: Do group members differentially evaluate men's and women's interaction, behavior, leadership, and performance? Do men and women communicate differently in groups? How are power and status allocated among men and women in groups? What roles and outcomes are valued most in groups based on their sex and gender composition?

Although feminists and their perspectives are often viewed as unitary, feminist theory is far from homogeneous. In the next section, we provide an overview of prominent theories in feminist scholarship (for a more thorough introduction, see Tong, 1998). To simplify a very complex field, we have divided the theories into two major categories. The first set of theories—which we have termed *individual differences theories*—have in common a focus on the psychological and epistemological differences between men and women as individuals. The second set of feminist theories—*structural inequality theories*—focus on systemic (economic, political, social) inequalities between men and women as members of society. We then introduce the reader to *multicultural or global feminism,* which addresses both individual and systemic elements and focuses on the racial and cultural diversity of women internationally.

Two caveats are necessary here. First, the two categories we have chosen are not exclusive divisions. Many of the theories address both individual and structural issues in analyzing differences between women and men. Hence, these categories reflect general, not specific orientations to feminism. Second, we clearly cannot do justice to *all* feminist theories but instead address the more prominent theories in each of these two categories.

Feminist Theoretical Perspectives

Individual Differences Feminist Theories

What we are calling individual differences feminist theories include those that focus on the psychological differences between women and men; they include psychoanalytic feminism, cultural feminism, standpoint theory, and postmodern feminism. Although these theories differ in important ways, they have in common the belief that women are likely to have a different perspective of the world than men. In general, these differences are attributed to the dissimilar roles men and women play in the social structure, in particular the sexual division of labor (men perform agentic tasks and roles, and women perform communal tasks and roles) as well as the fact that women do all or most of the parenting of children.

Psychoanalytic Feminism

Psychoanalytic feminism posits that women's ways of acting are "rooted deep in women's psyche and ways of thinking" (Tong, 1998, p. 5). These feminists believe family patterns and psychosexual development play a central role in explaining the differences between men and women. Although the roots of psychoanalytic feminism are in Freudian theory, much theory in this domain has developed as a critique and response to the misogynist basis of Freudian psychoanalysis (Adler, 1927; Horney, 1973; Mitchell, 1974).

Psychoanalytic theorists Dinnerstein (1977) and Chodorow (1978) claimed that much of what is wrong with gendered human relations can be traced to the fact that women do all or most of the parenting. Dinnerstein (1977) argued that men seek to dominate women in reaction to the all-powerful mother, and women, afraid of the powerful mother within themselves, seek to be controlled by men (Tong, 1998). Chodorow (1978) suggested that only boys fully separate from their mothers, which leads to their inability to relate deeply to others, whereas girls are able to develop deep emotional connections. This pattern—of women's desire for connection and men's desire for autonomy—continues to lead women to assume roles in the family and men to pursue positions in the workplace.

Cultural Feminism

Cultural feminism also focuses on the psychological and epistemological differences between women and men, but it places more emphasis on societal patterns and psychomoral development as the locus of women's and men's ways of thinking and acting. For example, Carol Gilligan (1982) challenged traditional theories of moral development (e.g., Freud, 1925/1962; Kohlberg, 1969), which hold that women are less morally developed than men. By describing women's different process of moral reasoning, Gilligan showed that women are differently, but not less morally developed than men. Similarly, Ruddick (1980) suggested that women's values, knowledge, and experiences could provide a moral alternative to masculine aggressive morality. She argued that maternal thinking, which teaches reconciliation, empathy, and respect for nature and humanity, could play a transformative role in our increasingly militarized society.

Feminist Standpoint Theorists

The work of psychoanalytic and cultural feminists was elaborated by standpoint theorists, who argued that women's experiences provided a unique epistemological position. Feminist standpoint theory, originally outlined by Hartsock (1983), argued that women's perspectives should be the starting point, not the ending point of human research. Standpoint theory suggested that knowledge is situated within individual experiences and that women's knowledge is shaped by material influences, history, and experiences. Hartsock (1998) indicated that the adoption of a standpoint "makes visible the inhumanity of relations among human beings and carries a historically liberatory role" (p. 229) that can generate both personal and societal transformation.

Postmodern Feminism

Not all feminist theorists think that *all* women experience reality in the same way. In particular postmodern and multicultural feminists (addressed later in the chapter) suggest that the very notion of the universal subject "woman" contributes to sexism and oppression. Postmodern feminists draw especially on ideas articulated by Lacan (1977), Derrida (1978), Foucault (1977, 1980), and de Beauvoir (1952/1974). Cixous (1981) and Irigaray (1985) viewed women's experiences as essentially different from men's and argued that the female body and sexuality are central to transforming the human experience.

In contrast, Julia Kristeva (1980) resisted identification of the feminine with women and the masculine with men. She suggested that the symbolic order is composed of the expression of both emotion and reason (Tong, 1998). Kristeva believed that truly liberated individuals could navigate both of these symbolic orders and thus bridge the masculine and the feminine.

Structural Inequality Feminist Theories

Instead of focusing on psychological and epistemological outcomes of men and women's different social and sexual roles, structural inequality feminists focus on the political, social, and economic structures that enforce and reify these roles and, as a consequence, afford men power over women. Still, the individual differences and structural inequality perspectives are not necessarily contradictory. They simply focus on different aspects of women's inequality. Liberal feminism, Marxist and socialist feminism, and radical feminism are representative feminist structural inequality theories.

Liberal Feminism

Liberal feminism is perhaps the most mainstream form of feminism. The feminist movements that took place in the 20th century were largely dominated by liberal feminist beliefs and represent what most people commonly think of as feminist theory. Liberal feminism is philosophically grounded in traditional liberal political theory and embraces the liberal values of universal human rationality, the essential equality of all people, and individual rights and equal treatment under the law. Early liberal feminist theorists included Mary Wollstonecraft and John Stuart Mill and Harriet Taylor Mill (see Jaggar, 1983).

Philosophically, liberal feminism understands the sexes to be essentially *similar* and gender to be a social construction. Hence, to the extent that women and men exhibit behavioral or psychological differences, this is a result of legal and economic systems that are created and maintained by rules and laws that privilege men and by a set of social values and norms that assign women less valued and powerful roles than men. Politically, liberal feminism has a reformist agenda, focusing on granting women equal rights as well as equal opportunities to pursue self-fulfillment.

Marxist and Socialist Feminism

Marxist and socialist feminists question the economic and social institutions usually taken for granted by liberal feminists and advocate a revolutionary rather than reformist agenda (cf. Hartmann, 1981; Jaggar, 1983; Rowbotham, 1973; Young, 1990). They understand the capitalist economic system as a set of power relations in which class oppression is the fundamental expression of exploitation (for a good collection of writings, see Engels, 1902/1942; Marx, 1834–1894/2000). Although this framework provided feminists with an elegant model of oppression to apply to women (Mitchell, 1971), a pure Marxist critique does not leave much room to theorize simultaneously about women's oppression under patriarchy (male-dominated structures and systems) and about working class oppression under capitalism (Hartmann, 1981; Young, 1990).

Socialist feminism, therefore, developed as a way of inserting specifically sex-based oppression into what is traditionally a sex-blind concept of class oppression within Marxism. Socialist feminists suggest that the union of capitalism and patriarchy oppresses women, in that capitalism is predicated on women performing unpaid labor in the private sphere. That is, current structures of production and reproduction act in concert to oppress women, and both these structures must change to achieve equality between men and women. Socialist feminists believe that this approach represents a unified feminist theory (Hartmann, 1981; Jaggar, 1983; Rowbotham, 1973; Young, 1990).

Radical Feminism

Radical feminism is generally harder to characterize than other schools of feminist thought because it represents a wide range of views and is not grounded in any identifiable philosophical or political tradition. To the extent that there are unifying principles of radical feminism, they are (1) that the oppression of women is the first and paradigmatic form of oppression, preceding and providing a model for all other forms of oppression; and (2) that the sex/gender system, which politically, socially, and economically privileges men and masculinity over women and femininity, constitutes the technology of women's oppression and must be eliminated (Jaggar & Rothenberg, 1984, see p. 86).

In terms of structural approaches to change within radical feminism, there are two main schools of thought. The first of these—radical *separatist* feminism—argues that there is no way for men and women to be liberated from their historical gendered roles in society without remaining continually at risk of co-optation by the patriarchal system if the male sex is not removed from the equation (e.g., Daly, 1978; French, 1985; Noddings, 1984). A second major school of radical feminist thought—radical *androgynous* feminism—takes the opposite approach, arguing that gender differences, in terms of both gendered characteristics and gendered labor and societal roles, are the root of the problem in the sex-gender system and instead advocates universal androgyny as the appropriate strategy to eliminate patriarchy (e.g., Bem, 1974; Firestone, 1970; Millet, 1970).

Multicultural and Global Feminism

Among those seeking to further decenter the notion of woman are multicultural and global feminists who straddle both the individual differences and structural inequality feminist perspectives. Multicultural/global feminists focus their attention on differences among women, particularly with respect to issues of race, sexuality, class, and nationality (see Shabat, 1998). Much feminist theory has been based on the observations of white, middle-class, heterosexual, Christian women in Western industrialized countries, who assumed that the process of overcoming oppression was the same for all women (Anzaldua & Moraga, 1981; Spelman, 1988).

Among the first to point out this apparent hypocrisy were black feminists. bell hooks (1990), for example, argued that no one form of oppression (racism, sexism, or classism) can be eliminated until all forms of oppression are eliminated. Lesbian feminists challenged the assumed normality of heterosexuality (Rich, 1980; Wittig, 1981), which they believe perpetuates female subordination by requiring women's identification with men.

Global feminists focus their attention on the oppression created by colonial and nationalist practices. Sometimes referred to as postcolonial feminism, these theories critiqued global political and economic policies that have divided the world into the First World and the Third World. For Third World feminists, political and economic discrimination (to which First World women often contribute) is much worse than gender discrimination. A central premise of global feminism is that all women are interconnected. Global feminists call on women to get involved in worldwide issues concerning women's sexuality and reproduction, as well as struggles for national liberation and economic development.

Summary

The individual differences feminist perspectives we discussed focus on the dissimilar perspectives and values of men and women, whereas the structural inequality feminist perspectives focus on the societal structures that afford men power over women. A multicultural feminist perspective focuses on both—how one's perspective and experiences stem from one's positions in the global community with respect to gender, race, class, and cultural structures. These perspectives offer different opportunities for small group research. For example, an individual differences feminist perspective would suggest that instead of focusing on task performance (a traditionally male or masculine value), researchers should focus on interpersonal relations within a group (or a traditionally female or feminine value). A structural inequality feminist perspective, on the other hand, may not question the basic assumptions or topics of mainstream small group research (i.e., task performance and productivity) but would instead focus on the influence of external structures on the internal divisions of labor and power within a group with respect to sex and gender. Table 7.1 presents a summary of basic assumptions of feminist perspectives on groups.

Research on Groups From a Feminist Perspective

In this section, we review relevant research that addresses the seven research questions pertaining to group structures, processes, outcomes, and practices. Much of this research was not conducted with an explicitly feminist aim or theoretical framework, but it addresses feminist concerns nonetheless. In a slight divergence from the structure of many of the other chapters, we organize our review first according to four major research foci of feminist-oriented research, and second according to the seven questions because we felt the foci provided a more descriptive framework for feminist group research than did the seven questions. The four foci of feminist-oriented group research that structure our review include: (1) communal and agentic behavior, (2) power and leadership, (3) group tasks and performance, and (4) implications for changes in groups over time. Within each of these sections, we explicitly indicate which of the seven questions we are addressing, although we sometimes answer them in a different order than might be found in other chapters and sometimes in sets of two or three rather than

Table 7.1   The Feminist Perspective

Definition of perspective	A feminist perspective seeks to eliminate oppressive practices toward women and other marginalized groups and replace them with relationships of equality
Key assumptions	• Men and women are equally capable and equally deserving • Internal and external factors influence gendered practices • Gender plays an important role in every group
Types of groups	Applicable to the study of any groups, especially those with mixed gender composition
Key theories	Psychoanalytic feminism, cultural feminism, standpoint feminism, postmodern feminism, liberal feminism, Marxist and socialist feminism, radical feminism, multicultural and global feminism
Dominant research methodologies	Laboratory investigations, observations and interviews, content analysis—both quantitative and qualitative methods are employed
Strengths	• Directs our attention to typically invisible groups and research topics • It is an interdisciplinary perspective focused on a single research goal • It has critical, practical, and activist underpinnings
Weaknesses	• Difficulty in moving beyond traditional male-centric definitions and models • Slow to translate perspectives into theoretical frameworks relevant for investigative work

singly. Table 7.2 also offers a summary of the answers to the seven questions from a feminist perspective.

Communal and Agentic Behavior in Groups

Research on communal and agentic behavior in groups best addresses Questions 1 and 4. Question 1 asks, *How does group composition impact group communication and behavior in groups?* Question 4 inquires, *What kinds of group interaction processes does a group carry out?* Indeed, research on communal/agentic behavior and interaction, and its connections to the sex composition of groups, is a major focus of research within the

Table 7.2   Key Findings of Feminist Perspective Research

Group composition	• Same-sex groups tend to engage in more gender stereotypical behavior than mixed-sex groups • Communication patterns differ in mixed-sex and same-sex groups; some research suggests less stereotyped behavior in mixed-sex groups, but other research shows more stereotyped behavior in mixed-sex groups (especially leadership behaviors) • Differences in task type affect how well men and women perform and how well same-sex versus mixed-sex groups perform
Group projects	There is little empirical research on this question; feminists would refocus and reframe this question to explore ways in which projects get gender typed, and how that gender-typing influences group interaction and performance
Group structure	• Men tend to use more autocratic leadership style and centralized leadership structure; women prefer more democratic style and decentralized leadership structure • Men emerge as leaders and task leaders more often than women • Male leaders are evaluated more favorably than female leaders
Interaction	• Men use more control-oriented communication; women use more affectively oriented interaction • In competitive situations, men use information to help their own position, and women share information more equally
Group action/ outcomes	There is little empirical research available from feminist perspective, so feminists might refocus and reframe this question to suggest that a reification of gendered interaction structures, relational patterns, power structures, social roles, and values result from group action
Change over time	This is not explicitly addressed in this perspective, but feminists might refocus and reframe this question to suggest that groups are likely to form when there is a relational, economic, social, or institutional reason to do so. Groups change and dissolve based on internal or external forces that act on the group
Ecology	• The anonymity of some technical environments may have advantages for women, but the power of reduced social cues may not be as great as originally proposed • In reframing this question, a feminist perspective might attend to how ecological factors influence gender-typing of interaction and performance

feminist perspective. Sex stereotypes and social roles associate women with communal characteristics and men with agentic characteristics (e.g., Bem, 1974; Eagly, 1987; Gilligan, 1982). Communal characteristics include being warm, focusing on interpersonal relations, and being giving and cooperative. Agentic characteristics include being independent, task-oriented, dominant, and competitive.

Individual difference feminists and structural inequality feminists agree that sex differences in communal and agentic orientations stem from structural forces (although the particular forces differ by theory, as reviewed). Individual difference feminists, however, tend to study sex differences as causal—something emanating from men and women, whose different styles can be observed in groups. For example, sociolinguistic or genderlect theories (Bem, 1975; Kendall & Tannen, 1997; Lakoff, 1975; Tannen, 1990) investigate how language interacts with gender identity to produce gendered outcomes. Structural inequality feminists study these sex differences as an outcome of social role expectations and differences between men and women in status and power. Theoretical frameworks in this tradition include social role theory (Eagly, 1987; Eagly, Wood, & Diekman, 2000) and status characteristics theory (Berger, Fisek, Norman, & Zelditch, 1977; Ridgeway, 1997, 2001a, 2001b; Ridgeway & Berger, 1986). (These two theories are discussed in more detail later in this chapter and in Chapter 5, this volume.) The study of differences in communal and agentic behavior tends to reflect an individual differences feminist perspective, although exceptions exist (e.g., Berdahl, 1996; Berdahl & Anderson, 2003).

Gender Composition Effects

Much research has examined how the sex composition of a group influences individual behavior and styles of interaction within it. Meta-analyses by Carli (1982) and by Anderson and Blanchard (1982) have demonstrated that all-female groups engage in relatively more positive socioemotional types of behavior than all-male groups, which engage in relatively more task-oriented and instrumental communicative behaviors. It should be noted, however, that in both types of groups, the highest percentage of behavior involves task-oriented contributions, and the second highest percentage involves positive socioemotional concerns.

Some feminists—particularly radical feminists—would challenge these findings and suggest that the distinction made between task-oriented and social-emotional behavior, so often linked to gender in groups, should be questioned. For example, criticisms have been directed at the distinction that Bales (1950) draws in his Interaction Process Analysis between instrumental and expressive acts. Specifically, Bales's classification of "agrees" and "disagrees" as expressive has come under fire (Wood & Rhodes, 1992). Although agreements and disagreements may have emotional consequences or may result from emotional experiences, they also serve task-oriented purposes, as they may operate to finalize a task suggestion or speed inclusion of an idea. Thus, research findings that suggest that female groups and group members focus on socioemotional concerns may be an artifact of Bales's coding system.

Although men and women often appear to behave in ways consistent with sex stereotypes in same-sex groups, evidence is mixed in terms of how they behave in mixed-sex groups. Much research suggests that people behave in less sex-stereotypic ways in mixed-sex groups (e.g., Aries, 1976; Berdahl & Anderson, 2003; Carli, 1982, 1989; Kerr & MacCoun, 1985; Piliavin & Martin, 1978; Taylor & Strassberg, 1986). For example, a pioneering study on gender and group interaction found that men engage in less competitive and more socioemotional behavior in the presence of women and that women engage in more competitive and less socioemotional behavior in the presence of men (Aries, 1976). That mixed-sex groups exhibit less sex-stereotyped behavior dovetails with findings that job satisfaction is higher within balanced-sex work groups than within single-sex work groups (Fields & Blum, 1997).

Other research, particularly that focusing on leadership emergence and participation in groups (reviewed in more detail later), suggests that men and women display more sex-stereotypic behavior as individuals in mixed-sex groups (e.g., Eagly & Karau, 1991; Graham & Papa, 1993; Samter & Burleson, 1990). Whether people display more or less sex-stereotypic behavior in groups may depend on the behavior in question (e.g., whether it is relative amounts of socioemotional or task-oriented behaviors within individuals or total amounts of influence and participation between them) or on the task at hand (e.g., whether it is unitary or divisible).

Sex Differences in Group Interaction and Behavior

Individual differences theories such as sociolinguistic and genderlect theories (Bem, 1975; Tannen, 1990), for example, are especially attentive to investigating differences in women's and men's communication and language. In terms of communication styles, men tend to score higher than women on measures of verbal aggressiveness and argumentativeness (Burgoon, Dillard, & Doran, 1983; Infante, 1982; Infante, Wall, Leap, & Danielson, 1984; Nicotera & Rancer, 1994). Even when it comes to using humor, men tend to be more aggressive by using humor to differentiate individuals, whereas women use humor for cohesion building (Robinson & Smith-Lovin, 2001). Women's interest in cohesion building also is a potential explanation for their tendency to ask significantly more probing questions, which are most likely to foster cooperation and connection, sharing of information, and increased participation by group members (Hawkins & Power, 1999; Meyers, Brashers, Winston, & Grob, 1997).

Men and women also tend to differ in predictable ways in terms of competitive and cooperative behavior in groups. During negotiations, women tend to behave more cooperatively than men, although they are similar in their levels of competitiveness (Walters, Stuhlmacher, & Meyer, 1998). Research also indicates that women are more likely to employ compromising strategies in a conflict, whereas men will tend to use competitive tactics (Gayle, Priess, & Allen, 1994). Men are more likely than women to use information that helps their own position and harms another's position in a competitive situation, whereas women are more likely to share all types of information equally (Deal, 2000).

Power and Leadership in Groups

Feminist-oriented research on power and leadership in groups is best suited to answer Questions 3, 5, and 7. Question 3 asks, *How are groups structured, what tools and technologies do they have access to, and how do these structures and technologies affect group interaction and performance?* Question 5 asks, *What results from group action?* Question 7 asks, *How does the group's ecology affect group interaction and performance?* According to a feminist perspective, group structures and technologies are believed to affect group interaction and performance, and group action results from gendered interaction structures, relational patterns, power structures, social roles, and values (see Table 7.2).

Group Structure and Leadership

Structural inequality feminist perspectives stress the importance of studying initially leaderless groups to examine how societal inequality is reflected in emergent leadership and power structures in groups. The general result of many studies of leadership emergence in mixed-sex groups is that men tend to be chosen as leaders more often than women when members are randomly assigned to groups and leaders are allowed to emerge (e.g., Eagly & Karau, 1991), although there is some evidence that gender (masculinity) rather than sex (maleness) drives this process (Kent & Moss, 1994). A meta-analysis (Carly & Eagly, 1999) showed that men are more likely to be chosen as leaders because their social roles encourage more task focus whereas women are more often relationally oriented.

Studies of communication and behavior in groups may reveal the processes that contribute to this outcome. Sociolinguistic and genderlect theories (Bem, 1975; Tannen, 1990), for example, seek to explain men's and women's communicative and/or language differences. Men tend to speak more, interrupt women more often than men, and are interrupted less often than women during group discussion, (e.g., Smith-Lovin & Brody, 1989; West & Zimmerman, 1983). Men and women are also perceived differently based on how they present information: Men generally were viewed as intelligent regardless of whether they used support or qualifiers, whereas women who provided no support and used qualifiers received lower intelligence and knowledgeability ratings (Bradley, 1981). Given these findings, some researchers have argued that gender differences in communication are due to relative status and power rather than to gender per se (Henley & Kramerae, 1991; Wheelan, 1996).

Whether this is due to social role expectations or to actual individual differences, men and women often engage in different leadership styles in small groups, which can affect the leadership structure of the group. Not only are men more likely to emerge as overall leaders, but they are also more likely to emerge as task leaders, whereas women are more likely to be maintenance or relational leaders (Eagly & Karau, 1991). Women leaders generally use democratic styles of leadership, focusing on participation and understanding, whereas men leaders tend to use autocratic styles of leadership, characterized by directives and aggressiveness (Eagly & Johnson, 1990). Still, Hawkins (1995) found that the group member who communicates the most task strategies to the group (regardless of gender) is most likely to emerge as the overall leader.

In groups and contexts in which the leadership structure is assigned rather than emergent, sex differences in behavior and styles tend to disappear. Walker, Illardi, McMahon, and Fennell (1996) demonstrated that men were five times more likely than women to exercise opinion leadership in mixed-sex groups, but sex differences vanished when leaders were assigned before group interaction. Similarly, studies of leadership in organizational settings, where leadership is formally assigned, fail to replicate many of the differences in behavior observed in women's and men's styles in student laboratory groups (cf. Eagly & Karau, 1991), suggesting that leadership role demands override expectations based on traditional sex roles in driving behavior in these contexts, and/or women feel a greater need to conform to male stereotypes in the organizational context (Fournier & Kelemen, 2001).

Research in this domain also indicates that there are differences in how men and women evaluate leadership. Several things can affect group members' perceptions and satisfaction with men or women leaders, such as negative attitudes, group composition, and loss or maintenance of reward power (Alderton & Jurma, 1980; Jurma & Wright, 1990). Lucas and Lovaglia (1998) found that women leaders were rated as being equally competent and willing to contribute as men leaders, however, unlike men leaders, women were also rated as more likable than other group members, and the members in groups led by women rated group performance lower than did those in groups led by men. Women leaders are especially likely to be evaluated negatively (compared to men) when they are in male-dominated roles or exhibit stereotypically masculine leadership styles (Eagly, Makhijani, & Klonsky, 1992).

Researchers studying groups from a feminist perspective have contemplated and examined possible solutions to the unequal structures and outcomes often experienced by women in a group context. For example, it may be possible to buffer groups from the impact of inequality in a culture or society at large by creating proximal cultures or environments, such as the organization, the extended family, or the neighborhood in which the group is embedded, cultures or environments that have values counter to this broader influence. Or, consistent with a liberal feminist perspective, social role theory suggests that women may benefit from longer-term group situations because with more time, women's actual abilities would outweigh initial judgments based on sex stereotypes (Eagly & Karau, 1991). Feminists also advocate providing women with information and training that would equalize their status and perceived expertise to that of men and allow the women to change existing structures (Kelly, Craig, & Spoor, 2003).

Group Action—Emergent Leadership

Much research on group action and gender in groups has focused on the frequency with which men and women participate and emerge as leaders in groups. The structural inequality feminist perspective is more prevalent in this domain than the individual differences feminist perspective, as evidenced by the two most popular theories used in this literature: social role theory (Eagly, 1987; Eagly et al., 2000) and status characteristics theory (Berger et al., 1977; Ridgeway, 1997, 2001a, 2001b). Social role theory is consistent with liberal feminism, as it assumes that men and women are basically similar but that sex differences in social roles outside a group drive expectations for men's and women's behavior within it, creating a traditional sexual division of labor whereby women assume communal (e.g., supportive) roles and men assume agentic (e.g., leadership) ones. Status characteristics theory is more consistent with a Marxist/socialist feminist perspective. Power and status differences between men and women in society are assumed to be imported into the group setting, where sex is used as a diffuse status cue and leads the group to expect men to be more competent than women.

Group Ecology

A burgeoning area of research that addresses a possible solution to sex inequality in mixed-sex groups is how the group's *technical environment* impacts communicative patterns of men and women. Several researchers have suggested that computer-mediated communication may reduce the impact of social cues on status-related behavior and outcomes in groups (Dubrovsky, Kiesler, & Sethna, 1991). The lack of social cues can encourage greater participation (Siegel, Dubrovsky, Kiesler, & McGuire, 1986) and minimize the potential disadvantages associated with a person's sex (Herschel, Cooper, Smith, & Arrington, 1994). The sense of anonymity encourages a feeling that ideas presented will be evaluated on their quality rather than the characteristics of the contributing individual (Jessup, Connolly, & Tansik, 1990).

Many women prefer interacting anonymously through collaborative group technology because it provides them the opportunity to communicate without being judged on the basis of sex (Gopal, Mirana, Robichaux, & Bostrom, 1997). In fact, women have demonstrated greater social interdependence in computer-mediated groups (Jaffe, Lee, Huang, & Oshagan, 1999). Still, although research shows that women are more likely to use strategies that maintain the reduced social cues of collaborative technology, men are more likely to seek ways to make computer-mediated interactions more like face-to-face interactions by providing clues or references to gender (Flanagin, Tiyaamornwong, O'Connor, & Seibold, 2002).

Despite theoretical advantages for women in a computer-mediated environment, it is still unclear whether these advantages are realized in practice. Some research indicates that women produce fewer messages in computer-mediated group meetings, expressing more opinions and agreements face-to-face (Adrianson, 2001). However, when *content* of messages was examined by Postmes and Spears (2002), they found that men dominated the discussion in terms of their communication style. Men were more autonomous, and women tended to be more dependent in their statements (Postmes & Spears, 2002). An interesting finding of this research was that stereotypical gendered behavior was more prominent when the gender of group members was not available, suggesting that the power of reduced social cues may not be as great as originally proposed.

Group Performance and Group Projects

Research from a feminist perspective on group performance and projects addresses part of Question 2 and Question 4 (group performance outcomes). Question 2 asks, *How do the group's projects affect interaction and performance?* Question 4 asks, *How does group performance result from group action?* In terms of Question 2, feminist researchers have been interested in exploring (1) ways in which group projects and tasks become gender typed, whether that typing is based on individual gender differences (individual differences perspective) or on more societal-level sex discrimination (structural inequality perspective); and (2) how the gender typing of group projects influences group interaction and performance.

Group Projects and Tasks

Feminist theorists would argue that tasks become gender typed due to relational and societal patterns, as well as the historical overrepresentation of one sex in a job. Tasks become male typed, for example, because predominantly men perform them. Individual differences feminists would argue that to the extent that sex stereotypes have been internalized and have created self-fulfilling prophecies of difference between men and women, groups with more men in them should perform better on male-typed tasks, and groups with more women in them should perform better on female-typed tasks (see Wood, 1987).

In addition, some structural inequality and global feminists would argue that tasks are gender typed by virtue of the power inherent in them. Tasks are male typed, for example, because they involve access to and control over resources and outcomes of importance to others. These feminists would be particularly concerned that men may attempt to usurp what power women accrue from specifically female-typed tasks or projects. Because structural inequality feminists are particularly interested in the division between public and private, and how reproduction supports that distinction to women's disadvantage (or, occasionally, advantage), they would be interested in examining how the type of project supports or hinders women's social or economic equality.

Second, both individual differences and structural inequality feminists would argue that gender typing of tasks and projects (whether through relational or structural means) influences group performance. These theorists suggest that any tasks that women commonly take responsibility for are gender typed as undervalued, private sphere, and without value within a capitalist system (Hartmann, 1981; Tong, 1998). Therefore, these feminists might be interested in examining how group projects are structured to lead group members to feel less alienated from group performance outcomes. Recent research on autonomous work groups or self-directed teams may be of particular interest, as they may serve to reduce group members' feelings of alienation (Cascio, 1995).

In this same vein, some feminist theorists from both of these perspectives would be particularly interested in reframing how traditionally male-typed tasks affect performance outcomes in groups of women. For example, Nelson (1988) and Martin and colleagues (e.g., Martin, 1992; Martin, Knopoff, & Beckman, 1988) have suggested that women-only companies have different starting assumptions, ground rules, cultures, and ways of conducting business than companies run by men. Research on women-only groups highlights the tensions between feminist organizing principles and traditional leadership structures (Bartunek, Walsh, & Lucey, 2000), and it is instructive regarding how groups can remain leaderless over time by maintaining flexibility in group processes (Booth-Butterfield & Booth-Butterfield, 1988; Counselman, 1991; Kees, 1999; Nelson, 1988; Wyatt, 2002). Hence, these feminists might ask the inverse question: How do interaction and the performance of gender in groups influence the projects they value and choose to pursue?

Group Performance

A feminist perspective is not as concerned as traditional group research with typical measures of group performance. However, this does not imply that feminists do not understand group performance to be relevant, only that current understandings of "performance" need to be expanded beyond simple task accomplishment.

Many feminists suggest that the traditional focus on task accomplishment as a group outcome demonstrates an androcentric and capitalistic bias in research on small groups. Others would challenge current definitions of performance, arguing that performance needs to be reconceptualized to include broader definitions of outcomes, such as member support and group well-being. For example, there are a number of fairly recent examples of researchers acknowledging the lack of emphasis on maintenance processes in general, and on the emotional processes of groups in particular (Kelly & Barsade, 2001; Meyers & Brashers, 1994; Moreland, 1987). Still other feminist theorists suggest that a focus on outcomes, and traditional performance outcomes in particular, eclipses the examination of group activities, such as communication and group maintenance processes, that go into the production of group outcomes. Radical feminists and some postmodern feminists would be interested in examining the emergence of a distinct communication style in all-female groups (Daly, 1978).

Much research on men's and women's task performance in groups has not come from a feminist perspective. That research which has come from a feminist perspective tends to critique the conclusions drawn from nonfeminist research. For example, early research found that all-male groups tend to outperform all-female groups (Hoffman, 1965). Wood's (1987) meta-analysis also acknowledged that, overall, male groups tend to outperform female groups but suggested that female groups' emphasis on social-emotional interaction benefits their performance on tasks that require high levels of social activity (e.g., decision-making tasks), whereas the relative emphasis of male groups on task-oriented interaction benefits their performance on tasks that require high levels of task behavior (e.g., brainstorming tasks). This hypothesis was also confirmed in the research of others (Hutson-Comeaux & Kelly, 1996; Wood, Polek, & Aiken, 1985). In a similar vein, Bowers, Pharmer, and Salas (2000) found that tasks that are well-defined, require little integration of information, and require simple responses may be better suited to same-sex groups, whereas tasks that involve limited data and require a great deal of computation and complex processes might be better suited to teams with more diverse membership. Wheelan (1996), however, suggested that differences in men's and women's group status, not gender composition, may be driving perceptions of group performance.

Group Change Over Time

Research on group change from within the feminist perspective addresses Question 6—*How does the group change over time?* Unlike much group research and theory, a feminist perspective offers many suggestions for how groups may form and change over time, particularly because a focus of this perspective is on improving women's status in social situations, and this takes time. The most explicit focus on group development comes from a structural inequality perspective, which addresses how external social dynamics influence group formation, member roles, and behavior within groups and how these external dynamics are likely to become reified or challenged in the small group context. Status characteristics theory (Berger et al., 1977), for example, predicts that status cues constrain behavior, reifying and legitimizing existing norms and inequitable power and status divisions, resulting in an entrenchment of gendered roles over time (Ridgeway, 1997, 2001a, 2001b). Social role theory (Eagly, 1987; Eagly et al., 2000) suggests that gender stereotypes are dynamic and predicts that sex differences will be challenged and will diminish over time as members gain experience with each other and make individualized rather than stereotypic assessments of behavior. An individual differences feminist perspective instead focuses on sex differences in perspectives and values and how these impact groups. Hence, theories such as sociolinguistic theory and genderlect theory, which assume that men's and women's communication and behavior differences are based in cultural and social experiences, hypothesize little change in groups' gendered practices over time.

A liberal feminist perspective would view groups as most likely to form when there is a rational reason—relational, economic, social, or institutional—for them to do so. Liberal feminists would probably assume that inaccurate sex stereotypes and gender-typed relational patterns influence initial group role assignments, patterns of interaction, and performance but that if these are corrected over time—through intervention or learning, for example—women can be expected to have equal opportunity in groups and to be as likely as men to emerge as leaders or in any other role. As for group dissolution, these feminists would assume that groups dissolve when there is no longer a rational reason for them to continue–when economic or interpersonal motives for continuation are no longer compelling, for example.

Marxist/socialist and global feminists, on the other hand, would suggest that groups are formed by those with capital or power and resource holders seeking to increase their wealth in some way. Thus, women are disadvantaged from the start in these groups, not only because of their lower power and status in society in general but also because of their relative position of laborer—and a female laborer at that—in a group run by a male capitalist (or perhaps First World women). Groups would dissolve when the capitalist male or First World woman controlling the group's resources (who may be its leader) decides it is beneficial for him or her to do so. It is also possible that groups dissolve when enough members grow resentful of the inequality and perceive themselves as having little to lose by revolting and trying to seize power over the group.

Still another view of group change is suggested by radical separatist feminists and some postmodern feminists. These theorists suggest that all-women groups may form as women choose to seek and define their own language and destinies, independent of men. Initially, all-women groups may merely adopt predominant models of group structure and interaction from the male-controlled world and culture that surrounds them. With enough isolation and time, however, they can be expected to develop their own unique, women-defined patterns of interaction and ways of doing things. If this vision and mode of operation remains valuable to members of women-only groups, they may not dissolve. Or they may dissolve to form new women-only groups or even to influence mixed-sex groups in ways defined by women.

Summary

This review of feminist-oriented research, and the accompanying refocusing and reframing of these questions, is an indication of both the richness of current scholarship in this area and the need for additional investigative work. As this review indicates, both theoretically and methodologically, feminist scholars are questioning conventional norms. In the next section, we describe more specifically the methodological choices of feminist scholars in the group research domain.

Feminist Methodological Perspectives

Feminist Research Practices

Feminist scholars in general have contributed a number of critiques of research practices in the social sciences and the humanities. In particular, feminists have noted that the topics (and conclusions) of science reflect the values and interests of dominant groups in our society (e.g., white males), and thus research may reinforce the structures that support men's dominance over women. Consequently, research in general, and much of small group research in particular, may not always adequately reflect the experiences of women or the issues of importance to them. Several feminist perspectives expand this critique to include more specific recommendations concerning ways of eliminating gender bias from research methods. These recommendations range from relatively minor corrections to mainstream research practices (e.g., liberal feminists, psychoanalytic feminists) to major paradigm shifts in what constitutes data (e.g., radical feminists, postmodern feminists).

A liberal feminist perspective, for example, emphasizes equality of participation for women and men at both the participant and the researcher level and encourages an acknowledgment of gender bias and work toward the elimination of this bias. The liberal feminist position has offered one of the most extensive critiques of the experimental research paradigm (see, e.g., Gray, 1995; Harding, 1987; Wallston & Grady, 1985). This critique acknowledges two primary biases in past research practices: the under-utilization of female participants and the lack of research in areas that may be of primary importance to women. This bias reveals itself both in the choice of topics of research (e.g., leadership rather than motherhood), the choice of materials (e.g., task content reflects material more familiar to men), and openness to certain results and conclusions from the research.

Psychoanalytic feminist scholars extended general psychoanalytic research, which involves understanding and synthesizing case histories of individuals. Chodorow (1989) noted that "psychoanalysis is the method and theory directed toward how we experience. . . unconscious fantasies and of how we construct and reconstruct our felt past in the present" (p. 4). She called for feminist research within a tradition that treated gender as a "social, cultural, and psychological phenomenon" (p. 5).

A Marxist-socialist feminist critique of method, like the liberal and psychoanalytic feminist critiques, also acknowledges the values and interests of the dominant groups in society as the main focus of research. However, the Marxist-socialist perspective also argues for a reduction or elimination of the hierarchical relationship between participants and the researcher (Oakley, 1988; Porter, 1999). Multicultural feminists also have noted that research tends both to measure other groups against standards driven by the dominant culture and to inaccurately represent other cultures (Few, Stephens, & Rouse-Arnett, 2003).

Radical and postmodern feminists argue that attempts to eliminate sex bias in current research practices, although appropriate, do not go far enough. Instead, these feminists argue that we must develop uniquely feminist approaches to science. The radical feminist perspective, for example, argues for the legitimization of alternative methods of data collection, such as the use of diaries and interviews rather than questionnaires and experiments (Campbell & Wasco, 2000; Gergen, 2001).

In general, feminist researchers from various perspectives have also been critical of the methods of other feminist researchers. Debates among feminist scholars about what constitutes data and knowledge (e.g., how should data be read or interpreted?) and how data and knowledge should be treated (e.g., what is truth?) are common across the different perspectives (e.g., Assiter, 1996; Butler, 1990; Fraser & Nicholson, 1990; Skeggs, 1995; Taylor & Rupp, 1993).

Feminist Choices of Method

A variety of methods have been used within feminist perspectives. For example, drawing from the work of MacKinnon (1989), some radical feminists have suggested that consciousness-raising groups and other methods of group-level data collection are appropriate for understanding women's lives (Campbell & Wasco, 2000). Focus group or "affinity group" discussions (e.g., Austen, Jefferson, & Thein, 2003) and support groups (Seiter, 1995) also are used to collect narrative data. These approaches allow for the development of connections between women and women's experiences in such a way that new perspectives may be revealed.

Similarly, in-depth interviewing is relatively common in feminist research (e.g., Burns, 2003; Chodorow, 1989; Foley & Faircloth, 2003; Riley, 2003).

For example, Mirchandani (2003) interviewed women about the "emotion work" of their professions in order to advance antiracist feminist theory. Ristock (2003) combined analyses from interviews of 80 lesbians who had experienced domestic violence and focus groups of 45 feminist service providers to assess the power dynamics in abusive same-sex relationships.

Other methods that are familiar to many researchers are found in feminist research, including conversation analysis (Christie, 2001; Ohara & Sullivan, 2003), discourse analysis (Riley, 2003; Todd & Fisher, 1988), ethnography (Anderson et al., 2003; Skeggs, 1995), case studies (Metcalf & Linstead, 2003), and fieldwork (McIntyre, 2003). Data analysis includes common methods of analyzing qualitative data. For example, grounded theory is one useful alternative in which data can be used to inform and extend theory (Austen et al., 2003; Kushner & Morrow, 2003). Research methods that are less traditional also have been explored and used in feminist research. For example, postmodern feminist Mary Gergen (2001) has infused social constructionist psychology with postmodern feminism, using analyses of women's autobiographies, transcripts of a monologue that she performed of a dialogue between Gergen and "Other," and fairly traditional surveys of college students. In addition to such alternative methods, feminist researchers also argue for the importance of including social context in research. Feminist scholars remind us to pay attention to the ways that context informs both participants' behavior and researchers' interests and investigations (Porter, 1999).

The debate among feminists concerning the relative value of quantitative versus qualitative methods has a fairly long history. Radical feminists initially criticized quantitative methods because the predetermined categories that were used to assess responses forced responders into narrow categories that might not adequately capture their unique experiences. Furthermore, these categories were generally established by male researchers and subsequently distorted or eclipsed women's experiences (Keller, 1985). Qualitative methods, in which themes and categories are revealed by the data rather than by the researcher, were seen as more appropriate for identifying new concepts and ideas represented in women's experience. Later feminist theorists noted, however, that because research participants in qualitative studies also tended to be white and middle class, the same biases that are prevalent in quantitative research also pervade qualitative methods (Cannon, Higgenbothan, & Leung, 1991). Today, most researchers agree that both quantitative and qualitative methods are subject to bias; neither one is more feminist than the other, and both are appropriate methods for understanding the human experience (Peplau & Conrad, 1989). In fact, a feminist perspective on research methods in general acknowledges the strengths and weaknesses of various research practices and approaches and encourages an owning up to these when choices are made (McGrath, Kelly, & Rhodes, 1993).

In sum, research practices across feminist perspectives incorporate qualitative and quantitative methods. Similarities in values include an emphasis on reflexivity (Mauthner & Doucet, 2003), including making clear what assumptions (and biases) might have guided the research as well as understanding and making explicit the challenges, successes, and failures of data collection (e.g., Williams & Lykes, 2003).

Contributions and Challenges of Feminist Group Research

Contributions of the Feminist Perspective

Perhaps one of the primary contributions of the feminist perspective is that it has helped to make visible groups that were previously (and sometimes still are) invisible in research designs. It has drawn our attention, not only to women, but to all oppressed, marginalized groups, whether identified by race, sexual preference, class, or other nonelite characteristics. It has allowed us to think about gender-inclusive views of groups so as to view "gender diversity as a resource and not a threat" (Sterk & Turner, 1994, p. 214).

A second contribution of this perspective is its interdisciplinary focus. Researchers and theorists who adopt a feminist view stem from many disciplines, including psychology, sociology, communication, political science, anthropology, economics, biology, history, fine arts, English, and music, among other disciplines. The feminist perspective on groups advocates few disciplinary boundaries, preferring instead to focus researchers on the single goal of defying oppressive social practices toward women and other marginalized groups (Bullis & Bach, 1996; Foss, 1997).

Finally, a third contribution of a feminist perspective is its activist underpinnings. Although it is true that not all feminist scholars take their research findings into the practical realm, all feminist scholarship (by its very nature) advocates for critique and change. In fact, Wyatt (2002) contended that feminist theory can provide a useful framework for investigating and helping social activist groups. Hence, feminist theory integrates both a practical and activist stance—a position that can be incorporated into any research that investigates groups (also see McIntyre, 2003; Taylor & Rupp, 1993; Williams & Lykes, 2003).

Challenges for the Feminist Perspective

Perhaps one of the greatest challenges of the feminist perspective is to move beyond traditional male-centered models and concepts—to avoid the "add women and stir" research practice. In the early years of feminist research, many of the studies of women's groups and issues were based on male-centric contexts such as task groups and male-dominated businesses and organizations (Wood, McMahan, & Stacks, 1984). Frequently, these studies focused on task-related performance or outcomes.

Some feminist researchers (as well as other group researchers) have suggested that this generally exclusive focus on task-oriented behaviors and groups may not be desirable or appropriate for the study of groups (Andrews, 1992; Meyers & Brashers, 1994; Scheerhorn, Geist, & Teboul, 1994). In part, this is because task-related processes such as decision making tend to privilege stereotypically male traits, such as competitiveness and win-lose orientations, and these traits then become accepted and privileged activities (Borisoff & Merrill, 1985). As an alternative, some scholars are suggesting that group researchers focus on other behavioral processes in groups (i.e., connectedness, cooperation, support, activism, egalitarianism, group-centered leadership) instead of concentrating their investigative efforts on decision-making activities (Armstrong & Priola, 2001; Bowers et al., 2000; Flanagin et al., 2002; Karakovsky & Elangovan, 2001; Schiller, 1997).

A second challenge for feminist researchers is to explain results from research that finds no evidence (or minimal evidence) of gender differences (e.g., Canary & House, 1993; Hyde & Plant, 1995). Explaining these conclusions is easier for structural inequality feminists than for individual differences theorists. Structural inequality feminists begin with the belief that women and men are essentially similar, capable, and deserving. Hence, if no differences are found between men and women in investigative work on groups, this finding can be explained by the less gender-laden structures that characterize these groups. For example, much research on groups is done with college students and involves hypothetical tasks. When no differences in men's and women's behavior are found, it may be because there were fewer power and status structures in these groups to impact members' behaviors, or because college students draw on fewer social, economic, and political structures in these types of groups—especially when engaged in hypothetical tasks. Or perhaps among college students, there are alternative proximal structures related to their educational experience (belief in greater equality, more interest in cooperation, fewer perceived status differences) that buffer gender-laden societal structures.

Individual differences feminist theorists have more difficulty with findings that show no evidence of gender differences because these perspectives focus primarily on psychological and epistemological dissimilarities between women and men. The sociolinguistic or genderlect feminist theorists contend, for example, that men and women grow up in, and exist in, different cultures (see Tannen, 1990; for a critique of Tannen's work, see Goldsmith & Fulfs, 1999). One way these feminists may explain a lack of differences is to conclude that the methods used were not appropriate, or the questions asked were unrealistic, or the population studied was inadequate or not suitable to the question being asked. As in all research, these critiques may be true.

Alternatively, these feminists might argue that differences between men and women are a matter of degree, not dichotomy (Duck & Wright, 1993; Wright, 1988). That is, both men and women will express task and relational communication in a group, but each sex may emphasize one category more than another. Similarly, some feminists might argue that actual differences between men and women are minimal and are really only evident at the extremes (Wood & Dindia, 1998). So, there may be a few men who are *only* agentic in their behavior in groups, and a few women who are *only* communal, but in general, the vast majority of men and women are both agentic and communal in groups. Hence, a finding of no differences in these group behaviors may be because there were no individuals displaying extreme gendered behavior.

Finally, although it may be true that many differences between women and men are minimal or relative (rather than dichotomous), it may also be the case that sometimes differences in degree are consequential (Wood & Dindia, 1998). For example, more extreme agentic behavior may lead to sexual harassment, or more extreme communal behavior may lead to staying in an abusive relationship. Although such differences may be found only among a small subset of men and women, and may reflect extreme positions, the consequences of these relative differences require researchers to assume a critical, activist stance.

Conclusion

Clearly, feminist theorizing is not univocal; there are many feminisms. Throughout this chapter, we have attempted to illustrate the many facets of a feminist perspective on groups. We have identified alternative feminist ways of viewing groups and current research trends and practices in the feminist domain. As indicated earlier, perhaps one of the greatest contributions of a feminist perspective on groups is that it forces us to question some of our most basic assumptions and beliefs about how groups form, function, and practice. As Spender (1980) suggested over two decades ago, "this is not to suggest that feminist research has the answers, only that it has opened up an area in which more, and more useful, answers might be found" (p. 50).

References

Adler, A. (1927). *Understanding human nature.* New York: Greenberg.

Adrianson, L. (2001). Gender and computer-mediated communication: Group processes in problem solving. *Computers in Human Behavior, 17,* 71–94.

Alderton, S. M., & Jurma, W. E. (1980). Genderless/gender-related task leader communication and group satisfaction: A test of two hypotheses. *Southern Speech Communication Journal, 46,* 48–60.

Anderson, J., Perry, J., Blue, C., Browne, A., Henderson, A., Khan, K. B. et al. (2003). Rewriting cultural safety within the postcolonial and postnational feminist project: Toward new epistemologies of healing. *Advances in Nursing Science, 26,* 196–214.

Anderson, L. R., & Blanchard, P. N. (1982). Sex differences in task and social-emotional behavior. *Basic and Applied Social Psychology, 3,* 109–139.

Andrews, P. H. (1992). Sex and gender differences in group communication: Impact on the facilitation process. *Small Group Research, 23,* 74–94.

Anzaldua, G., & Moraga, C. (Eds.). (1981). *This bridge called my back: Writings by radical women of color.* Watertown, MA: Persephone Press.

Aries, E. (1976). Interaction patterns and themes of male, female, and mixed groups. *Small Group Behavior, 7,* 7–18.

Armstrong, S. J., & Priola, V. (2001). Individual differences in cognitive style and their effects on task and social orientations of self-managed work teams. *Small Group Research, 32,* 283–312.

Assiter, A. (1996). *Enlightened women: Modernist feminism in a postmodern age.* New York: Routledge.

Austen, S., Jefferson, T., & Thein, V. (2003). Gendered social indicators and grounded theory. *Feminist Economics, 9,* 1–18.

Bales, R. F. (1950). *Interaction process analysis: A method for the study of small groups.* Cambridge, MA: Addison-Wesley.

Bartunek, J. M., Walsh, K., & Lucey, C. A. (2000). Dynamics and dilemmas of women leading women. *Organization Science, 11,* 589–610.

Bem, S. L. (1974). The measurement of psychological androgyny. *Journal of Consulting and Clinical Psychology, 45,* 196–205.

Bem, S. L. (1975). Androgyny vs. the tight little lives of fluffy women and chesty men. *Psychology Today, 9,* 58–62.

Berdahl, J. L. (1996). Gender and leadership in work groups: Six alternative models. *Leadership Quarterly, 7,* 21–40.

Berdahl, J., & Anderson, C. (2003). *Gender and leadership centralization in groups.* Unpublished manuscript.

Berger, J., Fisek, M. H., Norman, R. Z., & Zelditch, M., Jr. (1977). *Status characteristics and social interaction: An expectation states approach.* New York: Elsevier.

Booth-Butterfield, M., & Booth-Butterfield, S. (1988). Jock talk: Cooperation and competition within a university women's basketball team. In B. Bate & A. Taylor (Eds.), *Women communicating: Studies of women's talk* (pp. 177–198). Norwood, NJ: Ablex.

Borisoff, D., & Merrill, L. (1985). *The power to communicate: Gender differences as barriers.* Prospect Heights, IL: Waveland Press.

Bowers, C. A., Pharmer, J. A., & Salas, E. (2000). When member homogeneity is needed in work teams: A meta-analysis. *Small Group Research, 31,* 305–327.

Bradley, P. H. (1981). The folk-linguistics of women's speech: An empirical investigation. *Communication Monographs, 48,* 73–90.

Bullis, C., & Bach, B. W. (1996). Feminism and the disenfranchised: Listening beyond the "other." In E. B. Ray (Ed.), *Communication and disenfranchisement: Social health issues and implications* (pp. 3–28). Mahwah, NJ: Lawrence Erlbaum.

Burgoon, M., Dillard, J. P., & Doran, N. E. (1983). Friendly or unfriendly persuasion: The effects of violations of expectations by males and females. *Human Communication Research, 10,* 283–294.

Burns, M. (2003). Interviewing: Embodied communication. *Feminism & Psychology, 13,* 229–236.

Butler, J. (1990). *Gender trouble, feminism, and the subversion of identity.* New York: Routledge.

Campbell, R., & Wasco, S. M. (2000). Feminist approaches to social science: Epistemological and methodological tenets. *American Journal of Community Psychology, 28,* 773–791.

Canary, D. J., & House, K. S. (1993). Is there any reason to research sex differences in communication? *Communication Quarterly, 41,* 129–144.

Cannon, L. W., Higgenbothan, E., & Leung, M. L. A. (1991). Race and class bias in qualitative research on women. In M. M. Fonow & J. A. Cook (Eds.), *Beyond methodology: Feminist scholarship as lived research* (pp. 107–118). Bloomington: Indiana University Press.

Carli, L. L. (1982). *Are women more social and men more task oriented? A meta-analytic review of sex differences in group interaction, reward allocation, coalition formation, and cooperation in the Prisoner's Dilemma game.* Unpublished manuscript, University of Massachusetts-Amherst.

Carli, L. L. (1989). Gender differences in interaction style and influence. *Journal of Personality & Social Psychology, 56,* 565–576.

Carli, L. L., & Eagly, A. H. (1999). Gender effects on social influence and emergent leadership. In G. Powell (Ed.), *Handbook of gender and work* (pp. 203–222). Thousand Oaks, CA: Sage.

Cascio, W. F. (1995). Whither industrial and organizational psychology in a changing world of work? *American Psychologist, 50,* 928–939.

Chodorow, N. (1978). *The reproduction of mothering: Psychoanalysis and the sociology of gender.* Berkeley: University of California Press.

Chodorow, N. J. (1989). *Feminism and psychoanalytic theory.* New Haven, CT: Yale University Press.

Christie, C. (2001). *Gender and language: Towards a feminist pragmatics.* Edinburgh, UK: Edinburgh University Press.

Cixous, H. (1981). Castration or decapitation? *Signs: Journal of Women in Culture and Society, 7,* 41–55.

Counselman, E. F. (1991). Leadership in a long-term leaderless group. *Small Group Research, 22,* 240–257.

Daly, M. (1978). *Gyn/Ecology: The meta-ethics of radical feminism.* Boston: Beacon Press.

Deal, J. J. (2000). Gender differences in the intentional use of information in competitive negotiations. *Small Group Research, 31,* 702–723.

de Beauvoir, S. (1974). *The second sex* (H. M. Parshley, Trans.). New York: Vintage Books. (Original work published 1952)

Derrida, J. (1978). *Writing and difference* (A. Bass, Trans.). Chicago: University of Chicago Press.

Dinnerstein, D. (1977). *The mermaid and the minotaur: Sexual arrangements and human malaise.* New York: Harper.

Dubrovsky, V. J., Kiesler, S., & Sethna, B. N. (1991). The equalization phenomenon: Status effects in computer-mediated and face-to-face decision-making groups. *Human Computer Interaction, 6,* 119–146.

Duck, S., & Wright, P. (1993). Reexamining gender differences in same-gender friendships: A close look at two kinds of data. *Sex Roles, 28,* 709–727.

Eagly, A. E. (1987). *Sex differences in social behavior: A social role interpretation.* Hillsdale, NJ: Lawrence Erlbaum.

Eagly, A. H., & Johnson, B. T. (1990). Gender and leadership style: A meta-analysis. *Psychological Bulletin, 108,* 233–256.

Eagly, A. H., & Karau, S. J. (1991). Gender and the emergence of leaders: A meta-analysis. *Journal of Personality and Social Psychology, 60,* 685–710.

Eagly, A. H., Makhijani, M. G., Klonsky, B. G. (1992). Gender and the evaluation of leaders: A meta-analysis. *Psychological Bulletin, 111,* 3–22.

Eagly, A. H., Wood, W., & Diekman, A. B. (2000). Social role theory of sex differences and similarities: A current appraisal. In T. Eckes & H. Trautner (Eds.), *The developmental social psychology of gender* (pp. 123–174). Mahwah, NJ: Lawrence Erlbaum.

Engels, F. (1942). *The origin of the family, private property and the state.* New York: International Publishers Company. (Original work published 1902)

Few, A. L., Stephens, D. P., & Rouse-Arnett, M. (2003). Sister-to-sister talk: Transcending boundaries and challenges in qualitative research with Black women. *Family Relations, 52,* 205–215.

Fields, D. L., & Blum, T. C. (1997). Employee satisfaction in work groups with different gender composition. *Journal of Organizational Behavior, 18,* 181–196.

Firestone, S. (1970). *The dialectic of sex.* New York: Morrow.

Flanagin, A. J., Tiyaamornwong, V., O'Connor, J., & Seibold, D. R. (2002). Computer-mediated group work: The interaction of member sex and anonymity. *Communication Research, 29,* 66–93.

Foley, L., & Faircloth, C. A. (2003). Medicine as discursive resource: Legitimation in the work narratives of midwives. *Sociology of Health & Illness, 25,* 165–184.

Foss, S. K. (1997). Transforming rhetoric through feminist reconstruction: A response to the gender diversity perspective. *Women's Studies in Communication, 20,* 117–135.

Foucault, M. (1977). *Discipline and punish: The theory of the prison* (A. Sheridan, Trans.). London: Allen Lane.

Foucault, M. (1980). *Power/knowledge.* New York: Pantheon.

Fournier, V., & Kelemen, M. (2001). The crafting of community: Recoupling discourses of management and womanhood. *Human Relations, 8,* 267–290.

Fraser, N., & Nicholson, L. J. (1990). Social criticism without philosophy. In L. J. Nicholson (Ed.), *Feminism/postmodernism* (pp. 19–38). New York: Routledge.

French, M. (1985). *Beyond power: On women, men, and morals.* New York: Summit Books.

Freud, S. (1962). *Three essays on the theory of sexuality* (J. Strachey, Trans.). New York: Basic Books. (Original work published 1925)

Gayle, B. M., Priess, R. W., & Allen, M. (1994). Gender differences and the use of conflict strategies. In L. H. Turner & H. M. Sterk (Eds.), *Differences that make a difference: Examining the assumptions in gender research* (pp. 13–26). Westport, CT: Bergin & Garvey.

Gergen, M. (2001). *Feminist reconstructions in psychology: Narrative, gender, and performance.* Thousand Oaks, CA: Sage.

Gilligan, C. (1982). *In a different voice: Psychological theory and women's development.* Cambridge, MA: Harvard University Press.

Goldsmith, D. J., & Fulfs, P. A. (1999). "You just don't have the evidence": An analysis of claims and evidence in Deborah Tannen's *You just don't understand.* In M. E. Roloff (Ed.), *Communication yearbook* (Vol. 22, pp. 1–49). Thousand Oaks, CA: Sage.

Gopal, A., Mirana, S. M., Robichaux, B. P., & Bostrom, R. P. (1997). Leveraging diversity with information technology: Gender, attitude, and intervening influences in the use of group support systems. *Small Group Research, 28,* 29–71.

Graham, E. E., & Papa, M. J. (1993). Gender and function-oriented discourse in small groups: An examination of problem-solving processes and outcomes. In C. Berryman-Fink, D. Ballard-Reisch, & L. H. Newman (Eds.), *Communication and sex role socialization* (pp. 311–335). New York: Garland.

Gray, A. (1995). I want to tell you a story: The narratives of Video Playtime. In B. Skeggs (Ed.), *Feminist cultural theory: Processes and production* (pp. 153–168). New York: Manchester University Press.

Harding, S. (Ed.). (1987). *Feminism and methodology.* Bloomington: Indiana University Press.

Hartmann, H. (1981). The unhappy marriage of marxism and feminism: Towards a more progressive union. In L. Sargent (Ed.), *Women and revolution: A discussion of the unhappy marriage of marxism and feminism* (pp. 1–41). Boston: South End Press.

Hartsock, N. C. M. (1983). The feminist standpoint: Developing the ground for a specifically feminist historical materialism. In S. Harding & M. B. Hintikka (Eds.), *Discovering reality: Feminist perspectives on epistemology, methodology, metaphysics, and philosophy of science* (pp. 283–310). Boston: Reidel.

Hartsock, N. C. M. (1998). *The feminist standpoint revisited and other essays.* Boulder, CO: Westview.

Hawkins, K. (1995). Effects of gender and communication content on leadership emergence in small task-oriented groups. *Small Group Research, 26,* 234–249.

Hawkins, K., & Power, C. B. (1999). Gender differences in questions asked during small decision-making group discussions. *Small Group Research, 30,* 235–256.

Henley, N. M., & Kramerae, C. (1991). Gender, power, and miscommunication. In N. Coupland, H. Giles, & J. M. Wiemann (Eds.), *Miscommunication and problematic talk* (pp. 18–43). Newbury Park, CA: Sage.

Herschel, R. T., Cooper, T. R., Smith, L. F., & Arrington, L. (1994). Exploring numerical proportions in a unique context: The group support systems meeting environment. *Sex Roles, 31,* 99–123.

Hoffman, L. R. (1965). Group problem solving. In L. Berkowitz (Ed.), *Advances in experimental social psychology* (Vol. 2, pp. 99–132). New York: Academic Press.

hooks, b. (1990). *Yearning: Race, gender, and cultural politics.* Boston: South End Press.

Horney, K. (1973). *Feminine psychology.* New York: W. W. Norton.

Hutson-Comeaux, S. L., & Kelly, J. R. (1996). Sex differences in interaction style and group task performance: The process-performance relationship. *Journal of Social Behavior and Personality, 11,* 255–275.

Hyde, J. S., & Plant, E. A. (1995). Magnitude of psychological gender differences: Another side to the story. *American Psychologist, 50,* 159–161.

Infante, D. A. (1982). The argumentative student in the speech communication classroom: An investigation and implications. *Communication Education, 31,* 141–148.

Infante, D. A., Wall, C. H., Leap, C. J., & Danielson, K. (1984). Verbal aggression as a function of the receiver's argumentativeness. *Communication Research Reports, 1,* 33–37.

Irigaray, L. (1985). *This sex which is not one* (C Porter, Trans.). Ithaca, NY: Cornell University Press.

Jaffe, J. M., Lee, Y., Huang, L., & Oshagan, H. (1999). Gender identification, interdependence, and pseudonyms in CMC: Language patterns in an electronic conference. *The Information Society, 15,* 221–234.

Jaggar, A. M. (1983). *Feminist politics and human nature*. Totowa, NJ: Rowman & Allenheld.

Jaggar, A. M., & Rothenberg, P. S. (Eds.). (1984). *Feminist frameworks: Alternative theoretical accounts of the relations between women and men* (2nd ed.). New York: McGraw-Hill.

Jessup, L. M., Connolly, T., & Tansik, D. A. (1990). Toward a theory of automated group work: The deindividuating effects of anonymity. *Small Group Research, 21,* 333–348.

Jurma, W. E., & Wright, B. C. (1990). Follower reactions to male and female leaders who maintain or lose reward power. *Small Group Research, 21,* 97–112.

Karakovsky, L., & Elangovan, A. R. (2001). Risky decision making in mixed-gender teams: Whose risk tolerance matters? *Small Group Research, 32,* 94–111.

Kees, N. L. (1999). Women together again: A phenomenological struggle of leaderless women's groups. *Journal for Specialists in Group Work, 24,* 288–305.

Keller, E. F. (1985). *Reflections on gender and science*. New Haven, CT: Yale University Press.

Kelly, J. R., & Barsade, S. (2001). Mood and emotions in small groups and work teams. *Organizational Behavior and Human Decision Processes, 86,* 99–130.

Kelly, J. R., Craig, T. Y., & Spoor, J. S. (2003). *How cognitive centrality and gender affect perceptions of leadership, influence, and likability.* Unpublished manuscript.

Kendall, S., & Tannen, D. (1997). Gender and language in the workplace. In R. Wodak (Ed.), *Gender and discourse* (pp. 81–105). Thousand Oaks, CA: Sage.

Kent, R. L., & Moss, S. E. (1994). Effects of sex and gender role on leader emergence. *Academy of Management Journal, 37,* 1335–1346.

Kerr, N. L., & MacCoun, R. J. (1985). Role expectations in social dilemmas: Sex roles and task motivation in groups. *Journal of Personality and Social Psychology, 49,* 1547–1556.

Kohlberg, L. (1969). Stage and sequence: The cognitive-development approach to socialization. In D. A. Goslin (Ed.), *Handbook of socialization theory and research* (pp. 347–480). Chicago: Rand McNally.

Kristeva, J. (1980). *Desire in language*. New York: Columbia University Press.

Kushner, K. E., & Morrow, R. (2003). Grounded theory, feminist theory, and critical theory. *Advances in Nursing Science, 26,* 30–43.

Lacan, J. (1977). *Ecrits*. New York: W. W. Norton.

Lakoff, R. (1975). *Language and women's place*. New York: Harper & Row.

Lucas, J. W., & Lovaglia, M. J. (1998). Leadership status, gender, group size, and emotion in face-to-face groups. *Sociological Perspectives, 41,* 617–637.

MacKinnon, C. A. (1989). *Toward a feminist theory of the state*. Cambridge, MA: Harvard University Press.

Martin, J. (1992). *Cultures in organizations: Three perspectives*. New York: Oxford University Press.

Martin, J., Knopoff, K., & Beckman, C. (1988). An alternative to bureaucratic impersonality and emotional labor: Bounded emotionality at The Body Shop. *Administrative Science Quarterly, 43*, 429–469.

Marx, K. (2000). *Karl Marx: Selected writings* (2nd ed.). Oxford, UK: Oxford University Press. (Original work published in 1834–1894)

Mauthner, N. S., & Doucet, A. (2003). Reflexive accounts and accounts of reflexivity in qualitative data analysis. *Sociology, 37*, 413–431.

McGrath, J. E., Kelly, J. R., & Rhodes, J. E. (1993). A feminist perspective on research methodology: Some metatheoretical issues, contrasts, and choices. In S. Oskamp & M. Constanzo (Eds.), *The Claremont Symposium on Applied Social Psychology: Gender issues in contemporary society* (pp. 19–37). Newbury Park, CA: Sage.

McIntyre, A. (2003). Feminist fieldwork and political change. *Feminism & Psychology, 13*, 283–286.

Metcalf, B., & Linstead, A. (2003). Gendering teamwork: Re-writing the feminine. *Gender, Work, and Organization, 10*, 94–119.

Meyers, R. A., & Brashers, D. E. (1994). Expanding the boundaries of small group communication research: Exploring a feminist perspective. *Communication Studies, 45*, 68–85.

Meyers, R. A., Brashers, D. E., Winston, L., & Grob, L. (1997). Sex differences and group argument: A theoretical framework and empirical investigation. *Communication Studies, 48*, 19–41.

Millet, K. (1970). *Sexual politics.* Garden City, NY: Doubleday.

Mirchandani, K. (2003). Challenging racial silences in studies of emotion work: Contributions from anti-racist feminist theory. *Organization Studies, 24*, 721–742.

Mitchell, J. (1971). *Women's estate.* New York: Random House.

Mitchell, J. (1974). *Psychoanalysis and feminism.* New York: Vintage.

Moreland, R. L. (1987). The formation of small groups. In C. Hendrick (Ed.), *Review of personality and social psychology: Vol 8. Group processes* (pp. 80–110). Newbury Park, CA: Sage.

Nelson, M. W. (1988). Women's ways: Interactive patterns in predominantly female research teams. In B. Bate & A. Taylor (Eds.), *Women communicating: Studies of women's talk* (pp. 199–232). Norwood, NJ: Ablex.

Nicotera, A. M., & Rancer, A. S. (1994). The influence of sex on self-perceptions and social stereotyping of aggressive communication predispositions. *Western Journal of Communication, 58*, 283–307.

Noddings, N. (1984). *Caring: A feminine approach to ethics and moral education.* Berkeley: University of California Press.

Oakley, A. (1988). Interviewing women: A contradiction in terms. In H. Roberts (Ed.), *Doing feminist research* (pp. 30–61). New York: Routledge.

Ohara, Y., & Sullivan, S. (2003). Using conversation analysis to track gender ideologies in social interaction: Toward a feminist analysis of a Japanese phone-in consultation program. *Discourse and Society, 14*, 153–172.

Peplau, L. A., & Conrad, E. (1989). Beyond non-sexist research: The perils of feminist methods in psychology. *Psychology of Women Quarterly, 13,* 379–400.

Piliavin, J. A., & Martin, R. R. (1978). The effects of the sex composition of groups on style and social interaction. *Sex Roles, 4,* 281–296.

Porter, N. (1999). Reconstructing mountains from gravel: Remembering context in feminist research [Commentary]. *Psychology of Women Quarterly, 23,* 59–64.

Postmes, T., & Spears, R. (2002). Behavior on-line: Does anonymous computer communication reduce gender inequality? *Personality and Social Psychology Bulletin, 28,* 1073–1083.

Rich, A. (1980). Compulsory heterosexuality and lesbian existence. *Signs, 5,* 631–690.

Ridgeway, C. L. (1997). Interaction and the conservation of gender inequality: Considering employment. *American Sociological Review, 62,* 218–235.

Ridgeway, C. L. (2001a). The emergence of status beliefs: From structural inequality to legitimizing ideology. In J. T. Jost & B. Major (Eds.), *The psychology of legitimacy: Emerging perspectives on ideology, justice, and intergroup relations* (pp. 257–277). New York: Cambridge University Press.

Ridgeway, C. L. (2001b). Gender, status, and leadership. *Journal of Social Issues, 57,* 637–655.

Riley, S. C. E. (2003). The management of the traditional male role: A discourse analysis of the constructions and functions of provision. *Journal of Gender Studies, 12,* 99–113.

Ristock, J. L. (2003). Exploring dynamics of abusive lesbian relationships: Preliminary analysis of a multi-site, qualitative study. *American Journal of Community Psychology, 31,* 329–341.

Robinson, D. T., & Smith-Lovin, L. (2001). Getting a laugh: Gender, status, and humor in task discussions. *Social Forces, 80,* 123–158.

Rowbotham, S. (1973). *Woman's consciousness, man's world.* Harmondsworth, UK: Penguin.

Ruddick, S. (1980). *Maternal thinking: Toward a politics of peace.* Boston: Beacon Press.

Samter, W., & Burleson, B. R. (1990). Evaluations of communication skills as predictors of peer acceptance in a group living situation. *Communication Studies, 41,* 311–326.

Scheerhorn, D., Geist, P., & Teboul, J. B. (1994). Beyond decision making in decision-making groups: Implications for the study of group communication. In L. Frey (Ed.), *Group communication in context: Studies of natural groups* (pp. 247–262). Hillsdale, NJ: Lawrence Erlbaum.

Schiller, L. Y. (1997). Rethinking stages of development in women's groups: Implications for practice. *Social Work with Groups, 20*(3), 3–19.

Seiter, E. (1995). Mothers watching children watching television. In B. Skeggs (Ed.), *Feminist cultural theory: Process and production* (pp. 137–152). New York: Manchester University Press.

Shabat, E. (Ed.). (1998). *Talking visions: Multicultural feminism in a transnational age.* Cambridge: MIT Press.

Siegel, J., Dubrovsky, V. J., Kiesler, S., & McGuire, T. W. (1986). Group processes in computer-mediated communication. *Organizational Behavior and Human Decision Processes, 3,* 157–187.

Skeggs, B. (Ed.). (1995). *Feminist cultural theory: Process and production.* New York: Manchester University Press.

Smith-Lovin, L., & Brody, C. (1989). Interruptions in group discussions: The effects of gender and group composition. *American Sociological Review, 54,* 424–435.

Spelman, E. V. (1988). *Inessential woman: Problems of exclusion in feminist thought.* Boston: Beacon Press.

Spender, D. (1980). *Man made language.* London: Routledge & Kegan Paul.

Sterk, H. M., & Turner, L. H. (1994). Gender, communication, and community. In L. H. Turner & H. M. Sterk (Eds.), *Differences that make a difference: Examining the assumptions in gender research* (pp. 213–222). Westport, CT: Bergin & Garvey.

Tannen, D. (1990). *You just don't understand.* New York: Balantine.

Taylor, J. R., & Strassberg, D. S. 1986). The effects of sex composition on cohesiveness and interpersonal learning in short-term personal growth groups. *Psychotherapy: Theory, Research, Practice, Training, 23*(2), 267–273.

Taylor, V., & Rupp, L. J. (1993). Women's culture and lesbian feminist activism: A reconsideration of cultural feminism. *Signs: Journal of Women in Culture and Society, 19,* 32–61.

Todd, A. D., & Fisher, A. (Eds.). (1988). *Gender and discourse: The power of talk.* Norwood, NJ: Ablex.

Tong, R. P. (1998). *Feminist thought: A more comprehensive introduction* (2nd ed). Boulder, CO: Westview.

Walker, H. A., Illardi, B. C., McMahon, A. M., & Fennell, M. L. (1996). Gender, interaction, and leadership. *Social Psychology Quarterly, 59,* 255–272.

Wallston, B. S., & Grady, K. E. (1985). Integrating the feminist critique and the crisis in social psychology: Another look at research methods. In V. E. O'Leary, R. K. Unger, & B. S. Wallston (Eds.), *Women, gender, and social psychology* (pp. 7–33). Hillsdale, NJ: Lawrence Erlbaum Associates.

Walters, A. E., Stuhlmacher, A. F., & Meyer, L. L. (1998). Gender and negotiator competitiveness: A meta-analysis. *Organizational Behavior and Human Decision Processes, 76*(1), 1–29.

West, C., & Zimmerman, D. H. (1983). Small insults: A study of interruptions in cross-sex conversations between unacquainted persons. In B. Thorne, C. Kramarae, & N. Henley (Eds.), *Language, gender, and society* (pp. 102–117). Rowley, MA: Newbury House.

Wheelan, S. A. (1996). Effects of gender composition and group status differences on member perceptions of group developmental patterns, effectiveness, and productivity. *Sex Roles, 34,* 665–686.

Williams, J., & Lykes, M. B. (2003). Bridging theory and practice: Using reflexive cycles in feminist participatory action research. *Feminism & Psychology, 13,* 287–294.

Wittig, M. (1981). One is not born a woman. *Feminist Issues, 2,* 47–54.

Wood, J. T., & Dindia, K. (1998). What's the difference? A dialogue about differences and similarities between women and men. In D. J. Canary & K. Dindia (Eds.), *Sex differences and similarities in communication: Critical essays and empirical investigations of sex and gender in interaction* (pp. 19–39). Mahwah, NJ: Lawrence Erlbaum.

Wood, J. T., McMahan, E. M., & Stacks, D. W. (1984). Research on women's communication: Critical assessment and recommendations. In D. L. Fowlkes & C. S. McClure (Eds.), *Feminist visions: Toward a transformation of the liberal arts curriculum* (pp. 31–41). Tuscaloosa: University of Alabama Press.

Wood, W. (1987). Meta-analytic review of sex differences in group performance. *Psychological Bulletin, 102,* 53–71.

Wood, W., Polek, D., & Aiken, C. (1985). Sex differences in group task performance. *Journal of Personality and Social Psychology, 48,* 63–71.

Wood, W., & Rhodes, N. (1992). Sex differences in interaction style in task groups. In C. L. Ridgeway (Ed.), *Gender, interaction, and inequality* (pp. 97–121). New York: Springer-Verlag.

Wright, P. (1988). Interpreting research on gender differences in friendship: A case for moderation and a plea for caution. *Journal of Social and Personal Relationships, 5,* 367–373.

Wyatt, N. (2002). Foregrounding feminist theory in group communication research. In L. R. Frey (Ed.), *New directions in group communication* (pp. 43–56). Thousand Oaks, CA: Sage.

Young, I. (1990). Socialist feminism and the limits of dual systems theory. In I. Young, *Throwing like a girl and other essays in feminist philosophy and social theory* (pp. 21–35). Bloomington: Indiana University Press.

8

The Network Perspective on Small Groups

Theory and Research

Nancy Katz, David Lazer,
Holly Arrow, and Noshir Contractor

Abstract

This chapter provides a review of theory and research on small groups from the network perspective. First, a general summary of the social network perspective is provided. The primary theories that provide the intellectual underpinning of the network approach are identified, including theories of self-interest, theories of social exchange or dependency, theories of mutual or collective interest, cognitive theories, and theories of homophily. The dominant methods for conducting social network research are described. Then, empirical work focused on group-level network phenomena is reviewed. We articulate the primary substantive questions that still need to be addressed, as well as methodological refinements necessary to address them. Finally, we describe the benefits that can accrue to small group researchers who adopt a network perspective.

This chapter provides a broad review of the network perspective on small groups, with substantial attention to both theory and empirical findings. We trace the development of the network perspective from its early roots to its recent resurgence. The intended audience is small group researchers who are interested in how network ideas and methods can enhance their understanding of and traction on phenomena of interest. We hope to draw attention to the potential benefits of adopting a network perspective on small groups and to shape the direction in which this research stream evolves.

The chapter is organized into five sections. The first section is an introduction to the network perspective. Basic questions are addressed: What is a network? What are the essential dimensions along which networks meaningfully vary? How are networks measured? And what is the definition of a small group, from the network perspective? The second section is an overview of the core principles and the conceptual underpinnings of the network perspective, including theories of self-interest, theories of social exchange or dependency, theories of mutual or collective interest, cognitive theories, and theories of homophily. The third section is a chronological review of empirical research on networks and small groups. We include a number of studies that are not generally recognized as network research but have a significant (although typically overlooked) network component. We describe the relevant studies in some detail and provide an overview of the trajectory of the research. The fourth section is devoted to future directions. Here we define the substantive questions that need to be addressed, as well as methodological refinements necessary to sharpen our understanding of small group networks. Finally, in the conclusion, we specify the benefits that can accrue to small group researchers who adopt a network perspective. In Table 8.1 we summarize the main points of the chapter.

Introduction to the Network Perspective

What Is a Network?

A social network consists of a set of actors (*nodes*) and the relations (*ties* or *edges*) among these actors (Wasserman & Faust, 1994). The nodes may be individuals, groups, organizations, or societies. The ties may fall within a level of analysis (e.g., individual-to-individual ties) or may cross levels of analysis (e.g., individual-to-group ties). The defining feature of the network perspective is the conceptual building block of the tie—of individuals to individuals, groups to groups, or individuals to groups.

Table 8.1   The Network Perspective

Definition of perspective	The defining feature of the network perspective is the conceptual building block of the tie — of individuals to individuals, groups to groups, or individuals to groups
Key assumptions	The pattern of relationships has individual- and collective-level effects
Types of groups	There are two views of groups: (1) as emergent, within the network (e.g., clique analysis); and (2) as externally prescribed
Key theories	Theories of self-interest, theories of social exchange or dependency, theories of mutual or collective interest, cognitive theories, and theories of homophily
Dominant research methodologies	• Empirical work has focused on data collected from whole networks—that is, on every dyad within a bounded population, where advanced statistical approaches have been developed to deal with the interdependencies endemic in network data • Substantial research on egocentric data—the ties of particular individuals rather than the entire network • A long tradition of graph theory to describe the structure of networks • A tradition of experimental work, as well as emerging approaches using simulation modeling
Strengths	• Offers a tool for disaggregating many phenomena that have been studied at the group-level • Provides a coherent basis for measuring and understanding the group's context • Can help researchers integrate the internal workings of the group and the group's external environment • Allows a researcher to cross levels of analysis with relative ease • Provides tools for refined measurement of group interaction
Weaknesses	• Relative lack of longitudinal (dynamic) approaches to change in networks, although there has been increased attention to this issue in the last 5 years • Often difficult to distinguish the causal arrow between networks and the asserted effects of networks • Serious concerns about the reliability of (typically self-reported) relational data

What Are the Essential Dimensions Along Which Networks Vary?

Network researchers have examined a broad range of types of ties. These include: *communication ties* (such as who talks to whom, or who gives information or advice to whom); *formal ties* (such as who reports to whom); *affective ties* (such as who likes whom, or who trusts whom); *material* or *work flow ties* (such as who gives money or other resources to whom), *proximity ties* (who is spatially or electronically close to whom); and *cognitive ties* (such as who knows whom). Networks are typically *multiplex;* that is, actors share more than one type of tie. For example, two academic colleagues might have a formal tie (one is an assistant professor and reports to the other, who is the department chairperson), an affective tie (they are friends), and a proximity tie (their offices are two doors apart).

Network researchers have distinguished between *strong ties* (such as family and friends) and *weak ties* (such as acquaintances) (Granovetter, 1973, 1982). This distinction can involve a multitude of features, including affect, mutual obligations, reciprocity, and intensity. Strong ties are particularly valuable when an individual seeks socioemotional support, and they often entail a high level of trust. On the other hand, weak ties are more valuable when individuals are seeking diverse or unique information from someone outside their regular frequent contacts. This information could include new job or market opportunities.

Ties may be *nondirectional* (Joe attends a meeting with Jane) or vary in *direction* (Joe gives advice to Jane versus Joe gets advice from Jane). They may also vary in *content* (Joe talks to Jack about the weather and to Jane about sports), *frequency* (daily, weekly, monthly, etc), and *medium* (face-to-face conversation, written memos, e-mail, instant messaging, etc.). Finally, ties may vary in *sign*, ranging from positive (Joe likes Jane) to negative (Joe dislikes Jane).

How Are Networks Measured?

In a typical network study, every member of an organization is presented with a list of every other member of the organization.[1] Respondents are asked to put a checkmark next to every person on the list with whom they have contact. Respondents might also be asked to indicate how often they have contact, or the substance of those interactions. These self-report data are translated into a *sociogram,* using visualization software such as NetDraw (Borgatti, 2003), NetVis (Cummings, 2004), and Pajek (Batagelj & Mrvar, 2003). A sociogram is a visual display of all of the nodes and ties in a network. A sociogram can use a variety of algorithms to organize the layout of the nodes on the network visualization. Common layouts include random assignments, placing the nodes in a circle, arranging them based on certain attributes of the nodes (putting all females or all managers close to one another), or "annealing" the network, in which nodes that are tied (or more strongly tied) to one another are in closer proximity to each other than nodes that are not tied (or are more weakly tied) to them. The sociogram highlights whether there are many or few ties among organization members, the overall pattern of those ties, and where every individual respondent is situated in the network.

While the sociogram can provide a general sense of the network at a glance, researchers have developed a variety of metrics for quantifying important differences in network structure. Frequently used metrics include actor degree centrality (the extent to which actors send or receive direct ties), betweenness centrality (the extent to which actors have ties with others who are not directly connected), closeness centrality (the extent to which actors are directly or indirectly connected to the rest of the actors in the network), reciprocity (the extent to which there are mutual ties between actors), and transitivity (the extent to which actors who are connected to one another are also connected to the same other actors).

How Is a Group Defined
From the Network Perspective?

The construct of a *group,* when used in the social network literature, has had two primary meanings: (1) a group as a structural feature of a network or (2) a group as an exogenously determined or imposed category. According to the first meaning, groups (cliques) are subsets of fully connected or almost fully connected nodes within some population. That is, a group is an *emergent* phenomenon. An example would be the numerous social cliques identified in the classic anthropological study of a small city in the Deep South in the 1930s (Davis, Gardner, & Gardner, 1941). Membership in the cliques was inferred from the pattern of people's joint attendance at events like church suppers, card parties, and PTA meetings.

Methodologically, the study of group or subgroup formation requires a set of criteria for classifying a given set of relations as a group. Whereas the definition of a clique (a fully connected set of relations) is unproblematic in the case of binary choices (Wasserman & Faust, 1994), the issue of choosing cutoff values becomes more complex for rankings (e.g., Newcomb, 1961) or other valued measures and when one wishes to relax the balance-theory-inspired requirement of complete transitivity among all within-group relations. Freeman (1992) has tackled this problem by applying the distinction between strong and weak ties to distinguish subgroups within a larger network of ties in which they are embedded.

The second definition of a group is an exogenously determined category or boundary around a set of people (e.g., a corporation, a political party, or the residents of a city). In this context, network analysis is typically used to compare patterns of intra- versus intercategory communication. For example, in landmark works on social capital in communities (Bourdieu, 1985; Coleman, 1990; Putnam, 2000), group boundaries such as social class played a key role in creating denser subsidiary networks within classes. These dense networks facilitated both the diffusion of norms and the enforcement of those norms through the diffusion of reputations, iterated relationships, and threat of sanctions. The analogue in the small group arena would be groups with clearly defined boundaries and membership, such as the 14 men who worked together in the Bank Wiring observation room in one of the Hawthorne studies at the Western Electric plant (Homans, 1950). Members are viewed as belonging to one particular group (just as people are thought of as belonging to a particular social class or category), not as belonging to multiple overlapping groups.

Principles and Roots of the Network Perspective

Core Principles

The network approach spans a broad range of disciplines, including sociology, social psychology, mathematics, political science, anthropology, economics, and epidemiology. There is no single formal statement of the network perspective. Yet, there are certain core ideas that all or nearly all network scholars would likely endorse. Wellman (1988) has identified five fundamental principles that provide some "underlying intellectual unity" to the network approach.

First, people's behavior is best predicted by examining not their drives, attitudes, or demographic characteristics but rather the web of relationships in which they are embedded. That web of relationships presents opportunities and imposes constraints on people's behavior. If two people behave in a similar fashion, it is likely because they are situated in comparable locations in their social networks, rather than because they both belong to the same category (e.g., both are white women).

Second, the focus of analysis should be the relationships among units, rather than the units themselves or their intrinsic characteristics. Nothing can be properly understood in isolation or in a segmented fashion.

Third, analytic methods must not hinge on the conventional assumption of independence. A population or sample is defined relationally rather than categorically. Therefore, *inter*dependence among units is assumed.

Fourth, understanding a social system requires more than merely aggregating the dyadic ties. The flow of information and resources between two people depends not simply on their relationship to each other but on their relationships to everybody else. For example, it matters whether two people who communicate with each other are embedded within a cluster of individuals who also talk to one another or are embedded within two separate clusters that otherwise do not communicate at all (Burt, 1992).

Fifth, groups sometimes have fuzzy rather than firm boundaries. The building blocks of organizations are not discrete groups but rather overlapping networks. Individuals generally have cross-cutting relationships to a multitude of groups. Applying these five principles to small groups, a network study focuses on *relationships* among components in the group system—individual-to-individual ties within a group, individual-to-group ties, or group-to-environment ties—rather than on *features* of these components.

Theoretical Roots

How do network scholars explain why people create, maintain, dissolve, and possibly reconstitute network ties, and who is likely to form ties with whom? There are multiple schools of thought or "families of theories" (Monge & Contractor, 2003) within the network perspective, which approach this question from different vantage points. These include theories of self-interest, theories of social exchange or dependency, theories of mutual or collective interest, cognitive theories, and theories of homophily. We briefly describe each school, highlighting its intellectual forebears and its central theoretical mechanisms.

A large school of network researchers base their work on a rational *self-interest* paradigm. These scholars assume that people form dyadic and group ties in order to maximize their personal preferences and desires. The rational self-interest school within network research can be traced back to the work of sociologist James Coleman (1988). Coleman showed how—from two-actor interactions, with each actor operating out of self-interest—the basis for a social system (such as a small group) emerges. While each actor is trying to maximize his or her individual interests, at the same time, each is constrained because he or she is embedded in an interdependent relationship with the other. That relationship imposes limits on both actors' behavior and regulates the extent of self-seeking. These limits are counterbalanced by the increased access to resources each actor gets via the other.

Individuals consider the creation of ties as an investment in the accumulation of social resources or *social capital*. Social capital "is the sum of the resources, actual or virtual, that accrue to an individual or group by virtue of possessing a durable network of more or less institutionalized relationships of mutual acquaintance and recognition" (Bourdieu & Wacquant, 1992, p. 119). From a self-interest perspective, individuals expect to deploy this social capital (Coleman, 1988, 1990; Lin, 2001) and reap returns on their investment in the form of opportunities from which they can profit. For instance, Burt (1992, 1997, 1998, 2001) argues that *structural holes* in a network provide an opportunity for individuals to invest their social capital. Individuals fill a structural hole when they invest efforts to connect two or more others who are not directly connected. The return on their investment accrues from their ability to broker the flow of knowledge and information among those who are not directly connected.

A second school of network researchers draw on theories of *social exchange and dependency*. George Homans (1950) was a forebear of the social exchange school. Homans asserted that people establish ties to others with whom they can exchange valued resources. Whether a relationship will be sustained over time will depend on the payoffs to each of the two parties. With exchange theory, Homans sought to link the micro- to the macrolevel of analysis and show how the social structure arises from these one-on-one interactions. Richard Emerson (1972a, 1972b) enlarged the focus of exchange theory to look beyond the dyad at the network of relationships in which the dyad is embedded. Emerson examined exchanges and power dependences at both the interindividual and intergroup levels. He argued that when individuals or groups exchange valued resources, this is made possible due to a large-scale network of relationships.

Unlike theories of self-interest, an individual's motivation to create ties with others is not based on maximizing his or her personal investments. Instead, people are motivated to create ties based on their ability to minimize their dependence on others from whom they need resources and maximize the dependence of others who need resources they can offer. A social exchange calculus is often an optimal strategy to manage these dependencies. And these dependencies, social exchange theorists argue, constitute the glue that binds a group together. Several scholars have developed this perspective on dyads and groups into what is now commonly referred to as *network exchange theory* (Bienenstock & Bonacich, 1992, 1997; Cook, 1977, 1982; Cook & Whitmeyer, 1992; Willer & Skvoretz, 1997).

A third influential network perspective draws on theories of *mutual interest and collective action*. Its main premise is that "mutual interests and the possibility of benefits from coordinated action" (Marwell & Oliver, 1993, p. 2) often outweigh individual self-interest. Public goods theory, first articulated by Samuelson (1954), is one of the best developed theories of collective action. It was developed to explain the economics of collective versus private ownership of material infrastructure such as parks, bridges, and tunnels. More recently, it has been extended to explain the collective production and ownership of intellectual property (e.g., ideas, documents, decisions) such as those developed by small groups (Fulk, Flanagin, Kalman, Monge, & Ryan, 1996; Lessig, 2001; Monge et al., 1998).

Public goods theory seeks to explain the conditions under which group members contribute to the creation or maintenance of public goods so that everyone in the collective will be able to benefit from them. An important focus has been the role of communication networks in creating and maintaining these public goods. The calculus of mutual interest or collective action suggests that individuals do not create ties and coalesce into groups because it maximizes the self-interest of any individual within the group or even the exchange value between individuals in the group. Instead, the motivation to forge ties and form a group is to maximize their collective ability to leverage resources and mobilize for collective action in their environment. One of the defining features of a public good is the impossibility of exclusion (Hardin, 1982; Olson, 1965; Samuelson, 1954). That is, every member of the group has a right to benefit from the public good, irrespective of their contribution to its creation or maintenance. We know this phenomenon in the literature on group research as the "free rider" problem. Studying groups from a network perspective has the potential to enhance our understanding and management of free rider problems. For example, the literature on social capital (Bourdieu, 1985; Coleman, 1988) highlights the capacity of dense networks to reduce opportunistic behavior. If we view free riding as a kind of opportunistic behavior, this leads to testable hypotheses about how a group's network structure influences the effort level exerted by group members (Lazer & Katz, 2004).

A fourth network perspective on group research draws on a family of *cognitive theories*. Two of these theories are particularly relevant for the study of small groups: the theory of transactive memory systems and the theory of cognitive consistency. Although both theories focus on group members' cognitions, they differ in their explanation for why group members create and maintain their network ties. The theory of transactive memory explains that group members—each with his or her own set of skills and expertise—develop communication networks that help them identify and leverage the skills and expertise of others in the group (Hollingshead, 1998; Moreland, 1999; Wegner, 1987, 1995). These network ties facilitate the flows of knowledge within the group, thereby reducing the need for each group member to possess skills or expertise available elsewhere in the group. Hollingshead, Fulk, and Monge (2002) offer an intriguing argument for combining the explanatory mechanisms offered by transactive memory theory and public goods theory (previously described) to study the use of intranets or other knowledge repositories by groups.

Whereas the theory of transactive memory focuses on *what* members think other group members *know*, cognitive consistency theory focuses on *who* members think other group members *like*. Heider's (1958) balance theory posited that if two individuals were friends, they should have similar evaluations of an object. This model was extended and mathematically formulated by Harary, Norman, and Cartwright (1965). Holland and Leinhardt (1977) argued that the object could be a third person in a communication network. If the two individuals did not consistently evaluate the third person, they would experience a state of discomfort and would strive to reduce this cognitive inconsistency by altering their evaluations of either the third person or their own friendship. In common parlance, this argument is captured by the aphorism that "we like to be friends with friends of our friends" and that we experience tension when our friends are not friends with one another. In small groups, these affect ties (who likes whom) are an important explanation of the creation of communication ties within a group and the development of coalition within groups. Researchers have examined the effects of cognitive consistency on individuals' attitudes. For instance, Krackhardt and Kilduff (1990) report that members whose friends are friends with one another (they call this *schema consistent*) tend to be more satisfied than those whose friends did not get along with one another.

Fifth, a network perspective can help explain group communication on the basis of *homophily*. That is, members are more likely to create communication ties with other group members who they deem to be similar. In colloquial terms, we know this explanation by the phrase "birds of a feather flock together." Brass (1995b) observes that "similarity is thought to ease communication, increase predictability of behavior, and foster trust and reciprocity" (p. 51). Indeed the similarity attraction hypothesis (Byrne, 1971) is exemplified in the work of Sherif (1958), who suggested that individuals were more likely to select similar others because by doing so, they reduce the potential areas of conflict in the relationship.

A key issue for theories of homophily is determining the criteria used to evaluate similarity. Homophily has been studied on the basis of similarity in age, gender, education, prestige, social class, tenure, and occupation (Carley, 1991; Coleman, 1957; Ibarra, 1995; Laumann, 1966; Marsden, 1988; McPherson & Smith-Lovin, 1987). The theory of self-categorization (Turner & Oakes, 1986, 1989) offers important insights into which criteria are likely to be salient in judging similarity with other group members. Turner and Oakes argue that group members define their social identity through a process of self-categorization during which they classify themselves and others using categories such as age, race, and gender. The manner in which individuals categorize themselves influences the extent to which they associate with others who are seen as falling into the same category.

In today's increasingly virtual environments, group members often do not have access to visual cues, and hence, categories such as age and gender might become less salient than more abstract categories such as professional identity. As a result, groups where members perceive others as being similar are likely to have less conflict and more satisfaction. However, depending on the criteria used for judging similarity, these groups might also attenuate their exposure to diverse perspectives and hence impact their creativity (Brass, 1995a). A communication network perspective has the ability to explain (1) what criteria are used by group members to identify similar others and (2) how these criteria are invoked to create communication ties with similar others.

Empirical Research in the Network Perspective

In this section, we provide a chronological review of small group research that incorporates a network perspective. We draw from multiple disciplines, including social psychology, organizational behavior, administrative science, communication, anthropology, and sociology. (Table 8.2 provides a summary of the empirical findings that are reorganized based on the seven perspective questions that are serving as a guide for this volume.)

We distinguish between two general eras in the research: the 1930s to 1960s (the "early era") and the 1990s to 2000s (the "current era"). Some of the studies—largely those from the current era—are self-consciously network studies. In other words, the authors explicitly frame the research as "network research." Some of the studies—largely those from the early era—are not generally thought of as network research but in fact have a meaningful network component. It is our hope to raise awareness of the usually overlooked network features of several classic studies of small groups.

In understanding this research stream, it is important to be clear about what role network variables play in each study. In some studies, network ties constitute an input. In other studies, network ties constitute an output. Network ties can also mediate between inputs and outputs. Within each era, we organize the research into these three categories. Later, in our discussion of future research directions, we explore the implications of these analytic distinctions.

Table 8.2   Key Findings of Network Perspective Research

Group composition	• The greater the diversity of the group, the lower the interaction level • People choose to work in groups with people with whom they have prior ties and who are similar to themselves • The more prior relationships in a group, the greater the level of transactive memory within the group and the easier it is for members of the group to express disagreement
Group projects	• The greater the complexity of the task, the more likely a decentralized communication pattern will emerge within the group • Tasks interact with group structure in a variety of ways to affect performance (more below)
Group structure	• Group structure is conceived as the pattern of intragroup relationships • Technologies and resources may be conceived as nodes in the network • Norms are in part disseminated and enforced through social networks • When a group's task is relatively simple, a centralized pattern of ties among group members is more effective; when the task is complex, a decentralized pattern is more effective • Groups with centralized networks are more likely to produce a leader; the individual in the most central position is likely to emerge as the leader • When the information being conveyed among group members is relatively complex, strong ties are more effective than weak ties at conveying that information
Group interaction	The network perspective encompasses all dyadic-level interactions
Group action/outcomes	Results may be conceived at the nodal, group, or relational levels. For example: • At the nodal level: satisfaction, attitudes, effort • At the group level: performance • At the relational level: greater or lesser amount of ties inside and outside of groups
Change over time	• The role/impact of network ties depends on the point in the group's life; it is important to distinguish among ties that exist before the group is created; ties that exist during the group's work; and ties that remain after the group has completed its task

	• For self-formed groups (e.g., cliques), individuals who are similar will tend to be attracted to each other;
	• furthermore, mutual ties to third parties will predict the creation and the maintenance of ties between individuals
	• For exogenously formed groups, within-group ties will initially increase, and between-group ties will decrease—especially in a competitive environment
	• For groups with a novel task, the group's network will evolve from being low density, which enables exploratory group thinking, to high density, which enables execution
Ecology	• One can distinguish between individuals' ties to people outside the group and group-level ties to the outside
	• The density of a group's external ties can have either a positive or negative impact on group performance, depending on group autonomy and task overload
	• Ties to the larger organization can enhance a group's search capabilities and access to resources
	• Physical proximity is associated with a greater density of ties
	• Shared ties to individuals outside the group (embeddedness) regulates the effort level of group members

Early Era

Network as Input

In the 1950s and 1960s, Alex Bavelas and his colleagues at the MIT Group Networks Laboratory conducted a series of experiments on how networks shape group process. Bavelas and his colleagues manipulated the pattern of communication in small groups and measured the impact on individual and group functioning. The communication structure was determined by assigning participants (strangers to one another) to seats at adjoining cubicles and constraining who could pass messages to whom. Participants could not see one another but could slip written messages to certain other group members through slots in the walls. Figure 8.1 illustrates the types of network configurations studied for five-person groups. The researchers

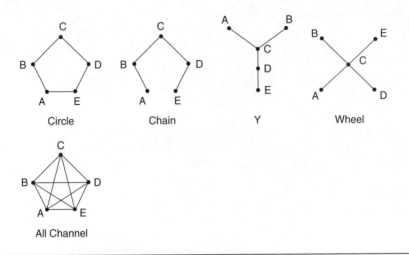

Figure 8.1   Sample of Five-Person Network Patterns

hoped to answer the question: What is the optimal network for group performance?

The MIT researchers found consistent differences in group outcomes based on how centralized the communication network was. Members of decentralized networks sent more messages, enjoyed the task more, made more errors, and were better at detecting and correcting errors. Members of centralized networks developed more differentiated role structures, with those in more central positions sending more messages, making fewer errors, and being designated leaders more often than those in peripheral positions (Bavelas, 1950; Bavelas & Barrett, 1951; Leavitt, 1951; Shaw, 1964).

The impact of centralization on task performance varied across studies based on task complexity, information distribution patterns, and the signal-to-noise ratio in the information. In simple information-gathering tasks, centralized networks were fastest. When the task required more complex processing, when information was distributed unevenly among members, or when the information was "noisy," groups with decentralized networks solved problems faster, showed more learning over time, and were better at detecting and correcting errors than groups with centralized networks (Shaw, 1964, 1971). Overall member satisfaction was higher in decentralized networks, regardless of variations in task features (Shaw, 1971).

The researchers also looked at the impact of changes over time in a group's communication network when the group's network was shifted from one pattern to another. The basic finding was that problem-solving patterns that developed under centralized structures were continued after a change to decentralized structure, although satisfaction improved. In what apparently was a contrast effect, this change increased satisfaction above the levels of groups that had a decentralized network throughout the experiment, while a change in the other direction (to greater centralization) resulted in the lowest measured levels of satisfaction, below groups that had a centralized network throughout the experiment (Cohen, 1962; Shaw, 1954, 1964, 1971).

Guetzkow and Simon (1955) extended these results by demonstrating that a critical mediating variable in the relationship between network structure and group performance was how the group chose to organize itself. Guetzkow and Simon replicated Leavitt's (1951) experiments, in which groups performing a simple task performed better in the wheel network than the circle or the all-channel networks. Guetzkow and Simon categorized groups based on the actual patterns of signal sending. That is, for any given communication network configuration that Bavelas and colleagues studied, there were a number of potential patterns that the groups could actually realize. The more channels in the assigned configuration, the more potential patterns. Some of those patterns might be inefficient, and some very efficient. Thus, for example, in the all-channel network, there was nothing to stop the group from performing the same way—and as well as—in the wheel network. The only reason the group did not, Guetzkow and Simon argued, is that in general all-channel groups tended to organize themselves inefficiently.

In groups that were structured as a wheel, the communication pattern that quickly emerged was a two-level hierarchy, with all information going to and from the hub. In the circle network, a variety of actual communication patterns emerged, but the ones that performed best—the three-level hierarchy (where, for example, the information flows between A and B, B and C, C and D, and D and E)—performed about as well as the wheel. In the all-channel network, there was an even greater variation of patterns, but the two- and three-level hierarchies in the all-channel networks performed as well as the wheel networks. In short, Guetzkow and Simon (1955) found that the performance advantage of the wheel was entirely due to the choices group members made about which communication channels to use. In the wheel, communication patterns were constrained so that group members had essentially no choice but the optimal pattern. For the circle and the all-channel networks, there were many suboptimal patterns, and many groups chose those suboptimal patterns.

At the same time that Bavelas and his colleagues were conducting experimental work, researchers at the Tavistock Institute in London were conducting field research that led to the development of the sociotechnical approach. The Tavistock researchers applied an implicit network perspective to the study of people, tasks, and technology. Studying groups in their natural settings, the researchers illustrated how the impact of a change in technology can be understood by considering how it affects the existing group structure, which they viewed as including the differentiated connections of workers to each other, their tools, and their tasks.

For example, Trist and Bamforth (1951) studied the introduction of new techniques for mining and their impact on the network of people, tools, and tasks. In contrast to earlier, nonmechanized "hand-got" mining methods, in which links among tasks, tools, and workers were coordinated into coherent and adaptive sociotechnical systems consisting of three to four men, the introduction of mechanization broke coordinating links among workers so that the production process and effective social organization were no longer compatible. Whereas the former cohesive structure allowed groups to adapt effectively to the changing demands of an extreme environment, the new system was brittle, greatly increasing the stress on the miners because of the constant threat of breakdown in the face of environmental challenges. Although the miners attempted to develop informal groups to counteract these problems, these network structures were strongly constrained by the physical and organizational context. The links and interdependencies among tasks and tools interacted with a severely constrained social structure to hamper productivity and produce widespread social and mental health problems among the miners.

Network as Output

How do groups and networks emerge in the first place? Several early studies shed light on this question. First was the classic Deep South study. In the 1930s, four researchers spent 18 months conducting a comprehensive study of the social structure in a small city in Mississippi (Davis et al., 1941; the fourth researcher was Davis's wife). The project, which was an early application of the methods of social anthropology to the study of modern society, explored the ways in which the social organization of the society governed behavior within and across caste (black/white) and class lines. These lines, in addition to gender boundaries and roles, formed the context in which smaller social groups (cliques) formed. These groups were homogeneous on caste and class dimensions and often on age, gender, and religious affiliation as well, a strong demonstration of the homophily principle.

One famous data set drawn from the Deep South study tracked the participation of 18 women in one or more of 14 events (e.g., church suppers, card parties, PTA meetings). Interviews indicated that the women belonged to one of two distinct cliques that partially overlapped in their social activities, and Davis et al. (1941) used the person-by-event matrix to classify each woman as a core, primary, or secondary member of one of the two cliques. Since that time, a series of researchers (e.g., Breiger, 1974; Freeman, 1992; Homans, 1950) have returned to this data set to test the usefulness of different ways of formalizing the concept of a social group. Theoretical conceptions of natural groups that require transitivity among all triads (if A has a tie to B and to C, then B must have a tie to C; Winship, 1977) do not fit the data set. Freeman (1992) demonstrated, however, that a sociological conception of the group based on Granovetter's distinction between strong and weak ties does allow for reliable detection of nonoverlapping groups without violating transitivity. Breiger (1974) viewed the data as an example of the "duality of persons and groups" because many of the events were meetings of distinguishably different groups. Thus, the same data set has been used to detect bounded "standing" groups with nonoverlapping membership (two distinct cliques), which nevertheless overlap strongly in their participation with "acting" groups of different types.

Two other early studies also focused on how networks of interaction arise among people who live in close proximity. The emergence of friendship groups from networks of interaction was studied by Newcomb and colleagues in a residence for university students (Newcomb, 1961) and in housing complexes by Festinger, Schacter, and Back (1950). The Newcomb study, which followed two sets of 17 men who were initially strangers, documented the chaining together over the course of 15 weeks of high-attraction dyads into triads, tetrads, and pentads, as the pattern of interpersonal attraction become increasingly ordered and complex. It documents how the evolution of both network and group structure was itself influenced by spatial proximity (roommates and those living on the same floor), similarity in values, and (in one set) the emergence of subgroup stereotypes based on demographic characteristics such as academic major and rural versus urban background. The hypotheses of the study were based on balance theory (Cartwright & Harary, 1956; Heider, 1946; Newcomb, 1953, 1981).

Work by Sherif and colleagues (Sherif, 1966; Sherif, Harvey, White, Hood, & Sherif, 1961) is another example of small group research that investigated network ties, although it is not conventionally recognized as network research. Most social psychologists think of the classic Robbers Cave study (Sherif et al., 1961) as documenting the emergence of intergroup hostility among two demographically identical groups of boys. That hostility was exacerbated by contact in competitive contexts, and it was eventually reversed through the need to work closely together to achieve superordinate goals. But the Robbers Cave study was in fact the third in a series of studies of how changes in group boundaries influenced networks of interpersonal attraction.

The first studies, conducted in 1949 and 1953 (summarized in Sherif, 1966), brought together two dozen boys age 11 to 12 from white, middle-class, Protestant families for a 3-week summer camp. At first, all boys were together in one bunkhouse. Once stable friendship clusters emerged, the boys were asked informally who their best friends were. The boys were then reassigned to two cabins, so that about two thirds of their best friends were in the other cabin. After the boys had adjusted to the change, they were asked again about who their best friends were in the entire camp (including both cabins). Although only one third of their cabin mates had been among their original choices, 95% of their subsequent choices were from within their cabin groups.

In the third (Robbers Cave) study (Sherif et al., 1961), the boys were divided into two cabins from the start (skipping the full group initial stage), and a stage of reintegration through superordinate goals and cooperative activities was added. After these cooperative activities, what had been an overwhelming percentage (more than 90%) of friendship choices within the separate groups of Eagles and Rattlers shifted back to a greater balance between groups, with intergroup choices accounting for a quarter to a third of all choices.

Network as Mediator Between Inputs and Outputs

Perhaps the earliest example of a network perspective on work groups can be found in the Hawthorne studies—a series of investigations of factors affecting work performance that took place in the late 1920s and early 1930s at the Western Electric Company in the Hawthorne Works in Chicago. Although the original studies were designed to look at the impact of lighting on worker productivity, the puzzling results directed the researchers' attention to the impact of the developing social network within groups of workers who were segregated for the purposes of the study. The researchers documented two effects that on the surface seemed contradictory.

The 14 men in the Bank Wiring Observation Room (Roethlisberger & Dickson; Homans, 1950) maintained a steady level of output despite management incentives designed to increase production. Networks of helping, job trading, friendship, and antagonism were documented, and analysis of these multiple networks revealed the existence of two cliques and several isolates. The helping and job-trading networks were part of a self-regulatory system that regulated output through the social sanctioning of men who violated group norms.

The five women in the Relay Assembly Room, however (Mayo, 1933), showed a consistent improvement in output over the course of 5 years. The development of network ties connecting the women was evidenced by, among other indicators, "the entertainment of each other in their respective homes, especially operatives one, two, three, and four" (p. 68). The results are consistent, however, when looked at from the perspective of how social structure can mediate between incentives and performance. The trajectory of improvement for the Relay Assembly women was only trivially affected by interventions such as the addition of a rest period and snacks, and later the removal of same.

Interestingly, research on small group networks was a fallow area in the 1970s and 1980s. What accounts for this lull? We cannot be sure, but we suspect two phenomena may have been operating. Social psychologists, who dominated the early era in research on small group networks, became increasingly focused on social cognition, a primarily individual-level phenomenon, and interest in groups waned in social psychology (Arrow, McGrath, & Berdahl, 2000; Moreland, Hogg, & Hains, 1994). Meanwhile, research on networks migrated to the field of sociology, where the focus was on macrolevels of analysis, such as the organization and the society, rather than on the small group.

Current Era

The last 15 years have seen a virtual tidal wave of network research. In particular, the social network construct of social capital has received tremendous attention since Putnam (1993). The popularity of network notions is now filtering down to the group level of analysis. Network researchers, traditionally focused on individual- and organizational-level networks (Cummings & Cross, 2003), are expanding their focus to include the networks within and among small groups. Small group researchers are curious to learn whether network methods might add to their understanding of and traction on small group phenomena. Thus, the two bifurcated streams of research—networks and small groups—are coming together again. In this section, we review recent research on small group networks. Again, we organize the research into three general categories: network as input, network as output, and network as mediator between input and output. Whenever possible, we highlight conceptual links between the early and the current eras.

Network as Input

Several researchers have returned to the question that Bavelas and his colleagues raised—What is the optimal network for group performance?—but broadened the scope of the investigation from laboratory experiments to field research. Sparrowe, Liden, Wayne, and Kraimer (2001) conducted a field study of 38 work groups in five organizations, where the groups were performing relatively complex tasks. The members of each group were asked how often they sought help or advice from one another on work-related matters. Supervisors provided assessments of each group's performance, including the quality, quantity, and timeliness of the work product and the levels of initiative and cooperation demonstrated by the group. Consistent with the early research at MIT, Sparrowe et al. found that groups with decentralized patterns of communication performed better than groups with centralized communication patterns.

Cummings and Cross (2003) found similar effects in their study of 182 project groups in a global telecommunications company. The groups had been nominated, based on outstanding performance, to participate in a company-wide reward program. The groups varied in size from 4 to 12 members and carried out complex, nonroutine work, such as new product development and internal improvement initiatives. Group members were asked to recall how often they communicated with one another over the course of the project. Controlling for the mean number of ties, Cummings and Cross found that a more hierarchical (as opposed to "flat") pattern of communication was associated with stronger group performance. On a more applied level, Lipman-Blumen and Leavitt (2001) have drawn on this type of centralization research to support their theory of high-performing "hot groups," whose success they attribute in part to their fluid, decentralized communication structures.

Other researchers have focused on the number rather than the pattern of communication links among group members. Baldwin, Bedell, and Johnson (1997) examined network ties within and among 62 MBA student groups of three to five members. Students were asked to identify who are "good friends, people you see socially outside of school" and who are "important sources of school-related advice." Baldwin et al. found that the friendship and advice ties within a group were positively associated with perceptions of group effectiveness, which in turn were positively associated with group grade. Reagans and Zuckerman (2001) drew on survey data collected from 224 corporate R&D groups in the mid-1980s. The groups came from 29 corporations, across seven industries. Reagans and Zuckerman analyzed the relationship between how often group members reported communicating with one another and group productivity as assessed by the group leader or manager. The researchers found the most productive groups were those with the most ties that cut across demographic boundaries, linking group members with different outlooks.

On a more theoretical level, Markovsky and colleagues have examined the conditions under which internal ties among group members could impair group performance. Markovsky et al. have considered subgroup formation as a source of friction that could degrade the overall solidarity of a larger unit. When people become involved in exclusive friendship cliques within a larger group, the unity of structure is disrupted (Markovsky & Chaffee, 1995; Markovsky & Lawler, 1994), and internal divisions between subgroups can weaken the group structure.

Gruenfeld, Mannix, Williams, and Neale (1996) examined related questions in an experimental study in which 71 three-person groups performed a decision task (solving a murder mystery). Groups were composed of either three familiars, two familiars and one stranger, or three strangers. A familiar was someone the participant defined as feeling "close to" or knowing "very well." In half of the groups, important clues were distributed evenly among the group members, and in half of the groups, information was distributed unevenly. Familiarity had a main effect on participants' perceptions of group process; familiar groups felt more comfortable working together and expressing disagreement. Familiarity also affected the groups' task strategy. Groups of familiars and mixed groups were more likely to pool their unique information, whereas groups of strangers were more likely to aggregate their individual choices and adopt the majority position. This difference in task strategy meant that groups of familiars and mixed groups performed best (identified the correct suspect) when information was distributed unevenly, and groups of strangers performed best when information was distributed evenly.

Network thinking has also influenced new conceptual models of groups. Building on the sociotechnical perspective, some researchers are reconceptualizing groups as a set of dynamic relations among people, tools, and tasks that form a complex system. Tschan and von Cranach (1996), for example, consider how tasks are connected to one another within the larger frameworks of group projects. Krackhardt and Carley (2003), in their PCANS (Precedence, Commitment, Assignment, Network, and Skill) model of organizational structure, develop a formalization of how people, tasks, and resources can be represented. Arrow et al. (2000) demonstrate how the full coordination network that constitutes the group structure can be decomposed into the networks that connect elements of a single type (people, tasks, or tools) and those that connect different types of nodes, providing network definitions of concepts such as the division of labor (the set of links that connect people to tasks) and roles (the set of links that connect people to tools and resources) and generating new constructs such as the *job network,* which specifies which tools and procedures are to be used to complete which tasks. The differential importance of the component networks within groups provides the basis for distinguishing among types of groups, such as task forces (in which the task and labor networks are primary), crews (in which the tool and job networks are primary), and teams (in which the member and role networks are primary).

The aforementioned studies focus on a group's internal network, that is, the pattern and number of ties among group members. Other studies, described later, focus on a group's external network, that is, the group's ties to individuals, groups, and organizations outside the group.

Ancona and Caldwell (1992) drew attention to the importance of a group's ties to its environment. Ancona and Caldwell developed a typology of 15 boundary-spanning behaviors, many of which involve the transfer of information and resources from outside the group. Research on interlocking boards of directors supports the notion that external group ties can play an important role in group success (e.g., Mizruchi, 1996) by providing useful knowledge from other boards (Davis, 1991; Haunschild, 1993). Some researchers, however, have reported mixed findings regarding the importance of boundary-crossing ties. Baldwin et al. (1997) found no relationship between a team's external ties and its performance. Sparrowe et al. (2001) found a strong *negative* relationship between a team's external ties and performance. Baldwin et al. suggest that their null findings simply reflect the fact that groups in their study had little need for external communication; due to the nature of the task, the configuration of internal ties was more important than external ties. In other words, a group's "need for external resources," as defined by the nature of the task, moderated the impact of external ties.

We believe work by Hansen (1999) and Haas (2002) may help resolve the discrepancy between Sparrowe et al.'s (2001) results (external ties can hurt a team's performance) and the other research suggesting external ties can be a valuable source of information and resources. Hansen found an interaction between tie strength and the complexity of information being transmitted. Weak ties worked best for bringing simple information from the external environment into the team. Complex information required the "bandwidth" of strong ties. Sparrowe et al.'s findings might be the result of not differentiating between strong and weak ties. Furthermore, Haas found that having many external ties may be either beneficial or harmful for a team depending on a number of factors, including autonomy and task overload. For teams with little autonomy or with overloaded members, communication initiated by the external environment negatively affected group performance.

External ties can influence group performance through other mechanisms in addition to information flow. Several researchers have examined the impact of intergroup ties on conflict. Nelson (1989) studied three to seven groups within each of 20 organizations. Nelson measured the number of strong and weak ties within and between the groups in each organization, based on frequency of contact. Nelson categorized each organization as either "high conflict" or "low conflict." High conflict was scored when one or more of the following conditions were present: There was recent turnover, pessimism about the organization's future due to infighting, inability to reach consensus on strategic or operational change, recent intervention by outsiders due to internal inability to make changes, or "easily identifiable opposing internal factions." Nelson found that low-conflict organizations had significantly more strong ties within and among groups.

One recent study looked at the impact of network ties on effort. Lazer and Katz (2004) found that when group members shared many overlapping external ties, they were less likely to free-ride on one another's efforts. In other words, structural embeddedness (Granovetter, 1985; Uzzi, 1996) regulated the effort level of group members. This finding highlights the broader trade-off groups face in having redundant external ties, which would limit opportunistic behavior, as compared to having nonredundant external ties, which would offer greater access to information and resources (Burt, 1992).

Network as Output

Several researchers have focused on the question: What conditions influence the emergence of a centralized pattern of ties? Building on work such as Tushman (1978) and Hirokawa, Ebert, and Hurst (1996) suggesting that people working on complex tasks are likely to use decentralized, consultative decision-making structures, Brown and Miller (2000) conducted an experiment to examine the impact of task complexity on network centralization. Forty-eight groups of four to five people were given the task of proposing policies for an early education program. All groups were given the same information, but groups differed in how they needed to process that information. Half of the groups were required to decide on six goals and two interventions for each goal. The other half were required to decide on two goals and one intervention for each goal. Brown and Miller videotaped the group discussions and coded the number of messages sent and received by each group member. The researchers found that groups assigned to the high-complexity version of the task developed less centralized communication patterns than groups assigned to the low-complexity version of the task.

Argote, Turner, and Fichman (1989) examined the impact of stress and tension on network centralization in 20 five-person groups. Argote et al. adopted a task first used by the MIT researchers, the common symbol task, where participants had to figure out which of five colors displayed on cards were commonly held by everyone in the group. Group performance was defined as the proportion of group members who gave the correct answer. Argote et al. found that groups experiencing high stress and tension developed more centralized communication networks, consistent with earlier research into threat-rigidity effects (Staw, Sandelands, & Dutton, 1981).

In a study that looked at both the emerging network and the impact of that network (hence, network as both output and input), Friedkin (1999) applied social influence network theory to account for the phenomenon of group polarization, which is a shift in member opinions after group discussion of an issue. In these experiments (with 50 four-person groups, 32 three-person groups, and 36 two-person groups), Friedkin manipulated the communication structure by constraining communication to telephones. That is, rather than the typical paradigm of social influence research, where all communication occurs at a collective level (e.g., Asch, 1951), communication in Friedkin's experiments was predominantly dyadic. Friedkin found an uneven distribution of influence, where participants influenced (and were influenced by) some people more than others. This resulted in an overall shift in opinions toward an emergent group norm based on this uneven influence, rather than simple convergence to the mean of members' prediscussion opinions.[2]

Network as Mediator Between Inputs and Outputs

One recent experimental study is noteworthy for pinning down causal relationships and mediating variables. Jehn and Shah (1997) conducted an experiment using 53 three-person groups. The study was a 2 x 2 factorial design; groups were composed of either friends or acquaintances and performed either a decision-making or a motor task. On both types of tasks, groups composed of friends outperformed groups composed of acquaintances. Jehn and Shah measured a number of potential mediating processes: information sharing, morale building, planning, critical evaluation, commitment, monitoring, and cooperation. The researchers found that information sharing and morale building mediated the relationship between friendship and performance on the motor task.

This recent era of research on the internal networks of small groups opens new vistas for fruitful investigation. The early experimental research that divided tasks into simple versus complex, although an important first step, undervalued variables that might interact with network structure to produce outcomes. The currently emerging framework—reconceptualizing groups as consisting of multiple component networks—will help us understand how the value of a particular network structure is contingent on the distribution of knowledge and other resources, as well as task structure.

Future Directions

Having summarized the existing studies, we now focus on the future of this research stream. In this section, we define the outstanding substantive questions that need to be addressed, as well as methodological refinements necessary to address them.

Research Questions

Social network analysis typically focuses on a single snapshot of the network. As we discuss later, it is critical that the methodology expand its repertoire of tools to understand networks over time. The lack of longitudinal analysis leads to questions regarding which is causally antecedent, the network or the hypothesized effects of the network (Lazer, 2001). We would distinguish among three conceptually distinct stages of a group's network: the network pregroup formation, the network during the group's existence, and network postgroup. Within each stage, there are substantive questions that need to be answered.

Network Pregroup

What is the pattern of prior connections among group members, and between group members and nonmembers? Does the network prior to the group have an impact on effectiveness independent of the network during the group process? In other words, do prior ties affect group functioning over and above the impact of communication during the group's life? What is the relationship between the network prior to the group and the network during the process? Networks tend to have some durability (Newcomb, 1961), and it seems likely the pregroup network is correlated with the network during the group process. This could have implications for task accomplishment; people might talk most with those they already know, even if the task demands that they talk mostly with group members they do not already know.

These pregroup issues then lead directly to questions around how groups are formed from the pregroup network (cf. Owens, Mannix, & Neale, 1998). Are group members self-selected? As noted previously in the discussion of homophily, self-selected groups will likely be more homogeneous. Do self-selected group members differ in other ways as well? How does selecting someone as a member of your group affect the evolving dyadic tie differently from simply finding yourself assigned together to the same group?

Network During Process and Outcomes

Most of the research on the relationship between outcomes and group network structure looks at the network during the process. However, because networks are dynamic, there is a significant possibility of a feedback loop between outcomes and the group network. (See, e.g., the feedback loop between team performance and cohesiveness, documented in Mullen & Copper's 1994 meta-analysis.) What might be the effects of a feedback process? One possibility is that misery (lack of success) breeds company (connectedness). Another possibility is that successful collaborations result in increased communication. Lack of success may lead to a vicious cycle of failure, leading to disconnectedness, leading to more failure, and so on.

Network Postgroup

What are the long-run effects of groups on the network? Arrow and Crosson (2003) found that once two people had been together in a group, the chances of their choosing to work together in a subsequent group increased. Similarly, Hinds, Carley, Krackhardt, and Wholey (2000) showed that people choose to work with people with whom they already have a strong working relationship. Furthermore, as noted previously, success may have a positive effect on the duration of relationships. How does the group outcome influence the future choices and options group members face in selecting groups to join?

Methodological Issues

There are three methodological issues that we feel need to be addressed to enhance the capacity of the network perspective. First, given the importance of taking the life cycle of a group into account when understanding its network, as previously discussed, tools must be developed that allow for the analysis of networks over time. The field has begun to wrestle with this issue, with the application of simulation analysis to study the dynamics of networks (Banks & Carley, 1996; Carley, 2003; Zeggelink, 1995) and the development of statistical methods, such as Monte Carlo maximum likelihood procedures, to examine longitudinal data (Huisman & Snijders, 2003; for a review, see Wasserman & Robins, in press). Although these new methodologies have yet to have a widespread impact on the field, they have the potential to be transformational.

Second, there are concerns with the reliability and validity of network data as they are currently collected. The vast majority of research on social networks relies on self-report data. A series of studies comparing self-report and observational relational data have found surprisingly large divergences between the two (Bernard, Killworth, & Sailer, 1980, 1982; Bernard, Killworth, & Cronenfeld, 1984; Marsden, 1990). Some researchers, such as Freeman, Romney, and Freeman (1987) have downplayed this concern, suggesting that observational data capture only a snapshot of interaction whereas self-report data provide a truer picture of the long-term social structure. Richards (1985) has argued that self-reported data capture perceptions about the network, and those perceptions are themselves theoretically important—a notion captured by W. I. Thomas's observation that "perceptions are real in their consequences even if they do not map one-to-one onto observed behaviors" (Krackhardt, 1987, p. 128). Most of the studies we cited in this chapter assume that self-report network data measure some long-run behavioral features of the network, per Freeman et al. We are less sanguine about—and believe much more attention must be paid to—the validation of self-reported network data.

Third, as noted early in the chapter, one of the fundamental assumptions of network analysis is the nonindependence of observations—that is, of both the nodes and the relations. One of the critical areas that has moved forward over the last few years, and needs to move farther still, is the development of statistical methods that capture the types of interdependencies that we know occur in social networks. Network methodologists have begun to develop techniques for the statistical modeling of social networks using Markov random graph models and the p^* family of models (Robins, Elliott, & Pattison, 2001; Wasserman & Pattison, 1996). These statistical models can detect whether an observed network exhibits certain hypothesized structural tendencies. These are important developments, and we assert that more progress is needed to propel the study of small group networks from a primarily descriptive focus to one that can be used to statistically confirm hypotheses about the structural tendencies of ties within groups (Contractor, Wasserman, & Faust, in press).

Conclusion

The use of social network analysis to study groups has begun to emerge from the sideline where it was relegated for decades. We think that this trend has significant merit, because social network analysis offers tools that can help small group researchers deal with challenges they currently face. For example, an increasing number of scholars have criticized the relative paucity of theory and research that attends to the group's external environment and how a group manages its relationship with strategic outsiders (e.g., Stohl & Putnam, 1994). The network perspective offers a coherent basis for measuring and understanding the group's context. The group's context is viewed as the larger social structure of connections among people, resources, and other collectives in which a group is embedded and to which it is connected. Network analysis offers an array of tools for investigating patterns of relations between a group and its external context.

More generally, a key benefit of the network approach is that it allows a researcher to cross levels of analysis with relative ease. Thus, one may examine the position of the team in an overarching network (e.g., Ancona, 1990), describe the internal structure of communication of a particular team (e.g., Sparrowe et al., 2001), or examine the position of a particular individual within the team (e.g., Bavelas, 1950).

On a related note, the network perspective can help researchers integrate the internal workings of the group and the group's external environment. Studies have generally focused on *either* the relationships among group members (e.g., cohesiveness, coordination, etc.) or on the group's relationship with outsiders, but relatively few studies link the internal and external perspectives (Ancona & Caldwell, 1992). Network methods can help researchers examine how a team's internal workings and its external environment interact. For example, Lazer and Katz (2004) found that group members' shared ties to friends outside the group influenced the extent of social loafing by group members.

Finally, network analysis offers techniques for identifying and exploring important features of small group interaction. While one such feature—centralization—has already received substantial attention, network techniques can help researchers assess other, potentially important features of small group interaction. For example, how do isolates (individuals without any ties) affect group functioning (e.g., Thomas-Hunt, Ogden, & Neale, 2003)? Do the capabilities of particular nodes (e.g., the central node) matter? As group membership changes over time, how do the addition and deletion of nodes—and the requisite reconfiguration of relationships—affect group dynamics?

Of course, like any conceptual framework, the network perspective has its limits. For example, the pattern of ties among group members is not always important; relationships among members of a tug-of-war team should matter far less than they do in a high-technology research and development team. However, we believe that as an approach to the study of small groups, social network analysis promises a particularly high yield to researchers.

Notes

1. There are also studies that examine *egocentric* networks, where a sample of individuals is selected and those individuals are asked about their relationships. This is particularly valuable in understanding certain features (e.g., interracial communication) of very large (e.g., societal) networks, where a complete census of the network is impossible (Marsden, 1988). Typically, in small group networks, a complete census of the group's network is possible and desirable.

2. This research raises an intriguing issue regarding the verisimilitude with "real world" small group phenomena—some of which occur through the types of dyadic interactions that Friedkin examined and some of which occur not on the dyadic but the group level.

References

Ancona, D. G. (1990). Outward bound: Strategies for team survival in the organization. *Academy of Management Journal, 33,* 334–365.

Ancona, D. G., & Caldwell, D. F. (1992). Bridging the boundary—external activity and performance in organizational teams. *Administrative Science Quarterly, 37,* 634–665.

Argote, L., Turner, M. E., & Fichman, M. (1989). To centralize or not to centralize: The effects of uncertainty and threat on group structure and performance. *Organizational Behavior and Human Decision Processes, 43,* 58–74.

Arrow, H., & Crosson, S. B. (2003). Musical chairs: Membership dynamics in self-organized group formation. *Small Group Research, 5,* 523–556.

Arrow, H., McGrath, J. E., & Berdahl, J. L. (2000). *Small groups as complex systems: Formation, coordination, development, and adaptation.* Thousand Oaks, CA: Sage.

Asch, S. (1951). Effects of group pressure upon the modification and distortion of judgments. In H. Guetzkow (Ed.), *Groups, leadership, and men.* Pittsburgh, PA: Carnegie Press.

Baldwin, T. T., Bedell, M. D., & Johnson, J. L. (1997). The social fabric of a team-based MBA program: Network effects on student satisfaction and performance. *Academy of Management Journal, 40,* 1369–1397.

Banks, D. L., & Carley, K. M. (1996). Models for network evolution. *Journal of Mathematical Sociology, 21,* 173–196.

Batagelj, V. A., & Mrvar, A. (2003). Pajek—Analysis and visualization of large networks. In M. Jünger & P. Mutzel (Eds.), *Graph drawing software* (pp. 77–103). Berlin: Springer.

Bavelas, A. (1950). Communication patterns in task-oriented groups. *Journal of the Acoustical Society of America, 22,* 723–730.

Bavelas, A., & Barrett, M. (1951). An experimental approach to organizational communication. *Personnel, 27,* 386–397.

Bernard, H., Killworth, P., & Sailer, L. (1980). Informant accuracy in social network data IV. *Social Networks, 2,* 191–218.

Bernard, H., Killworth, P., & Sailer, L. (1982). Informant accuracy in social network data V. *Social Science Research, 11,* 30–66.

Bernard, H. R., Killworth, P., & Cronenfeld, D. (1984). The problem of informant accuracy: The validity of retrospective data. *Annual Review of Anthropology, 13,* 495–517.

Bienenstock, E. J., & Bonacich, P. (1992). The core as solution to exclusionary networks. *Social Networks, 14,* 231–244.

Bienenstock, E. J., & Bonacich, P. (1997). Network exchange as a cooperative game. *Rationality and Society, 9,* 37–65.

Borgatti, S. (2003). NetDraw: Network visualization software. Retrieved from http://www.analytictech.com/netdraw.htm

Bourdieu, P. (1985). The forms of capital. In J. G. Richardson (Ed.), *Handbook of theory and research for the sociology of education* (pp. 241–258). New York: Greenwood.

Bourdieu, P., & Wacquant, L. J. D. (1992). *An invitation to reflexive sociology.* Chicago: University of Chicago Press.

Brass, D. J. (1995a). Creativity: It's all in your social network. In C. M. Ford & D. A. Gioia (Eds.), *Creative action in organizations* (pp. 94–99). London: Sage.

Brass, D. J. (1995b). A social network perspective on human resources management. *Research in Personnel and Human Resources Management, 13,* 39–79.

Breiger, R. (1974). The duality of persons and groups. *Social Forces, 53,* 181–190.

Brown, T. M., & Miller, C. E. (2000). Communication networks in task-performing groups: Effects of task complexity, time pressure, and interpersonal dominance. *Small Group Research, 31,* 131–157.

Burt, R. S. (1992). *Structural holes: The social structure of competition.* Cambridge, MA: Harvard University Press.

Burt, R. S. (1997). The contingent value of social capital. *Administrative Science Quarterly, 42,* 339–365.

Burt, R. S. (1998). The gender of social capital. *Rationality and Society, 10,* 5–46.

Burt, R. S. (2001). Structural holes versus network closure as social capital. In N. Lin, K. Cook, & R. S. Burt (Eds.), *Social capital: Theory and research,* (pp. 31–56). New York: Aldine de Gruyter.

Byrne, D. (1971). *The attraction paradigm.* New York: Academic Press.

Carley, K. M. (1991). A theory of group stability. *American Sociological Review, 56,* 331–354.

Carley, K. M. (2003). Dynamic network analysis. In R. Breiger & K. M. Carley (Eds.), *Summary of the NRC workshop on social network modeling and analysis.* Washington, DC: National Research Council.

Cartwright, D., & Harary, F. (1956). Structural balance—a generalization of Heider theory. *Psychological Review, 63,* 277–293.

Cohen, A. M. (1962). Changing small group communication networks. *Administrative Science Quarterly, 6,* 443–462.

Coleman, J. S. (1957). *Community conflict.* New York: Free Press.

Coleman, J. S. (1988). Social capital in the creation of human-capital. *American Journal of Sociology, 94,* S95–S120.

Coleman, J. S. (1990). *Foundations of social theory.* Cambridge: Belknap Press.

Contractor, N. S, Wasserman, S., & Faust, K. (in press). Testing multi-level, multi-theoretical hypotheses about organizational networks: An analytic framework and empirical example. *Academy of Management Review.*

Cook, K. S. (1977). Exchange and power in networks of interorganizational relations. *Sociological Quarterly, 18,* 62–82.

Cook, K. S. (1982). Network structures from an exchange perspective. In P. V. Marsden & N. Lin (Eds.), *Social structure and network analysis* (pp. 177–218). Beverly Hills, CA: Sage.

Cook, K. S., & Whitmeyer, J. M. (1992). Two approaches to social structure: Exchange theory and network analysis. *Annual Review of Sociology, 18,* 109–127.

Cummings, J. N. (2004). NetVis module—Dynamic visualization of social networks. Retrieved from http://www.netvis.org/

Cummings, J. N., & Cross, R. (2003). Structural properties of work groups and their consequences for performance. *Social Networks, 25,* 197–281.

Davis, A., Gardner, B. B., & Gardner, M. R. (1941). *Deep south: A social anthropological study of caste and class.* Chicago: University of Chicago Press.

Davis, G. F. (1991). Agents without principles—the spread of the poison pill through the intercorporate network. *Administrative Science Quarterly, 36,* 583–613.

Emerson, R. M. (1972a). Exchange theory, part I: A psychological basis for social exchange. In J. Berger, M. Zelditch, & B. Anderson (Eds.), *Sociological theories in progress* (pp. 38–57). Boston: Houghton Mifflin.

Emerson, R. M. (1972b). Exchange theory, part II: Exchange relations and networks. In J. Berger, M. Zelditch, & B. Anderson (Eds.), *Sociological theories in progress* (pp. 58–87). Boston: Houghton Mifflin.

Festinger, L., Schacter, S., & Back, K. (1950). *Social pressures in informal groups: A study of human factors in housing.* New York: Harper.

Freeman, L. C. (1992). The sociological concept of group—an empirical-test of two models. *American Journal of Sociology, 98,* 152–166.

Freeman, L. C., Romney, K. A., & Freeman, S. C. (1987). Cognitive structure and informant accuracy. *American Anthropologist, 89,* 310–325.

Friedkin, N. E. (1999). Choice shift and group polarization. *American Sociological Review, 64,* 856–875.

Fulk, J., Flanagin, A.J., Kalman, M. E., Monge, P. R., & Ryan, T. (1996). Connective and communal public goods in interactive communication systems. *Communication Theory, 6,* 60–87.

Granovetter, M. (1973). The strength of weak ties. *American Journal of Sociology, 81,* 1287–1303.

Granovetter, M. (1982). The strength of weak ties: A network theory revisited. In R. Collins (Ed.), *Sociological theory 1983* (pp. 105–130). San Francisco, CA: Jossey-Bass.

Granovetter, M. S. (1985). Economic action and social structure: The problem of embeddedness. *American Journal of Sociology, 91,* 481–510.

Gruenfeld, D., Mannix, E., Williams, K., & Neale, M. (1996). Group composition and decision making: How member familiarity and information distribution affect process and performance. *Organizational Behavior and Human Decision Processes, 67,* 1–15.

Guetzkow, H., & Simon, H. A. (1955). The impact of certain communication nets upon organization and performance in task-oriented groups. *Management Science, 1,* 233–250.

Haas, M. R. (2002). *Acting on what others know: Distributed knowledge and team performance.* Unpublished dissertation, Harvard University, Cambridge, MA.

Hansen, M. T. (1999). The search-transfer problem: The role of weak ties in sharing knowledge across organization subunits. *Administrative Science Quarterly, 44,* 82–111.

Harary, F., Norman, R. Z., & Cartwright, D. (1965). *Structural models: An introduction to the theory of directed graphs.* New York: John Wiley.

Hardin, R. (1982). *Collective action.* Baltimore, MD: John Hopkins University Press.

Haunschild, P. R. (1993). Interorganizational imitation: The impact of interlocks on corporate acquisition activity. *Administrative Science Quarterly, 38,* 564–592.

Heider, F. (1946). Attitudes and cognitive organization. *Journal of Psychology, 21,* 107–112.

Heider, F. (1958). *The psychology of interpersonal relations.* New York: John Wiley.

Hinds, P. J., Carley, K. M., Krackhardt, D., & Wholey, D. (2000). Choosing work group members: Balancing similarity, competence, and familiarity. *Organizational Behavior & Human Decision Processes, 81,* 226–251.

Hirokawa, R., Ebert, L., & Hurst, A. (1996). Communication and group decision-making effectiveness. In R. Y. Hirokawa & M. S. Poole (Eds.), *Communication and group decision making* (pp. 269–300). Thousand Oaks, CA: Sage.

Holland, P. W., & Leinhardt, S. (1977). Dynamic-model for social networks. *Journal of Mathematical Sociology, 5,* 5–20.

Hollingshead, A. B. (1998). Retrieval processes in transactive memory systems. *Journal of Personality and Social Psychology, 74,* 659–671.

Hollingshead, A. B., Fulk, J., & Monge, P. (2002). Fostering intranet knowledge-sharing: An integration of transactive memory and public goods approaches. In P. Hinds & S. Kiesler (Eds.), *Distributed work* (pp. 335–355). Cambridge: MIT Press.

Homans, G. (1950). *The human group.* New York: Harcourt, Brace.

Huisman, M., & Snijders, T. A. B. (2003). Statistical analysis of longitudinal network data with changing composition. *Sociological Methods and Research, 32,* 253–287.

Ibarra, H. (1995). Race, opportunity, and diversity of social circles in managerial networks. *Academy of Management Journal, 38,* 673–703.

Jehn, K. A., & Shah, P. P. (1997). Interpersonal relationships and task performance: An examination of mediating processes in friendship and acquaintance groups. *Journal of Personality and Social Psychology, 72,* 775–790.

Krackhardt, D. (1987). Cognitive social structures. *Social Networks, 9,* 109–134.

Krackhardt, D., & Carley, K. M. (2003). *PCANS model of structure in organizations* (CASOS working papers). Pittsburgh, PA: Carnegie-Mellon University.

Krackhardt, D., & Kilduff, M. (1990). Friendship patterns and culture: The control of organizational diversity. *American Anthropologist, 92,* 142–154.

Laumann, E. O. (1966). *Prestige and association in an urban community.* Indianapolis, IN: Bobbs-Merrill.

Lazer, D. M. (2001). The co-evolution of individual and network. *Journal of Mathematical Sociology, 25,* 69–108.

Lazer, D., & Katz, N. (2004). *Regulating opportunism: The role of embeddedness in teams* (Working paper). Cambridge, MA: Harvard University, John F. Kennedy School of Government.

Leavitt, H. J. (1951). Some effects of certain communication patterns on group performance. *Journal of Abnormal and Social Psychology, 46,* 38–50.

Lessig, L. (2001). *The future of ideas: The fate of the commons in a connected world.* New York: Random House.

Lin, N. (2001). *Social capital: A theory of social structure and action.* Cambridge, UK: Cambridge University Press.

Lipman-Blumen, J., & Leavitt, H. J. (2001). *Hot groups: Seeding them, feeding them, and using them to ignite your organization.* Oxford, UK: Oxford University Press.

Markovsky, B., & Chaffee, M. (1995). Social identification and solidarity: A reformulation. *Advances in Group Processes, 12,* 249–270.

Markovsky, B., & Lawler, E. J. (1994). A new theory of group solidarity. In B. Markovsky, K. Heimer, & J. O'Brien (Eds.), *Advances in group processes* (Vol. 11, pp. 113–137). Greenwich, CT: JAI Press.

Marsden, P. V. (1988). Homogeneity in confiding relations. *Social Networks, 10,* 57–76.

Marsden, P. V. (1990). Network data and measurement. *Annual Review of Sociology, 16,* 435–498.

Marwell, G., & Oliver, P. (1993). *The critical mass in collective action: A microsocial theory.* Cambridge, UK: Cambridge University Press.

Mayo, E. (1933). *The human problems of an industrial civilization.* New York: Viking Press.

McPherson, J. M., & Smith-Lovin, L. (1987). Homophily in voluntary organizations: Status distance and the composition of face to face groups. *American Sociological Review, 52,* 370–379.

Mizruchi, M. S. (1996). What do interlocks do? An analysis, critique, and assessment of research on interlocking directorates. *Annual Review of Sociology, 22,* 271–298.

Monge, P. R., & Contractor, N. (2003). *Theories of communication networks.* New York: Oxford University Press.

Monge, P. R., Fulk, J. K., Kalman, M., Flanagin, A. J., Parnassa, C., & Rumsey, S. (1998). Production of collective action in alliance-based interorganizational communication and information systems. *Organization Science, 9,* 411–433.

Moreland, R., Hogg, M., & Hains, S. (1994). Back to the future: Social psychological research on groups. *Journal of Experimental Social Psychology, 30,* 527–555.

Moreland, R. L. (1999). Transactive memory: Learning who knows what in work groups and organizations. In L. Thompson, D. Messick, & J. Levine (Eds.), *Sharing knowledge in organizations* (pp. 3–31). Mahwah, NJ: Lawrence Erlbaum.

Mullen, B., & Copper, C. (1994). The relation between group cohesiveness and performance: An integration. *Psychological Bulletin, 115,* 210–227.

Nelson, R. E. (1989). The strength of strong ties: Social networks and intergroup conflict in organizations. *Academy of Management Journal, 32,* 377–401.

Newcomb, T. M. (1953). An approach to the study of communicative acts. *Psychological Review, 4,* 183–214.

Newcomb, T. M. (1961). *The acquaintance process.* New York: Holt, Rinehart & Winston.

Newcomb, T. M. (1981). Heiderian balance as a group phenomenon. *Journal of Personality and Social Psychology, 40,* 862–867.

Olson, M., Jr. (1965). *The logic of collective action.* Cambridge, MA: Harvard University Press.

Owens, D., Mannix, E., & Neale, M. (1998). Strategic formation of groups: Issues in task performance and team member selection. *Research on Managing Groups and Teams, 1,* 149–165.

Putnam, R. D. (1993). *Making democracy work.* Princeton, NJ: Princeton University Press.

Putnam, R. D. (2000). *Bowling alone: The collapse and revival of American community.* New York: Simon & Schuster.

Reagans, R., & Zuckerman, E. W. (2001). Networks, diversity, and productivity: The social capital of corporate R&D teams. *Organization Science, 12,* 502–517.

Richards, W. D. (1985). Data, models, and assumptions in network analysis. In R. D. McPhee & P. K. Tompkins (Eds.), *Organizational communication: Themes and new directions* (pp. 109–147). Beverly Hills, CA: Sage.

Robins, G., Elliott, P., & Pattison, P. (2001). Network models for social selection processes. *Social Networks, 23,* 1–30.

Roethlisberger, F. J., & Dickson, W. J. (1939). *Management and the worker.* Cambridge, MA: Harvard University Press.

Samuelson, P. (1954). The pure theory of public expenditure. *Review of Economics and Statistics, 36,* 387–389.

Shaw, M. (1954). Some effects of unequal distribution of information upon group performance in various communication nets. *Journal of Abnormal and Social Psychology, 49,* 547–553.

Shaw, M. (1964). Communication networks. In L. Berkowitz (Ed.), *Advances in experimental psychology* (pp. 111–147). New York: Academic Press.

Shaw, M. (1971). *The psychology of small group behavior.* New York: McGraw-Hill.

Sherif, M. (1958). Superordinate goals in the reduction of intergroup conflicts. *American Journal of Sociology, 63,* 349–356.

Sherif, M. (1966). *In common predicament: Social psychology of intergroup conflict and cooperation.* Boston: Houghton Mifflin.

Sherif, M., Harvey, O. J., White, B. J., Hood, W. R., & Sherif, C. W. (1961). *Intergroup conflict and cooperation: The Robbers Cave Experiment.* Norman, OK: Institute of Social Relations.

Sparrowe, R. T., Liden, R. C., Wayne, S. J., & Kraimer, M. L. (2001). Social networks and the performance of individuals and groups. *Academy of Management Journal, 44,* 316–325.

Staw, B. M., Sandelands, L. E., & Dutton, J. E. (1981). Threat-rigidity effects in organizational behavior: A multi-level analysis. *Administrative Science Quarterly, 21,* 378–397.

Stohl, C., & Putnam, L. (1994). Group communication in context: Implications for the study of bona fide groups. In L. R. Frey (Ed.), *Group communication in context: Studies of natural groups* (2nd ed., pp. 285–292). Hillsdale, NJ: Lawrence Erlbaum.

Thomas-Hunt, M. C., Ogden, T. Y., & Neale, M. A. (2003). Who's really sharing? Effects of social and expert status on knowledge exchange within groups. *Management Science, 49,* 464–477.

Trist, E. L., & Bamforth, K. W. (1951). Social and psychological consequences of the longwall method of coal-getting. *Human Relations, 4,* 3–28.

Tschan, F., & von Cranach, M. (1996). Group task structure, processes, and outcome. In M. A. West (Ed.), *Handbook of work group psychology* (pp. 92–121). Chichester, UK: John Wiley.

Turner, J. C., & Oakes, P. J. (1986). The significance of the social identity concept for social psychology with reference to individualism, interactionism, and social influence. *British Journal of Social Psychology, 25,* 237–252.

Turner, J. C., & Oakes, P. J. (1989). Self-categorization theory and social influence. In P. B. Paulus (Ed.), *Psychology of group influence* (pp. 233–275). Hillsdale, NJ: Lawrence Erlbaum.

Tushman, M. (1978). Technical communication in R&D laboratories: The impact of project work characteristics. *Academy of Management Journal, 21,* 624–645.

Uzzi, B. (1996). The sources and consequences of embeddedness for the economic performance of organizations: The network effect. *American Sociological Review, 61,* 674–698.

Wasserman, S., & Faust, K. (1994). *Social network analysis.* Cambridge, UK: Cambridge University Press.

Wasserman, S., & Pattison, P. (1996). Logit models and logistic regressions for social networks: I. An introduction to Markov graphs and p*. *Psychometrika, 61,* 401–425.

Wasserman, S., & Robins, G. (in press). Introduction to random graphs, dependence graphs, and p^*. In P. J. Carrington, J. Scott, & S. Wasserman (Eds.), *Models and methods in social network analysis*. New York: Cambridge University Press.

Wegner, D. M. (1987). Transactive memory: A contemporary analysis of the group mind. In B. Mullen & G. Goethals (Eds.), *Theories of group behavior* (pp. 185–208). New York: Springer-Verlag.

Wegner, D. M. (1995). A computer network model of human transactive memory. *Social Cognition, 13*, 319–339.

Wellman, B. (1988). Structural analysis: From method and metaphor to theory and substance. In B. Wellman & S. Berkowitz (Eds.), *Social structures: A network approach* (pp. 19–61). Cambridge, UK: Cambridge University Press.

Willer, D., & Skvoretz, J. (1997). Network connection and exchange ratios: Theory, predictions, and experimental tests. *Advances in Group Processes, 14*, 199–234.

Winship, C. (1977). A distance model for sociometric structure. *Journal of Mathematical Sociology, 5*, 21–39.

Zeggelink, E. (1995). Evolving friendship networks: An individual-oriented approach implementing similarity. *Social Networks, 17*, 83–110.

9

Traces, Trajectories, and Timing

The Temporal Perspective on Groups

Holly Arrow, Kelly Bouas Henry,
Marshall Scott Poole, Susan Wheelan,
and Richard Moreland

Abstract

This chapter reviews empirical and theoretical literature that takes a temporal perspective on groups. The temporal perspective is process focused, treating groups as systems in which change occurs across multiple time scales. The review is organized around six themes that have been especially generative: (1) Time is socially constructed, (2) time is a resource, (3) time is a fundamental issue for theory and research, (4) groups change systematically over time, (5) group processes have temporal patterns, and (6) groups are complex systems characterized by nonlinear dynamics. We close by calling for continued theory and methodological developments to better integrate the disparate theories and findings found in literature inspired by the temporal perspective, and by identifying some changes in infrastructure that would facilitate this integrative process.

Most research on groups neglects the role of time.[1] This is not surprising. Studying groups is a resource-intensive process, and longitudinal designs make the resource problem worse. Moreover, time is a deeply problematic object of inquiry. All group processes unfold in time, which can be thought of as a ubiquitous context that is uncontrollable and impossible to replicate. These are not attractive attributes for scientists attempting to discover fundamental regularities in phenomena. As time unfolds and experience accumulates, groups change. Some of this change is systematic; some is idiosyncratic and particular. Some small group scholars are attracted by the challenging problems this poses, but many are not.

Serious attempts to tackle the mysteries of time and change in groups date back at least to Kurt Lewin, who coined the term *group dynamics*. His systems ideas about mutual, cross-level influence and quasi-stationary equilibria (Lewin, 1947a, 1947b) did not, however, inspire much empirical research. Why? Wheelan (1996) gives an ideological explanation, suggesting that the study of groups as systems was simply too difficult to reconcile with the concept of individual free will. Moreland (1996) proposes that the establishment of experimental methods as the standard paradigm in social psychology impeded progress in studying temporal processes. To this day, research by social psychologists strongly favors laboratory experiments over field studies of naturally occurring groups (Moreland, Hogg, & Hains, 1994), and ad hoc laboratory groups typically have no past and no anticipated future. Topics such as group development, which were once central to the field but are difficult to study in the laboratory, have in the past few decades been largely ignored or studied in clumsy ways (Moreland, 1996).

Scholars who prefer to study naturally occurring groups are more likely to grapple with change processes that unfold in the context of time as "history"—which is to say a cumulative, irreversible process. In the past few decades, such scholars are more often trained in disciplines such as communication or sociology or organizational behavior rather than social psychology. Case studies of naturally occurring groups provide a rich mine of data to guide our insights into temporal processes and help build theory (see, e.g., Frey, 2003; Hackman, 1990). However, systematic tests of theories about change processes remain difficult and rare.

In organizing and presenting the diverse body of work on issues of time or change in groups, we first define the scope of the chapter and identify six themes that have guided work that takes a temporal perspective on groups. Next, we review theoretical and empirical work tied to three different perspectives on time. We then move to the topic of change in groups, also organized into three sections based on different themes. We end the chapter with a discussion of possible future directions that identifies what we see as the primary challenges to be addressed in advancing our understanding of time and change in groups.

Definition, Scope, and Core Themes

The temporal perspective is a process-focused view that treats groups as systems in which change occurs across multiple time scales, generated both by endogenous processes and by forces external to the group. Time is viewed in a variety of ways: as a context, as a resource, as a moderator or mediator of other processes. Change is also viewed in a variety of ways: as progressive, contingent, episodic, or continuous; as endogenous or triggered by actors or events exogenous to the group. Although theories differ both in how they conceptualize time and in the specific dynamic variables of interest, they share an emphasis on describing temporal patterns and determining how variables interact and change over time within the group system or in its embedding context.

Literature reviewed for this chapter includes work that has time or change as a main focus. This includes studies of time pressure, temporal orientation, and scheduling, for example. In such studies, temporal factors may serve as the independent variable (e.g., time pressure), as a quasi-independent variable (early or late), or as a dependent variable (e.g., pacing or entrainment), or they may appear in several roles (e.g., impact of temporal orientation on scheduling; time allocation at different periods in a group's life). Along with the literature on small groups, we discuss some work that focuses on temporal issues in larger groups such as organizations.

Studies of how groups change may treat time as a mediator or moderator of other processes. Work that treats time as a mediator includes research on decision development, learning curves, and norm emergence. Work that treats time as a moderator includes, for example, studies of how the impact of communication medium differs in new and established groups, or how groups at different stages of group development respond to outsiders.

Scholarly work that falls under this perspective is spread over a number of literatures and advances a number of different theories. It includes some well-developed bodies of work that investigate a shared set of questions. Notable examples are work on group development (systematic patterns of change in a group as a whole over its life course) and decision development. Work on topics such as group socialization (the changing relationship between a member and the group) or group learning (how knowledge is accumulated and embedded in groups) form smaller bodies of work, often clustered around a few core authors and their collaborators and students. This Micronesia of infrequent larger islands, a few medium-size clusters, and

Table 9.1   The Temporal Perspective

Definition of perspective	This perspective includes research that has either time or change as its main object of study, or considers time as a mediator or moderator of other phenomena
Key assumptions	• Time is socially constructed • Time is a resource • Time is a problematic issue for theory and research • Groups change systematically over time • Group processes have temporal patterns • Groups are complex systems
Types of groups	The temporal perspective yields the greatest information when studying groups that have a history and future (e.g., sports teams, work groups, families, etc.).
Key theories	• Sequential, cyclic, and punctuated equilibrium theories of group development • Activity phase models • Group socialization model • Action theory • Structuration theory • Groups as complex systems
Dominant research methodologies	• Longitudinal studies of naturally occurring groups • Longitudinal laboratory simulations • Fine-grained study of real-time interaction, including short-term ad hoc groups
Strengths	• Provides a mechanism for integrating disparate findings across the groups literature • Provides a context for understanding limits of existing findings
Weaknesses	• Practical difficulties of longitudinal research • Lack of theoretical integration across studies • Theories lack specificity and are difficult to falsify • Methods suited for the study of processes over time are not well developed

numerous tiny islands is scattered across the whole breadth of the groups literature, which itself encompasses several academic disciplines. The basic characteristics of the temporal perspective are summarized in Table 9.1.

We have organized this review around six themes—three related primarily to time and three related primarily to change—that represent different aspects of this literature.

1. *Time is socially constructed.* This theme is central to work on the perception and understanding of time in groups. Studies that investigate the antecedents and consequences of different group conceptions of time fit this theme.

2. *Time is a resource.* Studies of how groups "manage" time and how time pressure (a resource shortage) affects group processes and outcomes fit this theme. It is inherent in all studies of how groups map activities to time.

3. *Time is a fundamental (and often problematic) issue for theory and research.* Scholars in several disciplines have noted that our conceptions of time shape the way we construct group theory, design research studies, and interpret our results.

4. *Groups change systematically over time; they develop.* This is the central theme of most group development work, which seeks to characterize the ways in which groups as systems change over time.

5. *Group processes have temporal patterns.* Work that fits this theme looks at the patterning of interaction in groups, including the sequencing of conversational turns, phases of group decision-making, and changing patterns in member-group relations.

6. *Groups are complex systems characterized by nonlinear dynamics.* Models of groups as complex systems share an emphasis on time and change at multiple levels. Many focus on causal forces that operate between levels of analysis, on discontinuous change, and on historical processes such as path dependence.

Time and Groups

The Social Construction of Time

Both the temporal perspectives of individual members and collective group norms about the meaning of time shape the way a group handles temporal matters. McGrath and Kelly (1986, p. 24) make the distinction between "objective" time measured by planetary orbits, calendars, and clocks, and "subjective" time as experienced psychologically by humans. The objective construction, which views time as a continuous and directional flow that can be measured as a regular succession of moments, is the dominant paradigm for Western culture. It is typically experienced by people living in the West as the "real and correct" notion of time, and thus it is often not recognized as a social construction. Yet, people perceive and relate to this continuum in a variety of ways.

A useful classification proposed by Ancona, Okhuysen, and Perlow (2001) identifies five types of time: clock time, cyclical time (such as the succession of seasons), two types of event time (predictable and unpredictable) and life cycle time, which refers to development progression within a finite life span. Two examples of predictable events that structure time are paydays and religious holidays. Examples of unpredictable events that become reference points for things that happen before and after would be major earthquakes or the September 11 attacks on New York and Washington in 2001.

One of the earliest studies of the social construction of time in a group is Roy's (1960) study of how four men counteracted the monotony of long hours of tedious machine work (objective time) by reconstructing time into a series of recurrent daily events, mostly organized around the procurement, sharing, stealing, and consumption of food and drink. The study illustrates how a group's construction of time can alter member experience and satisfaction.

A more common outcome variable in recent decades is group task performance, whether the focus is quality, quantity, or the ability to meet deadlines. Gersick's (1988, 1989) studies of task forces, for example, documented a shift in time perception at the midpoint of a group's time together. Before the midpoint, groups work at a relaxed pace, focus on the task in front of them, and pay relatively little attention to objective calendar or clock time. Time is a medium in which the group operates but is often not explicitly "managed." At the midpoint, the collective realization that half the group's time is "gone" catalyzes a new construction of time as a scarce and rapidly dwindling resource. For the rest of the group's life, time means "time left," sand in an hourglass that runs out as the deadline approaches (Gersick, 1989). A later study that measured attention to time in groups did not find the midpoint transition but documented steadily increasing attention to time as the deadline approaches (Waller, Zellmer-Bruhn, & Giambatista, 2002).

Groups working on different types of projects are liable to construct time and temporal markers differently. Groups that rely on external pacers, for example, such as task forces working against an externally imposed deadline, should have a very different conception of what constitutes "late," for example, than groups that are more internally focused (Ancona & Chong, 1996).

As Waller, Conte, Gibson, and Carpenter (2001) note, most work on the temporal perspective tends to assume a single, shared perception of time by all group members. Yet members may construct time differently. Waller et al. develop a series of propositions based on combining literature on time urgency (high versus low) and time perspective (future- versus present-oriented) to yield four individual-level prototypes: *organizers* (high time urgency, future oriented), *crammers* (high time urgency, present oriented), *visioners* (low time urgency, future oriented), and *relators* (low time urgency, present oriented). Waller et al. (2001) propose that under deadline conditions, teams composed of visioners and relators (both low urgency) will have difficulty meeting deadlines, whereas teams composed of organizers and crammers will not. The type of deadline should also matter, with "deep future" deadlines meshing better with teams composed of visioners and organizers and "shallow future" deadlines fitting teams of crammers and relators better. Finally, they propose that a temporal match between the time urgency and time perspective configuration of team members should have a positive impact on overall team performance.

Waller et al. (2001) also note that the prevalence of different time perspectives (past, present, or future) tends to vary across cultures (Hall, 1983), which suggests that groups of people from diverse cultural backgrounds will also likely be diverse in time perspective. Cultural differences in understanding of time, for example, result in different temporal patterns in the negotiation process (Faure & Sjostedt, 1993). The Western construction of time as a scarce commodity is less common in the Near East. Hence, negotiations among Westerners tend to have a quick pace and firm time frames, whereas people from the Near East tend to prefer a slower pace and looser, less-defined time frames.

Time as a Resource

The objective construction of time, which is strongly influenced by Newtonian conceptions (McGrath & Kelly, 1986), lends itself to economic metaphors of "time as money." As a scarce, valuable commodity, time should be used wisely, not wasted, and "saved" where possible. In work groups and organizations, this metaphor underlies notions of productivity and efficiency, which refer to the return on investment realized for a particular unit of time. This approach fits well with an input-process-output model of group functioning.

Viewing time as a resource makes it easier to study. Researchers can manipulate how much time different groups have to complete a task or can alter the amount of time a group has for successive tasks in an experiment, then observe how this affects interaction and performance. Kelly and colleagues (e.g., Kelly, Futoran, & McGrath, 1990; Kelly, Jackson, & Hutson-Comeaux, 1997; Kelly & Karau, 1993; Kelly & McGrath 1985) have produced a sophisticated body of work on this topic, which explores the impact of time pressure on individuals, dyads, and groups performing assigned tasks. Such studies illustrate the manipulation of objective time as an independent variable, the use of time allocation as an outcome variable, and the impact of sequencing, a "history" effect.

Experimental studies of time as a dependent variable typically look either at how a fixed amount of time is allocated or at how much time groups take to complete a task under different conditions—for example, communicating face-to-face (FTF) versus via a computer-mediated (CM) communication system such as e-mail, computer conferencing, or teleconferencing. The consistent finding is that CM groups take longer to complete a task than FTF groups (Hollingshead & McGrath, 1995; Rice, 1984; Weisband, 1992). When FTF and CM groups have the same fixed amount of time, FTF groups generate more words and communication "acts" in the same amount of time. They also allocate their available time differently, with FTF groups devoting proportionately more time to interpersonal, non-task activities (e.g., Hollingshead & McGrath, 1995; Lebie, Rhoades, & McGrath, 1996).

Viewed in conjunction with findings on the impact of time pressure, these results suggest that the different pattern of time allocation in CM and FTF groups is properly ascribed not to the medium per se but to how much time pressure the group experiences. CM groups with the same amount of objective time are actually under more time pressure than FTF groups because they are less efficient (i.e., they need more time for the same task).

Although a group's pattern of time allocation may emerge with little explicit discussion, activities related to deliberate time management of a task-oriented nature (e.g., planning, scheduling, prioritizing, goal setting) are found in many work groups (Fine, 1987; McGrath, 1990, 1991; Waller, 1997, 2000; Weingart, 1992; Weldon & Weingart, 1993). In a study of self-managed work teams, for example, Janicik and Bartel (2003) found that some teams were more likely than others to begin new projects with temporal planning, which involved such topics as allocation (how much time should be spent on each task?), scheduling (when must each task be completed?), and synchronization (what should each team member be doing when?). Teams that did more temporal planning tended to view time as a scarce resource, to develop norms that promoted attention to time, and to achieve greater coordination among team members and better team performance.

An interesting line of research on how groups manage their time investigates monochronic versus polychronic ways of organizing work. Hall (1983) uses these terms to distinguish cultures in which people tend to do one thing at a time (monochronic) or several things simultaneously (polychronic). The idea has also been applied to organizations (Schein, 1992) and treated as an individual difference (e.g., Kaufman-Scarborough & Lindquist, 1999). Applied to groups (Waller, 1997, 2000), it refers to a group's tendency to work on a single task at a time or multiple tasks simultaneously. The concept is not, however, a simple aggregation of individual tendencies, for a group can work on multiple tasks simultaneously by dividing them among members, all of whom work monochronically on one task at a time. Waller, Giambatista, and Zellmer-Bruhn (1999) found that groups that include a time-urgent member (someone who perceives time as an enemy and is highly aware of objective time) tend more toward monochronic behavior than groups that do not.

Work that fits the broad theme of "time as resource" can be arrayed along a continuum of increasing complexity using Ofori-Dankwa and Julian's (2001) four different levels of complexity in time research. Applied to time allocation, first-level studies look at quantitative differences in how much time is devoted to different activities, collapsed across the full interval measured. Hiltz, Johnson, and Turoff (1986), for example, found that CM groups had proportionately more task-oriented communication than FTF groups. This approach to aggregation presumes a stationary pattern and lends itself to cross-sectional research designs.

A second-level study (typical of much group development work) adds change as a possibility and considers that time allocation may vary across time within a group. Lebie and colleagues (1996) looked at time allocation (measured in terms of communication acts) in CM and FTF groups across a series of six work sessions and found that it varied both across communication media and across time. This study combined cross-sectional and repeated measures elements in the design and analyses. Considering polychronicity or monochronicity as an individual-level difference among members at the group level fits the next level of complexity because it introduces the possibility that different patterns of time allocation may occur simultaneously within a group. Fourth-level complexity involves attending to both multiple simultaneous processes and change over time. Ofori-Dankwa and Julian (2001, p. 426) identify as an example the (Waller et al., 1999) finding that individual-level temporal preferences trigger group-level monochronicity.

Time as a Fundamental Issue in Theory and Research

A growing chorus of scholars inspired by this theme is calling for more sophisticated attention to time in theory development and empirical research (e.g., Arrow, McGrath, & Berdahl, 2000; McGrath & Kelly, 1986; McGrath & Tschan, 2004b; Poole, Van de Ven, Dooley, & Holmes, 2000; Zaheer, Albert, & Zaheer, 1999). Responding to this call requires that we wean ourselves from the current overemphasis on cross-sectional "snapshot" studies. It also requires that we attend more closely to the timing and sequence of events. Taking account of time and change necessarily makes theories more complex, as is evident in Ofori-Dankwa and Julian's (2001) level-of-complexity typology. The fourth level of complexity includes the possibility of both multiple simultaneous streams of activity and change in these streams of activity over time.

In this section, we focus on two representative contributions that exemplify the theme of time as a fundamental issue in theory and research. The first is Zaheer et al.'s (1999) consideration of the role of time scales in theory and research design. The quantitative meaning of a time scale is the size of a temporal interval, whether objective or subjective. In group interaction, relevant time scales can range from split-second timing to hours, days, months, or even decades.

According to Zaheer and colleagues (1999), scholars need to attend to five types of time scales:

1. The *existence interval* is the time needed for one instance of a phenomenon to occur. Applied to stage theories of group development, for example, the existence interval would be the group's full life span.

2. The *observation interval* is the time over which a process is observed. For a group development study, the observation interval would be whatever segment of the group's life was captured in the study.

3. The *recording interval* is the frequency with which a phenomenon is measured. In a study of group development, this would refer to how often measurements of the group are taken.

4. The *aggregation interval* is the time scale across which recorded information is aggregated for analysis. The aggregation interval for a group development study might be either interval driven (e.g., 10-minute segments of conversation) or event driven (a single meeting of the group).

5. The *validity interval* defines the temporal boundaries of the theory—the time scale over which the theory holds. Specification of the validity interval clarifies the range of time scales to which a theory applies. For example, does it apply to groups that form and disband in a matter of minutes? To groups that persist for decades, such as families?

A theory is "time-scale complete" if it specifies time scale for all of its variables, relationships, and boundary conditions. Otherwise, researchers cannot make theory-driven choices of observation, recording, and aggregation intervals, and the criteria for evidence either in support of or contrary to theoretical predictions remain unclear.

Zaheer and colleagues (1999, p. 737) point out some parallels (and some differences) between levels of analysis and time scale issues. Group theorists are increasingly recognizing the need to specify the level of analysis—individual, group, or organization, for example—at which constructs "exist." Researchers are also increasingly exhorted to justify the aggregation of individual-level data to measure group-level constructs. Ideally, justification consists of both an aggregation model and evidence that the data conform to the model's requirements (Bliese, 2000). Applied to time scales, this suggests that researchers should give the reasoning behind and support for any decisions to aggregate across observations into "blocks" of time.

The second perspective discussed in this section is the social entrainment model (McGrath & Kelly, 1986), which fits the criteria for fourth-level complexity by including the simultaneous operation of multiple processes at different time scales and offers an illustration of how to address temporal issues in group theory. In their foundational work on the social psychology of time, McGrath and Kelly (1986, pp. 83–88) propose the following building blocks for a social entrainment model of interaction: rhythm, mesh, tempo, and pace. We explain each concept, then apply it to groups.

Rhythm refers to endogenous cyclic and developmental processes, from life span development to infradian (cycles with periods longer than a day), circadian (daily cycles), and ultradian (cycles shorter than a day). Applied to groups as the unit, this draws our attention to a host of different time scales at which different rhythms and cycles might be observed. Group development is the slowest rhythm; project cycles should take less time (unless the group is a short-term task force with a single project), whereas decision development can span a range from weeks (think juries) down to a matter of minutes.

Mesh is mutual entrainment or sychronization of rhythms within and across different time scales. For individual human beings, an example would be the coordination of heart rate (a faster rhythm) with respiration (a slower rhythm) and the entrainment of both heart rate and respiration to the sleep-wake circadian rhythm. At the group level, the emergence and maintenance of habitual routines can be considered a form of in-phase entrainment of activity across multiple individuals. In the banana time study (Roy, 1960, p. 162), fast-cycling verbal banter was triggered by and entrained to the slower rhythm of special "times" that physically interrupted work.

Tempo refers to the observed temporal patterns of behaviors that fluctuate across time. Applied to groups, an example would be the records of performance efficiency across different shifts and days of the week in teams working on a task such as printing (Guastello, 1995, pp. 188–195). Tempo corresponds to the actual time series measured, which may reflect the input of multiple cycles and rhythms that are or are not entrained, plus the impact of the final component in the model, pace.

Pace refers to external events and cycles that affect the rhythms, mesh, and tempo of the system of interest. In the printing group study, performance fluctuations emerged from the intersection of workers' endogenous circadian rhythms with changes in organizational structure imposed by management. External "pacers," such as frequent feedback about performance, can help a system maintain its rhythms. External perturbations such as changes in work assignments or deadlines can also disrupt a group's activity patterns.

The social entrainment model alerts us to the existence of temporal patterns at multiple time scales, from fast cycles to slower developmental processes, and to fluctuating patterns of behavior across time arising out of both entrainment of endogenous rhythms across scales and in response to external events that disrupt, regulate, or alter the timing or period of system rhythms.

As we turn to work that focuses explicitly on change over time, we make use of concepts from this section to sort out work that focuses on different time scales and that emphasizes, to varying degrees, endogenous, exogenous, and cross-level influences.

How Groups Change

Theories of change in groups address three key concepts: change, stability, and continuity. *Change* is an alteration in the nature of group interaction or performance, in the state of the group as a whole, or a second-order change in the patterning of group process. Shifting levels of dynamic variables over time serve as indicators of change processes.

Stability processes dampen fluctuations, maintaining groups in their current state, or restoring groups to a prior equilibrium, countering the impact of external or internal forces for change or transformation. *Continuity* occurs in groups that experience change while maintaining and reenacting consistent patterns and structure. Broad theories of dynamic processes in groups address the interplay of change and continuity, stability and instability, in groups that adjust to shifting forces while persisting across time as coherent collective entities.

In this section, we start with theories of group development, which consider how groups as a whole change across their full "life span." Next, we move to temporal patterning at shorter time scales or for a particular strand of group process. We end with complex systems models that link processes at different time scales and levels of analysis.

Systematic Change Over Time

The core theme in group-development research is that groups as a whole change systematically over time. Studies of group development span half a century and include impressionistic studies, which rely on experiences and reflections of observers (e.g., Bion, 1961; Rogers, 1970), empirical studies using observational systems (e.g., Bales, 1950; Dunphy, 1968; Gersick, 1988; Wheelan & McKeage, 1993), studies based on the examination of archival materials (e.g., Hare & Naveh, 1984; Worchel, 1994), and cross-sectional survey studies (e.g., Wheelan, Murphy, Tsumura, & Fried Kline, 1998). Although the proliferation of new theories has slowed since Hill and Gruner (1973) claim to have identified more than 100, theories developed in the past decade or so have introduced a variety of new themes and concepts of how change occurs. Because of the huge number of theories, some consolidation is needed to provide a coherent overview.

Two typologies of change theories provide frameworks for distinguishing among the plethora of group development models. The first, based on a review of theories in the social, biological, and physical sciences, identifies four distinct "motors" for generating change (Poole et al., 2000). *Life cycle* models describe the process of change as the unfolding of a prescribed sequence of stages following a program that is immanent within or imposed on the entity. *Teleological* models describe change as a purposeful movement of an entity toward one or more goals, with adjustments based on feedback from the environment. *Dialectical* models see change as emerging from conflict between opposing entities and eventual synthesis leading to the next cycle of conflict. *Evolutionary* models depict change as emerging from a repeated cycle of variation, selection, and retention and generally apply to change in a population rather than change within an entity over time. Theories of change often draw on more than one motor, allowing for 16 categories of theories based on different numbers (from none to all four) and combinations of motors.

A second framework (Arrow, 1997) distinguishes group development theories based on whether the primary forces promoting change and stability are internal or external to the group. Internal forces promoting change or stability often correspond to the social entrainment model's notion of rhythm—endogenous cyclic and developmental processes across multiple time scales, and mesh—synchronization of rhythms within and across different time scales (McGrath & Kelly, 1986). However, internal forces also include disruptions of rhythms (second-order change) that arise from within, such as those generated by a teleological motor. External forces promoting change or stability correspond to the social entrainment notion of pace—external events and cycles that affect the rhythms and mesh of the system of interest.

As seen in Table 9.2, we have expanded on the Arrow 2 x 2 table to include one more cell, for cycle models that do not envision continuity as part of the group pattern. We examine models and studies that fit these five categories in turn.

Table 9.2   Typology of Group Development Theories

Primary Source of Continuity	Primary Impetus for Change	
	Internal Forces	External Forces
Internal forces	Robust equilibrium (evolutionary motor)	Punctuated equilibrium (evolutionary, teleological)
External forces	Sequential stage (life cycle, dialectical)	Adaptive response (teleological motor)
Neither	Repeating cycle (dialectical motor)	

Source: Adapted from Arrow, 1997.

Robust Equilibrium Model

These models emphasize early change in the process of establishing a stable state, which is then maintained through a process of self-regulation that dampens or counters external disruption (Arrow, 1997). Change within the group is primarily apparent in the early phase of self-organization, and here, we can posit a modified evolutionary motor operating on the early variation provided by members. In this interpretation, groups start by exploring or "trying on" a variety of possible roles and norms and then select and retain a single structure. Bales (1955) found that in the first meetings of a group, a tentative group structure emerged, and then variations were often tried before the group settled into an equilibrated role structure (see also Gersick & Hackman's 1990 discussion of habitual routines in groups).

Groups may differ in how long they take to achieve stability, but once stability is achieved, further change is commonly viewed as requiring external intervention. Robust equilibrium models are implicit in much small group research that compares early and late periods or that contrasts structural elements that develop at different speeds. The presumption (often not articulated) is that once a group has emerged from its early period and finished "settling," the structure of interest will stay relatively constant.

Sequential Stage Models

These models identify a fixed sequence of qualitatively different stages through which a group passes as part of its naturally unfolding life cycle. This cycle corresponds to the slowest rhythm of change identified in the social entrainment model (McGrath & Kelly, 1986), and change is viewed as endogenous: No external cues are necessary for moving from one stage to the next. On the contrary, interventions by outsiders or other externalities may arrest the natural course of development so that a group becomes "stuck" in a particular stage and fails to progress. Members are presumed to be entrained to the same dominant focus of the group—which corresponds to a mesh process—although the stages vary in whether they emphasize in-phase (convergent) or anti-phase (conflictual) processes. Using the complexity classification, stage models exemplify Stage 2 theory, which includes multiple possible states visited at different times. Life cycle is the dominant motor, although a dialectical motor is sometimes evoked as a mechanism for moving from stage to stage (e.g., Bennis & Shepard, 1956).

Reviews of the group development literature (e.g., Lacoursiere, 1980; Tuckman, 1965; Tuckman & Jensen, 1977; Wheelan, 1994) report substantial evidence of patterns consistent with stage theory, although the number of stages proposed by individual scholars ranges from three (e.g., Hill & Gruner, 1973) to seven (e.g., Farrell, 1976). Here we describe the five-stage version that is most widely cited.

The initial stage focuses on issues of inclusion and dependency. Members attempt to identify behaviors acceptable to the leader and other group members, and early group meetings are characterized by member anxiety (Bion, 1961; Slater, 1966; Stock & Thelen, 1958). During the second stage of counterdependency and conflict, issues of power, authority, and competition are debated (Braaten, 1974/1975; Mann, Gibbard, & Hartman, 1967). Several theories suggest that these early struggles regarding authority and status are prerequisites for subsequent increases in cohesion and cooperation, (e.g., Dunphy, 1968; Mills, 1964; Tuckman & Jensen, 1977). Confrontations with the leader help establish solidarity and openness, and group members clarify areas of common values, which increases group stability (Theodorson, 1962).

As conflicts are resolved, the group moves to the third stage, devoted to the development of trust and characterized by more mature and open negotiation regarding goals and group structure, including roles and division of labor (Lundgren & Knight, 1978; Wheelan, 1990). This prepares the group for the fourth work stage, during which task orientation is high and ideas and feedback are exchanged openly (Bennis & Shepard, 1956; Tuckman, 1965). Groups that have a distinct ending point experience a fifth stage of termination, which may evoke disruption and conflict (Mann et al., 1967) but also the expression of positive feelings (Lundgren & Knight, 1978).

More sophisticated versions of stage theory allow for alterations of a fixed sequential progression (Bennis & Shepard, 1956; Mann et al., 1967; Wheelan, 1994). The smooth passage of groups in achieving the maturity of the work stage is not assumed. External disruption or membership change may arrest development or result in regression to a previous stage (Wheelan, 1994, p. 18). However, Hill and Gruner (1973) found that groups may also skip early stages if several of the members have been together in a previous group, demonstrating a "carryover" effect of member continuity.

Theories that explicitly integrate a dialectical motor as the mechanism for change provide an endogenous explanation for getting "stuck." Bennis and Shepard (1956, pp. 418–419) identify six stages in all, with two major stages and three subphases within each. The subphases fit neatly into a thesis, antithesis, and synthesis pattern, with opposing subgroups emerging in the antithesis subphases and the group achieving unity again in the synthesis subphases, led by members who serve as *catalysts*. Overly homogeneous groups, inadequate role differentiation, or failed role enactment may thus prevent a group from moving to the next stage (e.g., Bennis & Shepard, 1956; Kuypers, Davies, & Glaser, 1986).

A recent set of studies by Wheelan and colleagues illustrates a typical approach to studying group development. All 55,931 statements made by members of 16 experiential learning groups (whose total meeting time ranged from 4½ to 7½ hours) were coded, using categories derived from the group development literature: dependency, counterdependency, fight, flight, pairing, counterpairing, and work (Wheelan, Verdi, & McKeage, 1994). The proportion of statements in the various categories changed across time in similar ways and was consistent with expectations for groups in the early stages of development (Verdi & Wheelan, 1992; Wheelan & Kaeser, 1997).

Repeating Cycle Models

These models treat change as central to group process yet reject the notion of sequential progression. The endogenous rhythms they follow have cycle times shorter than the lifetime of the group, so that cycles repeat. The models differ in the complexity of cycles described and in their focus on what in the group is changing. All imply that resolution of certain issues is only temporary (Bion, 1961; Schutz, 1958). The oldest and simplest cycle model proposes that groups swing back and forth from focusing primarily on the task to focusing on socioemotional matters that preserve group solidarity (Bales, 1950). This rhythm continues for the life of the group.

A more recent cyclic model, based on a study of archival records of a wide variety of groups, proposes six stages through which groups cycle repeatedly (Worchel, 1994). Research based on this model demonstrates that the stage of group development affects the outgroup homogeneity effect and the prevalence of social loafing (Worchel, Coutant-Sassic, & Grossman, 1992) as well as the tendency to cooperate with ingroup and compete with outgroup members (Worchel, Coutant-Sassic, & Wong, 1993), illustrating the moderating effect of group stage on fundamental intra- and intergroup processes. In the *discontent* stage, the group is not a significant part of members' identities. Members feel alienated and participation is low. To move past this stage, the group needs a *precipitating event* that sparks renewed member interaction. As members coordinate a response to the event, they rediscover commonalities and develop hope that the group can change. As members renew their commitment, the group enters the *group identification* stage, during which the group defines (or redefines) its boundaries and makes sharp distinctions between members and outsiders. The group becomes an important part of member identity. As group and member identity solidifies, the group moves into the *group productivity* stage, marked by energetic collective work focused on reaching group goals. Boundaries weaken to allow the entry of new members who might help reach those goals. As the group achieves its goals and gains resources, it enters the *individuation* stage. Members demand recognition for their contributions. The group remains important to members, but they focus on their own needs. As member needs eclipse group needs in importance, intragroup competition increases, and the group begins to *decay*. As competition wanes and members put less energy into the group, alienation increases and the group returns to *discontent*.

Cyclic models emphasize endogenous processes, and the engine for change is oppositional tension. Thus, the dialectical motor is the best fit, although in the case of the simplest cycles, the movement is like a pendulum swing, with no true synthesis or progression. The most complex and fully dialectical model in this category proposes that groups change as they repeatedly explore three sets of paradoxes: the paradoxes of *belonging*, based on the tension between group and individual; the paradoxes of *engaging*, based on the tension between involvement and detachment; and the paradoxes of *speaking*, based on the tensions created by multiple sources and targets of influence (Smith & Berg, 1987).

Punctuated Equilibrium Models

The theory of punctuated equilibrium, originally developed to describe biological evolution, was applied first to organizational theory (e.g., Tushman & Romanelli, 1985) and then to small groups (Gersick, 1988). In the process, it shifted from a theory about change in populations to a theory about change within entities. The common feature is in the observed pattern of change—periods of stasis (or in some versions, incremental change) punctuated by short periods of radical change in which a group attempts to improve its fit with the demands of its embedding context.

Gersick (1988) found that groups quickly established a stable structure, which persisted until the midpoint of their time together, when the groups reorganized and established a new stable structure. During the first stable period, progress on the group task was relatively slow. During the second stable period, the project groups worked more effectively and achieved their goals and objectives. More general punctuated equilibrium models (Arrow, 1997; Gersick & Hackman, 1990) propose a pattern of longer stable periods punctuated by sudden, discontinuous intervals of instability and reorganization. Although change can be triggered by either internal or external forces, stability is seen to be maintained by processes internal to the group. The model combines evolutionary and teleological motors.

Adaptive Response Models

These models emphasize response to environmental opportunities and constraints as a guiding force in group change and continuity (Arrow, 1997). Developmental patterns are seen as contingent on the forces and incentives available to each group (McCollom, 1995; McGrath, 1991), leading to idiosyncratic patterns of development across groups, depending on whether the relevant embedding context is relatively stable or dynamic. The primary motor is teleological, as groups are seen as purposive entities pursuing a variety of goals. These models incorporate the notion of *equifinality,* which means that many paths can lead to the same destination. Time, interaction, and performance (TIP) theory (McGrath, 1991) proposes that groups typically pursue multiple concurrent projects related to three functions: task performance, member support, and group well-being. The sequence of transitions from different modes of activity will differ based on the nature of projects and obstacles a group encounters.

Challenges for Group Development Research

Taken as a whole, research concerning possible changes over time across a group's life span has demonstrated convincingly that groups change over time. Although researchers' methods and models have varied, empirical studies in this tradition look for and consistently find changes in groups over time. Evidence that task performance and work activity occur at higher levels later in a group's history, for example, has been found for an anthropological expedition, factory work groups, experiential groups (Hare, 1967, 1982), therapy and personal growth groups (Hill, 1974; Stiles, Tupler, & Carpenter, 1982), and a variety of task groups, from students completing a class project to bank officers designing a new product (Gersick, 1988, 1989).

Of course, this general finding is consistent with any number of previously presented models, most of which predict higher productivity in later periods of a group's life. For groups that experience repeated task cycles, better performance later in a group's life would also be expected on the basis of both individual and group-level learning with experience (Argote, 1993).

Although we can confidently assert that groups change over time, the timing, nature, and sequencing of these changes apparently differs between studies and sometimes between groups within a single study. We complete our overview of group development work by discussing how scholars have dealt with this puzzle.

Strategy 1: Treat between-group variability as uninteresting. If the primary goal is to find the "signal" of group development among the "noise" of individual variation, then variation can be treated as uninteresting, an indication of group-level idiosyncrasies overlaid on a central pattern. For example, groups may progress through the various stages at somewhat different rates. What matters is what they have in common, not how they are different.

Strategy 2: Define deviations from the pattern as evidence of problems or failures in a group. This shifts the emphasis from description to prescription and makes the model normative. Groups that follow the model are developing normally, whereas groups that do not are having problems. Failure to make the midpoint transition explains poor performance or group dissolution (Gersick 1988, 1989); failure to move beyond early stages demonstrates that a group has gotten "stuck" (Bennis & Shepard, 1956). For models that attribute systematic change to endogenous processes, idiosyncratic failures to fit can also be explained away based on externalities— unusual events in the group's context that throw it off the normative path.

Strategy 3: Make different paths part of the model. The adaptive response models are, essentially, contingency models that predict different paths among groups. Groups are seen as naturally coupled to their embedding contexts, so that change in the environment is part of the model, not a random intrusion. Contingency models allow for groups that are otherwise similar in nature to take different paths to the same goal. When data is examined group by group without imposing a set number or type of phases, but using a statistical model that detects breakpoints, different numbers and types of phases can be identified (e.g., Brower, 1986).

Strategy 4: Propose that different types of groups develop differently. This idea surfaces regularly in the literature, typically in the discussion section, where scholars toss out possible reasons that their findings differ from the patterns found in other studies. Careful elaboration of the idea that group type moderates group development has been seriously hampered, however, by the absence of a satisfactory typology of groups. Most typologies are ad hoc classifications based on different group purposes or projects, such as Tuckman's (1965) division of groups studied into the four "settings" of therapy groups, training groups, natural groups, and laboratory groups.

McGrath and colleagues (Arrow et al., 2000; McGrath & Tschan, 2004b) have proposed that qualitatively different developmental paths might be linked to different structural group types. Punctuated equilibrium patterns are proposed to be more common in task forces, which have a life span corresponding to the fixed interval for completing the task. Sequential stage or cycle patterns should be more common in longer-lived teams, which depend on a more elaborated structure of relations among members, and in clubs, which are organized to address member needs. Crews, assembled of members trained to perform clearly defined roles using specific tools, are expected to fit robust equilibrium or adaptive response patterns best.

Strategy 5: Assume researchers find different patterns because they attend to different aspects of groups. The developing relationship among members and leaders, for example, may exhibit a different pattern of change than the focal topic of group conversations or the way a group relates to its task or to other groups. In other words, researchers may be finding different patterns of development not only because they are studying different kinds of groups but also because they are selecting different aspects of these groups as indices of the development of the group as a system. Although the rhythms of change may be entrained, that does not mean that these rhythms cycle or develop at the same rate, so apparent differences could in part be an artifact of the choice of index, recording interval, and aggregation interval.

A recent study of a short-lived laboratory group demonstrates the impact of choosing different aggregation intervals. Chang, Bordia, and Duck (2003) coded the group's 40-minute conversation by dividing it alternately into two or four equal segments. The two-segment coding gave results consistent with expectations of the midpoint punctuated equilibrium model, whereas the four-segment coding found patterns that were, for the most part, consistent with expectations for a (quite rapid!) progression through a series of developmental stages.

Temporal Patterning in Group Process

Work reviewed in this section focuses on patterning across shorter time scales than the life span of group development, often attending to a particular thread of group activity or group structure. We adopt the convention suggested by McGrath & O'Connor (1996) of distinguishing between the developmental *stages* of the previous section and *phases* of an activity cycle.

Patterning Task Activity Within Task Cycles

Some of the earliest research on phase sequences was conducted by Bales and his colleagues (Bales 1950, 1953; Bales & Strodtbeck, 1951). After observing numerous laboratory groups, they described decision-making groups as moving through three phases, *orientation* (where the problem is discussed and the group organizes itself), *evaluation* (where the members consider alternatives and sometimes engage in conflict), and *control* (where the group centers on one option and attempts to take action). This phase model, like stage models in group development, assumes a life-cycle change motor—the unfolding of a sequence that is either logically determined or imposed on the group.

Later descriptive work provided evidence that groups do not necessarily follow a single fixed sequence of phases. Poole and colleagues (Poole, 1981; Poole & Roth, 1989) and Hirokawa and colleagues (Hirokawa, 1990; Orlitzky & Hirokawa, 2001) found that groups follow many decision paths. Normative prescriptions have also been adjusted: Although Hirokawa and colleagues found that some decision paths are better than others, no single sequence of phases is "best." Instead, many temporal patterns of decision making led to the same end result: good performance. The path chosen may depend on task features such as problem complexity (Nutt, 1984). Over the decades, work has thus shifted away from looking for the single "best path" to proposing that adapting activity patterns to match the task and contextual demands is essential to effective group performance (e.g., Ancona & Chong, 1996; Poole & De Sanctis, 1990). This indicates a corresponding shift to a more teleological focus on purposeful movement toward a goal, with changes inspired by feedback from the environment.

Researchers have also divided conflict interaction and negotiation into sequential periods with different behavioral patterns (Folger, Poole, & Stutman, 2004). Sheppard's (1984) phase analysis identified a four-step process as groups resolve conflicts. In the first three steps, group members develop a joint definition of the issue at hand, then move to a discussion of the alternative settlements, and finally select an alternative. The fourth phase is a period of reconciliation to the settlement. An alternative approach to defining phases focuses on the changing intensity of the conflict itself. Glasl (1982) describes the range of escalatory levels possible. At the first phase or level, parties are aware of tensions but try to handle them in a reasonable, controlled way. In the second phase, the relationship between the parties becomes the main source of tension and is characterized by distrust and lack of respect. At the third and highest phase, confrontations become aggressive and destructive. Glasl asserts that conflicts escalate from one phase to the next when parties pass an unspecified threshold of progressively extreme behavior. At higher levels, new dynamics emerge that make de-escalation very difficult.

The negotiation literature has noted distinctive temporal patterning when groups face deadlines for resolving a conflict and reaching agreement. Long periods of intransigence throughout the bulk of the negotiation process are followed by a flurry of concessions as a deadline approaches (Lim & Murnighan, 1994). Here the topics of change in groups and time in groups intersect. High time pressure increases both the number of negotiator concessions and cooperative acts and the likelihood of reaching an agreement (Stuhlmacher, Gillespie, & Champagne, 1998). Deadlines can improve outcomes for negotiators eager to reach agreement quickly because the passage of time is costly to them (Moore, 2004), and although many naive negotiators choose not to reveal a deadline to their opponent, the revelation can lead to a better outcome (Moore, 2003).

Sambamurthy and Poole (1992) studied the relationship of conflict-management stage sequences to consensus, perceived decision quality, and satisfaction with the decision process in computer-supported groups. They found that groups with the best outcomes first engaged in focused discussion of their decision, then moved to a period of open conflict and clash, and finally engaged in problem solving or negotiation to resolve the conflict. This resembles the normative stage sequence suggested as optimal in much of the negotiation literature (Holmes, 1992). Groups that never openly surfaced conflict, avoided it, or adopted win-lose orientations had significantly poorer results on all three dimensions.

Scholars interested in groups tackling problems or projects that are broader than a particular decision or conflict have also generated both descriptive and normative models. A standard proscription is that groups should begin with an *orientation* that serves as an anticipatory function—identifying goals and developing a plan to reach them. Next, the group should *enact* the plan. As the plan is executed, the group should *monitor* the results of its actions. Results should be compared to those anticipated by the plan, and the group should determine if their action has moved them closer to attaining the goal. If not, the group should *modify* the plan accordingly (Tschan, 2002). This pattern of orient-enact-monitor-modify (McGrath & Tschan, 2004b) is an information-processing model that sees change as teleological.

Empirical studies indicate that groups do not reliably follow this pattern and appear particularly reluctant to spend time planning before leaping into action (e.g., Hackman & Morris, 1975; Weingart, 1992). In line with normative prescriptions, groups that do plan ahead tend to perform better (e.g., Wittenbaum & Stasser, 1996). However, as with the decision-making literature, some suggest that the applicability of normative sequence rules may depend on context and task. In a static environment, taking time to gather information and consider alternatives makes sense. In a changing environment, it may be better to just act and see what happens, adjusting in "real-time" rather than planning (Eisenhardt & Sull, 2001).

A major focus of the social dilemma literature is how to encourage people to choose what is best for the group over more narrowly defined self-interest. Here, too, the idea of a normative sequence arises, with cooperation being more likely if goal definition and discussion of alternatives precedes action. Pruitt and Kimmel (1977) suggest that group members will not make a cooperative choice unless they have, first, adopted the goal of mutual cooperation and, second, developed the expectation that others will reciprocate cooperative choices. Consistent with this logic, Bouas and Komorita (1996) found that discussion of the dilemma prior to member choice fostered an expectation of cooperation, and only when that expectation had been created prior to choice were cooperation rates significantly improved in a laboratory social dilemma. Furthermore, Henry (2000) found that early perceptions of cooperation in a longitudinal social dilemma were also better predictors of later cooperation than group identification or previous group success.

Patterning Across Task Cycles

Some scholars have looked at temporal patterns of group performance in longer sequences and noted changes across cycles, such as cumulative improvement, progressive decline, or more complicated patterns of change. An example of progressive decline is groupthink (Janis, 1982). The more a group afflicted with groupthink invests in a poor course of action, the more committed it becomes, piling bad decision on bad decision. Groupthink develops when groups fail to properly evaluate alternatives and monitor the impact of decisions. In other words, the orient and monitor steps of the orient-enact-monitor-modify model (McGrath & Tschan, 2004b) are omitted or not executed properly.

Yet performance spirals can go in either direction. Initial success or failure can lead to both upward and downward performance spirals across multiple task cycles (Lindsley, Brass, & Thomas, 1995). In these spirals, group self-efficacy and performance increase or decrease in tandem through an amplifying positive feedback loop, in contrast to the pairing of inflated confidence and disastrous performance typical of groupthink. Second-order changes can occur when an efficacy-performance spiral reverses direction, is stopped though self-corrective action by the group, or ends because of ceiling or floor effects. Lindsley et al. explicitly distinguish these spirals from learning curves, a different kind of cumulative change pattern.

Although group performance on a new task can be expected to improve over successive task cycles simply on the basis of individual learning, group-level learning can also contribute to improvement (Argote, 1993). Prior individual experience (and associated learning) does not necessarily transfer to a group (e.g., Tuckman & Lorge, 1962), whereas group training does improve subsequent performance (Moreland, 1999), providing evidence that group-level processes, such as improved coordination and the development of transactive memory systems, are involved. The shape of group (and organizational) learning curves appears to be less consistent than individual learning curves, however, and some groups fail to show any improvement (Argote, 1993).

In social-dilemma tasks, when choice patterns over trial blocks are compared, the consistent finding is for cooperation to decline over trial blocks (Rapoport & Chammah, 1965; Isaac & Walker, 1988; Komorita, Parks, & Hulbert, 1992), although in a setting in which participants interact freely and choose their own partners, the opposite pattern of increasingly cooperative choices was observed (Arrow & Crosson, 2003; Crosson, Orbell, & Arrow, 2004). One key to interrupting or preventing the usual decline in cooperation lies in the microlevel pattern of member choices and strategies across time, a topic that fits our next theme of coordination of action across members within groups.

Process Coordination Among Members

A good deal of research has focused on how group members sequence and coordinate their actions. Early descriptive work looked at the patterning of conversation in groups that had either a general discussion task or a problem to solve to see whether, for example, a suggestion about the task or topic was followed by an evaluation about the suggestion, an alternate proposal, a request for more information, or some other sort of contribution (Bales, 1950). Later research on the issue of whether some sequences are better or worse has yielded mixed results. Tschan (2002) found that longer sequences were inversely related to performance (prior studies had found the opposite) and also that groups whose conversations showed a higher proportion of "ideal" cycles of orientation/planning-action-evaluation also performed better. This was consistent with prior findings that groups whose conversations better fit the normative pattern of problem statement-proposal-evaluation or question-answer-evaluation perform better (Stech, 1975).

The sequencing issue in iterated social dilemma choices is whether the cooperate or defect choice of one partner is followed by a matching or contrary choice by the other partner. Axelrod (1984) promotes tit-for-tat as a strategy that can moderate the typical decline in cooperation across trials and promote overall levels of cooperation, even if the other partner in the interaction is using a different strategy. Research by Komorita and colleagues (Komorita, Hilty, & Parks, 1991; Komorita et al., 1992; Parks, Henager, & Scamahorn, 1996) supports the idea embedded in tit-for-tat—that immediate reciprocation of cooperative choices by other members is crucial to achieving mutual cooperation—but found that retaliation for noncooperation can be delayed (although retaliation does need to occur at some point). Parks and Rumble (2001) found that delayed reciprocation of cooperative choice resulted in declines in cooperation across trials whereas immediate reciprocation of cooperation led to more stable, and in some cases increased cooperation over time.

In negotiation, the tit-for-tat strategy relies on sequential matching of actions, a form of "in phase" coordination also found in the negotiation literature. Weingart, Prietula, Hyder, and Genovese (1999) found that negotiators reciprocated both distributive and integrative tactical behavior over time. However, matching responses in negotiation tasks do not necessarily lead to better outcomes. Olekalns and Smith (2000) found that sequences that paired similar strategies (plus the frequency of contention) tended to yield impasses in negotiations; settlements were more likely with sequences that paired dissimilar strategies. There is also evidence that patterns for dealing with disagreements in groups affect other group processes. In a study of 10 quality-management teams, Kuhn and Poole (2000) found that group conflict-management styles that developed over several months or years influenced decision-making effectiveness.

In brainstorming research, attention has focused on the inherent coordination problem of having to take turns in a conversation. In other words, the issue is not the particular sequence of communications but the fact that there needs to be a sequence, that group members cannot all "have the floor" at the same time. Contrary to the expectation that groups should be better at generating ideas than individuals due to synergic group processes (Osborn, 1957), the consistent finding is that FTF groups generate fewer—and fewer original—ideas than the same number of individuals working independently (Diehl & Stroebe, 1987). Coordination problems appear to be a major reason. Hearing others talk interrupts one's own generation of ideas (production blocking), and the conversational constraint of having to take turns talking also slows down collective idea production. In other words, the forced mesh or synchronization of conversational rhythms at the group level disrupts the individual rhythm of idea generation.

In the early 1990s, Valacich and colleagues (Dennis & Valacich, 1993; Valacich, Wheeler, Mannecke, & Wachter, 1995) provided additional evidence for this interpretation in a series of studies contrasting groups who communicated face-to-face or via computer mediation. Computer-mediated communication (CM) eliminates production blocking by allowing group members to enter their ideas simultaneously, and CM idea-generation groups consistently outperform FTF groups in laboratory studies. However, in a study of quality-improvement teams in a natural setting, Jackson and Poole (2003) found that CM idea generation was no more productive than FTF idea generation. They also found that FTF idea-generation sessions were more efficient and led to more thorough discussion of ideas than CM sessions.

Emergence and Stabilization of New Structure

The development of structure in groups involves both the convergence of members on shared beliefs or behaviors and the divergence of members as they sort out into differentiated roles or status positions in the group. One consistent thread that runs through work on temporal aspects of structure is the contrast between fast and slow rhythms of emergence and stabilization.

Opp's (1982) norm formation theory distinguishes among the fast, top-down adoption of norms via what he calls *institutional* norm formation and the slower, more gradual, implicit process of *evolutionary* norm formation. The third route is explicit discussion and negotiation (*voluntary* norm formation), which may happen early in the life of a group or when a new issue not handled by existing norms surfaces. Bettenhausen and Murnighan (1985) also envision slow and fast processes, although they focus on whether members retrieve the same or different "scripts" for behavior at their initial interaction (the fast route) and on whether members' definitions of the situation match (which tends to become evident somewhat later in the group's life).

Expectation-states and dominance theorists (see Chapter 5) propose that demographically diverse groups (see Ridgeway, 1984) make status distinctions very quickly based on surface characteristics of members such as race, gender, and age, which are most salient in newer groups. In more homogeneous groups, however, status distinctions are proposed to emerge as the group interacts and members evaluate the relative quality and volume of member contributions to the discussion (Bales, Strodtbeck, Mills, & Roseborough, 1951). Not all homogeneous groups, however, demonstrate this slower pattern of differentiation. Fisek and Ofshe (1970), for example, found that a clear and persistent status differentiation was evident from the start in about half of the demographically homogeneous groups in their study.

Social role theory (Eagly, 1987) predicts that in demographically diverse groups, status and roles will be initially assigned according to stereotypes, following the same line of reasoning as expectation-states theory. However, as members get to know each other better, individuating information will cause members to adjust inaccurate assessments and reassign roles and status accordingly. Case studies indicate, however, that perceptions of performance tend to be distorted in ways that confirm the existing social order so that these adjustments do not necessarily take place. In the Robbers Cave study, for example, boys consistently overestimated the performance of high-status members and also tended to underestimate the scores of low-ranking members (Sherif, 1966, p. 77). This stabilizes and perpetuates the established hierarchy. The prediction that the impact of surface characteristics of members should fade over time while the impact of deeper characteristics such as attitudes and values increases (see Moreland & Levine, 1992) has, however, also garnered some empirical support (e.g., Harrison, Price, & Bell, 1998).

Cohesion, which holds a group and its members together, is commonly viewed as resulting at least in part from mutual attraction among group members. This attraction also has fast- and slow-developing elements. Cohesion based on social attraction forms quickly, as it involves simple attraction to a group prototype (Turner, Hogg, Oakes, Reicher, & Wetherell, 1987). Cohesion based on interpersonal attraction forms more slowly, as it involves an emergent mesh of feelings as members get to know each other (Hogg, 1992).

Habitual routines develop quickly in most groups and, according to standard accounts (e.g., Gersick & Hackman, 1990), are hard to change later on. Although rational models of orient-enact-monitor-modify indicate that groups should alter their behavior whenever feedback indicates they are not progressing expeditiously toward their goals, in practice, groups often cling to ineffective routines. Stabilized routines seem to "turn off" the teleological motor of goal-directed change, except during occasional windows of opportunity during which the group is more open to intervention (Hackman, 2002). External time pressure, like a looming deadline, may disrupt routine task execution (e.g., Gersick, 1988). Feldman (2000) challenges the standard view of habitual routines as changing mainly in response to a crisis, external shock, or intervention. She suggests that organizational routines, like other structures, are constantly being adjusted and altered based both on exogenous feedback and endogenous processes.

What forces stabilize group structures and make them resistant to change? Balance theory (Heider, 1958) proposes that balanced pairings of dyads create stability whereas unbalanced pairings, in which (for example) I dislike the friend of a friend, are inherently unstable. In an early study of emergent friendship cliques, Newcomb (1961) used balance theory to explain how, as high-attraction dyads became linked together in triads, the reinforcement of existing shared attitudes among larger numbers of people made change increasingly unlikely. Three decades later, Carley (1991) proposed that stability is maintained by the reinforcing nature of interaction on shared member knowledge structures, which in turn reinforces similar future interactions.

Ongoing Adjustments, Instability, and Discontinuities

Most theorizing and empirical research on structure focuses on the initial emergence of structure, emphasizes the stability of that structure, and pays little attention to later changes. In this section, we consider work that attends more to ongoing adjustments and discontinuities. We focus in particular on patterns of continuity and change in group composition and member-group relationships.

An analysis of how relationships between groups and their members might change over time can be found in Moreland and Levine's (1982) model of group socialization. That model embodies three psychological processes: evaluation, commitment, and role transition. Evaluation involves attempts by the group and the individual to assess and improve one another's rewardingness. Evaluation produces feelings of commitment, which rise and fall over time. When commitment reaches a critical level (a decision criterion), a role transition occurs. The relationship between the group and the individual is transformed, and both parties begin to evaluate one another again, often in new ways, continuing the cycle.

According to Moreland and Levine (1982), group membership begins with a period of *investigation,* when the group engages in recruitment and the individual (as a prospective member) engages in reconnaissance. If the commitment levels of both parties rise to their entry criteria, then the role transition of entry occurs, and the person becomes a new group member. Entry marks the end of investigation and the beginning of *socialization.* During socialization, the group and the individual try to change one another in ways that make their relationship more rewarding (Moreland & Levine, 1992). When these efforts succeed, the individual experiences assimilation, and the group experiences accommodation. If the commitment levels of both parties rise to their acceptance criteria, then the role transition of acceptance occurs, and the person becomes a full group member. Acceptance marks the end of socialization and the beginning of *maintenance*. During maintenance, the group and the individual negotiate about functional roles for the individual (e.g., leader) that might promote the achievement of group goals and satisfaction of personal needs. When role negotiation succeeds, the commitment levels of both parties rise, and maintenance continues, perhaps indefinitely. When role negotiation fails, however, commitment levels fall, and if they reach the divergence criteria of both parties, then the role transition of divergence occurs, and the individual becomes a marginal group member. Divergence marks the end of maintenance and the beginning of *resocialization*. Once again, the group and the individual try to change one another in ways that will make their relationship more rewarding. If enough (re)assimilation and (re)accommodation occur, then the commitment levels of both parties may rise again to their divergence criteria. In most cases, however, commitment levels continue to fall until they reach the exit criteria of the group and the individual. Group membership ends with a period of remembrance when both parties reflect on their relationship. These memories contribute to the group's traditions and to the departing member's reminiscences.

Moreland and Levine (2000) have related the socialization process to other group phenomena, such as composition, trust, innovation, culture, and intergroup relations. In other work, they generate and test hypotheses about specific aspects of the socialization process, such as unrealistic optimism among prospective group members and reactions to prospective and new group members among groups with different staffing levels.

Membership dynamics theory (Arrow & McGrath, 1995), which complements this model, proposes that groups always experience both pressures toward continuity and pressures toward change. Changes in membership may result from endogenous processes, as envisioned by the group socialization model, or from exogenous forces, such as members being fired, reassigned, or added to the group by powerful outsiders. Such changes destabilize the group structure and require a series of adjustments, which can bring a mixture of positive and negative effects.

The impact of membership change will vary depending on the number of members affected and their position in the existing status and role system. If the magnitude of member change is high enough, discontinuous change in the group system will result. The group may dissolve completely with no successor; fragments of the group may reform into a new group or groups; or the group system may persist with some sense of continuity but undergo a radical restructuring, reinventing itself with a new pattern of relations. Less dramatic membership change brings a mixture of benefits and costs. Moreland and Argote (2003), for example, argue that member change can benefit transactive memory at the level of a group's embedding organization but hurt transactive memory at the work-group level.

Lau and Murnighan (1998) introduce the metaphor of *fault lines* to suggest why groups differ in their propensity to splinter under pressure. They propose that when the distributions of member differences in a group align, distinct subgroups will form that cluster members who share the same sets of similarities within and differences between the subgroups. An example is a group that includes two younger black female clerical workers and two older white male plant managers. When differences do not align but are cross-cutting, fault lines will be weak because the "natural" divisions into subgroups will shift depending on what attributes are salient to members.

Work on the impact of turnover indicates how membership change affects another type of change over time, the learning curve. The typical finding is that turnover disrupts group learning, although somewhat paradoxically, the disruption appears to be more dramatic for simple as compared to more complex tasks (Argote, Insko, Yovetich, & Romero, 1995). One explanation is that for more complex tasks, innovation is a more important source of improvements. Consistent with this interpretation, member change can improve performance on creative tasks (Arrow & McGrath, 1993).

Some work on change in leadership over time focuses on the initial emergence of leaders. Factors such as the amount of participation (Burke, 1974) and the nature of a member's contributions (Schultz, 1986) have been found to predict who will take the role of leader in an initially leaderless group. Hollander's (1978) social exchange theory describes leaders as emerging after showing innovation in the solving of a difficult problem and demonstrating loyalty to the group. Leaders gain power if the solutions prove successful. They lose power if a failure is attributed to the leader's poor judgment, irresponsibility, or self-interested motivation.

The life cycle theory of leadership (Hersey & Blanchard, 1969), later revised and renamed situational leadership theory (Hersey & Blanchard, 1988), suggests that leadership styles are more or less effective depending on the level of development for a particular group member. The optimal level of task-oriented and relation-oriented behavior by leaders depends on the level of maturity and corresponding skill level of the subordinate, which is expected to change over time.

Charismatic leadership theorists, following a somewhat similar line of reasoning, suggest that personal identification of subordinates with leaders may be an important influence early in the relationship, but that later on internalization becomes more important (Conger & Kanungo, 1998). This echoes the pairing of faster versus slower processes seen in accounts of other aspects of group structure. Graen and Scandura's (1987) life cycle model,

PHASE, suggests a more extended dynamic interplay between leader and subordinate over time. This model skips over the issue of how individuals emerge as leaders in the first place, identifying the first phase of interaction between leaders and subordinates as a period of mutual evaluation of each other's motives, attitudes, and potential resources to be exchanged. In the second phase, the exchange arrangement between leader and subordinates is refined, and mutual trust is established. A third and final phase involves transforming the exchange relationship from a transactional to a more relational one based on commitment to the group's mission as the leader has defined it. Parallels with the group socialization model are evident.

Comments

The overall historical progression of much work on change processes exhibits a shift from early descriptive work to normative work on "best" sequences or patterns, and thence to a series of findings that call into question both the earlier descriptive models and the prescriptions of the normative models. Just as groups at the whole system level appear to change over time—but not necessarily in the same way or at the same rate—temporal patterns in group interaction and task activity appear to differ across tasks, across groups, and also across apparently similar groups doing identical tasks. A coherent story of how and why, one that accounts for the many exceptions and contingencies, is yet to emerge.

The general tendency in group research, as in most social science, has been to search for simple, straightforward patterns and theories. Seen as a whole, however, the accumulated findings on change in groups seem to be pushing us in the opposite direction. The complexity of observed patterns is increasingly clear. What is much less clear is what to make of these complexities. We turn next to work that attempts to grapple directly with complex dynamic patterns as a fundamental feature of small groups.

Groups as Complex Systems:
An Emerging Perspective on Groups

In recent years, a number of scholars have abandoned the quest for simplicity and have taken a different tack, treating groups as complex systems and developing theories and research methods commensurate with this complexity. These approaches argue that complexity is an inherent property of groups and that our theories must account for this complexity and its effects.

Theories and research that treat groups as complex systems share a set of assumptions:

1. Groups are influenced by a multitude of factors that interact in nonlinear fashion. Some theories assume these interactions are constituted by human action, which is inherently nondeterministic; others focus on recursive interactions that may follow simple rules. In both cases, the behavior of the system is viewed as often unpredictable and is marked by emergent phenomena that may move the group in novel or unintended directions.

2. Group systems are composed of multiple levels, both within the group and between the group and its environment, and cross-level influences are complex and nonlinear.

3. Group systems are not always well-behaved. Instead, they are often unpredictable, with behavior marked by discontinuities, critical incidents, path dependence, novelty, multiple causal factors operating unevenly on different levels and at different times in the group's history, and causal factors running on substantially different time scales.

Beyond these common points, complex systems theories of groups are quite diverse. Some are cast primarily in traditional, propositional terms; others use mathematical and simulation models. We start with propositional formulations and then discuss more formal representations.

Propositional Theories of Complex Group Systems

Action theory. Von Cranach (1996) articulated action theory to explain the complex interactions between group systems and other social systems and environments. He posited three principles: (1) the principle of *multilevel organization,* which states that humans and groups are organized on many levels, including the individual, group, and several societal levels; (2) the principle of *self-activity,* which states that individuals and social systems act on their own, on the basis of internal energy and internally stored information, in interaction with their environments; and (3) the principle of *historicity,* which states that human affairs can be understood only in the context of their previous history and embeddedness in the history of other systems.

Twenty-eight propositions based on these principles cover the nature of groups, the nature of group action in general, the nature of goal-directed action, and the relation of group structure to group process. Together, they portray the group as a self-organizing system that exists only by virtue of acting; when a group stops acting, it stops existing. Types of group actions include goal-directed, meaning-oriented, process-oriented, and agitated actions.

As groups act, they coevolve with other interlocking systems on multiple levels. Coevolution implies that as the group evolves, the structures involved both enable action and are themselves evolving as the group engages that action. For example, group action is organized by projecting task structure onto the group's structure (e.g., assigning different parts of the task to members on the basis of their role in the group). The group's structure may either be reinforced or changed by the work (e.g., a member who contributes a lot to a task may achieve higher status, thus changing the structure). This, in turn, may influence how the group projects future tasks onto its structure. The same sort of coevolution occurs for all systems involved in group action across levels of analysis. Thus, long- and short-term activities coevolve, the group and its members coevolve, the group coevolves with other groups it must coordinate with, activities in the group and other groups coevolve, and so on.

Group action involves both information processing and execution. Both occur at individual and intragroup levels as the group engages in activity cycles of varying lengths and levels of abstraction. Group structure results from the interaction of tasks, systems that encompass the group, member characteristics, traditions and history of the group, and environmental influences. Structure is implicated in action and is, in turn, an outcome of it. Action theory is a theoretical frame on which situated theories of group processes can be built, such as Tschan's (1995) model of the effects of communication on group task performance. Action theory has stimulated a good deal of research, mostly by European scholars.

Groups as complex systems. The groups as complex systems framework (Arrow et al., 2000) adapts ideas from the interdisciplinary field of complexity science to create an account of groups as open, adaptive systems that interact with the component systems (the members) who are partially embedded within them and with the multiple larger systems (organizations, neighborhoods, societies, economies) in which they are multiply embedded. The collective behavior of group-level activity emerges out of the interactions of group members, and the behavior of the collective evolves over time based in part on the constraints of the group's embedding contexts. The study of groups should thus attend to at least three levels of causal dynamics: the local dynamics of group interaction (where individual rhythms become entrained), the global dynamics of group development and change over time (the large-scale rhythm of the group plus the fluctuating tempos of behavior), and the contextual dynamics of changing environmental constraints (pacing cues) and group responses to these constraints (Arrow et al., 2000).

Group structure is a matrix of networks in which connections among members, tasks, tools, and information are established, enacted, and modified over time in response to changes in task, context, and experience. Group behavior is guided by the demands of group projects and member needs, and success in addressing these (sometimes conflicting) demands affects the viability and integrity of the group as a system.

The evolving collective behavior of the group cannot be deduced from nor reduced to the characteristics or individual behavior of the agents involved. In other words, system behavior depends not on the details of its components, but on the ensemble of nonlinear interactions among the components. Complex systems are hierarchically organized from more local to more global levels, and ordered behavior in such systems is generated and maintained by interaction among components both at one level and between different levels. This order is not imposed from outside the system but emerges out of system operation, a process called self-organization.

The nature of nonlinear interaction means that even when components follow simple rules of interaction, the details of local interactions cannot be predicted, and efforts to make such predictions are futile, like trying to forecast the weather beyond the horizon of a week or so. Despite the fundamental unpredictability at the level of local interaction, however, the behavior of the collective exhibits regularities that are much simpler than the myriad interactions from which this regular behavior emerges. This holds the promise that groups can be studied by focusing on the evolution of behavior at the level of interest, rather than trying to build up an understanding by the patient accumulation of detailed knowledge about the components of the system, and of the components of the components, and then trying to figure out how they might all interact.

When system constraints (or contextual variables; Arrow et al., 2000) differ across groups or change during the lifetime of a single group, this can trigger a shift to qualitatively different patterns (e.g., from repeating cycles to chaotic behavior), although some changes in contextual variables will trigger such bifurcations, and others will not. The impact of contextual variables on global behavior is not linear: Large changes in contextual variables at some ranges of values will have no discernable effect on group behavior, whereas small changes at some other ranges of values (near critical thresholds) will have dramatic effects on group behavior. Together, knowledge of characteristic dynamic patterns and knowledge of the range of contextual conditions that either evoke development along different paths or trigger abrupt changes in group behavior hold the promise of designing more effective interventions for groups.

Complexity principles applied to the study of groups thus suggest a number of propositions, including:

1. Interactions among group members should result in global patterns of behavior that arise from but are not deducible from individual member attributes or behavior.

2. A relatively small number of characteristic developmental patterns should be apparent among groups operating in similar conditions, although the details of how these patterns unfold (i.e., actual levels of variables, pacing) will vary.

3. Different constraints inherent in the group's operating environment will be associated with different characteristic patterns of development.

4. Groups can jump from one pattern to another in response to a change in operating conditions, but the magnitude of response will often not be proportional to the change.

McGrath and Tschan (2004a, 2004b) have synthesized action theory with complex systems theory to derive a multilevel theory of groups as complex action systems. This theory advances action theory by specifying the elements that compose groups (people, projects, technologies), levels of projects, and types of functions that group activity can serve. This theory and that of Arrow et al. offer a conceptualization of structure based on networks of mappings of elements; for example, a role network consists of a mapping of technologies/tools onto people. The network concept of structure is much more dynamic than those in most prior group research.

Structuration theory. Structuration theory considers how group activities are constituted through members' actions, explores the processes by which the production and reproduction of groups occurs, and identifies the factors that influence these processes (Poole, 1999; Poole & DeSanctis, 2003; Poole, Seibold, & McPhee, 1985, 1996).

The theory rests on a distinction between *system,* the observable pattern of relations in a group, and *structure,* the rules and resources members use to generate and sustain the group system. Sociologist Anthony Giddens (1984) characterizes structures as "recipes" for acting that consist of a configuration of rules and material and social resources used to bring about the action. Structuration theory construes the observable group system as a set of practices constituted by members' structuring behavior. The key to understanding this system lies not in surface-level behaviors or functions, but in the structures and structuring processes that support these. For example, a researcher using structuration theory would explore conflict management by asking questions such as: What rules and resources enable and guide conflict management? and Does group interaction give rise to other structuring processes that counteract or undermine the conflict management? Structurational research searches for a hidden order of structures and structuring processes underlying the observable group.

The central concept in the theory is *structuration,* which refers to the processes by which systems are produced and reproduced through members' use of rules and resources. This definition rests on several key arguments. First, not only is a system produced and reproduced through structuration, but the structures themselves are, too. Structures are *dualities:* They are both the medium and outcome of action. They are the medium of action because group members draw on structures to interact, but they are also its outcome because rules and resources exist only by virtue of being used in a practice. For instance, when a group takes a vote, it is employing the rules behind voting to act, but it is also reminding itself that these rules exist, working out a way of using the rules, and perhaps creating a special version of them. Hence, structures have a virtual existence; they exist in a continuous process of structuration.

Structuration theory attempts to shift the focus from systems or structures to structuration, which emphasizes the dynamic interrelationship of system and structure in interaction. Neither stability nor change is viewed as the basic state of a group. Each is explained in terms of the same model of continuous production and reproduction.

Structures are sometimes created "from scratch," but more often, groups appropriate them from existing institutional structures. Majority voting schemes, for example, are commonly used throughout democratic societies, so it is not surprising that members of groups carry this structure with them to other groups. The *appropriation* process, which adapts structural features to specific groups and circumstances and which may lead to structural innovation and change, is an important focus of research in structuration theory.

Two classes of factors influence structuration. The first class includes: *characteristics of the group and its situation* such as the group's tasks and the structures available in relevant institutions; members' *degree of insight* into the structures they use and the system as a whole; *differential distributions of resources,* which create power and status distinctions; and the *unintended consequences of action,* which arise as a result of the complexity of group systems and their environments.

The second set of influences on structuration is the dynamics through which different structural features mediate and interact with each other. Two types of structural dynamics can be distinguished: one structure *mediates* another when its production and reproduction involve the reproduction of the other. For example, the economic metaphor, in which choices are based on rationalistic cost-benefit calculations (see Lakoff & Johnson,

1980), often mediates decision rules in groups (Thibaut & Kelley, 1959). The second dynamic, *contradiction,* occurs when "the operation of one structural principle in the production of a societal system presumes that of another which tends to undermine it" (Giddens, 1979, p. 141). For example, numerous investigators have reflected on the contradiction between the social, collegial nature of group action and members' individualistic striving for control and personal position in groups (Smith & Berg, 1987).

Structuration theory has been applied in the study of argument and influence in groups (e.g., Poole et al., 1996), group use of information technology (e.g., DeSanctis & Poole, 1994; Majchrsak, Rice, Malhotra, & King, 2000; Poole & DeSanctis, 1990; Taylor, Groleau, Heaton, & Van Every, 2001), jury decision making (Keogh & Lake, 1993), and leadership (Kahai, Sosik, & Avolio, 1997). It attempts to mediate the tensions in group research between action and structure, micro- and macrolevels of analysis, and the group and its environment. It argues that complexity is a function of different ways in which structuring processes play out in particular contexts. A number of challenges facing structuration research, not the least of which is the difficulty of studying hidden deeper structures, are summarized in Poole (1999).

Formal Models of Complexity in Groups

Formal modeling has a long history in group research, and most dynamic models explore the complexity of group systems. Several strains of modeling can be distinguished. *Dynamic systems models* employ mathematical methods to represent systems of variables that represent key features of the process. These systems of equations are then used to derive trajectories of the values of these variables over time, giving a representation of the process generated by the mechanism built into the equations. Researchers can then compare the results of the modeling to data to ascertain how representative the model is. Examples of dynamic systems models include Leik's (Leik & Meeker, 1975) model of the distribution of acts in small groups, Fisek and Ofshe's (1970) model of the evolution of status structures in groups, and James A. Davis's (Davis & Leinhardt, 1972) models of balance in small groups and cliques.

Computational models simulate how a group system or parts of a system evolve over time. They differ from dynamic systems models in that they replicate the sequence of activities an individual or group undertakes rather than just calculating values of coevolving variables. Several different types of simulation models have been applied to issues of change in groups. Some simulations are mathematically based, such as Stasser's (1988) DISCUSS model, which simulates information flow and effects during group discussion;

Hastie, Penrod, and Pennington's (1983) JUS model, which simulates jury decision making; and Carley's (1991) model of group stability in society. Another option is cellular automata, which represent how interconnected units influence each other over time and have been employed by Latané (1996) to model the spread of ideas, emotions, and behaviors through a system. A third approach is systems dynamics simulation, which employs an algorithm applied by Forrester (1961; Sterman, 2000) to solve a system of differential equations that simulates a system. Contractor and Seibold (1993) used this approach to develop and test a self-organizing systems model of structuring processes in computer-supported groups.

Commonalities and Differences in Complexity Approaches

Although the connections among the lines of work discussed in this section are obvious, the approaches differ in whether they are stated in verbal or formal terms and in their perspective on complexity.

Action, complex systems, and structuration theories presume that human action is sufficiently complex that it cannot be fully captured by formal models. These theories argue that human interpretive and action processes are sufficiently varied that any formal representation captures only part of "what is there" and runs the risk of oversimplification. The power of human imagination is so great, these theories assert, that it is constantly creating new forms that could not be conceived in any formal model. Human action, constantly escaping the bounds of any formal theory, must be understood on its own terms, in theories cast in the same language that grounds human activity. In contrast, the modeling approaches argue that the ultimate goal is to capture the underlying rules of interaction that generate complex patterns, and they look for qualitative similarities among these patterns, depending on the value of contextual parameters. So long as we develop substantive models that can be compared with empirical evidence, we can build a firm foundation that accounts for the generation of complexity.

The approaches also differ in their attitude toward complexity. The complexity theory and modeling approaches presume that complexity emerges from simplicity, and vice versa. The power and potential insights of these approaches resides in their ability to show how seemingly complicated and inexplicable phenomena result from complex interactions among a few elements. Action and structuration theories treat complexity as a fundamental aspect of group life. Groups are messy, these theories hold, precisely because human action is spontaneous and indeterminate and because humans work with multiple levels of meaning and multiple projects and are members of multiple groups. Based on these assumptions, a good theory must be sufficiently flexible to capture the variegated constructs and influences involved in group activity. The challenge for approaches like action theory and structuration theory is to be complex enough to adequately capture group dynamics, but not so complex that the theory collapses of its own weight. Occam's razor is an important implement for such theories.

The challenge for modeling and complexity theory is to avoid simplifications that distort. Potential distortions in modeling include introducing restrictive assumptions and force-fitting theories into existing modeling techniques (McPhee & Poole, 1981). Verbal formulations of theories are more flexible and capable of capturing nuances of phenomena than are mathematical models, which require precise definitions of relations among variables. But although modeling does impose limitations on the form of theories, much progress has been made in developing diverse forms of models that can fit a wider variety of phenomena. As models become more complex, they will be able to incorporate key junctures, critical events, and causes operating at different rates and strengths, on different levels and at different times. If something can be described precisely in words, it can usually be modeled.

The Past, Present, and Future of Temporal Perspectives on Groups

Some of the key findings in this review are summarized under the seven questions in Table 9.3. Several challenges need to be addressed in advancing our understanding of time and change in groups: (1) theoretical integration and development, (2) unanswered (and often unasked) substantive questions about time and change in groups, and (3) a shift in research strategies and new resources to support this shift. A discussion of these issues will highlight strengths and weaknesses of the perspective, which are summarized in Table 9.1.

Theory

The body of literature that we have reviewed varies both in the degree to which it is theory driven and in the nature of the theories involved. Some areas, such as group development, are rich in models but need more theoretical integration. We need a meta-level framework that incorporates multiple paths of development and identifies factors that predispose groups toward one path or another—or that can shift a group from one path to another. Models that apply to different time scales or types of activity— group development, decision development, group learning, performance

Table 9.3   Key Findings of Temporal Perspective Research

Group composition	• Group members may differ in how they perceive and relate to time • Surface characteristics of members affect intragroup relations less over time • Established group members tend to attract similar new members; members who are different tend to leave • Alignment of member characteristics has implications for subgroup formation
Group structure	• Status based on surface characteristics is established quickly, but status can be earned over time by other means • Institutional norms form rapidly, evolutionary norms more slowly • Cohesion based on social attraction develops faster than cohesion based on personal attraction • Habitual routines form quickly but can be adjusted over time
Group projects	• Groups differ in whether they tackle projects using monochronic or polychronic strategies • Different types of project or tasks—such as decision making, negotiation, or performance tasks—are associated with different temporal patterning of activity • Task forces working on a single, unstructured project with a deadline often reorganize at the midpoint of their time together
Interaction	• Time management, recall of the past, and predicting the future help groups establish meaning of time and history • Groups create structure through iterative interaction • Interaction creates change through cycles of action, feedback, and modification • Conversation requires coordinated sequencing among members, which differs in face-to-face and computer-mediated contexts
Group action/ outcomes	• The sequencing of activities, especially planning, affects performance • Transactive memory systems develop over time • Learning curves can yield improved performance over time, while escalating commitment can yield reduced flexibility and a corresponding decline in performance • Longer communication periods increase the likelihood of a group discussing unshared information

	• Group focus on performance and quality of performance increases in later stages of development
Change over time	• The dominant stage model proposes that groups move through five stages of development: forming, storming, norming, performing, and adjourning
	• Cyclic models propose that groups deal repeatedly with the same issues in a new form
	• Punctuated equilibrium models suggest that groups alternate longer periods of stability with shorter periods of instability and reorganization
	• Contingency theories suggest that groups have varying functions as they move from project inception to completion
	• Temporal patterning decision path evolution models find that groups do not follow a consistent sequence of precise phases; however, task performance does tend to occur later in a group's development
Ecology	• Simple sources of influence combine over time to yield complex social phenomena
	• Older groups have more experience adapting to their embedding context, which can prevent dissolution of the group
	• Embedding contexts can trigger change that disrupts internal group processes geared toward stability

spirals, and structuration and microlevel action cycles in conversation—could also benefit from better integration, so that we have a better sense of the ways in which temporal patterns evident at different time scales mesh with or disrupt one another. Action theory, for example, asserts that processes for all subsystems and levels of analysis coevolve, but more specification is needed to help guide research on this process of coevolution.

Theories about group interaction and performance are also not time-scale complete: Most fail to address how or why a given set of relations will stabilize or change over time, and those that do often fail to specify how long or when such changes might be expected. Because of the failure to specify the validity interval in group-development theories, for example, researchers make wildly varying assumptions about how many stages might be expected in a group that meets for 40 minutes or 4 hours or 40 hours.

As suggested in the final section, we need theories that can account for the complexity that we observe. For behavior as complex and varied as group interaction, it seems likely that an adequate theory will need to incorporate all four motors of change. Of course, this will ultimately require an account of when, how, and why different motors of change become more or less important in the unfolding behavior of a group. Along with attending to change, we also need a better account of how groups maintain continuity in the face of changes in membership, task, and environmental context.

Unasked and Unanswered Questions

The evolution of work in this perspective has tended to follow a general sequence from more simple descriptive and normative models toward more complex and contingent models. Rather than the "one best" path, the evidence increasingly suggests that although there are many ways to go wrong in coordinating and sequencing group activity, there are multiple effective routes to effective performance as well. Here is a short selection of questions that we feel deserve more attention:

1. Why and how do groups develop differently? What contextual features make a particular pattern of development more or less likely? Might multiple different models of development apply simultaneously to different aspects of a group—in other words, does the observed pattern depend heavily on the observation and aggregation intervals and on the measurement indices that are chosen?

2. To what extent are change and continuity in different aspects of a group (interaction, task activity, membership roles and relations, routines and norms) linked or entrained together and how tightly? Do monochronic or polychronic strategies in one sphere of activity, for example, generalize to other spheres of activity? How do rhythms and changes in rhythms at different time scales and in different aspects of group process mesh together to yield global change? How are fast- and slow-developing elements of structure entrained to each other?

3. When groups change, what mechanisms underlie the transition from stability to instability and back again? What endogenous or exogenous triggers drive these transitions?

4. How does the type of group, the type of task, the group's relationship to its embedding context(s), and the expected duration of the group moderate patterns of development, stability, and change?

Research Strategies and Resources

To address the first set of questions, we need more longitudinal studies that gather data suited to testing a variety of development models, instead of more confirmatory studies that seek support for a single model. To address the second set of questions, we need more longitudinal studies that collect data on a variety of variables at different levels of resolution. We need to collect and examine process data with attention to sequencing and timing, and we also need to wean ourselves from an overreliance on "snapshot" studies. As Poole et al. (2000, p. 366) note, the event sequence data used in process research can be easily transformed into a form suitable for variance models, but the reverse is typically not true.

To address the third set of questions, we need to study groups for long enough that the slower developing aspects of structure have time to emerge. To address the fourth set of questions, we need to study groups that experience changes in task demands, membership, and other contextual features that are identified by theory to be good candidates to trigger either amplifying changes or to evoke homeostatic regulatory processes that cancel out the impact of any perturbation. Between-group designs are essential for studying the differences and similarities in patterns across groups, the last set of issues. This data also needs to be examined on a group-by-group basis, rather than collapsed together and averaged without checking the validity of any presumptions that groups of the "same" type will follow the "same" pattern at identical time scales.

This research will require sophisticated technologies. Recording equipment capable of capturing the verbal and nonverbal behavior of a sizable group that moves around from place to place is one ideal. Automated transcription of group discussions directly from media is also developing and will be important to future research.

Our methodological and statistical tools are sometimes not well matched to the kinds of questions asked by the temporal perspective. Many of the tools in our standard statistical tool kits are based on assumptions that, in general, do not hold for groups over time. Linear relations and independent observations cannot be assumed in such studies. Developments in time series analysis plus a host of new approaches in nonlinear dynamics hold promise, but many of these tools need to be adjusted and adapted to allow us to address substantive questions about groups. Methods specifically suited for the analysis of process data are discussed in Poole et al. (2000); they include phase analysis, Markov analysis, event time series analysis, and nonlinear systems analysis. Discussions of coding and interaction analysis can be found in Weingart (1997) and Neuendorff (2001). But much more work needs to be done to develop and refine methods suited for group research.

Of course, many scholars who take a temporal perspective would like to follow these guidelines more consistently, but they are hampered by the resource demands. To do rigorous analysis with a large sample of groups is a formidable task for an individual researcher or even a single research team. There is a need to find new and innovative ways to develop infrastructure for collaborative longitudinal and cross-sectional group research projects and to create opportunities for multiple researchers at multiple sites to study large numbers of groups over long periods of time. Developmental psychologists have overcome institutional barriers to conduct research that has followed individuals across the life span; we need to do the same for groups.

Time, change, development, and history affect how groups interact and how they perform. They moderate the relations among many variables of interest to those who study and work with groups. We hope that by drawing on past research as a source of lessons for the present, we can contribute to a future in which bridges are built across the archipelago of research on groups and there is time to provide a deeper understanding of time, change, and development in groups.

Note

1. We thank Bibb Latané for input during the early stages of this project. We also acknowledge valuable input from Joseph E. McGrath, Andrea B. Hollingshead, and our colleagues at the conference on Assessing Theory and Research in Groups. Support for this project was provided by National Science Foundation (grant SES 9986562, Social Psychology and Decision, Risk & Management Sciences Programs).

References

Ancona, D., & Chong, C. (1996). Entrainment: Pace, cycle, and rhythm in organizational behavior. *Research in Organizational Behavior, 18,* 251–284.

Ancona, D. G., Okhuysen, G. A., & Perlow, L. A. (2001). Taking time to integrate temporal research. *Academy of Management Review, 26*(4), 512–529.

Argote, L. (1993). Group and organizational learning curves: Individual, system, and environmental components. *British Journal of Social Psychology, 32*(1), 31–51.

Argote, L., Insko, C. A., Yovetich, N., & Romero, A. A. (1995). Group learning curves: The effects of turnover and task complexity on group performance. *Journal of Applied Social Psychology, 25*(6), 512–529.

Arrow, H. (1997). Stability, bistability, and instability in small group influence patterns. *Journal of Personality and Social Psychology, 72,* 75–85.

Arrow, H., & Crosson, S. B. (2003). Musical chairs: Membership dynamics in self-organized group formation. *Small Group Research, 5,* 523-556.

Arrow, H., & McGrath, J. E. (1993). Membership matters: How member change and continuity affect small group structure, process, and performance. *Small Group Research, 24,* 334–361.

Arrow, H., & McGrath, J. E. (1995). Membership dynamics in groups at work: A theoretical framework. In B. M. Staw & L. L. Cummings (Eds.), *Research in organizational behavior* (Vol. 17, pp. 373–411). Greenwich, CT: JAI Press.

Arrow, H., McGrath, J. E., & Berdahl, J. L. (2000). *Small groups as complex systems: Formation, coordination, development, and adaptation.* Thousand Oaks, CA: Sage.

Axelrod, R. (1984). *The evolution of cooperation.* New York: Basic Books.

Bales, R. F. (1950). *Interaction process analysis: A method for the study of small groups.* Chicago: University of Chicago Press.

Bales, R. F. (1953). The equilibrium problem in small groups. In T. Parsons, R. F. Bales, & E. A. Shils (Eds.), *Working papers in the theory of action* (pp. 111–161). Glencoe, IL: Free Press.

Bales, R. F. (1955). Adaptive and integrative changes as sources of strain in social systems. In A. P. Hare, E. F. Borgatta, & R. F. Bales (Eds.), *Small groups: Studies in social interaction* (pp. 127–131). New York: Knopf.

Bales, R. F., & Strodtbeck, F. L. (1951). Phases in group problem solving. *Journal of Abnormal and Social Psychology, 46,* 485–495.

Bales, R. F., Strodtbeck, F. L., Mills, T. M., & Roseborough, M. E. (1951). Channels of communication in small groups. *American Sociological Review, 16,* 461–468.

Bennis, W., & Shepard, H. (1956). A theory of group development. *Human Relations, 9,* 415–437.

Bettenhausen, K. L., & Murnighan, J. K. (1985). The emergence of norms in competitive decision-making groups. *Administrative Science Quarterly, 30,* 350–372.

Bion, W. (1961). *Experiences in groups.* New York: Basic Books.

Bliese, P. D. (2000). Within-group agreement, non-independence, and reliability: Implications for data aggregation and analysis. In K. J. Klein & S. W. Kozlowski (Eds.), *Multilevel theory, research, and methods in organizations* (pp. 349–381). San Francisco: Jossey-Bass.

Bouas, K. S., & Komorita, S. S. (1996). Group discussion and cooperation in social dilemmas. *Personality and Social Psychology Bulletin, 22,* 1144–1150.

Braaten, L. J. (1974/1975). Developmental phases of encounter groups: A critical review of models and a new proposal. *Interpersonal Development, 75,* 112–129.

Brower, A. M. (1986). Behavior changes in psychotherapy groups: A study using an empirically based statistical method. *Small Group Behavior, 17,* 164–185.

Burke, P. J. (1974). Participation and leadership in small groups. *American Sociological Review, 39,* 832–843.

Carley, K. M. (1991). A theory of group stability. *American Sociological Review, 56,* 331–354.

Chang, A., Bordia, P., & Duck, J. (2003). Punctuated equilibrium and linear progression: Toward a new understanding of group development. *Academy of Management Journal, 46,* 106–117.

Conger, J. A., & Kanungo, R. N. (1998). *Charismatic leadership in organizations.* Thousand Oaks, CA: Sage.

Contractor, H., & Seibold, D. R. (1993). Theoretical frameworks for the study of structuring processes in group decision support systems: Adaptive structuration theory and self-organizing systems theory. *Human Communication Research, 19,* 528–563.

Crosson, S. B., Orbell, J., & Arrow, H. (2004). "Social poker": A laboratory test of predictions from club theory. *Rationality and Society, 16*(2), 225–248.

Davis, J. A., & Leinhardt, S. (1972). The structure of positive interpersonal relations in small groups. In J. Berger, M. Zelditch, & B. Anderson (Eds.), *Sociological theories in progress* (pp. 218–251). Boston: Houghton Mifflin.

Dennis, A. R., & Valacich, J. S. (1993). Computer brainstorms: More heads are better than one. *Journal of Applied Psychology, 78,* 531–537.

DeSanctis, G., & Poole, M. S. (1994). Capturing the complexity in advanced technology use: Adaptive structuration theory. *Organization Science, 5,* 121–147.

Diehl, M., & Stroebe, W. (1987). Productivity loss in brainstorming groups: Toward the solution of a riddle. *Journal of Personality and Social Psychology, 53,* 497–509.

Dunphy, D. C. (1968). Phases, roles, and myths in self-analytic groups. *The Journal of Applied Behavioral Science, 4,* 195–225.

Eagly, A. H. (1987). *Sex differences in social behavior: A social-role analysis.* Hillsdale, NJ: Lawrence Erlbaum.

Eisenhardt, K. M., & Sull, D. N. (2001). Strategy as simple rules. *Harvard Business Review, 19,* 107–116.

Farrell, M. P. (1976). Patterns in the development of self-analytic groups. *Journal of Applied Behavioral Science, 12,* 523–542.

Faure, G. O., & Sjostedt, G. (1993). Culture and negotiation: An introduction. In G. O. Faure & J. Z. Rubin (Eds.), *Culture and negotiation* (pp. 1–13). Newbury Park, CA: Sage.

Feldman, M. S. (2000). Organizational routines as a source of continuous change. *Organization Science, 11*(6), 611–629.

Fine, G. A. (1987). *With the boys: Little League baseball and preadolescent culture.* Chicago: University of Chicago Press.

Fisek, M. H., & Ofshe, R. (1970). The process of status evolution. *Sociometry, 33,* 327–335.

Folger, J. P., Poole, M. S., & Stutman, R. (2004). *Working through conflict* (5th ed.). New York: Addison-Wesley Longman.

Forrester, J. W. (1961). *Industrial dynamics.* Cambridge, MA: Productivity Press.

Frey, L. R. (Ed.). (2003). *Group communication in context: Studies of bona fide groups* (2nd ed.). Mahwah, NJ: Lawrence Erlbaum.

Gersick, C. J. G. (1988). Time and transition in work teams: Toward a new model of group development. *Academy of Management Journal, 31,* 9–41.

Gersick, C. J. G. (1989). Marking time: Predictable transitions in task groups. *Academy of Management Journal, 32,* 274–309.

Gersick, C. J. G., & Hackman, J. R. (1990). Habitual routines in task-performing groups. *Organizational Behavior and Human Decision Processes, 47,* 65–97.

Giddens, A. (1979). *Central problems in social theory: Action, structure, and contradiction in social analysis.* Berkeley: University of California Press.

Giddens, A. (1984). *The constitution of society: Outline of the theory of structuration.* Berkeley: University of California Press.

Glasl, F. (1982). The process of conflict escalation and roles of third parties. In G. B. J. Bomers & R. Peterson (Eds.), *Conflict management and industrial relations* (pp. 119–140). Boston: Kluwer-Nijhoff.

Graen, G. B., & Scandura, T. (1987). Toward a psychology of dyadic organizing. *Research in Organizational Behavior, 9,* 175–208.

Guastello, S. J. (1995). *Chaos, catastrophe, and human affairs: Applications of nonlinear dynamics to work, organizations, and social evolution.* Mahwah, NJ: Lawrence Erlbaum.

Hackman, J. R. (Ed.). (1990). *Groups that work (and those that don't).* San Francisco: Jossey-Bass.

Hackman, J. R. (2002). *Leading teams: Setting the stage for great performances.* Boston: Harvard Business School Press.

Hackman, J. R., & Morris, C. H. (1975). Group tasks, group interaction process, and group effectiveness: A review and proposed integration. In L. Berkowitz (Ed.). *Advances in experimental social psychology,* (Vol. 8, pp. 45–99). New York: Academic Press.

Hall, E. T. (1983). *The dance of life: The other dimension of time.* Garden City, NY: Anchor Books.

Hare, A. P. (1967). Small group development in the relay assembly testroom. *Sociological Inquiry, 37,* 169–182.

Hare, A. P. (1982). *Creativity in small groups.* Beverly Hills, CA: Sage.

Hare, A. P., & Naveh, D. (1984). Group development at the Camp David Summit, 1978. *Small Group Behavior, 15,* 299–318.

Harrison, D. A., Price, K. H., & Bell, M. P. (1998). Beyond relational demography: Time and the effects of surface- and deep-level diversity on work group cohesion. *Academy of Management Journal, 41,* 96–107.

Hastie, R., Penrod, S. D., & Pennington, N. (1983). *Inside the jury.* Cambridge, MA: Harvard University Press.

Heider, F. (1958). *The psychology of interpersonal relations.* New York: John Wiley.

Henry, K. B. (2000). Perceptions of cooperation in a longitudinal social dilemma. *Small Group Research, 31,* 507–527.

Hersey, P., & Blanchard, K. H. (1969). Life cycle theory of leadership. *Training and Development Journal, 23,* 26–40.

Hersey, P., & Blanchard, K. H. (1988). *Management of organizational behavior* (5th ed.). Englewood Cliffs, NJ: Prentice Hall.

Hill, W. F. (1974). Systematic group development—SGD therapy. In A. Jacobs & W. Spradlin (Eds.), *The group as agent of change.* New York: Behavioral Publications.

Hill, W. F., & Gruner, L. (1973). A study of development in open and closed groups. *Small Group Behavior, 4,* 355–382.

Hiltz, S. R., Johnson, K., & Turoff, M. (1986). Experiments in group decision making, 1: Communications process and outcome in face-to-face vs. computerized conferences. *Human Communication Research, 13*(2), 225–252.

Hirokawa, R. Y. (1990). The role of communication in group decision-making efficacy: A task-contingency perspective. *Small Group Research, 21,* 190–204.

Hogg, M. A. (1992). *The social psychology of group cohesiveness: From attraction to social identity.* London: Harvester Wheatsheaf.

Hollander, E. P. (1978). *Leadership dynamics: A practical guide to effective relationships.* New York: Free Press.

Hollingshead, A. B., & McGrath, J. E. (1995). Computer-assisted groups: A Critical review of the empirical research. In R. L. Guzzo & E. Salas (Eds.), *Team effectiveness and decision-making in organizations* (pp. 46–78). San Francisco: Jossey-Bass.

Holmes, M. E. (1992). Phase structures in negotiation. In L. L. Putnam & M. E. Roloff (Eds.), *Communication and negotiation* (pp. 83–107). Newbury Park, CA: Sage.

Isaac, R. M., & Walker, J. M. (1988). Group size effects in public goods provision: The voluntary contributions mechanism. *Quarterly Journal of Economics, 103,* 179–199.

Jackson, M., & Poole, M. S. (2003). Idea generation in naturally occurring groups: Complex appropriation of a simple group procedure. *Human Communication Research, 29,* 560–591.

Janicik, G. A., & Bartel, C. A. (2003). Talking about time: Effects of temporal planning and time awareness norms on group coordination and performance. *Group Dynamics: Theory, Research, and Practice, 7,* 122–134.

Janis, I. L. (1982). *Groupthink.* Boston: Houghton Mifflin.

Kahai, S. S., Sosik, J. J., & Avolio, B. J. (1997). Effects of leadership style and problem structure on work group process and outcomes in an electronic meeting system environment. *Personnel Psychology, 50,* 121–146.

Kaufman-Scarborough, C., & Lindquist, J. D. (1999). Time management and polychronicity: Comparisons, contrasts, and insights for the workplace. *Journal of Managerial Psychology, 14,* 288–312.

Kelly, J. R., Futoran, G. C., & McGrath, J. E. (1990). Capacity and capability: Seven studies of entrainment of task performance rates. *Small Group Research, 21,* 283–314.

Kelly, J. R., Jackson, J. W., & Hutson-Comeaux, S. L. (1997). The effect of time pressure and task differences on influence modes and accuracy in problem-solving groups. *Personality and Social Psychology Bulletin, 23,* 10–22.

Kelly, J. R., & Karau, S. J. (1993). Entrainment of creativity in small groups. *Small Group Research, 24,* 179–198.

Kelly, J. R., & McGrath, J. E. (1985). Effects of time limits and task types on task performance and interaction of four-person groups. *Journal of Personality and Social Psychology 49,* 395–407.

Keogh, C. M., & Lake, R. (1993). Values as structuring properties in contract negotiations. In C. Conrad (Ed.), *The ethical nexus* (pp. 171–191). Norwood, NJ: Ablex.

Komorita, S. S., Hilty, J. A., & Parks, C. D. (1991). Reciprocity and cooperation in social dilemmas. *Journal of Conflict Resolution, 35,* 494–518.

Komorita, S. S., Parks, C. D., & Hulbert, L. G. (1992). Reciprocity and the induction of cooperation in social dilemmas. *Journal of Personality and Social Psychology, 62,* 607–617.

Kuhn, T., & Poole, M. S. (2000). Do conflict management styles affect group decision-making? Evidence from a longitudinal field study. *Human Communication Research, 26,* 558–590.

Kuypers, B., Davies, D., & Glaser, K. (1986). Developmental arrestations in self-analytic groups. *Small Group Behavior, 17,* 269–302.

Lacoursiere, R. B. (1980). *The life cycle of groups: Group developmental stage theory.* New York: Human Sciences Press.

Lakoff, G., & Johnson, M. (1980). *Metaphors we live by.* Chicago: University of Chicago Press.

Latané, B. (1996). Dynamic social impact: The creation of culture by communication. *Journal of Communication, 46,* 13–25.

Lau, D. C., & Murnighan, J. K. (1998). Demographic diversity and fault lines: The compositional dynamics of organizational groups. *Academy of Management Review, 23,* 325–340.

Lebie, L., Rhoades, J. A., & McGrath, J. E. (1996). Interaction process in computer-mediated and face-to-face groups. *Computer Supported Cooperative Work, 4*(2 & 3), 127–152.

Leik, R. K., & Meeker, B. F. (1975). *Mathematical sociology.* Englewood Cliffs, NJ: Prentice Hall.

Lewin, K. (1947a). Frontiers in group dynamics: Channels of group life: Social planning and action research. *Human Relations, 1,* 143–153.

Lewin, K. (1947b). Frontiers in group dynamics: Concept, method, and reality in social science: Social equilibria and social change. *Human Relations, 1,* 5–41.

Lim, S. A., & Murnighan, J. K. (1994). Phases, deadlines, and the bargaining process. *Oganizational Behavior and Human Decision Processes, 58,* 153–171.

Lindsley, D. H., Brass, D. J., & Thomas, J. B. (1995). Efficacy-performance spirals: A multilevel perspective. *Academy of Management Review, 20,* 645–678.

Lundgren, D., & Knight, D. (1978). Sequential stages of development in sensitivity training groups. *The Journal of Applied Behavioral Science, 14,* 204–222.

Majchrsak, A., Rice, R. E., Malhotra, A., & King, N. (2000). Technology adaptation: The case of a computer-supported inter-organizational virtual team. *MIS Quarterly, 24,* 569–600.

Mann, R., Gibbard, G., & Hartman, J. (1967). *Interpersonal style and group development.* New York: John Wiley.

McCollom, M. (1995). Reevaluating group development: A critique of familiar models. In J. Gillette & M. McCollom (Eds.), *Groups in context: A new perspective on group dynamics* (pp. 133–154). Lanham, MD: University Press of America.

McGrath, J. E. (1990). Time matters in groups. In J. Galegher & R. E. Kraut (Eds.), *Intellectual teamwork: Social and technological foundations of cooperative work* (pp. 23–61). Hillsdale, NJ: Lawrence Erlbaum.

McGrath, J. E. (1991). Time, interaction, and performance (TIP): A theory of groups. *Small Group Research, 22,* 147–174.

McGrath, J. E., & Kelly, J. R. (1986). *Time and human interaction: Toward a social psychology of time.* New York: Guilford Press.

McGrath, J. E., & O'Connor, K. M. (1996). Temporal issues in work groups. In M. A. West (Ed.), *Handbook of work group psychology* (pp. 25–52). Chichester, UK: John Wiley.

McGrath, J. E., & Tschan, F. (2004a). Dynamics in groups and teams: Groups as complex action systems. In M. S. Poole & A. H. Van de Ven (Eds.), *Handbook of organizational change and development* (pp. 50–72). Oxford, UK: Oxford University Press.

McGrath, J. E., & Tschan, F. (2004b). *Temporal matters in social psychology: Examining the role of time in the lives of groups and individuals.* Washington, DC: American Psychological Association.

McPhee, R. D., & Poole, M. S. (1981). Mathematical models in communication research. In M. Burgoon (Ed.), *Communication yearbook* (Vol. 5, pp. 159–191). New Brunswick, NJ: ICA-Transaction Press.

Mills, T. (1964). *Group transformations: An analysis of a learning group.* Englewood Cliffs, NJ: Prentice Hall.

Moore, D. A. (2003). *Myopic prediction, self-destructive secrecy, and the unexpected benefits of revealing final deadlines in negotiations.* Carnegie Mellon GSIA Working Paper.

Moore, D. A. (2004). The unexpected benefits of final deadlines in negotiation. *Journal of Experimental Social Psychology, 40,* 121–127.

Moreland, R. L. (1996). Lewin's legacy for small-groups research. *Systems Practice, 9,* 7–26.

Moreland, R. L. (1999). Transactive memory: Learning who knows what in work groups and organizations. In L. Thompson, D. Messick, & J. Levine (Eds.), *Shared cognition in organizations: The management of knowledge* (pp. 3–31). Mahwah, NJ: Lawrence Erlbaum.

Moreland, R. L., & Argote, L. (2003). Transactive memory in dynamic organizations. In R. Peterson & E. Mannix (Eds.), *Understanding the dynamic organization* (pp. 135–162). Mahwah, NJ: Lawrence Erlbaum.

Moreland, R. L., Hogg, M. A., & Hains, S. C. (1994). Back to the future: Social psychological research on groups. *Journal of Experimental Social Psychology, 30,* 527–555.

Moreland, R. L., & Levine, J. M. (1982). Socialization in small groups: Temporal changes in individual-group relations. In L. Berkowitz (Ed.), *Advances in experimental social psychology* (Vol. 15, pp. 137–192). New York: Academic Press.

Moreland, R. L., & Levine, J. M. (1992). The composition of small groups. In E. Lawler, B. Markovsky, C. Ridgeway, & H. Walker (Eds.), *Advances in group processes* (Vol. 9, pp. 237-280). Greenwich, CT.: JAI Press.

Moreland, R. L., & Levine, J. M. (2000). Socialization in organizations and work groups. In M. Turner (Ed.), *Groups at work: Theory and research* (pp. 69–112). Mahwah, NJ: Lawrence Erlbaum.

Newcomb, T. M. (1961). *The acquaintance process.* New York: Holt, Rinehart & Winston.

Neuendorff, K. (2001). *Content analysis.* Thousand Oaks, CA: Sage.

Nutt, P. C. (1984). Types of organizational decision processes. *Administrative Science Quarterly, 29,* 414–450.

Ofori-Dankwa, J., & Julian, S. D. (2001). Complexifying organizational theory: Illustrations using time research. *Academy of Management Review, 26*(3), 415–430.

Olekalns, M., & Smith, P. L. (2000). Understanding optimal outcomes: The role of strategy sequences in competitive negotiations. *Human Communication Research, 26,* 527–557.

Opp, K.-D. (1982). The evolutionary emergence of norms. *British Journal of Social Psychology, 21,* 139–149.

Orlitzky, M., & Hirokawa, R. Y. (2001). To err is human, to correct for it divine: A meta-analysis of research testing the functional theory of group decision-making effectiveness. *Small Group Research, 32,* 313–341.

Osborn, A. F. (1957). *Applied imagination.* New York: Scribner's.

Parks, C. D., Henager, R. F., & Scamahorn, S. D. (1996). Trust and reactions to messages of intent in social dilemmas. *Journal of Conflict Resolution, 40,* 134–151.

Parks, C. D., & Rumble, A. C. (2001). Elements of reciprocity and social value orientation. *Personality & Social Psychology Bulletin, 27,* 1301–1309.

Poole, M. S. (1981). Decision development in small groups I: A test of two models. *Communication Monographs, 48,* 1–24.

Poole, M. S. (1999). Theories of group communication. In L. Frey, D. Gouran, & M. S. Poole (Eds.), *Handbook of group communication theory and research* (pp. 37–70). Thousand Oaks, CA: Sage.

Poole, M. S., & DeSanctis, G. (1990). Understanding the use of decision support systems: The theory of adaptive structuration. In J. Fulk & C. Steinfield (Eds.), *Organizations and communication technology* (pp. 173–193). Newbury Park CA: Sage.

Poole, M. S., & DeSanctis, G. (2003). Structuration theory in information systems research: Methods and controversies. In M. E. Whitman & A. B. Woszczynski (Eds.), *Handbook for information systems research* (pp. 206–249). Hershey, PA: Idea Press.

Poole, M. S., & Roth, J. (1989). Decision development in small groups IV: A typology of group decision paths. *Human Communication Research, 15,* 323–356.

Poole, M. S., Seibold, D. R., & McPhee, R. D. (1985). Group decision-making as a structurational process. *Quarterly Journal of Speech, 71,* 74–102.

Poole, M. S., Seibold, D. R., & McPhee, R. D. (1996). The structuration of group decisions. In R. Y. Hirokawa & M. S. Poole (Eds.), *Communication and group decision-making* (2nd ed., pp. 114–146). Thousand Oaks, CA: Sage.

Poole, M. S., Van de Ven, A. H., Dooley, K., & Holmes, M. E. (2000). *Organizational change and innovation processes: Theory and methods for research.* New York: Oxford University Press.

Pruitt, D. G., & Kimmel, M. J. (1977). Twenty years of experimental gaming: Critique, synthesis, and suggestions for the future. *Annual Review of Psychology, 28,* 363–392.

Rapoport, A., & Chammah, A. M. (1965). *Prisoner's dilemma.* Ann Arbor: University of Michigan Press.

Rice, R. (1984). *The new media: Communication, research, and technology.* Beverly Hills, CA: Sage.

Ridgeway, C. L. (1984). Dominance, performance, and status in groups: A theoretical analysis. In E. J. Lawler (Ed.), *Advances in group processes* (Vol. 1, pp. 59–93). Greenwich, CT: JAI Press.

Rogers, C. (1970). *Carl Rogers on encounter groups.* New York: Harper &Row.

Roy, D. F. (1960). "Banana time": Job satisfaction and informal interaction. *Human Organization, 18,* 158–168.

Sambamurthy, V., & Poole, M. S. (1992). The effects of variations in capabilities of GDSS designs on the management of cognitive conflict in groups. *Information Systems Research, 3,* 224–251.

Schein, E. H. (1992). *Organizational culture and leadership* (2nd ed.). San Francisco: Jossey-Bass.

Schultz, B. (1986). Communicative correlates of perceived leaders in the small group. *Small Group Behavior, 17*(1), 51–65.

Schutz, W. (1958). *FIRO: A three dimensional theory of interpersonal behavior.* New York: Holt, Rinehart & Winston.

Sheppard, B. H. (1984). Third party conflict intervention: A procedural framework. In B. M. Staw & L. L. Cummings (Eds.), *Research in organizational behavior* (Vol. 6, pp. 41–190). Greenwich, CT: JAI Press.

Sherif, M. (1966). *In common predicament: Social psychology of intergroup conflict and cooperation.* Boston: Houghton Mifflin.

Slater, P. (1966). *Microcosm.* New York: John Wiley.

Smith, K. K., & Berg, D. N. (1987). *Paradoxes of group life: Understanding conflict, paralysis, and movement in group dynamics.* San Francisco: Jossey-Bass.

Stasser, G. (1988). Computer simulation as a research tool: The DISCUSS model of group decision making. *Journal of Experimental Social Psychology, 24,* 393–422.

Stech, E. L. (1975). An analysis of interaction structure in the discussion of a ranking task. *Speech Monographs, 37,* 249–256.

Sterman, J. (2000). *Business dynamics: Systems thinking and modeling for a complex world.* New York: Irwin.

Stiles, W. B., Tupler, L. A., & Carpenter, J. C. (1982). Participants' perceptions of self-analytic group sessions. *Small Group Behavior, 13,* 237–254.

Stock, D., & Thelen, H. (1958). *Emotional dynamics and group culture.* New York: New York University Press.

Stuhlmacher, A. F., Gillespie, T. L., & Champagne, M. V. (1998). The impact of time pressure in negotiation: A meta-analysis. *International Journal of Conflict Management, 9,* 97–116.

Taylor, J. R., Groleau, C., Heaton, L., & Van Every, E. (2001). *The computerization of work: A communication perspective.* Thousand Oaks, CA: Sage.

Theodorson, G. A. (1962). The function of hostility in small groups. *The Journal of Social Psychology, 256,* 57–66.

Thibaut, J. W., & Kelley, H. H, (1959). *The social psychology of groups.* New York: John Wiley.

Tschan, F. (1995). Communication enhances small group performance if it conforms to task requirements: The concept of ideal communication cycles. *Basic and Applied Social Psychology, 17,* 371–393.

Tschan, F. (2002). Ideal cycles of communication (or cognitions) in triads, dyads, and individuals. *Small Group Research, 33*(6), 615–643.

Tuckman, B. W. (1965). Developmental sequence in small groups. *Psychological Bulletin, 63,* 384–399.

Tuckman, B. W., & Jensen, M. A. C. (1977). Stages in small group development revisited. *Group and Organizational Studies, 2,* 419–427.

Tuckman, J., & Lorge, I. (1962). Individual ability as a determinant of group superiority. *Human Relations, 15,* 45–51.

Turner, J. C., Hogg, M. A., Oakes, P. J., Reicher, S. D., & Wetherell, M. S. (1987). *Rediscovering the social group: A self-categorization theory.* Oxford, UK: Basil Blackwell.

Tushman, M. L., & Romanelli, E. (1985). Organizational evolution: A metamorphosis model of convergence and reorientation. In B. M. Staw & L. L. Cummings (Eds.), *Research in organizational behavior* (Vol. 7, pp. 171–222). Greenwich, CT: JAI Press.

Valacich, J. S., Wheeler, B. C., Mennecke, B. E., & Wachter, R. (1995). The effects of numerical and logical group size on computer-mediated idea generation. *Organizational Behavior and Human Decision Processes, 62,* 318–329.

Verdi, A. F., & Wheelan, S. (1992). Developmental patterns in same-sex and mixed-sex groups. *Small Group Research, 23,* 256–278.

Von Cranach, M. (1996). Toward a theory of the acting group. In E. Witte & J. H. Davis (Eds.), *Understanding group behavior: Small group processes and interpersonal relations* (pp. 147–187). Hillsdale, NJ: Lawrence Erlbaum.

Waller, M. J. (1997). Keeping the pins in the air: How work groups juggle multiple tasks. In M. M. Beyerlein, D. A. Johnson, & S. T. Beyerlein (Eds.), *Advances in interdisciplinary studies of work teams* (Vol. 4, pp. 217–247). Greenwich, CT: JAI Press.

Waller, M. J. (2000). All in the timing: Team pacing behaviors in dynamic conditions. In C. L. Cooper & D. M. Rousseau (Eds.), *Trends in organizational behavior: Time in organizational behavior* (Vol. 7, pp. 37–43). Brisbane, Australia: Wiley.

Waller, M. J., Conte, J. M, Gibson, C. B., & Carpenter, M. A. (2001). The effect of individual perceptions of deadlines on team performance. *Academy of Management Review, 26,* 586–600.

Waller, M. J., Giambatista, R. C., & Zellmer-Bruhn, M. (1999). The effects of individual time urgency on group polychronicity. *Journal of Managerial Psychology, 13,* 244–256.

Waller, M. J., Zellmer-Bruhn, M. E., & Giambatista, R. C. (2002). Watching the clock: Group pacing behavior under dynamic deadlines. *Academy of Management Journal, 45*(5), 1046–1055.

Weingart, L. R. (1992). Impact of group goals, task component complexity, effort, and planning on group performance. *Journal of Applied Psychology, 77*(5), 682–693.

Weingart, L. R. (1997). How did they do that? The ways and means of studying group process. *Research in Organizational Behavior, 19,* 198–239.

Weingart, L. R., Prietula, M. J., Hyder, E. B., & Genovese, C. R. (1999). Knowledge and the sequential processes of negotiation: A Markov chain analysis of response-in-kind. *Journal of Experimental Social Psychology, 35,* 366–393.

Weisband, S. P. (1992). Group discussion and first advocacy effects in computer mediated and face-to-face decision making groups. *Organizational Behavior and Human Decision Processes, 53,* 352–380.

Weldon, E., & Weingart, L. R. (1993). Group goals and group performance. *British Journal of Social Psychology, 32,* 307–334.

Wheelan, S. A. (1990). *Facilitating training groups: A guide to leadership and verbal intervention skills.* New York: Praeger.

Wheelan, S. (1994). *Group processes: A developmental perspective.* Boston: Allyn & Bacon.

Wheelan, S. (1996). An initial exploration of the relevance of complexity theory to group research and practice. *Systems Practice, 9*(1), 49–70.

Wheelan, S., & Kaeser, R. M. (1997). The influence of task type and designated leaders on developmental patterns in groups. *Small Group Research, 28*(1), 94–121.

Wheelan, S., & McKeage, R. (1993). Developmental patterns in small and large groups. *Small Group Research, 24,* 60–83.

Wheelan, S., Murphy, D., Tsumura, E., & Fried Kline, S. (1998). Member perceptions of internal group dynamics and productivity. *Small Group Research, 29,* 371–393.

Wheelan, S., Verdi, A. F., & McKeage, R. (1994*). The group development observation system: Origins and applications.* Philadelphia: GDQ Associates.

Wittenbaum, G. M., & Stasser, G. (1996). Management of information in small groups. In J. L. Nye & A. M. Brower (Eds.), *What's social about social cognition?*

Social cognition research in small groups (pp. 3–28). Thousand Oaks, CA: Sage.

Worchel, S. (1994). You can go home again: Returning group research to the group context with an eye on developmental issues. *Small Group Research, 25,* 205–223.

Worchel, S., Coutant-Sassic, D., & Grossman, M. (1992). A developmental approach to group dynamics: A model and illustrative research. In S. Worchel, W. Wood, & J. A. Simpson (Eds.), *Group process and productivity.* Newbury Park, CA: Sage.

Worchel, S., Coutant-Sassic, D., & Wong, F. (1993). Toward a more balanced view of conflict: There is a positive side. In S. Worchel & J. A. Simplson (Eds.), *Conflict between people and groups.* Chicago: Nelson-Hall.

Zaheer, S., Albert, S., & Zaheer, A. (1999). Time scales and organizational theory. *Academy of Management Review, 24*(4), 725–741.

10

Small Groups From an Evolutionary Perspective

Linnda Caporael, David Sloan Wilson,
Charlotte Hemelrijk, and Kennon M. Sheldon

Abstract

This chapter discusses evolutionary approaches to small group research. It defines basic assumptions of the evolutionary perspective and then demarcates major debates within evolutionary theory relevant to the social scientific study of groups. Four distinct evolutionary perspectives on groups are defined and compared. Results of evolutionary research regarding group composition, typical group sizes, group interaction, outcomes, and development and change in groups are reviewed. We conclude with a discussion of strengths and weaknesses of the perspective and directions that future research may take.

In research on evolution, the small group is something of an anomaly, located somewhere between genes and cultures. Our species has lived in groups throughout its existence and is descended from a long line of primate species that also lived in groups. Until very recently (in evolutionary terms), we lived in small groups that are somewhat approximated by hunter-gatherer societies (Boehm, 2000; Kelly, 1995). The advent of agriculture resulted in a transformation of human society over a period of only a few thousand years (Diamond, 1997). Because genetic evolution is a relatively slow process, in some respects, we are adapted to a physical and social environment with origins in the past. However, individual learning and cultural change can themselves be described as evolutionary processes, resulting in rapid adaptation to modern environments. Studying human groups from an evolutionary perspective need not be confined to genetic evolution (Boyd & Richerson, 1985; Dunbar, Knight, & Power, 1999; Durham, 1991).

Although there are some common themes, the study of groups from an evolutionary viewpoint is best classified as an emerging perspective. Some evolutionists question whether groups are real, whereas others see groups as central to understanding humanity and have attempted to derive theories of how groups evolved and the impact of groups on evolution. Although to one outside the field evolution may seem a cut and dried theory, the study of evolution is in fact full of debate and has many different positions. Evolutionary thought relevant to groups is so broad and diverse that it cannot be summarized in a short article. This chapter will attempt to give readers an introduction to key positions and debates and to some conclusions drawn in this emerging research area. In writing this chapter, we have chosen to elide many differences among the authors and encourage readers to seek out the references we cite to understand the particularities and differences among us.

In the next section, we will discuss some basic assumptions of evolutionary thought and debates relevant to the evolutionary view of groups. Following this, we will distinguish four alternative evolutionary viewpoints that differ in terms of their definition of group, the degree of importance they accord to groups in the evolutionary process, and the specific aspects of groups they focus on. See Table 10.1. Following this, we will summarize representative findings related to those of the seven questions guiding this book that evolutionary research has addressed.

Central Issues in Evolutionary Thought on Groups

The defining construct of evolutionary approaches is natural selection through variation, selection, and retention (for an accessible overview of evolutionary theory, including a brief discussion of evolutionary psychology, see Sterelny & Griffiths, 1999). Heritable variations serve as the raw material for evolution. Generally, variation is assumed to be random. Selection refers to the idea that those variations best adapted to their environment are more likely to survive, reproduce, and pass on their genes to future generations. Retention indicates that there must be a mechanism for preserving and

Table 10.1   The Evolutionary Perspective

Definition of perspective	The evolutionary perspective does not constitute a single literature. There are diverse interpretations of Darwinism.

Key assumptions	• Adaptation (selection, variation, retention)
	• Two main approaches in human evolutionary theory:
	    Historical: Adaptations to past circumstances produce psychological mechanisms for group living
	    Functional: Groups are a by-product of individual behaviors to maximize reproductive potential

Types of groups	• Face-to-face groups • Nested hierarchy of groups: dyad, gossip group, primary network, intermediate group, tribe, societies
Key theories	• Machiavellian intelligence (gene's eye view) • Group selection • Coevolutionary theories • Niche construction
Dominant research methodologies	• Animal research (experimental and observational) • Conceptual analysis (philosophy of biology) • Historical/consilient research on human activities (war, religion) • Computer simulation and games
Strengths	• Potential to provide foundational principles on group structure • Potential to organize a large body of diverse findings about groups and provide novel hypotheses • New lens for understanding humans as fundamentally social beings
Weaknesses	• Very new area; widespread lack of integration across evolutionary perspectives, disciplines, vocabularies, acceptable research methods • Highly interactive with culture via high media profile and sociopolitical implications • Difficulty incorporating existing paleoanthropological evidence and lack of evidence about behavior in the past leads to multiple conceptual, theoretical, and methodological problems, including that the evolutionary past is not relevant

passing on variations, that is, the gene. However, there are different schools of thought about what the proper unit of analysis is and how the evolutionary process occurs. We will discuss different positions advanced by evolutionary theorists and use them to lay the groundwork for understanding different approaches to understanding groups through an evolutionary lens (Hemelrijk, 2002a, 2002b).

Not surprisingly, Charles Darwin (1859/1981) was the first to write about how groups might have shaped human cognitive and social behavior. According to him, those tribes with the most sagacious of men would make the best tools, overcome their enemies, and have the most children, would increase in number and replace other less sagacious tribes. The moral faculties were more troublesome for this view. Sympathetic and benevolent parents, those willing to sacrifice their lives rather than betray their comrades, were less likely to leave offspring than were those less eager to enter the fray. But Darwin overcame this difficulty by positing the "love of praise" and "the dread of blame" as the stimulus to the social virtues.

> A man who was not impelled by any deep, instinctive feeling, to sacrifice his life for the good of others, yet was roused to such actions by a sense of glory, would by his example excite the same wish for glory in other men, and would strengthen by exercise the noble feeling of admiration. He might thus do far more good to his tribe than by begetting offspring with a tendency to inherit his own high character. (p. 165)

Over generations, various factors would interact, resulting in the evolution of our "moral faculties." These would not give even a slight advantage to the individual man in begetting children. However, a tribe possessing men with high degrees of patriotism, obedience, courage, and sympathy; ready to sacrifice themselves for the common good, "would be victorious over most other tribes; and this would be natural selection" (p. 166).

Fast-forward 100 years. Wynne-Edwards (1962) argued that individuals would curb their own reproduction to maintain stable population levels, the result of an evolutionary process he called group selection. A "strong" version of group selection holds that individual interests are subordinate to the collective interests of the group. Natural selection results from selection between groups rather than of individuals.

Williams (1966), however, argued that most apparent instances of group selection could be explained more parsimoniously in terms of benefit to the gene, meaning that more copies of the individual's genes would be represented in succeeding generations. According to Williams, selection at the "genic level" could readily explain altruism between relatives because helping one's kin could mean that genes common to related individuals would benefit. Williams did admit, however, that human altruism might be an exception and speculated how it could evolve by group selection. Like Darwin, he agreed that there could be a "competition for goodwill" among unrelated individuals, and he imagined a primitive society where a good reputation based on altruism would pay off in terms of reciprocal exchanges, a theory later elaborated by Trivers (1971) as reciprocal altruism. Williams, however, concluded that apparent adaptations for group benefit would ultimately occur through the differential survival of individuals and would be designed for the perpetuation of the genes of the donor.

As the genes were the ultimate beneficiary, human altruism could not be considered an adaptation at the group level. By the 1970s, Williams's (1966) book became the standard account of neo-Darwinism, the claim that the genes were the only relevant level of analysis for understanding natural selection. This position is often called "the gene's eye view" or "the selfish gene" perspective.

The contrasting positions of Wynne-Edwards and Williams mark a debate important to evolutionary theories of groups. Most evolutionarily oriented psychologists follow Williams (1966) in rejecting group selection as an important force (Buss, 1999; Gaulin & McBurney, 2000), and groups are not even indexed in Barkow, Cosmides and Tooby's (1992) well-known book, *The Adapted Mind*. Donald Campbell (1975, 1982, 1983; 1990b; Campbell & Gatewood, 1994) was a notable exception. He wrote on the conflict between individual and group interests, clique selfishness undermining superordinate collective goals, and groups as "vehicles" for shared knowledge, among many other evolutionary topics (Caporael, 2001b). Early on, Campbell believed that humans had innate altruistic motives (Campbell, 1965), but he later recanted this view. Convinced that the gene's eye view supported the view of a basically selfish human nature, he argued that such self-interest was held in check by cultural norms that could evolve through cultural group selection (Campbell, 1975).

Wilson (Sober & Wilson, 1998; Wilson, 1975, 1983; Wilson & Sober, 1994) made the case that genes for altruism could increase in frequency as a result of selection at higher levels of organization, such as the group. Objections to the gene as the sole unit of selection grew out of the recognition that multilevel selection, which included group selection, was necessary for understanding the hierarchical and complex nature of biological phenomena (Buss, 1987; Maynard Smith & Szathmary, 1985). Wilson observed that self-sacrificial altruists will reproduce less than selfish egoists if the entire population is considered a single group. However, if the population is composed of subgroups with varying frequencies of altruists and egoists, and if groups with more altruists outreproduce groups with more egoists, then even if the frequency of altruists relative to egoists within the group declines, the frequency of altruists in the whole population can increase. Other evolutionists also opposed the view that genes were the only level of selection for various reasons (Eldredge, 1985; Lickliter & Honeycutt, 2003).

The contrast between individual and multilevel selection views is complicated by the fact that there is considerable variability in the basic units of evolution. Units in different evolutionary theories include genes, organisms, groups, entities in general, organisms-in-settings, and by-products of self-organizing systems. Even the term *gene*, long regarded as a basic unit, is no longer a definitive construct: Dennett (1995) advises his readers to think of "virtual genes" if they feel squeamish about genetic determinism. That is, the basis of heritability may be more complex than bits of genetic code.

Frequently, the choice of a unit of selection corresponds to a particular theoretical position. The gene's eye view points to genes (and sometimes individuals) as the unit of selection (Barkow et al., 1992; Buss, 1999). Groups plus other entities are associated with multilevel selection theories such as that described by Wilson and Sober (1994) and coevolutionary theories (Boyd & Richerson, 1985). Organisms-in-setting is a sign of constructionist approaches, which foreground the interactions of an organism and its immediate context as the unit of selection (Levins & Lewontin, 1985; Oyama, 1985). Systems and self-organizing approaches may combine all of the above units (Caporael & Baron, 1997; Hemelrijk, 2002a).

Theories may also vary with respect to how the concept of adaptation is used. Pan-adaptation is the assumption that a complex design results from natural selection. This is the widespread assumption in animal research, and there are advocates among human evolutionary theorists, as well (Barkow, 1989). In contrast, researchers on self-organizing systems posit that apparently complex social behavior may emerge interactively with only the simplest of rules built into an agent. Understanding how natural selection may operate on the products of such systems is one of the goals of this line of research (Hemelrijk, 1997; Latane & L'Herrou, 1996), which combines elements of adaptationist and emergent positions. These evolutionary approaches typically involve simulated agents (Hemelrijk, 1997) or situated robotics (Hendriks-Jansen, 1996).

Social Evolutionary Perspectives on Groups

Natural selection is a process that adapts organisms to their environments. For group living to evolve, the advantages would have to outweigh the disadvantages. Basically, individuals who grouped would have more offspring compared to individuals who lived solitary lives. Group living can be a hazardous to an animal's health. Parasites and disease spread more easily in groups than among solitary critters. Competition for mates and resources can lead to injury and death. Plus, there is always the problem of free riders. Nevertheless, often, it is adaptive to live in groups, and an enormous diversity of groupings has evolved across the animal kingdom (Boinski & Garber, 2000). Some creatures are highly organized to function adaptively at the group level. Others are marked by conflicts of interest among their members. Evolutionary biologists have made considerable progress understanding the nature of animal groups. Almost all the same principles can be used to understand the nature of human groups, although there are disagreements. Some researchers see solitary living as a primal state and grouping as a deviation that requires explanation (Dunbar, 1989); others ask if groups are "real" rather than a perceptual/linguistic illusion (Palmer, Fredrickson, & Tilley, 1997); and still others insist that some types of group living—and humans are among these—cannot be derived from solitary states (Caporael, Dawes, Orbell, & van de Kraght, 1989). Social evolutionary perspectives on groups can be categorized into four approaches emphasizing the different ways in which the group construct is used. The categorization, however, is a matter of convenience. Grouping in nature is multidimensional; it changes over time and over life span, and as a function of resources and of reproductive states (Avital & Jablonka, 2000; Sussman & Chapman, 2004).

Groups as Aggregates

Quite often, sociality may consist of little more than a group of opportunistic and individualistic cooperators (Norris & Schilt, 1988; Williams, 1966). A school of fish or a herd of fleet deer are aggregate groups. There may be safety in numbers, and the risks of predation might be spread out among a group of animals. As soon as the risks are reduced, the aggregate group breaks up. Some schools break up under the cover of darkness. African antelopes group when they live in the open, and they live solitary lives in forests where hiding is easier. Individuals that form opportunistic aggregates are adaptively specialized for knowing when to group and when to be solitary.

Groups are composed of interacting genetic competitors or rationally self-interested individuals. These approaches are common in evolutionary economics and evolutionary game theory, including studies modeling cooperation and competition (Axelrod, 1984, 1997; Gintis, 2000). Groups are viewed as aggregates of individuals (or dyads), with the assumption that the processes taking place in dyadic interaction scale up to large-group interaction. For example, cooperation in tit-for-tat games, which assume two players, is arguably a result of reciprocating behavioral control or feedback. A noncooperator on one round may be punished by her partner on the next when he fails to cooperate himself. Such control would be impossible in a large n-person game because the beneficiaries of cooperating activities may be spread out (giving rise to free riders).

"Players" in groups may also be categorized. In game theory, metaphors of "hawks" and "doves" may be used to describe the change in relative frequency of types in a structured game. In traditional evolutionary psychology (Buss, 1999; Tooby & Cosmides, 1992), groups may be based on gender or kinship. Many evolutionary researchers doubt that groups exist at all, arguing that their supposed entitativity is an artifact of human abilities to categorize (Palmer et al., 1997).

Cultural Evolution and Large-Scale Groups

Another approach incorporates culture as a crucial dimension for explaining human social behavior. The focus of interest is on human diversity as a function of the coevolution of both genetic and cultural influences. Durham (1976), for example, studied the distribution of adult lactose tolerance/intolerance (a biological trait) related to relying on milk and the use of milk products as a major source of nutrition (a cultural practice). The correspondence between long-term herding cultures and the ability to digest milk sugars illustrates the reciprocal relations between culture and genes. Such gene-culture coevolutionary theories do refer to subgroupings within a culture and to scenarios of prehistoric groups, but the focus is the application of evolutionary theory to explain within and between variations in societies.

Boyd and Richerson (1985) are well-known for elaborating gene-culture coevolutionary theories. In recent work, they argue that modern humans live in large-scale groups because of group selection on cultural variation, specifically, different institutional mechanisms that mimic small group living (Richerson & Boyd, 1999).

Self-Organizing Systems Approaches

There are a variety of systems approaches in evolutionary theorizing, all sharing an interest in self-organization and emergent interaction. In contrast to adaptationist approaches, which assume complex behavior must be influenced by genes inside the organism, self-organizing systems approaches start with computer models of agents (organisms) that are controlled by a few simple behavioral rules and obtain knowledge of their nearby environment only—in contrast to attaining global knowledge by individuals, as is assumed in optimality models. The challenge is to build "bottom up" models in which complex behavior emerges from simple organisms. The collection of agents themselves is "the group." Although the agents interact with their environment and other agents, their behavior is studied in the same way as in ethology. Results show that in these models, very simple agents generate complex social structures and that the same set of rules may lead to different patterns, depending on the past experience of different individuals, the demography of the population, or the distribution of food. There are few studies of the effects of self-organization in humans so far, but there are many such studies of insects and artificial systems (see Hemelrijk, 2002b, for a review).

Systems approaches challenge the implicitly accepted idea of "evolved complex mechanisms" with a parsimonious perspective that may turn out to be more appropriate for the human behavioral sciences. Instead of genes carrying the burden of explanation for complex behavior, simple behavioral rules or forms may evolve, with complex behavior and structure emerging as a product of interaction between the organism and the local environment. Such interactive emergence can be observed in artificial systems such as situated robotics (Hendriks-Jansen, 1996) and in real life (Thelen & Smith, 1994).

Small Group Models

Most explanations for the evolution of sociality have to do with defense from predators or cooperative foraging. But there can be other advantages to group living (Avital & Jablonka, 2000). Group members may learn vicariously about features of the local habitat such as locations for food. Slow-growing offspring may have special tutors and guards. Food may be regurgitated and shared. Some species even learn behavioral traditions exploiting novel resources. A common bird in Britain, the great tit, is famous for having learned to open the lids on milk bottles (when they were commonly delivered to people's front doors), a behavior that spread throughout the country.

There are other kinds of groups that cannot break up. The individuals that form such groups *must* be part of a group in order to reproduce and for the young to survive to reproductive age and start the cycle again. These groups are *obligately social* groups. They organize individual efforts and communication within the group, and they have tasks and roles for group members, as well as definable group boundaries (Brewer, 1997). In extreme cases such as wolf packs, naked mole rats, and meerkats (a social mongoose), only a breeding couple reproduce. Other group members contribute to the survival of the offspring.

In the human case, any work appealing to hunter-gatherer groups and ancestral environments could be said to have small groups as the basis of a model of human groups. However, surprisingly few models focus explicitly on the structural features of small groups and their connection to the evolution of social behavior or their relevance for large-scale groups.

The best known is Dunbar's (1993) work on the coevolution of language, neocortical size, and group size (summarized later). Boehm (2000) is also concerned with small groups; his interest in them is as the source of egalitarianism. Caporael (1997) problematizes the small group, theorizing how groups exist and coordinate behavior at all. Evolutionary perspectives on small groups also appear in management science. Campbell (1974, 1990a, 1994) influenced this work, which uses evolution either as a metaphor for institutional change or as an explanation for small group behavior (Baum & McKelvey, 1999).

The distinctions among these four positions are somewhat arbitrary and many studies could be classified into more than one category. However, they suggest the considerable diversity in disciplines and approaches to small groups from an evolutionary perspective, from claims that groups are not real to claims that individuals may be components of group "super-organisms." The following section summarizes evolutionary studies that address some of the seven basic questions that illustrate principles and thinking from diverse perspectives. In this section, we include relevant examples from studies of both human and nonhuman species. Comparisons across species, a tradition that was more common during past decades of psychological research than at present, can help convey the continuity and the complexity of evolutionary processes and outcomes. It might seem that by focusing on ancient environments, long-term evolution, and other species, the evolutionary perspective is only marginally relevant to the study of modern human groups. However, evolutionary thinking looks to the long term, and we believe the ensuing discussion will contribute to the same range of subjects and issues addressed by other perspectives on groups in the social sciences.

Results of Evolutionary Research on Small Groups

Evolutionary approaches to groups have not addressed all seven questions posed in this volume evenly. Evolutionary research naturally tends to emphasize questions related to the nature of individuals and their interrelationships

Table 10.2 Key Findings of Evolutionary Perspective Research

Group composition	• Kin and unrelated reciprocating individuals in face-to-face groups • Group size • Artificial agents • Nonhuman animals
Group structure	• Aggregates of minimally interacting actors or agents • Face-to-face groups in core configurations • Emergent group structures (e.g., dominance hierarchies) • Enormous between-species variability in group structures
Group projects	• Interface with habitat • Maximizing reproductive success
Interaction	• Conflict and cooperation • Clique selfishness • Imitation, social learning, and social control
Group action/outcomes	• Reproduction and survival to reproductive age • Coordination of activity and information transfer • Norms
Change over time	• Natural selection (variation, retention, selection) • Ontogeny • Cultural transmission and evolution
Ecology	• Groups serve as interface between individual and habitat • Niche construction (Organisms create and are shaped by niches resulting from organismic activity.) • Culture

in groups; how typical groups such as families, clans, and tribes influenced human evolution; the role of evolution in the creation of norms; the evolution of prosocial behavior and conflict; and groups as environments for individual evolution. See Table 10.2 for a summary of findings relevant to the seven questions.

Group Composition

Evolutionary studies have emphasized kinship, family role, and gender and their demographic distributions within groups as key variables affecting group interaction and thereby influencing adaptation and selection processes. Group size has also been a central object of interest.

In much evolutionary research, groups are taken for granted as a background against which social exchange, alliances, competition, mating, and other activities are played out. In traditional evolutionary psychology, environmental considerations such as the structure of relationships become important insofar as they identify adaptive problems and, therefore, hypotheses about cognitive design. This means that group attributes, specifically group attributes in the ancestral environment where human cognitive mechanisms evolved, are characteristically treated as independent variables, whereas cognitive design and associated characteristics are the dependent variables.

In the gene's eye view of evolution, performance is associated with reproduction, and interaction is frequently discussed in terms of altruism as opposed to self-interest. Kinship is a key factor of group composition in traditional evolutionary psychology. In general, groups pose different adaptive problems and opportunities for their individual members. Kin-based groups provide better opportunities for cooperative activities than do groups of unrelated individuals because individuals share, on average, copies of genes. Hence, human psychology is theoretically adapted to behave differently in different group contexts. We would expect distinct mechanisms for dealing with kin (and, indeed, for different kinds of kin), with mixed-sex groups, with all-male groups, and so forth. Geary (1998) provides an overall gene's-eye-view model of the mind in terms of mechanisms responsive to group categories. Considering the different kinds of individuals people might have encountered in the "environment of evolutionary adaptedness" (the environment in which selection for an adaptive trait actually occurred) can offer a good clue toward considering adaptive design. An important part of the gene's-eye view is that evolved psychology should reflect all and only those collections of individuals that recurred over evolutionary time. For example, adaptations for parental investment indicate that mothers (and fathers) and their offspring were together during long periods of their lives. Similarly, because the costs of assuming strangers are friendly when in fact they are hostile are likely to be far greater than the benefits lost from assuming strangers are unfriendly when they are not, we should expect particular caution with respect to strangers—in its extreme form, xenophobia.

Gender and age figure prominently in almost all evolutionary approaches, although with the exception of warfare (discussed later), there are few theories relevant to groups where gender and age are considered as demographic factors. In a study of primates by Hemelrijk and Luteijn (1998), the quality of social relationships was found to depend on the demographic distribution of males and females. It appears that female relationships are better (as measured by the degree of reciprocation of grooming among females) when there are relatively more males present among the adult members of the group. Females reciprocate grooming in proportion to the relative number of males that are present per female in the group. Reciprocation among females is weaker when there are fewer males per female. This is explained as a consequence of the intensity of competition among females for access to males. This competition is stronger if there are fewer males per female in a group, and in such a case, the quality of social relationships among females decreases.

The sex ratio of groups of primates, however, does not influence female relationships in groups of all species. It only influences female relationships in species in which females remain resident for the rest of their lives in their natal group. It does not hold for other species in which females migrate once they have become adult. This is understandable because in such female-transfer groups, instead of competing for access to males among themselves, females have the alternative option of simply finding males elsewhere.

Demography may influence the dominance structure of a group, particularly how youngsters may acquire high social rank or dominance. Datta (1992) developed a model showing that in fast-growing populations of primates (such as macaques), newborn female infants are protected by all family members against attacks by anyone (also other family members). Therefore, female infants have a higher dominance position than older sisters. In slowly growing populations, however, such protection is lacking due to the absence of sisters, and therefore, each individual fights for itself, and dominance positions are acquired in accordance with the fighting abilities of individual females.

Group size is another composition variable that has received much attention in evolutionary research. Group size is much easier to study in smaller, short-lived organisms than in primates, and research suggests size is implicated in fairly complex relationships. In ants, group size determines whether one or more of equidistant food sources of equal quality are exploited. If the group size is large, the colony exploits a single food source rather than many (Nicolis & Deneubourg, 1999), whereas small groups tend to exploit several food sources equally. The cause of this is that in large groups, the pheromonal reinforcement of the marking of a trail to a specific food source is much stronger than in small groups. This leads to greater uniformity in food exploitation.

In view of the common assumption among evolutionary researchers that humans have spent much of their evolutionary history in hunter-gatherer groups, it is somewhat surprising that there are not more theories specifically concerned with group size. Dyads are easily the most commonly studied interaction groups, deriving from work in evolutionary game theory (Lewontin, 1961; Trivers, 1971). Nevertheless, an important outcome of the game theory work is that humans are found to be far more cooperative than traditional notions of rational self-interest or selfish genes would suggest (Gintis, 2000). Social psychological research suggests that the level of analysis may be crucial for predicting competition. Insko and his colleagues show that groups are more competitive than individuals and that intergroup competition is stronger than intragroup competition (Wildschut, Pinter, Vevea, Insko, & Schopler, 2003).

Although most theories of groups can be classified as economic models of grouping, two similar theories are more specifically concerned with group structure. Dunbar (1993) and Caporael (1995, 1997) independently advanced models of typical group sizes that have evolved in human society. Dunbar identifies four group sizes that seem to represent typical groupings: gossip groups comprising two to four individuals, primary networks made up of bands of 30 to 50 individuals, intermediate groups of 100 to 200 individuals (corresponding to a village or lineage), and tribes of 500 to 2,500 individuals (the latter may be influenced by colonialism). Dunbar shows a correlation between mean group size and relative neocortical volume for several nonhuman primate species and argues that the same regression function underestimates human neocortical size, indicating that neocortical size is larger than would be expected on the basis of primate group size. In his view, gossip groups represent a shift in the evolution of humans from servicing social relationships with grooming, as is common in primates, to servicing them with useful information about the behavior of others in the groups.

Caporael (1995, 1997) proposes a model of face-to-face group structure with core subgroup configurations based on considerations of group size and modal tasks. Subgroup size and task requirements are used to jointly specify dominant forms of group interaction. For example, a dyad is a core configuration with a size of two and modal tasks that include interaction with an infant. A core configuration is an environment where certain capacities, such as finely tuned microcoordination (as used in interactional synchrony), can evolve. The other configurations are teams, demes, and macrodemes, analogous to the foraging parties, bands, and macrobands in anthropology. The basic hypothesis is that aspects of mental systems should correspond to features of modal tasks characteristic to configurations, which in turn are grounded in morphology and ecology. Caporael suggests that the core configuration model can explain previously unrelated findings in social psychology such as movement synchronies, distributed cognition, and social identity.

Group Structure

Evolutionary research has also addressed the issue of how group structures, particularly norms, develop and affect the evolutionary process.

One common way of viewing group structure from an evolutionary perspective is at the population level. This is done by considering the initial frequency distribution of the alternative genes in the population and modeling change over time in the distribution based on selection coefficients favoring one over the other. The genes are in individuals in a group, and the selection coefficients may or may not include the effects of interaction among individuals. These processes are also modeled using evolutionary games as an analogy to the analysis of population structure (both begin with binary processes as in coin flips). The games typically consist of two strategies, such as hawk and dove, and a payoff matrix motivates the interactions of the actors playing the strategies. Such games may highlight frequency-dependent selection, which is an effect of the group on the individual and arguably a type of group selection (Sober, 1984). Trivers' (1971) well-known work on the evolution of reciprocal altruism is based on the Prisoner's Dilemma. The matrix structure is such that it can promote cooperation, given low costs for helping, the ability to remember the source of aid, and future opportunities for reciprocation.

In gene-culture evolution theories, there may be little discussion of goal-oriented groups, but there are certainly implicit assumptions. For example, the imitation of practices and values is important in cultural evolution (Boyd & Richerson, 1985; Durham, 1991). Imitation is neither random nor passive. Rather various evolved decision rules, such as "copy the successful" or "copy the prestigious," bias what cultural variants are imitated and become more frequent in the culture. Norms and values evolve in this fashion.

Humans far surpass other animals in their use of culture and norms to guide behavior. According to Boehm (2000), human social groups are remarkable for the balance of power among their individual members, a balance that is achieved by effective coalitions against would-be alpha males. Such coalitions also occur among chimpanzees and baboons. The result is a form of guarded egalitarianism in which self-serving behaviors of all sorts are largely suppressed and the group behaves largely as a coordinated unit. If this scenario is correct, the ability to establish and enforce norms is part of a continuum between humans and nonhuman primates. One crucial difference between humans and nonhuman primates is that human cultural change is cumulative, one innovation providing the basis for subsequent innovations, which has not been observed in any other species (Tomasello, 1999). It is, therefore, a matter of contention whether the major features of human cultures and norms can still be explained within the framework of a gene-based version of the evolutionary approach.

The concept of human groups as moral communities (where morality is defined as "conformance to the rules of right conduct") has important implications for cultural transmission (Wilson, 2002). Behavioral variation can exist both between individuals within social groups and between social groups in a larger population. Differences between groups are often difficult to achieve and maintain when behaviors are coded directly by genes. However, cultural mechanisms reinforced by norms can cause even large groups to become behaviorally different from each other, and the same mechanisms maintain the differences despite the movement of individuals among groups (who abandon the customs of the old group and acquire the customs of the new group). Because natural selection is based on behavioral variation regardless of whether it is genetic or cultural in origin, norms and culturally acquired traits can result in forms of evolutionary change that could never happen by genetic evolution alone. Once again, these possibilities are best explored by thinking of culture and norms in conjunction with biological evolution rather than as a mysterious and ill-defined alternative (Boyd & Richerson, 1985; Wilson, 2002). So, for example, the tendencies to form and follow norms may be thought of as coevolutionary adaptations that contribute to complex cultural organizations and differentiations.

The study of culture and norms from an evolutionary perspective is relevant not only to the "big picture" of human evolution but also to the dynamics of social groups in everyday life. Social identity theory shows how easily people think of themselves as members of groups, especially in opposition to other groups (Abrams & Hogg, 1999). Social dilemma experiments demonstrate the fragility of cooperation in the absence of punishment but the ease with which it is achieved when the opportunity for punishment is allowed (e.g., Ostrom, Gardner, & Walker, 1994). A book aptly entitled *Order Without Law* (Ellickson, 1991) shows how people in small groups spontaneously establish, enforce, and largely abide by social norms in the absence of a formal legal system. Toqueville (1835/1990), the French social theorist who observed American democracy with such insight over a century ago, was equally perceptive about small-scale social groups in general when he said that "the village or township is the only association which is so perfectly natural that, wherever a number of men are collected, it seems to constitute itself" (p. 60). There is great opportunity for a synthesis between evolutionary biology and other perspectives in the social sciences to explain the mechanisms that people employ so naturally when they form into groups.

Hierarchical structure is another recurrent theme in the evolutionary perspective on groups. Dunbar (1993, 1996) and Caporael (1995, 1997) propose that groups are structured as a nested hierarchy of subgroups. Combining their two schemes, the dyad is nested within gossip groups, which are nested within primary networks, which are nested within intermediate groups, which are nested within tribes. Baum and Rao (2004) advance a theory of organization-environment coevolution as a nested hierarchy of evolutionary processes. Boyd and Richerson (1985) adopt a similar hierarchical structure in their argument that complex societies have a segmentary hierarchy. Although such hierarchies may have been functional in earlier phases of prehistory, they lead to inefficiencies in complex societies where subgroups subvert larger group goals, and changes of command are necessarily remote and lack the personal charisma of a leader.

Group Interaction

Humans engage in a number of group activities, including warfare and intergroup conflict; a range of cooperative activities, including hunting and mutual defense; and cooperative child-rearing, including care from distantly related or even unrelated group members.

Research on interaction such as conflict and prosocial behavior makes up a large part of the research involving evolutionary perspectives on social behavior. Most often, the group context is taken for granted, and theorizing is applied to "groups in general," which could include very large groups or populations. Nevertheless, interaction processes for groups in general must be based on cognitive mechanisms evolved and developed in small group contexts and then extended to larger groups. Research on prosocial behavior illustrates this type of work.

Prosocial behavior is a complex construct. At the behavioral level, this includes helping others in myriad ways, sometimes at a cost to oneself. At the psychological level, it includes wanting to help others as an end in itself, even the abandonment of self-will encouraged by many religions (Batson, 1991; Sober & Wilson, 1998; Wilson, 2002). At the social-structural level, it includes social systems that constrain people to behave prosocially whether they want to or not. For example, according to Rawls (1971), a just society is one that a person would design for him- or herself, subject to the constraint that the designer will be placed randomly within it. Such a society requires checks and balances to withstand the inevitable presence of antisocial behavior, which is adaptive to the individual in some contexts.

To pick a single example, males of many species have evolved to kill infants that are not their own offspring, which makes the mothers of the infants available for mating (Van Schaik & Janson, 2000). Males and females of the same species have evolved to protect their offspring, but they are not always successful. This is a clear example of how evolution can lead to conflicts of interest, behaviors that are bad for the group, and even individuals who act prosocially in some contexts (males protecting their own young) and antisocially in others (the same males attempting to kill the young of others).

All of these elements of prosociality can plausibly evolve through genetic and cultural evolution. In general, prosociality evolves when prosocial individuals manage to confine their interactions to each other, either avoiding antisocial individuals or withholding benefits from those who cannot be avoided. This general condition can be satisfied by many mechanisms that operate more or less strongly across the animal kingdom. Genetic relatedness constitutes one important mechanism. If helping has a genetic basis, then a genetic relative of a helper is also likely to be a helper, compared to an individual chosen at random from the population. Conversely, a genetic relative of a nonhelper is also more likely than chance to be a nonhelper. When relatives interact with each other, prosocial individuals become partially segregated from antisocial individuals automatically. This reasoning leads to a theory of nepotism (prosocial behaviors directed toward genetic relatives) that applies to humans and other species alike (Hamilton, 1964, 1975).

Other mechanisms allow tendencies toward prosocial behaviors to evolve among genetically unrelated individuals. If unrelated individuals learn each other's propensity to help, the helpers can form friendships with each other and force the nonhelpers to live a solitary existence or to interact with each other by default (Wilson & Dugatkin, 1997). If nonhelpers cannot be avoided, then conditional behavioral strategies can evolve that direct helpfulness toward helpers and nonhelpfulness toward nonhelpers (Axelrod, 1984; Dugatkin, 1997). Some of these mechanisms require a degree of cognitive sophistication (e.g., the ability to remember individuals and their past interactions), which may explain why our own species employs them so successfully.

Efforts to foster prosociality are more likely to succeed by providing the conditions that make prosocial behavior successful than by divorcing it from an evolutionary context. One example will illustrate how these ideas can be used to guide social science research on small human groups. In a recent study of American college students (Sheldon, Sheldon, & Osbaldiston, 2000), newly arrived freshmen were given a questionnaire measuring their degree of helpfulness. Primary participants were asked to select three friends or acquaintances (secondary participants) to fill out the questionnaire, with the understanding that there was also a game embedded in the questionnaire, a game with prizes. In the questionnaire, all participants completed the values measure (which yielded a significant intraclass correlation—*assortation* on the basis of values), and all made bids in 5 one-shot social dilemma games (i.e., with no feedback regarding the choices of other group members).

Participants could win prizes either by choosing to increase their individual point score (defect) or by increasing the group point score (cooperate). Game scores were then computed for each person, with reference to the participant's associated group members' bids. Although those with more prosocial values lost points within their groups, this disadvantage was mitigated by the fact that their groups as a whole were more cooperative: Those within more prosocial groups tended to receive higher individual game scores than those in less prosocial groups. The net advantage of prosociality depends on the degree to which prosocial individuals can recognize each other and form cooperating groups. The degree of assortation on shared values after a few months of college was weak—at 0.18—as far as correlations go, but it can be loosely compared to measures of shared genes (a proxy measure of shared values) where genealogical relatedness with first cousins is 0.25. Established human groups with a longer history of interactions presumably exhibit an even greater degree of assortation, although this needs to be tested. More research is needed to establish the psychological and social-structural mechanisms that increase prosocial assortation in an effort to make them work better.

The other side of the coin of prosocial behavior is conflict and warfare. For traditional evolutionary psychologists, outgroups are a continuing feature of the ancestral past and, consequently, some argue, so is warfare. In particular, the cognitive mechanisms that underlie intergroup conflict are believed to contribute to inclusive fitness. Warfare is in particular need of explanation because although between-group conflicts lead to within-group benefits, individuals' private interests are not self-evidently served by engaging in them. The costs of participating in intergroup conflict are high, possibly the cost of life, and a share of within-group benefits is likely to be less than the risks. Humans are unusual in that they form nonkin, male-based coalitions that engage in group-level cooperative activities. In particular, humans, across cultures and time, fight wars involving substantial numbers of individuals (Chagnon, 1988; Keegan, 1993; Tiger, 1969; Wrangham & Peterson, 1996).

A feature of warfare is that males involved in the conflict often rape females of the opposing group, to the winners' reproductive advantage. It has been argued that warfare is a result of adaptations specifically designed to facilitate ingroup cooperation for the purpose of outgroup exploitation. Tooby and Cosmides (1992) have argued that there is a domain-specific *coalitional psychology* specifically designed to solve the adaptive problems associated with intergroup conflict. A critical feature of this argument is that male reproductive success is limited by access to females. This model assumes that the reproductive benefits of warfare offset the potential costs, leading to a psychology of intergroup aggression. The widespread association between warfare and rape is consistent with this idea (Kurzban & Leary, 2001) as well as with other non-evolutionary explanations.

Two other important forms of group interaction are coordination and information transfer. Some animal studies are illustrative of evolutionary findings on these forms. Female guppies (*Poecilia reticulata*) have innate preferences for certain male characteristics such as body size and coloration. However, if a female guppy is allowed to observe another female choose one male over another, she develops a preference for the chosen male and others like him. This copying behavior is sufficiently strong to override the female's own innate preference. Remarkably, younger females copy older females but not the reverse (Dugatkin, 2000). Information transfer may also occur without direct imitation. For example, well-fed rats are neophobic; they resist foods with novel tastes and smells. Nutritionally stressed rats are neophilic; they sample novel foods and gradually incorporate those that do not make them sick into their diet. However, even a well-fed rat will be neophilic if it smells the novel food on the muzzle of another rat (discussed from an evolutionary perspective by Gaulin & McBurney, 2000). Rhesus monkeys sometimes give a call when they find food, bringing other monkeys to the scene. Hauser (1992) claims that if one monkey observes another fail to call after finding food, the former is likely to aggressively attack the latter. More generally, one reason that animals are highly sensitive to rewards and punishments in the laboratory is because in their natural competition, their fights among themselves can be seen as a kind of punishment, and incidental tolerance or grooming (in primates) can be seen as a possible form of reward.

The aforementioned examples clearly bear a resemblance to the acquisition and enforcement of behaviors that we associate with culture and norms in our own species, but they can be fully understood as biologically evolved adaptations. Other individuals are a rich source of information that can be obtained at lower cost than by interacting directly with the environment. Modifying the behavior of others with rewards and punishments can be highly advantageous. Thinking of culture and norms as coevolved adaptations in their own right, rather than alternatives to biology allows us to identify design features that might be missed otherwise. For example, accepting a new food only when smelled on the muzzle of another rat makes perfect sense from an adaptive standpoint. Similarly, in human societies, finding that another group member has already accepted a belief seems to heighten the attractiveness of that idea for those who newly encounter it.

Outcomes

By definition, successful group action results in survival and development to reproductive age of the individuals in the group. Shoaling, for example, leads to protection of group members (e.g., Landeau & Terborgh, 1986; Neil & Cullen, 1974). Among humans, if group action is unsuccessful, if there are too many unavoidable egoists, if wars and other intergroup conflicts are lost, then the minimal conditions for survival, reproduction, and development to reproductive age fail to be sustained, and the group and (less frequently) all its constituent members perish. The vulnerability of isolated humans or small groups of humans almost requires the concept of cultural group selection to explain why humans have been able to persist.

Time and Change

Time has several meanings for evolutionists—geological time, historical time, and lifetime. For the small hunter-gathering type groups of human prehistory, there would have been (ecologically dependent) minimal group size for the group to be self-sustaining. There would also have been maximum group size, constrained by ecological resources, and, according to several researchers, cognitive constraints as well (Caporael, 1995; Dunbar, 1993; Richerson & Boyd, 1999). The formation of subgroups in Caporael's (1997; Caporael & Baron, 1997) core configuration model is an ongoing dynamic process embedded in everyday task demands and activity. Groups form with respect to a task, dissolve, and reform for other tasks. Over evolutionary and cultural scales of time, groups form through the fissioning of large groups into smaller groups, with the development of the group being this activity sustained through generations.

From a historical perspective, the beginning of large-scale ultrasociality probably starts with settlements of related groups and the elaboration of nested hierarchy with cross-cutting group relationships. Urban life still has these elements, although overlaid with bureaucratic, efficiency-minded structures (that typically fail to achieve the promised efficiencies). Group fissioning still occurs in groups that have some freedom for self-organization such as scientists (Hull, 1988) and religious groups (Olsen, 1987).

Ecology and Environment

From a traditional evolutionary perspective, one meaning of ecology is a reference to the concept of the "environment of evolutionary adaptedness," that is, the ancestral past to which human minds are adapted. Some evolutionary psychologists believe that because humans now live in a world radically changed, human behavior may be maladapted. In contrast, human behavioral ecologists (Smith, Mulder, & Hill, 2001) argue that human behavior is adaptive (fitness maximizing) in current ecologies.

Another meaning of ecology refers to the role of the environment in natural selection. As we mentioned previously, self-organizing systems and natural selection via adaptation are sometimes thought of as opposing perspectives. However, self-organization and natural selection may work together, as illustrated in the following example (Hemelrijk, 2002b). In certain populations of a species, food scarcity may lead to an increase in the intensity of aggression via natural selection on the level of the individual because more intensely aggressive individuals are better able to grab the food. Environmental feedback from the spatial positioning of individuals of different dominance positions leads by self-organization to a steeper dominance hierarchy. This may be advantageous at a group level because during food scarcity, despotic societies may survive better than egalitarian ones because at least some females get enough food to reproduce, whereas in egalitarian societies, due to the equal division of food, none of the females can get sufficient food to reproduce. The difference between the two types of groups sets up the conditions for group selection. Under conditions of scarcity, egalitarian groups are likely to fail compared to despotic groups, where some limited reproduction continues to occur.

Conclusion and Future Directions

No single evolutionist would agree with our description and assessment of the evolutionary perspective on groups; indeed, none of the authors of this chapter are in complete agreement, either. Nevertheless, all are committed to the notion that an evolutionary approach merits more discussion and exploration. One strength of the evolutionary approach is in its potential to serve as a unifying theory and as a hybrid science across a wide variety of disciplines and methodological strategies (Caporael, 2001a). Where many other perspectives, such as the functional perspective, must qualify claims based on the type of task involved, the evolutionary perspective offers an explanation that is, for the most part, independent of the specific tasks a group performs. Because the evolutionary explanation is seated in human genetics and coevolved features of culture that are invariant across situations (e.g., prosociality), it offers explanations that are potentially more powerful than many other perspectives on groups.

The evolutionary perspective also shifts groups to front and center of understanding human psychology and social behavior generally (Caporael

2001a). Humans cannot survive and reproduce in the absence of a group. Human mental systems have evolved in groups, and we should expect that further research on groups from an evolutionary perspective will reveal a great deal about the mind that will be unexpected. At minimum, evolutionary theory can function as an imagination pump, back story, or standpoint on which to motivate middle-level theory and research. The last facility, however, also points to a weakness in evolutionary theorizing, and that is its well-known capacity to lend itself to evolutionary storytelling (Caporael, 1994; Kuper, 1988; Maynard Smith, 1987).

Issues to be resolved include questions about the grain of evolved traits. Should we expect them to be tightly integrated, large-grain capacities such as coalitional psychology, child rearing, or mate finding (Tooby & Cosmides, 1992)? Or are evolved traits largely small-grained, with components more like Lego blocks (Bechtel, 2003; Sher, 2003) that can be integrated through coevolutionary processes or by culture into many larger grain patterns, including a variety of group structures, functions, and activities? An analogy would be to several abilities (reading, bicycling, driving) that seem to be smaller-grained capacities available to be culturally reorganized. The issue of grain underlies questions about the flexibility of behavior in general.

Future directions for evolutionary perspectives on groups will have to include greater attention to the relations between theory and research. Basically, genetical evolutionary theory is one where the dependent variable—relative reproductive success of an alternative trait relative to other such traits—cannot be easily measured for human social traits. (The main independent variable—gene sequences for the trait in question—are not that measurable, either.) Although lab experiments and surveys done in the name of evolution have produced some interesting results, they may be more explicable in terms of media influence and current custom rather than Darwinism. A coevolutionary view of mind and culture removes issues of genetic determinism at the same time it muddies the waters. Little is known about how culture and biology come together to shape mental life or group life. Against these issues is the greater problem that the time scale of natural groups can be very long.

Overcoming these obstacles compels an interdisciplinary effort marked with substantial goodwill and intellectual generosity. Evolutionary approaches to groups will require new mixed-method, multimodel approaches (Tashakkori & Teddlie, 2003). These would include field observation, ethnography, computer simulations, focused experiments, and even robotic simulations. Despite the many challenges, however, the emerging evolutionary perspective promises a rich field of inquiry about fundamental properties of groups and mind.

References

Abrams, D., & Hogg, M. A. (1999). *Social identity and social cognition.* Malden, MA: Blackwell.

Avital, E., & Jablonka, E. (2000). *Animal traditions: Behavioural inheritance in evolution.* New York: Cambridge University Press.

Axelrod, R. (1984). *The evolution of cooperation.* New York: Basic Books.

Axelrod, R. (1997). *The complexity of cooperation: Agent-based models of competition and collaboration.* Princeton, NJ: Princeton University Press.

Barkow, J. H. (1989). *Darwin, sex, and status.* Toronto: University of Toronto Press.

Barkow, J. H., Cosmides, L., & Tooby, J. E. (Eds.). (1992). *The adapted mind.* New York: Oxford University Press.

Batson, C. (1991). The *altruism question: Towards a social-psychological answer.* Hillsdale, NJ: Lawrence Erlbaum.

Baum, J. A. C., & McKelvey, B. (Eds.). (1999). *Variations in organization science: In honor of Donald T. Campbell.* Thousand Oaks, CA: Sage.

Baum, J. A. C., & Rao, H. (2004). Evolutionary dynamics of organizational populations and communities. In M. S. Poole & A. H. Van de Ven (Eds.), *Handbook of organizational change and innovation* (pp. 212–258). New York: Oxford University Press.

Bechtel, W. (2003). Modules, brain parts, and evolutionary psychology. In S. J. Scher & F. Rauscher (Eds.), *Evolutionary psychology: Alternative approaches* (pp. 211–227). Dordrecht: Kluwer.

Boehm, C. (2000). *Hierarchy in the forest: The evolution of egalitarian behavior.* Cambridge, MA: Harvard University Press.

Boinski, S. & Garber, P. A. (Eds.). (2000). *On the move: How and why animals travel in groups.* Chicago: University of Chicago Press.

Boyd, R., & Richerson, P. J. (1985). *Culture and the evolutionary process.* Chicago: University of Chicago Press.

Brewer, M. B. (1997). On the social origins of human nature. In C. McGarty & A. Haslam (Eds.), *The message of social psychology* (pp. 54–62). Oxford, UK: Blackwell.

Buss, D. M. (1999). *Evolutionary psychology.* Boston: Allyn & Bacon.

Buss, L. W. (1987). *The evolution of individuality.* Princeton, NJ: Princeton University Press.

Campbell, D. T. (1965). Ethnocentric and other altruistic motives. In D. Levine (Ed.), *Nebraska symposium on motivation, 1965* (pp. 283–311). Lincoln: University of Nebraska Press.

Campbell, D. T. (1974). "Downward causation" in hierarchically organized biological systems. In F. Ayala & T. Dobzhansky (Eds.), *Studies in the philosophy of biology* (pp. 179–186). London: Macmillan.

Campbell, D. T. (1975). On the conflicts between biological and social evolution and between psychology and moral tradition. *American Psychologist, 30,* 1103–1126.

Campbell, D. T. (1982). Legal and primary-group social controls. *Journal of Social and Biological Structures, 5,* 431–438.

Campbell, D. T. (1983). The two distinct routes beyond kin selection to ultrasociality: Implications for the humanities and social sciences. In D. L. Bridgeman (Ed.), *The nature of prosocial development* (pp. 11–41). New York: Academic Press.

Campbell, D. T. (1990a). Asch's moral epistemology for socially shared knowledge. In I. Rock (Ed.), *The legacy of Solomon Asch* (pp. 39–55). Hillsdale, NJ: Lawrence Erlbaum.

Campbell, D. T. (1990b). Levels of organization, downward causation, and the selection-theory approach to evolutionary epistemology. In E. G. Tobach (Ed.), *Scientific methodology in the study of mind: Evolutionary epistemology* (pp. 1–15). Hillsdale, NJ: Lawrence Erlbaum.

Campbell, D. T. (1994). How individual and face-to-face group selection undermine firm selection in organizational evolution. In J. A. C. Baum & J. V. Singh (Eds.), *Evolutionary dynamics of organizations* (pp. 23–38). New York: Oxford University Press.

Campbell, D. T., & Gatewood, J. B. (1994). Ambivalently held group-optimizing predispositions. *Behavioral and Brain Sciences, 17,* 614.

Caporael, L. R. (1994). Of myth and science: Origin stories and evolutionary scenarios. *Social Science Information, 33,* 9–23.

Caporael, L. R. (1995). Sociality: Coordinating bodies, minds, and groups. *Psycoloquy [on-line serial], 6*(1).

Caporael, L. R. (1997). The evolution of truly social cognition: The core configurations model. *Personality and Social Psychology Review, 1,* 276–298.

Caporael, L. R. (2001a). Evolutionary psychology: Toward a unifying theory and a hybrid science. *Annual Review of Psychology, 52,* 607–628.

Caporael, L. R. (2001b). Natural tensions: Realism and constructivism. In D. L. Hull & C. M. Heyes (Eds.), *Selection theory and social construction: The evolutionary naturalistic epistemology of Donald T. Campbell.* Albany: State University of New York Press.

Caporael, L. R. (2001c). Parts and wholes: The evolutionary importance of groups. In C. Sedikides & M. B. Brewer (Eds.), *Individual self, relational self, and collective self* (pp. 241–258). Philadelphia: Psychology Press.

Caporael, L. R., & Baron, R. M. (1997). Groups as the mind's natural environment. In J. Simpson & D. Kenrick (Eds.), *Evolutionary social psychology* (pp. 317–343). Hillsdale, NJ: Lawrence Erlbaum.

Caporael, L. R., Dawes, R. M., Orbell, J. M., & van de Kragt, A. J. C. (1989). Selfishness examined: Cooperation in the absence of egoistic incentives. *Behavioral and Brain Sciences, 12,* 683–739.

Chagnon, N. (1988). Life histories, blood revenge, and warfare in a tribal population. *Science, 239,* 985–992.

Darwin, C. (1981). *The descent of man and selection in relation to sex.* Princeton, NJ: Princeton University Press. (Originally published 1859)

Datta, S. B. (1992). Effects of availability of allies on female dominance structure. In H. A. Harcourt & F. B. M. de Waal (Eds.), *Coalitions and alliances in human and in other animals* (pp. 61–82). Oxford, UK: Oxford University Press.

Dennett, D. C. (1995). *Darwin's dangerous idea.* New York: Simon & Schuster.

Diamond, J. (1997). *Guns, germs, and steel: The fates of human societies.* London: Random House.

Dugatkin, L. (2000). *The imitation factor.* New York: Simon & Schuster.

Dugatkin, L. A. (1997). The evolution of cooperation. *Bioscience, 47,* 355–362.

Dunbar, R. I. M. (1989). Selfishness reexamined. *Behavavioral and Brain Science, 12,* 700–702.

Dunbar, R. I. M. (1993). Coevolution of neocortical size, group size, and language in humans. *Behavioral and Brain Sciences, 16,* 681–735.

Dunbar, R. I. M (1996). *Grooming, gossip, and the evolution of language.* Cambridge, MA: Harvard University Press.

Dunbar, R. I. M., Knight, C., & Power, C. (Eds.). (1999). *The evolution of culture.* Edinburgh, UK: University of Edinburgh Press.

Durham, W. H. (1976). The adaptive significance of cultural behavior. *Human Ecology, 4,* 89–121.

Durham, W. H. (1991). *Coevolution: Genes, culture, and human diversity.* Stanford, CA: Stanford University Press.

Eldredge, N. (1985). *Unfinished synthesis: Biological hierarchies and modern evolutionary thought.* New York: Oxford University Press.

Ellickson, R. C. (1991). *Order without law: How neighbors settle disputes.* Cambridge, MA: Harvard University Press.

Gaulin, S. J. C., & McBurney, D. (2000). *Psychology: An evolutionary approach.* Upper Saddle River, NJ: Prentice Hall.

Geary, D. C. (1998). *Male, female: The evolution of human sex differences.* Washington, DC: American Psychological Association.

Gintis, H. (2000). *Game theory evolving.* Princeton, NJ: Princeton University Press.

Hamilton, W. D. (1964). The genetical evolution of social behavior. *Journal of Theoretical Biology, 7,* 1–52.

Hamilton, W. D. (1975). Innate social aptitudes in man, an approach from evolutionary genetics. In R. Fox (Ed.), *Biosocial anthropology* (pp. 133–155). London: Malaby Press.

Hauser, M. D. (1992). Costs of deception: Cheaters are punished in rhesus monkeys. *Proceedings of the National Academy of Sciences, 89,* 12137–12139.

Hemelrijk, C. K. (1997). *Cooperation without genes, games, or cognition.* In P. Husbands & I. Harvey (Eds.), *4th European Conference on Artificial Life* (pp. 511–520). Cambridge: MIT.

Hemelrijk, C. K. (2002a). Self-organization and natural selection in the evolution of complex despotic societies. *Biological Bulletin, 202,* 283–289.

Hemelrijk, C. K. (2002b). Understanding social behaviour with the help of complexity science (invited article). *Ethology, 108,* 655–671.

Hemelrijk, C. K., & Luteijn, M. (1998). Philopatry, male presence, and grooming reciprocation among female primates: A comparative perspective. *Behavioral Ecology and Sociobiology, 42*(3), 207–215.

Hendriks-Jansen, H. (1996). *Catching ourselves in the act.* Cambridge: MIT Press.

Hull, D. L. (1988). *Science as a process.* Chicago: University of Chicago Press.

Keegan, J. (1993). *A history of warfare.* New York: Knopf.

Kelly, R. L. (1995). *The foraging spectrum: Diversity in hunter-gatherer lifeways.* Washington, DC: Smithsonian Institution Press.

Kuper, A. (1988). *The invention of primitive society.* New York: Routledge.

Kurzban, R., & Leary, M. R. (2001). Evolutionary origins of stigmatization: The functions of social exclusion. *Psychological Bulletin, 127,* 187–208.

Landeau, L., & Terborgh, J. (1986). Oddity and the "confusion effect" in predation. *Animal Behaviour, 34,* 1372–1380.

Latane, B., & L'Herrou, T. (1996). Spatial clustering in the conformity game: Dynamic social impact in electronic groups. *Journal of Personality and Social Psychology, 70,* 1218–1230.

Levins, R., & Lewontin, R. (1985). *The dialectical biologist.* Cambridge, MA: Harvard University Press.

Lewontin, R. C. (1961). Evolution and the theory of games. *Journal of Theoretical Biology, 1,* 382–403.

Lickliter, R., & Honeycutt, H. (2003). Developmental dynamics: Toward a biologically plausible evolutionary psychology. *Psychological Bulletin, 129,* 839–835.

Maynard Smith, J. (1987). Science and myth. In N. Eldredge (Ed.), *The natural history reader in evolution* (pp. 222–229). New York City: Columbia University Press.

Maynard Smith, J., & Szathmary, E. (1985). *The major transitions in evolution.* New York: W. H. Freeman.

Neil, S. R., & Cullen, J. M. (1974). Experiments on whether schooling by their prey affects hunting behavior of cephalopods and fish predators. *Journal of Zoology London, 172,* 549–569.

Nicolis, S. C., & Deneubourg, J. L. (1999). Emerging patterns and food recruitment in ants: An analytical study. *Journal of Theoretical Biology, 198,* 575–592.

Norris, K. S., & Schilt, C. R. (1988). Cooperative societies in three-dimensional space: On the origins of aggregations, flocks, and schools, with special reference to dolphins and fish. *Ethology and Sociobiology, 9,* 149–179.

Olsen, C. L. (1987). The demography of colony fission from 1878–1970 among the Hutterites of North America. *American Anthropologist, 89,* 823–837.

Ostrom, E., Gardner, R., & Walker, J. M. (1994). *Rules, games, and common-pool resources.* Ann Arbor: University of Michigan Press.

Oyama, S. (1985). *The ontogeny of information.* New York: Cambridge University Press.

Palmer, C. T., Fredrickson, B. E., & Tilley, C. (1997). Categories and gatherings: Group selection and the mythology of cultural anthropology. *Evolution and Human Behavior, 18,* 291–308.

Rawls, J. (1971). *A theory of justice.* Cambridge, MA: Harvard University Press.

Richerson, P. J., & Boyd, R. (1999). Complex societies: The evolutionary origins of a crude superorganism. *Human Nature, 10,* 253–289.

Sheldon, K. M., Sheldon, M. S., & Osbaldiston, R. (2000). Prosocial values and group-assortation within an N-person Prisoner's Dilemma. *Human Nature, 11,* 387–404.

Sher, S. J. (2003, July). *How should we study the evolution of social cognition.* Paper presented at the EAESP Small Group Meeting on Social Cognition: Evolutionary and Cultural Perspectives, Budapest, Hungary.

Smith, E. A., Mulder, B., & Hill, K. (2001). Controversies in the evolutionary social sciences: A guide for the perplexed. *Trends in Evolution and Ecology, 16,* 128–135.

Sober, E. (1984). *The nature of selection.* Cambridge: MIT Press.

Sober, E., & Wilson, D. S. (1998). *Unto others: The evolution and psychology of unselfish behavior.* Cambridge, MA: Harvard University Press.

Sterelny, K., & Griffiths, P. E. (1999). *Sex and death.* Chicago: University of Chicago Press.

Tashakkori, A., & Teddlie, C. (Eds.). (2003). *Handbook of mixed methods in social and behavioral research.* Thousand Oaks, CA: Sage.

Thelen, E., & Smith, L. B. (1994). *A dynamic systems approach to the development of cognition and action.* Cambridge: MIT Press.

Tiger, L. (1969). *Men in groups.* New York: Random House.

Tocqueville, A. D. (1990). *Democracy in America.* Garden City, NJ: Anchor Books. (Original work published 1835)

Tomasello, M. (1999). *The cultural origins of human cognition.* Cambridge, MA: Harvard University Press.

Tooby, J. E., & Cosmides, L. (1992). The psychological foundations of culture. In J. H. Barkow, L. Cosmides, & J. E. Tooby (Eds.), *The adapted mind: Evolutionary psychology and the generation of culture* (pp. 19–136). Oxford, UK: Oxford University Press.

Trivers, R. L. (1971). The evolution of reciprocal altruism. *Quarterly Review of Biology, 46,* 35–57.

Van Schaik, C., & Janson, C. (Eds.). (2000). *Infanticide by males and its implications.* Cambridge, UK: Cambridge University Press.

Wildschut, T., Pinter, B., Vevea, J. L., Insko, C. A., & Schopler, J. (2003). Beyond the group mind: A quantitative review of the interindividual-intergroup discontinuity effect. *Psychological Bulletin, 129,* 698–722.

Williams, G. C. (1966). *Adaptation and natural selection.* Princeton, NJ: Princeton University Press.

Wilson, D. S. (1975). A theory of group selection. *Proceedings of the National Academy of Sciences, 72,* 143–146.

Wilson, D. S. (1983). The group selection controversy: History and current status. *Annual Review of Ecology and Systematics, 14,* 157–187.

Wilson, D. S. (2002). *Darwin's cathedral: Evolution, religion, and the nature of society.* Chicago: University of Chicago Press.

Wilson, D. S., & Dugatkin, L. A. (1997). Group selection and assortative interactions. *American Naturalist, 149,* 339–351.

Wilson, D. S., & Sober, E. (1994). Re-introducing group selection to the human behavioral sciences. *Behavioral and Brain Sciences, 17,* 585–654.

Wrangham, R., & Peterson, D. (1996). *Demonic males.* Boston: Houghton Mifflin.

Wynne-Edwards, V. C. (1962). *Animal dispersion in relation to social behavior.* London: Oliver and Boyd.

11

Touchstones

A Framework for Comparing Premises of Nine Integrative Perspectives on Groups

Janet Fulk and Joseph E. McGrath

Abstract

This chapter considers the nine perspectives with respect to a set of generic features that we refer to as touchstones. We ask what each of the perspectives says about: (1) the entity itself (i.e., group), including its formation and composition; (2) the context or setting within which that entity is embedded (i.e., issues regarding its boundaries and external influences on it); (3) the processes that take place in the group, both interaction patterns among members (e.g., interdependence, regulation of action) and psychological processes of members (e.g., cognitive, emotional, intentional); (4) the emergent properties, patterns, and/or outcomes of group existence and action; and (5) causality. Those comparisons show considerable similarity among various perspectives, as well as marked contrasts among others. The resulting picture of nine complementary but overlapping perspectives presents a much richer and more extensive picture of groups than any one of them alone.

The scope of this volume is awesome. Each chapter individually covers a vast terrain, and in combination, they demark the truly expansive domain of theory and research on groups. This is a unique, far-reaching, and quite remarkable compendium.

We undertook the daunting task of trying to compare and contrast the nine perspectives on the basis of a smaller set of features. Our intent was to select what seemed to be essential features of the content domain, but stated at an abstract or "meta" level. Inevitably, the inclusion and exclusion of features are to some degree biased by our own personal perspectives.

One key challenge has been that no reference points are truly ontology-free in themselves. Thus, the fit of the framework we employ to the complete set of perspectives is by nature less than perfect—fitting some ontological assumptions better than others. Nevertheless, we have tried to use these features as touchstones—referents against which each tradition may be compared and analyzed. (The term *touchstone* refers to a black stone that was used in ancient times to test for gold and silver by rubbing the purported rare metal stone against it.) We hope researchers will find that our touchstones offer additional insights.

Our presentation is organized around five major touchstones:

1. The Entity: How is the group formed and composed?

2. Context: How is the group situated with respect to group boundaries and to interaction with its external environment?

3. Processes: What is the nature of group interaction, and what role do psychological processes play?

4. Emergent properties, patterns, and/or outcomes: What does the group accomplish, and what does it leave behind?

5. Causality: What forms of causality apply and how do they operate?

In this chapter, we rely primarily on the content of the individual chapters in making our comparisons. References to the bulk of the research and theory we cite are found in the individual chapters of this volume, and our chapter merely highlights them. In a few cases, we have added information from work that does not appear in the chapters. In those cases, full references are provided at the end of the chapter.

We encourage you to employ your own personal touchstones as you explore these perspectives on the wonderfully vast realm of theory and research on groups.

The Entity

Our first touchstone asks: What processes were involved in getting the group formed, and how is it composed at any point in time? How do the perspectives differ in theorizing formative processes? What features of group composition are more or less important to research in each tradition? We begin our presentation with formation, then discuss composition. The framework proposed by Arrow, McGrath, and Berdahl (2000) organizes our discussion of this first touchstone.

Formation

Arrow et al. (2000) assert that groups can form "top down or bottom up" and by way of actions of people internal or external to the group. By crossing these two dimensions and looking at the extremes of each one, group formation can be categorized as (1) top down, by actions of some people who will not themselves be group members (as in the formation of task forces or teams in organizations); (2) top down, by actions of people who will themselves be group members (as when a person recruits others to join him/her in some group enterprise); (3) bottom up, by spontaneous actions of people who are in potential interactive relations to one another (e.g., formation of friendship groups by workmates); and (4) by the press of circumstances that induce interdependent action by people, who thereby become group members (e.g., joint actions by people trapped together under flood conditions). Thus, some groups initially are concocted (internally or externally), others emergent (spontaneous or circumstantial). These categories are not mutually exclusive except at the extremes; group formation often involves mixtures of two or more of these "pure types."

Functionalist research primarily has focused on concocted external groups, largely due to reliance on laboratory studies of ad hoc groups at a single point in time and on a single task. Despite this narrow band of research effort, the theories in this tradition are intended to be applicable to any goal-oriented group.

In the psychodynamic tradition, the group is not constituted of its members. Rather, the group emerges as members interact with each other and generate collective actions. Groups focus on therapy, learning, or development, whether they are concocted task-oriented work groups or whether they were brought together for some other reason.

For social identity and power traditions, groups are formed by the process of categorization, by any of the four types of formation processes.

Categorization may be made by external people (e.g., liberals versus neo-Nazis) or by group members themselves (e.g., concerned pit bull owners). Categorizations can be relatively enduring and self-selected (e.g., occupation), or circumstantial (passenger at an airport). The power tradition recognizes a wide variety of possible bases of formation. However, work in this tradition focuses attention less on initiation than on processes that occur *after* an initial group is formed, including also composition changes with entry and exit of members.

The network perspective includes both concocted groups based on exogenously applied boundaries and emergent groups based on intensity of interaction among subsets of individuals. Analytically, emergent groups are to some degree constructed because some criterion must be applied to communication intensity in order to identify who is part of a particular clique.

Not all socioevolutionary theorists admit that groups exist; some argue that "groups" are artifacts of natural human abilities to categorize phenomena. Those that argue for the existence of groups primarily focus on organized biological entities (interacting genetic competitors) that serve adaptive purposes for organisms. Adaptionist approaches see group formation as being influenced by genes. Systems approaches see formation of complex groups as having roots in a few simple rules or forms that are embellished with continuing interaction of the organism with the surrounding environment.

The symbolic/interpretive perspective views groups as emergent. Symbols are generative mechanisms for groups; symbols are shared and interpreted in order to generate a "common consciousness" that serves to unite separate individuals into a sense of being a group. Structuration approaches argue that groups are produced and reproduced through members' use of rules and resources. In the dialectical approach, a group is formed from the interplay of dialectical tensions, such as individuals simultaneously desiring to be leaders and followers.

The change perspective sees groups as sets of individuals that develop over time in response to both internal pressures and external forces. Individuals without prior history go through stages or cycles that are relatively predictable at the group level. These stages or cycles may be modified if members have prior history with each other. This perspective also argues, much like the network perspective, that during the formation stage, a group emerges from a network of social connections, but that groups are also influenced by the physical and social ecology in which they are embedded during the formation stage.

Feminist perspectives cover all four quadrants. Perhaps the most common perspective is external. In the Marxist view, distribution of capital is important, in that those with capital form the group (concocted, external).

Structural inequality views see how external dynamics can constrain behavior and thus reinforce existing roles and stereotypes. Liberal feminists see groups as forming when a reason exists and dissolving when that reason disappears. Radical separatist feminist theory sees groups as internal and emergent, filling the needs of women to define their own identities.

Composition

Arrow et al. (2000) argue that the important components of groups are:

1. *People,* who become the group's members. Members may be assigned, recruited, or may join incidental to other activities.

2. *Intentions/purposes,* which become the group's (and members') projects. Emergent groups generate their own purposes, concocted groups often have assigned goals, and circumstantial groups have their purposes thrust upon them by outside conditions. And,

3. *Technology* (both hard and soft) or tools, which provide the means by which the group's members will carry out their projects. Technology includes both software (e.g., procedures, protocols, norms) and hardware (e.g., physical tools such as computers and drill presses.) Technology may be assigned or borrowed (explicitly or implicitly), or it may be created or modified by the group either consciously or unconsciously.

Groups differ based on (1) what these components are and (2) how they are linked to each other, what Arrow et al. (2000) call member-task-tool networks. These networks themselves can be decomposed into subnetworks, such as task-tool or tool-tool. This conception of group composition aligns most clearly with the functional perspective. Nevertheless, it can be a useful schema for analysis, highlighting in particular how some perspectives differ fairly substantially from the functional view.

Member composition is an important theme in the functional, power, social identity, and feminist perspectives. Much functional research under combinatorial theories is concerned with determining which combinations of member abilities, traits, and psychological predispositions lead to more effective group decision-making and task performance and to better internal social relations. The power tradition adds a significant concern with member differences in power and status and how these also relate to intragroup cooperation and collective action. Value similarity is important to the negotiation tradition. In the social-dilemma literature, group size is a major variable, while member demographics have not been given much attention. Both power and functional perspectives have honed in on the effects of psychological diversity; cognitive diversity can improve decision quality whereas affective diversity can lead to nonproductive relational conflict. The social identity perspective is concerned with collective action, as is the power tradition, but the social identity perspective focuses more on the dynamic social identities that members embrace rather than on the members per se, except in cases where a social identity is directly tied to a demographic (e.g., race) or psychological (e.g., social values) characteristic of a member. Indeed, a hallmark of this tradition is depersonalization, in which an individual accepts the ingroup stereotype as the individual's own social identity, sacrificing his or her own unique characteristics.

Stereotypes are also the subject of feminist theory and research, but these stereotypes tend to be externally applied based on sex and gender status of individuals. Women are stereotyped as communal and men as agentic. Stereotypes both constrain behavior and are reinforced as individuals act them out. The balance of males and females in a group affects interaction patterns. Women tend to be more cooperative, and all-female groups are more attuned to socioemotional issues; men tend to speak more, interrupt more, and emerge as leaders. Many feminist theorists argue that such differences are more strongly rooted in differences in power and status than in innate differences between men and women.

Despite similar interests in compositional effects, these four traditions treat task and technology rather differently. For functional theory, task is an input variable; different tasks (e.g., complex versus simple) generate different processes, and different degrees of task-process fit produce different levels of performance. For power theory, different tasks have different levels of implied cooperativeness or competitiveness, due to differences in payoff functions for participants. Task may interact with member characteristics (e.g., risk aversion) to influence negotiation processes and outcomes. For social identity theory, task is less important in itself than in the social identity that might be created by competency at a particular task. The task can cue social identity (e.g., cooking dinner for children cues a parenting identity, and writing code cues a software engineer identity). Task scope relates to whether an individual assumes a relatively narrow identity (grader for a Professor X) versus a more general one (academic). Feminist research has found that simple tasks are better for same-sex groups, whereas mixed-sex groups bring a valuable cognitive diversity to complex tasks. One key feminist issue is that definitions of *task* and *effective task performance* themselves are biased toward male-oriented agentic activities rather than the socioemotional aspects in which women excel.

Technology has been more important for functional and feminist studies than for power or social identity. The exception is work by Postmes, Spears, and Lea (e.g., Postmes, 1996; Spears & Lea, 1992). Their SIDE (Social

Identity model of DEindividuation) argues that computer mediation can have very different effects on social influence, depending on the ability of the context to cue meaningful social identity. Computer mediation will increase social identity if the context cues common identity but will decrease social influence when a context highlights personal identity.

Functional and feminist research has looked at group processes and outcomes under different configurations of technology, including "soft" technologies such as brainstorming and "hard" technologies such as computer conferencing. Functionalists see technology as an input variable. Some feminist scholars argue that in anonymous computer conferencing, because sex is not salient and often not identifiable, individuals can communicate more effectively because their contributions are not judged based on their sex. Some research has supported this, but other research has found that sex differences in communication behavior are more rather than less exaggerated in mediated environments, perhaps to compensate for the lack of physical cues to sex. Some power research has studied the impact of technological mediation on bargaining processes and outcomes, but this has not been a central theme of this tradition.

The other four traditions have rather different approaches to people, tasks, tools and their interlinkages. The change tradition sees group composition as a dynamic blend of continuity and change. Over time, the mix of characteristics within the group will vary as membership changes. The effects of these variations may depend on where a group is in its own development cycle. Tasks also can be seen as sequences of activities (with recursivity) conducted at differential paces. Different groups develop different sequences; alternate paths to decision and action can be equally effective. Technology has not been a major theoretical focus, but some research has shown that technological mediation of communication is more effective for some stages in a group's life (e.g., when there is agreement on ends and means) than others (when a young group is figuring out what to do and who they are; Kraut, Galegher, & Egido, 1990). Other research has shown that, over time, differences between face–to–face and technology-mediated communication tend to fade, most likely because groups become acclimated to interacting via technology.

Socioevolutionary theory and research is not particularly concerned with tasks or technology, except to argue that survival is more likely when there are better matches of these features with group competencies and environmental demands. One approach to member composition is male/female ratios and how these affect reproduction and survival odds for a group. Other traits of interest include age, kinship, and altruism. Composition also matters in that good matches of the characteristics present within the group to the demands of the environment favor reproduction and survival.

For symbolic/interpretive theorists, members bring to the group communication traits and predispositions to symbolic behavior. Such variation can serve as a positive force by offering a diversity of symbolic resources to groups, or as a negative force by impeding symbolic activity. Tasks are socially constructed and interpreted through interaction and symbolic behavior. Symbolic behavior may vary by task, and both may be modified by culture. In direct contrast to the functionalist tradition, task and social aspects are not distinct, but rather they interpenetrate and are not readily separable. Technologies can be external resources that groups draw upon in their interaction and interpretation, as well as the subject of interpretation and symbolic behavior. Technologies also can be codified in rules that structure decision making, as in the technology of structuring an interaction via an agenda.

For psychodynamic theorists, composition both "matters not at all and it matters totally," according to McLeod and Kettner-Polley (Chapter 3, this volume). Because all human beings share universal instincts, composition does not matter. Yet, certain personal features can influence the emergence of "deep roles," including features such as sex, gender, status, national culture, and the valence different individuals hold toward different roles. A group's tasks are almost incidental because the major work of the group is the group itself. The task is to work through contrasting impulses and tensions. Although "hard" technologies have not played a role in research in this tradition, the "soft" technology of T-group training has been studied as a mechanism for triggering productive processes in groups.

Two aspects of group composition are important in the network perspective. First, group composition is linked to preexisting ties among subsequent group members. Second, there is more homophily within groups than between groups, and this homophily tends to increase over time. Task features (e.g., complexity) influence which pattern of network ties (e.g., centralized versus decentralized) will be more effective for a group and what type of individual tie (e.g., strong versus weak) will be most effective for information transfer. Some classic work (e.g., Tavistock Institute) has looked at how changes in technology affect group structure. More contemporary research is continuing this trend, for example, Barley's (1986) demonstration of significant changes in network role structure following implementation of new technology in medical teams.

Context

All of the perspectives acknowledge that groups are situated in and influenced by larger contexts. The perspectives differ in how they define that context and envision its implications for group processes and outcomes. Two key aspects of group context underlie these differences. The first is the nature of the boundaries that divide a group from its social, physical, and temporal contexts. What are these boundaries and how do they arise, what are their features, and how stable or dynamic are group boundaries? The second aspect is the role of external contexts in internal group functioning. How buffered are groups from their embedding contexts? How much, if at all, do groups act to shape their own external environments? What features and processes contribute to influences between the group and its environment?

Boundaries

Each perspective assumes that groups are bounded in space and/or time and in relation to other groups. Most theorists agree that there is some permeability to boundaries, permitting exchange and/or interaction between groups and contexts. Distinctions arise over ontological status of boundaries, features and dynamics.

Ontological status

Perhaps the most salient difference across the perspectives is whether group boundaries are real or imagined. The symbolic/interpretive perspective anchors the extreme of social constructivism, arguing that boundaries are symbolic-interpretive structures that are socially constructed and enacted, indeed, "imagined." Group members coalesce around common reference points created by manipulation of symbols. These reference points serve to link the individuals to something shared in common. Symbols can be social, physical, or temporal.

The psychodynamic perspective agrees that boundaries are interpsychic structures and that groups are defined not by their positions with respect to external references but rather by interactions and relationships among members. Nevertheless, the psychodynamic perspective does not embrace the full range of tenets of social construction so central to the symbolic/interpretive perspective. The psychodynamic tradition also highlights temporal boundaries much as the change perspective does, but with a more micro and narrow focus on starting and ending group sessions on time. The socioevolutionary perspective is divided in that not all evolutionists agree that groups exist, much less that they are key to understanding human behavior.

In the social identity and power perspectives, social boundaries can be created or changed primarily by changing categorization schemes. The power perspective argues that boundaries are established or modified by a group's "boundary rules." These rules define (1) who is and who is not in the group and (2) how easy it is to enter or exit the group.

One stream in the network perspective sees boundaries as exogenously determined. Classic intergroup studies demonstrate how changing an exogenous, concrete, physical boundary (which cabin each child slept in) had dramatic influence on intra- and intergroup behavior. Another stream, which examines cliques, focuses on emergent subgroups within collectives.

The functional, change, socioevolutionary, and feminist perspectives show less attention to the source of boundaries; instead, they focus on boundary activity, including influences from and exchanges with temporal, spatial, and social environments.

Features and Dynamics

The symbolic/interpretive and psychodynamic perspectives depart substantially from each other in characterizing interpsychic boundaries. The psychodynamic view is more concerned with dynamics within bounded groups than dynamics of the boundaries themselves. Boundaries are very clear; groups can be readily distinguished from their context, thus facilitating group identity. Boundaries are permeable and permit exchange between groups and their environments. Boundaries "contain" the energy and interaction of the group. In contrast, the symbolic/interpretive view presents boundaries as porous, negotiated, and dynamically produced and reproduced as members interact; hence, they are quite transient. The symbolic/interpretive perspective explicitly rejects the notion that boundaries in any way contain groups.

Similar to the symbolic/interpretive view, both the change and functional perspectives focus less on what boundaries may exist at a point in time than on how they change dynamically in relation to context. Both tend to see boundaries as relatively clear, demarcating groups from contexts. Boundaries are permeable. Groups emerge from embedding contexts and are influenced by those contexts. When groups dissolve, the members become reabsorbed into that context. This external view sees groups as going through cycles of interaction with their environments. Boundary activities are important factors in both traditions.

Yet, both the functional and change traditions have focused their research lens on looking inside the group. The environment is distinct from the group, and little attention is paid to how it (or the boundaries that separate it from the group) may coevolve over time with the group. One key aspect of this environment includes the temporal environment of pace, cycles, and rhythms, which Hollingshead et al. (Chapter 2, this volume) argue deserves considerably more attention in the functional perspective, along with additional functional research investigating the embeddedness of groups in larger systems.

For the socioevolutionary tradition, boundaries are based in resource niches and environmental features that favor particular clusterings of individuals. Organisms enforce boundaries to create outgroups, and they defend boundaries particularly strongly under conditions of resource scarcity. At the same time, genetic variations are created when outgroup members reproduce with ingroup members, increasing the likelihood of creating a variation that will increase the chances of group survival. The socioevolutionary view adds the concepts of birth, selection, death, and path dependency. The groups and configurations of groups that survive at any point in time are tied to historical forces, as well as to current resource niches, intergroup competition, and competition between global groups and bounded local groups embedded within them.

Strength of boundaries is important for establishing ingroup versus outgroup status and social identity in both the social identity and power traditions. Clear boundaries are thus central to both of these traditions. For the social identity perspective, boundaries separate distinct categories of people; categorization is at the heart of social identity.

For the social identity perspective, however, boundary behavior is indeed quite dynamic. Individuals progress through everyday life moving from one social category to another, for example, from mother to commuter to software engineer. Boundaries themselves can be fleeting; for example, when a game is over, a team dissipates and may not be reassembled again for any future interaction, or different teams may be formed out of the same pool of players. Social identities will shift in relation to such change.

The power perspective recognizes the nesting of groups that is so important to the socioevolutionary tradition, and social dilemma research and studies of collective action target some of the same part-whole conflicts found in the socioevolutionary approaches, while taking a decidedly more cognitive approach to understanding the motivations and dynamics.

Research on interlocking directorates is an example of how central to the network tradition is the premise of permeable boundaries and multiple overlapping group memberships. Boundaries defined by volume of communication among subsets of group members (cliques) are fluid, changing as individuals alter their communication with others in the group. The network perspective also emphasizes historical aspects in the form of preexisting ties at the time of group formation. Katz et al. (Chapter 8, this volume) also note that although theoretically the network perspective is interested in the impact of changes in the network over time, nevertheless the bulk of network research involves snapshots at a single point in time within an ongoing dynamic process.

Feminist scholarship also sees how the stereotypes, expectations, and power relations that exist in the embedding social systems influence group composition through highly permeable boundaries. The feminist perspective highlights how group processes and sexual stereotypes change or are reinforced over time by changes in the embedding social structures. Groups are far from impervious to such changes; indeed, one goal of feminist group research is to energize changes in the larger social systems for the purpose of improving not only individual life but also group interactions. Also, because groups appropriate sex-stereotypical behavior from the larger social context, internal group processes change in relation to external social change.

External Forces

The external environment is a source of information and resources that are important to the group's functioning and survival—a premise embodied in all perspectives. The symbolic/interpretive perspective goes one step further, arguing that contexts serve as interpretive frames and that groups actively try to manage that interpretive context though social and symbolic means. The perspectives differ in the way external forces are conceptualized, including (1) relative importance of internal versus external forces as energizing group action and (2) extent to which groups actively shape their environments.

Communication Across Boundaries

The functional, symbolic/interpretive, change, and network traditions consider frequency and scope of external communication to be important boundary activities. Interestingly, all four claim the same sets of research studies as within their own perspective. Despite research on external communication, the sources of group processes in the functional perspective are primarily internal, with external factors treated as moderating conditions. Similarly, the psychodynamic perspective offers stage or phase models of how the group matures based on natural human development. This view, consistent with the container metaphor, seeks to understand external influences on what are essentially internally driven processes. Within the change perspective, stage models of group change and continuity, even while recognizing external influences, nevertheless see change to be internally driven through a process that is both natural and gradual, what Arrow et al. (2000) assert is analogous to organismic development. By contrast, in other change models, including punctuated equilibrium, dynamic contingency, and decision development, external cues are triggers for change.

Research from social identity and power perspectives demonstrates that the mere existence of a categorized outgroup in the external environment influences interactions within the group. Furthermore, communication with other groups influences levels of intra- and intergroup competition and cooperation. In the network perspective, multiple overlapping group memberships integrate external forces into internal group functioning. In the feminist tradition, internal forces mimic and respond to external social structure, reproducing sex and gender relations in the broader society.

In the socioevolutionary tradition, environmental factors drive change in groups, especially resource availability. For example, groups that survive in scarcity conditions evolve mechanisms to protect reproductive females and vulnerable youth, who represent the future of the group. Some theorists in this tradition see culture and norms also as evolved adaptive mechanisms. From this view, groups can select useful variations not only by direct interaction with the environment but also by evolved rules such as "copy the successful."

By contrast, the symbolic/interpretive perspective sees typical external variables such as task, technology, and culture as socially constructed within the group through processes of appropriation of rules and resources. Such factors are not so much external as both internal and external.

Shaping the Environment

All of the perspectives regard the group as being embedded in multilayered (e.g., intergroup, institution, community) and multifaceted (e.g., task, physical, technology, temporal variables) environments. Interacting with the environment involves relations with multiple groups embedded in institutional and community settings and incorporates physical, technological, social, and temporal aspects. The social identity and power traditions focus most closely on other groups as external forces, whereas the other perspectives broaden the lens to other resources and constraints beyond other groups.

The change, functional, and network perspectives focus more on how groups are shaped by their environment than vice versa. The exception is research on external communication and weak ties, which incorporates active information-seeking outside the group. By contrast, symbolic/interpretive, power, and social identity theories consider that groups influence and actively manage their contexts, with both positive and negative consequences. Research in the coevolutionary tradition focuses most clearly on mutual shaping of group and context, whereas traditional evolutionary economics asserts a more environmentally and biologically deterministic stance. Socioevolutionary theories share with psychodynamic theory the premise that group interaction results from basic biological instincts, but psychodynamic theory focuses more on biological basis rather than environmental context.

Feminist theories vary on the question of when, whether, and how groups shape their environment. Some scholars advocate group solidarity among women and oppressed groups toward the goal of changing sexual stereotyping and associated power relations extant in the larger embedding context— conditions that serve as the instruments of their oppression. Other work challenges the notion that such stereotypes need necessarily follow from the context, arguing that women should not acquiesce to claims that they are relegated to acting out sexual stereotypes related to broader social status inequities. Rather, they should view themselves as empowered to control their own destinies.

Processes

A wide variety of different processes have been studied by group researchers. For this touchstone, we selected two general categories: interaction patterns and psychological processes. For interaction patterns, we narrow our discussion to two areas. First, how does each perspective theorize about cooperation, competition, and conflict? Second, what mechanisms do individuals and groups use to regulate the behavior of group members, such as roles, rules, norms, and power.

Interaction Patterns

Competition, Conflict, and Cooperation

Nowhere are competition, conflict, and cooperation more in the foreground than in the power and socioevolutionary traditions. For purposes of brevity, we highlight the premises, and describe only illustrative research findings for each tradition.

Four premises are particularly important to the power perspective. First, individuals pursue self-interest in their interactions with others. Second, group processes are driven by social dilemmas that pit the self-interests of the individual against the collective interests of the group, and/or the self-interests of a group against those of larger collectives or intergroups. Third, differences in power are a natural part of human groups and human institutions. Fourth, power can be used to create, sustain, or alleviate conflict.

A number of assertions follow from these premises and from associated research in the power tradition. The following are illustrative. Conflicts over resources lead to bargaining, social dilemmas, and coalition formation. Conflict related to the task can produce valuable syntheses, whereas relational conflict tends to reduce satisfaction and productivity. Aggregation rules provide structure and reduce conflict by defining the process by which decisions are made in the group. Cooperation is positively related to (1) pre-existing ties that provide shared metaknowledge of each other, (2) ability of the parties to communicate directly with one another, and (3) smaller group sizes. Power and status can reinforce each other.

Conflict is central to the socioevolutionary premises, as well. Interdependent and rationally self-interested individuals compete for survival. For some socioevolutionary theorists, this includes competition for selection between groups as well as between individuals, based on cultural variations across large-scale, usually regional groups. A key concern is how prosocial behavior evolves in the context of self-interested individuals. Interaction is seen as self-interest pitted against altruism. Among the findings are: Competition and conflict are stronger between groups than within groups. Between-group conflict can have benefits within-group, but such conflict may not be in the self-interest of any one individual because the costs of the conflict (e.g., loss of one's life in war) may be greater than that individual's portion of the collective benefits deriving from intergroup conflict. The evolution of cooperative behavior is positively related to (1) kinship and (2) cooperative individuals' withholding benefits from uncooperative and antisocial individuals. Furthermore, the cognitive sophistication found in humans (as opposed to most animals) is important for the evolution of prosocial behavior among unrelated individuals; humans rely on culture and norms to guide behavior much more than do other species. For example, because clique selfishness undermines collective goals, it is controlled by evolved cultural norms.

Social identity research has found that when individuals strongly identify with a group, they will sacrifice their own self-interests to help the group do better than another group. One rationale for this behavior is that depersonalization occurs when there is a strong ingroup, and this leads individuals to take the ingroup's interests as their own self-interests. For example, in wartime, when social identity is salient, a country's interests may be translated into the soldier's interest, even at the cost of his or her own life.

Feminist research has looked deeply into conflict, competition, and cooperation by males versus females in groups. Although women and men are similar in their levels of overall competitiveness in group interaction, women employ more compromise strategies whereas men employ more competitive tactics.

In general, women focus more on cooperation and reducing socioemotional conflict. Nevertheless, research has shown that men are less competitive in the presence of women, just as women are more competitive in the presence of men.

Functionalists view competition, conflict, and cooperation as processes that mediate input-output relationships. Regulation of these behaviors toward rationality should produce good decisions, such as social combination through voting, playing devil's advocate, or brainstorming techniques. The particular process that will be most effective depends on input factors as well as contingencies such as task complexity. Conflict, competition, and cooperation also arise naturally in groups and at different times in the life of a group. Conflict characterizes earlier stages when groups are little more than assemblages of self-interested individuals. More cooperative behavior emerges in later stages as groups develop a shared identity, interpersonal interactions become more regularized, and cohesion develops.

The change view shares this premise regarding group development. Conflict is necessary to season a group and regularize interaction both between group members at any one point in time and between different stages of group life over time. The group is a balance of forces that sustain coordinated action, including change versus stability and conflict versus cooperation.

For psychodynamic researchers, conflicts are intrapsychic. Yet, they are not idiosyncratic to each group member or to any one group. Rather, they involve universal issues related to instincts rooted in biology: survival and reproduction. In this sense, psychodynamic represents an intrapsychic version of socioevolutionary concerns. Conflicts manifest themselves in pressures and counterpressures in relation to libido, ego, and psychosexual tensions. Early work also focused on the problem of how groups can attend to both the task at hand and the socioemotional needs of members in the proper proportions required to sustain an equilibrium state.

The symbolic/interpretive perspective also focuses on dialectical tensions although it is less intrapsychic. Rituals are mechanisms for managing these dialectical tensions, rather than the psychodynamic focus on seeking the deep-seated sources of human frailty. For symbolic/interpretive theorists, competition exists over whose interpretation will become the group's interpretation. In essence, interpretations compete as much as individuals compete. Groups develop mechanisms for dealing with the inevitable conflicts over interpretations and symbolic behavior. Rules and procedures are created to serve as symbolic means for withdrawing from conflict and thus increase the group's ability to achieve consensus. Cooperation serves to highlight identity relative to outgroups. This identity is supported by shared languages, codes, rituals, and rites that are only accessible to and understandable by other members of the group.

Interdependence is the heart of network theory and research; it is represented in the ties that link different nodes. Individuals in a group can be tied by conflict, cooperation, or competition. One could create, for example, a conflict network based on who is in conflict with whom; similar networks could be created for competitive or cooperative ties. Beyond content, research has shown that some specific configurations of nodes are more likely to lead to cooperation and information sharing within the group than are other configurations. Furthermore, changing patterns of ties over time may be linked to interpersonal processes. For example, a conflict between A and B may sever their tie. Or, a new group member may spur a group to renegotiate their patterns of cooperation.

Mechanisms for Regulating Behavior of Group Members

All of the perspectives assert that the group employs mechanisms for regulating interaction, and that status, hierarchy, and power influence behavior in and of groups. Each focuses its lens somewhat differently, however. The social identity and psychodynamic perspectives devote relatively less attention to these phenomena. For psychodynamic scholars, status is seen as an emergent property, and roles are treated in the context of individuals having different valences to enter into a role. Although one important leadership role is to interpret overt behavior for its emotional significance to the group, group interaction is primarily seen as intrapsychic processes, such as projection and transference. For social identity theorists, emphasis is placed on ingroup versus outgroup as categories, with less attention to details of interaction within a group. A few findings have emerged, including that leaders who are prototypical are more influential and that collectivist cultures show higher conformity.

The symbolic/interpretive perspective proposes that symbolic processes are central to regulation of interaction. Roles are symbolically constructed and reconstructed by exchange of symbols. Norms are communicated and reinforced by stories; stories thus help to achieve symbolic convergence, which contributes to group stability. Humor is a mechanism to acknowledge disagreement in a nonthreatening way and thus can ameliorate some of the divisive tendencies associated with disagreements on values or appropriate behavior. By using symbolic processes to manage dialectical tensions, groups can achieve a degree of dynamic equilibrium. Shared interpretive schemes serve as integrating and conflict-reducing mechanisms. Norms, roles, rules, and shared schema are not so much fixed guidance systems as they are ongoing negotiations among group members in the continuous process of structuration.

For functionalists, regulation of interaction is a process that mediates between inputs and outputs. Mechanisms that control and regulate interaction serve key functions in groups. This includes, for example, procedural norms, conflict-management systems, and control systems. Within this regulation process, norms moderate the relationship between conflict and performance, in that some norms generate more constructive behavior than others. Also, different stages of group development are associated with different levels and types of regulation, as is also asserted by the change perspective. For both perspectives, consensual norms develop in later stages, along with negotiated roles, procedures, and status structures. There are multiple possible routes or sequences in developing structure. Progression toward group development need not be linear, nor must groups go through each and every stage. Furthermore, more enduring and stable status structures, roles, and norms may be different from the initial structures that are created rapidly in the very early phases on the basis of surface characteristics or institutional structures.

For the network perspective, the structure of a group is represented in the patterns of linkages across nodes. This structure both affects and is affected by regulatory mechanisms including norms, cohesion, and information-sharing patterns. A network structure may constrain and/or regulate interaction. For example, the presence of a gatekeeper will determine who receives what information and from whom. At the same time, regulatory mechanisms also can influence network structures. For example, an egalitarian norm can prevent the emergence of a gatekeeper in a network structure. Task structure moderates these relationships in that certain network structures are more suited to certain tasks. For example, when a task can be modularized such that each individual knows different things and does different subtasks, a communication network may be more sparsely connected than when a task generates high levels of reciprocal interdependence among group members. Group structures themselves can be decomposed into substructures such as cliques or triads. Substructure patterns can recursively influence overall group structure. Ties also exist to entities outside of the group, and these ties can regulate internal action such as effort levels.

Regulation of interaction is at the heart of the power perspective. The framework advanced by Lovaglia et al. (Chapter 5, this volume) to unify a diverse set of approaches to power, status, and conflict proposes that institutional rules structure interaction in groups. Boundary rules determine who is in and who is out of the group. Aggregation rules structure how the group will reach a decision that will be considered the choice of the group as a whole, for example, majority rule versus consensus. Aggregation rules need not apply to the whole of decision development; one rule may apply for the early part of decision making and another for a later point. Position rules structure the authority of the different positions in the group. They specify who has the most position or network power. Status, one's position in a network, regulates interactions in that those with higher status acquire higher power and prestige. Information rules determine who can know what and how that information is shared. Information asymmetries create the potential for differential control by one group member over another. The structure of a group evolves over time under the guidance of these evolving rules, including key features such as social roles, social norms, and sanctioning systems. The group's task is also important. The nature and structure of the task can change the importance of status characteristics and may imply different types of information structures, as is also argued in the network perspective.

From a feminist perspective, power and status are driving forces in regulating behavior in groups. Structural inequality theories argue that societal structures afford men power and status over women. This sex hierarchy is assimilated in the structure of groups. Sex, then, cues different expectations and behaviors for men and women in groups; the observed sex differences in communication and leadership are not due to sex per se but rather to relative status and power. Power and status cues in the group setting constrain behavior and thus reify the extant power structure, entrenching the sex hierarchy over time. In addition, tasks and roles are sex-typed based on their inherent power; the social and economic system assigns women the less powerful tasks and roles. Marxist feminist scholars further suggest that women are disadvantaged at the start in groups because they serve as laborers in groups run by male capitalists, or in some cases, First World women.

Psychoanalytic feminist theorists take a different view, arguing that a "powerful mother" arises as a result of female parenting. In reaction, men seek to dominate women when men become adults. Furthermore, women are afraid of the powerful mother within them, and as a result, they seek to be controlled by men. From this perspective, men and women both respond to nurturant matriarchy, in contrast to the structural equality perspective in which women are oppressed by social and economic patriarchy.

The socioevolutionary perspective steps back in time to ask: Where does the drive to organize by such hierarchies come from? This perspective begins with the premise that group structure is a nested hierarchy of subgroups in which higher-order groups influence lower-order groups (and vice versa in the case of the part-whole competition argument). Hierarchies have certain biological advantages. Steeper hierarchies are more adaptive under food scarcity because this means that at least some females will be sustained sufficiently to reproduce and thus ensure the survival of the species. Beyond biological survival and reproduction, group structure is also reproduced through daily practices. Culture and norms can be seen as biological adaptations that allow humans to learn by information exchange rather than by the more basic and more costly method of interacting directly with the environment. Rules such as "copy the successful" determine what imitations are incorporated into the culture as it evolves. Hierarchical configurations are also species specific, in part due to differences in the cultural mechanisms and the norms that sustain them. For some socioevolutionary theorists, culture and norms produce behavioral variations that go beyond those produced by biological evolution; thus, culture and biology interact to influence the nature and pace of evolution of groups. Some socioevolutionary theories also add that group size and task demands interact to specify a dominant form of interaction.

Psychological Processes

Psychological processes examined in the different perspectives cover the gamut of cognitive, emotional, and intentional processes. The different psychological processes receive varying levels of attention and theoretical prominence in the different traditions. The traditions also vary in their focus on individual versus collective psychological processes.

The most intense attention to deep emotions is found in the psychodynamic perspective. Indeed, a key tension facing both individuals and groups is between analysis and emotion. McLeod and Kettner-Polley (Chapter 3, this volume) point out that whereas Freud focused on the triumph of analysis over emotion, Moreno highlighted the triumph of emotion over analysis. Contrasting psychological pressures, for psychodynamic theorists, are at the heart of human groups. Psychological symptoms can be viewed as expressions of a compromise achieved between impulses and contrasting defensive forces. The psychodynamic perspective also delves most deeply into non-conscious processes. These include preconscious, subconscious, and unconscious aspects that are rooted in basic biological instincts common to all humans. Both the impulses and intrapsychic mechanisms to defend against them are genetic and appear as early as infancy. A main point of debate in the psychodynamic tradition has been the degree to which group dynamics do or do not closely mirror the contrasting tensions at the individual level. For at least one psychodynamic theorist, the existence of group mind based on universal human emotions is the essential definition of a group. The formation of a group mind is an emotional process, one that has alternatively been described as constructive by some theorists and destructive by others. Although there is no consensus on the existence of group mind, most theorists would agree that emotional contagion occurs within groups. As for intentionality, the psychodynamic perspective trains its lens more on nonconscious than intentional processes.

The socioevolutionary perspective, also based in biological mechanisms, nevertheless pays little to no attention to individual emotion or to psychological processes. At a general level, the socioevolutionary tradition asserts that universal interaction processes within and between groups are likely to be based in cognitive mechanisms that have evolved over time. Also, cognitive limitations constrain group size. Similar to the psychodynamic perspective, less attention is paid to intention than to random variation and biological evolution of group processes. By nature, humans and their groupings are driven by instincts for survival and reproduction, although these drives are not likely to be conscious and intentional.

According to Lovaglia et al. (Chapter 5, this volume), cognitions have not been seen as theoretically important in the power tradition but should be incorporated more closely in future research. Yet, a few findings in this tradition do involve cognitive aspects. For example, whereas cognitive conflict is associated with improved performance, affective conflict can have a deleterious effect on performance. In resource dilemmas and bargaining situations, cognitions such as egocentrism can reduce cooperation; self-efficacy and expectations of future interaction increase level of cooperation in social dilemmas. As for emotional factors, research has shown that strong emotional reactions occur in individuals who are the subject of coercive power, whereas positive emotions can accompany repeated exchange relations where there is mutual dependence. Lovaglia et al. argue that the role of affect is a promising area for future research. As with the socioevolutionary perspective, power theorists argue that individuals act in their own self-interest, but with the twist that this self-interest can be both conscious and intentional.

Whereas the psychodynamic perspective targets emotion, the social identity perspective clearly targets cognition. Social identity theory and research is concerned with the relationships between human cognitions and large-scale social processes. Key questions center on how a group's concern becomes the concern of the individual members. For example, why do individuals sacrifice self-interest in favor of the interests of a group to which they belong? What are the roots of depersonalization by which an ingroup stereotype becomes an individual's self-description? How do cultural variations such as individualism versus collectivism influence the relationship between individual and social self? Emotion and intention take a back seat to cognitive explanations in the social identity perspective. Social identity theory attempts to explain individual behavior that would be seen as irrational from a psychological point of view if it were divorced from its social context.

Most feminist theories assume that important psychological (and epistemological) differences exist between women and men and that these are reflected in both social identity and behavior (at both individual and group levels). Some individual difference feminist theories see such psychological differences as deeply rooted in one's sexual ascription and sexual identity and as linked, at least to some degree, to biological differences between men and women. Others attribute such differences to social sources that influence the cultural conditioning of women versus men. Structural inequality feminist theories look to external forces such as legal and economic systems for sources of intrapsychological differences between women and men. Postmodern feminist theory, which Meyers et al. (Chapter 7, this volume) classify as an individual differences perspective, starts with a very different premise than the other theories. Postmodern theories begin with the assumption that universal differences do not exist between the sexes, in that considerable variation occurs within each sex—intrasex variation is at least as great as variation between the sexes. Thus, each person has an opportunity to successfully navigate the worlds of both emotion and reason.

Functional theories focus heavily on psychological rationality in group processes. Nonrational processes such as groupthink and motivation to conform are regarded as defects. Individual differences in psychological processes play a secondary role and are often treated as personality traits, such as emotional stability, rather than as key input, process, or output variables. One clear exception is research on the effects of cognitive diversity and social anxiety on information sharing and group decision-making. Like power findings, emotional conflicts can reduce success of group efforts. Intentionality is largely assumed to be conscious and rational; groups are goal oriented, and effective groups understand both their goals and the mechanisms needed to achieve them. Effective groups manage processes to prevent nonrational elements from interfering in the group's goal accomplishment.

For symbolic/interpretive theorists, given-off (nonintentional) expressions are at least as important as given (intentional) ones. Indeed, symbolism is carried as often by unintentional messages as by intentional ones. Emotions play an important role for symbolic/interpretive theorists in several ways. People bring their own predispositions and preferences to the group situation, including, for example, emotional expressiveness. These individual differences also include variation in predisposition to symbolic behavior, as in communication apprehension. In addition, group actions affect member emotion, including even unwillingness to participate in groups, as in grouphate. A key challenge for groups is to balance attention to task (symbolically constructed) with attention to the socioemotional needs of members. Groups exhibit group-level emotions as well, such as group regret. Cognitions are also central, in that events and processes exist as interpretations in the individual mind and shared interpretations at the group level.

The network perspective does not include psychological processes in its core premises per se. However, psychological variables can play important roles in networks. For example, the content of ties may be shared emotion, cognition, intention, or interpretation. Different patterns of such ties can have implications for cohesion, conflict, cooperation, and performance. For example, unbalanced triads (e.g., two of the three linkages are positive emotional bonds, but the third is a negative emotional bond) will behave and perform quite differently than triads with all positive bonds, and both types will behave differently than triads with three negative emotional bonds. At the group level, a network can be described in relation to psychological processes. For example, psychological variables can include the density of emotional bonds among the members, the sharedness of cognitive models or interpretations, or the degree of convergence of intentions. The network perspective also draws attention to effects of reciprocated versus unreciprocated ties as in, for example, unreciprocated emotional attachment. For the network tradition, psychological processes are most likely to be found in either tie content or in group- or individual-level outcomes of a specific pattern of ties.

Change models of group development track how individual and group-level psychological processes vary as a group develops over time. The emotional component varies as individuals begin to develop attraction to the group and as anxiety levels related to inclusion and dependency are reduced. Anxiety and emotional conflict levels will increase at a very late stage if the group anticipates impending termination. Cognitive processes are implicated at all stages and are particularly important in the work orientation phase. Indeed, like the functional perspective, a key concern is how groups achieve a balance of task-oriented versus socioemotional psychological processes. Some change theories also look at variation in psychological processes over time without assuming a fixed, linear stage model. For change theorists, time is socially constructed and subjectively experienced, although it also may be linked to objective time. Research on habitual routines in groups highlights nonconscious and nonintentional processes in groups.

Emergent Properties, Patterns, and Outcomes

What results from group action and interaction? What does the group leave behind? Each perspective focuses on its own set of outcomes, although the concept of outcome in itself is conceptualized quite differently across perspectives. The symbolic/interpretive perspective focuses on structuration as a process rather than some fixed set of consequences. The variables of interest that shape and are shaped by symbolic communication and interpretive processing include culture, identity, group memory, meaning, and cohesion.

Cooperation, conflict, power, productivity, and quality of decision making are important outcomes in the power and change perspectives. Cooperation is of central importance for negotiation situations, where patterns of cooperation versus self-interest influence the nature of the benefits each participant acquires from the negotiation. In Prisoner's Dilemma, for example, the challenge is to achieve mutual cooperation in the context of a payoff system that heavily penalizes nonreciprocated cooperation and heavily rewards reciprocated cooperation. Cooperation in information-sharing tasks increases the amount of information shared in a group. On the flip side, conflict in resource allocation skews the final distribution of resources within and between groups. Quality of group decision-making takes the form of Pareto optimality in a negotiated agreement for the change perspective; "fairness" in the ultimatum game is a related concern in power theory and research. Another type of cooperation studied in both perspectives has been contribution to a public good, where the cooperation rate is an important predictor of future cooperation. Both perspectives exhibit concern for the institutional structure in which small groups operate and in which they negotiate roles, rules, and resource allocations. For the power perspective, power is both an outcome and a means. For the change perspective, stage models see productivity as becoming an important focus of group behavior during the latter stages of group development.

The functional perspective also focuses on models in which both performance and effectiveness of group decision-making are outcomes in later stages. Other features such as leadership and cohesion might be considered to be outcomes of earlier stages. The social identity perspective adds social identity as a key outcome variable, but also as a source of subsequent outcomes including intergroup differentiation and discrimination.

According to McLeod and Kettner-Polley (Chapter 3, this volume), concern with task performance is part of the psychodynamic perspective but is secondary to emotional and psychological outcomes. That is, performance can be an indicator of the emotional and psychological health of the group; the ability to perform well in work may result from increased insight and signal a change from obstructive to productive behavior.

Group performance is an outcome of interest in the network perspective; the nature of ties can influence performance either positively or negatively.

For example, increased density of ties tends to be linked to increased performance, unless the dense ties are hindrance ties, according to Katz et al. (Chapter 8, this volume). Network ties also influence leadership emergence, in that centralization is associated with production of the leadership in groups. Patterns of ties also influence information flow (internally and externally) and the locus of power in groups. The shape of the network can itself be an outcome. For example, homophilous persons tend to have different patterns of ties than heterophilous ones.

For individual difference feminist theorists, the psychological and epistemological differences between men and women in groups are outcomes of differences in men's (agentic) and women's (communal) roles, as well as resultant from the major parenting role assumed by women. Structural inequality feminist theorists see these sex differences as outcomes of differential social role expectations and differential power and status between men and women. The real outcome of concern is the reification of gendered patterns of interaction, power structures, roles, and social values. In contrast to functional theorists, many feminist theorists argue that a focus on task accomplishment as the key outcome in the study of groups reflects an androcentric and capitalistic bias.

Socioevolutionary theory is consistently focused on fitness and survival as the ultimate outcomes of group evolution. Groups that adapt and coevolve with their environments are the most fit, as are groups that are able to reproduce effectively. Some theories within the evolutionary tradition focus on cognitions as outcomes of adaptive processes in populations over time among humans. The "ancestral environment" in which cognitive abilities developed in the human species is an important predictor, whereas "cognitive design" is the outcome.

Causality

Much of the prior discussion has touched at least implicitly on the wide differences across the perspectives in causal premises. To bring these pieces together, this section presents a brief review of causal thinking expressed by the different perspectives. Not surprisingly, the functional and symbolic/interpretive differ most from each other.

The functional perspective explicitly addresses the four forms proposed by Aristotle. *Efficient* causality describes the means by which something is made to occur. *Material* causality concerns the material of which something is made—its composition. *Formal* cause inheres in the archetype, style, and defining features of an entity. *Final* cause is the purpose for which something is done. As Hollingshead et al. (Chapter 2, this volume) note, from the functional perspective, group processes are predicted to be an efficient cause of group performance, just as inputs are an efficient cause of group processes. This logic is reflected in the input-process-output model that characterizes much research in this tradition. The causal process flows in one direction, linearly, without recursivity. An exception to this general trend is McGrath and Hollingshead's (1994) task-media fit hypothesis. Groups are purposive and goal oriented in the sense of final causality; their purpose is to achieve some prespecified performance level or outcome state. Groups are different from each other based on the composition or raw inputs, as in material causality; different material causes are associated with different types of group processes. Regarding formal cause, groups are assumed to differ from each other based on designed features that distinguish one group from another group and from its environment, for example nominal versus Delphi group structures. The symbolic/interpretive perspective challenges the notion of efficient causation by the premise of interpenetration of means and ends in nonlinear, recursive structurational processes. Such processes also simultaneously and recursively link to other interaction forms such as dialectical tension. The material of which groups are made is not so much concrete as mental, in that different people and groups interpret phenomena in relation to their own cognitive and emotional states. In regard to final cause, to the extent that any group can be described as purposive, it is not necessarily prospectively so. Purposes may be constructed post hoc via attribution and retrospective sense-making. People can, of course, be purposively selected, gathered, and labeled a group. Nevertheless, most group processes (primarily symbol manipulation and interpretation) need not be directly related to the ostensible purpose assigned to the assemblage. Formal cause, in the sense of categories or types of groups, is not emphasized because each group is uniquely the product of its own symbol manipulation and interpretation.

The social identity perspective shares with symbolic/interpretive theory the notion that cognitive and emotional interpretations trump material features of the group or environment in influencing individual attitudes and behavior. For example, individuals assigned to membership in categories that had no basis in their relation to the concrete world (e.g., red versus blue) nevertheless found the category to be a significant source of social identity. Also, research has shown that when an individual believes that he or she is a member of a social category, the identity he or she feels with this category is an efficient cause of intergroup discrimination.

The power tradition involves several strands of research that come together in a perspective as a result of the subject of study rather than any particular doctrine of causation. One commonality from a biological perspective is that power is seen to arise naturally and inevitably as a way to organize human groupings. As humans build institutions, these institutions both shape and are shaped by the distribution of resources and power. In this view, biology, resource availability, and manipulation of symbols serve as efficient causes of the acquisition of power by individuals. The socio-evolutionary perspective shares the premise that power is a natural part of human groupings. The drive for power in any individual is the result of evolutionary forces that favor survival of the fittest as individuals and groups evolve slowly over long periods of time. Evolutionary processes may be seen as a formal cause of power differences across groups. Evolution is not seen as an external force, in the sense of an efficient cause, but rather as a constituent part, much as a plot is a formal cause of a dramatic work. Evolutionary processes lead to materially different groups as well, depending on how processes interact with different biological characteristics of different groups. Final cause is survival and reproduction.

One key difference in the change perspective compared to the others is that time is explicitly treated in causal fashion. Time is not something that occurs in the background. Instead, time is itself a significant efficient cause of group processes, either as a mediator variable or moderating influence. Although some change models envision a linear progression through a series of stages, others involve recursivity and nonlinearity. The progression through stages may be seen as a formal cause in the sense of a plot, except that to some degree, the focus is more on the plot than the completed dramatic work. The key organizing theme for the change tradition is that time plays an explicit role in theories of the group, although the specific role differs substantially across theories. Different theories have different ideas of material, efficient, and final causes.

Like the functional approach, psychodynamic theory sees groups as distinctly purposive in the sense of final cause. The goal of the group is to develop better insight and understanding via exploration of emotions. McLeod and Kettner-Polley (Chapter 3, this volume) describe a significant orientation to linear theories of group development. The development process is treated as a formal cause. At the same time, the perspective shares with the symbolic/interpretive and social identity perspectives the assumption that emotions are significantly implicated in group behavior. The psychodynamic tradition looks to the different psychological properties of individual members as material causes of different groups.

The network perspective offers an alternative way to represent relationships both within groups and between groups and the contexts in which they are embedded. Networks can be means or ends; networks may or may not exist for a purpose. The formal causes of networks are the nodes and linkages among the nodes. Perhaps the most central causal theme is that the material cause of a network is patterns of linkages across individual nodes; different arrangements produce different types of networks, such as centralized versus noncentralized.

In feminist theory, the sex composition of a group serves to distinguish one group from another. But material cause is more than just composition; it is also the enactment of sex-specific roles that naturally follow from "objective" sex composition. Efficient causes in feminist theory are the combinations of (1) member features (individual differences); (2) power and status differences in the group, which have been appropriated from social, legal, and economic contexts; and (3) observed sex-specific behavioral patterns such as agentic versus communal behaviors, or enactment of roles as independent leader versus dependent follower. Final causes vary by feminist theory. In the Marxist view, a final cause is the reinforcement of male domination, whereas in psychoanalytic feminist theory, a final cause is the resolution of issues related to the powerful mother. Many feminist theorists disagree that task performance is a final cause because this assumption privileges men, given the embedding social system. As to formal cause, feminist theorists look at selective properties of the group, preferring to isolate sex as the object of study. By implication, sex is the defining formal cause of group processes. Targeted views of formal cause are also found in power, social identity, and psychodynamic perspectives, whereas the functional and change traditions examine a broader range of defining features.

Conclusion

Preparation of this chapter has been a fascinating journey. The domains of the chapters are as vast as continents; exploring them is indeed a major expedition. A single chapter about each of these perspectives cannot do true justice to the depth and creativity of the theory and research in each tradition. Yet, the authors offer roadmaps that both satisfy intellectually and also energize our scholarly curiosity to delve even deeper into the terrain. The authors have provided exceptional cartography in the face of what is to some degree an arbitrary set of demarcations as to what constitutes a perspective. No better example can be found of the rich tapestries and creative insights created by truly interdisciplinary scholarship. In combination, this truly ambitious compendium demonstrates just how vast with riches is the study of groups today.

How might we use this bold endeavor and these panoramic chapters as models for future theory and research on groups? First and foremost, theorists can read work from a broad array of perspectives. Multidisciplinary and multitheoretical work seems likely to vastly enrich theory and research in this field. When theorists see commonalities and seek to understand diverse premises, our overall understanding of groups should deepen. As new touchstones are employed across an array of theories, new vistas become possible in groups theory and research. Second, key premises and assumptions differ across traditions, but they are often implicit, requiring the researcher to evaluate the different perspectives critically. To the extent that theorists can be explicit about assumptions, we can more rapidly come to understand the commonalities and differences among perspectives. Third, by focusing on similarities and dissimilarities across theories, traditions, and paradigms, we can develop a much more textured understanding.

Ivan Steiner (1974) once asked, rhetorically, in a title: "What ever happened to (the study of) the group . . . ?" This book suggests that a proper answer might be: "All sorts of interesting things!"

References

Arrow, H., McGrath, J., & Berdahl, J. (2000). *Small groups as complex systems: Formation, coordination, development, and adaptation.* Thousand Oaks, CA: Sage.

Barley, S. (1986). Technology as an occasion for structuring: Evidence from observations of CT scanners and the social ordering of radiology departments. *Administrative Science Quarterly, 31,* 78–108.

Kraut, R. E., Galegher, J., & Egido, C. (1990). Patterns of contact and communication in scientific research collaboration. In J. Galegher, R. E. Kraut, & C. Egido (Eds.), *Intellectual teamwork: Social and technological foundations of cooperative work.* Hillsdale, NJ: Lawrence Erlbaum.

McGrath, J. E., & Hollingshead, A. B. (1994). *Groups interacting with technology: Ideas, evidence, issues, and an agenda.* Thousand Oaks, CA: Sage.

Postmes, T. (1996). *Social influence in computer-mediated groups.* Amsterdam: University of Amsterdam.

Spears, R., & Lea, M. (1992). Social influence and the influence of the "social" in computer-mediated communication. In M. Lea (Ed.), *Contexts of computer-mediated communication* (pp. 30–65). Hemel Hempstead, UK: Harvester Wheatsheaf.

Steiner, I.D. (1974). Whatever happened to the group in social psychology? *Journal of Experimental Social Psychology, 10,* 94–108.

Author Index

Subject Index

About the Editors

Marshall Scott Poole (PhD, University of Wisconsin) is Professor of Communication and Information and Operations Management at Texas A&M University. He has conducted research and published extensively on the topics of group and organizational communication, computer-mediated communication systems, conflict management, and organizational innovation. He has coauthored or edited 10 books, including *Communication and Group Decision-Making, Research on the Management of Innovation, Organizational Change and Innovation Processes: Theory and Methods for Research,* and *Handbook of Organizational Change and Innovation.*

Andrea B. Hollingshead (PhD, University of Illinois) is Associate Professor of Psychology and Speech Communication at the University of Illinois, Urbana-Champaign. Her research investigates transactive memory and strategic information sharing in groups and organizations. She also studies the impacts of technology and the Internet on the ways that groups communicate, collaborate, and create community. She is coauthor of *Groups Interacting With Technology.*

About the Contributors

Dominic Abrams (PhD, University of Kent) is Professor of Psychology and Director of the Centre for the Study of Group Processes at the University of Kent. He studies the relationship between intra- and intergroup processes, processes of influence and regulation of group behavior, social identity, and social inclusion and exclusion.

Deborah G. Ancona (PhD, Columbia University) is the Seley Distinguished Professor of Management at the Sloan School of Management at MIT. She studies how teams manage both their internal and external dynamics to obtain high performance, as well as time and timing in organizations, including entrainment and temporal design.

Holly Arrow (PhD, University of Illinois, Urbana-Champaign) is a member of both the Psychology Department and the Institute for Cognitive and Decision Sciences at the University of Oregon. She studies the emergence and transformation of structure, including norms, influence hierarchies, and the cognitive networks of members in small groups.

Jennifer L. Berdahl (PhD, University of Illinois) is Assistant Professor of Management and Psychology at the University of Toronto. Her research investigates the social psychology of power in groups and organizations, gender and the emergence of leadership structures in small groups, and the effects of power on perceptions, emotions, and behaviors in small groups.

Dale Brashers (PhD, University of Arizona) is Associate Professor of Speech Communication at the University of Illinois, Urbana-Champaign. His research interests include decision making and uncertainty management in group and health contexts.

Linnda Caporael (PhD, University of California, Santa Barbara) is Professor of Science & Technology Studies at Rensselaer Polytechnic Institute. Her research interests are evolutionary theory and groups, cultural psychology, and social identity.

Jennifer R. Considine is a doctoral student in the Department of Communication at Texas A&M University. Her research interests include feminist approaches to the study of organizations, organizational spirituality, workplace religious discrimination, and interfaith dialogue.

Noshir Contractor (PhD, Annenberg School for Communication, University of Southern California) is Professor of Speech Communication and Psychology at the University of Illinois, Urbana-Champaign. He studies application of systems theories of complexity to communication, the role of emergent networks in and between organizations, and collaboration technologies in the workplace.

Larry Frey (PhD, University of Kansas) is Professor and Associate Chair of the Department of Communication at the University of Colorado at Boulder. His research seeks to understand how the participation of people (especially the underresourced and marginalized) in group communicative practices makes a difference in their individual and collective lives.

Janet Fulk (PhD, Ohio State University) is Professor of Communications in the Annenberg School for Communication and Professor of Management & Organization in the Marshall School of Business at the University of Southern California. Her research focuses on the role of communication and information technology in organizations.

Charlotte Hemelrijk (PhD, University of Utrecht; PhD, University of Zurich) is Assistant Professor in Theoretical Biology at the University of Groningen, the Netherlands. She studies self-organization of social behavior and its effect on evolution, using computer simulations and investigating hypotheses delivered by these models in real animals.

Kelly Bouas Henry (PhD, University of Illinois, Urbana-Champaign) is Assistant Professor of Psychology at Missouri Western State College. Her research focuses on a variety of group processes, with special emphasis on the dynamic aspects of group structure.

Steve Hinkle (PhD, University of North Carolina) was Professor of Psychology at Miami University in Oxford, Ohio, until his untimely death on October 19, 2002. His main research interests were motivational aspects of social identity theory, the relationship between individualism/collectivism and aspects of group processes, and the psychology of political action.

Randy Y. Hirokawa (PhD, University of Washington) is Professor and Chair in the Department of Communication Studies at the University of Iowa. His research focuses primarily on the relations between group communication processes and group decision-making effectiveness.

Michael A. Hogg (PhD, University of Bristol) is an Australian Professorial Fellow at the University of Queensland, with an honorary appointment as Visiting Professor of Psychology at the University of California, Santa Barbara. His research is on group processes, intergroup relations, social identity, and self-conception.

Karen A. Jehn (PhD, Northwestern University) is Professor of Social and Organizational Psychology at Leiden University, The Netherlands. She has researched workplace conflict as it relates to group processes and performance and is recently studying diversity and deviance.

Nancy Katz (PhD, Harvard University) is Associate Professor of Public Policy at the John F. Kennedy School of Government at Harvard University. Her research focuses on group dynamics, especially how to promote a healthy balance between cooperation and competition among members of a team.

Janice R. Kelly (PhD, University of Illinois) is Professor of Psychology at Purdue University. Her primary research interests include the effects of affective states and social factors (gender composition, degree of acquaintance) on group and dyadic interaction.

Richard Kettner-Polley (PhD, Harvard University) is Professor of Management and Dean of Doctoral Programs at Colorado Technical University in Colorado Springs. His research focuses on observational methods, field theory, organizational culture, and cross-cultural patterns of leadership and conflict. He is the long-time coeditor of *Small Group Research.*

David Lazer (PhD, University of Michigan) is Associate Professor of Public Policy at the Kennedy School of Government at Harvard University. He is cofounder and Associate Director of the National Center for Digital Government Research and Practice and has published numerous papers on intraorganizational, interorganizational, and international networks.

Michael Lovaglia (PhD, Stanford University) is Professor and Chair of the Department of Sociology at the University of Iowa. He investigates power and status processes, and his book, *The Personal Use of Social Psychology,* presents, in an accessible way, research that readers can use.

Elizabeth A. Mannix (PhD, University of Chicago) is Professor of Management and Organizations in the Johnson School of Management at Cornell University. Her current research includes work on knowledge sharing in virtual teams, the impact of types of diversity on team interaction and performance, and cross-cultural study of negotiation processes over time.

Joseph E. McGrath (PhD, University of Michigan) is Professor Emeritus of Psychology and Women's Studies at University of Illinois, Urbana-Champaign. His areas of research interest include theory and research on small groups, including groups interacting via computers; social psychological factors in stress; research methodology; gender issues in social psychology; and temporal processes in social psychological phenomena.

Poppy Lauretta McLeod (PhD, Harvard University) is Associate Professor of Organizational Behavior at the Weatherhead School of Management, Case Western Reserve University in Cleveland, Ohio. Her research focuses on decision making and communication in work teams, with particular emphasis on the role of technology.

Renee A. Meyers (PhD, University of Illinois) is Professor of Communication at the University of Wisconsin-Milwaukee. Her research investigates argument in group decision-making interactions and the impact of group argument on decision-making outcomes. Recently, she has been interested in studying communication processes in classroom groups.

Celia Moore is a doctoral candidate at the Rotman School of Management at the University of Toronto. She is interested in the role of leadership and resistance in the production of organizational culture, how power structures influence organizational life, and the content and outcomes of abusive supervision.

Richard Moreland (PhD, University of Michigan) is Professor of Psychology at the University of Pittsburgh, with a secondary appointment in the Katz School of Management there. He is interested in how groups change over time, including such phenomena as group formation and termination, group development, and group socialization.

Sabine Otten (PhD, University of Muenster) is Associate Professor of Psychology at the University of Groningen, The Netherlands. Her main research topics are the determinants of ingroup favoritism and outgroup derogation, the interplay between intra- and intergroup processes, and the impact of social identifications on aggressive interactions.

Paul B. Paulus (PhD, University of Iowa) is Professor and Chair of Psychology at the University of Texas at Arlington. His interests are in environmental psychology and group dynamics, with a recent research focus on group creativity, group decision-making, and group diversity.

Jennifer L. Peterson (PhD, University of Illinois) is Assistant Professor of Communication at the University of Wisconsin-Milwaukee. Her primary research interests include health communication, social support, and coping with illness, particularly in the case of people with rare or stigmatized illnesses, as well as the impact of technology on the support process.

Randall S. Peterson (PhD, University of California, Berkeley) is Associate Professor of Organizational Behavior at London Business School. His research investigates leadership in small organizational work teams, including the effects of performance feedback on future group interactions and performance and the effects of personality in leadership success.

John Rohrbaugh (PhD, University of Colorado) is Professor of Public Administration and Policy and Associate Dean of the Rockefeller College of Public Affairs and Policy, University at Albany (SUNY). He studies the problem-solving processes of management groups, executive teams, and expert task forces, with a focus on identifying methods to improve decision making.

Charles D. Samuelson (PhD, University of California, Santa Barbara) is Associate Professor of Psychology and Associate Department Head at Texas A&M University. His current areas of research include decision making in social dilemmas, cooperation and conflict in common-pool resource dilemmas, and computer-mediated communication in small groups.

Jane Sell (PhD, Washington State University) is Professor of Sociology at Texas A&M University. She is interested in conditions affecting legitimacy, disruptions to groups, and stereotyping and is presently investigating how initial interactions among group members might affect cooperation in subsequent social dilemmas.

Kennon M. Sheldon (PhD, University of California, Davis) is Associate Professor of Social/Personality Psychology at the University of Missouri-Columbia. His primary interests concern goals, motivation, well-being, and hierarchical models of personality and behavior, as summarized in his book, *Optimal Human Being: An Integrative Multi-level Perspective.*

Jennifer R. Spoor is a graduate student in Psychology at Purdue University. Her research interests include affect in groups, regulatory processes in groups, and group information processing.

Sunwolf (PhD, University of California, Santa Barbara; JD, University of Denver College of Law) is Assistant Professor of Interpersonal Communication at Santa Clara University. Her research examines jury deliberation, anticipatory regret in decision-making groups, facilitation, and social exclusion/inclusion in childhood peer groups.

ısan Wheelan (PhD, University of Wisconsin) is President of GDQ Associates, Inc. Until recently, she was Professor of Psychological Studies and Faculty Director of the Training and Development Center at Temple University. A licensed psychologist practicing in hospitals and clinics, she is engaged in research on group and organizational development.

David Sloan Wilson is Professor of Biology and Anthropology at Binghamton University. His research has focused on evolutionary bases of cooperation and collaboration in human societies.

Rick K. Wilson (PhD, Indiana University) is the Herbert S. Autrey Professor of Political Science at Rice University. His research, driven by behavioral game theory, investigates legislative political institutions, cross-national experimental economics, and bargaining behavior between individuals.

Gwen M. Wittenbaum (PhD, Miami University of Ohio) is Associate Professor of Communication at Michigan State University. Her research examines cognitive processes in small groups and strategic information sharing in decision-making groups.

Kay Yoon is a doctoral candidate in the Department of Speech Communication at University of Illinois, Urbana-Champaign. Her research interests include information sharing processes in small groups, expertise recognition in Transactive Memory Systems, and cultural diversity in task-performing groups.